# Philosophical Occasions
## 1912–1951

LUDWIG WITTGENSTEIN

# Philosophical Occasions
## 1912–1951

B
3376
W562
E5
1993

Edited by
James C. Klagge
and
Alfred Nordmann

WITHDRAWN
Regis College Library
15 ST. MARY STREET
TORONTO, ONTARIO, CANADA
M4Y 2R5

Hackett Publishing Company
Indianapolis & Cambridge

101405

Ludwig Wittgenstein: 1889–1951

Copyright © 1993 by Hackett Publishing Company, Inc.
All rights reserved
Printed in the United States of America

99 98 97 96 95 94 93 1 2 3 4 5 6 7 8 9 10

Design by Dan Kirklin

For further information, please address

Hackett Publishing Company, Inc.
P.O. Box 44937
Indianapolis, Indiana 46244-0937

**Library of Congress Cataloging-in-Publication Data**

Wittgenstein, Ludwig, 1889–1951.
[Selections. 1993]
Philosophical occasions, 1912–1951/Ludwig Wittgenstein; edited by
James C. Klagge and Alfred Nordmann.
p. cm.
Includes index.
ISBN 0-87220-155-4 (hard) ISBN 0-87220-154-6 (pbk.)
1. Philosophy. I. Klagge, James Carl, 1954– . II. Nordmann, Alfred,
1956– . III. Title.
B3376.W562E5 1993
192–dc20 92-38232
CIP

The paper used in this publication meets the minimum requirements of American National Standard for Information Sciences—Permanence of Paper for Printed Library Materials, ANSI Z39.48-1984.
∞

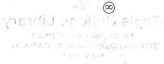

# Contents

# Editorial Preface

When Ludwig Wittgenstein died in 1951, his literary legacy consisted of one major published philosophical work, the *Tractatus Logico-Philosophicus*; a few minor publications; and a mass of papers—notes, typescripts, dictations—at various stages of revision, generally known as his *Nachlass* (legacy). In the past forty years, significant portions of this *Nachlass* have been published,[1] most notably the *Philosophical Investigations*, a volume that can rightfully claim to be close to something Wittgenstein might actually have published. Other books from the *Nachlass* range from the continuous record of first-draft thoughts of the *Notebooks: 1914–1916*, to the nearly completed *Philosophical Remarks*, to the topical selection from various sources of Wittgenstein's observations assembled as *Culture and Value*. From this series of book-length posthumous publications, fifteen as of 1992, emerges a faithful, though by no means complete, picture of Wittgenstein's lifelong philosophical activities.

In contrast to these volumes, there appeared, scattered far and wide throughout a variety of publications, a host of shorter writings—some published by Wittgenstein himself, others more or less independent fragments from his *Nachlass*, yet others records of Wittgenstein's lectures. The present volume gathers together all these shorter publications, adding only one as yet unpublished manuscript. As it turns out, however, the activity of two modest collectors may have produced an avenue in its own right into Wittgenstein's thought. From this series of short writings emerges a picture of Wittgenstein that is obviously far less detailed, but no less faithful, than the picture that emerges from the series of book-length publications: This collection spans a wide range of Wittgenstein's concerns, and it spans the whole of Wittgenstein's active philosophical life (1912–1951). It also exemplifies a considerable range of editorial stances toward Wittgenstein.

1. See von Wright's "The Wittgenstein Papers" in this volume, as well as our addendum to it, for an indication of what has been published so far from the *Nachlass*. Much of it, unedited and untranscribed, is available in microfilm or photocopy from the Cornell University library. Ultimately scholars hope for a complete critical edition, or at least transcription, of the *Nachlass*, but this will not happen soon. For a discussion of the need for such an edition, as well as the history of its pursuit, see Jaakko Hintikka's "An Impatient Man and His Papers," *Synthese*, v. 87, no. 2, May 1991, pp. 183-201.

The remainder of this preface tentatively identifies a few trajectories leading through this book, each tracing a dimension of Wittgenstein's work and its reception.

First, one might consider the range of subjects treated in this volume, which extends over almost the entirety of Wittgenstein's interests. We find reflections on ethics, language, logic, experience, culture, anthropology, and the nature of philosophy, and even comments on aesthetics and mathematics.

Second, this volume shows Wittgenstein engaged with a variety of academic *genres.* Three of the texts in this collection (Chapters 1, 4, and 8) were published by Wittgenstein during his lifetime—one of them (Chapter 4) a proper scholarly paper, the publication of which he later regretted. A fourth text (Chapter 3) provides the rationale for another publication of his—a spelling dictionary for elementary school students. There is first-draft writing (Chapter 12), and there is a corrected typescript (Chapter 9). There are attempts to present his views to a general audience (Chapters 5 and 14), but there are also expressions of profound scepticism concerning the very possibility of providing a systematic exposition of his views (Chapter 8). Indeed, much of his later writing appears to exemplify philosophy conceived as an unceasing activity rather than as the elaboration of a doctrine. This activity is perhaps best exemplified by those texts (Chapters 6, 11, and 13) which show Wittgenstein as a lecturer, thinking aloud and toward no definitive conclusion, for and with his students. While the decision to treat Wittgenstein the lecturer on a par with Wittgenstein the author can be justified by reference to his conception of philosophical activity, that decision is further confirmed by Norman Malcolm's report that Wittgenstein "had always regarded his lectures as a form of publication."[2]

Third, our volume shows Wittgenstein at various stages of his development, ranging from the self-assured tone of the young logician, to the incessant probing of his more mature style.

Fourth, the volume introduces us to Wittgenstein's personality. It shows him as a scrupulous elementary school teacher, as a lecturer and a writer searching for the right formulation, and as an intensely personal thinker. It shows his attempts to protect his integrity as a writer within the academic environment, and his relationships with his friends and colleagues.

2. Norman Malcolm, *Ludwig Wittgenstein: A Memoir,* 2nd edition, New York and Oxford: Oxford University Press, 1984, p. 48.

Finally, the book also shows a variety of responses *to* Wittgenstein—personal responses, on one level; scholarly and editorial responses, on another. There is G. E. Moore's intense struggle with Wittgenstein's thought, his unabashedly personal attempt to make sense of Wittgenstein within his own philosophical framework. Then there is the editorial posture of Rush Rhees—a student so deeply engrossed in Wittgenstein's thought that he takes an almost authorial role in presenting it. In contrast to both Moore and Rhees there is Heikki Nyman, who takes a strictly philological stance. Shying away from conjectures as to how to read Wittgenstein's text, Nyman aims for a scrupulous reproduction of the typescripts—reproductions that show the writer at work and present the texts as unfinished works in progress.

Various factors have conspired to make the editorial handling of Wittgenstein's *Nachlass* a matter of scholarly importance:

On the one hand, there is Wittgenstein's frustrating search for adequate formulations of his ideas, and his impatience with formulations, either his own or others', that do not "hit the nail on the head."[3] To understand Wittgenstein as he would want to be understood, we should focus on the works that came closest to passing muster with him. This suggests a conservative policy toward publishing material from the *Nachlass.* This collection provides some support for this conservative view: The letter to *Mind* and the anecdotes surrounding Wittgenstein's attitude toward the paper on logical form illustrate his worry about inadequate formulations.[4]

On the other hand, Wittgenstein's sometimes oracular, sometimes dialogical style makes the interpretation of even his most favored

3. See the Preface to the *Tractatus.* Wittgenstein's concern to hit the nail on the head contributed to the failure of the attempted collaboration of Wittgenstein and Friedrich Waismann in publishing a book-length exposition of Wittgenstein's views. For an account of this story, see A. Quinton's "Introduction" to Waismann's *Philosophical Papers,* Dordrecht, Holland: D. Reidel Publishing Company, 1977.

4. One of the reasons we scholars want to read the *Nachlass* is that we are very content with Wittgenstein's formulations—happy to read and quote them. The formulations seem perfectly adequate for our purposes. Indeed, when Wittgenstein is least satisfied we tend to be most satisfied, because he is least satisfied when he falls into the idiom that we find most familiar and understandable, and that he does not want to buy into. So what shall we make of the fact that he, and only he, is not content? Are we really keeping that in mind every time we quote something from the *Nachlass*? How would Wittgenstein scholarship be different if we decided to restrict ourselves to those formulations about which we are fairly confident that he considered them adequate?

formulations problematic. It often seems important to know the context in which a problem arose for Wittgenstein or to see an earlier, even if inadequate, elucidation of the problem, to be able to understand the merits of his ultimate treatment of the problem. And insofar as his philosophical "doctrine" recommends philosophy not as a doctrine at all, but as a kind of activity, it makes sense to examine Wittgenstein's notes, drafts, and constant reformulations in order to see such philosophical activity exemplified in his own case. Both these considerations suggest a more liberal policy toward publishing material from the *Nachlass.* Our edition also provides some support for defenders of this view. For example, the discussions of the alleged privacy of experience in the notes for the "Philosophical Lecture" and in Rhees's lecture notes provide genuine insight into and context for the remarks that went into the *Philosophical Investigations.*

If one takes the high editorial standard of the bilingual critical edition of the chapter on "Philosophy" and compares it to other publications from the *Nachlass,* one cannot help but notice omissions that need to be restored, editorial choices which ought to be scrutinized, and occasionally obvious errors of transcription from Wittgenstein's manuscripts—all of which argue for a critical edition of his complete works. In the meantime, and as a stopgap measure, we paired, sometimes for the first time, the German original and English translations, and provided or improved translations in the few cases where that was necessary; we restored some omissions (occasionally extensive) and corrected some errors; and at all times we tried, insofar as we were able, to produce the best text from the extant editions. More could be done, however, even with some of these texts.

These stopgap measures should not create the illusion that the already published work is sufficient for a detailed appreciation or investigation of Wittgenstein's thinking. To indicate the transitory character, as we hope it to be, of this volume in the publication history of Wittgenstein's *Nachlass,* we finally included an expanded and updated version of von Wright's archeological overview in "The Wittgenstein Papers."

Our sincere thanks are due to the executors of Wittgenstein's literary estate for permission to carry out this project, as well as to the editors, translators, and publishers who have allowed their work to be subsumed into this volume. We are particularly grateful to David G. Stern for his meticulous editing of the material in Chapters 10 and 14.

# Acknowledgments

1. Wittgenstein's review of P. Coffey, *The Science of Logic*, was originally published in *The Cambridge Review*, vol. 34, no. 853, March 6, 1913, p. 351. Reprinted by permission.
2. "Some Letters of Ludwig Wittgenstein," with commentary by W. Eccles, was originally published in *Hermathena*, vol. 97, 1963, pp. 57–65. Reprinted by permission.
3. Wittgenstein's "Geleitwort" and its English translation by Elisabeth Leinfellner were first published in the reissue of his *Wörterbuch für Volksschulen* (Vienna, Verlag Hölder-Pichler-Tempsky, 1977). The "Geleitwort" appeared on pp. xxv–xxx, and the translation on pp. xxxi–xxxv. © Verlag Hölder-Pichler-Tempsky, 1977. Reprinted by permission.
4. Wittgenstein's "Some Remarks on Logical Form" was originally published in *Proceedings of the Aristotelian Society, Supplementary Volume*, vol. 9, 1929, pp. 162–71. © The Aristotelian Society, 1929. Reprinted by courtesy of the editor.
5. Wittgenstein's "A Lecture on Ethics" was edited with the assistance of Rush Rhees and originally published in *The Philosophical Review*, vol. 74, January 1965, pp. 3–12. It is reprinted by permission of the publisher.
6. G. E. Moore's lecture notes with commentary were published in three parts as "Wittgenstein's Lectures in 1930–33," *Mind*, vol. 63, 1954, pp. 1–15 (part I) & 289–315 (part II); and vol. 64, 1955, pp. 1–27 (part III) & 264. We have incorporated into the text a few corrections Moore made as addenda. Reprinted by permission of Oxford University Press.
7. Wittgenstein's "Bemerkungen über Frazers *The Golden Bough*" was originally edited by Rush Rhees and appeared in *Synthese*, vol. 17, 1967, pp. 233–53. It is published here, with minor corrections, with the permission of Wittgenstein's literary executors.

   The English translation, "Remarks on Frazer's *Golden Bough*," was done by John Beversluis and originally appeared in *Wittgenstein: Sources and Perspectives*, edited by C. G. Luckhardt (Cornell University Press and Harvester-Wheatsheaf, 1979), pp. 61–81. Copyright © 1979 by Cornell University. Used by permission of the publishers, Cornell University Press and Harvester-

Wheatsheaf. Beversluis has slightly revised his translation for the present edition.

8. Wittgenstein's letter to the Editor of *Mind,* with the reply by R. B. Braithwaite, was published in *Mind,* vol. 42, no. 167, July 1933, pp. 415–16. Reprinted by permission of Oxford University Press.
9. Wittgenstein's "Philosophie" was edited by Heikki Nyman and published in *Revue Internationale de Philosophie,* vol. 43, no. 169, 1989, pp. 175–203. It is reprinted by permission.

   The English translation, "Philosophy," was done by C. G. Luckhardt and M. A. E. Aue and published in *Synthese,* vol. 87, April 1991, pp. 3–22. Reprinted by permission of Kluwer Academic Publishers. This translation © Kluwer Academic Publishers.
10. Wittgenstein's "Notes for Lectures on 'Private Experience' and 'Sense Data'" was originally edited, with some translation, by Rush Rhees and published in *The Philosophical Review,* vol. 77, 1968, pp. 275–320. It is reprinted by permission of the publisher. Some corrections and the insertions of additional material from MSS 148, 149, and 151, as well as some translation, have been carried out by David G. Stern. This material is published by permission of Wittgenstein's literary executors.
11. Rush Rhees's lecture notes were originally published in two parts in *Philosophical Investigations,* vol. 7, 1984, as "The Language of Sense Data and Private Experience—I," pp. 2–45 (lectures I–X), and "The Language of Sense Data and Private Experience—II," pp. 101–40 (lectures XI–XIX). Reprinted by permission. Copyright remains with Mrs. Peggy Rush Rhees.
12. L. Wittgenstein, "Ursache und Wirkung: Intuitives Erfassen," the German original, "Cause and Effect: Intuitive Awareness," the English translation by Peter Winch, editor's notes by Rush Rhees, as well as three appendices consisting of notes by Wittgenstein and lecture notes by Rhees, were first published in *Philosophia,* vol. 6, nos. 3–4, 1976, pp. 391–445. Reprinted by permission of the editor, Asa Kasher. Translations for Appendix B are newly provided by Peter Winch. Minor additions to Appendices A and B have been made from MS 159 and are published by permission of Wittgenstein's literary executors.

13. Yorick Smythies's notes were originally published as "A Lecture on Freedom of the Will" in *Philosophical Investigations,* vol. 12, no. 2, April 1989, pp. 85–100. Reprinted by permission. Minor corrections to the text have been made from Smythies's typescript. Copyright remains with Mrs. Peggy Rush Rhees.
14. Wittgenstein's "Notes for the 'Philosophical Lecture'" was edited from MS 166 by David G. Stern. It is published by permission of Wittgenstein's literary executors.
15. Wittgenstein's letters, with commentary by von Wright, were originally published under the title "Some Hitherto Unpublished Letters from Ludwig Wittgenstein to Georg Henrik von Wright" in *The Cambridge Review,* vol. 104, February 28, 1983, pp. 56–64. We have placed von Wright's comments, originally located at the end of the article, after the letters to which they relate. Reprinted by permission.
16. Georg Henrik von Wright's "The Wittgenstein Papers" originally appeared under the title "Special Supplement: The Wittgenstein Papers" in *The Philosophical Review,* vol. 78, no. 4, October 1969, pp. 483–503. It appeared in a revised and expanded version as "The Wittgenstein Papers," in von Wright's *Wittgenstein* (Basil Blackwell, 1982), pp. 35–62. It is published here, further revised and expanded, by permission of the two publishers and the author.

# Editorial Conventions

Introductions to the individual texts are printed in italics. Unsigned introductions have been written by the editors of this volume.

Catalogue numbers, such as TS 213 or MS 119, refer to Wittgenstein's typescripts or manuscripts as they have been catalogued by G. H. von Wright in his "The Wittgenstein Papers," printed as an appendix in this volume.

Those texts that Wittgenstein wrote in German have all been presented in German in this edition, and an English translation has been provided. Almost always this has been done by putting the German text on the lefthand page and the corresponding translation directly across from it on the righthand page. However, this has not proven to be possible in all cases. Where Wittgenstein alternated between German and English in a single text, we have opted to provide a continuous text in English, and for those portions of the English that are translations, the original German has been put into footnotes. Thus, it should always be the case that original and translation are simultaneously visible.

In his writings Wittgenstein sometimes would leave a space between consecutive paragraphs, and sometimes not. We have followed him in this where possible. The only problem arises for English translations. Since the German texts tend to run longer than the English translations, and since we have tried to keep the German and the English paragraphs aligned with each other, there are occasionally spaces between English paragraphs where there were none between the German paragraphs. In such cases the spacing of the German paragraphs is accurate.

Wittgenstein never used footnotes. All footnotes to texts in this volume were added either by previous editors of the material or by the editors of this volume. Those footnotes that end with "(eds.)" were inserted by the editors of this volume. In some cases, such as the third piece, all of the footnotes are those of the editors of this volume and are not specially flagged as such. Where we have presented parallel texts in German and in English, there may be a separate series of footnotes for each text, located at the bottom of the appropriate pages. However, in certain cases where the footnotes to the text present passages from other authors that Wittgenstein seems to have been commenting on, we have often presented these footnotes across the bottom of both the German and English pages. In these cases the footnotes will be separated from the texts by a line extending across both pages.

Square brackets "[ . . . ]" have been used by editors of the texts to indicate editorial insertions or conjectures.

For texts that have been reprinted from other sources we have tried to retain indication of the pagination of the original publication. Page numbers from the original publication are indicated in double brackets as follows: "⟦1⟧" and are located at the point in the line of text at which that page began. (In one case we have given pagination from two previous editions.) However, since our editions are occasionally more extensive than the original edition, the fact that some material follows a page indicator in our edition does not entail that it was on that page in the original edition. In the appendix "Additions and Corrections to the Texts" we have tried to indicate how our texts differ from earlier editions. In two cases we have included the pages of Wittgenstein's original typescript. In these cases the page numbers are indicated in the lefthand margin of the German text as follows: "S.1" (meaning: *Seite*/page 1), and if the page break occurred in the middle of our line of text, the point at which it occurred is indicated by a vertical rule: "|". We included manuscript pages only in cases where the earlier publication gave this information.

In the typesetting of Wittgenstein's texts, words printed in italics represent the fact that Wittgenstein has underlined them for emphasis. Those words he has double-underlined for added emphasis are printed in either small capitals or italic capitals. Broken underlining indicates Wittgenstein's dissatisfaction or uncertainty with a word or phrase, which he often expressed by wavy underlining. Wittgenstein used "// . . . //" to enclose variant drafts of words or phrases. Where he wrote alternative wording above the line, this has been indicated by editorial footnotes, or by actually typesetting the variant above the line (if his variant was *typed* above the line), or by using "/ . . . /" to enclose the variant.

Different extant editions adopted different editorial conventions. Therefore, the set of conventions adopted by us does not ensure uniformity on the question of what it means to reproduce Wittgenstein's text faithfully. Different editorial procedures remain distinctly discernible. These concern the selection of remarks, the extent to which variant formulations by Wittgenstein were considered, or the number and kind of editorial annotations. They also reach into typographical particulars. Most editors "silently" correct obvious spelling errors. However, these silent corrections only sometimes extend to the restitution of the German letter "ß". Wittgenstein used English-style quotation marks in his manuscripts and typescripts, even when writing in German. However, following the precedent of the bilingual edition of the *Tractatus Logico-Philosophicus*, published in consultation with Wittgenstein in 1922, we have chosen to typeset quotation marks in the German style for texts written in German and in the English style for texts written in or translated into English.

# 1

*Wittgenstein began his study of philosophy at Cambridge University in October of 1911. He worked closely with Bertrand Russell right from the start. In his second year of studies, at age twenty-three, he was asked to review a logic textbook for* The Cambridge Review. *This university periodical had previously published book reviews by serious logicians such as Philip Jourdain and Russell.*

*To appreciate Wittgenstein's approach fully, it helps to consider the character of the book under review and its author. After studying at the Catholic University of Louvain and translating into English a book entitled* Scholasticism, Old and New, *Professor Coffey of Maynooth College, Ireland, published in 1912* The Science of Logic. *He describes the aim of his treatise in the following terms:*

> *[. . .] modern writers on logic are inclined to discuss many problems which would find a more appropriate place in works on epistemology or ontology. [. . .] Philosophers who believe in the superiority of the Scholastic system, as compared with other systems now actually in vogue, recognize the need of applying the traditional principles of this system to modern conditions and problems. [. . .] The main body of the doctrine is, of course, derived from the study of Aristotelean and Scholastic authors; but [the author] wishes here to express his large indebtedness to those recent writers on logic from whose works he has derived much really valuable assistance.*[1]

*From among recent writers on logic, Coffey singles out six works, including Keynes's* Formal Logic *and Venn's* Empirical Logic. *While he does not make any reference to the modern mathematical logicians, Russell and Frege, his is a deliberate attempt to respond from an Aristotelean point of view to recent challenges by authors such as De Morgan, Jevons, Mill, and Whewell, discussing philosophers such as Kant and Hegel and physicists such as Mach and Kelvin, and fending off the claim that inductive reasoning should be treated statistically. Coffey would thus claim for himself that throughout the 831 pages of his two-volume work he has taken careful notice of much honest research, and perhaps he would contradict Wittgenstein on other issues, too.*[2]

1. *The Science of Logic,* volume 1, pp. viii f.

2. For example, as a Scholastic philosopher Coffey explicitly disagrees with some Idealists, in that he denies that reality is changed by becoming an object of our thoughts. See vol. 1, pp. 6f. and 30f., and vol. 2, pp. 152f.

*Other reviewers of* The Science of Logic *attempted to appreciate its merits and defects on the basis of its self-conscious alignment with the Aristotelean standpoint. For example, A. Wolf's scathing criticism of numerous particulars and of the book's "aggressively theological" character still ends on a conciliatory note:*

> *However, some of the views which appear to us erroneous may only serve as a special recommendation to some readers. And, in any case, from the standpoint of those who are specially interested in Scholastic logic and believe in Scholastic philosophy, Dr. Coffey's* Science of Logic *must certainly be commended as a highly successful enterprise.*[3]

*It is perhaps characteristic of Wittgenstein's approach that he does not even grant the division of standpoints into Aristotelean and modern, but that he needs only a fraction of Coffey's 831 pages to determine that this work and its traditional orientation do not measure up to the advanced standards of logic.*

*This book review was originally written in German and then translated into English by Wittgenstein and his friend David Pinsent,*[4] *to whom Wittgenstein later dedicated the* Tractatus. *The German original apparently has not survived. As Wittgenstein's "Notes on Logic" were not written until early October of 1913, this review stands as the earliest written record of Wittgenstein's philosophical views.*

*The Science of Logic:* an inquiry into the principles of accurate thought and scientific method. By P. Coffey, Ph.D. (Louvain), Professor of Logic and Metaphysics, Maynooth College. Longmans, Green & Co. 1912.

In no branch of learning can an author disregard the results of honest research with so much impunity as he can in Philosophy and Logic. To this circumstance we owe the publication of such a book as Mr Coffey's 'Science of Logic': and only as a typical example of the work of many logicians of to-day does this book deserve consideration. The author's Logic is that of the scholastic philosophers, and he

3. A. Wolf's review appeared in *Mind,* vol. 22, 1913, pp. 284–90. Cf. also B. H. Bode's review in the *Journal of Philosophy, Psychology and Scientific Methods,* vol. 10, 1913, pp. 132–35.

4. See the entry in Pinsent's diary for February 11th, 1913, p. 45 in *A Portrait of Wittgenstein as a Young Man,* ed., G. H. von Wright, Cambridge, Mass., and Oxford: Basil Blackwell, 1990.

makes all their mistakes—of course with the usual references to Aristotle. (Aristotle, whose name is so much taken in vain by our logicians, would turn in his grave if he knew that so many Logicians know no more about Logic to-day than he did 2,000 years ago). The author has not taken the slightest notice of the great work of the modern mathematical logicians—work which has brought about an advance in Logic comparable only to that which made Astronomy out of Astrology, and Chemistry out of Alchemy.

Mr Coffey, like many logicians, draws a great advantage from an unclear way of expressing himself; for if you cannot tell whether he means to say 'Yes' or 'No,' it is difficult to argue against him. However, even through his foggy expression, many grave mistakes can be recognised clearly enough; and I propose to give a list of some of the most striking ones, and would advise the student of Logic to trace these mistakes and their consequences in other books on Logic also. (The numbers in brackets indicate the pages of Mr Coffey's book—volume I.—where a mistake occurs for the first time; the illustrative examples are my own).

I. [36] The author believes that all propositions are of the subject-predicate form.

II. [31] He believes that reality is changed by becoming an object of our thoughts.

III. [6] He confounds the copula 'is' with the word 'is' expressing identity. (The word 'is' has obviously different meanings in the propositions—

'Twice two is four'
and 'Socrates is mortal.')

IV. [46] He confounds things with the classes to which they belong. (A man is obviously something quite different from mankind).

V. [48] He confounds classes and complexes. (Mankind is a class whose elements are men; but a library is not a class whose elements are books, because books become parts of a library only by standing in certain spatial relations to one another—while classes are independent of the relations between their members).

VI. [47] He confounds complexes and sums. (Two plus two is four, but four is not a complex of two and itself).

This list of mistakes could be extended a good deal.

The worst of such books as this is that they prejudice sensible people against the study of Logic.

LUDWIG WITTGENSTEIN.

# 2

# Some Letters of Ludwig Wittgenstein

*By* LUDWIG WITTGENSTEIN *and* WILLIAM ECCLES

My friendship with Ludwig Wittgenstein began when we met in the Grouse Inn, on the moors between Glossop and Hayfield in Cheshire in 1908. I was engaged on Dr Schuster's upper atmospheric meteorological research work, using box-kites carrying the various instruments. Wittgenstein arrived to do research on aeroplane design, also using kites for the purpose. We shared a room in the inn for meals and for our writing.

During the next three years, which Wittgenstein spent mainly in Manchester, we met very frequently, usually in my uncle's home. Engineering and other scientific matters were the normal subjects of our conversation but he was also interested in personal problems. Later, when he had moved to Cambridge, my wife and I provided for his visits to us a quiet room in our house, bare of ornamentation and with only the minimum of furniture. He had an unusual capacity for becoming lost in thought, and would not unnaturally be irritated if interrupted at such times. This partly explains the fact that some people found him difficult.

The following letters, while they make only occasional references to his philosophical work, throw some light on Wittgenstein as a person. (. . . My notes are enclosed in brackets.)

⟦58⟧ I

Written about July, 1912.

Wien, Alleegasse 16.

Dear E,

Thanks for your letter. I have thought about your question and hope you will be able to read the answer:

I think you ought to go to some *first class* German Works before you go in for a job in England, however good and independent it may be. If, however, you can not get into *first class* German works there seems to me to be no point in going to Germany at all. My reason is that you have got a very good memory for engineering matters and that. I am sure you will be able to make use of *any amount* of experience if once you are allowed to do as you like. This is not altogether a common place because most people (e.g. myself) can only make real use of a small amount of experience on their work because their experience is not so alive on them. I do not know if you understand what I mean and all that could much better be talked over. I am coming to Manchester about the 17th and hope sincerely to meet you there. My studies are going on very satisfactorily, and I have lots to tell you about them.

How is your bride?

L.W.

[This letter was in answer to a query about my future career on completion of my apprenticeship with the British Westinghouse Co. (now A.E.I., Manchester). I did not in fact take his advice as my firm doubled my salary when they heard of my proposed departure. 'Bride' should be 'fiancée'.]

## II

XVII Neuwaldeggerstrasse 38 Wien.
July, 1914.

Dear Eccles,

As you'll observe I am in Vienna again for a holiday. Thanks for your letter, your designs are splendid as far as I can judge. I will make a few remarks : re wardrobe—why is the horizontal crosspiece on the doors not in the ⟦59⟧ middle (from top to bottom), such that top and bottom panels are of same length? 2/ I think it might perhaps be more convenient to rest the wardrobe on a low (3″) foot V as is done on the manufacturer's design instead of the doors opening right on the carpet.

MEDICINE CHEST: Splendid.
DRESSING TABLE: "

I can't see any drawing of a bed, or do you wish to take the one which the furniture manufacturers submitted? If so *do* insist that they cut off all those measly fancy ends. And why should the bed stand on rollers? You're not going to travel about with it in your house!? By all means have the other things made after *your* design.

I hope the little stranger keeps well, and I hope he'll turn out to be a boy.

I am going for a journey in the middle of August and shall come to see you about the 10th of September. Remember me to your wife and Aunt, and I shall have lots of things to talk about when I see you next.

Yours ever,
L. W.

[This letter shows Wittgenstein's preference for functional design. So far as I know, the only ornamentation of which he could approve, was some pieces of classical statuary, such as he placed in the house he designed in Vienna, now a museum for him. He did not in fact come to see us because of the outbreak of war.]

## III

3/2/15.

Dear Eccles,

It's ages since we wrote to one another last, and I think it's very nice of me to start correspondence again. I dare say that you know that I joined our army as a vollunteer at the beginning of the war. I suppose you two are working for your country in some way or another. I am pretty well so far and have done a good deal of mathematical work during the last 6 months. How are you and how is Ada and Mrs. Moore, etc., etc.

⟦60⟧ I'm sending this letter via the Red Cross Geneve, Switzerland. Send your address the same way *soon.*

My address is:

K.u.K. Artilleriewerkstätte
der Festung Krakau
Feldpost No. 186.

Please remember me to everybody who likes to be reminded of my existence. So write soon and a lot.

Yours Ever,
Ludwig Wittgenstein.

P.S. I've forgotten your address so am sending this letter to Dr. Moore's place.

[Dr Moore was my uncle.]

## IV

10/3/25.

Dear Eccles,

I was more than pleased to hear from you, for some reason or other I was convinced that you either were killed in the war, or if alive, that you would hate Germans and Austrians so much that you would have no more intercourse with me. This seems extraordinary as my Cambridge friends are still writing to me and I to them, and the book which—as you perhaps remember I started writing before the war, was published three or four years ago in England (it is called 'Tractatus logico-philosophicus' and has been printed by Trench, Trubner & Co. London) This shows you that I'm alive. About the various events of my life I will not write now (I would have to write a book) except that at present I am elementary school teacher in the place where you addressed your letter to. I am awfully anxious to hear from you and all about you. Are Dr. & Mrs. Moore still alive? If so, please remember me to them and in fact to everybody who doesn't mind remembering me. I wish I could see you again before long, but when and where we can meet God knows. Perhaps we might manage to meet during the summer vacation, but I haven't got much time and *no* money to come to England as I have given *all* my money away, about 6 years ago. Last summer I should have come to England to see a friend of mine Mr. Keynes (whose name you may know) in Cambridge. He would have paid my expenses, but I resolved after all not to come, because I was so much ⟦61⟧ afraid that the long time and the great events (external and internal) that lie between us would prevent us from understanding one another. However now—or at least *to-day* I feel as if I might still be able to make myself understood by my old friends and if I get any opportunity I might—w.w.p. come and see you at Manchester.

In any case please write to me soon and long. Please excuse my faulty English I haven't even got a dictionary to look up words and correct the spelling.

Yours ever,
Ludwig Wittgenstein.
Otterthal Post Kirchberg am Wechsel
Nieder-Österreich, Austria

## V

[The following letter, from Wittgenstein's sister to me, witnesses to his ability to get on with children.

The money he gave away was a considerable private fortune.]

Dear Sir,

My mother whose eyes are rather weak, asked me to write to you instead of her and to thank you very much for your kind letter. We know your name very well, having heard it, as well as your uncle; often and often by my brother, while he was staying at Manchester. The direction the Austrian gentleman gave you is quite correct and I am sure Ludwig will have received your letter and will answer it by and by. To make it even more sure

I will send him the one you wrote to my mother. Ludwig is living in a very small mountain village as teacher in a children's school. When he came home from captivity (he had been taken prisoner by the Italians towards the end of the war) he gave all his money to his brothers and sisters and resolved to be a school master. I think he teaches wonderously well and the children are very fond of him. I do not think he intends going to England, but perhaps you might come to Austria to see him. We should all be very pleased to see you at our house, my mother especially, and we would show you the beauties of Vienna.

Yours very sincerely,
Hermine Wittgenstein.

Vienna IV, Argentinierstrasse 15.
March 12th, 1925.

⟦62⟧

## VI

7/5/25.

Dear E,

Thanks so much for your letter dated March 14th. Excuse me for letting you wait so long for an answer. I was very glad you wrote such a long letter, letting me know all about you but I'm afraid I can't write much in return about myself. All the things I should like to write about are so fearfully complicated much too complicated for my bad English—As to coming to England this summer I should like to see you and some other friends *very* much indeed and I think I will come and make use of your kind offer—but I'm not at all sure my visit will really be a success. England may not have changed since 1913 but *I* have. However, it is no use writing to you about that as I couldn't explain to you the exact nature of the change (though I perfectly understand it) you will see it yourself when I get there. I should like to come about the end of August. I'm awfully sorry I shall not see your aunt, Mrs. Moore, I liked her *very* much.

Now for your questions, I am not married and consequently haven't got children. My mother is getting very old. Bodily she is rather well, but her mind has suffered greatly from the sorrows and excitements of the war. My two brothers and myself were in the army, one was killed, the other one and myself were captive in Russia and Italy and my mother didn't know for many months whether we were alive or dead.—

Please remember me to your wife and to Dr. Moore.

Yours ever,
Ludwig Wittgenstein.

## VII

Post Stamp 12/9/25.

Post Card entitled 'OTTERTHAL' Post Kirchberg am Wechsel N.Oe. showing the school where he taught.

D.E.,

I'm trying the old job again as you can gather from this postcard. However I don't feel so miserable now, as I have decided to come to you if the worst came to the ⟦63⟧ worst, which it certainly will sooner or later. Please remember me to your wife, give my affectionate greetings to your children and give Hugh a sound thrashing in my name.

Yours ever,
L. Wittgenstein.

[He came straight to us when he reached England and stayed for some days. It was during this period that he obtained his first copy of the English edition of his *Tractatus.* The 'sound thrashing' is not to be taken literally, as other references to our children show.]

## VIII

Trinity College, Cambridge.
10/3/31.

My dear E,

I have been very busy this term and though I've very often thought of writing to you I always put it off. Just before Xmas I was elected to a research fellowship of Trinity College which means: no more financial difficulties for 5 years and that I can devote my time to the work I want to do. As a matter of fact my capacity for the particular kind of work, in all probability, will have left me in 2 or 3 years and then I shall probably resign my fellowship. What with lecturing and my own work I'm too busy to get away from Cambridge during term time. I haven't even been to London once, but we could arrange to meet there some day, whereas its impossible for me to come to Timperley, and as soon as term is over I rush home to Vienna where several people want to see me (not that they have any very good reason, but they do).

I am going down for the Easter vacation on Friday and coming up again about the 20th of April. Let me know if you ever come to London. Weekends would be no good for me as they are my busiest time, but Wednesdays and Thursdays (particularly the latter) would do.

Let me know about your work etc. I hope your family is well, please remember me to all of them. A man I should like *very* much to hear from is Jim Bamber, I wrote to him about 6 months ago but got no reply. If you happen to see him, please remember me to him and if he ⟦64⟧ has got my letter and not answered it for sheer laziness tell him that I think he is a beast.

Yours,
L. Wittgenstein.

[Jim Bamber referred to above, was technician in the Manchester University engineering laboratory; he assisted Wittgenstein in his jet engine experiments.]

## IX

Trinity College.
30/10/31

My dear E,

Thanks so much for your letter, I am just now very busy indeed, so its quite impossible for me to come, say, to Manchester. But what about meeting in London, don't you ever, in the course of your business, go there? Let me know if you do. Perhaps also we could meet when you are on your way to Russia.

I am quite well and very busy writing. As to the newspaper cutting; imagine, I opened your letter standing by the fireplace, the cutting dropped out and straight into the fire, so that I don't know anything about it, except what you write in your letter—I can quite imagine what it must be like to know that your old Coleraine home is broken up. I should feel the same if this happened to my parents' house in Vienna.

I should like to see your children again, especially Hugh.

In my last letter I asked you to let me know something about Jim Bamber. *Please try to see him if you ever get to Manchester:* or write to him, I want to hear about him or from him. After all he was one of the very few people with whom I got on well during my Manchester period.

Let me hear from you again and whether there is any chance of seeing you in London (or Cambridge).

Yours ever,
L. Wittgenstein.

P.S. What you write about enjoying life 100% seems to me humbug. The above——

[I was, in fact, too busy to visit Cambridge at the time because of work in Russia connected with a large factory in the Urals.

Wittgenstein had visited my Coleraine home with me before the 1914–18 war.]

⟦65⟧

## XI

81, East Road, Cambridge.
27/3/39.

My dear Eccles,

Thank you for your letter, yes its me—I should very much like to see you, and curiously enough I was talking to someone about you yesterday. I'd like to come to you in the Easter vac. which is on now, but I think it will probably be impossible, I'm waiting for my naturalisation to go through. I applied for it about 10 months ago and it's due now. If I can get my (British) passport in a week or two from now I shall try to go to Vienna with it for a week or two to see my sisters who live there and are in a difficult and dangerous situation. For although I can't really help them they will be glad to see me again.

Having got the professorship is very flattering and all that but it might have been very much better for me to have got a job opening and closing crossing gates. I don't get any kick out of my position (except what my vanity and stupidity sometimes gets).

Well perhaps I can see you in the summer vac. if not now. I'd like to see your children too, particularly Hugh.

So long and thanks again for your letter. Please remember me to Mrs. Eccles.

Yours ever,
L. Wittgenstein.

# 3

*Within a month after he returned from World War I Wittgenstein gave away his considerable fortune, and by September 1919 he enrolled in a Teachers Academy to train for the profession of elementary school teacher. He worked as a teacher from the fall of 1920 until the spring of 1926. These years finally saw the publication, in 1922, of the* Tractatus Logico-Philosophicus, *which he had completed before becoming a teacher. But during those years he also produced a slim spelling dictionary for elementary school students, published in 1926 as the* Wörterbuch für Volksschulen. *The following provides a detailed description of the events and considerations that preceded the composition of this dictionary.*[1] *While it reads like a preface to the work, this* "Geleitwort" *was never meant to be published as part of the* Wörterbuch.[2] *Instead, it was submitted along with the manuscript to a board of education which had to determine the suitability of this dictionary for the elementary schools. The purpose of the* Geleitwort *was to convince the board that "the compiled dictionary is adapted to the children's vocabulary and to the individual age groups."*[3] *Even though school inspector Eduard Buxbaum was none too impressed and requested a number of changes, only some of these changes were made, and the book was soon published with the ministry's approval. There is no evidence that it was ever adopted as a teaching aid.*

*The* "Geleitwort" *consists of six typewritten pages, which were carefully transcribed for this edition,*[4] *preserving even the majority of Witt-*

1. For further historical detail compare Adolf Hübner's preface (in English and German) in the 1977 reprint of the *Wörterbuch* by its original publisher, Hölder-Pichler-Tempsky, in Vienna. Compare also Konrad Wünsche's *Der Volksschullehrer Ludwig Wittgenstein,* Frankfurt: Suhrkamp, 1985.

2. Some biographers have erroneously suggested that its publication was somehow suppressed; compare e.g. Ray Monk, *Ludwig Wittgenstein: The Duty of Genius,* New York: Free Press and London: Jonathan Cape, 1990, pp. 227f.

3. From a letter to Wittgenstein by his publisher, dated April 21, 1925. The publisher adds: "We ask that in the preface you return to this thought which is, in any event, already taken into account in your manuscript." The letter is reproduced in Adolf Hübner's preface to the 1977 reprint, *op. cit.*, pp. x and xxi.

4. For a facsimile reprint of the *"Geleitwort"* see the edition cited in the first note. All notes to the transcription and to the translation by Elisabeth Lein-

*genstein's spelling and typing errors, as well as grammatical mistakes.*[5] *Even though the* "Geleitwort" *addresses some of the more principled issues associated with the* Wörterbuch, *the* Wörterbuch *itself bears considerable interest. Among its entries is* "das Kochinchinahuhn *[a Vietnamese chicken],*" *but between* "der Philister *[philistine]*" *and* "der Phosphor *[phosphorus]*" *one will look in vain for* "die Philosophie", *and between* "logieren = wohnen *[to reside]*" *and* "die Lohe : Gerberlohe *[blaze : tan]*" *there is no entry for* "die Logik." *Another remarkable feature is that the* Wörterbuch *makes considerable allowances for the Austrian* Mundart *or spoken dialect, even to the point where it blurs the grammatically crucial distinction between the dative and the accusative cases.*[6]

---

fellner were added by the editors of the present edition. The marginal arabic page numbers for the German text refer to Wittgenstein's typescript, the intralineal roman page numbers refer to the pages in the reprint of the *Wörterbuch* (first note above).

5. To be sure, the grammatical mistakes may simply be matters of oversight or mere typing mistakes, after all. In particular, Wittgenstein often forgets the comma which opens a minor clause; he also writes *"ich habe erlebt, das"* instead of *dass* or *daß*. Compare also note 3 to the English translation of the *"Geleitwort."*

6. Compare, for example, the entry: "im = in dem, in der Mundart: 'in', z.B.: 'I woar in Zimmer'."

S.1 # GELEITWORT zum Wörterbuch für Volksschulen

Das vorliegende Wörterbuch soll einem dringenden Bedürfnis des gegenwärtigen Rechtschreibunterrichtes abhelfen. Es ist aus der Praxis des Verfassers hervorgegangen: Um die Rechtschreibung seiner Klasse zu bessern, schien es dem Verfasser notwendig, seine Schüler mit Wörterbüchern[1] zu versehen, um sie in den Stand zu setzen, sich jederzeit über die Schreibung eines Wortes zu unterrichten; und zwar, erstens, auf möglichst rasche Weise, zweitens aber auf eine Weise, die es möglich macht sich das gesuchte Wort dauernd einzuprägen. Hauptsächlich beim Schreiben und Verbessern der Aufsätze wird die Schreibung der Wörter dem Schüler zur intressanten[2] und dringenden Frage. Das häufige Befragen des Lehrers oder der Mitschüler stört die Mitschüler bei ihrer Arbeit, leistet auch einer gewissen Denkfaulheit Vorschub und die Information durch den Mitschüler ist überdies häufig falsch. Ausserdem aber hinterlässt die mündliche Mitteilung einen viel schwächeren Eindruck im Gedächtnis als das gesehene Wort. Nur das Wörterbuch macht es möglich, den Schüler für die Rechtschreibung seiner Arbeit voll verantwortlich zu machen, denn es gibt ihm ein sicheres Mittel seine Fehler zu finden und zu verbessern, wenn er nur will. Es ist aber unbedingt nötig, dass der Schüler seinen Aufsatz selbständig verbessert. Er soll sich als alleiniger Verfasser seiner Arbeit fühlen und auch allein für sie verantwortlich sein. Auch setzt nur die selbstständige[3] Verbesserung den Lehrer in den Stand, sich ein richtiges Bild von den Kenntnissen und der Intelligenz des Schülers zu machen. Das Vertauschen der Hefte und gegenseitige Verbessern der Arbeiten liefert ein sozusagen verschwommenes Bild von den Fähigkeiten der Klasse. Aus der Arbeit des Schülers A will ich nicht zugleich

1. The last letter was added by hand.

2. The spelling 'intressant' is colloquial but not correct. In the *Wörterbuch* the word is correctly spelled 'interessant.'

3. Either the third 's' was corrected from a 'v' or Wittgenstein intended to delete the 's' by blotting it out with a 'v'. The correct spelling of the word is 'selbständig' as Wittgenstein spelled three lines above. 'Selbstständig' is a common mistake.

# Preface to the *Dictionary for Elementary Schools*

The goal of this dictionary is to fill an urgent need with respect to the present teaching of orthography. It is a result of the author's practical experiences: In order to improve orthographical writing in his class and, in order to enable students to inform themselves about the spelling of a word, the author found it necessary to supply them with dictionaries. Firstly, such a dictionary should enable the student to look up a word as quickly as possible. Secondly, the way in which the dictionary informs the student should enable him to retain the looked-up word permanently. The spelling of words becomes an interesting and urgent problem for the student mainly when it comes to the writing and correcting of compositions. But the frequent questioning of the teacher, or of the fellow students, disturbs the other students in their work. This questioning of students and teacher also promotes a certain mental sluggishness. Moreover, the information given by another student is often wrong. Besides, oral information leaves a much weaker imprint on the memory than a word which one has seen. Only a dictionary makes it possible to hold the student completely responsible for the spelling of what he has written because it furnishes him with reliable measures for finding and correcting his mistakes, provided he has a mind to do so. It is, however, absolutely necessary that the student corrects his composition on his own. He should feel that he is the only author of his work and he alone should be responsible for it. It is also this independent correction that enables the teacher to get a correct picture of the student's knowledge and of his mental capacities. The exchange of exercise-books and the reciprocal correction of compositions results in a blurred image, so to speak, of the abilities of the class. From student A's work I do not want to learn at the same time of student B's knowledge. What student B knows I want to learn from student B's work. It has sometimes been maintained that this reciprocal correction results in a correct picture of the class's general level. But even that is not true. It would be true only if each student would correct the compositions of all the other students. This, of course, is not possible. I also believe that the teacher should not be interested in such an average spelling; it is not

erfahren, was der Schüler B kann, sondern das will ich aus der Arbeit des B ersehen. Und die gegenseitige Verbesserung gibt nicht einmal, wie manchmal behauptet wird, ein richtiges Bild über das allgemeine
S.2 Niveau der Klasse | ⟦xxvi⟧ (dazu müsste jeder Schüler die Arbeiten aller seiner Mitschüler verbessern, was natürlich nicht möglich ist). Auch ist, glaube ich, eine solche Durchschnittsrechtschreibung nicht das, was den Lehrer interessieren soll; denn nicht die Klasse[4] soll richtig schreiben lernen, sondern *jeder* Schüler! also war den Schülern ein Wörterbuch in die Hand zu geben; denn auch ein Wörterheft, wie[5] es vielfach empfohlen wird,[6] erfüllt unseren Zweck nicht. Im Wörterheft werden für jeden Anfangsbuchstaben einige Seiten freigelassen und in dem verfügbaren Raum tragen die Schüler gelegentlich wichtige Wörter ein, in der Reihenfolge, wie sie der Unterricht ergibt. Ein solches Heft mag für manche Zwecke gut sein, aber zum Nachschlagen, als Ersatz des Wörterbuches, taugt es nicht, denn es enthält entweder viel zu wenig Wörter, oder das Aufsuchen wird ungeheuer zeitraubend, also praktisch unmöglich. Also ein Wörter*buch*,[7] aber welches?[8] Es kommen nur die beiden Wörterbücher des Schulbücher-Verlages in Betracht. Die grosse Ausgabe desselben, die ich im Folgenden der Kürze halber „das grosse Wörterbuch" nennen will, hat für meinen Zweck verschiedene Nachteile. Erstens ist es zu umfangreich und infolgedessen unserer Landbevölkerung vielfach zu teuer; zweitens ist es infolge seines Umfangs für die Kinder schwer zu gebrauchen; drittens enthält es eine grosse Menge von Wörtern die das Kind nie gebraucht — insbesondere viele Fremdwörter — dagegen enthält es viele Wörter nicht, die für die Kinder notwendig wären. Dies sind zum Teil solche Wörter die vielleicht ihrer Einfachheit halber nicht aufgenommen wurden, z.B.: „dann", „wann", „mir", „dir", „du", „in", u.a. — Aber gerade diese einfachsten Wörter werden von den Kindern sehr häufig falsch geschrieben und sind die[9] Gelegenheit zu den bedauerlichsten Fehlern. Anderenteils vermissen wir im grossen Wörterbuch viele Zusammensetzungen und

4. The typescript contains a stray mark: 'nicht"die Klasse'.
5. Here, a typo was blotted out in the typescript.
6. The comma was added by hand.
7. The italicized part of the word was underlined (apparently by hand) in the typescript.
8. The '?' is missing in the typescript. Instead, an extremely faint period was apparently added by hand.
9. A second 'die' was crossed out by hand.

*the class* that should learn how to spell but each *individual* student! Thus it was necessary to put a dictionary into the students' hands. Sometimes, the use of an exercise-book containing wordlists is recommended, but even such a notebook does not fulfill our goal. In such a book of wordlists one leaves some pages empty for each initial letter. The student occasionally enters important words into the available space in the same order in which those words occur during the lessons. Such a collection of wordlists might be helpful for some ⟦xxxii⟧ purposes, but it is useless as a substitute for a dictionary if one wants to look up a word, for it either does not contain enough words or the looking up of words takes an enormously long time and becomes, thus, practically impossible. Hence [there is the need for] a dictionary in *book form*—but which one? Only the two dictionaries that have been published by the Schulbücher Verlag can be considered. The large edition of this dictionary—from now on I will call it the "large dictionary" for short—has various disadvantages with respect to my purposes. Firstly, it is too voluminous and, therefore, often too expensive for our rural population. Secondly, because of its bulk it is hard to use for the children. Thirdly, it contains a large number of words that the child never uses, especially many foreign words.[1] On the other hand, it lacks many words which are necessary for the children. Partly those are words that have not been included perhaps because of their commonness, e.g. *dann* [*then,* etc.], *wann* [*when,* etc.], *mir* [*me,* Dative], *dir* [*you,* Dative], *in* [*in, into,* etc.], etc. But it is exactly those most common words that are frequently misspelled by the children, and they are the occasion of the most deplorable mistakes. On the other hand, we look in vain in the large dictionary for many compounds and decompositions of compounds. But those things belong in a dictionary for elementary schools because children recognize them as such only with difficulty. Thus, it often does not occur to them to look up the base noun of a compound (e.g. *Rauchfang* [*chimney*]—the children say *Raufang*). Or they recognize the word to be a compound but make an error when they decompose it. E.g. for the word *Einnahme* [*receiving, receipt, capture,* etc.] they look up *ein* [*a, one, in,* etc.] and *Name* [*name*], etc. For these reasons, the large dictionary was not suitable for my purposes. But the short edition was entirely useless because it lacked most of the common

1. Some of the foreign words included in Wittgenstein's *Wörterbuch* are '*das Kolophonium = Geigenharz* [rosin],' '*der Kognac* [cognac],' '*die Induktion, der Induktor* [induction, inductor].'

Abteilungen,[10] die darum in ein Wörterbuch für Volksschulen gehören, weil die Kinder sie schwer als solche erkennen und darum häufig nicht auf den Gedanken komme die Stammwörter nachzuschlagen (z.B. „Rauchfang" — die Kinder sagen „Raufang").[11] Oder sie erkennen das Wort als Komposition, irren sich aber bei seiner Auflösung und schlagen etwa für das Wort „Einnahme" „ein"[12] und ⟦xxvii⟧ „Name" nach etz.etz. Aus den angeführten Gründen war das
S.3 grosse | Wörterbuch für meinen Zweck nicht geeignet; die kleine Ausgabe aber ist[13] gänzlich unbrauchbar: denn es fehlen in ihr die allermeisten einfachen und wichtigen Wörter des täglichen Lebens; ja dieses Büchlein ist beinahe nur ein Fremdwörterbuch, also gerade das was ich nicht brauchen konnte. In dieser Not entschloss ich mich dazu, meinen Schülern (der 4. Klasse einer 5 klassigen Schule) ein Wörterbuch zu diktieren. Dieses Wörterbuch umfasste cca 2500 Stichwörter. Ein Wörterbuch von noch geringeren Umfange hätte seinen Zweck nicht erfüllt. Wer in der Praxis steht, [14] kann sich einen Begriff von der Schwierigkeit dieser Arbeit machen,[15] die ja dazu führen soll, dass[16] jeder Schüler ein sauberes und womöglich fehlerfreies Wörterbuch erhält, denn um das zu erreichen, muss der Lehrer beinahe jedes Wort bei jedem Schüler kontrollieren. (Stichproben genügen nicht. Von den Anforderungen[17] an die Disziplin will ich nicht reden). Als dieses Wörterbüchlein nach mehrmonatlicher Arbeit fertig war, zeigte es sich nun, dass die Arbeit der Mühe wert gewesen war, denn die Besserung in der Rechtschreibung war erstaunlich. Das Orthographische Gewissen war geweckt worden. Aber dieses Verfahren, sich ein Wörterbuch selbst anzulegen, ist doch im allgemeinen nicht durchführbar, insbesondere nicht an niederorganisierten Schulen und auch an höher organisierten ist es so zeitraubend und schwierig, dass diese Nachteile reichlich die Vorteile aufwiegen, die ein selbst angelegtes Wörterbuch ja zweifellos vor dem

10. Instead of 'Abteilungen (sections, departments)' Wittgenstein probably meant to write 'Ableitungen (derivatives, decompositions)'.

11. ').' are missing in the typescript. Instead, there appears to be a handwritten comma beneath the closing quotation marks.

12. The closing quotation mark was added by hand.

13. The word 'ist' was added by hand.

14. The comma was added by hand.

15. The comma was added by hand.

16. The second 's' was added by hand.

17. A letter was blotted out.

and important words of everyday life. Indeed, this little volume is almost a glossary of only foreign words and, thus, something I could not use. In this distressing situation I made up my mind to dictate[2] to my students (the fourth grade of a school with five grades) a dictionary. This dictionary contained about 2,500 entries. A dictionary of an even smaller size would not have served its purpose. He who works at the practical level is able to understand the difficulties of this work. Because the result should be that each student receives a clean and, if at all possible, correct copy of the dictionary, and in order to reach that goal the teacher has to control almost every word each student has written. (It is not enough to take samples. I do not even want to talk about the demands on discipline.) When, after several months[3] of work, this little dictionary was finished it appeared that the work had been worthwhile: the improvement of spelling was astonishing. The orthographic conscience had been awakened! But ordinarily this procedure of writing a dictionary by oneself is not feasible, especially at the elementary school ⟦xxxiii⟧ level. But also at the level of the secondary schools this procedure would have the disadvantage of being time-consuming and difficult, and those disadvantages would amply outweigh the advantages which, without doubt, such a self-composed dictionary

2. The last two words are underlined by hand, and there is a large exclamation mark at the margin. These marks are presumably those of school inspector Eduard Buxbaum, who found this passage rather puzzling, trying to explain it away in his report on the *Wörterbuch*: "From a procedural standpoint one has to say that it is strange that the author says in the preface that he has dictated the dictionary to his students. One obviously has to understand this in the following way: Words that are already known to the children, have previously been written down by them, and have been treated in accordance with the method of 'cued' word memorization, are written down again from dictation in order to control how well the students spell" (quoted by Hübner in *Wörterbuch für Volksschulen, op. cit.*, pp. xi and xxii). In fact, Wittgenstein is to be taken quite literally in this passage. He spent several months dictating a spelling dictionary of about three thousand words to one of his classes. At least one student's copy of this *Diktierbüchlein* exists today. As Wünsche points out, it still contains spelling mistakes (*Der Volksschullehrer Wittgenstein, op. cit.*, pp. 93–95).

3. This word is liberally underlined by hand with a large exclamation mark at the margin. Both marks are again presumably by Eduard Buxbaum, who complains in his report about Wittgenstein's nonidiomatic expression: "By no means should the mistake to write *'eine mehrmonatliche Arbeit'* instead of saying *'eine Arbeit von vielen Monaten'* creep into a dictionary of the German language, not even into the preface." (Cf. Hübner in *Wörterbuch, op. cit.*, pp. xi and xii.)

fertig gekauften hat. So kam ich dazu, das vorliegende Wörterbuch zu schreiben.

Die Probleme, die sich bei der Zusammenstellung des Wörterbuches ergeben, betreffen[18] die Auswahl und die Anordnung der Wörter. Für die Auswahl der Wörter waren mir folgende Gesichtspunkte massgebend:

1.) In das Wörterbuch sollen nur solche, aber alle solche Wörter aufgenommen werden, die österreichsichen Volksschülern geläufig sind. Also auch viele gute deustche Wörter nicht, die in Oesterreich ungebräuchlich sind; z.B. abgefeimt, äffen, bosseln, erkleklich, etz.etz. Mit dem Raum ist zu sparen, da grosser Umfang das Nachschlagen erschwert und das Buch verteuert. Andererseits ist, im Rahmen der dem Schüler geläu⟦xxviii⟧figen Wörter, möglichste Vollständigkeit allein schon deshalb erforderlich, weil häufiges vergebliches Nachschlagen den Schüler unsicher macht und dazu führt, dass er das Wörterbuch nicht mehr um Rat fragt.

S.4 2.) Kein Wort ist zu einfach um aufgenommen zu werden — denn ich habe erlebt, das „wo“ mit Dehnungs-h und „was“ mit ss geschrieben wurde.

3.) Zusammensetzungen sind aufzunehmen, wo sie entweder vom Kinde schwer als solche erkannt werden oder wo das Nachschlagen der Stammwörter leicht zu Fehlern führt.

4.) Fremdwörter sind aufzunehmen, wenn sie allgemein gebräuchlich sind. Ihre Verdeutschung ist zu geben, wo sie nicht zu umständlich oder unverständlicher ist, als das Fremdwort.

5.) Ausdrücke der Mundart sind nur soweit aufzunehmen, als sie in die gebildete Sprache Eingang gefunden haben, wie zum Bsp. Heferl, Packel, Lacke, u.a.

In einzelnen Fällen ist es freilich schwer zu entscheiden, ob ein Wort aufzunehmen ist, oder nicht. Weit schwieriger aber sind die Fragen die die Anordnung der Wörter aufwirft. Für die Anordnung nämlich sind ausser dem Grundsatz der alphabetischen Ordnung verschieden einander kreuzende Prinzipien massgebend und welches im gegebenen Fall das bestimmende Prinzip sein soll, hängt nicht selten von der subjektiven Auffassung des Verfassers ab. Ein solches Prinzip ist es z.B., die abgeleiteten Wörter dem Stammwort anzugliedern (d.h.: nur das Stammwort ist Stichwort,[19] die anderen Wörter reihen sich

18. This word was later inserted (between lines) with the typewriter.
19. The comma was added by hand.

would have had over a ready-made and bought one. Those were the reasons that caused me to write the dictionary under consideration. The problems that arise with the composition of the dictionary concern the selection and the arrangement of the words. For the selection of words the following viewpoints were essential for me:

1.) Only those words that the students of Austrian elementary schools are familiar with should be listed in the dictionary; with respect to those words the listing should be complete. Thus, also many good German words which are not used in Austria, like *abgefeimt* [*crafty, cunning,* etc.], *äffen* [*mock, ape,* etc.], *bosseln* [*emboss, mould,* etc.], *erkleklich* [*erklecklich; considerable,* etc.], etc., should not be entered. One has to save space, since great bulk will make the looking up of words more difficult and the book more expensive. Regarding words the student is familiar with, on the other hand, it is necessary that the dictionary be as complete as possible for many reasons, not the least of which is: if the student often looks up words in vain he will become insecure, with the end result being that he will no longer consult the dictionary.

2.) No word is too common to be entered, since I have experienced that *wo* [*where,* etc.] has been written with the "*h*" that indicates a long vowel, and *was* [*what,* etc.] with "*ss*".

3.) Compounds should be entered if it is either difficult for the child to recognize them as such or if the looking up of the base word easily leads to mistakes.

4.) Foreign words should be entered if they are used universally. They should be translated into German if this is not too cumbersome and if the translation is not less understandable than the foreign word itself.

5.) Dialectal expressions should be entered only insofar as they have been admitted into the educated language, like e.g. *Heferl* [*Häferl; mug, little pot,* etc.], *Packel* [*small parcel*], *Lacke* [*puddle,* etc.].

In some cases it is indeed difficult to decide whether or not a word should be entered into the dictionary. Much more difficult, however, are the questions which arise concerning the arrangement of the words. Namely, for the arrangement certain principles that clash with one another are essential, in addition to the principle of alphabetic order. Which principle should be the determining one in each given case depends quite often on the subjective ⟦xxxiv⟧ view of the author. Such a principle is e.g. to group the derivatives after the base word (that is, only the base word functions as key-word, all the other words [derivatives] follow the key-word on the same line or on the following

ihm in der gleichen Zeile, oder in den folgenden Zeilen an; im letzteren Falle sind die folgenden Zeilen hineingerückt.) Mit diesem Grundsatz kreuzt sich der Grundsatz der alphabetischen Ordnung. Wie sind z.B. die Wörter „alt", „Altar", „Alter",[20] „Altertum", „altertümlich" anzuordnen? Hier haben wir die alphabetische Ordnung; sie hat den Nachteil, dass „alt" und „Alter", die doch zusammengehören, durch ein Wort von heterogener Bedeutung getrennt sind. Die Zusammenziehung verwandter Wörter ist aber schon aus Gründen der Raumersparnis erwünscht. Nun würde dieser Grundsatz aber erfordern, dass auch „Altertum" und „altertümlich" dem Wort „alt" angegliedert werden, also vor das ⟦xxix⟧ Wort „Altar" rücken;[21] diese Anordnung aber erschiene doch wieder unnatürlich und würde das Finden der komplizierten Ableitungen sehr erschweren. Ich habe die Worte in diesem Falle so angeordnet:

*alt* das Alter
der *Altar*
S.5 Das *Altertum,* altertümlich
etz.[22]

Ich habe dieses Beispiel hier angeführt, weil es zeigt, wie die Anordnung der Wörter von verschiedenen Gesichtspunkten beherrscht wird, deren Berechtigungen oft[23] schwer gegen einander abzuwägen sind. Mancher würde vielleicht den Grundsatz der alphabetischen Ordnung als alleinherrschenden empfehlen (so ist er z.B. im Weideschen Wörterbuch durchgeführt). Aber die rein alphabetische Ordnung, wo sie heterogene Wörter zwischen eng verwandte einschiebt, stellt meiner Meinung nach a.d.[24] Abstraktionsvermögen des Kindes zu hohe Anforderungen und ist aus Gründen des Wortverständnisses und der — überaus wichtigen Raumersparnis oft nicht zu empfehlen. Und ebenso führt jedes Festhalten an einem starren Prinzip zu unserem Zwecke nicht entsprechenden Anordnungen und muss aufgegeben werden — sosehr dadurch auch die Arbeit des Verfassers erleichtert würde. Vielmehr ist es nötig, immer wieder Kompromisse zu

20. Capitalization was added by hand.
21. The semicolon was added by hand.
22. In the typescript the three italicized words are double underlined by hand.
23. Misspelled in the typescript.
24. This abbreviation for 'an das' was inserted by hand.

lines. In the latter case the following lines are indented.) This principle clashes with the principle of alphabetic order. E.g. how should one arrange the words *alt* [*old,* etc.], *Altar* [*altar*], *Alter* [*old age,* etc.], *Altertum* [*antiquity,* etc.], *altertümlich* [*antique,* etc.]. Here we could use alphabetic order, but alphabetic order has the disadvantage that *alt* and *Alter* which belong together are separated by a word with a heterogenous meaning. But the saving of space makes it desirable to group related words together. But this principle would demand that also *Altertum* and *altertümlich* are grouped after *alt,* i.e. they should be moved before the word *Altar.* However, this arrangement would appear to be unnatural, and the finding of complicated derivatives would become very difficult. In this case I have arranged the words in the following manner:

*alt,* das Alter
der *Altar*
D[d]as *Altertum,* altertümlich
etc.

I have mentioned this example because it shows how the arrangement of the entries is governed by various principles. It is often difficult to justify one principle in relation to another. Some would perhaps recommend that the principle of alphabetic order should be the only governing principle. (This principle is e.g. carried out in Weide's dictionary.) But if the purely alphabetic order inserts a heterogenous word between closely related ones, then in my opinion the alphabetic order demands too much from a child's power of abstraction. Thus, because of the comprehension of words and the highly important saving of space, the purely alphabetic order often cannot be recommended. Equally, each instance of clinging to a dogmatic principle leads to an arrangement that does not suit our purpose and has to be abandoned—even if this would make the author's work much easier. Rather, it is necessary to compromise again and again. In some instances, the introduction of a derivative after the base word leads easily to confusions; in other instances, this danger does not exist. In some cases the base word is not commonly used at all—its derivative, however, is in common usage. In such cases it is advisable to put the derivative in front of the base word. In some instances one has to put a configuration of words besides the lexical entry which explains the

schliessen. In einem Fall führt das Angliedern der Ableitung an das Stammwort leicht zu Verwechslungen, im anderen ist diese Gefahr nicht vorhanden; in manchen Fällen ist das Stammwort ganz ungebräuchlich,[25] die Ableitung dagegen gebräuchlich und es empfiehlt sich, diese jenem voranzustellen; hier ist eine Komposition neben das Stichwort zu setzen, weil es dessen Bedeutung klar macht und vor Missverständnissen bewahrt, dort ist dies überflüssig; etz. etz. Es würde mich zu weit führen, meine Anordnung in einer grösseren Anzahl von Fällen zu rechtfertigen. Ich habe sie mir in jedem einzelnen Falle genau und lange überlegt. Immer wider kreuzen sich psychologische Grundsätze (wo wird der Schüler das Wort suchen, wie wird er am besten vor Verwechslungen bewahrt, etz) mit grammatikalischen (Stammwort, Ableitung),[26] mit typographischen ([27]Raumausnützung, ⟦xxx⟧ Uebersichtlichkeit des Satzbildes, etz.) So kommt es, dass dem oberflächlichen Beurteiler auf Schritt und Tritt scheinbar willkürliche Inkonsequenzen entgegentreten, die aber durch Kompromisse zwischen den massgebenden Gesichtspunkten bedingt sind.

Den Fettdruck habe ich, ausser zur Hervorhebung der Stichwörter überall dort gebraucht, wo ich Wörter oder einzelne Buchstaben
S.6 be-|sonders auffällig machen wollte. Die Gründe dürften in jedem besonderen Falle nicht schwer verständlich sein. Auch hier aber war es nicht angezeigt, nach *einem*[28] Prinzip allein zu entscheiden, ob ein Wort oder Buchstabe fett zu drucken sei, oder nicht. (etwa alle Stammwörter fett zu drucken, die Ableitungen aber nicht).

Das ß[29] habe ich, wo es für die alphabetische Ordnung der Wörter massgebend war, als einfachen s-Laut behandelt. Die gewöhnliche Anordnung, die es dem ss anschliesst, schien mir in einer grossen Anzahl von Fällen unnatürlich und geeignet den Kindern das Finden eines Wortes zu erschweren; so z.B. wenn[30] sich zwischen „aus" und „aussen" die Wörter „ausgiebig", „Auskunft", „Ausnahme", etz. einschieben. Der Schüler liest „aus", findet bei „ause" nichts und denkt sich, „ah dann weiss ich ohnehin schon, wie „ausen" geschrieben wird." Freilich entsteht auch durch meine Anordnung manches Unnatürliche, weil das -ß- in der gegegenwärtigen Rechtschreibung

25. The comma was added by hand.
26. The comma was added by hand.
27. The '(' is missing in the typescript.
28. The italicized word was underlined in the typescript, perhaps by hand.
29. This letter was drawn in by hand after Wittgenstein deleted another sign.
30. The faintly legible word 'wenn' was inserted by hand between lines.

meaning of the lexical entry and prevents misunderstandings. In other cases this is superfluous, etc. It would be too much if I would justify my groupings for a larger number of cases. In each ⟦xxxv⟧ individual case I have pondered the grouping thoroughly for a long time. Again and again psychological principles (where will the student look for the word, how does one guard him against confusions in the best possible manner) clash with grammatical ones (base word, derivative) and with the typographical utilization of space,[4] with the well-organized appearance of the printed page, etc. Thus it happens that the superficial critic will meet with seemingly arbitrary inconsistencies everywhere, but those inconsistencies are caused by compromises between essential viewpoints.

Aside from emphasizing the key-words, I have also used boldface in all those cases where I wanted to make words or single letters especially conspicuous. It should not be difficult to understand the reasons in each individual case. But also here it was not advisable to decide on the basis of one single principle whether or not a word should be printed in boldface (e.g. to print all base words in boldface, but not the derivatives).

The letter "*ß*" I have treated as a simple *s*-sound when the alphabetic order of words was the determining factor. The normal arrangement where it follows "*ss*" seemed to me to be unnatural in a great number of cases. It also seemed likely to make the search for a word more difficult for the children, e.g. when between *aus* [*from, out,* etc.] and *aussen* [*außen; out, outside,* etc.] the words *ausgiebig* [*plentiful,* etc.], *Auskunft* [*information,* etc.], *Ausnahme* [*exception,* etc.], etc. are inserted. The student reads *aus,* finds nothing under *ause,* and thinks, "Oh, I know already how *ausen* is spelled".[5] It is not to be denied, however, that my arrangement produces some unnatural groupings

4. A line was drawn in the left margin of the typescript from nine lines up (*neben das Stichwort . . .* [*in front of the base word . . .*]) to here.

5. The *Wörterbuch* ends up listing the terms in the following order: *aus, Ausdehnung, . . . außen, außer, . . . ausführlich, . . . ausgiebig, . . . Auskunft, . . . Ausnahme,* etc.

als ein sz und als -ſs-[31] gebraucht wird und also in jedem dieser beiden Fälle an eine andere Stelle des Alphabets gehörte.
Noch ein Wort über die Vorausstellung des Artikels vor das Stichwort: Ich glaube, dass diese das Verständnis[32] erleichtert und manchen Irrtümern vorbeugt. Ich habe allen Hauptwörtern (mit Ausnahme einiger Zusammensetzungen) den Artikel beigefügt, da er das Hauptwort als solches hervorhebt. Der nachgestellte Artikel aber wird vom Kinde leicht übersehen, oder fälschlich auf das ihm folgende Wort bezogen. Die Uebersichtlichkeit der Kolumne dürfte durch die neue Anordnung nicht gelitten haben.

Otterthal 22.4.1925.

Der Verfasser.

31. As above, the two letters were drawn in by hand, the first after deletion of another sign. While the 'ß' is still used in contemporary German, the second letter has become obsolete. Originally, the 'ß' designated 'sz' while the other letter represented a double-s. The modern 'ß' conflates these usages.
32. Two letters blotted out (the word previously read "Unverständnis").

since, according to present orthography, "ſʒ" is used for "*sz*" and for "ſs". In each of those two cases "ſʒ" would take a different place in the alphabet.[6]

Let me add a word about putting the article in front of an entry. I believe that this facilitates comprehension and prevents errors. I have added the article to all nouns (with the exception of some compounds) since the article sets off the noun as such. If one puts the article behind the noun it is easily overlooked by the child or the child relates it erroneously to the following word. I do not believe that the readability of the column has suffered from this new arrangement.

Otterthal, April 22, 1925.

The author.

6. Modern German typeface contains the letter 'ß' which is taken to represent an 'ss' but which occasionally also phonetically represents the sound of 'sz'. In the older Fraktur typeface employed in the *Wörterbuch* that letter looks more like 'sz' but also represents both sounds. Wittgenstein here confronts the problem of how to alphabetize this letter: should alphabetization follow the phonetic distinction between the sounds of 'ss' and 'sz', should it follow orthographic convention and always treat the 'ß' or the 'ſʒ' as a form of 'ss', or should it for didactic purposes treat this letter like a single 's'? While most dictionaries adopt the second option, Wittgenstein follows the third. The German original of this text shows that the problem is further complicated by the fact that at the time when Wittgenstein was writing handwritten orthography contained different letters for 'ss' and 'sz'.

# 4

*This invited paper was written in 1929 for the Joint Session of the Aristotelian Society and the Mind Association. Though it was published in the proceedings, Wittgenstein decided not to deliver it at the session. Instead he spoke on an entirely different topic—generality and infinity in mathematics. Wittgenstein made it very clear, in his 1933 letter to* Mind *(Chapter 8 in this volume) and in comments to his friends, that he thought the paper was quite worthless.*[1]

1. This information, as well as other anecdotes concerning this paper and its substitute lecture, can be found in G.E.M. Anscombe's note published with an earlier reprint of this piece in *Essays on Wittgenstein's 'Tractatus'*, eds. I. Copi and R. Beard, New York: Macmillan, and London: Routledge & Kegan Paul, 1966, p. 31; Wittgenstein's letter to Russell (R. 54, July 1929) in *Letters to Russell, Keynes, and Moore,* Ithaca, N.Y.: Cornell University Press, and Oxford: Basil Blackwell, 1974, p. 99; G. E. Moore's comments in his "Wittgenstein's Lectures in 1930–33," p. 47 of Chapter 6 in this volume; F. R. Leavis's recollection of the night before Wittgenstein was supposed to deliver the paper, in "Memories of Wittgenstein," in *Recollections of Wittgenstein,* ed. R. Rhees, New York and Oxford: Oxford University Press, 1984, pp. 60–61; and Karl Britton's recollection in "Portrait of a Philosopher," in *Wittgenstein: The Man and His Philosophy,* ed. K. T. Fann, New York: Dell, 1967, p. 58.

# Some Remarks on Logical Form

*By* L. WITTGENSTEIN

Every proposition has a content and a form. We get the picture of the pure form if we abstract from the meaning of the single words, or symbols (so far as they have independent meanings). That is to say, if we substitute variables for the constants of the proposition. The rules of syntax which applied to the constants must apply to the variables also. By syntax in this general sense of the word I mean the rules which tell us in which connections only a word gives sense, thus excluding nonsensical structures. The syntax of ordinary language, as is well known, is not quite adequate for this purpose. It does not in all cases prevent the construction of nonsensical pseudopropositions (constructions such as "red is higher than green" or "the Real, though it is an *in itself,* must also be able to become a *for myself*", etc.).

If we try to analyze any given propositions we shall find in general that they are logical sums, products or other truthfunctions of simpler propositions. But our analysis, if carried far enough, must come to the point where it reaches propositional forms which are not themselves composed of simpler propositional forms. We must eventually reach the ultimate connection of the terms, the immediate connection which cannot be broken without ⟦163⟧ destroying the propositional form as such. The propositions which represent this ultimate connexion of terms I call, after B. Russell, atomic propositions. They, then, are the kernels of every proposition, *they* contain the material, and all the rest is only a development of this material. It is to them we have to look for the subject matter of propositions. It is the task of the theory of knowledge to find them and to understand their construction out of the words or symbols. This task is very difficult, and Philosophy has hardly yet begun to tackle it at some points. What method have we for tackling it? The idea is to express in an appropriate symbolism what in ordinary language leads to endless misunderstandings. That is to say, where ordinary language disguises logical structure, where it allows the formation of pseudopropositions, where it uses one term in an infinity of different meanings, we must replace it by a symbolism which gives a clear picture of the logical structure, excludes pseudopropositions, and uses its terms unambiguously. Now we can only substitute a clear symbolism for the unprecise one by inspecting the phenomena which we want to describe, thus trying to understand their logical multiplicity. That is to say, we can only arrive at a correct analysis by, what might be called, the logical investigation of the phenomena themselves, *i.e.*, in a certain sense *a posteriori*, and not by conjecturing about *a priori* possibilities. One is often tempted to ask from an *a priori* standpoint: What, after all, *can* be the only forms of atomic propositions, and to answer, *e.g.*, subject-predicate and relational propositions with two or more terms further, perhaps, propositions relating predicates and relations to one another, and so on. But this, I believe, is mere playing with words. An atomic form cannot be foreseen. And it would be surprising if the actual ⟦164⟧ phenomena had nothing more to teach us about their structure. To such conjectures about the structure of atomic propositions, we are led by our ordinary language, which uses the subject-predicate and the relational form. But in this our language is misleading: I will try to explain this by a simile. Let us imagine two parallel planes, I and II. On plane I figures are drawn, say, ellipses and rectangles of different sizes and shapes, and it is our task to produce images of these figures on plane II. Then we can imagine two ways, amongst others, of doing this. We can, first, lay down a law of projection—say that of orthogonal projection or any other—and then proceed to project all figures from I into II, according to this law. Or, secondly, we could proceed thus: We lay down the rule that every ellipse on plane I is to appear as a circle in plane II, and every rectangle as a square in II. Such a way of representation may be convenient for us if for some reason we prefer to draw only circles and squares on plane II. Of course, from these images the exact shapes of the original figures on plane I cannot be immediately inferred. We can only gather from them that the original was an ellipse or a rectangle. In order to get in a single instance at the determinate shape of the original we would have to know the individual method by which, *e.g.*, a particular ellipse is projected into the circle before me. The case of ordinary language is quite analogous. If the facts of reality are the ellipses and rectangles on plane I the subject-predicate and relational forms correspond to the circles and squares in plane II. These forms are the norms of our particular language into which we project in *ever so many different* ways *ever so many different* logical forms. And for this very reason we can draw no conclusions—except very vague ones—from the use of these ⟦165⟧ norms as to the actual logical form of the phenomena described. Such forms as "This paper is boring", "The weather is fine", "I am lazy", which have nothing whatever in common with one another, present themselves as subject-predicate propositions, *i.e.*, apparently as propositions of the same form.

If, now, we try to get at an actual analysis, we find logical forms which have very little similarity with the norms of ordinary language. We meet with the forms of space and time with the whole manifold of spatial and temporal objects, as colours, sounds, etc., etc., with their gradations, continuous transitions, and combinations in various proportions, all of which we cannot seize by our ordinary means of expression. And here I wish to make my first definite remark on the logical analysis of actual phenomena: it is this, that for their representation numbers (rational and irrational) must enter into the structure of the atomic propositions themselves. I will illustrate this by an example. Imagine a system of rectangular axes, as it were, cross wires, drawn in our field of vision and an arbitrary scale fixed. It is clear that we then can describe the shape and position of every patch of colour in our visual field by means of statements of numbers which have their significance relative to the system of co-ordinates and the unit chosen. Again, it is clear that this description will have the right logical multiplicity, and that a description which has a smaller multiplicity will not do. A simple example would be the representation of a patch P by the expression "[6–9, 3–8]" and of a proposition ⟦166⟧

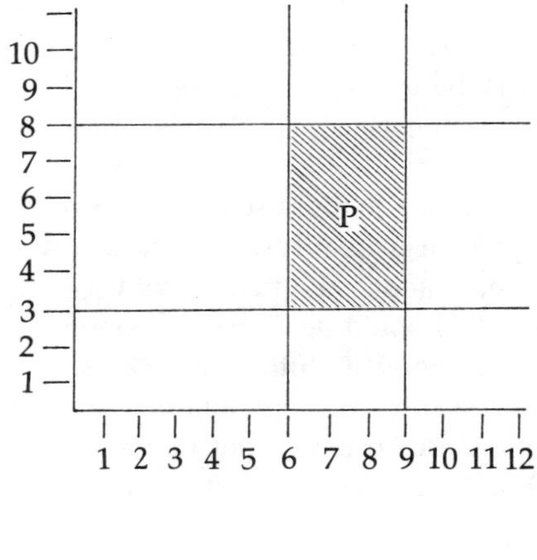

about it, *e.g.*, P is red, by the symbol "[6–9, 3–8] R", where "R" is yet an unanalyzed term ("6–9" and "3–8" stand for the continuous interval between the respective numbers). The system of co-ordinates here is part of the mode of expression; it is part of the method of projection by which the reality is projected into our symbolism. The relation of a patch lying between two others can be expressed analogously by the use of apparent variables. I need not say that this analysis does not in any way pretend to be complete. I have made no mention in it of time, and the use of two-dimensional space is not justified even in the case of monocular vision. I only wish to point out the direction in which, I believe, the analysis of visual phenomena is to be looked for, and that in this analysis we meet with logical forms quite different from those which ordinary language leads us to expect. The occurrence of numbers in the forms of atomic propositions is, in my opinion, not merely a feature of a special symbolism, but an essential and, consequently, unavoidable feature of the representation. And numbers will have to enter these forms when—as we should say in ordinary language—we are ⟦167⟧ dealing with properties which admit of gradation, *i.e.*, properties as the length of an interval, the pitch of a tone, the brightness or redness of a shade of colour, etc. It is a characteristic of these properties that one degree of them excludes any other. One shade of colour cannot simultaneously have two different degrees of brightness or redness, a tone not two different strengths, etc. And the important point here is that these remarks do not express an experience but are in some sense tautologies. Every one of us knows that in ordinary life. If someone asks us "What is the temperature outside?" and we said "Eighty degrees", and now he were to ask us again, "And is it ninety degrees?" we should answer, "I told you it was eighty." We take the statement of a degree (of temperature, for instance) to be a *complete* description which needs no supplementation. Thus, when asked, we say what the time is, and not also what it isn't.

One might think—and I thought so not long ago—that a statement expressing the degree of a quality could be analyzed into a logical product of single statements of quantity and a completing supplementary statement. As I could describe the contents of my pocket by saying "It contains a penny, a shilling, two keys, and nothing else". This "and nothing less" is the supplementary statement which completes the description. But this will not do as an analysis of a statement of degree. For let us call the unit of, say, brightness *b* and let

E(*b*) be the statement that the entity E possesses this brightness, then the proposition E(2*b*), which says that E has two degrees of brightness, should be analyzable into the logical product E(*b*) & E(*b*), but this is equal to E(*b*); if, on the other hand, we try to distinguish between the units and consequently write E(2*b*) = E(*b*′) & E(*b*″), we assume ⟦168⟧ two different units of brightness; and then, if an entity possesses one unit, the question could arise, which of the two—*b*′ or *b*″—it is; which is obviously absurd.

I maintain that the statement which attributes a degree to a quality cannot further be analyzed, and, moreover, that the relation of difference of degree is an internal relation and that it is therefore represented by an internal relation between the statements which attribute the different degrees. That is to say, the atomic statement must have the same multiplicity as the degree which it attributes, whence it follows that numbers must enter the forms of atomic propositions. The mutual exclusion of unanalyzable statements of degree contradicts an opinion which was published by me several years ago and which necessitated that atomic propositions could not exclude one another. I here deliberately say "exclude" and not "contradict", for there is a difference between these two notions, and atomic propositions, although they cannot contradict, may exclude one another. I will try to explain this. There are functions which can give a true proposition only for one value of their argument because—if I may so express myself—there is only room in them for one. Take, for instance, a proposition which asserts the existence of a colour R at a certain time T in a certain place P of our visual field. I will write this proposition "R P T", and abstract for the moment from any consideration of how such a statement is to be further analyzed. "B P T", then, says that the colour B is in the place P at the time T, and it will be clear to most of us here, and to all of us in ordinary life, that "R P T & B P T" is some sort of contradiction (and not merely a false proposition). Now if statements of degree were analyzable—as I used to think—we could explain this contradiction by saying that the colour R con-⟦169⟧tains all degrees of R and none of B and that the colour B contains all degrees of B and none of R. But from the above it follows that no analysis can eliminate statements of degree. How, then, does the mutual exclusion of R P T and B P T operate? I believe it consists in the fact that R P T as well as B P T are in a certain sense *complete.* That which corresponds in reality to the function "( ) P T" leaves room only for one entity—in the same sense, in fact, in which we say that there is room for one person only in a chair. Our symbolism, which allows us to form the sign of the logical product of "R P T" and "B P T", gives here no correct picture of reality.

I have said elsewhere that a proposition "reaches up to reality", and by this I meant that the forms of the entities are contained in the form of the proposition which is about these entities. For the sentence, together with the mode of projection which projects reality into the sentence, determines the logical form of the entities, just as in our simile a picture on plane II, together with its mode of projection, determines the shape of the figure on plane I. This remark, I believe, gives us the key for the explanation of the mutual exclusion of R P T and B P T. For if the proposition contains the form of an entity which it is about, then it is possible that two propositions should collide in this very form. The propositions, "Brown now sits in this chair" and "Jones now sits in this chair" each, in a sense, try to set their subject term on the chair. But the logical product of these propositions will put them both there at once, and this leads to a collision, a mutual exclusion of these terms. How does this exclusion represent itself in symbolism? We can write the logical product of the two propositions, *p* and *q*, in this way:—⟦170⟧

| p | q | |
|---|---|---|
| T | T | T |
| T | F | F |
| F | T | F |
| F | F | F |

What happens if these two propositions are R P T and B P T? In this case the top line "T T T" must disappear, as it represents an impossible combination. The true possibilities here are—

| R P T | B P T |
|---|---|
| T | F |
| F | T |
| F | F |

That is to say, there *is* no logical product of R P T and B P T in the first sense, and herein lies the exclusion as opposed to a contradiction. The contradiction, if it existed, would have to be written—

| R P T | B P T | |
|---|---|---|
| T | T | F |
| T | F | F |
| F | T | F |
| F | F | F |

but this is nonsense, as the top line, "T T F," gives the proposition a greater logical multiplicity than that of the actual possibilities. It is, of course, a deficiency of our ⟦171⟧ notation that it does not prevent the formation of such nonsensical constructions, and a perfect notation will have to exclude such structures by definite rules of syntax. These will have to tell us that in the case of certain kinds of atomic propositions described in terms of definite symbolic features certain combinations of the T's and F's must be left out. Such rules, however, cannot be laid down until we have actually reached the ultimate analysis of the phenomena in question. This, as we all know, has not yet been achieved.

# 5

*Wittgenstein gave a lecture on ethics to the Heretics Society in Cambridge on November 17th, 1929, at the invitation of C. K. Ogden. The Heretics Society was a general audience that had no particular interest or training in philosophy. David Pinsent, Wittgenstein's friend, had been a member when he was at Cambridge. Previous speakers included Bertrand Russell, H. G. Wells, and Virginia Woolf.*[1] *Several weeks later Wittgenstein discussed the contents of the lecture with members of the Vienna Circle.*[2]

*What is printed here is a typescript (TS 207) for the lecture. The typescript was written in English and bears no title. There is also a handwritten manuscript that differs in some ways from the typescript.*[3]

1. The date comes from Desmond Lee's Introduction to *Wittgenstein's Lectures: Cambridge, 1930–1932,* Totowa, N.J.: Rowman and Littlefield, and Oxford, Basil Blackwell, 1980, p. xv. The date of November 1930 given by Brian McGuinness in a footnote on p. 77 of *Wittgenstein and the Vienna Circle,* ed. B. McGuinness, New York: Barnes and Noble, and Oxford: Basil Blackwell, 1979, has been acknowledged by McGuinness, in a personal communication, to be a misprint. Other information comes from M. Drury, "Some Notes on Conversations with Wittgenstein," *Recollections of Wittgenstein,* ed. R. Rhees, p. 82; *A Portrait of Wittgenstein as a Young Man,* ed. G. H. von Wright, pp. xiv and 4 n.2; and Ray Monk, *Ludwig Wittgenstein: The Duty of Genius,* p. 276.

2. See the brief account recorded by Friedrich Waismann in *Wittgenstein and the Vienna Circle,* pp. 79 and 92–93.

3. See von Wright's comments in "The Wittgenstein Papers," published in this volume, pp. 487 and 496–497.

# A Lecture on Ethics

Before I begin to speak about my subject proper let me make a few introductory remarks. I feel I shall have great difficulties in communicating my thoughts to you and I think some of them may be diminished by mentioning them to you beforehand. The first one, which almost I need not mention, is that English is not my native tongue and my expression therefore often lacks that precision and subtlety which would be desirable if one talks about a difficult subject. All I can do is to ask you to make my task easier by trying to get at my meaning in spite of the faults which I will constantly be committing against the English grammar. The second difficulty I will mention is this, that probably many of you come up to this lecture of mine with slightly wrong expectations. And to set you right in this point I will say a few words about the reason for choosing the subject I have chosen: When your former secretary honoured me by asking me to read a paper to your society, my first thought was that I would certainly do it and my second thought was that if I was to have the ⟦4⟧ opportunity to speak to you I should speak about something which I am keen on communicating to you and that I should not misuse this opportunity to give you a lecture about, say, logic. I call this a misuse, for to explain a scientific matter to you it would need a course of lectures and not an hour's paper. Another alternative would have been to give you what's called a popular-scientific lecture, that is a lecture intended to make you believe that you understand a thing which actually you don't understand, and to gratify what I believe to be one of the lowest desires of modern people, namely the superficial curiosity about the latest discoveries of science. I rejected these alternatives and decided to talk to you about a subject which seems to me to be of general importance, hoping that it may help to clear up your thoughts about this subject (even if you should entirely disagree with what I will say about it). My third and last difficulty is one which, in fact, adheres to most lengthy philosophical lectures and it is this, that the hearer is incapable of seeing both the road he is led and the goal which it leads to. That is to say: he either thinks: "I understand all he says, but what on earth is he driving at" or else he thinks "I see what he's driving at, but how on earth is he going to get there." All I can do is again to ask you to be patient and to hope that in the end you may see both the way and where it leads to.

I will now begin. My subject, as you know, is Ethics and I will adopt the explanation of that term which Professor Moore has given in his book *Principia Ethica.* He says: "Ethics is the general enquiry into what is good." Now I am going to use the term Ethics in a slightly wider sense, in a sense in fact which includes what I believe to be the most essential part of what is generally called Aesthetics. And to make you see as clearly as possible what I take to be the subject matter of Ethics I will put before you a number of more or less synonymous expressions each of which could be substituted for the above definition, and by enumerating them I want to produce the same sort of effect which Galton produced when he took a number of photos of different faces on the same photographic plate in order to get the picture of the typical features they all had in common. And as by showing to you such a collective photo I could make you see what is the typical ⟦5⟧—say—Chinese face; so if you look through the row of synonyms which I will put before you, you will, I hope, be able to see the characteristic features they all have in common and these are the characteristic features of Ethics. Now instead of saying "Ethics is the enquiry into what is good" I could have said Ethics is the enquiry into what is valuable, or, into what is really important, or I could have said Ethics is the enquiry into the meaning of life, or into what makes life worth living, or into the right way of living. I believe if you look at all these phrases you will get a rough idea as to what it is that Ethics is concerned with. Now the first thing that strikes one about all these expressions is that each of them is actually used in two very different senses. I will call them the trivial or relative sense on the one hand and the ethical or absolute sense on the other. If for instance I say that this is a *good* chair this means that the chair serves a certain predetermined purpose and the word good here has only meaning so far as this purpose has been previously fixed upon. In fact the word good in the relative sense simply means coming up to a certain predetermined standard. Thus when we say that this man is a good pianist we mean that he can play pieces of a certain degree of difficulty with a certain degree of dexterity. And similarly if I say that it is *important* for me not to catch cold I mean that catching a cold produces certain describable disturbances in my life and if I say that this is the *right* road I mean that it's the right road relative to a certain goal. Used in this way these expressions don't present any difficult or deep problems. But this is not how Ethics uses them. Supposing that I could play tennis and one of you saw me playing and said "Well, you play pretty badly" and suppose I answered "I know, I'm playing badly but I don't want to play any better," all the other man could say would be "Ah then that's all right." But suppose I had told one of you a preposterous lie and he came up to me and said "You're behaving like a beast" and then I were to say "I know I behave badly, but then I don't want to behave any better," could he then say "Ah, then that's all right"? Certainly not; he would say "Well, you *ought* to want to behave better." Here you have an absolute judgment of value, whereas the first instance was one of a relative judgment. The essence of this difference seems to be obviously this: Every judg-⟦6⟧ment of relative value is a mere statement of facts and can therefore be put in such a form that it loses all the appearance of a judgment of value: Instead of saying "This is the right way to Granchester," I could equally well have said, "This is the right way you have to go if you want to get to Granchester in the shortest time"; "This man is a good runner" simply means that he runs a certain number of miles in a certain number of minutes, etc. Now what I wish to contend is that, although all judgments of relative value can be shown to be mere statements of facts, no statement of fact can ever be, or imply, a judgment of absolute value. Let me explain this: Suppose one of you were an omniscient person and therefore knew all the movements of all the bodies in the world dead or alive and that he also knew all the states of mind of all human beings that ever lived, and suppose this man wrote all he knew in a big book, then this book would contain the whole description of the world; and what I want to say is, that this book would contain nothing that we would call an *ethical* judgment or anything that would logically imply such a judgment. It would of course contain all relative judgments of value and all true scientific propositions and in fact all true propositions that can be made. But all the facts described would, as it were, stand on the same level and in the same way all propositions stand on the same level. There are no propositions which, in any absolute sense, are sublime, important, or trivial. Now perhaps some of you will agree to that and be reminded of Hamlet's words: "Nothing is either good or bad, but thinking makes it so." But this again could lead to a misunderstanding. What Hamlet says seems to imply that good and bad, though not qualities of the world outside us, are attributes to our states of mind. But what I mean is that a state of mind, so far as we mean by that a fact which we can describe, is in no ethical sense good or bad. If for instance in our world-book we read the description of a murder with all its details physical and psychological, the mere description of these facts will contain nothing which we could call an *ethical* proposition. The murder will be on exactly the same level as any other event, for instance the falling of a stone. Certainly the reading of this description might cause us pain or rage or any other emotion, or we might read about the pain or rage caused by ⟦7⟧ this murder in other people when they heard of it, but there will simply be facts, facts, and facts but no Ethics. And now I must say that if I contemplate what Ethics really would have to be if there were such a science, this result seems to me quite obvious. It seems to me obvious that nothing we could ever think or say should be *the* thing. That we cannot write a scientific book, the subject matter of which could be intrinsically sublime and above all other subject matters. I can only describe my feeling by the metaphor, that, if a man could write a book on Ethics which really was a book on Ethics, this book would, with an explosion, destroy all the other books in the world. Our words used as we use them in science, are vessels capable only of containing and conveying meaning and sense, *natural* meaning and sense. Ethics, if it is anything, is supernatural and our words will only express facts; as a teacup will only hold a teacup full of water [even] if I were to pour out a gallon over it. I said that so far as facts and propositions are concerned there is only relative value and relative good, right, etc. And let me, before I go on, illustrate this by a rather obvious example. The right road is the road which leads to an arbitrarily predetermined end and it is quite clear to us all that there is no sense in talking about the right road apart from such a predetermined goal. Now let us see what we could possibly mean by the expression, "*the* absolutely right road." I think it would be the road which *everybody* on seeing it would, *with logical necessity,* have to go, or be ashamed for not going. And similarly the *absolute good,* if it is a describable state of affairs, would be one which everybody, independent of his tastes and inclinations, would *necessarily* bring about or feel guilty for not bringing about. And I want to say that such a state of affairs is a chimera. No state of affairs has, in itself, what I would like to call the coercive power of an absolute judge. Then what have all of us who, like myself, are still tempted to use such expressions as "absolute good," "absolute value," etc., what have we in mind and what do we try to express? Now whenever I try to make this clear to myself it is natural that I should recall cases in which I would certainly use these expressions and I am then in the situation in which you would be if, for instance, I were to give you a lecture on the psychology of pleasure. What you would do then ⟦8⟧ would be to try and recall some typical situation in which you always felt pleasure. For, bearing this situation in mind, all I should say to you would become concrete and, as it were, controllable. One man would perhaps choose as his stock example the sensation when taking a walk on a fine summer's day. Now in this situation I am, if I want to fix my mind on what I mean by absolute or ethical value. And there, in my case, it always happens that the idea of one particular experience presents itself to me which therefore is, in a sense, my experience *par excellence* and this is the reason why, in talking to you now, I will use this experience as my first and foremost example. (As I have said before, this is an entirely personal matter and others would find other examples more striking.) I will describe this experience in order, if possible, to make you recall the same or similar experiences, so that we may have a common ground for our investigation. I believe the best way of describing it is to say that when I have it *I wonder at the existence of the world.* And I am then inclined to use such phrases as "how extraordinary that anything should exist" or "how extraordinary that the world should exist." I will mention another experience straight away which I also know and which others of you might be acquainted with: it is, what one might call, the experience of feeling *absolutely* safe. I mean the state of mind in which one is inclined to say "I am safe, nothing can injure me whatever happens." Now let me consider these experiences, for, I believe, they exhibit the very characteristics we try to get clear about. And there the first thing I have to say is, that the verbal expression which we give to these experiences is nonsense! If I say "I wonder at the existence of the world" I am misusing language. Let me explain this: It has a perfectly good and clear sense to say that I wonder at something being the case, we all understand what it means to say that I wonder at the size of a dog which is bigger than anyone I have ever seen before or at any thing which, in the common sense of the word, is extraordinary. In every such case I wonder at something being the case which I *could* conceive *not* to be the case. I wonder at the size of this dog because I could conceive of a dog of another, namely the ordinary size, at which I should not wonder. To say "I wonder at such and such being the case" has only sense if I can imagine it not to be the ⟦9⟧ case. In this sense one can wonder at the existence of, say, a house when one sees it and has not visited it for a long time and has imagined that it had been pulled down in the meantime. But it is nonsense to say that I wonder at the existence of the world, because I cannot imagine it not existing. I could of course wonder at the world round me being as it is. If for instance I had this experience while looking into the blue sky, I could wonder at the sky being blue as opposed to the case when it's clouded. But that's not what I mean. I am wondering at the sky being *whatever it is*. One might be tempted to say that what I am wondering at is a tautology, namely at the sky being blue or not blue. But then it's just nonsense to say that one is wondering at a tautology. Now the same applies to the other experience[s] which I have mentioned, the experience of absolute safety. We all know what it means in ordinary life to be safe. I am safe in my room, when I cannot be run over by an omnibus. I am safe if I have had whooping cough and cannot therefore get it again. To be safe essentially means that it is physically impossible that certain things should happen to me and therefore it's nonsense to say that I am safe *whatever* happens. Again this is a misuse of the word "safe" as the other example was of a misuse of the word "existence" or "wondering." Now I want to impress on you that a certain characteristic misuse of our language runs through *all* ethical and religious expressions. All these expressions *seem*, prima facie, to be just *similes*. Thus it seems that when we are using the word *right* in an ethical sense, although, what we mean, is not right in its trivial sense, it's something similar, and when we say "This is a good fellow," although the word good here doesn't mean what it means in the sentence "This is a good football player" there seems to be some similarity. And when we say "This man's life was valuable" we don't mean it in the same sense in which we would speak of some valuable jewelry but there seems to be some sort of analogy. Now all religious terms seem in this sense to be used as similes or allegorically. For when we speak of God and that he sees everything and when we kneel and pray to him all our terms and actions seem to be parts of a great and elaborate allegory which represents him as a human being of great power whose grace we try to win, etc., etc. But this allegory also describes the experience[s] which I ⟦10⟧ have just referred to. For the first of them is, I believe, exactly what people were referring to when they said that God had created the world; and the experience of absolute safety has been described by saying that we feel safe in the hands of God. A third experience of the same kind is that of feeling guilty and again this was described by the phrase that God disapproves of our conduct. Thus in ethical and religious language we seem constantly to be using similes. But a simile must be the simile for *something*. And if I can describe a fact by means of a simile I must also be able to drop the simile and to describe the facts without it. Now in our case as soon as we try to drop the simile and simply to state the facts which stand behind it, we find that there are no such facts. And so, what at first appeared to be a simile now seems to be mere nonsense. Now the three experiences which I have mentioned to you (and I could have added others) seem to those who have experienced them, for instance to me, to have in some sense an intrinsic, absolute value. But when I say they are experiences, surely, they are facts; they have taken place then and there, lasted a certain definite time and consequently are describable. And so from what I have said some minutes ago I must admit it is nonsense to say that they have absolute value. And I will make my point still more acute by saying "It is the paradox that an experience, a fact, should seem to have supernatural value." Now there is a way in which I would be tempted to meet this paradox. Let me first consider, again, our first experience of wondering at the existence of the world and let me describe it in a slightly different way; we all know what in ordinary life would be called a miracle. It obviously is simply an event the like of which we have never yet seen. Now suppose such an event happened. Take the case that one of you suddenly grew a lion's head and began to roar. Certainly that would be as extraordinary a thing as I can imagine. Now whenever we should have recovered from our surprise, what I would suggest would be to fetch a doctor and have the case scientifically investigated and if it were not for hurting him I would have him vivisected. And where would the miracle have got to? For it is clear that when we look at it in this way everything miraculous has disappeared; unless what we mean by this term is merely that a fact has not yet been explained by ⟦11⟧ science which again means that we have hitherto failed to group this fact with others in a scientific system. This shows that it is absurd to say "Science has proved that there are no miracles." The truth is that the scientific way of looking at a fact is not the way to look at it as a miracle. For imagine whatever fact you may, it is not in itself miraculous in the absolute sense of that term. For we see now that we have been using the word "miracle" in a relative and an absolute sense. And I will now describe the experience of wondering at the existence of the world by saying: it is the experience of seeing the world as a miracle. Now I am tempted to say that the right expression in language for the miracle of the existence of the world, though it is not any proposition *in* language, is the existence of language itself. But what then does it mean to be aware of this miracle at some times and not at other times? For all I have said by shifting the expression of the miraculous from an expression *by means of* language to the expression *by the existence* of language, all I have said is again that we cannot express what we want to express and that all we *say* about the absolute miraculous remains nonsense. Now the answer to all this will seem perfectly clear to many of you. You will say: Well, if certain experiences constantly tempt us to attribute a quality to them which we call absolute or ethical value and importance, this simply shows that by these words we *don't* mean nonsense, that after all what we mean by saying that an experience has absolute value *is just a fact like other facts* and that all it comes to is that we have not yet succeeded in finding the correct logical analysis of what we mean by our ethical and religious expressions. Now when this is urged against me I at once see clearly, as it were in a flash of light, not only that no description that I can think of would do to describe what I mean by absolute value, but that I would reject every significant description that anybody could possibly suggest, *ab initio,* on the ground of its significance. That is to say: I see now that these nonsensical expressions were not nonsensical because I had not yet found the correct expressions, but that their nonsensicality was their very essence. For all I wanted to do with them was just *to go beyond* the world and that is to say beyond significant language. My whole tendency and I believe the tendency of all men who ever tried ⟦12⟧ to write or talk Ethics or Religion was to run against the boundaries of language. This running against the walls of our cage is perfectly, absolutely hopeless. Ethics so far as it springs from the desire to say something about the ultimate meaning of life, the absolute good, the absolute valuable, can be no science. What it says does not add to our knowledge in any sense. But it is a document of a tendency in the human mind which I personally cannot help respecting deeply and I would not for my life ridicule it.

LUDWIG WITTGENSTEIN

# 6

*In 1911 G. E. Moore was appointed University Lecturer in Moral Sciences at Cambridge, and Wittgenstein attended some of his lectures on psychology in 1912. Moore developed such a high opinion of Wittgenstein's abilities in the following years that in April of 1914, in response to Wittgenstein's requests, he travelled to Norway, where Wittgenstein was then living, to have Wittgenstein explain his latest ideas.*[1]

*Moore became Professor of Philosophy at Cambridge in 1925, and upon his retirement from that position in 1939, Wittgenstein assumed the Professorship.*

*Lecture notes by students and friends are an inherently problematic source of information about Wittgenstein's views. Note-takers have invariably commented on their own difficulty in understanding Wittgenstein's ideas, and hence their own uncertainty about having reported them accurately. It is helpful, therefore, when notes from different people can be consulted. The interested reader can compare these notes with those taken by John King and Desmond Lee in 1930–1932 and those taken by Alice Ambrose in 1932–1933.*[2]

*In his lectures Wittgenstein used the logical notation of* Principia Mathematica,[3] *and Moore presumed its familiarity to his readers. In this notation,* 'p ⊃ q' *means* 'if p is true then q is true', 'p . q' *means* 'both p and q are true', 'p v q' *means* 'either p or q or perhaps both are true', '~p' *means* 'p is false', 'fa' *means* 'the thing named by "a" has the property of being f', '(x) . fx' *means* 'all things have the property of being f', and '(∃x) . fx' *means* 'there is at least one thing that has the property of being f'. *Wittgenstein uses* 'p = q' *to mean* 'p and q are either both true or both false' *although that is not how it is used in* Principia.

1. That the enthusiasm for this visit came mainly from Wittgenstein rather than Moore can be gauged by Wittgenstein's letters M.2–M.7 to Moore in *Letters to Russell, Keynes and Moore,* pp. 145–49. Wittgenstein's philosophical ideas at this time are preserved in "Notes Dictated to G. E. Moore in Norway," Appendix II of *Notebooks: 1914–1916,* 2nd edition, Chicago: University of Chicago Press, and Oxford: Basil Blackwell, 1979, pp. 108–19.

2. See *Wittgenstein's Lectures: Cambridge, 1930–1932,* ed. D. Lee; and Part I of *Wittgenstein's Lectures: Cambridge, 1932–1935,* ed. A. Ambrose, Totowa, N.J.: Rowman and Littlefield, and Oxford: Basil Blackwell, 1979.

3. By A. N. Whitehead and B. Russell, published in three volumes by Cambridge University Press, 1st edition 1910, 2nd edition 1927. See especially pp. 4–17 of Chapter I of the Introduction to vol. I.

# Wittgenstein's Lectures in 1930–33

*By* G. E. MOORE

In January, 1929, Wittgenstein returned to Cambridge after an absence of more than fifteen years. He came with the intention of residing in Cambridge and pursuing there his researches into philosophical problems. Why he chose Cambridge for this latter purpose I do not know: perhaps it was for the sake of having the opportunity of frequent discussion with F. P. Ramsey. At all events he did in fact reside in Cambridge during all three Full Terms of 1929, and was working hard all the time at his researches.[1] He must, however, at some time during that year, have made up his mind that, besides researching, he would like to do a certain amount of lecturing, since on 16th October, in accordance with his wishes, the Faculty Board of Moral Science resolved that he should be invited to give a course of lectures to be included in their Lecture List for the Lent Term of 1930.

During this year, 1929, when he was researching and had not begun to lecture, he took the Ph.D. degree at Cambridge. Having been entered as an "Advanced Student" during his previous period of residence in 1912 and 1913, he now found that he was entitled to submit a dissertation for the Ph.D. He submitted the *Tractatus* and Russell and I were appointed to examine him. ⟦2⟧ We gave him an oral examination on 6th June, an occasion which I found both pleasant and amusing. We had, of course, no doubt whatever that his work deserved the degree: we so reported, and when our report had been approved by the necessary authorities, he received the degree in due course.

In the same month of June in which we examined him, the Council

1. The statement in the Obituary notice in *The Times* for 2nd May, 1951, that he arrived in Cambridge in 1929 "for a short visit" is very far from the truth. Fortunately I kept a brief diary during the period in question and can therefore vouch for the truth of what I have stated above about his residence in 1929, though there is in fact other evidence.

of Trinity College made him a grant to enable him to continue his researches. (They followed this up in December, 1930, by electing him to a Research Fellowship, tenable for five years, which they afterwards prolonged for a time.)

In the following July of 1929 he attended the Joint Session of the Mind Association and Aristotelian Society at Nottingham, presenting a short paper entitled "Some Remarks on Logical Form". This paper was the only piece of philosophical writing by him, other than the *Tractatus,* published during his life-time. Of this paper he spoke in a letter to MIND (July, 1933) as "weak"; and since 1945 he has spoken of it to me in a still more disparaging manner, saying something to the effect that, when he wrote it, he was getting new ideas about which he was still confused, and that he did not think it deserved any attention.

But what is most important about this year, 1929, is that in it he had frequent discussions with F. P. Ramsey—discussions which were, alas! brought to an end by Ramsey's premature death in January, 1930.[2] Ramsey had written for MIND (October 1923, p. 465) a long Critical Notice of the *Tractatus;* and subsequently, during the period when Wittgenstein was employed as a village-schoolmaster in Austria, Ramsey had gone out to see him, in order to question him as to the meaning of certain statements in the *Tractatus.* He stayed in the village for a fortnight or more, having daily discussions with Wittgenstein. Of these ⟦3⟧ discussions in Austria I only know that Ramsey told me that, in reply to his questions as to the meaning of certain

2. In the Preface to his posthumously published *Philosophical Investigations,* where Wittgenstein acknowledges his obligations to Ramsey (p. x), Wittgenstein himself says that he had "innumerable" discussions with Ramsey "during the last two years of his life", which should mean both in 1928 and in 1929. But I think this must be a mistake. I imagine that Wittgenstein, trusting to memory alone, had magnified into a series of discussions continuing for two years, a series which in fact only continued for a single year. It will be noticed that in the letter from Ramsey himself which I am about to quote, and which is dated 14th June, 1929, Ramsey states that he had been in close touch with Wittgenstein's work "during the last two terms", *i.e.* during the Lent and May terms of 1929, implying that he had not been in close touch with it in 1928. And though I do not know where Wittgenstein was in 1928, he certainly was not resident in Cambridge where Ramsey was resident, so that it is hardly possible that they can have had in that year such frequent discussions as they certainly had in 1929. [In 1928 Wittgenstein was in Vienna completing a house for his sister Gretl that he had designed with his friend Paul Engelmann. (eds.)]

statements, Wittgenstein answered more than once that he had forgotten what he had meant by the statement in question. But after the first half of the discussions at Cambridge in 1929, Ramsey wrote at my request the following letter in support of the proposal that Trinity should make Wittgenstein a grant in order to enable him to continue his researches.

"In my opinion Mr. Wittgenstein is a philosophic genius of a different order from any one else I know. This is partly owing to his great gift for seeing what is essential in a problem and partly to his overwhelming intellectual vigour, to the intensity of thought with which he pursues a question to the bottom and never rests content with a mere possible hypothesis. From his work more than that of any other man I hope for a solution of the difficulties that perplex me both in philosophy generally and in the foundations of Mathematics in particular.

"It seems to me, therefore, peculiarly fortunate that he should have returned to research. During the last two terms I have been in close touch with his work and he seems to me to have made remarkable progress. He began with certain questions in the analysis of propositions which have now led him to problems about infinity which lie at the root of current controversies on the foundations of Mathematics. At first I was afraid that lack of mathematical knowledge and facility would prove a serious handicap to his working in this field. But the progress he has made has already convinced me that this is not so, and that here too he will probably do work of the first importance.

"He is now working very hard and, so far as I can judge, he is getting on well. For him to be interrupted by lack of money would, I think, be a great misfortune for philosophy."

The only other thing I know about these discussions with Ramsey at Cambridge in 1929 is that Wittgenstein once told me that Ramsey had said to him "I don't like your method of arguing".

Wittgenstein began to lecture in January, 1930, and from the first he adopted a plan to which he adhered, I believe, throughout his lectures at Cambridge.[3] His plan was only to lecture once a week in

3. Professor von Wright has subsequently informed me that I was mistaken in believing this: that in 1939, Wittgenstein lectured twice a week and held no discussion class; and that in the Easter Term of 1947, he both gave two lectures a week and also held a discussion class. I have also remembered that at one time (I do not know for how long) he gave, besides his ordinary lectures, a special set of lectures for mathematicians. [This was in 1932–33. See Part IV of *Wittgenstein's Lectures: Cambridge, 1932–1935*, ed. A. Am-

every week of Full Term, but on a later day in each week to hold a discussion class at which what he had said in that week's lecture could be discussed. At first both lecture and discussion class were held in an ordinary lecture-room in the University Arts School; but very early in the first term Mr. R. E. Priestley (now Sir Raymond Priestley), who was then ⟦4⟧ Secretary General of the Faculties and who occupied a set of Fellows' rooms in the new building of Clare, invited Wittgenstein to hold his discussion classes in these rooms. Later on, I think, both lectures and discussion classes were held in Priestley's rooms, and this continued until, in October, 1931, Wittgenstein, being then a Fellow of Trinity, was able to obtain a set of rooms of his own in Trinity which he really liked. These rooms were those which Wittgenstein had occupied in the academic year 1912–13, and which I had occupied the year before, and occupied again from October, 1913, when Wittgenstein left Cambridge and went to Norway. Of the only two sets which are on the top floor of the gate-way from Whewell's Courts into Sidney Street, they were the set which looks westward over the larger Whewell's Court, and, being so high up, they had a large view of sky and also of Cambridge roofs, including the pinnacles of King's Chapel. Since the rooms were not a Fellow's set, their sitting-room was not large, and for the purpose of his lectures and classes Wittgenstein used to fill it with some twenty plain cane-bottomed chairs, which at other times were stacked on the large landing outside. Nearly from the beginning the discussion classes were liable to last at least two hours, and from the time when the lectures ceased to be given in the Arts School they also commonly lasted at least as long. Wittgenstein always had a blackboard at both lectures and classes and made plenty of use of it.

I attended both lectures and discussion classes in all three terms of 1930 and in the first two terms of 1931. In the Michaelmas term of 1931 and the Lent term of 1932 I ceased, for some reason which I cannot now remember, to attend the lectures[4] though I still went to the discussion classes; but in May 1932, I resumed the practice of attending the lectures as well, and throughout the academic year 1932–33 I attended both. At the lectures, though not at the discussion classes, I took what I think were very full notes, scribbled in

---

brose. (eds.)]

4. In fact Wittgenstein did not hold lectures during those terms. See his letter of 23.8.31 to Moore (M.17) in *Letters to Russell, Keynes and Moore,* p. 159. (eds.)

note-books of which I have six volumes nearly full. I remember Wittgenstein once saying to me that he was glad I was taking notes, since, if anything were to happen to him, they would contain some record of the results of his thinking.

My lecture-notes may be naturally divided into three groups, to which I will refer as (I), (II) and (III). (I) contains the notes of his lectures in the Lent and May terms of 1930; (II) those of his lectures in the academic year 1930–31; and (III) those of lectures which he gave in the May term of 1932, after I had resumed attending, as well as those of all the lectures he gave in the academic year 1932–33. The distinction between the three ⟦5⟧ groups is of some importance, since, as will be seen, he sometimes in later lectures corrected what he had said in earlier ones.

The chief topics with which he dealt fall, I think, under the following heads. First of all, in all three periods he dealt (A) with some very general questions about language, (B) with some special questions in the philosophy of Logic, and (C) with some special questions in the philosophy of Mathematics. Next, in (III) and in (III) alone, he dealt at great length, (D) with the difference between the proposition which is expressed by the words "I have got toothache", and those which are expressed by the words "You have got toothache" or "He has got toothache", in which connexion he said something about Behaviorism, Solipsism, Idealism and Realism, and (E) with what he called "the grammar of the word 'God' and of ethical and aesthetic statements". And he also dealt, more shortly, in (I) with (F) our use of the term "primary colour"; in (III) with (G) some questions about Time; and in both (II) and (III) with (H) the kind of investigation in which he was himself engaged, and its difference from and relation to what has traditionally been called "philosophy".

I will try to give some account of the chief things he said under all these heads; but I cannot possibly mention nearly everything, and it is possible that some of the things I omit were really more important than those I mention. Also, though I tried to get down in my notes the actual words he used, it is possible that I may sometimes have substituted words of my own which misrepresent his meaning: I certainly did not understand a good many of the things he said. Moreover, I cannot possibly do justice to the extreme richness of illustration and comparison which he used: he was really succeeding in giving what he called a "synoptic" view of things which we all know. Nor can I do justice to the intensity of conviction with which he said everything which he did say, nor to the extreme interest which he excited in his hearers. He, of course, never read his lectures: he had not, in fact, written them out, although he always spent a great deal of time in thinking out what he proposed to say.

(A) He did discuss at very great length, especially in (II), certain very general questions about language; but he said, more than once, that he did not discuss these questions because he thought that language was the subject-matter of philosophy. He did not think that it was. He discussed it only because he thought that particular philosophical errors or "troubles in our thought" were due to false analogies suggested by our actual use of expressions; and he emphasized that it was only necessary ⟦6⟧ for him to discuss those points about language which, as he thought, led to these particular errors or "troubles".

The general things that he had to say about language fall naturally, I think, under two heads, namely (*a*) what he had to say about the meaning of single words, and (*b*) what he had to say about "propositions".

(*a*) About the meaning of single words, the positive points on which he seemed most anxious to insist were, I think, two, namely ($\alpha$) something which he expressed by saying that the meaning of any single word in a language is "defined", "constituted", "determined" or "fixed" (he used all four expressions in different places) by the "grammatical rules" with which it is used in that language, and ($\beta$) something which he expressed by saying that every significant word or symbol must essentially belong to a "system", and (metaphorically) by saying that the meaning of a word is its "place" in a "grammatical system".

But he said in (III) that the sense of "meaning" of which he held these things to be true, and which was the only sense in which he intended to use the word, was only one of those in which we commonly use it: that there was another which he described as that in which it is used "as a name for a process accompanying our use of a word and our hearing of a word". By the latter he apparently meant that sense of "meaning" in which "to know the meaning" of a word means the same as to "understand" the word; and I think he was not quite clear as to the relation between this sense of "meaning" and that in which he intended to use it, since he seemed in two different places to suggest two different and incompatible views of this relation, saying in (II) that "the rules applying to negation actually describe my experience in using 'not', *i.e.* describe my understanding of the word", and in one place in (III), on the other hand, saying, "perhaps there is a causal connection between the rules and the feeling we have when we hear 'not'". On the former occasion he added that "a logical investigation doesn't teach us anything about the meaning of negation: we can't get any clearer about its meaning. What's difficult is to make the rules explicit".

Still later in (III) he made the rather queer statement that "the idea of meaning is in a way obsolete, except in such phrases as 'this means the same as that' or 'this has no meaning'", having previously said in (III) that "the mere fact that we have the expression 'the meaning' of a word is bound to lead us wrong: we are led to think that the rules are responsible to something not a rule, whereas they are only responsible to rules".

As to ($\alpha$) although he had said, at least once, that the meaning ⟦7⟧ of a word was "constituted" by the grammatical rules which applied to it, he explained later that he did not mean that the meaning of a word *was* a list of rules; and he said that though a word "carried its meaning with it", it did not carry with it the grammatical rules which applied to it. He said that the student who had asked him whether he meant that the meaning of a word *was* a list of rules would not have been tempted to ask that question but for the false idea (which he held to be a common one) that in the case of a substantive like "the meaning" you have to look for something at which you can point and say "This is the meaning". He seemed to think that Frege and Russell had been misled by the same idea, when they thought they were bound to give an answer to the question "What *is* the number 2?" As for what he meant by saying that the meaning of a word is "determined by" (this was the phrase which he seemed to prefer) the "grammatical rules" in accordance with which it is used, I do not think he explained further what he meant by this phrase.

($\beta$) As to what he meant by saying that, in order that a word or other sign should have meaning, it must belong to a "system", I have not been able to arrive at any clear idea. One point on which he insisted several times in (II) was that if a word which I use is to have meaning, I must "commit myself" by its use. And he explained what he meant by this by saying "If I commit myself, that means that if I use, *e.g.* 'green' in this case, I have to use it in others", adding "If you commit yourself, there are consequences". Similarly he said a little later, "If a word is to have significance, we must commit ourselves", adding "There is no use in correlating noises to facts, unless we commit ourselves to using the noise in a particular way again—unless the correlation has consequences", and going on to say that it must be possible to be "led by a language". And when he expressly raised, a little later, the question "What is there in this talk of a 'system' to which a symbol must belong?" he answered that we are concerned with the phenomenon of "being guided by". It looked, therefore, as if one use which he was making of the word "system" was such that in order to say that a word or other sign "belonged to a system", it was not only necessary but *sufficient* that it should be used in the same way on several different occasions. And certainly it would be natural to say that a man who habitually used a word in the same way was using it "systematically".

But he certainly also frequently used "system" in such a sense that *different* words or other expressions could be said to belong to the *same* "system"; and where, later on, he gave, as ⟦8⟧ an illustration of what he meant by "Every symbol must essentially belong to a system", the proposition "A crotchet can only give information on what note to play in a system of crotchets", he seemed to imply that for a sign to have significance it is *not* sufficient that we should "commit ourselves" by its use, but that it is also necessary that the sign in question should belong to the same "system" with other signs. Perhaps, however, he only meant, not that for a sign to have *some* meaning, but that for *some* signs to have *the significance which they actually have in a given language,* it is necessary that they should belong to the same "system" with other signs. This word "system" was one which he used very very frequently, and I do not know what conditions he would have held must be satisfied by two different signs in order that they may properly be said to belong to the same "system". He said in one place in (II) that the "system of projection" by which "2 + 3" can be projected into "5" is "in no way inferior" to the "system" by which "II + III" can be projected into "IIIII", and I think one can see, in this case, that "2 + 3 = 5" can be properly said to belong to the same "system" as, *e.g.* "2 + 2 = 4", and also can properly be said to belong to a different "system" from that to which "II + III = IIIII" and "II + II = IIII" both belong, though I have no clear idea as to the sense in which these things can properly be said. Nor do I know whether Wittgenstein would have held, *e.g.* that in the case of *every* English word, it could not have the significance which it actually has in English unless it belonged to the same "system" as other English words, or whether he would have held that this is only true of *some* English words, *e.g.* of the words "five" and "four", and of the words "red" and "green".

But besides these two positive things, ($\alpha$) and ($\beta$), which he seemed anxious to say about the meaning of words, he also insisted on three negative things, *i.e.* that three views which have sometimes been held are mistakes. The first of these mistakes was (γ) the view that the meaning of a word was some image which it calls up by association—a view to which he seemed to refer as the "causal" theory of meaning. He admitted that sometimes you cannot understand a word unless it calls up an image, but insisted that, even where this is the case, the image is just as much a "symbol" as the word is. The second mistake was (δ) the view that, where we can give an "ostensive" definition of a word, the object pointed at is the meaning of the word. Against this view, he said, for one thing, that, in such a case "the gesture of pointing together with the object pointed at can be ⟦9⟧ used *instead* of the word", *i.e.* is itself something which has meaning and has the same meaning as the word has. In this connexion he also pointed out that you may point at a red book, either to show the meaning of "book" or to show the meaning of "red", and that hence in "This is a book" and "This is the colour 'red'", "this" has quite a different meaning; and he emphasized that, in order to understand the ostensive definition "This is 'red'", the hearer must already understand what is meant by "colour". And the third mistake was (ϵ) that a word is related to its meaning in the same way in which a proper name is related to the "bearer" of that name. He gave as a reason for holding that this is false that the bearer of a name can be ill or dead, whereas we cannot possibly say that the meaning of the name is ill or dead. He said more than once that the bearer of a name can be "substituted" for the name, whereas the meaning of a word can never be substituted for that word. He sometimes spoke of this third mistake as the view that words are "representative" of their meanings, and he held that in no case is a word "representative" of its meaning, although a proper name is "representative" of its bearer (if it has one). He added in one place: "The meaning of a word is no longer for us an object corresponding to it."

On the statement "Words, except in propositions, have no meaning" he said that this "is true or false, as you understand it"; and immediately went on to add that, in what he called "language games", single words "have meanings by themselves", and that they may have meaning by themselves even in our ordinary language "if we have provided one". In this connexion he said, in (II), that he had made a mistake (I think he meant in the *Tractatus*) in supposing that a proposition must be complex. He said the truth was that we can replace a proposition by a simple sign, but that the simple sign must be "part of a system".

(*b*) About "propositions", he said a great deal in many places as to answers which might be given to the question "What is a proposition?"—a question which he said we do not understand clearly. But towards the end of (III) he had definitely reached the conclusion "It is more or less arbitrary what we call a 'proposition'", adding that "therefore Logic plays a part different from what I and Russell and Frege supposed it to play"; and a little later he said that he could not give a general definition of "proposition" any more than of "game": that he could only give examples, and that any line he could draw would be "arbitrary, in the sense that nobody would have ⟦10⟧ decided whether to call so and so a 'proposition' or not". But he added that we are quite right to use the word "game", so long as we don't pretend to have drawn a definite outline.

In (II), however, he had said that the word "proposition", "as generally understood", includes both "what I call propositions", also "hypotheses", and also mathematical propositions; that the distinction between these three "kinds" is a "logical distinction", and that therefore there must be some grammatical rules, in the case of each kind, which apply to that kind and not to the other two; but that the "truth-function" rules apply to all three, and that that is why they are all called "propositions".

He went on to illustrate the difference between the first two kinds by saying that "There seems to me to be a man here" is of the first kind, whereas "There is a man here" is a "hypothesis"; and said that one rule which applies to the first and not to the second is that I can't say "There seems to me to seem to me to be a man here" whereas I can say "There seems to me to be a man here". But, soon after, he said that the word "proposition" is used in *two* different ways, a wider and a narrower, meaning by the wider that in which it included all three of the kinds just distinguished, and by the narrower, apparently, that in which it included the first two kinds, but not the third. For propositions in this narrower sense he seemed later very often to use the expression "experiential propositions", and accordingly I will use this expression to include propositions of both the first two kinds. The things which he had to say about experiential propositions, thus understood, were extremely different from those which he had to say about the third kind; and I will therefore treat these two subjects separately.

($\alpha$) Of experiential propositions he said in (I) that they could be "compared with reality" and either "agreed or disagreed with it". He pointed out very early something which he expressed by saying "Much of language needs outside help", giving as an example your use of a specimen of a colour in order to explain what colour you want a wall painted; but he immediately went on to say (using "language" in a different sense) that in such a case the specimen of a colour is "a part of your language". He also pointed out (as in the *Tractatus*) that you can assert a proposition or give an order without using any words or symbols (in the ordinary sense of "symbol"). One of the most striking things about his use of the term "proposition" was that he apparently so used it that in giving an order you are necessarily expressing a "proposition", although, of course, an order can ⟦11⟧ be neither true nor false, and can be "compared with reality" only in the different sense that you can look to see whether it is carried out or not.

About propositions, understood in this sense, he made a distinction in (II) between what he called "the sign" and what he called "the symbol", saying that whatever was necessary to give a "sign" significance was a part of "the symbol", so that where, for instance, the "sign" is a sentence, the "symbol" is something which contains both the sign and also everything which is necessary to give that sentence sense. He said that a "symbol", thus understood, *is* a "proposition" and "cannot be nonsensical, though it can be either true or false". He illustrated this by saying that if a man says "I am tired" his mouth is part of the symbol; and said that any explanation of a sign "completes the symbol".

Here, therefore, he seemed to be making a distinction between a proposition and a sentence, such that no sentence can be identical with any proposition, and that no proposition can be without sense. But I do not think that in his actual use of the term "proposition" he adhered to this distinction. He seemed to me sometimes so to use "proposition" that every significant sentence *was* a proposition, although, of course, a significant sentence does not contain everything which is necessary to give it significance. He said, for instance, that signs with different meanings must *be* different "symbols". And very often he seemed to me to follow the example of Russell in the Introduction to *Principia Mathematica* in so using the word "proposition" that "propositions", and not merely sentences, could be without sense; as, for instance, when he said at the beginning of (II) that his object was to give us some "firm ground" such as "If a proposition has a meaning, its negation must have a meaning". And, towards the end of (III), in connexion with the view at which he had then arrived that the words "proposition", "language" and "sentence" are all "vague", he expressly said that the answer to the question whether, when you say "A unicorn looks like this" and point at a picture of a unicorn, the picture is or is not a part of the proposition you are making, was "You can say which you please". He was, therefore, now rejecting his earlier view that a proposition must contain everything which is necessary to make a sentence significant, and seemed to be implying that the use of "proposition" to mean the same as "sentence" was a perfectly correct one.

In connexion with the *Tractatus* statement that propositions, in the "narrower" sense with which we are now concerned, are ⟦12⟧ "pictures", he said he had not at that time noticed that the word "picture" was vague; but he still, even towards the end of (III), said that he thought it "useful to say 'A proposition is a picture *or something like one*'" although in (II) he had said he was willing to admit that to call a proposition a "picture" was misleading; that propositions are not pictures "in any ordinary sense"; and that to say that they are, "merely stresses a certain aspect of the grammar of the word 'proposition'—merely stresses that our uses of the words 'proposition' and 'picture' follow similar rules".

In connexion with this question of the similarity between experiential "propositions" and pictures, he frequently used the words "project" and "projection". Having pointed out that it is paradoxical to say that the words "Leave the room" is a "picture" of what a boy does if he obeys the order, and having asserted that it is, in fact, *not* a "picture" of the boy's action "in any ordinary sense", he nevertheless went on to say that it is "as much" a picture of the boy's action as "2 + 3" is of "5", and that "2 + 3" really is a picture of "5" "*with reference to a particular system of projection*", and that this system is "in no way inferior" to the system in which "II + III" is projected into "IIIII", only that "the method of projection is rather queer". He had said previously that the musical signs "♯" and "♭" are obviously not pictures of anything you do on the keyboard of a piano; that they differ in this respect from what, *e.g.* "" would be, if you had the rule that the second crotchet is to stand for the white key on the piano that is to the right of that for which the first crotchet stands, and similarly for the third and second crotchet; but nevertheless, he said, "♯" and "♭" "work in exactly the same way" as these crotchets would work, and added that "almost all our words work as they do". He explained this by saying that a "picture" must have been given by an explanation of how "♯" and "♭" are used, and that an explanation is always of the same kind as a definition, *viz.* "replacing one symbol by another". He went on to say that when a man reads on a piano from a score, he is "led" or "guided" by the position of the crotchets, and that this means that he is "following a general rule", and that this rule, though not "contained" in the score, nor in the result, nor in both together, must be "contained" in his intention. But he said, that though the rule is "contained" in the intention, the intention obviously does not "contain" any *expression* of the rule, any more than, when I read aloud, I am ⟦13⟧ conscious of the rules I follow in translating the printed signs into sounds. He said that what the piano-player does is "to see the rule in the score", and that, even if he is playing automatically, he is still "guided by" the score, provided that he *would* use the general rule to judge whether he had made a mistake or not. He even said in one place that to say that a man is "guided" by the score "means" that he *would justify* what he played by reference to the score. He concluded by saying that, if he plays correctly, there is *a* "similarity" between what he does on the piano and the score, "though we usually confine 'similarity' to projection according to certain rules only"; and that in the same sense there is *a* "similarity" between automatic traffic-signals and the movements of traffic which are guided by them. Later on he said that for any sign whatever there *could* be a method of projection such that it made sense, but that when he said of any particular expression "That means nothing" or "is nonsense", what he meant was "*With the common method of projection* that means nothing", giving as an instance that when he called the sentence "It is due to human weakness that we can't write down all the cardinal numbers" "meaningless", he meant that it is meaningless if the person who says it is using "due to human weakness" as in "It's due to human weakness that we can't write down a billion cardinal numbers". Similarly, he said that surely Helmholtz must have been talking nonsense when he said that in happy moments he could imagine four-dimensional space, because *in the system he was using* those words make no sense, although "I threw the chalk into four-dimentional space" would make sense, if we were not using the words on the analogy of throwing from one room into another, but merely meant "It first disappeared and then appeared again". He insisted more than once that we are apt to think that we are using a new system of projection which would give sense to our words, when in fact we are not using a new system at all: "any expression" he said "*may* make sense, but you may think you are using it with sense, when in fact you are not".

One chief view about propositions to which he was opposed was a view which he expressed as the view that a proposition is a sort of "shadow" intermediate between the expression which we use in order to assert it and the fact (if any) which "verifies" it. He attributed this view to W. E. Johnson, and he said of it that it was an attempt to make a distinction between a proposition and a sentence. (We have seen that he himself had in (II) made a different attempt to do this.) He said that it regarded the supposed "shadow" as something "similar" to the fact ⟦14⟧ which verifies it, and in that way different from the expression which expresses it, which is not "similar" to the fact in question; and he said that, even if there were such a "shadow" it would not "bring us any nearer to the fact", since "it would be susceptible of different interpretations just as the expression is". He said, "You can't give any picture which can't be misinterpreted" and "No interpolation between a sign and its fulfilment does away with a sign". He added that the only description of an expectation "which is relevant for us" is "the expression of it", and that "the expression of an expectation contains a description of the fact that would fulfil it", pointing out that if I expect to *see a red patch* my expectation is fulfilled if and only if I do *see a red patch,* and saying that the words "see a red patch" have the same meaning in both expressions.

Near the beginning of (I) he made the famous statement, "The sense of a proposition is the way in which it is verified"; but in (III) he said this only meant "You can determine the meaning of a proposition by asking how it is verified" and went on to say, "This is necessarily a mere rule of thumb, because 'verification' means different things, and because in some cases the question 'How is that verified?' makes no sense". He gave as an example of a case in which that question "makes no sense" the proposition "I've got toothache", of which he had already said that it makes no sense to ask for a verification of it—to ask "How do you know that you have?" I think that he here meant what he said of "I've got toothache" to apply to all those propositions which he had originally distinguished from "hypotheses" as "what I call propositions"; although in (II) he had distinguished the latter from "hypotheses" by saying that they had "a definite verification or falsification". It would seem, therefore, that in (III) he had arrived at the conclusion that what he had said in (II) was wrong, and that in the case of "what he called propositions", so far from their having "a definite verification", it was senseless to say that they had a verification at all. His "rule of thumb", therefore, could only apply, if at all, to what he called "hypotheses"; and he went on to say that, in many cases, it does not apply even to these, saying that statements in the newspapers could verify the "hypothesis" that Cambridge had won the boat race, and that yet these statements "only go a very little way towards explaining the meaning of 'boat-race'"; and that similarly "The pavement is wet" may verify the proposition "It has been raining", and that yet "it gives very little of the grammar of 'It has been raining'". He went on to say "Verification determines the meaning of a proposition ⟦15⟧ only where it gives the grammar of the proposition in question"; and in answer to the question "How far is giving a verification of a proposition a grammatical statement about it?" he said that, whereas "When it rains the pavement gets wet" is not a grammatical statement at all, if we say "The fact that the pavement is wet is a *symptom* that it has been raining" this statement is "a matter of grammar".

⟦II/289⟧ ($\beta$) The third kind of "proposition" mentioned in Part I (p. 55), of which at the very beginning of (I) Wittgenstein gave mathematical propositions as an example, saying that they are a "very different sort of instrument" from, *e.g.* "There is a piece of chalk here", and of which he sometimes said that they are not propositions at all, were those which have been traditionally called "necessary", as opposed to "contingent". They are propositions of which the negation would be said to be, not merely false, but "impossible", "unimaginable", "unthinkable" (expressions which he himself often used in speaking of them). They include not only the propositions of pure Mathematics, but also those of Deductive Logic, certain propositions which would usually be said to be propositions about colours, and an immense number of others.

Of these propositions he undoubtedly held that, unlike "experiential" propositions, they cannot be "compared with reality", and do not "either agree or disagree" with it. But I think the most important thing he said about them, and certainly one of the most important things he said anywhere in these lectures, was an attempt to explain exactly how they differed from experiential propositions. And this attempt, so far as I can see, consisted in maintaining with regard to them two things, *viz.* ($\beta'$) that the sentences, which would commonly be said to express them, do in fact, when used in this way, "say nothing" or "are without sense", and ($\beta''$) that this supposed fact that ⟦290⟧ such sentences, when so used, are without sense, is due to the fact that they are related in a certain way to "rules of grammar". But *what,* precisely, was the relation to grammatical rules, which he held to be the reason why they had no sense? This question still puzzles me extremely.

For a time I thought (though I felt that this was doubtful) that he held so-called necessary propositions to be *identical* with certain grammatical rules—a view which would have yielded the conclusion that sentences, which would commonly be said to express necessary propositions, are in fact always merely expressing rules of grammar. And I think he did in fact hold that the very same expressions, which would commonly be said to express necessary propositions, can also be properly used in such a way that, when so used, they merely express rules of grammar. But I think he must have been aware (though I think he never expressly pointed this out) that, if so, then, *when* such expressions are being used merely to express rules of grammar they are being used in a very different way from that in which, on his view, they are being used when they would commonly be said to be expressing necessary propositions. For he certainly held, if I am not mistaken, of *all* expressions which would commonly be said to be expressing necessary propositions, what in the *Tractatus* he had asserted to be true of the particular case of "tautologies", *viz.* both (1) that, when so used, they are "without sense" and "say nothing", and (2) that, nevertheless, they are, in a certain sense "true", though he made plain, in these lectures, that he thought that the sense in which they are "true" was very different from that in which experiential propositions may be "true". (As I have said (p. 56), he seemed to me often to use the words "proposition" and "sentence" as if they meant the same, perhaps partly because the German word "Satz" may be properly used for either; and therefore often talked as if sentences could *be* "true".) But of the same expressions, when used, as he thought they might be, merely to express rules, though he might perhaps have said that they "say nothing", since he insisted strongly of one particular class of them, namely, those which express rules of deduction, that they are neither true nor false, he cannot, I think, have held that they are "without sense"; indeed he said, at least once, of an expression which would commonly be said to express a necessary proposition, "if it is to have any meaning, it must be a mere rule of a game"—thus implying that, if it is used to express a rule, it has a meaning. But in what sense was he using "rules", when he insisted that his own "rules of inference" were neither true ⟦291⟧ nor false? I think this is an important question, because he seems to me to have used the expression "rules of grammar" in two different senses, the difference between which he never expressly pointed out, and one of which is such that a grammatical rule, in that sense, will be true or false. He often spoke as if rules of grammar *allowed* you to use certain expressions and *forbade* you to use others, and he gave me the impression that, when so speaking, he was giving the name of "rules" to actual statements that you are allowed or forbidden to use certain expressions—that, for instance, he would have called the statement, "You can't say 'Two men *was* working in that field'" a rule of English grammar. This use of "can't" is, indeed, one which is quite natural and familiar in the case of rules of games, to which he constantly compared rules of grammar; *e.g.* a chessplayer might quite naturally say to an opponent, who was a beginner and was not yet familiar with the rules of chess, "You can't do that" or "You can't make that move", if the beginner moved a pawn, from its position at the beginning of the game, three squares forward instead of only two. But, if we so use "rule" that the expression "You can't do that", when thus used, is expressing a rule, then surely a rule *can* be true or false; for it is possible to be mistaken as to whether you can or can't make a certain move at chess, and "You can't do that" will be true, if it is an *established* rule in chess not to make the kind of move in question, and will be false if there is no such established rule. But if we ask: What is the rule which *is* established in such a case? we come upon a very different sense of "rule"; for the answer to this question will consist in describing or specifying a way in which somebody *might* act, whether anybody ever does so act or not; and with this sense of "rule" it seems to me obvious that a rule cannot be true or false, and equally obvious that any expression which specifies it will have sense. In the case of rules of grammar, the possible action which such a rule specifies, will, of course, be a way of using words or forms of sentence in speaking or writing; and I think that the fact that "rule" may be used in this sense, in which a "rule" can obviously be neither true nor false, may have been partly responsible for Wittgenstein's assertion that his "rules of inference" were neither true nor false. It is perhaps worth noting that the statement that such a rule is an *established* rule in a given language, (as is implied for English by, *e.g.*, the statement, "You can't say 'Two men *was* working in that field' "), which really is true or false, is, of course, an experiential proposition about the way in which words or forms of sentence are actually used in the ⟦292⟧ language in question; and that, therefore, if we suppose that the very same expression which is sometimes used to express a necessary proposition can also be used to express such an experiential proposition, then the ways in which it is used in these two cases must be very different; just as the ways in which the same expression is used, if used sometimes to express a necessary proposition and sometimes merely to specify a possible way of speaking or writing, must also be very different.

I think, therefore, that Wittgenstein cannot possibly have held that expressions which are being used in the way in which they would commonly be said to be expressing necessary propositions, are being used in the same way in which they are being used when used to express rules of grammar. But, if so, to *what* relation to rules of grammar did he hold it was due that expressions which are being used in the former way, have no sense? I am still extremely puzzled as to the answer to this question, for the following reason.

He seemed often to suggest that any sentence which is "constructed in accordance with" (this is his own phrase) the rules of grammar of the language to which the sentence belongs, always has sense; *e.g.* that any English sentence which is constructed in accordance with the rules of English grammar, has sense. But, if so, since he held that, *e.g.* the sentences "2 + 2 = 4" or "The proposition with regard to any two propositions that they are not both false follows logically from the proposition that they are both true", both of which would certainly be commonly said to express necessary propositions, are, when so used, without sense, he must have held that these two sentences, when so used, are not constructed in accordance with the rules of English grammar. Can he possibly have held that they are not? I think it is possible he did; but I do not know. But in the passage which I have already quoted (p. 58) about Helmholtz's statement that he could imagine the fourth dimension, he seemed to be saying that if Helmholtz was "projecting" the sentence "I can imagine a piece of chalk being thrown into the fourth dimension" "with the common method of projection", then he was talking nonsense, but that if he had been "projecting" that sentence in an unusual way, so that it meant the same as "I can imagine a piece of chalk first disappearing and then appearing again", then he would have been talking sense. But is not "projecting with the common method of projection" merely a metaphorical way of saying "using in accordance with the established rules of grammar"? If so, then Wittgenstein was here saying that a sentence used in accordance with the ⟦293⟧ established rules of grammar may nevertheless *not* make sense, and even implying that, in particular cases, the fact that it does not make sense is (partly) due to the fact that it *is* being used in accordance with the usual rules. I think, however, that possibly he intended to distinguish between "projecting with the common method" and "using in accordance with the usual rules", since he insisted strongly in at least one passage that any rule can be "interpreted" in different ways, and also (if I have not misunderstood him) that it is impossible to add to any rule an unambiguous rule as to how it is to be interpreted. Possibly, therefore, he meant by "projecting with the common method", *not* "using in accordance with the usual rules", but "*interpreting* in the usual manner"—a distinction which would apparently allow him to hold that, when Helmholtz uttered his nonsensical sentence, he was *not* using that sentence in accordance with the usual rules, though he *was* interpreting in the usual manner the rules, whatever they may have been, in accordance with which he was using it. But I am very puzzled as to how this distinction could be used. Suppose, for instance, a person were to use "I can imagine a piece of chalk being thrown into the fourth dimension" in such a way that it meant the same as "I can imagine a piece of chalk first disappearing and then appearing again", how on earth could anyone (including the person in question) possibly decide whether in such a case the speaker or writer was doing what Wittgenstein called elsewhere "changing his grammar", *i.e.* using the first expression *not* in accordance with the usual rules, but in accordance with rules such that it meant the same as the second means, or whether he was merely "interpreting" in an unusual way the rules, whatever they may have been, in accordance with which he was using the first expression? I suspect, therefore, that when Wittgenstein said that Helmholtz must have been using the "common method of projection", when he uttered his nonsensical sentence, he was not distinguishing this from using the sentence in accordance with the ordinary rules, and was therefore implying that a sentence constructed in accordance with the ordinary rules might nevertheless be without sense. But, if so, his view may have been that, *e.g.* "2 + 2 = 4", when used in the way in which it would commonly be said to express a necessary proposition, *is* used in accordance with the ordinary rules of grammar, and is nevertheless "without sense", and is so partly *because* it *is* used in accordance with the ordinary rules; for he certainly would not have denied that that expression *might* be used in such a way that it had sense. But I do not know whether this was his view or not.

⟦294⟧ But finally there is still another reason why I am puzzled as to what his view was about sentences, which would commonly be said to express necessary propositions. His view was, if I am right, one which he expressed by the use of the expressions, ($\beta'$) "without sense", as equivalent to which he often used the expressions "nonsense", "meaningless", and even "useless" and ($\beta''$) "rules of grammar"; and these two expressions were used by him constantly throughout these lectures. And my last puzzle is due to the facts that I think there is reason to suspect that he was not using either expression in any ordinary sense, and that I have not been able to form any clear idea as to how he was using them.

($\beta'$) With regard to the expression "without sense" I think there is no doubt that he was using it in the same way in which he used it in the *Tractatus,* 4.461, when he said that a "tautology" is without sense (sinnlos). In that passage he gave as an example of the supposed fact that a "tautology" is without sense the statement "I know nothing about the weather, if I know that either it is raining or it is not"; and in these lectures he used a very similar example to show the same thing. Also in that passage of the *Tractatus* he said that a "tautology" "says nothing", and seemed to mean by this the same as what he meant by saying that it was "without sense"; and this expression he also used in these lectures, and apparently in the same sense. And I think it is clearly true that we could say correctly of a man who only knew that either it was raining or it was not, that he knew nothing *about the present state of the weather.* But could we also say correctly of such a man that he knew *nothing at all*? I do not think we could; and yet, so far as I can see, it is only if we could say this correctly that we should be justified in saying that the sentence "Either it is raining or it is not" "says nothing" or is "without sense". I think, therefore, that Wittgenstein can only have been right in saying that "tautologies" and other sentences, which would commonly be said to express necessary propositions, are "without sense" and "say nothing", if he was using these two expressions in some peculiar way, different from any in which they are ordinarily used. So far as I can see, if we use "make sense" in any way in which it is ordinarily used, "Either it's raining or it's not" *does* make sense, since we should certainly say that the meaning of this sentence is different from that of "Either it's snowing or it's not", thus implying that since they have different meanings, both of them have *some* meaning; and similarly, if "say nothing" is used in any sense in which it is ordinarily used, Wittgenstein's ⟦295⟧ proposition in *Tractatus* 5.43 that "All the 'Sätze' of Logic say the same, namely, nothing" seems to me to be certainly untrue. And that he was using these expressions in some peculiar way seems to me to be also suggested by the fact that in *Tractatus* 4.461, he seems to be saying that "contradictions" are "without sense" in the same sense in which "tautologies" are, in spite of the fact that in the very same passage he asserts that the latter are "unconditionally true", while the former are "true under no condition". But, if he was using these expressions (and also "meaningless" and "nonsense", which, as I have said, he often used as equivalent to them) in some peculiar sense, what was that sense? Later in (III) he expressly raised the questions "What is meant by the decision that a sentence makes or does not make sense?" and "What is the criterion of making sense?" having said that, in order to answer these questions, he must "plunge into something terrible", and that he must do this in order to "put straight" what he had just been saying, which, he said, he had not "put correctly". In trying to answer these questions or this question (for I think he was using the two expressions to mean the same) he said many things, including the statement that he had himself been "misled" by the expression "sense"; and he went on to say that his present view was that "'sense' was correlative to 'proposition'" (meaning, apparently, here by "proposition" what he had formerly called "proposition in the narrower sense", *i.e.* "experiential proposition", thus excluding, *e.g.*, mathematical "propositions") and that hence, if "proposition" was not "sharply bounded", "sense" was not "sharply bounded" either. He went on to say about "proposition" the things which I have already quoted (p. 55); and then implied that where we say "This makes no sense" we always mean "This makes nonsense *in this particular game*"; and in answer to the question "Why do we call it 'nonsense'? what does it mean to call it so?" said that when we call a sentence "nonsense", it is "because of some similarity to sentences which have sense", and that "nonsense always arises from forming symbols analogous to certain uses, where they have no use". He concluded finally that "'makes sense' is vague, and will have different senses in different cases", but that the expression "makes sense" is useful just as "game" is useful, although, like "game", it "alters its meaning as we go from proposition to proposition"; adding that, just as "sense" is vague, so must be "grammar", "grammatical rule" and "syntax".

But all this, it seems to me, gives no explanation of how he was ⟦296⟧ using the expression "without sense" in the particular case of "tautologies" and other sentences which would commonly be said to express necessary propositions: it only tells us that he might be using it in a different sense in that case from that in which he used it in other cases. The only explanation which, so far as I know, he did give as to how he was using it in the particular case of "tautologies", was where he asked in (III), "What does the statement that a tautology 'says nothing' mean?" and gave as an answer, that to say that "$q \supset q$" "says nothing" means that $p \,.\, (q \supset q) = p$; giving as an example that the logical product "It's raining and I've either got grey hair or I've not" = "It's raining". If he did mean this, and if, as he seemed to be, he was using "says nothing" to mean the same as "is without sense", one important point would follow, namely, that he was not using "without sense" in the same way in the case of "tautologies" as in the case of "contradictions", since he would certainly not have said that $p \,.\, (q \,.\, \sim q) = p$. But it gives us no further explanation of how he *was* using "without sense" in the case of "tautologies". For if he was using that expression in any ordinary way, then I think he was wrong in saying that "It's raining, and I've either got grey hair or I've not" = "It's raining", since, in any ordinary usage, we should say that the "sense" of "either I've got grey hair or I've not" was different from that of, *e.g.*, "either I'm six feet high or I'm not", and should not say, as apparently he would, that both sentences say nothing, and therefore say the same.

In connexion with his use of the phrase "without sense", one other thing which he said or implied more than once should, I think, be mentioned, because it may give a partial explanation of why he thought that both "contradictions" and "tautologies" are without sense. He said in (I) that "the linguistic expression" of "This line can be bisected" is "'This line *is* bisected' has sense", while at the same time insisting that "the linguistic expression" of "This line is infinitely divisible" is not "'This line is infinitely divided' has sense" (he held that "this line *is* infinitely divided" is senseless) but is "an infinite possibility in language". He held, therefore, that in many cases the "linguistic expression" of "It is possible that *p* should be true" or "should have been true" is "The sentence '*p*' has sense". And I think there is no doubt that he here meant by "possible" what is commonly called, and was called by him on a later occasion, "logically possible". But to say that a sentence "*p*" is the "linguistic expression" of a *proposition* "*q*", would ⟦297⟧ naturally mean that the sentence "*p*" and the *sentence* "*q*" have the same meaning, although for some reason or other "*p*" can be called a "linguistic expression", though the sentence "*q*" can not. And that he did hold that, if an expression "*p*" is "the linguistic expression" of a *proposition* "*q*", then the expression "*p*" and the *expression* "*q*" have the same meaning was also suggested by a passage late in (III), where, having explained that by "possible" he here meant "logically possible", he asked the question "Doesn't 'I can't feel his toothache' mean that 'I feel his toothache' has no sense?" obviously implying that the right answer to this question is "Yes, it does". And he also, in several other places, seemed to imply that "*p* can't be the case", where this means "It is logically impossible that *p* should be the case" means the same as "The sentence '*p*' has no sense". I think that his view in the *Tractatus* that "contradictions" are "without sense" (sinnlos) may have been a deduction from this proposition. But why should he have held that "tautologies" also are "without sense"? I think that this view of his may have been, in part, a deduction from the conjunction of the proposition that "It is logically impossible that *p*" means the same as "The sentence '*p*' has no sense" with his principle, which I have already had occasion to mention (pp. 55–56), and which he said "gave us some firm ground", that "If a proposition has meaning, its negation also has meaning", where, as I pointed out, he seemed to be using "proposition" to mean the same as "sentence". For it is logically impossible that the negation of a tautology should be true, and hence, if it is true that "It is logically impossible that *p*" means the same as "The sentence '*p*' has no sense", then it will follow from the conjunction of this proposition with his principle, that a "tautology" (or should we say "any sentence which expresses a tautology"?) also has none. But why he thought (if he did) that "It is logically impossible that *p*" means the same as "The sentence '*p*' has no sense", I cannot explain. And it seems to me that if, as he certainly held, the former of these two propositions entails the latter, then the sentence "It is logically impossible that *p*" must also have no sense; for can this sentence have any sense if the sentence "*p*" has none? But, if "It is logically impossible that *p*" has no sense, then, so far as I can see, it is quite impossible that it can mean the same as "The sentence '*p*' has no sense", for this latter expression certainly has sense, if "having sense" is being used in any ordinary way.

($\beta''$) With regard to the expressions "rules of grammar" or "grammatical rules" he pointed out near the beginning of (I), ⟦298⟧ where he first introduced the former expression, that when he said "grammar should not allow me to say 'greenish-red'", he was "making things belong to grammar, which are not commonly supposed to belong to it"; and he immediately went on to say that the arrangement of colours in the colour octahedron "is really a part of grammar, not of psychology"; that "There is such a colour as a greenish blue" is "grammar"; and that Euclidean Geometry is also "a part of grammar". In the interval between (II) and (III) I wrote a short paper for him[5] in which I said that I did not understand how he was using the expression "rule of grammar" and gave reasons for thinking that he was not using it in its ordinary sense; but he, though he expressed approval of my paper, insisted at that time that he was using the expression in its ordinary sense. Later, however, in (III), he said that "any explanation of the use of language" was "grammar", but that if I explained the meaning of "flows" by pointing at a river "we shouldn't naturally call this a rule of grammar". This seems to suggest that by that time he was doubtful whether he was using "rule of grammar" in quite its ordinary sense; and the same seems to be suggested by his saying, earlier in (III), that we should be using his "jargon" if we said that whether a sentence made sense or not depended on "whether or not it was constructed according to the rules of grammar".

I still think that he was not using the expression "rules of grammar" in any ordinary sense, and I am still unable to form any clear idea as to how he was using it. But, apart from his main contention (whatever that may have been) as to the connexion between "rules of grammar" (in his sense) and necessary propositions, there were two things upon which he seemed mainly anxious to insist about "rules of

5. For more on this paper and Wittgenstein's reply to it see John King's notes recorded on pp. 97–98 of *Wittgenstein's Lectures: Cambridge, 1930–1932*, ed. D. Lee. (eds.)

grammar", namely ($\gamma'$), that they are all "arbitrary" and ($\gamma''$) that they "treat only of the symbolism"; and something ought certainly to be said about his treatment of these two points.

As for ($\gamma'$) he often asserted without qualification that all "rules of grammar" are arbitrary. But in (II) he expressly mentioned two senses of "arbitrary" in which he held that some grammatical rules are *not* arbitrary, and in one place in (III) he said that the sense in which all were arbitrary was a "peculiar" one. The two senses, of which he said in (II) that some grammatical rules were *not* arbitrary in those senses, were (1) a sense in which he said that rules about the use of single words were always "in part" *not* arbitrary—a proposition which he thought followed from his proposition, which I have mentioned before ⟦299⟧ (p. 52), that all single words are significant only if "we commit ourselves" by using them, and (2) a sense in which to say that a rule is an established rule in the language we are using is to say that it is not arbitrary: he gave, as an example, that if we followed a rule according to which "hate" was an intransitive verb, this rule would be arbitrary, whereas "if we use it in the sense in which we do use it", then the rule we are following is not arbitrary. But what, then, was the sense in which he held that all grammatical rules *are* arbitrary? This was a question to which he returned again and again in (II), trying to explain what the sense was, and to give reasons for thinking that in that sense they really are arbitrary. He first tried to express his view by saying that it is impossible to "justify" any grammatical rule—a way of expressing it to which he also recurred later; but he also expressed it by saying that we can't "give reasons" for grammatical rules, soon making clear that what he meant by this was that we can't give reasons for *following* any particular rule rather than a different one. And in trying to explain why we can't give reasons for following any particular rule, he laid very great stress on an argument, which he put differently in different places, and which I must confess I do not clearly understand. Two of the premisses of this argument are, I think, clear enough. One was (1) that any reason "would have to be a description of reality": this he asserted in precisely those words. And the second was (2) that "any description of reality must be capable of truth and falsehood" (these again were his own words), and it turned out, I think, that part of what he meant by this was that any false description must be significant. But to complete the argument he had to say something like (what again he actually said in one place) "and, if it were false, it would have to be said in a language not using this grammar"; and this is what I do not clearly understand. He gave as an illustration of his meaning that it cannot be because of a "quality in reality" that "I use sweet" in such a way that "sweeter" has meaning, but "identical" in such a way that "more identical" has none; giving as a reason "If it were because of a 'quality' in reality, it must be possible to say that reality hasn't got this quality, which grammar forbids". And he had said previously "I can't say what reality would have to be like, in order that what makes nonsense should make sense, because in order to do so I should have to use this new grammar". But, though I cannot put clearly the whole of his argument, I think one important point results from what I have quoted—a point which he himself never expressly pointed out. It results, ⟦300⟧ namely, that he was using the phrases "description of reality" and "quality in reality" in a restricted sense—a sense, such that no statement to the effect that a certain expression is actually used in a certain way is a "description of reality" or describes "a quality in reality". He was evidently so using these terms that statements about the actual use of an expression, although such statements are obviously experiential propositions, are not to be called "descriptions of reality". He was confining the term "descriptions of reality" to expressions in which no term is used as a name for itself. For if he were not, it is obviously perfectly easy to say what reality would have to be like in order that "more identical", which is nonsense, should make sense: we can say that if "more identical" were used to mean what we now mean by "sweeter", then it would make sense; and the proposition that "more identical" is used in that way, even if it is a false one (and I do not know for certain that the very words "more identical" are not used in that way in *e.g.* some African language) it is certainly not one which English grammar "forbids" us to make—it is certainly untrue that the sentence which expresses it has no significance in English.

It seems, therefore, that though in (II) he had said that what he meant by saying that all "grammatical rules" are "arbitrary" was that we cannot "give reasons" for following any particular rule rather than a different one, what he meant was only that we cannot give reasons for so doing which are both (*a*) "descriptions of reality" and (*b*) "descriptions of reality" *of a particular sort, viz.* descriptions of reality which do not *mention,* or say anything *about,* any particular word or other expression, though of course they must *use* words or other expressions. And that this was his meaning is made, I think, plainer from a passage late in (III) in which he compared rules of deduction with "the fixing of a unit of length" (or, as he said later, a "standard" of length). He there said "The reasons (if any) for fixing a unit of length do not make it 'not arbitrary', in the sense in which a statement that so and so is the length of this object is not arbitrary", adding "Rules of deduction are analogous to the fixing of a unit of length", and (taking "3 + 3 = 6" as an instance of a rule of deduction) "'3 + 3 = 6' is a rule as to the way we are going to talk . . . it is a preparation for a description, just as fixing a unit of length is a preparation for measuring". He seemed, therefore, here to be admitting that reasons *of a sort* can sometimes be given for following a particular "grammatical rule", only not reasons of the special sort which a well-conducted operation of measurement may give (once the meaning of "foot" ⟦301⟧ has been fixed), for, *e.g.*, the statement that a particular rod is less than four feet long. He did in fact mention in this connexion that some "grammatical rules" follow from others; in which case, of course, that they do so follow may be given as a reason for speaking in accordance with them. In this case, however, he would no doubt have said that the reason given is not a "description of reality". But it is obvious that reasons which are, in any ordinary sense, "descriptions of reality" can also be given for following a particular rule; *e.g.* a particular person may give, as a reason for calling a particular length a "foot", the "description of reality" which consists in saying that that is how the word "foot", when used for a unit of length, is generally used in English. And, in this case, of course, it may also be said that the reason why the word "foot" was originally used, in English, as a name for the particular length which we do in fact so call, was that the length in question is not far from the length of those parts of a grown man's body which, in English, are called his "feet". In these cases, however, I think he might have urged with truth both (*a*) that the reason given, though a "description of reality", is a description which "mentions" or says something *about* the word "foot" and does not merely *use* that word, and also (*b*) that it is not a reason for following the rule of calling that particular length a "foot" in the same sense of the word "reason" as that in which a well-conducted measurement may give a "reason" for the statement that a particular rod is less than four feet long. It is surely obvious that a "reason" for *acting* in a particular way, *e.g.* in this case, for using the word "foot" for a particular length, cannot be a reason for so doing in the same sense of the word "reason" as that in which a reason for thinking that so and so is the case may be a reason for so thinking. I think, therefore, if all these explanations are given, it becomes pretty clear in what sense Wittgenstein was using the word "arbitrary" when he said that all grammatical rules were arbitrary.

But there remains one thing which he said in this connexion which has puzzled me extremely. He actually introduced his comparison between rules of deduction and the fixing of a unit of length by saying: "The statement that rules of deduction are neither true nor false is apt to give an uncomfortable feeling." It appeared, therefore, as if he thought that this statement that they are neither true nor false followed from the statement that they are arbitrary, and that the comparison of them with the fixing of a unit of length would tend to remove this uncomfortable feeling, *i.e.* to make you see that they really are neither true nor false.

⟦302⟧ Now, in connexion with his comparison between rules of deduction and the fixing of a unit of length, he gave (among other examples) as an example of a rule of deduction "3 + 3 = 6", and said a good deal about this example. And it certainly does give me a very uncomfortable feeling to be told that "3 + 3 = 6" is neither true nor false. But I think this uncomfortable feeling only arises because one thinks, if one is told this, that the *expression* "3 + 3 = 6" is being used in the way in which it most commonly is used, *i.e.* in the way in which it would commonly be said to be expressing a necessary proposition. And I think this uncomfortable feeling would completely vanish if it were clearly explained that the person who says this, is *not* using the expression "3 + 3 = 6" in this way, but in the very different way which I tried to distinguish above (p. 62), *i.e.* the way in which it is merely used to specify a possible way of speaking and writing, which might or might not be actually adopted, although in this case the rule of speaking and writing in the way specified is, as a matter of fact, a well-established rule. I said that Wittgenstein never, so far as I knew, in these lectures expressly distinguished these two different ways of using the same expression (*e.g.* the expression "3 + 3 = 6"), but that I thought he did hold that, *e.g.* the expression "3 + 3 = 6" could be properly used in the second way as well as in the first, and that his thinking this might be partly responsible for his declaration that rules of deduction are neither true nor false (p. 63). For it seemed to me quite obvious that, if the expression "3 + 3 = 6" is used in this second way, then it cannot possibly be either true or false. But I cannot help thinking that in this passage in (III) in which he compared rules of deduction with the fixing of a unit of length, he actually meant to say that even when used in the first way, *i.e.* in the way in which it would commonly be said to express a necessary proposition, it still expresses neither a true nor a false proposition.

In what he actually said about "3 + 3 = 6" in this passage, I think it is necessary to distinguish three different propositions which he made, of which the first two seem to me certainly true, but the third not to follow from the first two, and to be extremely doubtful. (1) He began by asking the question, "Is 'I've put 6 apples on the mantel-piece' the same as 'I've put 3 there, and also another 3 there'?" and then, after pointing out that counting up to 3 in the case of each of two different groups, and arriving at the number "6" by counting *all* the apples, are "three different experiences", he said "You can imagine putting two groups of 3 there, and then finding only 5". And the two ⟦303⟧ propositions which seem to me certainly true are (*a*) that you can imagine this which he said you can imagine, and (*b*) (which he also said) that "3 + 3 = 6" does not "prophesy" that, when you have had the two experiences of counting up to 3 in the case of each of two groups of apples which you certainly have put on the mantel-piece, you will also have the third experience of finding that there are 6 there, when you come to count *all* the apples that are there; or, in other words, he was saying that the proposition "3 + 3 = 6" is quite consistent with finding, by your third experience of counting, that there are only 5 there. This second proposition seems to me also true, because it seems to me clear that it is a mere matter of experience, that when you have put two groups of 3 apples on a mantel-piece, you will, under the circumstances Wittgenstein was considering (*e.g.* that no apple has been taken away) find that there are 6 there; or, in other words, it is a mere matter of experience that apples don't simply vanish with no apparent cause; and it surely should be obvious that "3 + 3 = 6" certainly entails no more than that, *if* at any time there were in any place two different groups, each numbering 3 apples, then *at that time* there were 6 apples in the place in question: it entails nothing about any future time. But (2) Wittgenstein went on to add that if, on having put two groups of 3 on the mantel-piece, and finding that there were only 5 there, you were to say (as you certainly might under the circumstances he was considering) "one must have vanished", this latter statement "*only means* 'If you keep to the arithmetical rule "3 + 3 = 6"' you *have to say* 'One must have vanished'".

And it is this assertion of his that, under the supposed circumstances, "One must have vanished" *only means* that, if you keep to a certain rule, you must *say so,* which seems to me questionable and not to follow from the two true propositions I have given under (1). (He had already said something similar in (I) in connexion with his very paradoxical proposition that Euclidean Geometry is "a part of grammar"; for he there said that what Euclid's proposition "The three angles of a triangle are equal to two right angles" asserts is "If by measurement you get any result for the sum of the three angles other than 180°, you *are going to say* that you've made a mistake".)

But I have been a good deal puzzled as to what he meant and implied by this assertion that, under these circumstances the words "One must have vanished" *only mean* "If you keep to the arithmetical rule '3 + 3 = 6', you have to say so". And, of course, my view that it is very doubtful whether what he ⟦304⟧ meant and implied is true depends on my view as to what he did mean and imply.

Of course, the circumstances under which he said that "One must have vanished" *only means* this, are extremely unusual: possibly they never have happened and never will happen: but, as I have said, I fully agree with him that they *might* happen—that I can *imagine* their happening; and the question whether, if they did, then the words "One must have vanished" would *only mean* what he says, seems to me to raise an extremely important question, which does not only concern what would happen under these extremely unlikely circumstances, but concerns what is the case under circumstances which constantly do occur.

I will first try to state as accurately as I can what I take to be the circumstances he was supposing, and I will put them in the form of what he was supposing would be true of me, if I had been in those circumstances. He was supposing, I take it, (1) that I should know, because I had counted correctly, that I did put on the mantel-piece two groups of apples, each of which contained 3 apples and no more, (2) that I should know, by counting *at a subsequent time,* that there were *at that time* only 5 apples on the mantel-piece, (3) that I should also know, because I was watching all the time, that nothing had happened which would account in any normal way for the fact that, though I put 3 + 3 there, there are only 5 there now, *e.g.* I should know, in this way, that nobody had taken one away, that none had fallen off the mantel-piece, and that none had visibly flown away, and finally, (4) (and this, if I am not mistaken, was very essential to his point) that I should *not* know, by any operation of counting performed either by myself or by any other person who had told me his result, that I did put 6 apples on the mantel-piece, so that, if I asserted that I did put 6, this could only be a deduction from the proposition that I did put 3 + 3 there, which (1) asserts that I *have* found to be true by counting.

Under the circumstances stated in (1) and (3) I certainly should be very much surprised to find that what is stated in (2) was true, and I might quite naturally assert that one must have vanished, though I think I might equally naturally express my surprise by the use of words which contain no "must", *e.g.* by saying "Why! one has vanished!" And it is under these circumstances, if I am not mistaken, that Wittgenstein was asserting that if I did use the words "One must have vanished" to make an assertion, these words would "*only mean*" "If I keep to the arithmetical rule '3 + 3 = 6' I have to say that one must have vanished".

⟦305⟧ And, first of all, I have felt some doubts on two separate points as to what he meant by the words "you have to say so". The first is this. I at first thought that he might be using the words "say so", rather incorrectly, to mean "say *the words* 'One must have vanished'" (or, of course, any equivalent words, *e.g.* in another language). But I now think there is no reason to suppose that he was not using the word "say" quite correctly (*i.e.* as we usually do), to mean the same as "assert", and there is some positive reason to suppose that he was doing so. One positive reason is that, among the circumstances which he was supposing was that which I have called (1), *viz.* that I should *know* that I did put 3 + 3 apples on the mantel-piece; and I think he was certainly supposing that if I knew this, I should not merely say the words "I put 3 + 3 there", but should *assert* that I did—a proposition which does not seem to me certainly true, though, if I knew it, I should certainly be *willing* to assert it, unless I wanted to tell a lie. The second point is this: What did he mean by "have to" in "I should *have to* say so"? These words might naturally mean that I should be failing to keep to the rule "3 + 3 = 6" if I merely failed to assert that one must have vanished—if, for instance, I merely made no assertion. But I feel sure he did not mean to assert that I should be failing to keep to the rule (which I will in future call, for short, "violating" the rule) if I merely omitted to say that one must have vanished. I think he certainly meant that I should be violating the rule only if I made some assertion the making of which was inconsistent with asserting that one must have vanished, *e.g.* if I asserted that none had vanished.

If I am right on these two points, his view as to what the words "One must have vanished" would "only mean" under the supposed circumstances, could be expressed more clearly as the view that these words would only mean "If I assert that I put 3 + 3 on the mantel-piece, I shall be keeping to the rule '3 + 3 = 6' if I also assert that one must have vanished, and shall be violating that rule, if I make any assertion the making of which is inconsistent with asserting that one must have vanished". And I will, in future, assume that this was his view.

But now the question arises: Why should he have held that, under the supposed circumstances, the words "One must have vanished" would "only mean" a proposition which mentioned the arithmetical proposition "3 + 3 = 6"? How does "6" come in? I think the answer to this question is that he was assuming that among the propositions from which, under the ⟦306⟧ supposed circumstances, the proposition that one had vanished would be a deduction (the "must have", of course, indicates, as "must" often does, that it would be a deduction from *some* propositions) would be not only the propositions given as known by me in (1), (2) and (3) of my description of the circumstances, but also the proposition "I put 6 apples on the mantel-piece", which, according to (4) in my description is *not* known by me as a result of any operation of counting, but only, if at all, as a deduction from "I put 3 + 3". And I think his reason for asserting that, under the supposed circumstances "One must have vanished" would "only mean" what he said it would only mean, was that he was supposing that this sentence "I put 6 on the mantel-piece" would *not,* under the circumstances described in (1) and (4), mean what it would mean if I had discovered, by counting *all* the apples I was putting on the mantel-piece, that I was putting 6, but, since I had not done this, would "only mean" "I shall be keeping to the rule '3 + 3 = 6', if I assert that I put 6, and shall be violating that rule if I make any assertion inconsistent with asserting that I put 6"—a proposition which to avoid clumsy repetitions, I will in future call "B". I think, therefore, he was implying that under the circumstances (1) and (4), the words "I put 6 apples on the mantel-piece" would "only mean" B. And I think the important question raised by his assertion as to what "One must have vanished" would "only mean" under circumstances (1), (2), (3) and (4), is this question as to whether, under circumstances (1) and (4), which might quite often occur, "I put 6" would "only mean" B—"only mean" being used, of course, in the same sense (whatever that may have been) in which he used it with regard to "One must have vanished".

But then the question arises: In what sense was he using the expression "only mean"? If any one tells us that, under the circumstances (1) and (4), the sentence "I put 6 on the mantel-piece", if used to make an assertion, would "only mean" B, I think the most natural interpretation of these words would be that anyone who, under circumstances (1) and (4), used this sentence to make an assertion would be using it to assert B. But I think it is quite incredible that any one would ever actually use the expression "I put 6" to assert B; and equally incredible that any one would ever use the expression "One must have vanished" to assert what Wittgenstein said would be their "only meaning" under circumstances (1), (2), (3) and (4). In both cases the assertion which is said to be the "only meaning" of a given expression is an assertion *about* the ordinary meaning ⟦307⟧ of the expression in question, to the effect that you will be speaking in accordance with a certain rule if you use the expression in question to assert what it would be usually used to mean, and will be violating that rule if you make any assertion inconsistent with that ordinary meaning. And I think it is quite incredible that anybody would ever use a given expression to make such an assertion *about* the ordinary meaning of the expression in question; and, in both our cases, quite clear that anybody who did use the expression in question to make an assertion, would be using it to *make* the assertion which it would ordinarily mean, and not to make the assertion *about* its ordinary meaning which Wittgenstein said or implied would be its "only meaning" under the circumstances described. And I do not think that he ever meant to make either of these incredible statements: he was not intending to say that the sentence "One must have vanished" ever would be used, or could be properly used, to make the assertion which he says would be its "only meaning" under the supposed circumstances. But, if so, how was he using the expression "only mean"? I think he was using it, not in its most natural sense, but loosely, in a more or less natural sense, to say that the assertion which he said would be its "only meaning" under the circumstances described, would be *the* true proposition which resembled most closely a proposition which he held to be false, but which he knew was commonly held to be true. In the case of "I put 6", if he implied, as I think he did, that, under circumstances (1) and (4), "I put 6" would "only mean" B, the proposition which he held to be false was the proposition that if I put 3 + 3, it is *necessarily* also true that I put 6, and the proposition which he held to be *the* true proposition which most closely resembled this false proposition, and which might therefore have misled those who think to be true this proposition which he held to be false, was that, if "I put 3 + 3" was true, then B would be true. I think, in fact, he was holding that the proposition that in putting 3 + 3 on the mantel-piece, I was *necessarily* putting 6 there, was false; that I can imagine that in putting 3 + 3 there, I was *e.g.* only putting 5, and that, if there ever were 3 + 3 on the mantel-piece, nevertheless, if anybody had counted correctly how many there were altogether *at that very time,* he would possibly have found that there were only 5.

But whether or not he held, as I think he did, that in putting 3 + 3 apples on the mantel-piece, I was not necessarily putting 6, I think it is quite certain that he held another proposition, about the relation of which to this one I am not clear. He held, ⟦308⟧ namely, that the expression "3 + 3 = 6" is *never* used in Arithmetic, not therefore even when it would commonly be held to express a necessary proposition, to express a proposition from which it follows that if I put 3 + 3, I necessarily put 6. And this view seems to me to follow from his two views (1) that (as is suggested by his phrase "the arithmetical *rule* '3 + 3 = 6'") the expression "3 + 3 = 6", as used in Arithmetic, *always* only expresses a "rule of grammar", and (2) that rules of grammar "treat only of the symbolism". I shall shortly have to point out that there seems to me to be a serious difficulty in understanding exactly what he meant by saying that, *e.g.* "3 + 3 = 6" "treats only of the symbolism"; but I think there is no doubt he meant at least this: that you will be speaking in accordance with that rule if, when you *assert* that you put 3 + 3, you also *assert* that you put 6, and violating it if, having *asserted* the former, you make any assertion the making of which is incompatible with asserting the latter, but that it by no means follows that, if you keep to the rule, what you assert will be *true,* nor yet that, if you violate it, what you assert will be *false:* in either case, he held, what you assert *may* be true, but also *may* be false. And I think his reason for this view of his can be made plainer by noticing that since (as he implies by his phrase "the arithmetical rule '3 + 3 = 6'") "3 + 3 = 6" is a well-established rule (if a rule of grammar at all), it will follow that, if you keep to that rule, you will be using language "correctly" (or, with his use of "grammar", speaking "grammatically"), and that, if you violate it will be speaking "incorrectly" (or, with his use of "grammar", guilty of bad grammar); and that from the fact that you are using language correctly, in the sense of "in accordance with an established rule", it by no means follows that what you assert, by this correct use of language, is "correct" in the very different sense in which "That is correct" = "That is true", nor from the fact that you are using language incorrectly that what you assert by this incorrect use of language is "incorrect" in the very different sense in which "That is incorrect" = "That is false". It is obvious that you may be using language just as correctly when you use it to assert something false as when you use it to assert something true, and that when you are using it incorrectly, you may just as easily be asserting something true by this incorrect use as something false. It by no means follows, for instance, from the fact that you are using the word "foot" "correctly", *i.e.* for the length for which it is usually used in English, that when you make such an assertion as "This rod is ⟦309⟧ less than four feet long", your assertion is true; and, if you were to use it "incorrectly" for the length which is properly called in English an "inch" or for that which is properly called a "yard", it would by no means follow that any assertion you made by this incorrect use of the word "foot" was false. I think Wittgenstein thought that similarly you will be using the phrase "I put 6" correctly, if, when you assert that you put 3 + 3, you also assert that you put 6, and incorrectly if, when you assert that you put 3 + 3, you deny that you put 6, or even assert that it is possible that you did not put 6; and that this is *the* true proposition which has led people to assume, what he thought false, that the expression "3 + 3 = 6" is used in Arithmetic to express a proposition from which it follows that if I put 3 + 3, I necessarily put 6.

And I think this view of his also gives the chief explanation of what he meant by the puzzling assertion that 3 + 3 = 6 (and *all* rules of deduction, similarly) is neither true nor false. I think what he chiefly meant by saying this was not, as I suggested above (p. 62) that 3 + 3 = 6 was a "rule" in the sense in which rules can obviously be neither true nor false, but that he was using "true" in a restricted sense, in which he would have said that 3 + 3 = 6 was only "true" if it followed from it (as he denied to be the case) that if I put 3 + 3 on the mantel-piece, I necessarily put 6; in a sense, therefore, in which, even if, as I suggested (p. 63), he sometimes used "rule" in a sense in which the proposition "You can't *say* that you put 3 + 3, and *deny* that you put 6"—a proposition which he held to be true in any ordinary sense, he would nevertheless have said that this proposition was not "true", because it was a proposition about how words are actually used. I think he was using "true" and "false" in a restricted sense, just as he was using "description of reality" in a restricted sense (above, p. 71), *i.e.* in a sense in which no propositions about how words are used can be said to be "true" or "false".

And the reason why I think it very doubtful whether he was right in holding (if he did hold) that it is not true that in putting 3 + 3 on the mantel-piece, I necessarily also put 6, is that I do not think I can imagine that in putting 3 + 3, I was not putting 6. I have already said (p. 74) that I agree with him that I can imagine that, having put 3 + 3 there, I should find at *a subsequent time* that there were only 5 there, even under the circumstances described in (3) of my description of the circumstances he was supposing: I can imagine, I think, that one has really vanished. But it seems to be quite a different question whether I can ⟦310⟧ imagine that, in putting 3 + 3, I was not putting 6, or that, if at any time there were 3 + 3 on the mantel-piece, there were *at that time* not 6 there. I admit, however, that the propositions that I was putting 6, or that there were 6 on the mantel-piece, do seem to me to entail that, *if* anybody had counted correctly, he would have found that there were 6; I am, therefore, implying that I cannot imagine these hypothetical propositions not to be true: but I do not think I can imagine this. And I also can see no reason to think that the expression "3 + 3 = 6" is never used in Arithmetic to express a proposition from which it follows that if I put 3 + 3, I put 6. I am not convinced that this expression, in Arithmetic, *always* only expresses a "grammatical rule", *i.e.* a rule as to what language it will be correct to use, even if it sometimes does. Wittgenstein has not succeeded in removing the "uncomfortable feeling" which it gives me to be told that "3 + 3 = 6" and "($p \supset q \,.\, p$) entails $q$" are neither true nor false.

($\gamma''$) As for the proposition that rules of grammar "treat only of the symbolism", he never, at least while I was present, expressly pointed out that such an expression as "2 = 1 + 1" can be used to express at least three very different propositions. It can be used (1) in such a way that anybody could understand what proposition or rule it was being used to express, provided only he understood how the sign "=" was being used, and did not understand either the expression "2" or the expression "1 + 1" except as names for themselves (what has been called "autonymously"). But it can be used (2) in such a way that nobody could understand what proposition or rule it was being used to express, unless he understood non-autonymously both the sign "=" and also the expression "1 + 1", but need not understand the expression "2" other than autonymously. Or (3) it can be used in such a way that nobody could understand what proposition or rule it was being used to express, unless he understood non-autonymously *both* the expression "2" and the expression "1 + 1", as well as the expression "=". But, though he did not expressly point out that *e.g.* "2 = 1 + 1" could be used in each of these three very different ways, he said things which seem to me to imply the view that in Arithmetic it was *only* used in the first way. He said, for instance, in (II) "To explain the meaning of a sign means only to substitute one sign for another", and again, later on, "An explanation of a proposition is always of the same kind as a definition, *i.e.* replacing one symbol by another". In making these statements, he seems to me to have been confusing the true proposition that ⟦311⟧ you can only explain the meaning of one sign by *using* other signs, with the proposition, which seems to me obviously false, that, when you explain the meaning of one sign by *using* another, all you are asserting is that the two signs have the same meaning or can be substituted for one another: he seems in fact to have been asserting that propositions, which are in fact of form (2), are only of form (1). And this mistake seems to be responsible for the astounding statement which he actually made in (III) that Russell has been mistaken in thinking that "= Def." had a different meaning from "=". It seems to me obvious that a statement can only be properly called a "definition" or "explanation" of the meaning of a sign, if, in order to understand what statement you are making by the words you use, it is necessary that the hearer or reader should understand the *definiens,* and not merely take it as a name for itself. When, for instance, *Principia Mathematica* defines the meaning of the symbol "$\supset$" by saying that "$p \supset q$" is to mean "$\sim p \vee q$", it is surely obvious that nobody can understand what statement is being made as to how "$\supset$" will be used, unless he understands the expression "$\sim p \vee q$", and does not take it merely as a name for itself; and that therefore the statement which is being made is not merely a statement of form (1), to the effect that the two different expressions "$p \supset q$" and "$\sim p \vee q$" have the same meaning or can be substituted for one another, but a statement of form (2), *i.e.* that the *definiens*

"$\sim p \vee q$" is *not* being used autonymously, though the *definiendum* "⊃" *is* being used autonymously.

But the most serious difficulty in understanding what he meant by saying that, *e.g.* "3 + 3 = 6" "treats only of the symbolism" seems to me to arise from a question with which he only dealt briefly at the end of (I), and with which he there dealt only in a way which I certainly do not at all completely understand; namely, the question: Of *what* symbols did he suppose that "3 + 3 = 6" was treating? He did indeed actually assert in (III) that the proposition "red is a primary colour" was a proposition about the word "red"; and, if he had seriously held this, he might have held similarly that the proposition or rule "3 + 3 = 6" was merely a proposition or rule about the particular expressions "3 + 3" and "6". But he cannot have held seriously either of these two views, because the *same* proposition which is expressed by the words "red is a primary colour" can be expressed in French or German by words which say nothing about the English word "red"; and similarly the *same* proposition or rule which is expressed by ⟦312⟧ "3 + 3 = 6" was undoubtedly expressed in Attic Greek and in Latin by words which say nothing about the Arabic numerals "3" and "6". And this was a fact which he seemed to be admitting in the passage at the end of (I) to which I refer. In this passage, which he introduced by saying that he would answer objections to the view (which he held) that the arithmetical calculus "is a game", he began by saying, very emphatically, that it is *not* a game "with ink and paper"; by which he perhaps meant (but I do not know) that it is not a game with the Arabic numerals. He went on to say that Frege had concluded from the fact that Mathematics is not a game "with ink and paper" that it dealt not with the symbols but with "what is symbolised"—a view with which he apparently disagreed. And he went on to express his own alternative view by saying "What is essential to the rules is the logical multiplicity which all the different possible symbols have in common"; and here, by speaking of "all the different possible symbols", I take it he was admitting, what is obvious, that the *same* rules which are expressed by the use of the Arabic numerals may be expressed by ever so many different symbols. But if the rules "treat only of the symbolism" how can two rules which treat of *different* symbols, *e.g.* of "3" and "III", possibly be the *same* rule? I suppose he must have thought that we use the word "same" in such a sense that two rules, which are obviously *not* the same, in that they treat of different symbols, are yet said to be the same, provided only that the rules for their use have the same "logical multiplicity" (whatever that may mean). But he never, I think, at least while I was present, returned to this point, or tried to explain and defend his view.

He did, however, in this passage, compare the rules of Arithmetic to the rules of chess, and used of chess the phrase, "What is characteristic of chess is the logical multiplicity of its rules" just as he used of Mathematics the phrase "What is essential to its rules is the logical multiplicity which all the different possible symbols have in common". I doubt, however, whether he was right in what he meant by saying "*What* is characteristic of chess is the logical multiplicity of its rules", which, of course, implies that this is sufficient to characterise chess. He was undoubtedly right in saying that the material and the shape of which the different pieces are commonly made is irrelevant to chess: chess could certainly be played with pieces of any material and any shape, *e.g.* with pieces of paper which were all of the same shape. But if by "the rules of chess" he meant, as I think he probably did, the rules which govern the moves which ⟦313⟧ may be made by pieces of different sorts, *e.g.* by pawns and bishops, and was suggesting that the "logical multiplicity" of the rules which govern the possible moves of a pawn and a bishop is sufficient to distinguish a pawn from a bishop, I think he was wrong. The rule that a pawn can only make certain moves certainly, I think, does not mean that any piece the rules for the moves of which have a certain "logical multiplicity" (whatever that may mean) may only make the moves in question, even if he was right in holding that the rules for the moves of pawns have a different "logical multiplicity" from those for the moves of bishops; and similarly in the case of all the other different kinds of pieces. Though a pawn is certainly not necessarily distinguished from a bishop or a knight by its shape, as it usually is, it seems to me that it is necessarily distinguished by the positions which it may occupy at the beginning of the game, so that a rule which states that pawns can only make such and such moves, states that pieces which occupy certain positions at the beginning of the game can only make such and such moves; and similarly with all the other different kinds of piece: they are all necessarily distinguished from one another by the positions which they occupy at the beginning of the game, where "necessarily" means that it would not be chess that you were playing, if the pieces to which different kinds of move are allowed, did not occupy certain positions relatively to one another at the beginning of the game. Of course, if you did play chess with pieces of paper which were all of the same shape, it would be necessary that the pieces should have some mark to show what positions they had occupied at the beginning of the game, as might be done, for instance, by writing "pawn" on those pieces which had occupied certain positions, and, *e.g.* "bishop" on those which had occupied others; and it would also be necessary to distinguish by some mark (what is usually done by a difference of colour) those pieces which belonged to one of the two players from those which belonged to the other, as could, *e.g.* be easily done by writing a "0" on all the pieces which belonged to one player, and a "+" on all which belonged to the other. I think, therefore, he was probably wrong in holding, as he apparently did, that the rules of chess are completely analogous, in respect of their relation to "logical multiplicity", to what he held to be true of the rules of Arithmetic.

There remains one other matter which should be mentioned in treating of his views about necessary propositions. He made a good deal of use, especially in (II) in discussing rules of deduction, ⟦314⟧ of the expression "internal relation", even asserting in one place "What justifies inference is an internal relation". He began the discussion in which he made this assertion by saying that "following" is called a "relation" as if it were like "fatherhood"; but said that where, for example, it is said that a proposition of the form "$p \vee q$" "follows" from the corresponding proposition of the form "$p \,.\, q$", the so-called "relation" is "entirely determined by the two propositions in question", and that, this being so, the so-called "relation" is "entirely different from other relations". But it soon became plain that, when he said this about "following", it was only one of the proper uses of the word "follow" in English, as between two propositions, of which he was speaking, namely, that use which is sometimes called "follows logically": he did, in fact, constantly use the word "inference" as if it meant the same as "deductive inference". How he made plain that what he was talking of as "following" was only "following logically", was that he immediately went on to say that the kind of "following" of which he was speaking, and which he exemplified by the sense in which any proposition of the form "$p \vee q$" "follows" from the corresponding proposition of the form "$p \,.\, q$", was "quite different" from what is meant when, *e.g.* we say that a wire of a certain material and diameter *can't* support a piece of iron of a certain weight—a proposition which he actually expressed in the next lecture (quite correctly according to English usage) as the proposition that "it *follows* from the weight of the piece of iron and the material and diameter of the wire, that the wire will break if you try to support that piece of iron by it". He went on to express the difference between these two uses of "follow", by saying that, in the case of the wire and the piece of iron, both (*a*) "it remains *thinkable* that the wire will not break", and (*b*) that "from the weight of the piece of iron and the material and diameter of the wire *alone,* I can't know that the wire will break", whereas in the case of a proposition of the form "$p \vee q$" and the corresponding proposition of the form "$p\ .\ q$" "following" is an "internal relation", which, he said; means "roughly speaking" "that it is *unthinkable* that the relation should not hold between the terms". And he immediately went on to say that the *general* proposition "$p \vee q$ follows from $p\ .\ q$" "is not wanted"; that "if you can't see", by looking at two propositions of these forms that the one follows from the other, "the general proposition won't help you"; that, if I say of a proposition of the form "$p \vee q$" that it follows from the corresponding proposition of the form "$p\ .\ q$" "everything here is ⟦315⟧ useless, except the two propositions themselves"; and that if another proposition were needed to justify our statement that the first follows from the second, "we should need an infinite series". He finally concluded "A rule of inference" (meaning "deductive inference") "never justifies an inference".

In the next lecture, which he began, as he often did, by repeating (sometimes in a slightly different form and, if necessary, with added explanations and corrections) the main points which he had intended to make at the end of the preceding one, he said that to say of one proposition "$q$" that it "follows" from another "$p$" "*seems* to say that there is a relation between them which justifies passing from one to the other", but that "what makes one suspicious about this is that we perceive the relation by merely looking at the propositions concerned—that it is 'internal' and not like the proposition that 'This wire will break' follows from the weight of the iron and the material and diameter of the wire"; and here he immediately went on to add that the expression "internal relation" is misleading, and that he used it "only because others had used it"; and he proceeded to give a slightly different formulation of the way in which the expression had been used, *viz.* "A relation which holds if the terms are what they are, and which cannot therefore be imagined not to hold". He also, shortly afterwards, gave some further explanation of what he had meant by saying that if a rule were needed to justify the statement that one proposition follows [logically] from another, we should need an infinite series. He said that if a rule *r*, were needed to justify an inference from *p* to *q*, *q* would follow from the conjunction of *p* and *r*, so that we should need a fresh rule to justify the inference from this conjunction to *q*, and so on *ad infinitum.* Hence, he said, "an inference can only be justified by what we see", and added that "this holds throughout Mathematics". He then gave his truth-table notation for "$p \vee q$" and "$p \,.\, q$", and said that the "criterion" for the statement that the former follows from the latter was that "to every T in the latter there corresponds a T in the former". He said that, in saying this, he had stated "a rule of inference", but that this rule was only a "rule of grammar" and "treated only of the symbolism". A little later he said that the relation of "following" can be "represented" by "tautologies" (in his special sense), but that the tautology "$(p \,.\, q) \supset (p \vee q)$" does not *say* that $p \vee q$ follows from $p \,.\, q$, because it says nothing, but that the fact that it is a tautology *shews* that $p \vee q$ follows from $p \,.\, q$. And a little later still he said that the relation of following "can be seen by ⟦316⟧ looking at the *signs*", and seemed to identify this with saying that it is "internal"; and the fact that he here said that it can be seen by looking at the *signs,* whereas he had previously said that it can be seen by looking at the *propositions,* seems to me to shew that, as I said (p. 56) seemed to be often the case, he was identifying "sentences" with "propositions". Finally he introduced a new phrase, in explanation of his view that the expression "internal relation" is misleading, saying that internal and external relations are "categorically" different; and he used the expression "belong to different categories" later on in (III), where he said that "follows" and "implies" (a word which he here used, as Russell had done, as if it meant the same as the *Principia* symbol "⊃") "belong to different categories"; adding the important remark that whether one proposition "follows" from another "cannot depend at all upon their truth or falsehood", and saying that it only depends on "an internal *or grammatical* relation".

⟦III/1⟧ (B) In the case of Logic, there were two most important matters with regard to which he said that the views he had held when he wrote the *Tractatus* were definitely wrong.

(1) The first of these concerned what Russell called "atomic" propositions and he himself in the *Tractatus* had called "Elementar-

sätze". He said in (II) that it was with regard to "elementary" propositions and their connexion with truth-functions or "molecular" propositions that he had had to change his opinions most; and that this subject was connected with the use of the words "thing" and "name." In (III) he began by pointing out that neither Russell nor he himself had produced any examples of "atomic" propositions; and said that there was something wrong indicated by this fact, though it was difficult to say exactly what. He said that both he and Russell had the idea that non-atomic propositions could be "analysed" into atomic ones, but that we did not yet know what the analysis was: that, *e.g.* such a proposition as "It is raining" might, if we knew its analysis, turn out to be molecular, consisting, *e.g.* of a conjunction of "atomic" propositions. He said that in the *Tractatus* he had objected to Russell's assumption that there certainly were atomic propositions which asserted two-termed relations—that he had refused to prophesy as to what would be the result of an analysis, if one were made, and that it might turn out that no atomic proposition asserted less than *e.g.* a ⟦2⟧ four-termed relation, so that we could not even talk of a two-termed relation. His present view was that it was senseless to talk of a "final" analysis, and he said that he would now treat as atomic all propositions in the expression of which neither "and", "or", nor "not" occurred, nor any expression of generality, provided we had not expressly given an exact definition, such as we might give of "It's rotten weather", if we said we were going to use the expression "rotten" to mean "both cold and damp".

In saying this he seemed to me to be overlooking both the fact that a man often says that he is going to use an expression in a certain definite way and then does not in fact so use it, and also the fact that many common words, *e.g.* father, mother, sister, brother, etc., are often so used that such a sentence as "This is my father" undoubtedly expresses a molecular proposition, although a person who so uses it has never expressly stated that he will so use it. These two facts, however, of course, do not prove that he was wrong in thinking that it is senseless to talk of a "final" or "ultimate" analysis.

(2) The second important logical mistake which he thought he had made at the time when he wrote the *Tractatus* was introduced by him in (III) in connexion with the subject of "following" (by which he meant, as usual, *deductive* following or "entailment"—a word which I think he actually used in this discussion) from a "general" proposition to a particular instance and from a particular instance to a "general" proposition. Using the notation of *Principia Mathematica*, he

asked us to consider the two propositions "$(x) . fx$ entails $fa$" and "$fa$ entails $(\exists x) . fx$". He said that there was a temptation, to which he had yielded in the *Tractatus,* to say that $(x) . fx$ is identical with the logical product "$fa . fb . fc \ldots$", and $(\exists x) . fx$ identical with the logical sum "$fa \vee fb \vee fc \ldots$"; but that this was in both cases a mistake. In order to make clear exactly where the mistake lay, he first said that in the case of such a universal proposition as "Everybody in this room has a hat" (which I will call "A"), he had known and actually said in the *Tractatus,* that, even if Smith, Jones and Robinson are the only people in the room, the logical product "Smith has a hat, Jones has a hat and Robinson has a hat" cannot possibly be identical with A, because in order to get a proposition which entails A, you obviously have to add "and Smith, Jones and Robinson are the only people in the room". But he went on to say that if we are talking of "individuals" in Russell's sense (and he actually ⟦3⟧ here mentioned atoms as well as colours, as if they were "individuals" in this sense), the case is different, because, in that case, there is no proposition analogous to "Smith, Jones and Robinson are the only people in the room". The class of things in question, if we are talking of "individuals", is, he said, in this case, determined not by a proposition but by our "dictionary": it is "defined by grammar". *E.g.* he said that the class "primary colour" is "defined by grammar", not by a proposition; that there is no such proposition as "red is a primary colour", and that such a proposition as "In this square there is one of the primary colours" really is identical with the logical sum "In this square there is either red or green or blue or yellow"; whereas in the case of Smith, Jones and Robinson, there is such a proposition as "Smith is in this room" and hence also such a proposition as "Smith, Jones and Robinson are the only people in this room". He went on to say that one great mistake which he made in the *Tractatus* was that of supposing that in the case of *all* classes "defined by grammar", general propositions were identical either with logical products or with logical sums (meaning by this logical products or sums of the propositions which are values of $fx$) as, according to him, they really are in the case of the class "primary colours". He said that, when he wrote the *Tractatus,* he had supposed that *all* such general propositions were "truth-functions"; but he said now that in supposing this he was committing a fallacy, which is common in the case of Mathematics, *e.g.* the fallacy of supposing that $1 + 1 + 1 \ldots$ is a sum, whereas it is only a *limit,* and that $\frac{dx}{dy}$ is a quotient, whereas it also is only a *limit.*

He said he had been misled by the fact that $(x) . fx$ can be replaced by $fa . fb . fc \ldots$, having failed to see that the latter expression is not always a logical product: that it is only a logical product if the dots are what he called "the dots of laziness", as where we represent the alphabet by "A, B, C . . .", and therefore the whole expression can be replaced by an enumeration; but that it is not a logical product where, *e.g.* we represent the cardinal numbers by 1, 2, 3 . . . , where the dots are not the "dots of laziness" and the whole expression can not be replaced by an enumeration. He said that, when he wrote the *Tractatus,* he would have defended the mistaken view which he then took by asking the question: How can $(x) . fx$ possibly entail $fa$, if $(x) . fx$ is not a logical product? And he said that the answer to this question is that where $(x) . fx$ is not a logical product, the proposition "$(x) . fx$ entails $fa$" is "taken as a primary ⟦4⟧ proposition", whereas where it is a logical product this proposition is deduced from other primary propositions.

The point which he here made in saying that where we talk of the cardinal numbers we are not talking of a logical product was a point which he had made earlier, in (I), though he did not there point out that in the *Tractatus* he had made the mistake of supposing that an infinite series was a logical product—that it *could* be enumerated, though we were unable to enumerate it. In this passage in (I) he began by saying that by the proposition "there are an infinite number of shades of grey between black and white" we "mean something entirely different" from what we mean by *e.g.* "I see three colours in this room", because, whereas the latter proposition can be verified by counting, the former can not. He said that "There are an infinite number" does not give an answer to the question "How many are there?" whereas "There are three" does give an answer to this question. He went on to discuss infinite divisibility in the case of space, and said (as I have already mentioned p. 67), that the "linguistic expression" of "This line can be bisected" was "The words 'This line has been bisected' have sense", but that the "linguistic expression" of "This line can be infinitely divided" is certainly not "The words 'This line has been infinitely divided' have sense". He said that if we express "has been bisected", "has been trisected", "has been quadrisected", etc., by $f(1 + 1), f(1 + 1 + 1), f(1 + 1 + 1 + 1)$, etc., we see that an internal relation holds between successive members of this series and that the series has no end; and he concluded by saying that the "linguistic expression" of an infinite possibility is an infinite possibility in language. He also pointed out that $\Sigma 1 + \frac{1}{2} + \frac{1}{4} \ldots$ approaches a limit, whereas a logical product does not approach any limit. And he said finally that the cases to which the *Principia* notations $(x) . \phi x$ and $(\exists x) . \phi x$ apply, *i.e.* cases in which the former can be regarded as a logical product and the latter as a logical sum of propositions of the form $\phi a$, $\phi b$, $\phi c$, etc., are comparatively rare; that oftener we have propositions, such as "I met a man", which do not "presuppose any totality"; that the cases to which the *Principia* notations apply are only those in which we could give proper names to the entities in question; and that giving proper names is only possible in very special cases.

Besides these two cardinal cases, in which he said that the views which he had held at the time when he wrote the *Tractatus* were certainly wrong, I think that the chief logical points which he made were as follows.

⟦5⟧ (3) One point which he made was that Russell was quite wrong in supposing that, if expressions of the form "$p \supset q$" are used with the meaning which is given to "$\supset$" in *Principia Mathematica*, then it follows that from a false proposition we *can infer* every other proposition, and that from a true one we *can infer* any other true one. He said that Russell's holding this false opinion was partly due to his supposing that "$p \supset q$" can be translated by "If $p$, then $q$". He said that we never use "*If p, then q*" to mean merely what is meant by "$p \supset q$"; and that Russell had admitted this, but still maintained that in the case of what he called "formal implications", *i.e.* propositions of the form $(x) . \phi x \supset \psi x$, such a proposition can be properly translated by "If . . . , then . . .". Wittgenstein said that this also was a mistake, giving as a reason that if, *e.g.* we substitute "is a man" for $\phi$ and "is mortal" for $\psi$, then the mere fact that there were no men would verify $(x) . \phi x \supset \psi x$, but that we never so use "If . . . , then . . ." that the mere fact that there were no men would verify "If anything is a man, then that thing is mortal".

(4) He also, on more than one occasion, said something about Sheffer's "stroke notation", and, on one occasion, about Tarski's "3-valued" Logic.

About the former he said that it resembled what are called mathematical "discoveries" in respect of the fact that Sheffer had no rule for discovering an answer to the question "Is there only one logical constant?" whereas there is a rule for discovering, *e.g.* the answer to a multiplication sum. He said that, where there is no rule, it is misleading to use the word "discovery", though this is constantly done. He said that Russell or Frege might quite well have used the expression "$p|q$" as short for "$\sim p \,.\, \sim q$", and yet still maintained that they had two primitive ideas, "and" and "not", and not one only. Plainly, therefore, he thought that Sheffer, though he admitted that Sheffer had actually defined "$p|q$" as meaning "$\sim p \,.\, \sim q$", had done something else. But what else? He said that Sheffer's "discovery" consisted in finding a "new aspect" of certain expressions. But I am sorry to say that I did not and do not understand what he meant by this.

On Tarski's 3-valued Logic he said that it was all right "as a calculus"—that Tarski had really "discovered" a new calculus. But he said that "true" and "false" could not have in it the meaning which they actually have; and he particularly emphasized that Tarski had made the mistake of supposing that his third value, which he called "doubtful", was identical with what we ordinarily mean by "doubtful."[6]

⟦6⟧ (C) Of problems which are specifically problems in the philosophy of Mathematics, I think that those which he most discussed are the three following. But in this case I should like to remind the reader of what I said in my first article (p. 50) that I cannot possibly mention nearly everything which he said, and that it is possible that some things which I omit were really more important than what I mention; and also to give the warning that in this case it is particularly likely that I may have misunderstood or may misrepresent him, since my own knowledge of Mathematics is very small. But I think that what I say will at least give some idea of the *kind* of questions which he was eager to discuss.

(1) In (I) he said that there were two very different kinds of proposition used in Mathematics, "neither of them at all like what are usually called propositions". These were (1) propositions proved by a

6. ⟦264⟧ It has been pointed out to me that I made a great mistake in speaking of "Tarski's 3-valued Logic", since the calculus in question was invented solely by Professor J. Lukasiewicz, and Tarski had no hand whatever in its invention. I did not know this at the time, and I think I must have been misled into my mistake by Wittgenstein himself, since, on looking up my notes of the passage in question, I find no name mentioned except Tarski's, which is mentioned three times. Of course I cannot be certain that Wittgenstein did not also mention Lukasiewicz: he certainly did at one point speak of "they", as if Tarski was not the only person involved: but I think he must at least have supposed that Tarski was partly responsible for the calculus, even if he did not suppose him to be its sole author. I am now informed, on unimpeachable evidence, that Tarski had no hand whatever in the invention.

chain of equations, in which you proceed from axioms to other equations, by means of axioms, and (2) propositions proved by "mathematical induction". And he added in (III) that proofs of the second kind, which he there called "recursive proofs", are not proofs in the same *sense* as are proofs of the first kind. He added that people constantly commit the fallacy of supposing that "true", "problem", "looking for", "proof" always mean the same, whereas in fact these words "mean entirely different things" in different cases.

As an example of a proposition of the second kind he took the Associative Law for the addition of numbers, namely, "$a + (b + c) = (a + b) + c$"; and he discussed the proof of this proposition at considerable length on two separate occasions, first in (I) and then later in (III). On both occasions he discussed a proof of it given by Skolem, though in (I) he did not expressly say that the proof discussed was Skolem's. He said in (I) that the proof seemed to assume at one point the very proposition which it professed to prove, and he pointed out in (III) that in one of the steps of his proof Skolem did actually assume the Associative Law. He said that since Skolem professed to be giving a proof, one would have expected him to prove it from other formulae, but that in fact the proof begins in an entirely different way, namely with a definition—the definition "$a + (b + 1) = (a + b) + 1$"; and he maintained both in (I) and in (III) that it was quite unnecessary for Skolem to assume the Associative Law in one step of his proof, saying in (I) that the proof "really rests entirely on the definition", and in (III) that you don't in fact use the Associative Law in the proof at ⟦7⟧ all. He wrote the proof "in his own way" in order to show this, saying that if you write the definition in the form "$\phi 1 = \psi 1$", then all that is proved is the two formulae $(a) \phi(c + 1) = \phi c + 1$ and $(b) \psi(c + 1) = \psi c + 1$, and that to prove these two formulae is the same thing as what is called "proving the Associative

---

Lukasiewicz invented the calculus and published an account of it in 1920, before he was even acquainted with Tarski.

On looking at my notes, to find what (so far as they can be trusted) Wittgenstein had said on this first matter, I found that I had badly misrepresented him on another. I represent him as saying that Tarski had called the third value in the calculus "doubtful". But this is a complete mistake. What he actually said was that Tarski had chosen a particular letter to represent the third value, because he supposed this value to "correspond" to "possible", and that it did not in fact so correspond. He said nothing whatever about "doubtful", but only about "possible". The substitution of "doubtful" for "possible" seems to have been a piece of great carelessness on my part.

Law *for all numbers*". He went on to say that the fact that this proof proves all we want "shows that we are not dealing with an extension at all"; that instead of talking of a *finite part* of the series "1, 2, 3 . . .", on the one hand, and of the *whole* series on the other hand, we should talk of a bit of the series and of *the Law which generates it*; that proving the Associative Law "for *all* numbers" can't mean the same sort of thing as proving it, *e.g.* for three numbers, since, in order to do this latter, you would have to give a separate proof for each of the three; and that what we have in the proof is a general *form* of proof for *any* number. Finally he said that the generality which is misleadingly expressed by saying that we have proved the Associative Law for "*all* cardinals", really comes in in the definition, which might have been written in the form of a series, *viz.* "1 + (1 + 1) = (1 + 1) + 1" "1 + (2 + 1) = (1 + 2) + 1" "2 + (1 + 1) = (2 + 1) + 1" *and so on*; and that this series is not a logical product of which the examples given are a part, but a *rule,* and that "the examples are only there to explain the rule".

(2) Another problem in the philosophy of Mathematics, which he discussed on no less than three separate occasions, was what we are to say of the apparent question "Are there anywhere in the development of $\pi$ three consecutive 7's?" (Sometimes he took the question "Are there *five* consecutive 7's?" instead of "Are there three?") He first dealt with this apparent question in (I), in connexion with Brouwer's view that the Law of Excluded Middle does not apply to some mathematical propositions; *i.e.* that some mathematical propositions are neither true nor false; that there is an alternative to being either true or false, *viz.* being "undecidable". And on this occasion he said that the words "There are three consecutive 7's in the development of $\pi$" are nonsense, and that hence not only the Law of Excluded Middle does not apply in this case, but that no laws of Logic apply in it; though he admitted that if someone developed $\pi$ for ten years and actually found three consecutive 7's in the development, this would prove that there were three consecutive 7's *in a ten years' development,* and seemed to be admitting, therefore, that it is possible that there might be. The next time he discussed the question, early in (III), he said that if anyone actually found three consecutive 7's this would prove that there are, but that ⟦8⟧ if no one found them that wouldn't prove that there are not; that, therefore, it is something for the truthof which we have provided a test, but for the falsehood of which we have provided none; and that therefore it must be a quite different

sort of thing from cases in which a test for both truth and falsehood is provided. He went on to discuss the apparent question in a slightly new way. He said we seem to be able to define $\pi'$ as the number which, if there are three consecutive 7's in the development of $\pi$, differs from $\pi$ in that, in the place in which three consecutive 7's occur in $\pi$, there occur in it three consecutive 1's instead, but which, if there are not, does not differ from $\pi$ at all; and that we seem to be able to say that $\pi'$, so defined, either is identical with $\pi$ or is not. But he said here that, since we have no way of finding out whether $\pi'$ is identical with $\pi$ or not, the question whether it is or not "has no meaning"; and, so far as I can see, this entails the same view which he had expressed in (I), *viz.* that the words "There are *not* three consecutive 7's anywhere in the development of $\pi$" have no meaning, since, if these words had a meaning, it would seem to follow that "$\pi' = \pi$" also has one, and that therefore the question "Is $\pi'$ identical with $\pi$?" also has one. In the second passage in (III) in which he discussed this apparent question he expressly said that though the words (1) "There are five consecutive 7's in the first thousand digits of $\pi$" have sense, yet the words (2) "there are five consecutive 7's *somewhere* in the development" have none, adding that "we can't say that (2) makes sense because (2) follows from (1)". But in the very next lecture he seemed to have changed his view on this point, since he there said "We ought not to say 'There are five 7's in the development' has no sense", having previously said "It has whatever sense its grammar allows", and having emphasized that "it has a very curious grammar" since "it is compatible with there not being five consecutive 7's in any development you can give". If it has sense, although a "very curious" one, it does presumably express a proposition to which the Law of Excluded Middle and the other rules of Formal Logic do apply; but Wittgenstein said nothing upon this point. What he did say was that "All big mathematical problems are of the nature of 'Are there five consecutive 7's in the development of $\pi$?'" and that "they are therefore quite different from multiplication sums, and not comparable in respect of difficulty".

He said many other things about this question, but I cannot give them all, and some of them I certainly did not and do not understand. But one puzzling thing which he seemed to say in (III) was that, if we express the proposition that there is, in ⟦9⟧ the development of $\pi$, a number of digits which is immediately followed by five consecutive 7's, by "$(\exists n) . fn$", then there are two conceivable ways of proving

$(\exists n) . fn$, namely, (1) by *finding* such a number, and (2) by proving that $\sim(\exists n) . fn$ is self-contradictory; but that the $(\exists n) . fn$ proved in the latter way could not be the same as that proved in the former. In this connexion he said that there is no "opposite" to the first method of proof. He said also that "$\exists n$" means something different where it is possible to "look for" a number which proves it, from what it means where this is not possible; and, generally, that "The proof of an existence theorem gives the meaning of 'existence' in that theorem", whereas the meaning of "There's a man in the next room" does not depend on the method of proof.

(3) This last problem is connected, and was connected by him, with a general point which he discussed more than once in connexion with the question "How can we look for a method of trisecting an angle by rule and compasses, if there is no such thing?" He said that a man who had spent his life in trying to trisect an angle by rule and compasses would be inclined to say "If you understand both what is meant by 'trisection' and what is meant by 'bisection by rule and compasses', you must understand what is meant by 'trisection by rule and compasses'" but that this was a mistake; that we can't imagine trisecting an angle by rule and compasses, whereas we can imagine dividing an angle in into eight equal parts by rule and compasses; that "looking for" a trisection by rule and compasses is not like "looking for" a unicorn, since "There are unicorns" has sense, although in fact there are no unicorns, whereas "There are animals which show on their foreheads a construction by rule and compasses of the trisection of an angle" is just nonsense like "There are animals with three horns, but also with only one horn": it does not give a description of any possible animal. And Wittgenstein's answer to the original question was that by proving that it is impossible to trisect an angle by rule and compasses "we change a man's idea of trisection of an angle" but that we should say that what has been proved impossible is the very thing which he had been trying to do, because "we are willingly led in this case to identify two different things". He compared this case to the case of calling what he was doing "philosophy", saying that it was not the same kind of thing as Plato or Berkeley had done, but that we may feel that what he was doing "takes the place" of what Plato and Berkeley did, though it is really a different thing. He illustrated the same ⟦10⟧ point in the case of the "construction" of a regular pentagon, by saying that if it were proved to a man who had

been trying to find such a construction that there isn't any such thing, he would say "That's what I was trying to do" because "his idea has shifted on a rail on which he is ready to shift it". And he insisted here again that (*a*) to have an idea of a regular pentagon and (*b*) to know what is meant by constructing by rule and compasses, *e.g.* a square, do not in combination enable you to know what is meant by constructing, by rule and compasses, a regular pentagon. He said that to explain what is meant by "construction" we can give two series of "constructions", *viz.* (*a*) equilateral triangle, regular hexagon, etc., and (*b*) square, regular octagon, etc., but that neither of these would give meaning to the construction of a regular pentagon, since they don't give any rule which applies to the number 5. He said that in a sense the result wanted is clear, but the means of getting at it is not; but in another sense, the result wanted is itself not clear, since "constructed pentagon" is not the same as "measured pentagon" and that whether the same figure will be both "depends on our physics": why we call a construction a construction of a regular pentagon is "because of the physical properties of our compasses, etc."

In (I) he had said that in the case of Logic and Mathematics (and "Sense-data") you can't know the same thing in two independent ways; and that it was in the case of "hypotheses" and *nowhere else,* that there are different evidences for the same thing. But in (III) he said that even in the case of hypotheses, *e.g.* the proposition that there is a cylindrical object on the mantel-piece, he himself preferred to say that if the evidence was different, the proposition was also different, but that "you can say which you please". He did not say whether, in the case of Logic and Mathematics also, he now held that "you can say which you please".

(D) He spent, as I have said in my first article (p. 50), a great deal of time on this discussion, and I am very much puzzled as to the meaning of much that he said, and also as to the connexion between different things which he said. It seems to me that his discussion was rather incoherent, and my account of it must be incoherent also, because I cannot see the connexion between different points which he seemed anxious to make. He said very early in the discussion that the whole subject is "extraordinarily difficult" because "the whole field is full of misleading notations"; and that its difficulty was shown by the fact that the ⟦11⟧ question at issue is the question between

by the fact that the ⟦11⟧ question at issue is the question between Realists, Idealists and Solipsists. And he also said, more than once, that many of the difficulties are due to the fact that there is a great temptation to confuse what are merely experiential propositions, which might, therefore, not have been true, with propositions which are necessarily true or are, as he once said, "tautological or grammatical statements". He gave, as an instance of a proposition of the latter sort, "I can't feel your toothache", saying that "If you feel it, it isn't mine" is a "matter of grammar", and also that "I can't feel your toothache" means the same as "'I feel your toothache' has no sense"; and he contrasted this with "I hear my voice coming from somewhere near my eyes", which he said we think to be necessary, but which in fact is not necessary "though it always happens". In this connexion he gave the warning "Don't be prejudiced by anything which *is* a fact, but which *might* be otherwise". And he seemed to be quite definite on a point which seems to me certainly true, *viz.* that I might see without physical eyes, and even without having a body at all; that the connexion between seeing and physical eyes is merely a fact learnt by experience, not a necessity at all; though he also said that "the visual field" has certain internal properties, such that you can describe the motion of certain things in it as motions towards or away from "your eye"; but that here "your eye" does not mean your physical eye, nor yet anything whatever which is *in* the visual field. He called "your eye", in this sense, "the eye of the visual field", and said that the distinction between motion towards it and away from it was "on the same level" as "the distinction between 'curved' and 'straight'".

However, he began the discussion by raising a question, which he said was connected with Behaviourism, namely, the question "When we say 'He has toothache' is it correct to say that his toothache is only his behaviour, whereas when I talk about my toothache I am not talking about my behaviour?"; but very soon he introduced a question expressed in different words, which is perhaps not merely a different formulation of the same question, *viz.* "Is another person's toothache 'toothache' in the same sense as mine?" In trying to find an answer to this question or these questions, he said first that it was clear and admitted that what verifies or is a criterion for "I have toothache" is quite different from what verifies or is a criterion for "He has toothache", and soon added that, since this is so, the *meanings* of "I have toothache" and "he has toothache" must be different. In this connexion he said later, first, that the ⟦12⟧ meaning of "verification" is different, when we speak of verifying "I have" from what it is when we speak of verifying "He has", and then, later still, that there is no such thing as a verification for "I have", since the question "How do you know that you have toothache?" is nonsensical. He criticized two answers which might be given to this last question by people who think it is not nonsensical, by saying (1) that the answer "Because I feel it" won't do, because "I feel it" means the same as "I have it", and (2) that the answer "I know it by inspection" also won't do, because it implies that I can "look to see" whether I have it or not, whereas "looking to see whether I have it or not" has no meaning. The fact that it is nonsense to talk of verifying the fact that I have it, puts, he said, "I have it" on "a different level" in grammar from "he has it". And he also expressed his view that the two expressions are on a different grammatical level by saying that they are not both values of a single propositional function "*x* has toothache"; and in favour of this view he gave two definite reasons for saying that they are not, namely, (1) that "I don't know whether I have toothache" is always absurd or nonsense, whereas "I don't know whether he has toothache" is not nonsense, and (2) that "It seems to me that I have toothache" is nonsense, whereas "It seems to me that he has" is not.

He said, that when he said this, people supposed him to be saying that other people never really have what he has, but that, if he did say so, he would be talking nonsense; and he seemed quite definitely to reject the behaviourist view that "he has toothache" means only that "he" is behaving in a particular manner; for he said that "toothache" doesn't in fact only mean a particular kind of behaviour, and implied that when we pity a man for having toothache, we are not pitying him for putting his hand to his cheek; and, later on, he said that we *conclude* that another person has toothache from his behaviour, and that it is legitimate to conclude this on the analogy of the resemblance of his behaviour to the way in which we behave when we have toothache. It seemed, therefore, that just as to his first question he meant to give definitely the answer "No", so to his second question he meant to give definitely the answer "Yes"; the word "toothache" is used in the same sense when we say that he has it (or "you have it") as when we say that I have it, though he never expressly said so; and though he seemed to throw some doubt on whether he meant this by saying "I admit that other people do have toothache—this having *the meaning which we have given it*".

⟦13⟧ It seemed, therefore, that he did not think that the difference between "I have toothache" and "He has toothache" was due to the fact that the word "toothache" was used in a different sense in the two sentences. What then was it due to? Much that he said seemed to suggest that his view was that the difference was due to the fact that in "He has toothache" we were necessarily talking of a physical body, whereas in "I have toothache" we were not. As to the first of these two propositions he did not seem quite definite; for though at first he said that "my voice" means "the voice which comes from my mouth", he seemed afterwards to suggest that in "He has toothache" (or "You have") we were not necessarily referring to a *body,* but might be referring only to a *voice,* identified as "his" or "yours" without reference to a body. But as to the second proposition, the one about "I have toothache", the point on which he seemed most anxious to insist was that what we call "having toothache" is what he called a "primary experience" (he once used the phrase "direct experience" as equivalent to this one); and he said that "what characterizes 'primary experience'" is that in its case "'I' does not denote a possessor". In order to make clear what he meant by this he compared "I have toothache" with "I see a red patch"; and said of what he called "visual sensations" generally, and in particular of what he called "the visual field", that "the idea of a person doesn't enter into the description of it, just as a [physical] eye doesn't enter into the description of what is seen"; and he said that similarly "the idea of a person" doesn't enter into the description of "having toothache". How was he here using the word "person"? He certainly meant to deny that the idea of a physical body enters necessarily into the description; and in one passage he seemed to imply that he used "person" to mean the same as "physical body", since he said "A description of a sensation does not contain a description of a sense-organ, nor, *therefore,* of a person". He was, therefore, still maintaining apparently that one distinction between "I have toothache" and "He has toothache" was due to the fact that the latter necessarily refers to a physical body (or, perhaps, to a voice instead) whereas the former does not. But I think this was not the only distinction which he had in mind, and that he was not always using "person" to mean the same as physical body (or, perhaps, a voice instead). For he said that "Just as no [physical] eye is involved in seeing, so no Ego is involved in thinking or in having toothache"; and he quoted, with apparent approval, Lichtenberg's saying "Instead of 'I think' we ought ⟦14⟧ to say 'It thinks'" ("it" being used, as he said, as

"Es" is used in "Es blitzet" [it rains]); and by saying this he meant, I think, something similar to what he said of "the eye of the visual field" when he said that it is not anything which is *in* the visual field. Like so many other philosophers, in talking of "visual sensations" he seemed not to distinguish between "what I see" and "my seeing of it"; and he did not expressly discuss what appears to be a possibility, namely, that though no person enters into what I see, yet some "person" other than a physical body or a voice, may "enter into" my seeing of it.

In this connexion, that in "I have toothache" "I" does not "denote a possessor", he pointed out that, when I talk of "*my* body", the fact that the body in question is "mine" or "belongs to me", cannot be verified by reference to that body itself, thus seeming to imply that when I say "This body belongs to me", "me" is used in the second of the senses which he distinguished for "I", *viz.* that in which, according to him, it does not "denote a possessor". But he did not seem to be quite sure of this, since he said in one place "*If* there is an ownership such that I possess a body, this isn't verified by reference to a body", *i.e.* that "This is *my* body" can't possibly mean "This body belongs to this body". He said that, where "I" is replaceable by "this body" "I" and "he" are "on the same [grammatical] level". He was quite definite that the word "I" or "any other word which denotes a subject" is used in "two utterly different ways", one in which it is "on a level with other people", and one in which it is not. This difference, he said, was a difference in "the grammar of our ordinary language". As an instance of one of these two uses, he gave "I've got a match-box" and "I've got a bad tooth", which he said were "on a level" with "Skinner has a match-box" and "Skinner has a bad tooth". He said that in these two cases "I have . . ." and "Skinner has . . ." really were values of the same propositional function, and that "I" and "Skinner" were both "possessors". But in the case of "I have toothache" or "I see a red patch" he held that the use of "I" is utterly different.

In speaking of these two senses of "I" he said, as what he called "a final thing", "In one sense 'I' and 'conscious' are equivalent, but not in another", and he compared this difference to the difference between what can be said of the pictures on a film in a magic lantern and of the picture on the screen; saying that the pictures in the lantern are all "on the same level" but that the picture which is at any given time on the screen is not "on the same level" with any of them, and that if we were to ⟦15⟧ use "conscious" to say of one of the pictures in the lantern that it was at that time being thrown on the screen, it would be meaningless to say of the picture on the screen that it was "conscious". The pictures on the film, he said, "have neighbours", whereas that on the screen has none. And he also compared the "grammatical" difference between the two different uses of "I" with the difference between the meaning of "has blurred edges" as applied to the visual field, and the meaning of the same expression as applied to any drawing you might make of the visual field: your drawing might be imagined to have sharp edges instead of blurred ones, but this is unimaginable in the case of the visual field. The visual field, he said, has no outline or boundary, and he equated this with "It has no sense to say that it has one".

In connexion with his statement that "I", in one of its uses, is equivalent to "conscious", he said something about Freud's use of the terms "conscious" and "unconscious". He said that Freud had really discovered phenomena and connexions not previously known, but that he talked as if he had found out that there were in the human mind "unconscious" hatreds, volitions, etc., and that this was very misleading, because we think of the difference between a "conscious" and an "unconscious" hatred as like that between a "seen" and an "unseen" chair. He said that, in fact, the grammar of "felt" and "unfelt" hatred is quite different from that of "seen" and "unseen" chair, just as the grammar of "artificial" flower is quite different from that of "blue" flower. He suggested that "unconscious toothache", if "unconscious" were used as Freud used it, might be necessarily bound up with a physical body, whereas "conscious toothache" is not so bound up.

As regards Solipsism and Idealism he said that he himself had been often tempted to say "All that is real is the experience of the present moment" or "All that is certain is the experience of the present moment"; and that any one who is at all tempted to hold Idealism or Solipsism knows the temptation to say "The only reality is the present experience" or "The only reality is *my* present experience". Of these two latter statements he said that both were equally absurd, but that, though both were fallacious, "the idea expressed by them is of enormous importance". Both about Solipsism and about Idealism he had insisted earlier that neither of them pretends that what it says is learnt by experience—that the arguments for both are of the form "you can't" or "you must", and that both these expressions "cut [the statement in question] out of our language". ⟦16⟧ Elsewhere he said that both Solipsists and Idealists would say they "couldn't imagine it otherwise", and that, in reply to this, he would say, "If so, your statement has no sense" since "nothing can characterize reality, except as opposed to something else which is not the case". Elsewhere he had said that the Solipsist's statement "Only my experience is real" is absurd "as a statement of fact", but that the Solipsist sees that a person who says "No: my experience is real too" has not really refuted him, just as Dr. Johnson did not refute Berkeley by kicking a stone. Much later he said that Solipsism is right if it merely says that "I have toothache" and "He has toothache" are "on quite a different level", but that "if the Solipsist says that he has something which another hasn't, he is absurd and is making the very mistake of putting the two statements on the same level". In this connexion he said that he thought that both the Realist and the Idealist were "talking nonsense" in the particular sense in which "nonsense is produced by trying to express by the use of language what ought to be embodied in the grammar"; and he illustrated this sense by saying that "I can't feel his toothache" means "'I feel his toothache' has no sense" and therefore does not "express a fact" as "I can't play chess" may do.

(E) He concluded (III) by a long discussion which he introduced by saying "I have always wanted to say something about the grammar of ethical expressions, or, *e.g.* of the word 'God'". But in fact he said very little about the grammar of such words as "God", and very little also about that of ethical expressions. What he did deal with at length was not Ethics but Aesthetics, saying, however, "Practically everything which I say about 'beautiful' applies in a slightly different way to 'good'". His discussion of Aesthetics, however, was mingled in a curious way with criticism of assumptions which he said were constantly made by Frazer in the "Golden Bough", and also with criticism of Freud.

About "God" his main point seemed to be that this word is used in many *grammatically* different senses. He said, for instance, that many controversies about God could be settled by saying "I'm not using the word in such a sense that you can say . . .", and that different religions "treat things as making sense which others treat as nonsense, and don't merely deny some proposition which another religion affirms"; and he illustrated this by saying that if people use "god" to mean something like a human being, then "God has four arms" and

⟦17⟧ "God has two arms" will both have sense, but that others so use "God" that "God has arms" is nonsense—would say "God *can't* have arms". Similarly, he said of the expression "the soul", that sometimes people so use that expression that "the soul is a gaseous human being" has sense, but sometimes so that it has not. To explain what he meant by "grammatically" different senses, he said we wanted terms which are not "comparable", as *e.g.* "solid" and "gaseous" are comparable, but which differ as, *e.g.* "chair" differs from "permission to sit on a chair", or "railway" from "railway accident".

He introduced his whole discussion of Aesthetics by dealing with one problem about the meaning of words, with which he said he had not yet dealt. He illustrated this problem by the example of the word "game", with regard to which he said both (1) that, even if there is something common to all games, it doesn't follow that this is what we mean by calling a particular game a "game", and (2) that the reason why we call so many different activities "games" need not be that there is anything common to them all, but only that there is "a gradual transition" from one use to another, although there may be nothing in common between the two ends of the series. And he seemed to hold definitely that there is nothing in common in our different uses of the word "beautiful", saying that we use it "in a hundred different games"—that, *e.g.* the beauty of a face is something different from the beauty of a chair or a flower or the binding of a book. And of the word "good" he said similarly that each different way in which one person, A, can convince another, B, that so-and-so is "good" fixes the meaning in which "good" is used in that discussion—"fixes the grammar of that discussion"; but that there will be "gradual transitions", from one of these meanings to another, "which take the place of something in common". In the case of "beauty" he said that a difference of meaning is shown by the fact that "you can say more" in discussing whether the arrangement of flowers in a bed is "beautiful" than in discussing whether the smell of lilac is so.

He went on to say that specific colours in a certain spatial arrangement are not merely "symptoms" that what has them *also* possesses a quality which we call "being beautiful", as they would be, if we meant by "beautiful", *e.g.* "causing stomachache", in which case we could learn by experience whether such an arrangement did always cause stomachache or not. In order to discover how we use the word "beautiful" we need, he said, to consider (1) what an actual aesthetic controversy or ⟦18⟧ enquiry is like, and (2) whether such enquiries are in fact psychological enquiries "though they look so very different". And on (1) he said that the actual word "beautiful" is hardly ever used in aesthetic controversies: that we are more apt to use "right", as, *e.g.* in "That doesn't look quite right yet", or when we say of a proposed accompaniment to a song "That won't do: it isn't right". And on (2) he said that if we say, *e.g.* of a bass "It is too heavy; it moves too much", we are not saying "If it moved less, it would be more agreeable to me": that, on the contrary, that it should be quieter is an "end in itself", not a means to some other end; and that when we discuss whether a bass "will do", we are no more discussing a psychological question than we are discussing psychological questions in Physics; that what we are trying to do is to bring the bass "nearer to an ideal", though we haven't an ideal before us which we are trying to copy; that in order to show what we want, we might point to another tune, which we might say is "perfectly right". He said that in aesthetic investigations "the one thing we are not interested in is causal connexions, whereas this is the only thing we are interested in in Psychology". To ask "Why is this beautiful?" is not to ask for a causal explanation: that, *e.g.* to give a causal explanation in answer to the question "Why is the smell of a rose pleasant?" would not remove our "aesthetic puzzlement".

Against the particular view that "beautiful" means "agreeable" he pointed out that we may refuse to go to a performance of a particular work on such a ground as "I can't stand its greatness", in which case it is disagreeable rather than agreeable; that we may think that a piece of music which we in fact prefer is "just nothing" in comparison to another to which we prefer it; and that the fact that we go to see "King Lear" by no means proves that that experience is agreeable: he said that, even if it is agreeable, that fact "is about the least important thing you can say about it". He said that such a statement as "That bass moves too much" is not a statement about human beings at all, but is more like a piece of Mathematics; and that, if I say of a face which I draw "It smiles too much", this says that it could be brought closer to some "ideal", not that it is not yet agreeable enough, and that to bring it closer to the "ideal" in question would be more like "solving a mathematical problem". Similarly, he said, when a painter tries to improve his picture, he is not making a psychological experiment on himself, and that to say of a door "It is top-heavy" is to say what is wrong with it, *not* what impression ⟦19⟧ it gives you. The question of Aesthetics, he said, was not "Do you like this?" but "*Why* do you like it?"

What Aesthetics tries to do, he said, is to give *reasons, e.g.* for having this word rather than that in a particular place in a poem, or for having this musical phrase rather than that in a particular place in a piece of music. Brahms' *reason* for rejecting Joachim's suggestion that his Fourth Symphony should be opened by two chords was not that that wouldn't produce the feeling he wanted to produce, but something more like "That isn't what I meant". *Reasons,* he said, in Aesthetics, are "of the nature of further descriptions": *e.g.* you can make a person see what Brahms was driving at by showing him lots of different pieces by Brahms, or by comparing him with a contemporary author; and all that Aesthetics does is "to draw your attention to a thing", to "place things side by side". He said that if, by giving "reasons" of this sort, you make another person "see what you see" but it still "doesn't appeal to him", that is "an end" of the discussion; and that what he, Wittgenstein, had "at the back of his mind" was "the idea that aesthetic discussions were like discussions in a court of law", where you try to "clear up the circumstances" of the action which is being tried, hoping that in the end what you say will "appeal to the judge". And he said that the same sort of "reasons" were given, not only in Ethics, but also in Philosophy.

As regards Frazer's "Golden Bough", the chief points on which he seemed to wish to insist were, I think, the three following. (1) That it was a mistake to suppose that there was *only one* "reason", in the sense of "motive", which led people to perform a particular action—to suppose that there was "one motive, which was *the* motive". He gave as an instance of this sort of mistake Frazer's statement, in speaking of Magic, that when primitive people stab an effigy of a particular person, they believe that they have hurt the person in question. He said that primitive people do not *always* entertain this "false scientific belief", though in some cases they may: that they may have quite different reasons for stabbing the effigy. But he said that the tendency to suppose that there is "one motive which is *the* motive" was "enormously strong", giving as an instance that there are theories of play each of which gives *only one* answer to the question "Why do children play?" (2) That it was a mistake to suppose that *the* motive is always "to get something useful". He gave as an instance of this mistake Frazer's supposition that "people at a certain stage thought it useful to kill a person, in order to get a good crop". (3) That it was a ⟦20⟧ mistake to suppose that why, *e.g.* the account of the Beltane Festival "impresses us so much" is because it has "developed from a festival in which a real man was burnt". He accused Frazer of thinking that this was the reason. He said that our puzzlement as to why it impresses us is not diminished by giving the *causes* from which the festival arose, but is diminished by finding other similar festivals: to find these may make it seem "natural", whereas to give the causes from which it arose cannot do this. In this respect he said that the question "Why does this impress us?" is like the aesthetic questions "Why is this beautiful?" or "Why will this bass not do?"

He said that Darwin, in his "expression of the Emotions", made a mistake similar to Frazer's, *e.g.* in thinking that "because our ancestors, when angry, wanted to bite" is a sufficient explanation of why we show our teeth when angry. He said you might say that what is satisfactory in Darwin is not such "hypotheses", but his "putting the facts in a system"—helping us to make a "synopsis" of them.

As for Freud, he gave the greater part of two lectures to Freud's investigation of the nature of a "joke" (Witz), which he said was an "aesthetic investigation". He said that Freud's book on this subject was a very good book for looking for philosophical mistakes, and that the same was true of his writings in general, because there are so many cases in which one can ask how far what he says is a "hypothesis" and how far merely a good way of representing a fact—a question as to which he said Freud himself is constantly unclear. He said, for instance, that Freud encouraged a confusion between getting to know the *cause* of your laughter and getting to know the *reason* why you laugh, because what he says sounds as if it were science, when in fact it is only a "wonderful representation". This last point he also expressed by saying "It is all excellent similes, *e.g.* the comparison of a dream to a rebus". (He had said earlier that all Aesthetics is of the nature of "giving a good simile".) He said that this confusion between *cause* and *reason* had led to the disciples of Freud making "an abominable mess": that Freud did not in fact give any method of analysing dreams which was analogous to the rules which will tell you what are the causes of stomachache; that he had genius and therefore might sometimes by psycho-analysis find the *reason* of a certain dream, but that what is most striking about him is "the enormous field of psychical facts which he arranges".

As for what Freud says about jokes, he said first that Freud makes the two mistakes (1) of supposing that there is something ⟦21⟧ common to all jokes, and (2) of supposing that this supposed common character is the meaning of "joke". He said it is not true, as Freud supposed, that *all* jokes enable you to do covertly what it would not be seemly to do openly, but that "joke", like "proposition", "has a rain-

anxious to insist was perhaps that psycho-analysis does not enable you to discover the *cause* but only the *reason* of, *e.g.* laughter. In support of this statement he asserted that a psycho-analysis is successful only if the patient agrees to the explanation offered by the analyst. He said there is nothing analogous to this in Physics; and that what a patient agrees to can't be a *hypothesis* as to the *cause* of his laughter, but only that so-and-so was the *reason* why he laughed. He explained that the patient who agrees did not think of this reason at the moment when he laughed, and that to say that he thought of it "subconsciously" "tells you nothing as to what was happening at the moment when he laughed".

(F) In (I), rather to my surprise, he spent a good deal of time in discussing what would usually be called a question about colours, namely, the question how the four "saturated" colours, pure yellow, pure red, pure blue and pure green, which he called "primary", are distinguished from those "saturated" colours which are not "primary". He drew a circle on the blackboard to represent the arrangement of the saturated colours, with a vertical diameter joining "yellow" at the top to "blue" at the bottom, and a horizontal diameter joining "green" on the left to "red" on the right. And he seemed to be maintaining with regard to these four colours that they are distinguished from the other saturated colours in the two following ways, *viz.* (1) that the sense in which any purple is "between" pure red and pure blue, and in which any orange is "between" pure yellow and pure red is very different from the sense of "between" in which pure red is "between" any orange and any purple; a difference which he also expressed by saying that whereas an orange can be properly called a "mixture" of yellow and red, red cannot possibly be called a "mixture" of orange and purple; and (2) that whereas pure red can be properly said to be "midway" between pure yellow and pure blue, there is no colour which is "midway" between pure red and pure blue, or "midway" between pure yellow and pure red, etc. He said that, for these reasons, the arrangement of the saturated colours in a square, with the four "primaries" at the four corners, is a better picture of their relations than the arrangement of them in a circle. ⟦22⟧ I say only that he *seemed* to be making these assertions, because he emphasized from the beginning that "primary" is not an adjective to "colour" in the sense in which "black" may be an adjective to "gown", but that the distinction between "primary" and "not primary" is a "logical" distinction—an expression which he explained later on by saying that, just as sounds are not distinguished from colours by the fact that something is true of the one which is not true of the other, so red, blue, green and yellow are not distinguished from the other saturated colours by the fact that anything is true of them which is not true of the others. He emphasized to begin with that the sentences "blue is not primary" and "violet is primary" are both of them "nonsense", and I think there is no doubt he held that, since this is so, their contradictories "blue is primary" and "violet is not primary" are also nonsense, though there is a sense in which the two last are true, and the two former false. In other words, I think he certainly held that "blue is primary" is a "necessary proposition"—that we can't imagine its not being true—and that therefore, as he said (p. 102), it "has no sense". It would seem to follow that if, as he seemed to be, he was really talking about the *colours,* red, blue, green and yellow, all that he said about them was "nonsense". According to what he said elsewhere, he could only have been talking sense, if he was talking, not about the colours, but about certain words used to express them; and accordingly he did actually go on to say that "red is primary" was only a proposition about the use of the English word "red", which, as I said (p. 83), he cannot seriously have held. The question I am here raising is the question which I discussed at length in my second article, and I have nothing to add except to give one quotation which I ought to have given there. He actually said, in one place in (II), "What corresponds to a necessity in the world must be what in language seems an arbitrary rule". I do not think he had succeeded in getting quite clear as to what relation he wished to assert to hold between what he called "rules of grammar", on the one hand, and "necessary propositions", on the other.

(G) With questions about Time he dealt, at considerable length, in two places in (III).

The earlier discussion was in connexion with his view that the "troubles in our thought" which he was concerned to remove, arise from our thinking that sentences which we do not use with any practical object, sound as if they "ought to have sense", ⟦23⟧ when in fact they have none. And in this connexion his main point seemed to be that, since we talk of Time "flowing" as well as of a river "flowing", we are tempted to think that Time "flows" in a certain "direction", as a river does, and that therefore it has sense to suppose that Time might flow in the opposite direction, just as it certainly has sense to suppose that a river might. He said, in one place, that some philosophers have actually made the muddle of thinking that Time has a "direction" which might conceivably be reversed. Later on he made a distinction, as to the meaning of which I am not clear, between what he called "memory-time" and what he called "information-time", saying that in the former there is only earlier and later, not past and future, and that it has sense to say that I remember that which in "information-time" is future. This distinction seemed to be connected with one he had made earlier, when he said that, if we imagine a river with logs floating down it at equal spatial distances from one another, the interval between the time at which, *e.g.* the 120th log passed us and that at which, *e.g.* the 130th passed, might *seem* to be equal to that between the time at which the 130th passed us and that at which the 140th passed us, although, *measured by a clock,* these intervals were not equal. He went on to ask: "Supposing all events had come to an end, what is the criterion for saying that Time would have come to an end too, or that it still went on?" and to ask: "If there were no events earlier than a hundred years ago, would there have been no time before that?" He said that what we need to do is to notice how we use the expression "Time"; and that people ask "Has Time been created?" although the question "Has 'before' been created?" has absolutely no meaning.

But he said a good many things in this discussion which I have failed to understand, and I may easily have omitted points which he would have considered of the first importance.

In his second discussion he was trying to show what was wrong with the following statement which Russell made in his *Outline of Philosophy*: "Remembering, which occurs now, cannot possibly . . . prove that what is remembered occurred at some other time, because the world might have sprung into being five minutes ago, . . . full of acts of remembering which were entirely misleading."[7] But I cannot help thinking that, in what he said about this statement, he made two quite definite mistakes as to what Russell was implying by it. In order to explain why I think so I must, however, first explain what I take it that Russell was implying.

7. Bertrand Russell, *Outline of Philosophy,* London: George Allen & Unwin, 1927, ch. I. (eds.)

⟦24⟧ It will be noted that Russell speaks as if "acts of remembering" could be "entirely misleading"; and he seems not to have noticed that we so use the term "remember" that if an act, which resembles an act of remembering, turns out to be entirely misleading, we say that it was not an act of remembering. For instance "I remember that I had breakfast this morning" is so used that, if it turns out that I did not have breakfast this morning, it *follows logically* that I do *not* remember that I did: from "I remember that I had it" it *follows logically* that I did have it, so that "acts of remembering, which are entirely misleading" is a contradiction in terms; if an act is entirely misleading, it is not an act of remembering. It is plain, therefore, that Russell was using the expression "acts of remembering" in a different sense from any in which it can be correctly used; and his view could be more correctly expressed as the view that it is *logically possible* that we never remember anything. I say "logically possible", because when he says "the world *might* have sprung into being five minutes ago", I think he certainly means by "might", merely that it is *logically possible* that it did.

Now Wittgenstein pointed out, quite justly, that when Russell says "The world might have sprung into being five minutes ago" his choice of "five minutes ago" as the time when the world might have "sprung into being" is "arbitrary": Russell's view requires that it is equally true that it might have "sprung into being" two minutes ago or one minute ago, or, says Wittgenstein, that it might have begun to exist *now*: he actually said that Russell *ought* to have said "The world might have been created *now*". And I think it is true that Russell does imply this. But Wittgenstein said that in the statement quoted, Russell was "committing the precise fallacy of Idealism". And surely this is a complete mistake! From what I have quoted (p. 102) it appears clear that what Wittgenstein regarded as the "fallacy of Idealism" was some such statement as "It is logically *im*possible that anything should be real except the present experience". And Russell's statement certainly does not imply this. It looks to me as if, for the moment, Wittgenstein was confusing the two entirely different propositions, (1) "It is logically possible that nothing exists except the present experience" which Russell may be said to imply, and (2) "It is logically *im*possible that anything should exist except the present experience", which he certainly does not imply.

But it seems to me that he also made another complete mistake as to what Russell's view implied; and this was a criticism into which he went at some length. He began by asking us to ⟦25⟧ consider the question "What is the verification for the proposition 'The world began to exist five minutes ago'?" saying that, if you admit no criterion for its truth, that sentence is "useless", or, as he afterwards said, "meaningless". And his criticism of Russell here consisted in saying that "Russell is refusing to admit as evidence for 'the world began more than five minutes ago' what we all admit as such evidence, and is therefore making that statement meaningless". He compared Russell's statement to the statement "There is a rabbit between A and B, whenever nobody is looking" which he said "seems to have sense, but is in fact meaningless, because it cannot be refuted by experience". But surely Russell would admit and can perfectly consistently admit, that some of those events, which he calls incorrectly "acts of remembering" do constitute very strong evidence that the world existed more than five minutes ago. He is not concerned to deny that they constitute *strong* evidence, but only that they constitute *absolutely conclusive* evidence—that they "prove" that it did. In other words, he is only asserting that it is *logically possible* that the world did not. Wittgenstein seems to me to have overlooked the distinction between denying that we have *any* evidence which Russell does not do, and denying that we have *absolutely conclusive* evidence, which I think Russell certainly meant to do.

But later on Wittgenstein seemed to me to be suggesting another quite different argument, which, if he did mean what he seemed to mean, and if what he seemed to mean is true, would really be a valid refutation of Russell's statement. He introduced again the phrase "memory-time", saying that a certain order of events might be so called, and then going on to say that all these events "approach a point such that it will have no sense to say 'B occurred after the present in memory-time'"; that "now" "should be a point in an order"; and that when we say "The clock is striking now", "now" means "the present of our memory-time", and cannot mean, *e.g.* "at 6:07" because it has sense to say "It is 6:07 *now*". I think all this suggests that his view was that "now", in the sense in which we commonly use it, and in which Russell was undoubtedly using it, has a meaning such that part of what we are saying when we say that an event is happening "now", is that it was preceded by other events which we remember; and, if this is true, it would certainly follow that Russell was wrong in implying that it is logically possible that nothing should have happened before *now*.

⟦26⟧ (H) I was a good deal surprised by some of the things he said about the difference between "philosophy" in the sense in which what he was doing might be called "philosophy" (he called this "modern philosophy"), and what has traditionally been called "philosophy". He said that what he was doing was a "new subject", and not merely a stage in a "continuous development"; that there was now, in philosophy, a "kink" in the "development of human thought", comparable to that which occurred when Galileo and his contemporaries invented dynamics; that a "new method" had been discovered, as had happened when "chemistry was developed out of alchemy"; and that it was now possible for the first time that there should be "skilful" philosophers, though of course there had in the past been "great" philosophers.

He went on to say that, though philosophy had now been "reduced to a matter of skill", yet this skill, like other skills, is very difficult to acquire. One difficulty was that it required a "sort of thinking" to which we are not accustomed and to which we have not been trained—a sort of thinking very different from what is required in the sciences. And he said that the required skill could not be acquired merely by hearing lectures: discussion was essential. As regards his own work, he said it did not matter whether his results were true or not: what mattered was that "a method had been found".

In answer to the question why this "new subject" should be called "philosophy" he said in (III) that though what he was doing was certainly different from what, *e.g.* Plato or Berkeley had done, yet people might feel that it "takes the place of" what they had done—might be inclined to say "This is what I really wanted" and to identify it with what they had done, though it is really different, just as (as I said above, p. 96) a person who had been trying to trisect an angle by rule and compasses might, when shown the proof that this is impossible, be inclined to say that this impossible thing was the very thing he had been trying to do, though what he had been trying to do was really different. But in (II) he had also said that the "new subject" did really resemble what had been traditionally called "philosophy" in the three respects that (1) it was very general, (2) it was fundamental both to ordinary life and to the sciences, and (3) it was independent of any special results of science; that therefore the application to it of the word "philosophy" was not purely arbitrary.

He did not expressly try to tell us exactly what the "new method" which had been found was. But he gave some hints ⟦27⟧ as to its nature. He said, in (II), that the "new subject" consisted in "something like putting in order our notions as to what can be said about the world", and compared this to the tidying up of a room where you have to move the same object several times before you can get the room really tidy. He said also that we were "in a muddle about things", which we had to try to clear up; that we had to follow a certain instinct which leads us to ask certain questions, though we don't even understand what these questions mean; that our asking them results from "a vague mental uneasiness", like that which leads children to ask "Why?"; and that this uneasiness can only be cured "either by showing that a particular question is not permitted, or by answering it". He also said that he was not trying to teach us any new facts: that he would only tell us "trivial" things—"things which we all know already"; but that the difficult thing was to get a "synopsis" of these trivialities, and that our "intellectual discomfort" can only be removed by a synopsis of *many* trivialities—that "if we leave out any, we still have the feeling that something is wrong". In this connexion he said it was misleading to say that what we wanted was an "analysis", since in science to "analyse" water means to discover some new fact about it, *e.g.* that it is composed of oxygen and hydrogen, whereas in philosophy "we know at the start all the facts we need to know". I imagine that it was in this respect of needing a "synopsis" of trivialities that he thought that philosophy was similar to Ethics and Aesthetics (p. 106).

I ought, perhaps, finally to repeat what I said in my first article (p. 51), namely, that he held that though the "new subject" must say a great deal about language, it was only necessary for it to deal with those points about language which have led, or are likely to lead, to definite philosophical puzzles or errors. I think he certainly thought that some philosophers now-a-days have been misled into dealing with linguistic points which have no such bearing, and the discussion of which therefore, in his view, forms no part of the proper business of a philosopher.

# 7

*In 1890, James George Frazer published the first volume of* The Golden Bough, *but his anthropological study of magic and religion was not completed until 1915, when the first volumes had already appeared in a third revised edition, while a twelfth volume provided bibliography and general index to the entire work. As famous and influential as his magisterial treatment soon became, Wittgenstein never read it in its entirety. In his recollection of "Conversations with Wittgenstein" M. O'C. Drury reports this for the year 1931: "Wittgenstein told me he had long wanted to read Frazer's* The Golden Bough *and asked me to get hold of a copy out of the Union Library and read it out loud to him. I got the first volume of the full edition and we continued to read from it for some weeks. He would stop me from time to time and make comments on Frazer's remarks."*[1]

*From this first encounter with Frazer stems part I of the following collection of remarks. The remarks occur intermittently throughout a manuscript volume that Wittgenstein kept for the first half of 1931 (MS 110). He later grouped them together and incorporated them into a larger typescript of altogether 771 pages (TS 221). In this typescript, the longest section on Frazer runs for ten pages and represents the bulk of part I. It is followed by three shorter sets of remarks from the same typescript.*

*The remarks in part II stem from a second encounter with Frazer. According to Rush Rhees, Wittgenstein received a much-abbreviated one-volume edition, his personal copy of* The Golden Bough, *in 1936.*[2] *Thus "not earlier than 1936 and probably after 1948"*[3] *Wittgenstein made pencil notes on scraps of paper referring to particular pages in this abbreviated edition. They were probably meant for insertion into the pages of that book (they are now known as MS 143). Part II consists of these notes.*

*The "Remarks on Frazer's* Golden Bough*" were first edited and published in 1967 by Rush Rhees in the journal* Synthese. *Rhees later prepared a bilingual book edition*[4] *which leaves out a considerable num-*

1. In *Recollections of Wittgenstein,* ed. R. Rhees, p. 119.
2. Ibid., p. 220.
3. Rush Rhees in "Introductory Note," *Synthese,* vol. 17, 1967, p. 234.
4. Published in Retford, England, by Brynmill, 1979. The italicized intralineal page references in our German text are to this edition (pp. 1–18).

*ber of the remarks he had earlier included. Some of the later editions followed Rhees's earlier format; others adopted his later cuts. From the various extant editions, we have tried to produce as comprehensive and faithful a text as possible, placing the contentious remarks (pp. 136–141, 150–155 below) in brackets.*[5] *We also followed the practice of earlier editors by reproducing some of the passages from Frazer's book to which Wittgenstein appears to refer. However, while previous editors make reference only to Wittgenstein's own one-volume edition,*[6] *we also include in brackets the corresponding volume and page numbers for the large standard edition of* The Golden Bough.[7]

*While the extant editions disagree about what to include and what to leave out of Wittgenstein's remarks, most reproduce a short sequence of remarks which appears in his manuscript around the place where he turns to Frazer, but which he did not incorporate into the typescript because he considered them bad (in his manuscript he labeled them with an 'S' for* 'schlecht'*):*[8]

> *I now believe that it would be right to begin my book with remarks about metaphysics as a kind of magic.*
>
> *But in doing this I must not make a case for magic nor may I make fun of it.*
>
> *The depth of magic should be preserved.—*
>
> *Indeed, here the elimination of magic has itself the character of magic.*

5. Aside from the editions already mentioned and the translation by John Beversluis, we consulted the edition by Joachim Schulte in Ludwig Wittgenstein, *Vortrag über Ethik und andere kleine Schriften,* Frankfurt: Suhrkamp, 1989, pp. 29–46, compare pp. 141f.

6. James George Frazer, *The Golden Bough,* abbreviated one-volume edition, London: Macmillan, 1922 (with various reprints thereafter).

7. James George Frazer, *The Golden Bough: A Study in Magic and Religion,* third edition, 12 volumes, London: Macmillan, 1966.

8. The German reads as follows:

> Ich glaube jetzt, daß es richtig wäre, mein Buch mit Bemerkungen über die Metaphysik als eine Art von Magie zu beginnen.
>
> Worin ich aber weder der Magie das Wort reden noch mich über sie lustig machen darf.
>
> Von der Magie müßte die Tiefe behalten werden.—
>
> Ja, das Ausschalten der Magie hat hier den Charakter der Magie selbst.

*For, back then, when I began talking about the* 'world' *(and not about this tree or table), what else did I want but to keep something higher spellbound in my words?*

---

Denn, wenn ich damals anfing, von der "*Welt*" zu reden (und nicht von diesem Baum oder Tisch), was wollte ich anderes, als etwas Höheres in meine Worte bannen.

# Bemerkungen über Frazers *Golden Bough*

## I

Man muß beim Irrtum ansetzen und ihn in die Wahrheit überführen.

D.h., man muß die Quelle des Irrtums aufdecken, sonst nützt uns das Hören der Wahrheit nichts. Sie kann nicht eindringen, wenn etwas anderes ihren Platz einnimmt.

Einen von der Wahrheit zu überzeugen, genügt es nicht, die Wahrheit zu konstatieren, sondern man muß den *Weg* vom Irrtum zur Wahrheit finden.

Ich muß immer wieder im Wasser des Zweifels untertauchen.

Frazers Darstellung der magischen und religiösen Anschauungen der Menschen ist unbefriedigend: sie läßt diese Anschauungen als *Irrtümer* erscheinen.

So war also Augustinus im Irrtum, wenn er Gott auf jeder Seite der *Confessionen* anruft?

Aber — kann man sagen — wenn er nicht im Irrtum war, so war es doch der Buddhistische Heilige — oder welcher immer — dessen Religion ganz andere Anschauungen zum Ausdruck bringt. Aber *keiner* von ihnen war im Irrtum, außer wo er eine Theorie aufstellte.

Schon die Idee, den Gebrauch — etwa die Tötung des Priesterkönigs — ⟦235⟧erklären zu wollen, scheint mir verfehlt. Alles, was Frazer tut, ist, sie Menschen, die so ähnlich denken wie er, plausibel zu machen. Es ist sehr merkwürdig, daß alle diese Gebräuche endlich sozusagen als Dummheiten dargestellt werden.

Nie wird es aber plausibel, daß die Menschen aus purer Dummheit all das tun.

Wenn er uns z.B. erklärt, der König müsse in seiner Blüte getötet werden, ⟦*2*⟧ weil nach den Anschauungen der Wilden sonst seine Seele nicht frisch erhalten würde, so kann man doch nur sagen: wo jener Gebrauch und diese Anschauung zusammengehn, dort entspringt nicht der Gebrauch der Anschauung, sondern sie sind eben beide da.

# Remarks on Frazer's *Golden Bough*

## I

One must start out with error and convert it into truth.

That is, one must reveal the source of error, otherwise hearing the truth won't do any good. The truth cannot force its way in when something else is occupying its place.

To convince someone of the truth, it is not enough to state it, but rather one must find the *path* from error to truth.

I must plunge into the water of doubt again and again.

Frazer's account of the magical and religious views of mankind is unsatisfactory: it makes these views look like *errors*.

Was Augustine in error, then, when he called upon God on every page of the *Confessions*?

But—one might say—if he was not in error, surely the Buddhist holy man was—or anyone else—whose religion gives expression to completely different views. But *none* of them was in error, except when he set forth a theory.

The very idea of wanting to explain a practice—for example, the killing of the priest-king—seems wrong to me. All that Frazer does is to make them plausible to people who think as he does. It is very remarkable that in the final analysis all these practices are presented as, so to speak, pieces of stupidity.

But it will never be plausible to say that mankind does all that out of sheer stupidity.

⟦62⟧ When, for example, he explains to us that the king must be killed in his prime, because the savages believe that otherwise his soul would not be kept fresh, all one can say is: where that practice and these views occur together, the practice does not spring from the view, but they are both just there.

Es kann schon sein, und kommt heute oft vor, daß ein Mensch einen Gebrauch aufgibt, nachdem er einen Irrtum erkannt hat, auf den sich dieser Gebrauch stützte. Aber dieser Fall besteht eben nur dort, wo es genügt, den Menschen auf seinen Irrtum aufmerksam zu machen, um ihn von seiner Handlungsweise abzubringen. Aber das ist doch bei den religiösen Gebräuchen eines Volkes nicht der Fall, und *darum* handelt es sich eben um *keinen* Irrtum.

Frazer sagt, es sei sehr schwer, den Irrtum in der Magie zu entdecken — und darum halte sie sich so lange — weil z.B. eine Beschwörung, die Regen herbeiführen soll, früher oder später gewiß als wirksam erscheint. Aber dann ist es eben merkwürdig, daß die Menschen nicht früher daraufkommen, daß es ohnehin früher oder später regnet.

Ich glaube, daß das Unternehmen einer Erklärung schon darum verfehlt ist, weil man nur richtig zusammenstellen muß, was man *weiß*, und nichts dazusetzen, und die Befriedigung, die durch die Erklärung angestrebt wird, ergibt sich von selbst.

Und die Erklärung ist es hier gar nicht, die befriedigt. Wenn Frazer anfängt und uns die Geschichte von dem Waldkönig von Nemi erzählt, ⟦*3*⟧ so tut er dies in einem Ton, der zeigt, daß er fühlt und uns fühlen lassen will, daß hier etwas Merkwürdiges und Furchtbares geschieht. Die Frage aber „warum geschieht dies?" wird eigentlich dadurch beantwortet: Weil es furchtbar ist. Das heißt, dasselbe, was uns bei diesem Vorgang furchtbar, großartig, schaurig, tragisch, etc., nichts weniger als trivial und bedeutungslos vorkommt, *das* hat diesen Vorgang ins Leben gerufen.

⟦236⟧ Nur *beschreiben* kann man hier und sagen: so ist das menschliche Leben.

---

1. See Sir James George Frazer, *The Golden Bough*, p. 264 [iii, 422]: "But reflection and enquiry should satisfy us that to our predecessors we are indebted for much of what we thought most our own, and that their errors were not wilful extravagances or the ravings of insanity, but simply hypotheses, justifiable as such at the time when they were propounded, but which a fuller experience has proved to be inadequate. It is only by the successive testing of hypotheses and rejection of the false that truth is at last elicited. After all, what we call truth is only the hypothesis which is found to work best. Therefore in reviewing the opinions and practices of ruder ages and

It can indeed happen, and often does today, that a person will give up a practice after he has recognized an error on which it was based. But this happens only when calling someone's attention to his error is enough to turn him from his way of behaving. But this is not the case with the religious practices of a people and *therefore* there is *no* question of an error.[1]

Frazer says that it is very hard to discover the error in magic—and that is why it has lasted so long—because, for example, an incantation that is supposed to bring rain certainly seems efficacious sooner or later.[2] But then it is surely remarkable that people don't realize earlier that sooner or later it's going to rain anyhow.

I believe that the attempt to explain is already therefore wrong, because one must only correctly piece together what one *knows,* ⟦63⟧ without adding anything, and the satisfaction being sought through the explanation follows of itself.

And the explanation isn't what satisfies us here at all. When Frazer begins by telling us the story of the King of the Wood of Nemi, he does this in a tone which shows that he feels, and wants us to feel, that something strange and dreadful is happening. But the question "why does this happen?" is properly answered by saying: Because it is dreadful. That is, precisely that which makes this incident strike us as dreadful, magnificent, horrible, tragic, etc., as anything but trivial and insignificant, is also *that* which has called this incident to life.

Here one can only *describe* and say: this is what human life is like.

---

races we shall do well to look with leniency upon their errors as inevitable slips made in the search for truth, and to give them the benefit of that indulgence which we ourselves may one day stand in need of: *cum excusatione itaque veteres audiendi sunt*".

2. See Frazer, p. 59 [i, 242]: "A ceremony intended to make the wind blow or the rain fall, or to work the death of an enemy, will always be followed, sooner or later, by the occurrence it is meant to bring to pass; and primitive man may be excused for regarding the occurrence as a direct result of the ceremony, and the best possible proof of its efficacy."

Die Erklärung ist im Vergleich mit dem Eindruck, den uns das Beschriebene macht, zu unsicher.

Jede Erklärung ist ja eine Hypothese.

Wer aber, etwa, von der Liebe beunruhigt ist, dem wird eine hypothetische Erklärung wenig helfen. — Sie wird ihn nicht beruhigen.

Das Gedränge der Gedanken, die nicht herauskönnen, weil sich alle vordrängen wollen und so am Ausgang verkeilen.

Wenn man mit jener Erzählung vom Priesterkönig von Nemi das Wort „die Majestät des Todes" zusammenstellt, so sieht man, daß die beiden Eins sind.
Das Leben des Priesterkönigs stellt das dar, was mit jenem Wort gemeint ist.

Wer von der Majestät des Todes ergriffen ist, kann dies durch so ein Leben zum Ausdruck bringen. — Dies ist natürlich auch keine Erklärung, sondern setzt nur ein Symbol für ein anderes. Oder: eine Zeremonie für eine andere.

Einem religiösen Symbol liegt keine *Meinung* zu Grunde.
Und nur der Meinung entspricht der Irrtum.

Man möchte sagen: Dieser und dieser Vorgang hat stattgefunden; lach', wenn Du kannst.

⟦*4*⟧ Die religiöse Handlung, oder das religiöse Leben des Priesterkönigs ist von keiner anderen Art, als jede echt religiöse Handlung heute, etwa ein Geständnis der Sünden. Auch dieses läßt sich „*erklären*" und läßt sich nicht erklären.

In effigie verbrennen. Das Bild des Geliebten küssen. Das basiert *natürlich nicht* auf einem Glauben an eine bestimmte Wirkung auf den Gegen⟦237⟧stand, den das Bild darstellt. Es bezweckt eine Befriedigung und erreicht sie auch. Oder vielmehr, es *bezweckt* gar nichts; wir handeln eben so und fühlen uns dann befriedigt.

Man könnte auch den Namen der Geliebten küssen, und hier wäre die Stellvertretung durch den Namen klar.

Compared with the impression which the thing described makes on us, the explanation is too uncertain.

Every explanation is after all an hypothesis.

But an hypothetical explanation will be of little help to someone, say, who is upset because of love.—It will not calm him.

The crowd of thoughts which cannot come out, because they all want to rush forward and thus get stuck in the exit.

If a narrator places the priest-king of Nemi and "the majesty of death" side by side, he realizes that they are the same.
The life of the priest-king shows what is meant by that phrase.

Someone who is affected by the majesty of death can give expression to this through such a life.—This, of course, is ⟦64⟧ also no explanation, but merely substitutes one symbol for another. Or: one ceremony for another.

No *opinion* serves as the foundation for a religious symbol.
And only an opinion can involve an error.

One would like to say: This and that incident have taken place; laugh, if you can.

The religious actions, or the religious life, of the priest-king are no different in kind from any genuinely religious action of today, for example, a confession of sins. This, too, admits of being '*explained*' and not explained.

Burning in effigy. Kissing the picture of one's beloved. That is *obviously not* based on the belief that it will have some specific effect on the object which the picture represents. It aims at satisfaction and achieves it. Or rather: it *aims* at nothing at all; we just behave this way and then we feel satisfied.

One could also kiss the name of one's beloved, and here it would be clear that the name was being used as a substitute.

Der selbe Wilde, der, anscheinend um seinen Feind zu töten, dessen Bild durchsticht, baut seine Hütte aus Holz wirklich und schnitzt seinen Pfeil kunstgerecht und nicht in effigie.

Die Idee, daß man einen leblosen Gegenstand zu sich herwinken kann, wie man einen Menschen zu sich herwinkt. Hier ist das Prinzip das, der Personifikation.

Und immer beruht die Magie auf der Idee des Symbolismus und der Sprache.

Die Darstellung eines Wunsches ist, eo ipso, die Darstellung seiner Erfüllung.

Die Magie aber bringt einen Wunsch zur Darstellung; sie äußert einen Wunsch.

Die Taufe als Waschung. — Ein Irrtum entsteht erst, wenn die Magie wissenschaftlich ausgelegt wird.

Wenn die Adoption eines Kindes so vor sich geht, daß die Mutter es durch ihre Kleider zieht, so ist es doch verrückt zu glauben, daß hier ein *Irrtum* vorliegt und sie glaubt, das Kind geboren zu haben.

⟦*5*⟧ Von den magischen Operationen sind die zu unterscheiden, die auf einer falschen, zu einfachen, Vorstellung der Dinge und Vorgänge beruhen. Wenn man etwa sagt, die Krankheit ziehe von einem Teil des Körpers in den andern, oder Vorkehrungen trifft, die Krankheit abzuleiten, als wäre sie eine Flüssigkeit oder ein Wärmezustand. Man macht sich dann also ein falsches, das heißt hier, unzutreffendes Bild.

Welche Enge des seelischen Lebens bei Frazer! Daher: Welche Unmöglichkeit, ein anderes Leben zu begreifen, als das englische seiner Zeit!

⟦238⟧ Frazer kann sich keinen Priester vorstellen, der nicht im Grunde ein englischer Parson unserer Zeit ist, mit seiner ganzen Dummheit und Flauheit.

Warum sollte dem Menschen sein Name nicht heilig sein können. Ist er doch einerseits das wichtigste Instrument, das ihm gegeben wird, anderseits wie ein Schmuckstück, das ihm bei der Geburt umgehangen wird.

Wie irreführend die Erklärungen Frazers sind, sieht man — glaube ich — daraus, daß man primitive Gebräuche sehr wohl selbst er-

The same savage, who stabs the picture of his enemy apparently in order to kill him, really builds his hut out of wood and carves his arrow skillfully and not in effigy.

The idea that one can summon an inanimate object to oneself as one can summon a person. Here the principle is that of personification.

And magic is always based on the idea of symbolism and language.

The representation of a wish is, *eo ipso,* the representation of its realization.

⟦65⟧ But magic brings a wish to representation; it expresses a wish.

Baptism as washing.—An error arises only when magic is interpreted scientifically.

If the adoption of a child proceeds in such a way that the mother draws it from under her clothes,[3] it is surely insane to believe that an *error* is present and that she believes she has given birth to the child.

Operations which depend on a false, overly simple idea of things and processes are to be distinguished from magical operations. For example, if one says that the illness is moving from one part of the body to another, or takes precautions to divert the illness as if it were a liquid or a condition of warmth. One is then creating a false picture for oneself, which, in this case, means a groundless one.

What a narrow spiritual life on Frazer's part! As a result: how impossible it was for him to conceive of a life different from that of the England of his time!

Frazer cannot imagine a priest who is not basically a present-day English parson with the same stupidity and dullness.

Why shouldn't it be possible for a person to regard his name as sacred? It is certainly, on the one hand, the most important instru-

3. See Frazer, p. 15 [i, 74]: ". . . in Bulgaria and among the Bosnian Turks . . . a woman will take a boy whom she intends to adopt and push or pull him through her clothes; ever afterwards he is regarded as her very son, and inherits the whole property of his adoptive parents."

dichten könnte und es müßte ein Zufall sein, wenn sie nicht irgendwo wirklich gefunden würden. Das heißt, das Prinzip, nach welchem diese Gebräuche geordnet sind, ist ein viel allgemeineres als Frazer es erklärt und in unserer eigenen Seele vorhanden, so daß wir uns alle Möglichkeiten selbst ausdenken könnten. — Daß etwa der König eines Stammes für niemanden sichtbar bewahrt wird, können wir uns wohl vorstellen, aber auch, daß jeder Mann des Stammes ihn sehen soll. Das letztere wird dann gewiß nicht in irgendeiner mehr oder weniger zufälligen Weise geschehen dürfen, sondern er wird den Leuten *gezeigt* werden. Vielleicht wird ihn niemand berühren dürfen, vielleicht aber jeder berühren *müssen*. Denken wir daran, daß nach Schuberts Tod sein Bruder Partituren Schuberts in kleine Stücke zerschnitt und seinen Lieblingsschülern solche Stücke von einigen Takten gab. Diese Handlung, als Zeichen der Pietät, ist uns *ebenso* verständlich, wie die andere, die Partituren unberührt, niemandem zugänglich, aufzubewahren. Und hätte Schuberts Bruder die Partituren verbrannt, so wäre auch das als Zeichen der Pietät verständlich.

Das Zeremonielle (heiße oder kalte) im Gegensatz zum Zufälligen (lauen) charakterisiert die Pietät.

⟦*6*⟧ Ja, Frazers Erklärungen wären überhaupt keine Erklärungen, wenn sie nicht letzten Endes an eine Neigung in uns selbst appellierten.

Das Essen und Trinken ist mit Gefahren verbunden, nicht nur für den Wilden, sondern auch für uns; nichts natürlicher, als daß man sich vor diesen schützen will; und nun könnten wir uns selbst solche Schutzmaßnahmen ausdenken. — Aber nach welchem Prinzip erdichten wir sie? Offenbar danach, daß alle Gefahren der Form nach auf einige sehr einfache reduziert werden, die dem Menschen ohne weiteres sichtbar sind. Also nach dem selben Prinzip, nach dem die ungebildeten Leute unter uns sagen, die Krankheit ziehe sich vom Kopf in die Brust etc., etc. ⟦239⟧ In diesen einfachen Bildern wird natürlich die Personifikation eine große Rolle spielen, denn, daß Menschen (also Geister) dem Menschen gefährlich werden können, ist jedem bekannt.

Daß der Schatten des Menschen, der wie ein Mensch ausschaut, oder sein Spiegelbild, daß Regen, Gewitter, die Mondphasen, der Jahreszeitwechsel, die Ähnlichkeit und Verschiedenheit der Tiere unter einander und zum Menschen, die Erscheinungen des Todes, der Geburt und des Geschlechtslebens, kurz alles, was der Mensch

ment which is given to him, and, on the other, like a piece of jewelry hung around his neck at birth.

One sees how misleading Frazer's explanations are—I believe—by noting that one could very easily invent primitive practices oneself, and it would be pure luck if they were not actually found somewhere. That is, the principle according to which these practices are arranged is a much more general one than in Frazer's explanation and it is present in ⟦66⟧ our own minds, so that we ourselves could think up all the possibilities.—We can easily imagine, for example, that the king of a tribe is kept hidden from everyone, but also that every man in the tribe must see him. Certainly, then, the latter will not be left to happen in some more or less chance manner, but he will be *shown* to the people. Perhaps no one will be allowed to touch him, but perhaps everyone *must* touch him. Recall that after Schubert's death his brother cut some of Schubert's scores into small pieces and gave such pieces, consisting of a few bars, to his favorite pupils. This act, as a sign of piety, is *just as* understandable to us as the different one of keeping the scores untouched, accessible to no one. And if Schubert's brother had burned the scores, that too would be understandable as a sign of piety.

The ceremonial (hot or cold) as opposed to the haphazard (lukewarm) characterizes piety.

Indeed, if Frazer's explanations did not in the final analysis appeal to a tendency in ourselves, they would not really be explanations.

There are dangers connected with eating and drinking, not only for savages, but also for us; nothing is more natural than the desire to protect oneself from these; and now we could devise such preventative measures ourselves.—But according to what principle are we to invent them? Obviously, according to the one by which all dangers are reduced to the form of a few very simple ones which are immediately evident to man. Hence the same principle according to which uneducated people among us say that the illness is moving from the head into the chest, etc., etc. Personification will, of course, play a large role in these simple pictures, for, as everyone knows, men (hence spirits) can become dangerous to mankind.

It goes without saying that a man's shadow, which looks like him, or his mirror-image, the rain, thunderstorms, the phases of the moon, the changing of the seasons, the way in which animals are similar to and different from one another and in relation to man, the phenomena of death, birth, and ⟦67⟧ sexual life, in short, everything we observe around us year in and year out, interconnected in so many

jahraus jahrein um sich wahrnimmt, in mannigfaltigster Weise mit einander verknüpft, in seinem Denken (seiner Philosophie) und seinen Gebräuchen eine Rolle spielen wird, ist selbstverständlich, oder ist eben das, was wir wirklich wissen und interessant ist.

Wie hätte das Feuer oder die Ähnlichkeit des Feuers mit der Sonne verfehlen können auf den erwachenden Menschengeist einen Eindruck zu machen. Aber nicht vielleicht „weil er sich's nicht erklären kann" (der dumme Aberglaube unserer Zeit) — denn wird es durch eine „Erklärung" weniger eindrucksvoll? —

Die Magie in „Alice in Wonderland" beim Trocknen durch Vorlesen des Trockensten was es gibt.

Bei der magischen Heilung einer Krankheit *bedeutet* man ihr, sie möge den Patienten verlassen.

⟦7⟧ Man möchte nach der Beschreibung so einer magischen Kur immer sagen: Wenn *das* die Krankheit nicht versteht, so weiß ich nicht, *wie* man es ihr sagen soll.

Nichts ist so schwierig, wie Gerechtigkeit gegen die Tatsachen.

Ich meine nicht, daß gerade das *Feuer* Jedem einen Eindruck machen muß. Das Feuer nicht mehr, wie jede andere Erscheinung, und die eine Erscheinung Dem, die andere Jenem. Denn keine Erscheinung ist an sich besonders geheimnisvoll, aber jede kann es uns werden, und das ist eben das Charakteristische am erwachenden Geist des Menschen, daß ihm eine Erscheinung bedeutend wird. Man könnte fast sagen, der Mensch sei ein zeremonielles Tier. Das ist wohl teils falsch, teils unsinnig, aber es ist auch etwas Richtiges daran.

Das heißt, man könnte ein Buch über Anthropologie so anfangen: Wenn man das Leben und Benehmen der Menschen auf der Erde betrachtet, so sieht man, daß sie außer den Handlungen, die man tierische ⟦240⟧ nennen könnte, der Nahrungsaufnahme, etc., etc., etc., auch solche ausführen, die einen eigentümlichen Charakter tragen und die man rituelle Handlungen nennen könnte.

Nun aber ist es Unsinn, so fortzufahren, daß man als das Charakteristische *dieser* Handlungen sagt, sie seien solche, die aus fehlerhaften Anschauungen über die Physik der Dinge entsprängen. (So tut es Frazer, wenn er sagt, Magie sei wesentlich falsche Physik, bzw. falsche Heilkunst, Technik, etc.)

Vielmehr ist das Charakteristische der rituellen Handlung gar keine Ansicht, Meinung, ob sie nun richtig oder falsch ist, obgleich eine Meinung — ein Glaube — selbst auch rituell sein kann, zum Ritus gehören kann.

different ways, will play a part in his thinking (his philosophy) and in his practices, or is precisely what we really know and find interesting.

How could fire or the similarity of fire to the sun have failed to make an impression on the awakening mind of man? But perhaps not "because he can't explain it" (the foolish superstition of our time)—for will an 'explanation' make it less impressive?—

The magic in *Alice in Wonderland:* of drying out by reading the driest thing there is.[4]

With the magical healing of an illness, one *directs* the illness to leave the patient.

After the description of any such magical treatment, one always wants to say: If the illness doesn't understand *that,* I don't know *how* one should tell it to leave.

Nothing is so difficult as doing justice to the facts.

I don't mean that just *fire* must make an impression on everyone. Fire no more than any other phenomenon, and one thing will impress this person and another that. For no phenomenon is in itself particularly mysterious, but any of them can become so to us, and the characteristic feature of the awakening mind of man is precisely the fact that a phenomenon comes to have meaning for him. One could almost say that man is a ceremonial animal. That is, no doubt, partly wrong and partly nonsensical, but there is also something right about it.

That is, one could begin a book on anthropology by saying: When one examines the life and behavior of mankind throughout the world, one sees that, except for what might be called animal activities, such as ingestion, etc., etc., etc., men also perform actions which bear a characteristic peculiar to themselves, and these could be called ritualistic actions.

But then it is nonsense for one to go on to say that the characteristic feature of *these* actions is the fact that they arise from faulty views about the physics of things. (Frazer does this when he says that magic is essentially false physics or, as the case may be, false medicine, technology, etc.)

⟦68⟧ Rather, the characteristic feature of ritualistic action is not at all a view, an opinion, whether true or false, although an opinion—a belief—can itself be ritualistic or part of a rite.

4. Lewis Carroll, *Alice in Wonderland,* chap. III.

Wenn man es für selbstverständlich hält, daß sich der Mensch an seiner Phantasie vergnügt, so bedenke man, daß diese Phantasie nicht wie ein gemaltes Bild oder ein plastisches Modell ist, sondern ein kompliziertes Gebilde aus heterogenen Bestandteilen: Wörtern und Bildern. Man wird dann das Operieren mit Schrift- und Lautzeichen nicht mehr in Gegensatz stellen zu dem Operieren mit „Vorstellungsbildern" der Ereignisse.

Wir müssen die ganze Sprache durchpflügen.

⟦*8*⟧ Frazer: „That these observances are dictated by fear of the ghost of the slain seems certain. . . ." Aber warum gebraucht Frazer denn das Wort „ghost"? Er versteht also sehr wohl diesen Aberglauben, da er ihn uns mit einem ihm geläufigen abergläubischen Wort erklärt. Oder vielmehr, er hätte daraus sehen können, daß auch in uns etwas für jene Handlungsweisen der Wilden spricht. — Wenn ich, der ich nicht glaube, daß es irgendwo menschlich-übermenschliche Wesen gibt, die man Götter nennen kann — wenn ich sage: „ich fürchte die Rache der Götter", so zeigt das, daß ich damit etwas meinen kann, oder einer Empfindung Ausdruck geben kann, die nicht notwendig mit jenem Glauben verbunden ist.

Frazer wäre im Stande zu glauben, daß ein Wilder aus Irrtum stirbt. In den Volksschullesebüchern steht, daß Attilla seine großen Kriegszüge unternommen hat, weil er glaubte, das Schwert des Donnergottes zu besitzen.

⟦241⟧ Frazer ist viel mehr savage, als die meisten seiner savages, denn diese werden nicht so weit vom Verständnis einer geistigen Angelegenheit entfernt sein, wie ein Engländer des 20sten Jahrhunderts. *Seine* Erklärungen der primitiven Gebräuche sind viel roher, als der Sinn dieser Gebräuche selbst.

Die historische Erklärung, die Erklärung als eine Hypothese der Entwicklung ist nur *eine* Art der Zusammenfassung der Daten — ihrer Synopsis. Es ist ebensowohl möglich, die Daten in ihrer Beziehung zu einander zu sehen und in ein allgemeines Bild zusammenzufassen, ohne es in Form einer Hypothese über die zeitliche Entwicklung zu tun.

Identifizierung der eigenen Götter mit Göttern anderer Völker. Man überzeugt sich davon, daß die Namen die gleiche Bedeutung haben.

If one holds it as self-evident that people delight in their imagination, one should bear in mind that this imagination is not like a painted portrait or plastic model, but a complicated pattern made up of heterogeneous elements: words and pictures. One will then no longer place operating with written and phonetic symbols in opposition to operating with 'mental images' of events.

We must plow through the whole of language.

Frazer: ". . . That these observances are dictated by fear of the ghost of the slain seems certain. . . ."[5] But why then does Frazer use the word 'ghost'? He thus understands this superstition very well, since he explains it to us with a superstitious word he is familiar with. Or rather, this might have enabled him to see that there is also something in us which speaks in favor of those savages' behavior.—If I, a person who does not believe that there are human-superhuman beings somewhere which one can call gods—if I say: "I fear the wrath of the gods," that shows that I can mean something by this, or can give expression to a feeling which is not necessarily connected with that belief.

Frazer would be capable of believing that a savage dies because of an error. In books used in primary schools it is said that Attila had undertaken his great military campaigns because he believed that he possessed the sword of the god of thunder.

Frazer is much more savage than most of his savages, for they are not as far removed from the understanding of a spiritual matter as a twentieth-century Englishman. *His* explana⟦69⟧tions of primitive practices are much cruder than the meaning of these practices themselves.

The historical explanation, the explanation as an hypothesis of development, is only *one* way of assembling the data—of their synopsis. It is just as possible to see the data in their relation to one another and to embrace them in a general picture without putting it in the form of an hypothesis about temporal development.

Identifying one's own gods with the gods of other peoples. One convinces oneself that the names have the same meaning.

5. See Frazer, p. 212 [iii, 166].

„Und so deutet das Chor auf ein geheimes Gesetz" möchte man zu der Frazer'schen Tatsachensammlung sagen. Dieses Gesetz, diese Idee, *kann* ich nun durch eine Entwicklungshypothese darstellen oder auch, analog dem Schema einer Pflanze, durch das Schema einer religiösen Zeremonie, ⟦*9*⟧ oder aber durch die Gruppierung des Tatsachenmaterials allein, in einer „*übersichtlichen*" Darstellung.

Der Begriff der übersichtlichen Darstellung ist für uns von grundlegender Bedeutung. Er bezeichnet unsere Darstellungsform, die Art, wie wir die Dinge sehen. (Eine Art der ‚Weltanschauung', wie sie scheinbar für unsere Zeit typisch ist. Spengler.)

Diese übersichtliche Darstellung vermittelt das Verständnis, welches eben darin besteht, daß wir die „Zusammenhänge sehen". Daher die Wichtigkeit des Findens von *Zwischengliedern.*

Ein hypothetisches Zwischenglied aber soll in diesem Falle nichts tun, als die Aufmerksamkeit auf die Ähnlichkeit, den Zusammenhang, der *Tatsachen* lenken. Wie man eine interne Beziehung der Kreisform zur Ellipse dadurch illustrierte, daß man eine Ellipse allmählich in einen Kreis überführt; *aber nicht um zu behaupten, daß eine gewisse Ellipse tatsächlich, historisch, aus einem Kreis entstanden wäre* (Entwicklungs⟦242⟧hypothese), sondern nur um unser Auge für einen formalen Zusammenhang zu schärfen.

Aber auch die Entwicklungshypothese kann ich als weiter nichts sehen, als eine Einkleidung eines formalen Zusammenhangs.

* * *

⟦*10*⟧ Ich möchte sagen: nichts zeigt unsere Verwandtschaft mit jenen Wilden besser, als daß Frazer ein ihm und uns so geläufiges Wort wie ‚ghost' oder ‚shade' bei der Hand hat, um die Ansichten dieser Leute zu beschreiben.

(Das ist ja doch etwas anderes, als wenn er etwa beschriebe, die Wilden bilden sich ein, daß ihnen ihr Kopf herunterfällt, wenn sie einen Feind erschlagen haben. Hier hätte *unsere Beschreibung* nichts Abergläubisches oder Magisches an sich.)

Ja, diese Sonderbarkeit bezieht sich nicht nur auf die Ausdrücke ‚ghost' und ‚shade', und es wird viel zu wenig Aufhebens davon gemacht, daß wir das Wort ‚Seele', ‚Geist' (‚spirit') zu unserem eigenen gebildeten Vokabular zählen. Dagegen ist es eine Kleinigkeit, daß wir nicht glauben, daß unsere Seele ißt und trinkt.

In unserer Sprache ist eine ganze Mythologie niedergelegt.

"And so the chorus points to a secret law" one feels like saying to Frazer's collection of facts. I *can* represent this law, this idea, by means of an evolutionary hypothesis, or also, analogously to the schema of a plant, by means of the schema of a religious ceremony, but also by means of the arrangement of its factual content alone, in a '*perspicuous*' representation.

The concept of perspicuous representation is of fundamental importance for us. It denotes the form of our representation, the way we see things. (A kind of 'World-view' as it is apparently typical of our time. Spengler.)

This perspicuous representation brings about the understanding which consists precisely in the fact that we "see the connections". Hence the importance of finding *connecting links.*

But an hypothetical connecting link should in this case do nothing but direct the attention to the similarity, the relatedness, of the *facts.* As one might illustrate an internal relation of a circle to an ellipse by gradually converting an ellipse into a circle; *but not in order to assert that a certain ellipse actually, historically, had originated from a circle* (evolutionary hypothesis), but only in order to sharpen our eye for a formal connection.

⟦70⟧ But I can also see the evolutionary hypothesis as nothing more, as the clothing of a formal connection.

* * *

I should like to say: nothing shows our kinship to those savages better than the fact that Frazer has on hand a word as familiar to himself and to us as 'ghost' or 'shade' in order to describe the views of these people.

(That is certainly something different than were he to describe, for example, the savages as imagining that their heads will fall off when they have killed an enemy. Here *our description* would contain nothing superstitious or magical in itself.)

Indeed, this peculiarity relates not only to the expressions 'ghost' and 'shade', and much too little is made of the fact that we count the words 'soul' and 'spirit' as part of our educated vocabulary. Compared with this, the fact that we do not believe that our soul eats and drinks is a trifling matter.

An entire mythology is stored within our language.

Austreiben des Todes oder Umbringen des Todes; aber anderseits wird er als Gerippe dargestellt, als selbst in gewissem Sinne tot. „As dead as death." ‚Nichts ist so tot wie der Tod; nichts ist so schön wie die Schönheit selbst.' Das Bild, worunter man sich hier die Realität denkt, ist, daß die Schönheit, der Tod, etc. die reinen (konzentrierten) Substanzen sind, während sie in einem schönen Gegenstand als Beimischung vorhanden sind. — Und erkenne ich hier nicht meine eigenen Betrachtungen über ‚Gegenstand' und ‚Komplex'?

In den alten Riten haben wir den Gebrauch einer äußerst ausgebildeten Gebärdensprache.

Und wenn ich in Frazer lese, so möchte ich auf Schritt und Tritt sagen: Alle diese Prozesse, diese Wandlungen der Bedeutung, haben wir noch ⟦243⟧ in unserer Wortsprache vor uns. Wenn das, was sich in der letzten Garbe verbirgt, der ‚Kornwolf' genannt wird, aber auch diese Garbe selbst, ⟦*11*⟧ und auch der Mann, der sie bindet, so erkennen wir hierin einen uns wohlbekannten sprachlichen Vorgang.

* * *

Ich könnte mir denken, daß ich die Wahl gehabt hätte, ein Wesen der Erde als die Wohnung für meine Seele zu wählen, und daß mein Geist dieses unansehnliche Geschöpf als seinen Sitz und Aussichtspunkt gewählt hätte. Etwa, weil ihm die Ausnahme eines schönen Sitzes zuwider wäre. Dazu müßte freilich der Geist seiner selbst sehr sicher sein.

Man könnte sagen „jeder Aussicht ist ein Reiz abzugewinnen", aber das wäre falsch. Richtig ist, zu sagen, jede Aussicht ist bedeutsam für den, der sie bedeutsam sieht (das heißt aber nicht, sie anders sieht als sie ist). Ja, in diesem Sinne ist jede Aussicht gleich bedeutsam.

Ja, es ist wichtig, daß ich auch die Verachtung jedes Andern für mich mir zu eigen machen muß, als einen wesentlichen und bedeutsamen Teil der Welt von meinem Ort gesehen.

To drive out or slay death; but on the other hand it is represented as a skeleton, as itself dead in a certain sense. "As dead as death." "Nothing is as dead as death; nothing is as beautiful as beauty itself." The picture in terms of which one conceives of reality here is such that beauty, death, etc. are the pure (concentrated) substances, while they are present in a beautiful object as an admixture.—And do I not recognize here my own observations about 'object' and 'complex'?

In the ancient rites we have the use of an extremely developed gesture-language.

And when I read Frazer, I continually would like to say: We still have all these processes, these changes of meaning, before us in our verbal language. When what hides in the last sheaf of corn is called the 'Corn-wolf', but also this sheaf itself as ⟦71⟧ well as the man who binds it, we recognize herein a familiar linguistic occurrence.[6]

* * *

I could imagine that I had had the choice of picking a creature of the earth as the dwelling place for my soul, and that my spirit had chosen this unattractive creature as its residence and vantage point. Perhaps because the anomaly of a beautiful residence would be repugnant to it. One's spirit would certainly have to be very sure of itself to do this.

One could say "every view has its charm", but that would be false. The correct thing to say is that every view is significant for the one who sees it as significant (but that does not mean, sees it other than it is). Indeed, in this sense, every view is equally significant.

It is indeed important that I must also make my own the contempt that anyone may have for me, as an essential and significant part of the world as seen by me.

6. See Frazer, p. 449 [vii, 273]: "In various parts of Mecklenburg, where the belief in the Corn-wolf is particularly prevalent, every one fears to cut the last corn, because they say that the Wolf is sitting in it; . . . the last bunch of standing corn is itself commonly called the Wolf, and the man who reaps it . . . is himself called Wolf. . . ."

Wenn es einem Menschen freigestellt wäre, sich in einen Baum eines Waldes gebären zu lassen: so gäbe es Solche, die sich den schönsten oder höchsten Baum aussuchen würden, solche, die sich den kleinsten wählten, und solche, die sich einen Durchschnitts- oder minderen Durchschnittsbaum wählen würden, und zwar meine ich nicht aus Philistrosität, sondern aus eben dem Grund, oder der Art von Grund, warum der Andre den höchsten gewählt hat. Daß das Gefühl, welches wir für unser Leben haben, mit dem eines solchen Wesens, das sich seinen Standpunkt in der Welt wählen konnte, vergleichbar ist, liegt, glaube ich, dem Mythus — oder dem Glauben — zu Grunde, wir hätten uns unsern Körper vor der Geburt gewählt.

* * *

⟦*12*⟧ Ich glaube, das Charakteristische des primitiven Menschen ist es, daß er nicht aus *Meinungen* handelt (dagegen Frazer).

Ich lese, unter vielen ähnlichen Beispielen, von einem Regenkönig in Afrika, zu dem die Leute um Regen bitten, *wenn die Regenperiode kommt.* ⟦244⟧ Aber das heißt doch, daß sie nicht eigentlich meinen, er könne Regen machen, sonst würden sie es in den trockenen Perioden des Jahres, in der das Land „a parched and arid desert" ist, machen. Denn wenn man annimmt, daß die Leute einmal aus Dummheit dieses Amt des Regenkönigs eingesetzt haben, so ist es doch gewiß klar, daß sie schon vorher die Erfahrung hatten, daß im März der Regen beginnt und sie hätten dann den Regenkönig für den übrigen Teil des Jahres funktionieren lassen. Oder auch so: Gegen morgen, wenn die Sonne aufgehen will, werden von den Menschen Riten des Tagwerdens zelebriert, aber nicht in der Nacht, sondern da brennen sie einfach Lampen.

[Wenn ich über etwas wütend bin, so schlage ich manchmal mit meinem Stock auf die Erde oder an einen Baum etc. Aber ich glaube doch nicht, daß die Erde schuld ist oder das Schlagen etwas helfen kann. „Ich lasse meinen Zorn aus." Und dieser Art sind alle Riten. Solche Handlungen kann man Instinkt-Handlungen nennen. — Und

---

7. See ibid., p. 107 [ii, 2]: ". . . the Kings of the Rain, *Mata Kodou,* who are credited with the power of giving rain at the proper time, that is, the rainy season. Before the rains begin to fall at the end of March the country is a parched and arid desert; and the cattle, which form the people's chief wealth, perish for lack of grass. So, when the end of March draws on, each house-

If a man were given the choice to be born in one tree of a forest, there would be some who would seek out the most beautiful or the highest tree, some who would choose the smallest, and some who would choose an average or below average tree, and I certainly do not mean out of philistinism, but rather for exactly the same reason, or kind of reason, that the other had chosen the highest. That the feeling which we have for our lives is comparable to that of such a being who could choose for himself his viewpoint in the world underlies, I believe, the myth—or the belief—that we had chosen our bodies before birth.

* * *

I believe that the characteristic feature of primitive man is that he does not act from *opinions* (contrary to Frazer).

I read, among many similar examples, of a Rain-King in Africa to whom the people pray for rain *when the rainy period* ⟦72⟧ *comes.*[7] But surely that means that they do not really believe that he can make it rain, otherwise they would do it in the dry periods of the year in which the land is "a parched and arid desert". For if one assumes that the people formerly instituted this office of Rain-King out of stupidity, it is nevertheless certainly clear that they had previously experienced that the rains begin in March, and then they would have had the Rain-King function for the other part of the year. Or again: toward morning, when the sun is about to rise, rites of daybreak are celebrated by the people, but not during the night, when they simply burn lamps.[8]

[When I am furious about something, I sometimes beat the ground or a tree with my walking stick. But I certainly do not believe that the ground is to blame or that my beating can help anything. "I am venting my anger". And all rites are of this kind. Such actions may be called Instinct-actions.—And an historical explanation, say, that I or

---

holder betakes himself to the King of the Rain and offers him a cow that he may make the blessed waters of heaven to drip on the brown and withered pastures."

8. Ibid., pp. 78–79 [i, 312ff].

eine historische Erklärung, etwa daß ich früher oder meine Vorfahren früher geglaubt haben, das Schlagen der Erde helfe etwas, sind Spiegelfechtereien, denn sie sind überflüssige Annahmen, die *nichts* erklären. Wichtig ist die Ähnlichkeit des Aktes mit einem Akt der Züchtigung, aber mehr als diese Ähnlichkeit ist nicht zu konstatieren.

Ist ein solches Phänomen einmal mit einem Instinkt, den ich selber besitze, in Verbindung gebracht, so ist eben dies die gewünschte Erklärung; d.h. die, welche diese besondere Schwierigkeit löst. Und eine weitere Forschung über die Geschichte meines Instinkts bewegt sich nun auf andern Bahnen.

Kein geringer Grund, d.h. überhaupt kein *Grund* kann es gewesen sein, was gewisse Menschenrassen den Eichbaum verehren ließe, sondern nur das, daß sie und die Eiche in einer Lebensgemeinschaft vereinigt waren, also nicht aus Wahl, sondern, wie der Floh und der Hund, mit einander entstanden. (Entwickelten die Flöhe einen Ritus, er würde sich auf den Hund beziehen.)

Man könnte sagen, nicht ihre Vereinigung (von Eiche und Mensch) hat zu diesen Riten die Veranlassung gegeben, sondern, in gewissem Sinne, ihre Trennung. ⟦245⟧ Denn das Erwachen des Intellekts geht mit einer Trennung von dem ursprünglichen *Boden*, der ursprünglichen Grundlage des Lebens vor sich. (Die Entstehung der *Wahl*.)

(Die Form des erwachenden Geistes ist die Verehrung.)]

## II

[S.168. Dies ist natürlich nicht so, daß das Volk glaubt, der Herrscher habe diese Kräfte, der Herrscher aber sehr wohl weiß, daß er sie nicht hat, oder es nur dann nicht weiß, wenn er ein Schwachkopf oder ein Narr ist. Sondern die Notion von seiner Kraft ist natürlich so eingerichtet, daß sie mit der Erfahrung — des Volkes und seiner — übereinstimmen kann. Daß dabei irgendeine Heuchelei eine Rolle spielt, ist nur wahr, sofern sie überhaupt bei dem meisten was Menschen tun nahe liegt.

my ancestors previously believed that beating the ground does help is shadow-boxing, for it is a superfluous assumption that explains *nothing.* The similarity of the action to an act of punishment is important, but nothing more than this similarity can be asserted.

Once such a phenomenon is brought into connection with an instinct which I myself possess, this is precisely the explanation wished for; that is, the explanation which resolves this particular difficulty. And a further investigation about the history of my instinct moves on another track.

It was not a trivial reason, for really there can have been no *reason,* that prompted certain races of mankind to venerate the ⟦73⟧ oak tree, but only the fact that they and the oak were united in a community of life, and thus that they arose together not by choice, but rather like the flea and the dog. (If fleas developed a rite, it would be based on the dog.)

One could say that it was not their union (the oak and man) that has given rise to these rites, but in a certain sense their separation. For the awakening of the intellect occurs with a separation from the original *soil,* the original basis of life. (The origin of *choice.*)

(The form of the awakening spirit is veneration.)]

## II

[p.168.[9] It is, of course, not so that the people believe that the ruler has these powers, and the ruler knows very well that he doesn't have them, or can only fail to know it if he is an imbecile or a fool. But the notion of his power is, of course, adapted in such a way that it can harmonize with experience—the people's as well as his own. That some hypocrisy thereby plays a role is true only insofar as it generally lies close at hand with most things people do.

9. Ibid., p. 168 [iii, 1]: "At a certain stage of early society the king or priest is often thought to be endowed with supernatural powers or to be an incarnation of a deity, and consistently with this belief the course of nature is supposed to be more or less under his control. . . ."

S.169. Wenn ein Mensch in unserer (oder doch meiner) Gesellschaft zu viel lacht, so presse ich halb unwillkürlich die Lippen zusammen, als glaubte ich die seinen dadurch zusammen halten zu können.

S.170. Der Unsinn ist hier, daß Frazer es so darstellt, als hätten diese Völker eine vollkommen falsche (ja wahnsinnige) Vorstellung vom Laufe der Natur, während sie nur eine merkwürdige Interpretation der Phänomene besitzen. D.h., ihre Naturkenntnis, wenn sie sie niederschrieben, würde von der unsern sich nicht *fundamental* unterscheiden. Nur ihre *Magie* ist anders.

⟦246⟧ S.171. ". . . a network of prohibitions and observances, of which the intention is not to contribute to his dignity, . . . ." Das ist wahr und falsch. Freilich nicht die Würde des Schutz der Person, wohl aber die — sozusagen — natürliche Heiligkeit der Gottheit in ihm.]

⟦*13*⟧ So einfach es klingt: der Unterschied zwischen Magie und Wissenschaft kann dahin ausgedrückt werden, daß es in der Wissenschaft einen Fortschritt gibt, aber nicht in der Magie. Die Magie hat keine Richtung der Entwicklung, die in ihr selbst liegt.

[S.179. Wievielmehr Wahrheit darin, daß der Seele dieselbe Multiplizität gegeben wird, wie dem Leib, als in einer modernen verwässerten Theorie.

Frazer merkt nicht, daß wir da Platos und Schopenhauers Lehre vor uns haben.

Alle kindliche (infantile) Theorien finden wir in der heutigen Philosophie wieder; nur nicht mit dem Gewinnenden des Kindlichen.]

---

10. Ibid., p. 169 [iii, 3f.]: "In ancient times, he was obliged to sit on the throne for some hours every morning, with the imperial crown on his head, but to sit altogether like a statue, without stirring either hands or feet, head or eyes, nor indeed any part of his body, because, by this means, it was thought that he could preserve peace and tranquillity in his empire. . . ."

11. Ibid., p. 170 [iii, 5]: "The power of giving or withholding rain is ascribed to him, and he is the lord of the winds. . . ."

12. Ibid., p. 171 [iii, 8]: "A king of this sort lives hedged in by a ceremonious etiquette, a network of prohibitions and observances, of which the intention is

p.169.[10] When a man laughs too much in our company (or at least in mine), I half-involuntarily compress my lips, as if I believed I could thereby keep his closed.

p.170.[11] The nonsense here is that Frazer represents these people as if they had a completely false (even insane) idea of ⟦74⟧ the course of nature, whereas they only possess a peculiar interpretation of the phenomena. That is, if they were to write it down, their knowledge of nature would not differ *fundamentally* from ours. Only their *magic* is different.

p.171.[12] ". . . a network of prohibitions and observances, of which the intention is not to contribute to his dignity . . ." That is true and false. Certainly not the dignity of protection of the person, but perhaps—so to speak—the natural sanctity of the divinity in him.]

As simple as it sounds: the distinction between magic and science can be expressed by saying that in science there is progress, but in magic there isn't. Magic has no tendency within itself to develop.

[p.179.[13] How much more truth there is in this view, which ascribes the same multiplicity to the soul as to the body, than in a modern watered-down theory.

Frazer doesn't notice that we have before us the teaching of Plato and Schopenhauer.

We find every childlike (infantile) theory again in today's philosophy, only not with the winning ways of the childlike.]

---

not to contribute to his dignity, much less to his comfort, but to restrain him from conduct which, by disturbing the harmony of nature, might involve himself, his people, and the universe in one common catastrophe. Far from adding to his comfort, these observances, by trammelling his every act, annihilate his freedom and often render the very life, which it is their object to preserve, a burden and sorrow to him."

13. Ibid., p. 179 [iii, 28]: "The Malays conceive the human soul as a little man . . . who corresponds . . . to the man in whose body he resides. . . ."

S.614. Das Auffallendste schiene mir außer den Ähnlichkeiten die Verschiedenheit aller dieser Riten zu sein. Es ist eine Mannigfaltigkeit von Gesichtern mit gemeinsamen Zügen, die da und dort immer wieder auftauchen. Und was man tun möchte ist, Linien ziehen, die die gemeinsamen Bestandteile verbinden. Es fehlt dann noch ein Teil der Betrachtung und es ist der, welcher dieses Bild mit unsern eigenen Gefühlen und Gedanken in Verbindung bringt. Dieser Teil gibt der Betrachtung ihre Tiefe.

In allen diesen Gebräuchen sieht man allerdings etwas, der Ideenassoziation *ähnliches* und mit ihr verwandtes. Man könnte von einer Assoziation der Gebräuche reden.

⟦247⟧ S.618. Nichts spricht dafür, warum das Feuer mit solchem Nimbus umgeben sein sollte. Und, wie seltsam, was heißt es eigentlich, „es schien vom Himmel gekommen zu sein"? von welchem Himmel? Nein es ist gar nicht selbstverständlich, daß das Feuer so betrachtet wird — aber es wird eben so betrachtet.

⟦*14*⟧ Hier scheint die Hypothese erst der Sache Tiefe zu geben. Und man kann sich an die Erklärung des seltsamen Verhältnisses von Siegfried und Brunhild im neuen Nibelungenlied erinnern. Nämlich, daß Siegfried Brunhilde schon früher einmal gesehen zu haben scheint. Es ist nun klar, daß, was diesem Gebrauch Tiefe gibt, sein *Zusammenhang* mit dem Verbrennen eines Menschen ist. Wenn es bei irgendeinem Fest Sitte wäre, daß Menschen (wie beim Roß-und-Reiter-Spiel) auf einander reiten, so würden wir darin nichts sehen als eine Form des Tragens, die an das Reiten des Menschen auf einem Pferd erinnert; wüßten wir aber, daß es unter vielen Völkern Sitte gewesen wäre, etwa Sklaven als Reittiere zu benützen, und so beritten gewisse Feste zu feiern, so würden wir jetzt in dem harmlosen Gebrauch unserer Zeit etwas Tieferes und weniger Harmloses sehen. Die Frage ist: haftet dieses — sagen wir — Finstere dem

14. In Chapter LXII: The Fire Festivals of Europe.

15. Frazer, p. 618 [x, 148]: ". . . As soon as any sparks were emitted by means of the violent friction, they applied a species of agaric which grows on old birch trees, and is very combustible. This fire had the appearance of being immediately derived from heaven, and manifold were the virtues ascribed to it. . . ."

16. Ibid., p. 618 [x, 148]: ". . . the person who officiated as master of the feast produced a large cake baked with eggs and scalloped round the edge,

p.614.[14] Besides these similarities, what seems to me to be most striking is the dissimilarity of all these rites. It is a multiplicity of faces with common features which continually emerges here and there. And one would like to draw lines connecting these common ingredients. But then one part of our account would still be missing, namely, that which brings this picture into connection with our own feelings and thoughts. This part gives the account its depth.

In all these practices one, of course, sees something that is *similar* to the association of ideas and related to it. One could speak of an association of practices.

⟦75⟧ p.618.[15] Nothing accounts for why the fire should be surrounded by such a nimbus. And, how strange, what does it really mean "it had the appearance of being derived from heaven"? from which heaven? No, it is not at all self-evident that fire is looked at in this way—but that's just how it is looked at.

Here the hypothesis seems to give the matter depth for the first time. And one can recall the explanation of the strange relationship between Siegfried and Brunhilde in the new *Nibelungenlied.* Namely, that Siegfried seems to have already seen Brunhilde before. It is now clear that what gives this practice depth is its *connection* with the burning of a man.[16] If it were the custom at some festival for the men to ride on one another (as in the game of horse and rider), we would see nothing in this but a form of carrying which reminds us of men riding horseback; but if we knew that among many peoples it had been the custom, say, to employ slaves as riding animals and, so mounted, to celebrate certain festivals, we would now see something deeper and less harmless in the harmless practice of our time. The question is: does the sinister, as we may call it, attach to the practice of the Beltane Fire Festival in itself, as it was carried on one hundred years ago, or is the Festival sinister only if the hypothesis of its origin

---

called *am bonnach beal-tine—i.e.,* the Beltane cake. It was divided into a number of pieces, and distributed in great form to the company. There was one particular piece which whoever got was called *cailleach beal-tine—i.e.,* the Beltane *carline,* a term of great reproach. Upon his being known, part of the company laid hold of him and made a show of putting him into the fire . . . And while the feast was fresh in people's memory, they affected to speak of the *cailleach beal-tine* as dead."

Gebrauch des Beltane Feuers, wie er vor 100 Jahren geübt wurde, an sich an, oder nur dann, wenn die Hypothese seiner Entstehung sich bewahrheiten sollte. Ich glaube es ist offenbar die innere Natur des neuzeitlichen Gebrauchs selbst, die uns finster anmutet, und die uns bekannten Tatsachen von Menschenopfern weisen nur die Richtung in der wir den Gebrauch ansehen sollen. Wenn ich von der innern Natur des Gebrauchs rede, meine ich alle Umstände, in denen er geübt wird und die in dem Bericht von so einem Fest nicht enthalten sind, da sie nicht sowohl in bestimmten Handlungen bestehen, die das Fest charakterisieren, als in dem was man den Geist des Festes nennen könnte, welcher beschrieben würde indem man z.B. die Art von Leuten beschriebe, die daran teilnehmen, ihre übrige Handlungsweise, d.h. ihren Charakter; die Art der Spiele, die sie sonst spielen. Und man würde dann sehen, daß das Finstere im Charakter dieser Menschen selbst liegt.

⟦248/*15*⟧ S.619. Hier sieht etwas aus wie die Überreste eines Losens. Und durch diesen Aspekt gewinnt es plötzlich Tiefe. Würden wir erfahren, daß der Kuchen mit den Knöpfen in einem bestimmten Fall etwa ursprünglich zu Ehren eines Knopfmachers zu seinem Geburtstag gebacken worden sei, und sich der Gebrauch dann in der Gegend erhalten habe, so würde dieser Gebrauch tatsächlich alles „Tiefe" verlieren, es sei denn daß es in seiner gegenwärtigen Form an sich liegt. Aber man sagt in so einem Fall oft: „dieser Gebrauch ist *offenbar* uralt". Woher weiß man das? Ist es nur, weil man historisches Zeugnis über derartige alte Gebräuche hat? Oder hat es noch einen andern Grund, einen, den man durch Introspektion gewinnt? Aber auch wenn die vorzeitliche Herkunft des Gebrauchs und die Abstammung von einem finstern Gebrauch historisch erwiesen ist, so ist es doch möglich, daß der Gebrauch heute *gar nichts* mehr finsteres an sich hat, daß nichts von dem vorzeitlichen Grauen an ihm hängen geblieben ist. Vielleicht wird er heute nur mehr von Kindern geübt, die im Kuchenbacken und Verzieren mit Knöpfen wetteifern. Dann liegt das Tiefe also nur im Gedanken an jene Abstammung. Aber diese kann doch ganz unsicher sein und man möchte sagen: „Wozu sich über eine so unsichere Sache Sorgen machen" (wie eine rückwärts schauende Kluge Else). Aber solche Sorgen sind es nicht. — Vor allem: woher die Sicherheit, daß ein solcher Gebrauch uralt sein muß (was sind unsere Daten, was ist die Verification)? Aber haben wir denn eine Sicherheit, können wir uns nicht darin irren und des Irrtums historisch überführt werden?

turns out to be true? I believe it is clearly the inner nature of the modern practice itself which seems sinister to us, and the familiar facts of human sacrifice only indicate the lines along which we should view the practice. When I speak of the inner nature of the ⟦76⟧ practice, I mean all circumstances under which it is carried out and which are not included in a report of such a festival, since they consist not so much in specific actions which characterize the festival as in what one might call the spirit of the festival; such things as would be included in one's description, for example, of the kind of people who take part in it, their behavior at other times, that is, their character; the kind of games which they otherwise play. And one would then see that the sinister quality lies in the character of these people themselves.

p.619.[17] We see something here that looks like the last vestige of drawing lots. And, through this aspect, it suddenly gains depth. If we were to learn that the cake with the knobs had, in a particular case, originally been baked, say, in honor of a button-maker on his birthday and that this practice had been preserved in the region, this practice would in fact lose all 'depth', unless this depth is embedded in the present form of the practice itself. But in such a case one often says: "this practice is *obviously* ancient". How does one know that? Is it only because one has historical evidence about ancient practices of this kind? Or does it have yet another reason which one arrives at through introspection? But even if both the prehistoric origin of the practice and its derivation from an earlier practice are proven historically, it is nevertheless possible that the practice has *nothing whatever* sinister about it today, that nothing of the prehistoric horror remains attached to it. Perhaps today it is engaged in only by children who compete in baking cakes and decorating them with knobs. Then the depth lies only in thinking about that derivation. But this can still be very uncertain and one would like to say: "Why worry about so uncertain a matter?" (like a backwards-looking Clever Elsie[18]). But it

17. Ibid., p. 619 [x, 150]: ". . . they divide the cake into so many portions, as similar as possible to one another in size and shape, as there are persons in the company. They daub one of these portions all over with charcoal, until it be perfectly black. They put all the bits of the cake into a bonnet. Every one, blindfold, draws out a portion. He who holds the bonnet, is entitled to the last bit. Whoever draws the black bit, is the *devoted* person who is to be sacrificed to *Baal*. . . ."

18. See "Clever Elsie," #34 in Grimms' *Tales.* (eds.)

Gewiß, aber ⟦*16*⟧ es bleibt dann doch immer etwas, dessen wir sicher sind. Wir würden dann sagen: „Gut, in diesem einen Fall mag die Herkunft anders sein, aber im allgemeinen ist sie sicher die vorzeitliche." Was uns dafür *Evidenz* ist, das muß die Tiefe dieser Annahme enthalten. Und diese Evidenz ist wieder eine nicht-hypothetische psychologische. Wenn ich nämlich sage: das Tiefe in diesem Gebrauch liegt in seiner Herkunft *wenn* sie sich so zugetragen hat. So liegt also entweder das Tiefe in dem Gedanken an so eine Herkunft, oder das Tiefe ist selbst nur hypothetisch und man kann nur sagen: *Wenn* es sich so zugetragen hat, so war das eine finstere tiefe ⟦249⟧ Geschichte. Ich will sagen: Das Finstere, Tiefe liegt nicht darin, daß es sich mit der Geschichte dieses Gebrauchs so verhalten hat, denn vielleicht hat es sich gar nicht so verhalten; auch nicht darin, daß es sich vielleicht oder wahrscheinlich so verhalten hat, sondern in dem, was mir Grund gibt, das anzunehmen. Ja woher überhaupt das Tiefe und Finstere im Menschenopfer? Denn sind es nur die Leiden des Opfers, die uns den Eindruck machen? Krankheiten aller Art, die mit ebensoviel Leiden verbunden sind, rufen diesen Eindruck *doch* nicht hervor. Nein, dies Tiefe und Finstere versteht sich nicht von selbst wenn wir nur die Geschichte der äußeren Handlung erfahren, sondern *wir* tragen es wieder hinein aus einer Erfahrung in unserm Innern.

Die Tatsache, daß das Los durch einen Kuchen gezogen wird, hat auch etwas besonders schreckliches (beinahe wie der Verrat durch einen Kuß), und daß uns das besonders schrecklich anmutet, hat wieder eine wesentliche Bedeutung für die Untersuchung solcher Gebräuche.

Es ist, wenn ich so einen Gebrauch sehe, von ihm höre, wie wenn ich einen Mann sehe wie er bei geringfügigem Anlaß streng mit einem andern spricht, und aus dem Ton der Stimme und dem Gesicht merke, daß dieser Mann bei gegebenem Anlaß furchtbar sein kann. Der Eindruck, den ich hier erhalte, kann ein sehr tiefer und außerordentlich ernster sein.

Die *Umgebung* einer Handlungsweise.

Eine Überzeugung liegt jedenfalls den Annahmen über den Ursprung des Beltanefestes — z.B. — zu Grunde; die ist, daß solche Feste nicht von einem Menschen, sozusagen aufs Geratewohl, erfunden werden, sondern ⟦*17*⟧ eine unendlichviel breitere Basis brauchen, um sich zu erhalten. Wollte ich ein Fest erfinden, so würde

is not that kind of worry.—Above all: where do we get the certainty that such a practice must be ancient (what are our data, ⟦77⟧ what is the verification)? But are we certain then? might we not be mistaken and convicted of our mistake by history? Certainly, but then there still remains something of which we are certain. We would then say: "Good, the origin may be different in this case, but in general it is surely prehistoric." Whatever we regard as *evidence* for this must include the depth of this assumption. And this evidence is again non-hypothetical, psychological. That is, when I say: the depth in this practice lies in its origin *if* it did come about in this way, then the depth lies either in the thought of such an origin, or the depth is itself hypothetical, and one can only say: *If* it happened that way then it was a deep and sinister business. I want to say: The deep, the sinister, do not depend on the history of the practice having been like this, for perhaps it was not like this at all; nor on the fact that it was perhaps or probably like this, but rather on that which gives me grounds for assuming this. Indeed, how is it that in general human sacrifice is so deep and sinister? For is it only the suffering of the victim that makes this impression on us? There are illnesses of all kinds which are connected with just as much suffering, *nevertheless* they do not call forth this impression. No, the deep and the sinister do not become apparent merely by our coming to know the history of the external action, rather it is *we* who ascribe them from an inner experience.

The fact that the lots are drawn by the use of a cake is particularly horrible (almost like betrayal with a kiss), and that it strikes us this way is again of fundamental importance for the investigation of such practices.

When I see such a practice, or hear of it, it is like seeing a man speaking harshly to someone else over a trivial matter, and noticing from his tone of voice and facial expression that this man can on occasion be terrible. The impression that I receive here can be very deep and extraordinarily serious.

The *surroundings* of a way of acting.

In any case, a conviction serves as the basis for the assumptions about the origin of, for example, the Beltane Festival; ⟦78⟧ namely, that such festivals are not made up by one person, so to speak, at random, but rather need an infinitely broader basis if they are to be preserved. If I wanted to make up a festival, it would die out very

es baldigst aussterben oder aber solcherweise modifiziert werden, daß es einem allgemeinen Hang der Leute entspricht.

Was aber wehrt sich dagegen anzunehmen, das Beltanefest sei immer in der gegenwärtigen (oder jüngstvergangenen) Form gefeiert worden? Man möchte sagen: Es ist zu sinnlos um so erfunden worden zu sein. Ist es nicht, wie wenn ich eine Ruine sehe und sage: das muß einmal ein Haus gewesen sein, denn niemand würde einen so beschaffenen Haufen ⟦250⟧ behauener und unregelmäßiger Steine errichten? Und wenn gefragt würde: Woher weißt Du das?, so könnte ich nur sagen: meine Erfahrung mit den Menschen lehrt es mich. Ja selbst da wo sie wirklich Ruinen bauen, nehmen sie die Formen von eingestürzten Häusern her.

Man könnte es auch so sagen: Wer uns mit der Erzählung vom Beltanefest einen Eindruck machen wollte, brauchte jedenfalls die Hypothese von seiner Herkunft nicht zu äußern, sondern er brauchte uns nur das Material (das zu dieser Hypothese führt) vorlegen und nichts weiter dazu sagen. Nun möchte man vielleicht sagen: „Freilich, weil der Hörer, oder Leser, den Schluß selber ziehen wird!“ Aber muß er diesen Schluß explizite ziehen? also, überhaupt, ziehen? Und was ist es denn für ein Schluß? Daß das oder jenes *wahrscheinlich* ist?! Und wenn er den Schluß selber ziehen kann, wie soll ihm der Schluß einen Eindruck machen? was ihm den Eindruck macht muß doch das sein, was *er* nicht gemacht hat! Impressioniert ihn also erst die geäußerte Hypothese (ob von ihm oder andern geäußert), oder schon das Material zu ihr? Aber könnte ich da nicht ebensogut fragen: Wenn ich sehe wie Einer umgebracht wird — impressioniert mich da einfach, was ich sehe oder erst die Hypothese, daß hier ein Mensch umgebracht wird?

Aber es ist ja nicht einfach der Gedanke an die mögliche Herkunft des Beltanefestes welche den Eindruck mit sich führt sondern, was man die ungeheure Wahrscheinlichkeit dieses Gedankens nennt. Als das was vom Material hergenommen ist.

So wie das Beltanefest auf uns gekommen ist, ist es ja ein Schauspiel und ähnlich wie wenn Kinder Räuber spielen. Aber doch nicht so. Denn ⟦*18*⟧ wenn es auch abgekartet ist, daß die Partei die das Opfer rettet gewinnt, so hat doch, was geschieht, noch immer einen Temperamentszusatz, den die bloße schauspielerische Darstellung nicht hat. — Aber auch wenn es sich bloß um eine ganz kühle Darstellung handelte, würden wir uns doch beunruhigt fragen: Was

quickly or be modified in such a manner that it corresponds to a general inclination of the people.

But what prevents us from assuming that the Beltane Festival has always been celebrated in its present (or very recent) form? One would like to say: it's too foolish for it to have been invented in this form. Isn't that like my seeing a ruin and saying: that must have been a house at one time, for nobody would have put up such a heap of hewn and irregular stones? And if I were asked: How do you know that? I could only say: from my experience with people. Indeed, even in places where people actually build ruins, they take the form of collapsed houses.

One might also put it this way: Anyone who wanted to make an impression on us with the story of the Beltane Festival need not advance the hypothesis of its origin in any case, he need only lay before us the material (which leads to this hypothesis) and say nothing further. One might now perhaps like to say: "Of course, because the listener or reader will draw the conclusion himself!" But must he draw this conclusion explicitly? therefore, draw it at all? And what kind of conclusion is it? That this or that is *probable*?! And if he can draw the conclusion himself, how is the conclusion to make an impression on him? Whatever makes an impression on him must surely be something that *he* has not made. Is he impressed for the first time by hearing the hypothesis expressed (whether by himself or someone else), or already by the material that leads to it? But couldn't I just as well ask: If I see someone being killed,—is what makes an impression on me simply what I see, or is it only the hypothesis that here a man is being killed?

But it is not simply the thought of the possible origin of the Beltane Festival that carries with it the impression, but rather ⟦79⟧ what is called the enormous *probability* of this thought. As that which is derived from the material.

As it has come down to us, the Beltane Festival is indeed a play, and is similar to children playing robbers. But surely not. For although it has been prearranged that the party who rescues the victim wins, nevertheless what takes place still has an addition of temperament which the mere dramatic presentation does not have.—But even if it were merely a question of a wholly cool performance, we would still uneasily ask ourselves: What about this presentation, what is its *meaning*?! And it

soll diese Darstellung, was ist ihr *Sinn*?! Und sie könnte uns abgesehen von jeder Deutung dann durch ihre eigentümliche Sinnlosigkeit beunruhigen. (Was zeigt, welcher Art der Grund so einer Beunruhigung sein kann.) Würde nun etwa eine harmlose Deutung gegeben: Das Los werde einfach geworfen, damit man das Vergnügen hätte, jemandem damit drohen zu können ins Feuer geworfen zu werden, was nicht angenehm sei; so wird das Beltanefest viel ähnlicher ⟦251⟧ einer jener Belustigungen wo einer der Gesellschaft gewisse Grausamkeiten zu erdulden hat und die so wie sie sind ein Bedürfnis befriedigen. Und das Beltanefest würde durch so eine Erklärung auch wirklich jedes Geheimnisvolle verlieren, wenn es eben nicht selbst in der Handlung wie in der Stimmung von solchen gewöhnlichen Räuberspielen etc. abwiche.

Ebenso, daß Kinder an gewissen Tagen einen Strohmann verbrennen, auch wenn dafür keine Erklärung gegeben würde, könnte uns beunruhigen. Seltsam, daß *ein Mensch* festlich von ihnen verbrannt werden sollte! Ich will sagen: die Lösung ist nicht beunruhigender als das Rätsel.

Warum soll es aber nicht wirklich nur (oder doch zum Teil) der *Gedanke* sein, der mir den Eindruck gibt? Sind denn Vorstellungen nicht furchtbar? Kann mir bei dem Gedanken, daß der Kuchen mit den Knöpfen einmal dazu gedient hat das Todesopfer auszulosen, nicht schaurig zumut werden? Hat nicht der *Gedanke* etwas Furchtbares? — Ja, aber das was ich in jenen Erzählungen sehe, gewinnen sie doch durch die Evidenz, auch durch solche, die damit nicht unmittelbar verbunden zu sein scheint; durch den Gedanken an den Menschen und seine Vergangenheit, durch all das Seltsame, das ich in mir und in den Andern sehe, gesehen und gehört habe.

[S.640. Das kann man sich sehr gut denken — und als Grund wäre etwa angegeben worden, daß die Schutzheiligen sonst gegeneinander ziehen würden, und daß nur einer die Sache dirigieren könne. Aber auch das wäre nur eine nachträgliche Ausdehnung des Instinkts.

Alle diese *verschiedene* Gebräuche zeigen, daß es sich hier nicht um die Abstammung des einen vom andern handelt, sondern um einen gemeinsamen Geist. Und man könnte alle diese Zeremonien selber erfinden (erdichten). Und der Geist aus dem man sie erfände wäre eben ihr gemeinsamer Geist.

could then make us uneasy owing to its peculiar meaninglessness, irrespective of any interpretation. (Which shows the kind of basis such uneasiness can have.) Suppose now, for example, that a harmless interpretation were given: They simply cast lots so that they would have the pleasure of threatening someone with being thrown into the fire, which is not pleasant; in this way the Beltane Festival becomes much more like one of those amusements where one of the company has to endure certain forms of cruelty which, such as they are, satisfy a need. By means of such an explanation, the Beltane Festival would indeed lose all of its mysterious character if it did not itself deviate from such ordinary games of robbers, etc. in its action and mood.

Just as the fact that on certain days children burn a straw-man could make us uneasy, even if no explanation for it were given. Strange that they should burn *a man* as part of the festivities! I want to say: the solution is no more disturbing than the riddle.

But why shouldn't it really be only (or certainly in part) the *thought* which gives me the impression? For aren't ideas terrible? Can't I be horrified by the thought that the cake with the knobs has at one time served to select by lot the sacrificial victim? Doesn't the *thought* have something terrible about it?—Yes, but what I see in those stories is nevertheless acquired through the evidence, including such evidence as does not appear to be directly connected with them,—through the thoughts of man and his past, through all the strange things I see, and have seen and heard about, in myself and others.

⟦80⟧ [p.640[19] One can very well imagine that—and perhaps the reason given might have been that the patron saints would otherwise pull against one another, and that only one could direct the matter. But this too would only be a later extension of instinct.

All these *different* practices show that it is not a question of the derivation of one from the other, but of a common spirit. And one could invent (devise) all these ceremonies oneself. And precisely that spirit from which one invented them would be their common spirit.

19. See p. 640 [cf. x, 275, 279]: "Various rules were also laid down as to the kind of persons who might or should make the need-fire. Sometimes it was said that the two persons who pulled the rope which twirled the roller should always be brothers or at least bear the same baptismal name . . ."

⟦252⟧ S.641. Die Verbindung von Krankheit und Schmutz. „Von einer Krankheit reinigen."

Es liefert eine einfache, kindliche Theorie der Krankheit, daß sie Schmutz ist, der abgewaschen werden kann.

Wie es ‚infantile Sexualtheorien' gibt, so überhaupt infantile Theorien. Das heißt aber nicht, daß alles, was ein Kind tut, *aus* einer infantilen Theorie als seinen Grund hervorgegangen ist.

Das Richtige und Interessante ist nicht zu sagen: das ist aus dem hervorgegangen, sondern: es könnte so hervorgegangen sein.

S.643. Daß das Feuer zur Reinigung gebraucht wurde, ist klar. Aber nichts kann wahrscheinlicher sein, als daß die denkenden Menschen Reinigungszeremonien, auch wo sie ursprünglich nur als solche gedacht gewesen wären, später mit der Sonne in Zusammenhang gebracht haben. Wenn sich einem Menschen ein Gedanke aufdrängt (Feuer-Reinigung) und einem ein anderer (Feuer-Sonne) was kann wahrscheinlicher sein, als daß sich einem Menschen beide Gedanken aufdrängen werden. Die Gelehrten die immer eine Theorie haben möchten!!!

Die *gänzliche* Zerstörung durch das Feuer, anders als durch Zerschlagen, Zerreißen etc., muß den Menschen aufgefallen sein.

Auch wenn man nichts von einer solchen Verbindung des Reinigung und Sonne Gedankens wüßte, könnte man annehmen, daß er irgendwo wird aufgetreten sein.

⟦253⟧ S.680. ‚Soul-stone'. Da sieht man wie eine solche Hypothese arbeitet.

---

20. Ibid., pp. 640–641 [cf. x, 289]: ". . . as soon as the fire on the domestic hearth had been rekindled from the need-fire, a pot full of water was set on it, and the water thus heated was afterwards sprinkled upon the people infected with the plague or upon the cattle that were tainted by the murrain."

21. Ibid., p. 643 [x, 330f.]: ". . . Dr. Westermarck has argued powerfully in favour of the purificatory theory alone. . . . However, the case is not so clear as to justify us in dismissing the solar theory without discussion. . . ."

p.641.[20] The connection between illness and dirt. "To cleanse of an illness."

It affords a simple, childlike theory of illness, that it is dirt which can be washed off.

Just as there are 'infantile theories of sex', so there are infantile theories in general. But that doesn't mean that everything a child does has arisen *out of* an infantile theory as its basis.

The correct and interesting thing to say is not: this has arisen from that, but: it could have arisen this way.

p.643.[21] That fire was used for purification is clear. But nothing can be more probable than the fact that later on thinking people brought purification ceremonies into connection with the sun, even where the ceremonies had originally been thought of only as purificatory. When one thought forces itself ⟦81⟧ upon one person (fire-purification) and a different thought upon another (fire-sun), what can be more probable than the fact that both thoughts will force themselves upon a single person. The learned who would always like to have a theory!!!

That fire destroys things *completely,* unlike battering, tearing them to pieces, etc., must have attracted the attention of people.

Even if one didn't know that the thoughts purification and sun had been connected, one could assume this to have arisen somewhere.

p.680.[22] 'Soul-stone.' Here one sees how such an hypothesis works.

---

22. Ibid., p. 680 [xi, 156]: ". . . in New Britain there is a secret society. . . . On his entrance into it every man receives a stone in the shape either of a human being or of an animal, and henceforth his soul is believed to be knit up in a manner with the stone."

S.681. Das würde darauf deuten, daß hier eine Wahrheit zu Grunde liegt und kein Aberglaube. (Freilich ist es dem dummen Wissenschaftler gegenüber leicht in den Geist des Widerspruchs zu verfallen.) Aber es kann sehr wohl sein, daß der völlig enthaarte Leib uns in irgendeinem Sinne den Selbstrespekt zu verlieren verleitet. (Brüder Karamazoff.) Es ist gar kein Zweifel, daß eine Verstümmelung, die uns in unseren Augen unwürdig, lächerlich, aussehen macht, uns allen Willen rauben kann uns zu verteidigen. Wie verlegen werden wir manchmal — oder doch viele Menschen (ich) — durch unsere physische oder ästhetische Inferiorität.]

p.681.[23] That would point to the fact that here truth rather than superstition lies at the basis. (Of course, it is easy to fall into the spirit of contradiction when face to face with the stupid scientist.) But it may very well be the case that the completely shaved body induces us in some sense to lose our self-respect. (Brothers Karamazov.) There is no doubt whatever that a mutilation which makes us appear unworthy or ridiculous in our own eyes can completely deprive us of the will to defend ourselves. How embarrassed we sometimes become—or at least many people (I)—by our physical or aesthetic inferiority.]

23. Ibid., p. 680–681 [xi, 158]: ". . . it used to be thought that the maleficent powers of witches and wizards resided in their hair, and that nothing could make any impression on the miscreants so long as they kept their hair on. Hence in France it was customary to shave the whole bodies of persons charged with sorcery before handing them over to the torturer."

# 8

*Wittgenstein's letter to the philosophical journal* Mind *was written in response to R. B. Braithwaite's article, "Philosophy," pp. 1–32 in* University Studies.[1] *Braithwaite offered an overview of the progress of philosophical studies at Cambridge since the First World War. His account of Wittgenstein's thought (pp. 18–32) includes both the* Tractatus *and various ideas he is said to have propounded since his return to Cambridge, especially concerning grammatical rules, the nature of a proposition, the verification principle, and solipsism.*[2]

*Richard Braithwaite was, in 1933, a Fellow of King's College and University Lecturer in Moral Science at Cambridge. He had presumably attended Wittgenstein's classes in the early 1930's. Braithwaite was appointed Knightsbridge Professor of Moral Philosophy in 1953, a position he held until his retirement in 1967.*

12*th April*, 1933.

TO THE EDITOR OF "MIND".

DEAR SIR,

I have been reading Mr. Braithwaite's article in the recently published book, *Cambridge University Studies*, with some alarm, in particular what he there represents as being my present views on questions of philosophy. I have been doing research in philosophy during the last four years, but have not published any of my work, except, at the very beginning of that period, a short (and weak) article in the *Proceedings of the Aristotelian Society*. Now had I published my thoughts in print I should not trouble you with this letter. For any serious reader could then look up what my views were in my own publication. As it is, if he is interested in what I think, his only source

1. Edited by H. von Wright, and published in London by Ivor Nicholson and Watson, 1933.

2. This information comes from G. Frongia and B. McGuinness, *Wittgenstein: a Bibliographical Guide*, Cambridge, Mass., and Oxford: Basil Blackwell, 1990, pp. 69–70. See also Wittgenstein's letter (M.19), to G. E. Moore, editor of *Mind*, concerning some trivial details about the proofs for the letter, in *Letters to Russell, Keynes and Moore*, p. 160.

is Mr. Braithwaite's article. And therefore I must warn such a reader that I disclaim all responsibility for the views and thoughts which Mr. Braithwaite attributes to me. Part of his statements can be taken to be inaccurate representations of my views, others again clearly contradict them.

⟦416⟧ That which is retarding the publication of my work, the difficulty of presenting it in a clear and coherent form, *a fortiori* prevents me from stating my views within the space of a letter. So the reader must suspend his judgement about them.

Yours truly,
LUDWIG WITTGENSTEIN.

Cambridge,
*27th May,* 1933.

TO THE EDITOR OF "MIND".

DEAR SIR,

Dr. Wittgenstein has been good enough to show me his letter published above. I should be sorry if it were thought that Dr. Wittgenstein was responsible for any of the statements in my article. I had hoped that my opening paragraph would make it clear that the article stated only what impression the various Cambridge philosophers had made upon me. But, since Dr. Wittgenstein fears that there may be some doubt as to his responsibility, I now regret not having explicitly cautioned the reader against accepting uncritically my account of views which have not been published by their authors in printed form.

The extent to which I have misrepresented Dr. Wittgenstein cannot be judged until the appearance of the book which we are all eagerly awaiting.

Yours truly,
R. B. BRAITHWAITE.

King's College,
Cambridge.

# 9

*The following chapter—entitled "Philosophie" by Wittgenstein himself—comes from TS 213, Wittgenstein's so-called "Big Typescript". The Big Typescript, constructed by Wittgenstein in 1933, is some 768 pages long and is organized into chapters and sections. It may have been considered by Wittgenstein to be a finished piece of work. But in any case dissatisfaction supervened, as he soon began to make extensive revisions to the first two-thirds of the work—first in the typescript itself, but then later in new manuscripts. Rush Rhees edited and published a sort of descendant of TS 213—*Philosophical Grammar*—which was constructed out of the new revisions of the first two-thirds of the typescript, plus the last third of the typescript, which was never revised by Wittgenstein. All but four chapters of TS 213 appear in some form in the published work—one of the four is this chapter on "Philosophy".*[1] *It is Wittgenstein's most sustained attempt to elucidate his conception of philosophy.*

*Some of the writings in the present collection afford an opportunity to see how Wittgenstein worked, weeding through previous notebooks, manuscripts, and typescripts, grouping together related remarks. The following chapter shows that Wittgenstein already drew on MS 110 (also a source for Part I of the "Remarks on Frazer's Golden Bough") as he was composing these remarks on 'philosophy'. There are other echoes to previous chapters in this text, and it is perhaps not surprising that the interrelatedness of a variety of themes should become particularly obvious as Wittgenstein elaborates his conception of philosophy.*

*The fact that Wittgenstein had begun revising TS 213, including this chapter, makes the job of editing this material for publication especially difficult. This task of editing was carried out in exemplary fashion by*

1. This information comes from Anthony Kenny, "From the Big Typescript to the Philosophical Grammar," in *Essays on Wittgenstein in Honour of G. H. von Wright, Acta Philosophica Fennica,* vol. 28, 1976, pp. 41–53. The four missing chapters ("Expectation, Wish etc.", "Philosophy", "Phenomenology", and "Idealism, etc.") would come between Chapter II ("Generality") and Chapter III ("The Foundations of Mathematics") of Part II of Rhees's published edition.

*Heikki Nyman.*[2] *(Wittgenstein emphasizes certain words by spacing the letters. This convention has been followed in the English as well as in the German. Recall that broken underlining indicates Wittgenstein's dissatisfaction with a word or phrase.)*

2. For a facsimile reproduction of p. 419 of the typescript, see *Revue Internationale de Philosophie,* vol. 43, 1989, p. 172. For some of the story behind Nyman's editorial standards, see G. H. von Wright's "The Wittgenstein Papers," published in this volume, p. 504 n. 18 *infra.*

# Philosophie

§§ 86–93 (S. 405–435)
aus dem sogenannten
„Big Typescript“
(Katalognummer 213)

S.406

## 86

SCHWIERIGKEIT DER PHILOSOPHIE, NICHT DIE INTELLEKTUELLE SCHWIERIGKEIT DER WISSENSCHAFTEN, SONDERN DIE SCHWIERIGKEIT EINER UMSTELLUNG. WIDERSTÄNDE DES *WILLENS* SIND ZU ÜBERWINDEN.

Wie ich oft gesagt habe, führt die Philosophie mich zu keinem Verzicht, da ich mich nicht entbreche, etwas zu sagen, sondern eine gewisse Wortverbindung als sinnlos aufgebe. In anderem Sinne aber erfordert die Philosophie dann eine Resignation, aber des Gefühls, nicht des Verstandes. Und das ist es vielleicht, was sie Vielen so schwer macht. Es kann schwer sein, einen Ausdruck nicht zu gebrauchen, wie es schwer ist, die Tränen zurückzuhalten, oder einen Ausbruch des Zorns //der Wut//.

/(Tolstoi: die Bedeutung (Bedeutsamkeit) eines Gegenstandes liegt in seiner allgemeinen Verständlichkeit. — Das ist wahr und falsch. Das, was den Gegenstand schwer verständlich macht ist — wenn er bedeutend, wichtig, ist — nicht, dass irgendeine besondere Instruktion über abstruse Dinge zu seinem Verständnis erforderlich wäre, sondern der Gegensatz zwischen dem Verstehen des Gegenstandes
S.407 und dem, was die meisten Men-|schen sehen *wollen*. Dadurch kann gerade das Naheliegendste am allerschwersten verständlich werden. Nicht eine Schwierigkeit des Verstandes, sondern des Willens ist zu überwinden.)/

Die Arbeit an der Philosophie ist — wie vielfach die Arbeit ?in der Architektur — eigentlich mehr die //eine// Arbeit an Einem selbst.

# Philosophy

## Sections 86–93 (pp. 405–35) of the so-called "Big Typescript" (Catalog Number 213)

### 86

DIFFICULTY OF PHILOSOPHY NOT THE INTELLECTUAL DIFFICULTY OF THE SCIENCES, BUT THE DIFFICULTY OF A CHANGE OF ATTITUDE. RESISTANCES OF THE *WILL* MUST BE OVERCOME.

As I have often said, philosophy does not lead me to any renunciation, since I do not abstain from saying something, but rather abandon a certain combination of words as senseless. In another sense, however, philosophy requires a resignation, but one of feeling and not of intellect. And maybe that is what makes it so difficult for many. It can be difficult not to use an expression, just as it is difficult to hold back tears, or an outburst of anger //rage//.

/(Tolstoy: the meaning (meaningfulness) of a subject lies in its being generally understandable.—That is true and false. What makes a subject difficult to understand—if it is significant, important—is not that some special instruction about abstruse things is necessary to understand it. Rather it is the contrast between the understanding of the subject and what most people *want* to see. Because of this the very things that are most obvious can become the most difficult to understand. What has to be overcome is not a difficulty of the intellect, but of the will.)/

Work on philosophy is—as work in[?] architecture frequently is—actually more of a //a kind of// work on oneself. On one's own con-

An der eignen Auffassung. Daran, wie man die Dinge sieht. (Und was man von ihnen verlangt.)

Beiläufig gesprochen, hat es in //nach// der alten Auffassung — etwa der, der (grossen) westlichen Philosophen — zwei Arten von Problemen ⟦178⟧ im wissenschaftlichen Sinne gegeben //zweierlei Arten von Problemen . . . .//: wesentliche, grosse, universelle, und unwesentliche, quasi accidentelle Probleme. Und dagegen ist unsere Auffassung, dass es kein g r o s s e s, wesentliches Problem im Sinne der Wissenschaft gibt.

⟦179⟧
S.408

## 87

DIE PHILOSOPHIE ZEIGT DIE IRREFÜHRENDEN ANALOGIEN IM GEBRAUCH UNSRER SPRACHE AUF.

Ist die Grammatik, wie ich das Wort gebrauche, nur die Beschreibung der tatsächlichen Handhabung der Sprache //Sprachen//? So dass ihre Sätze eigentlich wie Sätze einer Naturwissenschaft aufgefasst werden könnten?

Das könnte man die descriptive Wissenschaft vom Sprechen nennen, im Gegensatz zu der vom Denken.

Es könnten ja auch die Regeln des Schachspiels als Sätze aus der Naturgeschichte des Menschen aufgefasst werden. (Wie die Spiele der Tiere in naturgeschichtlichen Büchern beschrieben werden.)

Wenn ich einen philosophischen Fehler rektifiziere und sage, man hat sich das immer so vorgestellt, aber so ist es nicht, so zeige ich immer auf eine Analogie //so muss ich immer . . . . . zeigen//, nach
S.409 der | man sich gerichtet hat, und, dass diese Analogie nicht stimmt. // . . . so muss ich immer eine Analogie aufzeigen, nach der man gedacht hat, die man aber nicht als Analogie erkannt hat.//

Die Wirkung einer in die Sprache aufgenommenen falschen Analogie: Sie bedeutet einen ständigen Kampf und Beunruhigung (quasi einen ständigen Reiz). Es ist, wie wenn ein Ding aus der Entfernung ein Mensch zu sein scheint, weil wir dann Gewisses nicht wahrnehmen, und in der Nähe sehen wir, dass es ein Baumstumpf ist. Kaum entfernen wir uns ein wenig und verlieren die Erklärungen aus dem

ception. On the way one sees things. (And what one demands of them.)

Roughly speaking, in //according to// the old conception—for instance that of the (great) western philosophers—there have been two kinds of problems in fields of knowledge //twofold kinds of problems. . . .//: essential, great, universal, and inessential, quasi-accidental problems. And against this stands our conception, that there is no such thing as a great, essential problem in the sense of "problem" in the field of knowledge.

## 87

PHILOSOPHY SHOWS THE MISLEADING ANALOGIES IN THE USE OF LANGUAGE.

Is grammar, as I use the word, only the description of the actual ⟦6⟧ handling of language //languages//? So that its propositions could actually be understood as the propositions of a natural science?

That could be called the descriptive science of speaking, in contrast to that of thinking.

Indeed, the rules of chess could be taken as propositions from the natural history of man. (As the games of animals are described in books on natural history.)

If I correct a philosophical mistake and say that this is the way it has always been conceived, but this is not the way it is, I always point to an analogy //I must always point to . . . .// that was followed, and show that this analogy is incorrect. //. . . . I must always point to an analogy according to which one had been thinking, but which one did not recognize as an analogy.//

The effect of a false analogy taken up into language: it means a constant battle and uneasiness (as it were, a constant stimulus). It is as if a thing seemed to be a human being from a distance, because we don't perceive anything definite, but from close up we see that it is a tree stump. The moment we move away a little and lose sight of the explanations, one figure appears to us; if after that we

Auge, so erscheint uns eine Gestalt; sehen wir daraufhin näher zu, so sehen wir eine andere; nun entfernen wir uns wieder, etc. etc..

⟦180⟧ (Der aufregende Charakter der grammatischen Unklarheit.)

Philosophieren ist: falsche Argumente zurückweisen.

Der Philosoph trachtet, das erlösende Wort zu finden, das ist das Wort, das uns endlich erlaubt, das zu fassen, was bis jetzt[1] immer, ungreifbar, unser Bewusstsein belastet hat.
(Es ist, wie wenn man ein Haar auf der Zunge liegen hat; man spürt es, aber kann es nicht erfassen //ergreifen// und darum nicht loswerden.)

Der Philosoph liefert uns das Wort, womit man //ich// die Sache ausdrücken und unschädlich machen kann.

S.410 (Die Wahl unserer Worte ist so wichtig, weil es gilt, die Physiognomie der Sache genau zu treffen, weil nur der genau gerichtete Gedanke auf die richtige Bahn führen kann. Der Wagen muss haargenau auf die Schiene gesetzt werden, damit er richtig weiterrollen kann.)

Eine der wichtigsten Aufgaben ist es, alle falschen Gedankengänge so charakteristisch auszudrücken, dass der Leser sagt „ja, genau so habe ich es gemeint“. Die Physiognomie jedes Irrtums nachzuzeichnen.

Wir können ja auch nur den Andern eines Fehlers überführen, wenn er anerkennt, dass dies wirklich der Ausdruck seines Gefühls ist. // . . . wenn er diesen Ausdruck (wirklich) als den richtigen Ausdruck seines Gefühls anerkennt.//

⟦181⟧ Nämlich, nur wenn er ihn als solchen anerkennt, ist er der richtige Ausdruck. (Psychoanalyse.)

Was der Andre anerkennt, ist die Analogie die ich ihm darbiete, als Quelle seines Gedankens.

1. Handwritten alternative: dahin.

look more closely, we see a different figure; now we move away again, etc., etc.

(The irritating character of grammatical unclarity.)

Philosophizing is: rejecting false arguments.

The philosopher strives to find the liberating word, that is, the word that finally permits us to grasp what up until now[1] has intangibly weighed down our consciousness.

(It is as if one had a hair on one's tongue; one feels it, but cannot grasp //seize// it, and therefore cannot get rid of it.)

The philosopher delivers the word to us with which one //I// can express the thing and render it harmless.

(The choice of our words is so important, because the point is to hit upon the physiognomy of the thing exactly, because only the exactly aimed thought can lead to the correct track. The car must be placed on the tracks precisely so, so that it can keep rolling correctly.)

⟦7⟧ One of the most important tasks is to express all false thought processes so characteristically that the reader says, "Yes, that's exactly the way I meant it". To make a tracing of the physiognomy of every error.

Indeed we can only convict someone else of a mistake if he acknowledges that this really is the expression of his feeling. //. . . . if he (really) acknowledges this expression as the correct expression of his feeling.//

For only if he acknowledges it as such, is it the correct expression. (Psychoanalysis.)

What the other person acknowledges is the analogy I am proposing to him as the source of his thought.

1. Handwritten alternative: then.

⟦182⟧
S.411

## 88

WOHER DAS GEFÜHL DES FUNDAMENTALEN UNSERER GRAMMATISCHEN UNTERSUCHUNGEN?

(Es beschäftigen uns Fragen verschiedener Art, etwa „wie gross ist das spezifische Gewicht dieses Körpers“, „wird es heute schön bleiben“, „wer[2] wird als nächster zur Tür hereinkommen“, etc.. Aber unter unseren Fragen finden sich solche von besonderer Art. Wir haben hier ein anderes Erlebnis. Die Fragen scheinen fundamentaler zu sein als die anderen. Und nun sage ich; wenn wir dieses Erlebnis haben, dann sind wir an der Grenze der Sprache angelangt.).[3]

Woher nimmt die Betrachtung ihre Wichtigkeit, da sie doch nur alles Interessante, d.h. alles Grosse und Wichtige, zu zerstören scheint? (Gleichsam alle Bauwerke; indem sie nur Steinbrocken und Schutt übrig lässt.)

Woher nimmt die Betrachtung ihre Wichtigkeit:[4] die uns darauf aufmerksam macht, dass man eine Tabelle auf mehr als eine Weise brauchen kann, dass man sich eine Tabelle als Anleitung zum Gebrauch einer Tabelle ausdenken kann, dass man einen Pfeil auch
S.412 als Zeiger der Richtung von | der Spitze zum Schwanzende auffassen kann, dass ich eine Vorlage auf mancherlei Weise als Vorlage benützen kann?

⟦183⟧ Wir führen die Wörter von ihrer metaphysischen, wieder auf ihre richtige[5] Verwendung in der Sprache zurück.

(Der Mann, der sagte, man könne nicht zweimal in den gleichen Fluss steigen, sagte etwas Falsches; man kann zweimal in den gleichen Fluss steigen.)

Und so sieht die Lösung aller philosophischen Schwierigkeiten aus. Ihre[6] Antworten müssen, wenn sie richtig sind, hausbacken und

2. In the typescript originally: er. The initial letter „w“ is a handwritten addendum.

3. Handwritten marginal note: gehört zu „müssen“, „können“.

4. The typescript has: ihre Wichtigkeit:, die.

5. Handwritten alternative: normale. There is a handwritten wavy line under “richtige”: ~~~~~

6. Handwritten alternative: Unsere.

## 88

WHERE DOES THE FEELING THAT OUR GRAMMATICAL INVESTIGATIONS ARE FUNDAMENTAL COME FROM?

(Questions of different kinds occupy us, for instance "What is the specific weight of this body", "Will the weather stay nice today", "Who[2] will come through the door next", etc. But among our questions there are those of a special kind. Here we have a different experience. The questions seem to be more fundamental than the others. And now I say: if we have this experience, then we have arrived at the limits of language.)[3]

Where does our investigation get its importance from, since it seems only to destroy everything interesting, that is, all that is great and important? (As it were all the buildings, leaving behind only bits of stone and rubble.)

Whence does this observation derive its importance:[4] the one that points out to us that a table can be used in more than o n e way, that one can think up a table that instructs one as to the use of a table? The observation that one can also conceive of an arrow as pointing from the tip to the tail, that I can use a model as a model in different ways?

⟦8⟧ What we do is to bring words back from their metaphysical to their correct[5] use in language.

(The man who said that one cannot step into the same river twice said something wrong; one c a n step into the same river twice.)

And this is what the solution of all philosophical difficulties looks like. Their[6] answers, if they are correct, must be homespun and

2. In the original typescript: he. The word "who" is a handwritten alteration.

3. Handwritten marginal note: belongs to "must", "can".

4. The typescript has: its importance:, the.

5. Handwritten alternative: normal. There is a handwritten wavy line under "correct": ~~~~~~

6. Handwritten alternative: our.

gewöhnlich sein.[7] Aber man muss sie im richtigen Geist anschauen, dann macht das nichts.[8]

Woher nehmen //nahmen// die alten philosophischen Probleme ihre Bedeutung?

Der Satz der Identität z.B. schien eine fundamentale Bedeutung zu haben. Aber der Satz, dass dieser „Satz" ein Unsinn ist, hat diese Bedeutung übernommen.

Ich könnte fragen: Warum empfinde ich einen grammatischen Witz in gewissem Sinne als tief? (Und das ist natürlich die philosophische Tiefe.)

Warum empfinden wir die Untersuchung der Grammatik als fundamental?

(Das Wort „fundamental" kann auch nichts metalogisches, oder philosophisches bedeuten, wo es überhaupt eine Bedeutung hat.).[9]

⟦184⟧ Die Untersuchung der Grammatik ist im selben Sinne fun-
S.413 damental, wie | wir die Sprache fundamental — etwa ihr eigenes Fundament — nennen können.

Unsere grammatische Untersuchung unterscheidet sich ja von der eines Philologen etc.; uns interessiert z.B. die Übersetzung von einer Sprache in andre, von uns erfundene Sprachen. Überhaupt interessieren uns Regeln, die der Philologe gar nicht betrachtet. Diesen Unterschied können wir also wohl hervorheben.

Anderseits wäre es irreführend zu sagen, dass wir das Wesentliche der Grammatik behandeln (er, das Zufällige).

„Aber das ist ja nur eine äussere Unterscheidung //ein äusserer Unterschied//". Ich glaube, eine andere gibt es nicht.

7. Handwritten alternative: gewöhnliche & triviale sein.
8. At the end of the remark there is the handwriting: <[„Schlichter Unsinn"].
9. The parentheses are a handwritten addition.

ordinary.[7] But one must look at them in the proper spirit, and then it doesn't matter.[8]

Where do //did// the old philosophical problems get their importance from?

The law of identity, for example, seemed to be of fundamental importance. But now the proposition that this "law" is nonsense has taken over this importance.

I could ask: why do I sense a grammatical joke as being in a certain sense deep? (And that of course is what the depth of philosophy is.)

Why do we sense the investigation of grammar as being fundamental?

(When it has a meaning at all, the word "fundamental" can also mean something that is not metalogical, or philosophical.)[9]

The investigation of grammar is fundamental in the same sense in which we may call language fundamental—say its own foundation.

Our grammatical investigation differs from that of a philologist, etc.: what interests us, for instance, is the translation from one language into other languages we have invented. In general the rules that the philologist totally ignores are the ones that interest us. Thus we are justified in emphasizing this difference.

On the other hand it would be misleading to say that we deal with the essentials of grammar (he, with the accidentals).

"But that is only an external differentiation //an external difference//." I believe there is no other.

7. Handwritten alternative: ordinary and trivial.
8. At the end of the remark there is the handwriting: <["plain nonsense"].
9. The parentheses are a handwritten addition.

Eher könnten wir sagen, dass wir doch etwas Anderes Grammatik nennen, als er. Wie wir eben Wortarten unterscheiden, wo für ihn kein Unterschied (vorhanden) ist.

Die Wichtigkeit der Grammatik ist die Wichtigkeit der Sprache.

Man könnte auch ein Wort z.B. ‚rot' wichtig nennen insofern, als es oft und zu Wichtigem gebraucht wird, im Gegensatz etwa zu dem Wort ‚Pfeifendeckel'. Und die Grammatik des Wortes ‚rot' ist dann wichtig, weil sie die Bedeutung des Wortes ‚rot' beschreibt.

(Alles, was die Philosophie tun kann ist, Götzen zerstören. Und das heisst, keinen neuen — etwa in der „Abwesenheit eines Götzen" — zu schaffen.)

⟦185⟧
S.414

## 89

METHODE DER PHILOSOPHIE: DIE ÜBERSICHTLICHE DARSTELLUNG DER GRAMMATISCHEN //SPRACHLICHEN// TATSACHEN.
DAS ZIEL: DURCHSICHTIGKEIT DER ARGUMENTE. GERECHTIGKEIT.[10]

Es hat Einer gehört, dass der Anker eines Schiffes durch eine Dampfmaschine aufgezogen werde. Er denkt nur an die, welche das Schiff treibt (und nach welcher es Dampfschiff heisst) und kann sich, was er gehört hat, nicht erklären. (Vielleicht fällt ihm die Schwierigkeit auch erst später ein.) Nun sagen wir ihm: Nein, es ist nicht d i e s e Dampfmaschine, sondern ausser ihr gibt es noch eine Reihe anderer an Bord und eine von diesen hebt den Anker. — War sein Problem ein philosophisches? War es ein philosophisches, wenn er von der Existenz anderer Dampfmaschinen auf dem Schiff gehört hatte und nur daran erinnert werden musste? — Ich glaube, seine Unklarheit hat zwei Teile: Was der Erklärende ihm als Tatsache mitteilt, hätte der Fragende sehr wohl als Möglichkeit sich selber ausdenken können, und seine Frage in bestimmter Form, statt in der des blossen Zugeständnisses der Unklarheit vorlegen können. Diesen Teil des Zweifels hätte er selber beheben können, dagegen konnte ihn Nachdenken nicht über die Tatsachen belehren. Oder: Die Be-
S.415 unruhigung, | die davon herkommt, dass er die Wahrheit nicht wusste, konnte ihm kein Ordnen seiner Begriffe nehmen.

10. Under the title, in handwriting: ¥ S. 40/3?.

Rather we could say that we are calling something else grammar than he is. Even as we differentiate kinds of words where for him there is no difference (present).

The importance of grammar is the importance of language.

⟦9⟧ One could also call a word, for instance 'red', important insofar as it is used frequently and for important things, in contrast, for instance, to the word 'pipe-lid'. And then the grammar of the word 'red' is important because it describes the meaning of the word 'red'.

(All that philosophy can do is to destroy idols. And that means not creating a new one—for instance as in "absence of an idol".)

## 89

THE METHOD OF PHILOSOPHY: THE PERSPICUOUS REPRESENTATION OF GRAMMATICAL //LINGUISTIC// FACTS.
THE GOAL: THE TRANSPARENCY OF ARGUMENTS. JUSTICE.[10]

Someone has heard that the anchor of a ship is hauled up by a steam engine. He only thinks of the one that powers the ship (and because of which it is called a steamship) and cannot explain to himself what he has heard. (Perhaps the difficulty doesn't occur to him until later.) Now we tell him: No, it is not t h a t steam engine, but besides it a number of other ones are on board, and one of these hoists the anchor.—Was his problem a philosophical one? Was it a philosophical one if he had already heard of the existence of other steam engines on the ship and only had to be reminded of it?—I believe his confusion has two parts: what the explainer tells him as fact the questioner could easily have conceived as a possibility by himself, and he could have posed his question in a definite form instead of in the form of a mere admission of confusion. He could have removed this part of his doubt by himself; however, reflection could not have instructed him about the facts. Or: the uneasiness that comes from not having known the truth was not removable by any ordering of his concepts.

10. Under the title, in handwriting: ¥ p. 40/3?. This is a reference to page 40 of the typescript. Wittgenstein had apparently wanted to include a remark or a part of one from page 40 on this page.

Die andere Beunruhigung und Unklarheit wird durch die Worte „hier stimmt mir etwas nicht" gekennzeichnet und die Lösung, durch (die Worte): „Ach so. Du meinst nicht d i e Dampfmaschine" oder — für einen andern Fall — „. . . . Du meinst mit Dampfmaschine nicht nur Kolbenmaschine".

⟦186⟧ Die Arbeit des Philosophen ist ein Zusammentragen von Erinnerungen zu einem bestimmten Zweck.

Eine philosophische Frage ist ähnlich der, nach der Verfassung einer bestimmten Gesellschaft. — Und es wäre etwa so, als ob eine Gesellschaft ohne klar geschriebene Regeln zusammenkäme, aber mit einem Bedürfnis nach solchen; ja, auch mit einem Instinkt, durch welchen sie gewisse Regeln in ihren Zusammenkünften beobachten //einhalten//; nur, dass dies dadurch erschwert wird, dass nichts hierüber klar ausgesprochen ist und keine Einrichtung getroffen, die die Regeln deutlich macht. //klar hervortreten lässt.// So betrachten sie tatsächlich Einen von ihnen als Präsidenten, aber er sitzt nicht oben an der Tafel, ist durch nichts kenntlich und das erschwert die Verhandlung. Daher kommen wir und schaffen eine klare Ordnung: Wir setzen den Präsidenten an einen leicht kenntlichen Platz und seinen Sekretär zu ihm an ein eigenes Tischchen und die übrigen gleichberechtigten Mitglieder in zwei Reihen zu beiden Seiten des Tisches etc. etc..

Wenn man die Philosophie fragt: „w a s  i s t — z. B. — Substanz?", so wird um eine Regel gebeten. Eine allgemeine Regel, die für das Wort „Substanz" g i l t, d.h.: nach welcher ich zu spielen entschlossen bin. — Ich will sagen: die Frage „was ist . . . ." bezieht sich nicht auf S.416 einen | besonderen — praktischen — Fall, sondern wir fragen sie von unserem Schreibtisch aus. Erinnere Dich nur an den Fall des Gesetzes der Identität, um zu sehen, dass es sich bei der Erledigung einer philosophischen Schwierigkeit nicht um das Aussprechen neuer Wahrheiten über den Gegenstand der Untersuchung (der Identität) handelt.

Die Schwierigkeit besteht nur[11] darin, zu verstehen, was uns die Festsetzung einer Regel hilft. Warum die uns beruhigt, nachdem wir so ⟦187⟧ schwer[12] beunruhigt waren. Was uns beruhigt ist offenbar,

11. Handwritten alternative: nun.
12. Handwritten alternative: tief.

The other uneasiness and confusion is characterized by the words "Something's wrong here" and the solution is characterized by (the words): "Oh, you don't mean t h a t steam engine" or—in another case—". . . . By 'steam engine' you don't mean just a piston engine."

The work of the philosopher consists in assembling reminders for a particular purpose.

A philosophical question is similar to one about the constitution of a particular society.—And it would be as if a society came together ⟦10⟧ without clearly written rules, but with a need for them; indeed also with an instinct according to which they observed //followed// certain rules at their meetings; but this is made difficult by the fact that nothing is clearly expressed about this and no arrangement is made which clarifies //brings out clearly// the rules. Thus they in fact view one of them as president, but he doesn't sit at the head of the table and has no distinguishing marks, and that makes doing business difficult. Therefore we come along and create a clear order: we seat the president in a clearly identifiable spot, seat his secretary next to him at a little table of his own, and seat the other full members in two rows on both sides of the table, etc., etc.

If one asks philosophy: "W h a t is—for instance—substance?" then one is asking for a rule. A general rule, which is v a l i d for the word "substance", i.e., a rule according to which I have decided to play.—I want to say: the question "What is . . . ." doesn't refer to a particular—practical—case, but we ask it sitting at our desks. Just remember the case of the law of identity in order to see that taking care of a philosophical problem is not a matter of pronouncing new truths about the subject of the investigation (identity).

The difficulty lies only[11] in understanding how establishing a rule helps us. Why it calms us after we have been so profoundly[12] uneasy. Obviously what calms us is that we see a system which (systematically)

11. Handwritten alternative: now.
12. Handwritten alternative: deeply.

dass wir ein System sehen, das diejenigen Gebilde (systematisch) ausschliesst, die uns immer beunruhigt haben, mit denen wir nichts anzufangen wussten und die wir doch respektieren zu müssen glaubten. Ist die Festsetzung einer solchen grammatischen Regel in dieser Beziehung nicht wie die Entdeckung einer Erklärung in der Physik? z. B., des Copernicanischen Systems? Eine Ähnlichkeit ist vorhanden. — Das Seltsame an der philosophischen Beunruhigung und ihrer Lösung möchte scheinen, dass sie ist, wie die Qual des Asketen, der, eine schwere Kugel unter Stöhnen stemmend, da stand und den ein Mann erlöste, indem er ihm sagte: „lass' sie fallen". Man fragt sich: Wenn Dich diese Sätze beunruhigen, Du nichts mit ihnen anzufangen wusstest, warum liessest Du sie nicht schon früher fallen, was hat Dich daran gehindert? Nun, ich glaube, es war das falsche System, dem er sich anbequemen zu müssen glaubte, etc..[13]

(Die besondere Beruhigung, welche eintritt, wenn wir einem Fall, den wir für einzigartig hielten, andere ähnliche Fälle an die Seite stellen können, tritt in unseren Untersuchungen immer wieder ein, wenn wir zeigen, dass ein Wort nicht nur e i n e Bedeutung (oder, nicht nur zwei) hat, sondern in fünf oder sechs verschiedenen (Bedeutungen) gebraucht wird.)

S.417 Die philosophischen Probleme kann man mit den Kassenschlössern vergleichen, die durch Einstellen eines bestimmten Wortes oder einer bestimmten Zahl geöffnet werden, sodass keine Gewalt die Tür öffnen kann, ehe gerade dieses Wort getroffen ist, und ist es getroffen, jedes Kind sie öffnen kann. // . . . und ist es getroffen, keinerlei Anstrengung nötig ist, die Tür //sie// zu öffnen.//

⟦188⟧ Der Begriff der übersichtlichen Darstellung ist für uns von grundlegender Bedeutung. Er bezeichnet unsere Darstellungsform, die Art, wie wir die Dinge sehen. (Eine Art der ‚Weltanschauung', wie sie scheinbar für unsere Zeit typisch ist. Spengler.)

Diese übersichtliche Darstellung vermittelt das Verstehen //Verständnis//, welches eben darin besteht, dass wir die „Zusammenhänge sehen". Daher die Wichtigkeit der Z w i s c h e n g l i e d e r. //des Findens von Z w i s c h e n g l i e d e r n.//

13. At the end of the remark there is a handwritten addition: Henne & Kreidestrich.

excludes those structures that have always made us uneasy, those we were unable to do anything with, and which we still thought we had to respect. Isn't the establishment of such a grammatical rule similar in this respect to the discovery of an explanation in physics, for instance, of the Copernican system? A similarity exists.—The strange thing about philosophical uneasiness and its resolution might seem to be that it is like the suffering of an ascetic who stood raising a heavy ball, amid groans, and whom someone released by telling him: "Drop it." One wonders: if these sentences make you uneasy and you didn't know what to do with them, why didn't you drop them earlier, what stopped you from doing it? Well, I believe it was the false system that he thought he had to accommodate himself to, etc.[13]

(The particular peace of mind that occurs when we can place other similar cases next to a case that we thought was unique, occurs again and again in our investigations when we show that a word doesn't have ⟦11⟧ just o n e meaning (or just two), but is used in five or six different ways (meanings).)

Philosophical problems can be compared to locks on safes, which can be opened by dialing a certain word or number, so that no force can open the door until just this word has been hit upon, and once it is hit upon any child can open it. //. . . . and if it is hit upon, no effort at all is necessary to open the door//it//.//

The concept of a perspicuous representation is of fundamental significance for us. It earmarks the form of account we give, the way we look at things. (A kind of 'world-view', as is apparently typical of our time. Spengler.)

This perspicuous representation produces just that comprehension //understanding// which consists in "seeing connections". Hence the importance of i n t e r m e d i a t e c a s e s //of finding i n t e r m e d i a t e c a s e s.//

13. At the end of the remark there is a handwritten addition: hen and chalk-line.

Der Satz ist vollkommen logisch analysiert, dessen Grammatik vollkommen klargelegt ist. Er mag in welcher Ausdrucksweise immer hingeschrieben oder ausgesprochen sein.

Unserer Grammatik fehlt es vor allem an Übersichtlichkeit.

Die Philosophie darf den wirklichen //tatsächlichen// Gebrauch der Sprache // . . . darf, was wirklich gesagt wird// in keiner Weise antasten, sie kann ihn //es// am Ende also nur beschreiben.

Denn sie kann ihn auch nicht begründen.

S.418 Sie lässt alles wie es ist.
Sie lässt auch die Mathematik wie sie ist (jetzt ist) und keine mathematische Entdeckung kann sie weiter bringen.
Ein „führendes Problem der mathematischen Logik“ (Ramsey) ist ein Problem der Mathematik wie jedes andere.

(Ein Gleichnis gehört zu unserem Gebäude; aber wir können auch aus ihm keine Folgen ziehen; es führt uns nicht über sich selbst hinaus, sondern muss als Gleichnis stehen bleiben. Wir können keine Folgerun⟦189⟧gen daraus ziehen. So, wenn wir den Satz mit einem Bild vergleichen (wobei ja, was wir unter ‚Bild‘ verstehen, schon früher //vorher// in uns festliegen muss) oder, wenn ich die Anwendung der Sprache mit der, etwa, des Multiplikationskalküls vergleiche.
Die Philosophie stellt eben alles bloss hin und erklärt und folgert nichts.)

Da alles offen daliegt, ist auch nichts zu erklären. Denn was etwa nicht offen daliegt, interessiert uns nicht. // . . . ., denn, was etwa verborgen ist . . . .//
Die Antwort auf die Frage nach der Erklärung der Negation ist wirklich: verstehst Du sie denn nicht? Nun, wenn Du sie verstehst, was gibt es da noch zu erklären, was hat eine Erklärung da noch zu tun?

Wir müssen wissen, was Erklärung heisst. Es ist die ständige Gefahr, dieses Wort in der Logik in einem Sinn verwenden zu wollen, der von der Physik hergenommen ist.

A sentence is completely logically analyzed when its grammar is laid out completely clearly. It might be written down or spoken in any number of ways.

Above all, our grammar is lacking in perspicuity.

Philosophy may in no way interfere with the real //actual// use of language //. . . . with what is really said//; it can in the end only describe it.

For it cannot give it any foundation either.

It leaves everything as it is.

It also leaves mathematics as it is (is now), and no mathematical discovery can advance it.

A "leading problem of mathematical logic" (Ramsey) is a problem of mathematics like any other.

(A simile is part of our edifice; but we cannot draw any conclusions from it either; it doesn't lead us beyond itself, but must remain standing as a simile. We can draw no inferences from it. As when we compare a sentence to a picture (in which case, what we understand by 'picture' must already have been established in us earlier //before//) or when I compare the application of language with, for instance, that of the calculus of multiplication.

⟦12⟧ Philosophy simply puts everything before us, and neither explains nor deduces anything.)

Since everything lies open to view there is nothing to explain either. For what might not lie open to view is of no interest to us. //. . . . , for what is hidden, for example, is. . . .//

The answer to the request for an explanation of negation is really: don't you understand it? Well, if you understand it, what is there left to explain, what business is there left for an explanation?

We must know what explanation means. There is a constant danger of wanting to use this word in logic in a sense that is derived from physics.

Methodologie,[14] wenn sie von der Messung redet, sagt nicht, aus welchem Material etwa wir den Massstab am Vorteilhaftesten her-
S.419 stellen, um dies | und dies Resultat zu erzielen; obwohl doch das auch zur Methode des Messens gehört. Vielmehr interessiert diese Untersuchung bloss, unter welchen Umständen wir sagen, eine Länge, eine Stromstärke, (u.s.w.) sei gemessen. Sie will die, von uns bereits verwendeten, und geläufigen, Methoden tabulieren, um dadurch die Bedeutung der Worte „Länge", „Stromstärke", etc. festzulegen.)

Wollte man T h e s e n in der Philosophie aufstellen, es könnte nie über sie zur Diskussion kommen, weil Alle mit ihnen einverstanden wären.

⟦190⟧ Das Lernen der Philosophie ist w i r k l i c h ein Rückerinnern. Wir erinnern uns, dass wir die Worte wirklich auf diese Weise gebraucht haben.[15]

Die philosophisch wichtigsten Aspekte der Dinge //der Sprache// sind durch ihre Einfachheit und Alltäglichkeit verborgen.

(Man kann es nicht bemerken, weil man es immer (offen) vor Augen hat.)

Die eigentlichen Grundlagen seiner Forschung fallen dem Menschen gar nicht auf. Es sei denn, dass ihm d i e s einmal aufgefallen //zum Bewusstsein gekommen// ist. (Frazer etc. etc..)

Und das heisst, das Auffallendste (Stärkste) fällt ihm nicht auf.

(Eines der grössten Hindernisse für die Philosophie ist die Erwartung neuer tiefer //unerhörter// Aufschlüsse.)

Philosophie könnte man auch das nennen, was v o r allen neuen Entdeckungen und Erfindungen möglich //da// ist.

S.420 Das muss sich auch darauf beziehen, dass ich keine Erklärungen der Variablen „Satz" geben kann. Es ist klar, dass dieser logische Begriff, diese Variable, von der Ordnung des Begriffs „Realität" oder „Welt" sein muss.

14. Before the remark, in handwriting in the margin: VII 7.
15. In handwriting, in the margin: VII 164.

When[14] methodology talks about measurement, it does not say which material would be the most advantageous to make the measuring stick of in order to achieve this or that result: even though this too, after all, is part of the method of measuring. Rather this investigation is only interested in the circumstances under which we say that a length, the strength of a current (etc.) is measured. It wants to tabulate the methods which we already used and are familiar with, in order to determine the meaning of the words "length", "strength of current", etc.)

If one tried to advance t h e s e s in philosophy, it would never be possible to debate them, because everyone would agree to them.

Learning philosophy is r e a l l y recollecting. We remember that we really used words in this way.[15]

The aspects of things //of language// which are philosophically most important are hidden because of their simplicity and familiarity.
(One is unable to notice something because it is always (openly) before one's eyes.)

The real foundations of his inquiry do not strike a man at all. Unless t h a t fact has at some time struck him //he has become aware of//. (Frazer, etc., etc.)
And this means he fails to be struck by what is most striking (powerful).

(One of the greatest impediments for philosophy is the expectation of new, deep //unheard of// elucidations.)

⟦13⟧ One might also give the name philosophy to what is possible //present// b e f o r e all new discoveries and inventions.

This must also relate to the fact that I can't give any explanations of the variable "sentence". It is clear that this logical concept, this variable, must belong to the same order as the concept "reality" or "world".

14. Before the remark, in handwriting in the margin: VII 7.
15. In handwriting, in the margin: VII 164.

Wenn Einer die Lösung des ‚Problems des Lebens' gefunden zu haben glaubt, und sich sagen wollte, jetzt ist alles ganz leicht, so brauchte er sich zu seiner Widerlegung nur erinnern, dass es eine Zeit gegeben hat, wo diese ‚Lösung' nicht gefunden war; aber auch zu der Zeit musste man leben können und im Hinblick auf sie erscheint die gefundene Lösung wie ⟦191⟧ //als// ein Zufall. Und so geht es uns in der Logik. Wenn es eine ‚Lösung' der logischen (philosophischen[16]) Probleme gäbe, so müssten wir uns nur vorhalten, dass sie ja einmal nicht gelöst waren (und auch da musste man leben und denken können). — — —

Alle Überlegungen können viel hausbackener angestellt werden, als ich sie in früherer Zeit angestellt habe. Und darum brauchen in der Philosophie auch keine neuen Wörter angewendet werden, sondern die alten, gewöhnlichen Wörter der Sprache reichen aus. //die alten reichen aus.//

(Unsere Aufgabe ist es nur, gerecht zu sein. D.h., wir haben nur die Ungerechtigkeiten der Philosophie aufzuzeigen und zu lösen, aber nicht neue Parteien — und Glaubensbekenntnisse — aufzustellen.)

(Es ist schwer, in der Philosophie nicht zu übertreiben.)

(Der Philosoph übertreibt, schreit gleichsam in seiner Ohnmacht,
S.421 so | lange er den Kern der Konfusion noch nicht entdeckt hat.)

Das philosophische Problem ist ein Bewusstsein der Unordnung in unsern Begriffen, und durch Ordnen derselben zu heben.

Ein philosophisches Problem ist immer von der Form: „Ich kenne mich einfach nicht aus".

Wie ich Philosophie betreibe, ist es ihre ganze Aufgabe, den Ausdruck so zu gestalten, dass gewisse Beunruhigungen //Probleme // verschwinden. (Hertz.))

⟦192⟧ Wenn ich Recht habe, so müssen sich philosophische Probleme wirklich restlos lösen lassen, im Gegensatz zu allen andern.

16. In the typescript presumably mistakenly: Philosophischen.

If someone believes he has found the solution to the 'problem of life' and tried to tell himself that now everything is simple, then in order to refute himself he would only have to remember that there was a time when this 'solution' had not been found; but at that time too one had to be able to live, and in reference to this time the new solution appears like //as// a coincidence. And that's what happens to us in logic. If there were a 'solution' of logical (philosophical[16]) problems then we would only have to call to mind that at one time they had not been solved (and then too one had to be able to live and think).— — —

All reflections can be carried out in a much more homespun manner than I used to do. And therefore no new words have to be used in philosophy, but rather the old common words of language are sufficient. //the old ones are sufficient//

(Our only task is to be just. That is, we must only point out and resolve the injustices of philosophy, and not posit new parties—and creeds.)

(It is difficult not to exaggerate in philosophy.)

(The philosopher exaggerates, shouts, as it were, in his helplessness, so long as he hasn't yet discovered the core of his confusion.)

The philosophical problem is an awareness of disorder in our concepts, and can be solved by ordering them.

A philosophical problem always has the form: "I simply don't know my way about."

As I do philosophy, its entire task consists in expressing myself in such a way that certain troubles //problems// disappear. ((Hertz.))

If I am correct, then philosophical problems must be completely solvable, in contrast to all others.

16. In the typescript presumably mistakenly: Philosophical.

Wenn ich sage: Hier sind wir an der Grenze der Sprache, so scheint //klingt// das immer, als wäre hier eine Resignation nötig, während im Gegenteil volle Befriedigung eintritt, da keine Frage übrig bleibt.

Die Probleme werden im eigentlichen Sinne aufgelöst — wie ein Stück Zucker im Wasser.

/Die Menschen, welche kein Bedürfnis nach Durchsichtigkeit ihrer Argumentation haben, sind für die Philosophie verloren./

⟦193⟧
S.422

## 90

PHILOSOPHIE.
DIE KLÄRUNG DES SPRACHGEBRAUCHES. FALLEN DER SPRACHE.

Wie kommt es, dass die Philosophie ein so komplizierter Bau //Aufbau// ist. Sie sollte doch gänzlich einfach sein, wenn sie jenes Letzte, von aller Erfahrung Unabhängige ist, wofür Du sie ausgibt. — Die Philosophie löst die Knoten in unserem Denken auf; daher muss ihr Resultat einfach sein, ihre Tätigkeit aber so kompliziert wie die Knoten, die sie auflöst.

Lichtenberg: „Unsere ganze Philosophie ist Berichtigung des Sprachgebrauchs, also, die Berichtigung einer Philosophie, und zwar der allgemeinsten.“

(Die Fähigkeit[17] zur Philosophie besteht[18] in der Fähigkeit,[19] von einer Tatsache der Grammatik einen starken und nachhaltigen Eindruck zu empfangen.).[20]

Warum die grammatischen Probleme so hart und anscheinend un-
S.423 ausrott-|bar sind — weil sie mit den ältesten Denkgewohnheiten, d.h.

17. Handwritten alternative (with an unbroken wavy line under the original word): Veranlagung.
18. Handwritten alternative (with an unbroken wavy line under the original word): liegt.
19. Handwritten alternative (suspending the broken underlinings): Empfänglichkeit.
20. Handwritten marginal remark: zu ‚Witz‘, ‚Tiefe‘.

If I say: here we are at the limits of language, then it always seems ⟦14⟧ //sounds// as if resignation were necessary, whereas on the contrary complete satisfaction comes, since n o question remains.

The problems are dissolved in the actual sense of the word—like a lump of sugar in water.

/People who have no need for transparency in their argumentation are lost to philosophy./

## 90

PHILOSOPHY.
THE CLARIFICATION OF THE USE OF LANGUAGE. TRAPS OF LANGUAGE.

How is it that philosophy is such a complicated building //structure//. After all, it should be completely simple if it is that ultimate thing, independent of all experience, that it claims to be.—Philosophy unravels the knots in our thinking; hence its results must be simple, but its activity is as complicated as the knots that it unravels.

Lichtenberg: "Our entire philosophy is correction of the use of language, and therefore the correction of a philosophy, and indeed of the most general philosophy."

(The capacity[17] for philosophy consists[18] in the ability[19] to receive a strong and lasting impression from a grammatical fact.)[20]

Why are grammatical problems so tough and seemingly ineradicable?—Because they are connected with the oldest thought habits, i.e.,

17. Handwritten alternative (with an unbroken wavy line under the original word): talent.
18. Handwritten alternative (with an unbroken wavy line under the original word): lies.
19. Handwritten alternative (suspending the broken underlining): susceptibility.
20. Handwritten marginal remark: for 'humor', 'depth'.

mit den ältesten Bildern, die in unsere Sprache selbst geprägt sind, zusammenhängen. ((Lichtenberg.))

/Das Lehren der Philosophie hat dieselbe ungeheure Schwierigkeit, welche der Unterricht in der Geographie hätte, wenn der Schüler eine ⟦194⟧ Menge falsche und viel zu einfache //und falsch vereinfachte// Vorstellungen über den Lauf und Zusammenhang der Flussläufe //Flüsse// und Gebirgsketten //Gebirge// mitbrächte./

/Die Menschen sind tief in den philosophischen d.i. grammatischen Konfusionen eingebettet. Und, sie daraus zu befreien, setzt voraus, dass man sie aus den ungeheuer mannigfachen Verbindungen herausreisst, in denen sie gefangen sind. Man muss sozusagen ihre ganze Sprache umgruppieren. — Aber diese Sprache ist ja so entstanden //geworden//, weil Menschen die Neigung hatten — und haben — so zu denken. Darum geht das Herausreissen nur bei denen, die in der einer instinktiven Auflehnung gegen //Unbefriedigung mit// die Sprache leben. Nicht bei denen, die ihrem ganzen Instinkt nach in der Herde leben, die diese Sprache als ihren eigentlichen Ausdruck geschaffen hat./

Die Sprache hat für alle die gleichen Fallen bereit; das ungeheure Netz gut erhaltener //gangbarer[21]// Irrwege. Und so sehen wir also Einen nach dem Andern die gleichen Wege gehen und wissen schon, wo er jetzt abbiegen wird, wo er geradeaus fortgehen wird, ohne die Abzweigung zu bemerken, etc. etc.. Ich sollte also an allen den Stellen, wo falsche Wege abzweigen, Tafeln aufstellen, die über die gefährlichen Punkte hinweghelfen.

S.424 Man hört immer wieder die Bemerkung, dass die Philosophie eigentlich keinen Fortschritt mache, dass die gleichen philosophischen Probleme, die schon die Griechen beschäftigten, uns noch beschäftigen. Die das aber sagen, verstehen nicht den Grund, warum es so ist //sein muss//. Der ist aber, dass unsere Sprache sich gleich geblieben ist und uns immer wieder zu denselben Fragen verführt. Solange es ein Verbum ‚sein' geben wird, ⟦195⟧ das zu funktionieren scheint wie ‚essen' und ‚trinken', solange es Adjektive ‚identisch', ‚wahr', ‚falsch', ‚möglich' geben wird, solange von einem Fluss der Zeit und von einer Ausdehnung des Raumes die Rede sein wird,

21. In the typescript mistakenly: ganzbarer.

with the oldest images that are engraved into our language itself. ((Lichtenberg.))

/Teaching philosophy involves the same immense difficulty as instruction in geography would have if a pupil brought with him a mass of false and far too simple //and falsely simplified// ideas about the course and connections of the routes of rivers //rivers// and mountain chains //mountains//./

/People are deeply imbedded in philosophical, i.e., grammatical confusions. And to free them from these presupposes pulling them out of the immensely manifold connections they are caught up in. One must ⟦15⟧ so to speak regroup their entire language.—But this language came about //developed// as it did because people had—and have—the inclination to think in this way. Therefore pulling them out only works with those who live in an instinctive state of rebellion against //dissatisfaction with// language. Not with those who following all of their instincts live within the herd that has created this language as its proper expression./

Language contains the same traps for everyone; the immense network of well-kept //passable[21]// false paths. And thus we see one person after another walking the same paths and we know already where he will make a turn, where he will keep on going straight ahead without noticing the turn, etc., etc. Therefore wherever false paths branch off I should put up signs which help one get by the dangerous places.

One keeps hearing the remark that philosophy really makes no progress, that the same philosophical problems that had occupied the Greeks are still occupying us. But those who say that don't understand the reason it is //must be// so. The reason is that our language has remained the same and seduces us into asking the same questions over and over. As long as there is a verb 'to be' which seems to function like 'to eat' and 'to drink', as long as there are adjectives like 'identical', 'true', 'false', 'possible', as long as one talks about a flow of time and an expanse of space, etc., etc., humans will continue to

21. In the typescript the word for "passable" was misspelled.

u.s.w., u.s.w., solange werden die Menschen immer wieder an die gleichen rätselhaften Schwierigkeiten stossen, und auf etwas starren, was keine Erklärung scheint wegheben zu können.

Und dies befriedigt im Übrigen ein Verlangen nach dem Überirdischen //Transcendenten//, denn, indem sie die „Grenze des menschlichen Verstandes" zu sehen glauben, glauben sie natürlich, über ihn hinaus sehen zu können.

Ich lese „. . . philosophers are no nearer to the meaning of ‚Reality' than Plato got, . . .". Welche seltsame Sachlage. Wie sonderbar, dass Plato dann überhaupt so weit kommen konnte! Oder, dass wir dann nicht weiter kommen konnten! War es, weil Plato so gescheit war?

Der Konflikt, in welchem wir uns in logischen Betrachtungen immer wieder befinden, ist wie der Konflikt zweier Personen, die miteinander einen Vertrag abgeschlossen haben, dessen letzte Formulierungen in leicht missdeutbaren Worten niedergelegt sind, wogegen die Erläuterungen zu diesen Formulierungen alles in unmissverständlicher Weise erklären. Die eine der beiden Personen nun hat ein kurzes Gedächtnis, vergisst die Erläuterungen immer wieder, miss-
S.425 deutet die Bestimmungen des | Vertrages und kommt //gerät daher// fortwährend in Schwierigkeiten. Die andere muss immer von frischem an die Erläuterungen im Vertrag erinnern und die Schwierigkeit wegräumen.

Erinnere Dich daran, wie schwer es Kindern fällt, zu glauben, (oder einzusehen) dass ein Wort wirklich zwei ganz verschiedene Bedeutungen hat //haben kann//.

⟦196⟧ Das Ziel der Philosophie ist es, eine Mauer dort zu errichten, wo die Sprache ohnehin aufhört.

Die Ergebnisse der Philosophie sind die Entdeckung irgend eines schlichten Unsinns, und Beulen, die sich der Verstand beim Anrennen an die Grenze //das Ende// der Sprache geholt hat. Sie, die Beulen, lassen uns den Wert jener Entdeckung verstehen. //erkennen.//

Welcher Art ist unsere Untersuchung? Untersuche ich die Fälle, die ich als Beispiele anführe, auf ihre Wahrscheinlichkeit? oder Tatsächlichkeit? Nein, ich führe nur an, was möglich ist, gebe also grammatische Beispiele.

bump up against the same mysterious difficulties, and stare at something that no explanation seems able to remove.

And this by the way satisfies a longing for the supra-natural //transcendental//, for in believing that they see the "limits of human understanding" of course they believe that they can see beyond it.

I read ". . . . philosophers are no nearer the meaning of 'Reality' than Plato got. . . .". What a strange state of affairs. How strange in that case that Plato could get that far at all! Or, that we were not able to get farther! Was it because Plato was so smart?

The conflict in which we constantly find ourselves when we undertake logical investigations is like the conflict of two people who have concluded a contract with each other, the last formulations of which are expressed in easily misunderstandable words, whereas the explanations of these formulations explain everything unmistakably. Now one of the ⟦16⟧ two people has a short memory, constantly forgets the explanations, misinterprets the conditions of the contract, and continually gets //therefore continually runs// into difficulties. The other one constantly has to remind him of the explanations in the contract and remove the difficulty.

Remember what a hard time children have believing (or accepting) that a word really has //can have// two completely different meanings.

The aim of philosophy is to erect a wall at the point where language stops anyway.

The results of philosophy are the uncovering of one or another piece of plain nonsense, and are the bumps that the understanding has got by running its head up against the limits //the end// of language. These bumps let us understand //recognize// the value of the discovery.

What kind of investigation are we carrying out? Am I investigating the probability of cases that I give as examples, or am I investigating their actuality? No, I'm just citing what is possible and am therefore giving grammatical examples.

Philosophie wird nicht in Sätzen, sondern in einer Sprache niedergelegt.

Wie Gesetze nur Interesse gewinnen, wenn die Neigung besteht, sie zu übertreten, //wenn sie übertreten werden// so gewinnen gewisse grammatische Regeln erst dann Interesse, wenn die Philosophen sie übertreten möchten.

S.426 Die Wilden haben Spiele (oder wir nennen es doch so), für die sie keine geschriebenen Regeln, kein Regelverzeichnis besitzen. Denken wir uns nun die Tätigkeit eines Forschers, die Länder dieser Völker zu bereisen und Regelverzeichnisse für ihre Spiele anzulegen. Das ist das ganze Analogon zu dem, was der Philosoph tut. ((Warum sage ich aber nicht: Die Wilden haben Sprachen (oder wir . . . . .), . . . . keine geschriebene Grammatik haben . . . .")).[22]

⟦197⟧
S.427

## 91

DIE PHILOSOPHISCHEN PROBLEME TRETEN UNS IM PRAKTISCHEN LEBEN GAR NICHT ENTGEGEN (WIE ETWA DIE DER NATURLEHRE), SONDERN ERST, WENN WIR UNS BEI DER BILDUNG UNSERER SÄTZE NICHT VOM PRAKTISCHEN ZWECK, SONDERN VON GEWISSEN ANALOGIEN IN DER SPRACHE LEITEN LASSEN.

Was zum Wesen der Welt gehört, kann die Sprache nicht ausdrücken. Daher kann sie nicht s a g e n, dass Alles fliesst. Nur was wir uns auch anders vorstellen könnten, kann die Sprache sagen.

Dass Alles fliesst, muss im Wesen der Berührung der Sprache mit der Wirklichkeit liegen. Oder besser: dass Alles fliesst, muss im Wesen der Sprache liegen. Und, erinnern wir uns: im gewöhnlichen Leben fällt uns das nicht auf — sowenig, wie die verschwommenen Ränder unseres Gesichtsfelds („weil wir so daran gewöhnt sind", wird Mancher sagen). Wie, bei welcher Gelegenheit, glauben wir denn darauf aufmerksam zu werden? Ist es nicht, wenn wir Sätze gegen die Grammatik der Zeit bilden wollen?

Wenn man sagt, dass ‚alles fliesst', so fühlen wir, dass wir gehindert sind, das Eigentliche, die eigentliche Realität festzuhalten. Der

22. In the typescript the parentheses are missing at the end of the remark.

Philosophy is not laid down in sentences but in a language.

Just as laws only become interesting when there is an inclination to transgress them //when they are transgressed// certain grammatical rules are only interesting when philosophers want to transgress them.

Savages have games (that's what we call them, anyway) for which they have no written rules, no inventory of rules. Let's now imagine the activity of an explorer, who travels through the countries of these peoples and takes an inventory of their rules. This is completely analogous to what the philosopher does. ((But why don't I say: savages have languages (that's what we . . . . ) . . . . without a written grammar?))[22]

⟦17⟧ 91

WE DON'T ENCOUNTER PHILOSOPHICAL PROBLEMS AT ALL IN PRACTICAL LIFE (AS WE DO, FOR EXAMPLE, THOSE OF NATURAL SCIENCE). WE ENCOUNTER THEM ONLY WHEN WE ARE GUIDED NOT BY PRACTICAL PURPOSE IN FORMING OUR SENTENCES, BUT BY CERTAIN ANALOGIES WITHIN OUR LANGUAGE.

Language cannot express what belongs to the essence of the world. Therefore it cannot *say* that everything flows. Language can only say what we could also imagine differently.

That everything flows must lie in how language touches reality. Or better: that everything flows must lie in the nature of language. And, let's remember: in everyday life we don't notice that—as little as we notice the blurred edges of our visual field ("because we are so used to it", some will say). How, on what occasion, do we think we start noticing it? Isn't it when we want to form sentences in opposition to the grammar of time?

When someone says 'everything flows', we feel that we are hindered in pinning down the actual, the actual reality. What goes on on the

22. In the typescript the parentheses are missing at the end of the remark.

Vorgang auf der Leinwand entschlüpft uns eben, weil er ein Vorgang |
S.428 ist. Aber wir beschreiben doch etwas; und ist das ein anderer Vorgang? Die Beschreibung steht doch offenbar gerade mit dem Bild auf der Leinwand in Zusammenhang. Es muss dem Gefühl unserer Ohnmacht ein falsches Bild zugrunde liegen. Denn was wir beschreiben wollen können, das können wir beschreiben.

Ist nicht dieses falsche Bild das eines Bilderstreifens, der so geschwind vorbeiläuft, dass wir keine Zeit haben, ein Bild aufzufassen.

Wir würden nämlich in diesem Fall geneigt sein, dem Bilde nachzulaufen. Aber dazu gibt es ja im Ablauf eines Vorgangs nichts analoges.

⟦198⟧ Es ist merkwürdig, dass wir das Gefühl, dass das Phänomen uns entschlüpft, den ständigen Fluss der Erscheinung, im gewöhnlichen Leben nie spüren, sondern erst, wenn wir philosophieren. Das deutet darauf hin, dass es sich hier um einen Gedanken handelt, der uns durch eine falsche Verwendung unserer Sprache suggeriert wird.

Das Gefühl ist nämlich, dass die Gegenwart in die Vergangenheit schwindet, ohne dass wir es hindern können. Und hier bedienen wir uns doch offenbar des Bildes eines Streifens, der sich unaufhörlich an uns vorbeibewegt und den wir nicht aufhalten können. Aber es ist natürlich ebenso klar, dass das Bild missbraucht ist. Dass man nicht sagen kann „die Zeit fliesst“ wenn man mit „Zeit“ die Möglichkeit der Veränderung meint.

Dass uns nichts auffällt, wenn wir uns umsehen, im Raum herumsehen, unseren eigenen Körper fühlen etc. etc., das zeigt, wie natürlich uns eben diese Dinge sind. Wir nehmen nicht wahr, dass wir den Raum perspek-|tivisch sehen oder dass das Gesichtsbild gegen den Rand zu in irgendeinem Sinne verschwommen ist. Es fällt uns nie auf und kann uns nie auffallen, weil es d i e Art der Wahrnehmung ist. Wir denken nie darüber nach, und es ist unmöglich, weil es zu der Form unserer Welt keinen Gegensatz gibt.

Ich wollte sagen, es ist merkwürdig, dass die, die nur den Dingen, nicht unseren Vorstellungen, Realität zuschreiben, sich in der Vorstellungswelt so selbstverständlich bewegen und sich nie aus ihr heraussehnen.

screen escapes us precisely because it is something going on. But we are describing something; and is that something else that is going on? The description is obviously linked to the very picture on the screen. There must be a false picture at the bottom of our feeling of helplessness. For what we want to describe we can describe.

Isn't this false picture that of a strip of film that runs by so quickly that we don't have any time to perceive a picture?

For in this case we would be inclined to chase after the picture. But in the course of something going on there is nothing analogous to that.

It is remarkable that in everyday life we never have the feeling that the phenomenon is getting away from us, that appearances are continually flowing, but only when we philosophize. This points to the fact that we are dealing here with a thought that is suggested to us through a wrong use of our language.

For the feeling is that the present vanishes into the past without our being able to stop it. And here we are obviously using the picture of a strip that constantly moves past us and that we can't stop. But of course ⟦18⟧ it's just as clear that the picture is being misused. That one cannot say "time flows" if by "time" one means the possibility of change.

That we don't notice anything when we look around, look around in space, feel our own bodies, etc., etc., shows how natural these very things are to us. We don't perceive that we see space perspectivally or that the visual image is in some sense blurred near its edge. We don't notice this, and can never notice it, because it is *the* mode of perception. We never think about it, and it is impossible, because the form of our world has no contrary.

I wanted to say that it is odd that those who ascribe reality only to things and not to our mental images move so self-confidently in the world of imagination and never long to escape from it.

D.h., wie selbstverständlich ist doch das Gegebene. Es müsste mit allen Teufeln zugehen, wenn das das kleine, aus einem schiefen Winkel aufgenommene Bildchen wäre.

Dieses Selbstverständliche, *das Leben*, soll etwas Zufälliges, Nebensächliches sein; dagegen etwas, worüber ich mir normalerweise nie den Kopf zerbreche, das Eigentliche!

⟦199⟧ D.h., das, worüber hinaus man nicht gehen kann, noch gehen will, wäre nicht die Welt.

Immer wieder ist es der Versuch, die Welt in der Sprache abzugrenzen und hervorzuheben — was aber nicht geht. Die Selbstverständlichkeit der Welt drückt sich eben darin aus, dass die Sprache nur sie bedeutet, und nur sie bedeuten kann.

Denn, da die Sprache die Art ihres Bedeutens erst von ihrer Bedeutung, von der Welt, erhält, so ist keine Sprache denkbar, die nicht diese Welt darstellt.

In den Theorien und Streitigkeiten der Philosophie finden wir die Worte, deren Bedeutungen uns vom alltäglichen Leben her wohlbekannt sind, in einem ultraphysischen Sinne angewandt.

S.430 Wenn die Philosophen ein Wort gebrauchen und nach seiner Bedeutung forschen, muss man sich immer fragen: wird denn dieses Wort in der Sprache, die es geschaffen hat //für die es geschaffen ist//, je tatsächlich so gebraucht?

Man wird dann meistens finden, dass es nicht so ist, und das Wort gegen seine normale //entgegen seiner normalen// Grammatik gebraucht wird. („Wissen“, „Sein“, „Ding“.)

(Die Philosophen sind oft wie kleine Kinder,[23] die zuerst mit ihrem Bleistift beliebige[24] Striche auf ein Papier kritzeln und nun //dann// den Erwachsenen fragen „was ist das?“ — Das ging so zu: Der Erwachsene hatte dem Kind öfters etwas vorgezeichnet und gesagt: „das ist ein Mann“, „das ist ein Haus“, u.s.w.. Und nun macht das Kind auch Striche und fragt: was ist nun *das*?)

23. Handwritten alternative: Den <Philosophen> geht es oft wie den kleinen Kindern----.

24. Handwritten alternative: irgend welche.

I.e., how self-evident is the given. Things would have to have come to a pretty pass for that to be just a tiny photograph taken from an oblique angle.

What is self-evident, *life*, is supposed to be something accidental, unimportant; by contrast something that normally I never worry my head about is what is real!

I.e., what one neither can nor wants to go beyond would not be the world.

Again and again there is the attempt to define the world in language and to display it—but that doesn't work. The self-evidence of the world is expressed in the very fact that language means only it, and can only mean it.

As language gets its way of meaning from what it means, from the world, no language is thinkable which doesn't represent this world.

In the theories and battles of philosophy we find words whose meanings are well-known to us from everyday life used in an ultra-physical sense.

When philosophers use a word and search for its meaning, one must always ask: is this word ever really used this way in the language which created it //for which it is created//?

Usually one will then find that it is not so, and that the word is used against //contrary to// its normal grammar. ("Knowing", "Being", "Thing".)

(Philosophers are often like little children,[23] who first scribble ⟦19⟧ random[24] lines on a piece of paper with their pencils, and now //then// ask an adult "What is that?"—Here's how this happened: now and then the adult had drawn something for the child and said: "That's a man", "That's a house", etc. And then the child draws lines too, and asks: now what's *that*?)

23. Handwritten alternative: (Philosophers) often behave like little children . . . .

24. Handwritten alternative: some.

⟦200⟧
S.431

## 92

METHODE IN DER PHILOSOPHIE.
MÖGLICHKEIT DES RUHIGEN FORTSCHREITENS.

Die eigentliche Entdeckung ist die, die mich fähig macht, mit dem Philosophieren aufzuhören, wann ich will.

Die die Philosophie zur Ruhe bringt, so dass sie nicht mehr von Fragen gepeitscht ist //wird//, die sie selbst in Frage stellen.

Sondern es wird jetzt an Beispielen eine Methode gezeigt, und die Reihe dieser Beispiele kann man abbrechen //kann abgebrochen werden//.

Richtiger hiesse es aber: Es werden Probleme gelöst (Beunruhigungen //Schwierigkeiten// beseitigt), nicht ein Problem.

Die Unruhe in der Philosophie kommt daher, dass die Philosophen die Philosophie falsch ansehen, falsch sehen, nämlich gleichsam in (unendliche) Längsstreifen zerlegt, statt in (endliche) Querstreifen. Diese Umstellung der Auffassung macht die grösste Schwierigkeit. Sie wollen also gleichsam den unendlichen Streifen erfassen, und
S.432 klagen, | dass es //dies// nicht Stück für Stück möglich ist. Freilich nicht, wenn man unter einem Stück einen endlosen Längsstreifen versteht. Wohl aber, wenn man einen Querstreifen als Stück //ganzes, definitives Stück// sieht. — Aber dann kommen wir ja mit unserer Arbeit nie zu Ende! Freilich //Gewiss// nicht, denn sie hat ja keins.

(Statt der turbulenten Mutmassungen und Erklärungen wollen wir ruhige Darlegungen[25] //Konstatierungen// sprachlicher Tatsachen ge⟦201⟧ben. //von sprachlichen Tatsachen geben.//) //wollen wir die ruhige Feststellung[26] sprachlicher Tatsachen.//

Wir müssen die ganze Sprache durchpflügen.

25. Handwritten alternative: Erwägung.

26. Originally in the typescript: Festsetzung. But Wittgenstein crossed out "setzung" and replaced it by "stellung."

## 92

METHOD OF PHILOSOPHY.
THE POSSIBILITY OF CALM PROGRESS.

The real discovery is the one that makes me capable of stopping doing philosophy when I want to.

The one that gives philosophy peace, so that it is no longer //being// tormented by questions which bring *itself* in question.

Instead, we now demonstrate a method by examples; and one can break off the series of examples //and the series of examples can be broken off//.

But more correctly, one should say: Problems are solved (uneasiness //difficulties// eliminated), not a *single* problem.

Unrest in philosophy comes from philosophers looking at, seeing, philosophy all wrong, i.e., cut up into (infinite) vertical strips, as it were, rather than (finite) horizontal strips. This reordering of understanding creates the *greatest* difficulty. They want to grasp the infinite strip, as it were, and complain that it //this// is not possible piece by piece. Of course it isn't, if by 'a piece' one understands an endless vertical strip. But it is, if one sees a horizontal strip as a piece //a whole, definite piece//.—But then we'll never get finished with our work! Of course //certainly// not, because it doesn't have an end.

(Instead of turbulent conjectures and explanations, we want to give calm demonstrations[25] //statements// of linguistic facts //about linguistic facts//.) //we want the calm noting[26] of linguistic facts.//

We must plow though the whole of language.

25. Handwritten alternative: reflection.
26. Originally in the typescript: establishment.

(Die meisten Menschen, wenn sie eine philosophische Untersuchung anstellen sollen,[27] machen es wie Einer, der äusserst nervös einen Gegenstand in einer Lade sucht. Er wirft Papiere aus der Lade heraus — das Gesuchte mag darunter sein — blättert hastig und ungenau unter den übrigen. Wirft wieder einige in die Lade zurück, bringt sie mit den andern durcheinander, u.s.w.. Man kann ihm dann nur sagen: Halt, wenn Du s o suchst, kann ich Dir nicht suchen helfen. Erst musst Du anfangen, in vollster Ruhe methodisch eines nach dem andern zu untersuchen; dann bin ich auch bereit, mit Dir zu suchen und mich auch in der Methode nach Dir zu richten.)

⟦202⟧
S.433

## 93

DIE MYTHOLOGIE IN DEN FORMEN UNSERER SPRACHE.
((PAUL ERNST.))

In den alten Riten haben wir den Gebrauch einer äusserst ausgebildeten Gebärdensprache.

Und wenn ich in Frazer lese, so möchte ich auf Schritt und Tritt sagen: Alle diese Prozesse, diese Wandlungen der Bedeutung, haben wir noch in unserer Wortsprache vor uns. Wenn das, was sich in der letzten Garbe verbirgt, der ‚Kornwolf' genannt wird, aber auch diese Garbe selbst, und auch der Mann der sie bindet, so erkennen wir hierin einen uns wohlbekannten sprachlichen Vorgang.

Der Sündenbock, auf den man seine Sünde legt und der damit in die Wüste hinausläuft, — ein falsches Bild, ähnlich denen, die die philosophischen Irrtümer verursachen.

Ich möchte sagen: nichts zeigt unsere Verwandtschaft mit jenen Wilden besser, als dass Frazer ein ihm und uns so geläufiges Wort wie „ghost" oder „shade" bei der Hand hat, um die Ansichten dieser Leute zu beschreiben.

S.434 (Das ist ja doch etwas anderes, als wenn er etwa beschriebe, die Wilden bildeten //bilden// sich ein, dass ihnen ihr Kopf herunterfällt, wenn sie einen Feind erschlagen haben. Hier hätte u n s e r e B e s c h r e i b u n g nichts Abergläubisches oder Magisches an sich.)

27. Unclear in the typescript. The typewriting gives the impression that the original "wollen" was to be changed to "sollen" by typing over the "w".

(When most people ought to[27] engage in a philosophical investigation, they act like someone who is looking for an object in a drawer ⟦20⟧ very nervously. He throws papers out of the drawer—what he's looking for may be among them—leafs through the others hastily and sloppily. Throws some back into the drawer, mixes them up with the others, and so on. Then one can only tell him: Stop, if you look in that way, I can't help you look. First you have to start to examine one thing after another methodically, and in peace and quiet; then I am willing to look with you and to direct myself with you as model in the method.)

## 93

THE MYTHOLOGY IN THE FORMS OF OUR LANGUAGE. ((PAUL ERNST.))

In ancient rites we find the use of an extremely well-developed language of gestures.

And when I read Frazer, I would like to say again and again: All these processes, these changes of meaning, we have right in front of us even in our language of words. If what is hidden in the last sheaf is called the 'Cornwolf', as well as the sheaf itself, and also the man who binds it, then we recognize in this a linguistic process we know well.

The scapegoat, on which one lays one's sins, and who runs away into the desert with them—a false picture, similar to those that cause errors in philosophy.

I would like to say: nothing shows our kinship with those savages better, than that Frazer has at hand a word like "ghost" or "shade", which is so familiar to him and to us, to describe the views of these people.

(This is quite different than if he were to relate, for instance, that the savages imagined //imagine// that their head falls off when they have slain an enemy. Here our description would contain nothing superstitious or magical.)

27. Unclear textual point in the typescript. The typewriting gives the impression that the original words "want to" were overstruck to produce "ought to".

Ja, diese Sonderbarkeit bezieht sich nicht nur auf die Ausdrücke „ghost“ und „shade“, und es wird viel zu wenig Aufhebens davon gemacht, dass wir das Wort „Seele“, „Geist“ („spirit“) zu unserem eigenen gebildeten Vokabular zählen. Dagegen ist es eine Kleinigkeit, dass wir nicht glauben, dass unsere Seele isst und trinkt.

⟦203⟧ In unserer Sprache ist eine ganze Mythologie niedergelegt.

Austreiben des Todes oder Umbringen des Todes; aber anderseits wird er als Gerippe dargestellt, also selbst in gewissem Sinne tot. „As dead as death“. ‚Nichts ist so tot wie der Tod; nichts so schön wie die Schönheit selbst!‘ Das Bild, worunter man sich hier die Realität
reinen (konzentrierten)
denkt ist, dass die Schönheit, der Tod, etc. die reine (konzentrierte)
Substanzen sind
Substanz ist, während sie in einem schönen Gegenstand als
sind
Beimischung vorhanden ist. — Und erkenne ich hier nicht meine eigenen Betrachtungen über ‚Gegenstand‘ und ‚Komplex‘? (Plato.)

Die primitiven Formen unserer Sprache: Substantiv, Eigenschaftswort und Tätigkeitswort zeigen das einfache Bild, auf dessen Form sie alles zu bringen sucht.

Solange man sich unter der Seele ein Ding, einen Körper vorstellt, der in unserem Kopfe ist, solange ist diese Hypothese nicht gefährlich. Nicht in der Unvollkommenheit und Rohheit unserer Mo-
S.435 delle | liegt die Gefahr, sondern in ihrer Unklarheit (Undeutlichkeit). Die Gefahr beginnt, wenn wir merken, dass das alte Modell nicht genügt, es nun aber nicht ändern, sondern nur gleichsam sublimieren. Solange ich sage, der Gedanke ist in meinem Kopf, ist alles in Ordnung; gefährlich wird es, wenn wir sagen, der Gedanke ist nicht in meinem Kopfe, aber in meinem Geist.

Indeed, this oddity refers not only to the expressions "ghost" and "shade", and much too little is made of it that we include the words "soul" and "spirit" in our own educated vocabulary. Compared to this it is insignificant that we do not believe that our soul eats and drinks.

An entire mythology is laid down in our language.

⟦21⟧ Driving out death or killing death; but on the other hand it is portrayed as a skeleton, and therefore as dead itself, in a certain sense. "As dead as death." 'Nothing is as dead as death; nothing as beautiful as beauty itself!' The picture according to which reality is thought of here is that beauty, death, etc., is the pure (concentrated) substance, whereas in a beautiful object it is contained as an admixture.—And don't I recognize here my own observations about 'object' and 'complex'? (Plato.)

are the pure (concentrated) substances they are

The primitive forms of our language: noun, adjective and verb, show the simple picture into whose form language tries to force everything.

So long as one imagines the soul as a *thing*, a *body*, which is in our head, this hypothesis is *not* dangerous. The danger of our models does not lie in their imperfection and roughness, but in their unclarity (fogginess).

The danger sets in when we notice that the old model is not sufficient but then we don't change it, but only sublimate it, as it were. So long as I say the thought is in my head, everything is all right; things get dangerous when we say that the thought is not in my head, but in my spirit.

# 10

*This is a revised and expanded version of material previously edited by Rush Rhees. The notes are undated, but Rhees thinks they were begun in late 1934 or early 1935 and finished in March 1936; von Wright's catalogue dates the first notebook to 1934–5 and the last to 1936. They must have been prepared in connection with the lectures on the same topics that Wittgenstein gave during 1935–6. Although he did not lecture from notes, "what he said was both a revision and discussion of what he had thought and written in preparing."*[1]

*This edition consists of a much fuller transcription of Wittgenstein's discussion of sense data and private language in the three manuscript notebooks that Rhees used (MSS 148, 149, and 151). Rhees omitted nearly half of the source material, dropping sentences, paragraphs, and lengthy passages without any indication of the breaks. This not only left out much material that is interesting in its own right, it also made it impossible to follow Wittgenstein's train of thought. In an appendix at the end of this volume is a list of the new and substantially revised paragraphs in this edition. Like Rhees, I have left out two lengthy discussions of the philosophy of mathematics that are clearly separated from the rest of the text in the manuscripts; the location of these passages is indicated by means of footnotes in the body of the text.*

*Wittgenstein alternated between English and German when writing these notes. Translations of the German passages have been supplied in the main body of the text, with the German original in footnotes.*

*Like Rhees, I have not indicated the places where Wittgenstein's spelling has been corrected, and I have inserted additional punctuation, especially commas, question marks, and quotation marks, where they seemed to be needed, though I have not been quite as liberal as he was. While I have included Wittgenstein's alternate drafts of a single passage when they seemed to be of interest, many purely stylistic variants have been omitted. Similarly, while deletions, marginalia, and diagrams in the text are referred to where they seem particularly relevant, they have*

1. Rhees's "Note on the Text," *The Philosophical Review,* 1968, p. 272. Rhees's note contains further discussion of the source of these notes and the context in which they were composed.

*not been systematically included. Editorial conjectures and expansions (occasionally nontrivial) of Wittgenstein's abbreviations are indicated by means of square brackets.*[2]

DAVID G. STERN

2. The transcription and additional translations were originally produced in 1984 from a microfilm of the Wittgenstein papers at the University of California, Berkeley, and revised in 1992, using the microfilm at the University of Iowa. I would like to thank Guenter Zoeller for checking my transcription and translation of the German text and Kathleen Schmidt for helping me check the transcription against the microfilm.

# Notes for Lectures on "Private Experience" and "Sense Data"

The experience of fright appears (when we philosophize) to be an amorphous experience behind the experience of starting.

All I want to say is that it is misleading to say that the word "fright" signifies something which goes along with the experience of expressing fright.

There is here again the queer case of a difference between what we say, when we actually try to see what happens, and what we say when we think about it (giving over the reins to language).

The "far away" look, the dreamy voice, seem to be only means for conveying the real inner feeling.

"Therefore there must be something else" means nothing unless it expresses a resolution to use a certain mode of expression.

Suppose you tried to separate the feeling which music gives you from hearing music.

Say and mean "long, long ago—", "lang ist es her—" and now put instead of these words new ones with many more syllables and try if you can [to] put the same meaning into the words. Put instead of the copula a very long word say "Kalamazoo".

Puell*a*, Poet*a*.[1] "'Masculine' and 'feminine' *feeling*" 'attached' to *a*.

Aren't there two (or more) ways to any event I might describe?

1. These are the Latin words for "girl" (a feminine noun) and "poet" (a masculine noun).

We say 'making this gesture isn't all'. The first answer is: We are talking about the *experience* of making this gesture. Secondly: it is true that different experiences can be described by the same gesture; but not in the sense that one is the pure one and the others consist . . .

What's it like to at one time notice /hear/ the particular timbre of a sound and at another time hear just the sound as such?[2]

"I call this impression 'blue' ".[3]

How, then, can one describe the exact experience in 'Poet*a*' etc.?[4]

The philosophical problem is: "What is it that puzzles me about /in/ this matter?"

To give names is to label things; but how does one label impressions?

The eye and the world.[5]

The masculine *a* and the feminine *a*.[6]

Some things can be said about the /particular/ determinate experience and besides this there seems to be something, the most essential part of it, which cannot be described.[7]

We say here that a name is given to a particular impression. And this is strange and problematic. For it seems as though the impression were something too ethereal to be named. (Marrying a woman's wealth.)[8]

2. Wie ist es, wenn man einmal die besondere Klangfarbe eines Tones merkt /hört/ und anderemal nur den Klang als solchen?
3. „Ich nenne diesen Eindruck ‚blau' ".
4. Wie kann man denn die genaue Erfahrung in ‚Poet*a*' etc. beschreiben?
5. Das Auge und die Welt.
6. Das männliche *a* und das weibliche *a*.
7. Es läßt sich über die besondere /bestimmte/ Erfahrung einiges sagen und außerdem scheint es etwas, und zwar das Wesentlichste, zu geben, was sich nicht beschreiben läßt.
8. Man sagt hier, daß ein bestimmter Eindruck benannt wird. Und darin liegt etwas seltsames und problematisches. Denn es ist als wäre der Eindruck etwas zu ätherisches um ihn zu benennen. (Den Reichtum einer Frau heiraten).

You say you have an intangible impression. I am not doubting what you say. But I question whether you have said anything by it. I.e., what was the point of uttering these words, in what game?[9]

⟦276⟧ It is as though, if /although/ you can't tell me exactly what happens inside you, you can nevertheless tell me something general about it. By saying e.g. that you are having an impression which can't be further described.

As it were: There *is* something further about it, only you *can't say* it; you can only make the general statement.

It is this idea /form of expression/ which plays hell with us.

"There is not only the gesture but a particular feeling which I can't describe": instead of that you might have said: "I am trying to point out a feeling to you"—this would be a grammatical remark showing how my information is meant to be used. This is almost similar as though I said: "This I call 'A' and I am pointing out a *colour* to you and not a shape."

How can one point to the colour and not to the shape? Or to the feeling of toothache and not to the tooth, etc.?

What does one call "describing a feeling to someone"?

"Never mind the shape,—look at the *colour*!"

"Was there a feeling of pastness when you said you remembered . . . ?"

'I know of none'.

How does one point to a number, draw attention to a number, *mean* a number?

How do I call a taste "lemon taste"? Is it by having that taste and saying the words: "I call this taste . . . "?

9. Du sagst, Du hast einen ungreifbaren Eindruck. Ich bezweifle nicht, was Du sagst. Aber ich frage, ob Du damit etwas gesagt hast. D.h., wozu hast Du diese Worte geäußert, in welchem Spiel?

And can I give a name to my *own* taste experience without giving the taste a common name which is to be used in common language? —"I give my feeling a name, nobody else can know what the name means".

A [slave][10] has to remind me of something and isn't to know what he reminds me of.

I note down a word in my diary which serves to bring back a taste.[11]

"I use the name for the impression directly and not in such a way that anyone else can understand it."

Buying something from oneself. Going through the operations of buying.

My right hand selling to my left hand.

Feeling—(thought.) Transference.[12]

A good way of naming a colour would be to write its name in an ink of the corresponding colour.[13]

'I name the feeling'.—I don't quite know how you do this, what use you are making of the word /name/.

"I'm giving the feeling which I have just /I'm having/ now a name."— I don't quite know what you are doing.

One might say: "What is the use of talking of our feeling at all. Let us devise a language which really only says what can be understood". Thus I am not to say "I have a feeling of pastness": But . . .

"This pain I call 'toothache' and I can never make him understand what it means."

10. [Sklave]

11. The two and a half pages of sketchy diagrams and drawings that follow in the original have been omitted.

12. Gefühle—(Gedanken.) Übertragung.

13. Eine gute Art, eine Farbe zu benennen, wäre, in einer entsprechend gefärbten Tinte den Namen schreiben.

We are under the impression that we can point to the pain, as it were unseen by the other person, and name it.

For what does it mean that this pain /feeling/ is the meaning of this name?

Or, that the pain is the bearer of the name?

It is the substantive 'pain' which puzzles us. This substantive seems to produce an illusion. What would things look like if we expressed pains by moaning and holding the painful spot?

Or that we utter the word pain pointing to a spot.

"But the point is that we should say 'pain' when there really is pain." But how am *I* to know if there really is pain? If what I feel really is pain? Or if I really have a *feeling*?—

It is very useful to consider: How would I express in a language of gestures: "I wasn't in pain, but was acting as though I were."[14]

"Surely it isn't enough that he moans, I must be able to describe the state when he moans and hasn't got pains."

"He has pains, says he has pains and saying 'pains' *he means his* pains". How does he *mean* his pains by the word 'pain' or 'toothache'?

"He says 'I see green' and means the colour he sees".—If asked afterwards "what did you mean by 'green'?" he might answer 'I meant this colour', pointing to it.

"In my own case I know that when I say 'I have pain' this utterance is accompanied by something;—but is it also accompanied by something in another man?"

In as much as his utterance needn't be accompanied by *my* pain I may say that it isn't accompanied by anything.

"I know what I mean by 'toothache' but the other person can't *know* it."

14. Es ist sehr nützlich zu bedenken: Wie würde ich in einer Gebärdensprache ausdrücken: „ich hatte keine Schmerzen, aber stellte mich, als ob ich welche hätte"?

As[15] negation: "The deuce he is. . . ."

The philosophy of a tribe which uses /knows/ only the expression "I'll be damned if . . ." for negation.[16]

It's all very well to say . . .[17]

"One can never see a whole body; rather, always only a part of its surface."[18,19]

"Wouldn't one like to know with real certainty whether the other had pains?"

Feeling of pastness. "The experiences bound up with the gesture etc. aren't the experience of pastness, for they could be there without the feeling of pastness."—"But, on the other hand, would it be that experience of pastness without those experiences bound up with the gesture?"—Why should we say that the characteristic /essential/ part is the part outside these experiences? Isn't the experience at least partially described if I have described the gestures etc.?

In this way also: The words "long long ago" sometimes evoke a particular feeling in me. Sometimes they don't. But when they do evoke it, then they, their tone, are part of the characteristic experience.[20]

Speaking to others and to myself.
"If I have *a certain* experience, I give myself the sign. . . ."[21]

15. Als
16. Die Philosophie eines Stammes, der als Negation nur den Ausdruck benutzt /kennt/: "I'll be damned if . . ."
17. On a beau dire . . .
18. „Man kann nie einen ganzen Körper sehen sondern nur immer einen Teil seiner Oberfläche."
19. At this point in the manuscript, there is a separately paginated sequence of 47 pages of notes on the philosophy of mathematics.
20. Auch so: Die Worte „lang ist es her—" rufen in mir manchmal ein bestimmtes Gefühl wach. Manchmal nicht. Aber wenn sie es wachrufen, so sind sie, ihr Ton, Teil der charakteristischen Erfahrung.
21. Sprechen mit Andern und mit mir selbst.
„Wenn ich *eine gewiße* Erfahrung habe, gebe ich mir das Zeichen . . ."

When one says "I talk to myself" one generally means just that one speaks and is the only person listening.

If I look at something red and say to myself, this is red, am I giving myself information? Am I communicating a personal experience to myself? Some people philosophizing might be ⟦277⟧ inclined to say that this is the only real case of communication of personal experience because only I know what I really mean by "red."

Remember in which special cases only it has sense to inform another person that the colour which he sees now is red.

One doesn't say to one's self "This is a chair.—Oh really?"

How then can I give an experience (say, a pain) a name? Isn't it as if I wanted to, so to speak, put a hat on it?[22]

Let's suppose one said "One can only put a hat on it indirectly". Then I would ask: Do you believe that one would have got the idea of speaking of someone that way if one hadn't thought that one can put a hat on a person in pain? Yes, saying that one could only indirectly put a hat on the pain makes it look as if there nevertheless were a direct way which would now indeed be unquestionable.[23]

The difficulty is that we feel that we have said something about the nature of pain when we say that one person can't have another person's pain. Perhaps we shouldn't be inclined to say that we had said anything physiological or even psychological, but something metapsychological, metaphysical. Something about the essence, nature, of pain as opposed to its causal connections to other phenomena.

It seems to me as though it would be not false but nonsense to say "I feel his pains," but as though this were because of the nature of

22. Wie kann ich denn einer Erfahrung (etwa einem Schmerz) einen Namen geben? Ist es nicht als wollte ich ihm, etwa, einen Hut aufsetzen?

23. Nehmen wir an, man sagte: „Man kann ihm nur indirekt einen Hut aufsetzen" so würde ich fragen: Glaubst du, daß man je auf die Idee gekommen wäre, davon zu reden, wenn man nicht daran gedacht hätte, daß man dem Menschen, der Schmerz hat, einen Hut aufsetzen kann? Ja, sagen, man könne dem Schmerz nur indirekt einen Hut aufsetzen, macht es erscheinen, als gäbe es dennoch einen direkten Weg, der nun tatsächlich nicht fragbar sei.

pain, of the person etc. as though, therefore, this statement were ultimately a statement about the nature of things.

So we speak for example of an asymmetry in our mode of expression and we look on it as a mirror image of the essence of the things.[24]

Intangibility of impressions. (Anguish). Some we should say were more tangible than others. Seeing more tangible than a faint pain; and this more tangible than a vague fear, longing etc.

In what way are these intangible experiences less easy to communicate, to describe, than the 'simpler' ones?

In what way do we use the phrase: "This experience is difficult to describe".

And can it even be impossible to describe certain experiences?

What sense does it make to say: this experience is not describable? We would like to say: it is too complex, too subtle.[25]

"This experience is not communicable, but *I* know it—because I have it."[26]

"There is the experience and the description of the experience.— So it cannot be a matter for indifference whether the other has the same experience as I or not; and therefore what matters when I talk to myself must be my experience. It must be a decisive factor that I know this experience (whereas I am not directly acquainted with the other's experience)."[27]

24. Es scheint mir etwa, als wäre es zwar nicht falsch sondern unsinnig zu sagen „ich fühle seine Schmerzen," aber als wäre dies so infolge der Natur des Schmerzes, der Person etc. Als wäre also jene Aussage letzten Endes doch eine Aussage über die Natur der Dinge.

Wir sprechen also etwa von einer Asymmetrie unserer Ausdrucksweise und fassen diese auf als ein Spiegelbild des Wesens der Dinge.

25. Was für einen Sinn hat es zu sagen, diese Erfahrung ist nicht beschreibbar? Wir möchten sagen: sie ist zu komplex, zu subtil.

26. „Diese Erfahrung ist nicht mitteilbar, aber *ich* kenne sie,—weil ich sie habe."

27. „Es gibt die Erfahrung, und die Beschreibung der Erfahrung. —Daher kann es nicht gleichgültig sein, ob der Andere dieselbe Erfahrung hat wie ich, oder nicht;—und daher muß es, wenn ich mit mir selbst rede, auf meine Erfahrung ankommen. Es muß dabei eine entscheidende Rolle spielen, daß ich diese Erfahrung kenne (während ich mit der des Andern nicht direkt vertraut bin)."

Can one say: "In what I say of someone else's experience, that experience (itself) does not play any part. But in what I say of my experience the experience itself does play a part?"

"I speak about my experience, so to say, in its presence."[28]

As if someone were to say: "There isn't only the description of the table, but also the table".[29]

"There isn't only the word 'toothache', there's also such a thing as toothache itself//————there's also toothache."[30]

It seems that since I cannot, for example, describe an experience, but have it, it follows that I can *know* it more exactly than anyone else. But what does knowing an experience mean, if it doesn't mean describing it and doesn't mean having it?

Is there a *knowledge* of experience that we cannot communicate?[31]

Does it make sense to say "I know this experience better //more exactly// than anyone else can know it"? Are there experiences which the other person can know just as well as I and those which he cannot? Does this mean: he can't have this very same intricate experience?—It would mean: "He can have it, but we can never /can't/ know that he has had just /exactly/ this one". E.g., it seems as though we could say: "We can, in a sense, know that he sees precisely this monochrome, smooth, red surface, but not that he sees exactly

28. Kann man sagen: „In dem das, was ich über die Erfahrung des Andern sage, spielt solche Erfahrung (selbst) nicht hinein. In dem das, was ich über meine Erfahrung sage, spielt diese Erfahrung selbst hinein?"

„Ich spreche über meine Erfahrung, sozusagen, in ihrer Anwesenheit."

29. Wie wenn jemand sagen würde: „Es gibt nicht nur die Beschreibung des Tisches sondern auch den Tisch."

30. „Es gibt nicht nur das Wort ‚Zahnschmerz', es gibt auch etwas wie /such a thing as/ den Zahnschmerz selbst."//————es gibt auch Zahnschmerzen."

31. Es scheint, daß, da ich etwa eine Erfahrung nicht beschreiben kann, sie aber habe, daß ich sie daher genauer *kennen* kann als irgend ein Anderer. Aber was heißt, die Erfahrung kennen, wenn es nicht heißt, sie beschreiben und nicht heißt, sie haben?

Gibt es eine *Kenntnis* der Erfahrung, die wir nicht mitteilen können?

this *glimmering*. Because the exact visual image of the glimmering cannot be described.[32]

There is, after all, also the case in which we can describe a visual image more exactly by means of a painted picture than by means of words.[33]

Consider this: "One can describe a figure more accurately with the help of numerical values than without them."[34]

But the experience which I *have* seems, in a certain sense, to take the place of a description of this experience. "It is its own description."[35]

Aren't we mixing up two things here: the compositeness of experience and what one could call its original flavour /tone/? Its own natural colour.[36]

The conception is that only a part of the original experience is preserved in the process of communication, and something else is lost. Namely "its timbre" or whatever one wants to call it. Here it

32. Hat es Sinn zu sagen „ich kenne diese Erfahrung besser //genauer// als irgend ein Anderer sie kennen kann"? Gibt es Erfahrungen, die der Andere ebensogut kennen kann wie ich, und solche, die er nicht so gut kennen kann? Heißt das: er kann diese selbe komplizierte Erfahrung nicht haben? — Es heißt wohl: „Er kann sie haben, aber wir können nie /nicht/ wissen, daß er gerade /genau/ diese gehabt hat". Z.B. scheint es, als könnten wir sagen: „Wir können in einen Sinn wissen, daß er gerade diese einfarbige, glatte, rote Fläche sieht, aber nicht, daß er genau dieses *Flimmern* sieht. Weil sich das genaue Gesichtsbild beim /des/ Flimmern/s nicht beschreiben läßt.

33. Es gibt ja auch den Fall, in dem wir ein Gesichtsbild genauer durch ein gemaltes Bild als durch Worte beschreiben können.

34. Wie ist es damit: „Man kann eine Figur genauer mit Hilfe von Maßzahlen als ohne diese beschreiben".

35. Aber die Erfahrung, die ich *habe*, scheint eine Beschreibung dieser Erfahrung, in gewissem Sinne, zu ersetzen. „Sie ist ihre eigene Beschreibung."

36. Vermischen wir hier nicht zwei Dinge: die Zusammengesetztheit der Erfahrung und, was man ihren ursprünglichen Geschmack/Ton /flavour/ nennen könnte? Ihre eigentliche natürliche Farbe.

strikes one as though one could only convey the coloured drawing and the other inserts *his* colours in it. But that is, naturally, (a) deception.[37]

But couldn't we really say that we had produced a picture in the other by means of our description but that we cannot know whether this picture is now precisely the same as our own? Let us think here of the use of the word 'same' in such sentences as: "These circles are, to all appearances, entirely the same".[38]

It is relevant to this that we don't usually experience our visual image as something in us, like say a pain in the eye, that we are however inclined to think according to this picture when we philosophize.[39]

The 'if-sensation'. Compare with the 'table-sensation'. There is the question "What's the table sensation like?" and the answer is a picture of a table. In what sense is the if-sensation analogous to the table-sensation? Is there a description of this sensation and *what do we call a description of it*? Putting the gestures instead of the sensations means just giving the nearest rough description there is of the experience.

Example.

("I have a peculiar feeling of pastness in my wrist.")

37. Es ist die Auffassung, daß von der ursprünglichen Erfahrung nur ein Teil bei /in/ der Mitteilung erhalten bleibt, und etwas anderes von ihr verloren geht. Nämlich eben ‚ihr timbre', oder wie man es nennen möchte. Es kommt Einem hier so vor, als könnte man sozusagen nur die farbene Zeichnung vermitteln, und der Andere setzte in sie *seine* Farben ein. Aber das ist natürlich (eine) Täuschung.

38. Aber können wir nicht wirklich sagen, wir hätten in dem Anderen durch unsere Beschreibung ein Bild hervorgebracht, aber wir können nicht wissen, ob dieses Bild nun genau das gleiche ist wie das unsere? Denken wir hier an den Gebrauch des Wortes gleich in solchen Sätzen wie: „Diese Kreise sind dem Augenschein nach ganz gleich".

39. Hierher gehört auch, daß wir gewöhnlich unser Gesichtsbild nicht als etwas in uns empfinden wie etwa einen Schmerz in Auge, daß wir aber, wenn wir philosophieren, geneigt sind, diesem Bild gemäß zu denken.

6)[40] "We shall never know whether he meant this or that". C died after the training in that room. We say: Perhaps he would have reacted like B when taken into the daylight. But we shall never know.

α) We should say this question was decided if he arose from his grave and we then made the experiment with him. Or his ghost appeared to us in a spiritualist séance and told us that he has a certain experience.

β) We don't accept any evidence. But what if we didn't accept the evidence in 5 either and said (something like) "we can't be sure that he is the identical man who was trained in the room" or: "he is the identical man but we can't know whether he *would have* behaved like this in the past time when he was trained."

7) We introduce a new notation for the expression "If P happens then always (as a rule) Q happens. P didn't happen this time and Q didn't happen". We say instead: "If P had happened Q would have happened". E.g. "If the gunpowder is dry under these circumstances a spark of this strength explodes it. It wasn't dry this time and didn't explode under the same circumstances". We say instead "If the gunpowder had been dry this time it would have exploded". The point of this notation is that it nears the form of this proposition very much to the form: "The gunpowder was dry this time so it exploded". I mean the new form doesn't stress the fact that it did not explode but, we might say, paints a vivid picture of it exploding this time. We could imagine a form of expression in a picture language corresponding to the two kinds of notations in the word language. The second notation will be particularly appropriate e.g. if we wish to give a person a shock by making him vividly imagine that which would have happened, stressing only slightly that it didn't happen.

8 Someone might say to us: "But are you sure that the second sentence means just what the first one means and not just something similar or that and something else as well?" (Moore) I should say: I'm talking of the case where it means just this, and this seems to me an important case (which you concede by saying what you have said). But of course I don't say that it isn't used in other ways as well and then we'll have to talk about these other cases separately.

9 Someone says "Lowering one's voice sometimes means that what you say is less important than the rest, in other cases you lower your

40. This series of remarks presumably continues a sequence of remarks that were numbered 1)–5), but they are not part of the source manuscripts, and I have been unable to locate them elsewhere in the Wittgenstein papers.

voice to show that you wish to draw special attention to what you now say."

We must be clear that our examples are not preparations to the analysis of the actual meaning of the expression so-and-so (Nicod) but giving them effects that "analysis".

Have we now shown that to say in 5) "We can't know whether he would have behaved . . ." makes no sense? We should say the sentence /to say this sentence/ under these circumstances has lost its /the/ point which it would have had under other circ[umstance]s but this doesn't mean that we can't give it another point.

10) We say "We can't know whether this spark would have been sufficient to ignite that mixture; because we can't reproduce the exact mixture not having the exact ingredients or not having a balance to weigh them etc., etc." But suppose we could reproduce all the circumstances and someone said "we can't know whether it would have exploded", and being asked why he said "Because we can't know whether *under these circumstances* it would have exploded *then.*" This answer would set our head whirling. We would feel he wasn't playing the same game with that expression as we do. We should be inclined to say "This makes no sense!" And this means that we are at a loss not knowing what reasonings, what actions, go with this expression. Moreover we believe that he made up a sentence analogous to sentences used in certain lang[uage] games not noticing that he took the *point* away.

In which case do we say that a sentence has point? That comes to asking in which case do we call something a language game. I can only answer: Look at the family of language games, that will show you whatever can be shown about the matter.

12) (The private visual image.) B is trained to describe his afterimage when he has looked say into a bright red light. He is made to look into the light, then to shut his eyes and he is then asked "What do you see?" This question before was put to him only if he looked at physical objects. We suppose he reacts by a description of what he sees with closed eyes.—But halt! This description of the training seems wrong for what if I had had to describe my own, not B's, training. Would I then also have said: "I reacted to the question by . . ." and not rather: "When I had closed my eyes I saw an image and described it." If I say "I saw an image and described it" I say this as opposed to the case where /in which/ I gave a description without seeing an image. (I might have lied or not). Now we could of course also distinguish these cases if B describes an afterimage. But we don't

wish to consider now cases in which the mechanism of lying plays any part. For if you say "I always know whether I am lying but not whether the other person is", I say: in the case I'm considering I can't be said to *know* that I'm not lying, or let us say not saying the untruth, because the dilemma [of either] saying the truth or the untruth is in this case unknown to me. Remember that when I'm asked "What do you see here?" I don't always ask myself: "Now shall I say the truth or something else?" If you say "but surely if you in fact speak the truth then you did see something and you saw what you said you saw". I answer: How can I know that I see what I say I see? Do I have a criterion or use one for the colour I see actually being red?

13) We imagine that the expression "I can't see what you see" has been given sense by explaining it to mean: "I can't see what you see, being in a different position relative to the object we are looking at", or ". . . having not as good eyes as you", or ". . . having found as in . . . that B sees something which we don't though we look at the same object" etc. "I can't see your afterimage" might be explained to mean "I can't see what you see if I close my eyes", meaning you say you see a red circle, I see a yellow one.
14) Identity of physical objects, of shapes, colours, dreams, toothache.
15) (The object we see.) The physical object and its appearance. Form of expression: different views of the same phy[sical] object are different objects seen. We ask "What do you see?" and he can either answer "a chair", or "this" (and draw the particular view of the chair). So we are now inclined to say that each man sees a different object and one which no other person sees, for even if they look at the same chair from the same spot it may appear different to them and the objects before the other mind's eye I can't look at.
16) ⟦278⟧ (I can't know whether he sees anything at all or only behaves as I do when I see something.) There seems to be an undoubted asymmetry in the use of the word "to see" (and all words relating to personal experience). One can /is inclined to/ state this in the way that "I know when I see something by just seeing it, without hearing what I say or observing the rest of my behaviour, whereas I know *that* he sees and *what* he sees only by observing his behaviour, i.e. indirectly."

(*a*) There is a mistake in this, viz.: "I know what I see because I see it." What does it mean to know that?

(*b*) It is true to say that my reason for saying that I see is not the observation of my behaviour. But this is a gramm[atical] prop[osition.]

(*c*) It seems to be an imperfection that I can only know ———— [indirectly that he sees]. But this is just the way we use the word ———— ["see"]. Could we then ———— [say I know directly that he sees] if we would? Certainly.[41]

Does /Should we say that/ the person who has not learned the language knows that he sees red but can't express it?—Or should we say: "He knows what he sees but can't express it"?—So, besides seeing it, he also knows what he sees?

Imagine we described a totally different experiment, say this, that I sting someone with a needle and observe whether he cries out or not /makes a sound or not/. Then surely it would interest us if the subject whenever we stung him saw, say, a red circle. And we would distinguish the case when he cried out and saw a circle from the case when he cried out and didn't see one.

This case is quite straightforward and there is no problem about it /seems to be nothing problematic about it./

If I say "I tell myself that I see red, I tell myself what I see" it seems that after having told myself I now know better what I see, am better acquainted with it, than before. (Now in a sense this may be so . . . )

"When he asked me what colour I saw, I guessed what he meant /wanted to know/ and told him."

"It is not enough to distinguish between the cases in which B or I say that I see red and do see red, and the case [in which] I say this but don't see red, but we must distinguish between the cases in which I see red, say I see red and mean to describe what I see and the cases in which I don't mean this."

Consider the case in which I don't say what I see in words but by pointing to a sample. Here again I distinguish now between the case in which I 'just meant by pointing' and the case in which I *see* and point.

Now suppose I asked: "How do I know that I see, and that I see red? I.e., how do I know that I do what you call seeing and seeing

41. The manuscript contains only the dashes, not the words suggested in brackets.

red?" For we use the words 'seeing' and 'red' between us in a game we play with one another.

Don't you say: 'In order to be a description of our personal experience what we say must not be just our reaction but must be *justified*'? But does the justification need another justification?

Suppose, we play the game 2 and B calls out the word "red". Suppose A now asks B: "do you only say 'red' or did you really see it?"

"Surely there are two phenomena: one, just speaking, the other, seeing and speaking accordingly." Answer: Certainly we speak of these two cases but we shall here have to show how these expressions are used; or, in other words, how they are taught. For the mere fact that we possess a picture of them does not help us as we must describe in what way this picture is used. More especially as we are inclined to assume a use different from the actual one.

We have therefore to explain under what conditions we say: "I say 'red' but don't see red" or "I say 'red' and see red", or "I said 'red' but didn't see red" etc. etc.

Imagine that saying red was often followed by some agreeable event. We found that the child enjoyed that event and often instead of 'green' said 'red'. We would use this reaction to play another lang[uage] game with the child. We would say "you cheat, it's red". Now again we are dependent upon the subsequent reactions of the child.

Such games are actually played with children: Telling a person the untruth and enjoying his surprise at finding out what really happened.

But couldn't we imagine some kind of perversity in a child which made it say 'red' when it saw green and v[ice] v[ersa] and at the same time this not being discovered because it happened to see red in those cases where we say 'green'?

But if here we talk of perversity, we could /might/ also assume that we all were perverse. For how are we, or B, ever to find out that he is perverse?

The idea is, that he finds out (and we do) when later on he learns how the word 'perverse' is used and then he remembers that he was that way all along.

Imagine this case: The child looks at the lights, says the name of the right colour to himself in an aside and then, loud, the wrong word. It chuckles while doing so. This is, one may say, a rudimentary form of cheating. One might even say: "This child is going to be a liar". But if it had not said the aside but only imagined itself pointing to one colour on the chart and then said the wrong word,—was this cheating too?

Can a child cheat like a banker without the knowledge of the banker?

"I can assure you that before when I said 'I see red' I saw black".

"He tells us his private experience, that experience which nobody but he knows anything about".

"Surely his memory is worth more than our indirect criteria, as only he could know what he saw."

But let us see;—we sometimes say outside philosophy such things as "of course only he knows how he feels" /or "I can't know what you feel"./ Now how do we apply such a statement? Mostly it is an expression of helplessness like "I don't know what to do". But this helplessness isn't due to an unfortunate metaphysical fact, 'the privacy of personal experience', or it would worry us constantly. Our expression is comparable to this: "What's done can't be undone!"

We also say to the doctor "Surely I must know whether I have pains or not!" How do we use this statement?

"All right, if we can't talk in this way about someone else, I can certainly say of myself that *I* either saw red at that time or didn't /had some other experience./ I may not remember now, but at the time I saw one thing or the /an/ other!" This is like saying "one of these two pictures must have fitted." And my answer is not that perhaps neither of them fits but that I'm not yet clear about what 'fitting' in this case means.

Now is it the same case, are these different cases: A blind man sees everything just as we do but he acts as a blind man does and on the other hand he sees nothing and acts as a blind man does. At first sight we should say: here we have obviously two clearly different cases although we admit that we can't know which we have before us. I should say: We obviously use two different pictures which one /we/

could describe like this: . . . But we use the pictures in such a way that the two games 'come to the same'.

By the way,—would you say that he surely /certainly/ knew that he was blind if he was so? Why do you feel more reluctant about this statement?

"Surely he knew that he saw red but he couldn't say so!"—Does that mean "Surely he saw, knew that he saw the colour which we call 'red' " . . . —or would you say it means "he knew that he saw *this* colour" (pointing to a red patch). But did he, while he knew it, point to this patch?

Use of: "He knows what colour he sees," "I know what colour I saw," etc.

"Darkening of memory"[42] does this expression make sense and in what cases? And isn't, on the other hand, the picture which we use quite clear in all cases?

The case of old people usually having /getting/ memories of the time in which they learnt to speak and understand speech:

a) They say or paint that such and such things have happened although other records always contradict them.

b) The memories agree with the records. Only in this case shall we say that they remember.

Suppose they paint the scenes they say they remember and paint the faces being dark,—shall we say that they saw them that dark or that the colour had become darker in their memory?

How do we know what colour a person sees? By the sample he points to? And how do we know what relation the sample is meant to have to the original? Now are we to say "We never know . . ."? Or had we better cut these "We never know" out of our language and consider how as a matter of fact we are wont to use the word "to know"?

⟦279⟧ What if someone asked: "How do I know that what I call seeing red isn't an *entirely* different experience every time? and that I

42. „Nachdunkeln der Erinnerung“

am not deluded into thinking that it is the same or nearly the same?" Here again the answer "I can't know" and the subsequent removal of the question.

Is it ever true that when I call a colour 'red' I serve myself of memory?? /make use of memory?/

To use the memory of what happened when we were taught language is all right as long as we don't think that this memory teaches us something essentially private.

"A rod has one length or another however we find it out". Here again the picture I1.

"Though he can't say what it is he sees while he is learning No.1, he'll tell us afterwards what he saw." We mix this case up with the one: "When his gag will have been removed he'll tell us what he saw".

What does it mean, 'to tell someone what one sees'? Or (perhaps), 'to show someone what one sees'?

When we say 'He'll tell us what he saw' we have an idea that then we'll know what he *really* saw in a direct way ("at least if he isn't lying").

"He is in a better position to say what he sees than we are."—That depends.—

If we say "he'll tell us what he saw," it is as though he would make use of language which we had never taught him.

It is as if now we have got an *insight* into something which before we had only seen from the outside.

Inside and outside!

"Our teaching /training/ connects the word 'red' (or is meant to connect it) with a particular impression of his (a private impression, an impression in him). He then communicates this impression—indirectly, of course—through the medium of speech."

Where is our idea of direct and indirect communication taken from?

How, if we said, as we sometimes might be inclined: "We can only hope that this indirect way of communicating really succeeds".

We see the facts about the usage of our words crookedly as /so/ long as we are still tempted here to talk of direct and indirect.

As long as you use the picture direct-indirect in this case you can't trust yourself about judging the grammatical situation rightly otherwise [in other ways].

Is telling what one sees something like turning one's inside out? And learning to say what one sees, learning to let others see inside us?

"We teach him to make us see what he sees." He seems in an indirect way to show us *the object* which he sees, the object which is before his mind's eye. "We can't look at it, it is in him."

The idea of the private *object* of vision. Appearance, sense datum.

The visual field. (Not to be confused with visual space.)

Telling someone what one sees seems like showing him, if indirectly, the object which is before one's mind's eye.

The idea of the object before one's mind's eye is firmly tied up with the idea of a comparison of such objects in different persons compared to which the comparison really used is an indirect one.

Whence the idea of the privacy of sense data?

"But do you really wish to say that they are not private? That one person can see the picture before the other person's eye?"

Surely you wouldn't think that *telling* someone what one sees is a /could be a/ more direct way of communicating than showing him by pointing to a sample!

"He'll tell us later what it was he saw" means that we'll get to know in a (comparatively) direct and a sure way what he saw as opposed to the guesses we could make before.

We don't realise that the answer he gives us now is only part of a game like No.1, only more complicated.

We don't deny that he can remember having dreamt so-and-so before he was born. Denying this to us would be like denying that he can *say* he remembers having dreamt so-and-so before he was born.

I.e. we don't deny that he can make this move but we say that the move alone or together with all the sensations feelings etc. he might have while he is making it does not tell us what game it is a move of /to what game the move belongs/.

We might e.g. never try to connect up a statement of this sort with anything past (in another sense). We might treat it as an interesting phenomenon and possibly connect it up with the person in a Freudian way or on the other hand we may look for some phenomena in the brain of the embryo which might be called dreams etc. etc. . . Or we may just say: "old people are liable to say such things" and leave it at that.

Suppose now someone remembered that yesterday he called red 'green' and vice versa but that this didn't appear as he also saw green what today he sees red and vice versa. Now here is a case in which we might be inclined to say that we learn from him today something about the working of his mind yesterday, that yesterday we judged by the outside while today we are allowed to look at the inside of what happened. It is as though we looked back but now got a glance at something that was closed to us /covered up/ yesterday.

⟦280⟧ If I say what it is I see, how do I compare what I say with what I see in order to know whether I say the truth?

Lying about what I see, you might say, is knowing what I see and saying something else. Supposing I said it just consists of saying to myself 'this is red' and aloud 'this is green.'

Compare lying and telling the truth in the case of telling what colour you see, with the case of describing a picture which you saw, or telling the right number of things you had to count.

Collating what you say and what you see.

Is there always a collating?

Or could one call it giving a picture of the colour I see if I say the word red? Unless it be a picture by its connections with a sample.

But isn't it giving a picture if I point to a sample?

"What I show *reveals* what I see"—in what sense does it do that? The idea is that now you can so to speak look inside me. Whereas I only reveal to you what I see in a game of revealing and hiding which is altogether played with signs of one category. "Direct-indirect."

We are thinking of a game in which there is an inside in the normal sense.

We must get clear about how the metaphor of revealing (outside and inside) is actually applied by us; otherwise we shall be tempted to look for an inside behind that which in our metaphor is the inside.

We are used to describing the case by means of a picture which, say, contains 3 steps. But when we think about language we forget how this picture is actually applied in practical cases. We then are often tempted to apply it as it wasn't originally meant and are puzzled about a third step in the facts.

"I see a particular sense datum/image /thing/ and say a particular thing". This is all right if I realise the way in which I specify what I see and what I say.

"If he had learned to show me (or tell me) what he sees, he could now show me." Certainly—but what is it like to show me what he sees? It is pointing to something under particular circumstances. Or is it something else (don't be misled by the idea of indirectness)?

You compare it with such a statement as: "If he had learned to open up, he could now open up and show me what's inside /I could now see what's inside/." I say yes, but remember what opening up in this case is like.

⟦281⟧ But what about the criterion whether there is anything inside or not? Here we say "I know there's something inside in *my* case. And this is how I know of the 'inside' at all first hand." //"And this is how I have first hand knowledge of the inside at all."// "This is how I know about an inside and am led to suppose it in the other person too."

Further, we are not inclined to say that only hitherto we have not known the inside of another person, but that the idea of this knowledge is bound up with the idea of myself.

"So if I say 'he has toothache' I am supposing that he has what I have when I have toothache." Suppose I said: "If I say 'I *suppose* he has toothache' I am supposing that he has what I have if I have toothache"—this would be like saying "If I say 'this cushion is red' I mean that it has the same color which the sofa has if it is red." But this isn't what I intended /was meant/ to say with the first sentence. I wished to say that talking about his toothache at all was based upon a supposition, a supposition which by its very essence could not be verified.

But if you look closer you will see that this is an entire misrepresentation of the use of the word 'toothache.'

---

Can two people have the same afterimage?

Language game: 'Description of imaginings /the picture before one's mind's eye.'/

Can two persons have the same picture before their mind's eye?

In which case would we say that they had two images exactly alike but not identical?

---

The fact that two ideas seem here inseparably bound up suggests to us that we are dealing with one idea only and not with two and that by a queer trick our language suggests a totally different structure of grammar than the one actually used. For we have the sentence that only I can know directly my experience and only indirectly the experience of the other person. Language suggests 4 possible configurations but rules out 2. It is as though I had used the 4 letters a, b, c, d to denote two objects only but by my notation somehow suggesting that I am talking of 4.

It seems as though I wished to say that to me L.W. something applied which does not apply to other people. That is, there seems to be an asymmetry.

I *express* things asymmetrically and could express them symmetrically; only then one would see what facts prompt us to the asymmetrical expression.

I do this by spreading the use of the word "I" over all human bodies as opposed to L.W. alone.

⟦282⟧ I want to describe a situation in which I should not be tempted to say that I assumed or believed that the other had what I have. Or, in other words, a situation in which we would not [speak] of *my consciousness* and *his consciousness.* And in which the idea would not occur to us that we could only be conscious of our own consciousness.

The idea of the ego inhabiting a body to be abolished.

If what[ever] consciousness [there is] spreads over all human bodies, then there won't be any temptation to use the word 'ego.'

Let's assume that hearing was done by no organ of the body we know of . . .

Let us imagine the following arrangement: . . .

If it is absurd to say that I only know that *I* see but not that the others do—isn't this at any rate less absurd than to say the opposite?

Is it impossible to imagine a philosophy that would be the diametrical opposite of solipsism?[43]

43. Ist eine Philosophie undenkbar, die das diametrale Gegenteil des Solipsismus ist?

The idea of the constituent of a fact: "Is my person (or a person) a constituent of the fact that I see or not?" This expresses a question concerning the symbolism just as if it were a question about nature.

"It thinks". Is this proposition true and "I think" false?[44]

Lang[uage] game: I paint, for myself, what I see. The picture doesn't contain *me.*

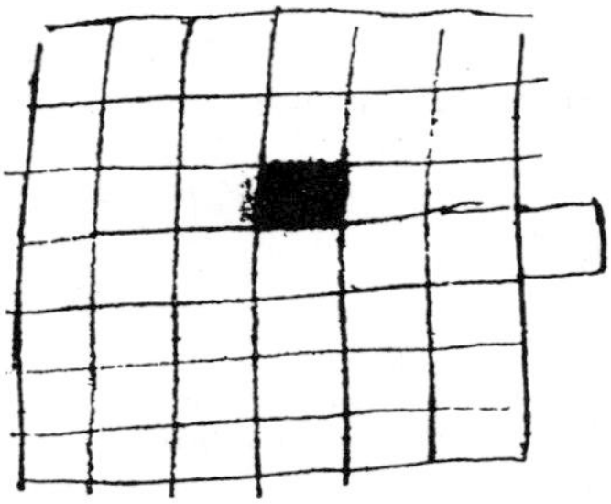

A board game, in fact chess, but the board has a square which must never be used. This may be misleading.

A board game in which only one man is said to play, the other to 'answer'.

What if the other person always correctly described what I saw and imagined, would I not say he knows what I see?—"But what if he describes it wrongly on some occasion? Mustn't I say he was mistaken?" Why should I say this and not, rather, he has forgotten the meanings of his words?

"But after all, only I can finally decide whether what he said is right. We can't assume that *he* knows what I see and *I don't!*" We can also do this!

Can a man doubt whether what he sees is red or green? (Elaborate this.)

⟦283⟧ "Surely if he knows anything he must know what he sees!"—It is true that the game of "showing or telling what one sees" is one of the most fundamental language games; which means that what we in ordinary life call using language mostly presupposes this game.

44. „Es denkt". Ist dieser Satz wahr und „ich denke" falsch?

I can for what I see use the impersonal form of description, and the fact that I say "for what I see" doesn't say at all that after all this is only a disguised personal description! For I just expressed myself in *our* ordinary form of expression, in English.

Is a cube an extremely regular symmetrical body, or the irregular thing that I see if I look at it from an angle? What should I emphasize? Should I say: it is primarily irregular but one could represent it as something regular, irregularly projected, or: it is primarily regular but irregularly projected?[45]

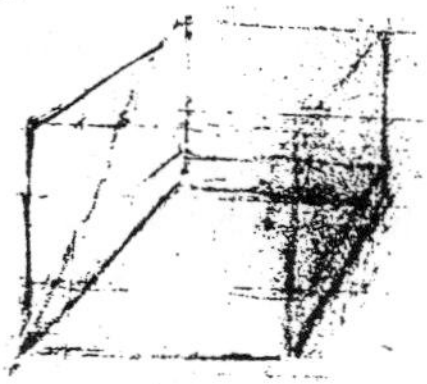

What's the difference between my being angry and he being angry? If I wish to write down my experiences the two experiences that I am angry and that he is angry are absolutely, entirely different (although the words used for describing them are very similar. I might, therefore, naturally object to this way of expression.)

"A cube has 9 real edges and 3 imaginary ones".[46]

If I write down my own experiences nothing is more natural than to refer by "I" only to my body (or: LW's body) as opposed to other bodies, but not to distinguish my toothache from his by the words "I" and "he".

The usual game played with the word "toothache" involves the distinction of *bodies* which have the toothache.

Does the solipsist also say that only he can play chess?

45. Ist ein Würfel ein äußerst regelmäßiger symmetrischer Körper, oder das Unregelmäßige, was ich sehe, wenn ich ihn von einer Ecke aus sehe? Was soll ich hervorheben? Soll ich sagen: er sei primär unregelmäßig aber man könne ihn als etwas Regelmäßiges unregelmäßig projiziert darstellen, oder er sei primär regelmäßig aber unregelmäßig projiziert?

46. „Ein Würfel hat 9 reelle Kanten und 3 imaginäre".

But he will say that behind the sentence 'I see . . .' when he says it and it's true, there stands something which does not stand behind "he sees" or "I see" when the other man says it.

I'll start with a description of what 'I see' but in impersonal form.

"I speak" and "the other speaks" are two totally different experiences.[47]

I say "it's nice" then I say "*I* said that". Thereby I have—neither to myself nor to the other—*said* who has uttered it. I have said it to him.[48]

"But how do I know that *I* have spoken if not in the peculiar experience of speaking?"[49]

The word "I" does not designate a person.[50]

Remember that whatever the word 'I' means to you, to the other man it *shows* /draws his attention to/ a human body, and is of no value otherwise.

Does it make sense to say the star stays at the same point?[51]

I could write a book on physics in which every sentence starts with "I remember".

Could one say: Here the sentences are all directly backed by real experience or by primary reality.

We must be misled in a queer way!

"Surely," I want to say, "if I'm to be quite /really/ frank I must say that I have something which nobody has."—But who's I?—Hell! I

47. „Ich spreche" und „der Andere spricht" sind zwei total verschiedene Erfahrungen.

48. Ich sage „Es ist schön", dann sage ich „das hatte *ich* gesprochen". Damit habe ich weder mir noch dem Andern *gesagt*, wer es gesprochen hat. Ich habe es ihm gesagt.

49. „Aber woher weiß ich, daß *ich* gesprochen habe, wenn nicht in der eigentümlichen Erfahrung des Sprechens?"

50. Das Wort „Ich" bezeichnet keine Person.

51. Hat es einen Sinn zu sagen, der Stern bleibt beim gleichen Punkt?

don't express myself properly, but there's *something!* You can't deny that there is my personal experience and that this in a most important sense *has no neighbour.*—But you don't mean that it *happens* to be alone but that its grammatical position is that of having no neighbour.

"But somehow our language doesn't bring it out that there is something unique, namely real present experience, and do you just wish me to /advise me to/ resign myself to that?"

(A philosophical book might be entitled "the wonders of the jungle".)

(Funny that in ordinary life we never feel that we have to resign ourselves to something by using ordinary language!)

How is it that the utterance,[52] I might propose for those sentences which describe my personal experience does /do/ not really quite satisfy me?

Partly because of what we call "imagining that the other person sees (feels) pain".

We [too] are inclined to use the same picture for both processes.[53]

---

Now imagine this: as soon as ever he has learnt enough of language to express it, he tells us that he saw blue when he said "red" in No. 1.

This sounds as if, then, we really ought to be convinced that he saw blue etc.

The person who paints his memories.

It reminds one misleadingly of "as soon as ever he had learnt enough of their language, the stranger informed his hosts of . . ."

This hangs together with the idea that the child remembers before it says that it does.

52. Aussprechung

53. [Auch] wir sind geneigt, dasselbe Bild für beide Vorgänge zu verwenden.

Consider the case of the child drawing /painting/ its memories. It has painted a blue light instead of a red one.

Augustine, about expressing the wishes inside him.

Why shouldn't we consider the case that the child learns to think and always assume that it had a private language before it learnt ours. Only: what do we mean by *learning* the language? In what sense can we be said to teach the child the natural gesture-language? Or *can't* we teach him that?

Can't the child learn to wish for an apple by learning to *draw* an apple?

Circle and ellipse. Should I say "he saw the circle as an ellipse yesterday" or "this is how he represented a circle on the following day".[54]

(Remembering that one thought so-and-so. "I don't remember him but I know, remember, that he struck me as being a fool.")[55]

"He mostly sees red where we see red."

The normal use of the expression "he sees [red][56] where . . ." is this: We take it as the criterion for meaning the same by 'red' as we do, that as a rule he agrees with us in giving the same names to the colours of objects as we do. If then in a particular instance he says something is red where we should say that it's green, we say he sees it different from us.

Notice how in such a case we would behave. We should look for a cause of his different judgment, and if we had found one we should certainly be inclined to say he saw red where we saw green. It is further clear that even before ever finding such a ⟦284⟧ cause we might under circumstances be inclined to say this. But also that we can't give a strict rule for. . . .

54. Kreis und Ellipse. Soll ich sagen „er hat den Kreis gestern als Ellipse gesehen" oder „so stellte er den folgenden Tag einen Kreis dar".

55. (Sich daran erinnern, das und das gedacht zu haben. „Ich erinnere mich nicht an ihn, aber ich weiß, erinnere mich, daß er mir einen dümmlichen Eindruck gemacht hat.")

56. The text reads "green" here, but this was probably a slip.

Consider this case: someone says "it's queer /I can't understand it/, I see everything red blue today and vice versa." We answer "it must look queer!" He says it does and, e.g., goes on to say how cold the glowing coal looks and how warm the clear (blue) sky. I think we should under these or similar circumst[ances] be incl[ined] to say that he saw red what we saw [blue].[57] And again we should say that we know that he means by the words 'blue' and 'red' what we do as he has always used them as we do.

On the other hand: Someone tells us today that yesterday he always saw everything red blue, and v[ice] v[ersa]. We say: But you called the glowing coal red, you know, and the sky blue. He answers: That was because I had also changed the names. We say: But didn't it feel very queer? and he says: No, it seemed all perfectly ordinary /natural/. Would we in this case too say: . . . .?

Case of contradicting memory images: tomorrow he remembers this, the day after tomorrow something else.

The whole trend, to show that the expression "letting one look into his soul," is often misleading.

Back to the example of the after image /or No. 1./ We can say that these cases are not cases of communic[ation] of personal exp[erience] if there were no pers[onal] exp[erience] but only the 'outward signs.'

Now I ask what are our criteria for there being or there having been a pers[onal] exp[erience] besides the expression? And the answer seems to be that for the outsider //the other man// the criteria are indeed more outside expressions, but that I myself know whether I have an experience or not; in particular, whether I see red or not.

But let me ask: what is knowing that I see red like? I mean: look at something red, 'know that it is red,' and ask yourself /observe //mark/// what you're doing. Don't you mean seeing red and impressing it on your mind that you are doing so? But there are, I suppose, several things that you are doing: You probably *say* to yourself the word 'red' or 'this is red' or something of the sort, or perhaps glance from the

57. The text reads "green," but this is because Wittgenstein had changed an earlier use of "green" to "blue" but failed to make the change here.

red object to another red one which you're taking to be the paradigm of red, and suchlike. On the other hand you just intently stare at the red thing.

⟦285⟧ In part of their uses the expression[s] "visual image" and "picture" run parallel; but where they don't, the analogy which does exist tends to delude us.

Taut[ology].

The grammar of 'seeing red' connected to the expression of seeing red closer than one thinks.

"You talk as though one couldn't /can't/ see a red patch if one can't say that one does; as if seeing something was saying that one sees it". "Seeing something" of course doesn't mean the same as saying that one sees something but the senses of these expressions are closer related than it might appear to you.

We say a blind man does not see anything. But not only do we say so but he too says that he does not see. I don't mean "he agrees with us that he does not see," "he doesn't dispute it," but rather: he too describes the facts in this way, having learned the same language as we have. Now whom do we call blind, what is our criterion for blindness? A certain kind of behaviour. And if the person behaves in that particular way, we not only call him blind but teach him to call himself blind. And in *this* sense his behaviour also determines the meaning of blindness for *him.* But now you will say: "Surely blindness isn't a behaviour; it's clear that a man can behave like a blind man and not be blind. Therefore 'blindness' means something different; his behaviour only helps him to understand what we *mean* by 'blindness.' The outward circumstances are what both he and we know. Whenever he behaves in a certain way, we say that he sees nothing and he notices that a certain private experience of his coincides with all these cases and thereby knows /so concludes/ that we mean this experience of his by saying that he sees nothing."

The idea is that we teach a person the meaning of expressions relating to personal experiences *indirectly.* Such an indirect mode of teaching we could imagine as follows. I teach a child the names of colours and a game, say, of bringing objects of a certain colour when 'the name of the colour' is called out. I don't however teach him the colour names by pointing to a sample which I and he see and saying, e.g., the word red. Instead I have various spectacles ⟦286⟧ each of which, when I look through it, makes me see the white paper in a different colour. These spectacles are also distinguished by their outside appearance: the one that makes me see red has circular glasses another one elliptical ones, etc. I now teach the child in this way: that when I see it putting the circular ones on its nose I say the word 'red,' when the elliptical ones 'green,' and so forth. This one might call teaching the child the meanings of the colour names in an indirect way, because one could here /in this case/ say that I led the child to correlate the word 'red' with something that I didn't see but hoped the child would see if it looked through the circular glasses. And this way is indirect as opposed to the direct way of pointing to a red object etc.

(Mind-reading)

From this it should follow that we sometimes rightly, sometimes wrongly, teach a man to say that he is blind: for what if he saw all the time but nevertheless behaved exactly like a blind man?—Or should we say: "Nature wouldn't play such a trick on us!"

We can see here that we don't quite understand the real use of the expression "to see something" or "to see nothing."

And what is so misleading to us when we consider this use is the following. We say, "Surely we can see something without ever saying or showing that we do, and on the other hand we can say that we see so-and-so without seeing it; therefore seeing is *one* process and expressing that we see another, and all that they have to do with each other is that they sometimes coincide—they have the same connections as being red and being sweet. Sometimes what is red is sweet—etc." Now this is obviously not quite true and not quite false. It seems somehow that we look at the use of these words with some prejudice. It is clear that we in our language use the words 'seeing red' in such a way that we can say "he /*A*/ sees red but doesn't show it"; on the other hand it is easy to see that we would have no use for these words if their application was severed from the criteria of behaviour. That is to say: to the language game which we play with these words it is both essential that the people who play it (should) behave in the particular way we call expressing /saying, showing/ what they see, and also that sometimes and under certain circumstances they should more or less entirely conceal what they see.

⟦287⟧ Balance. The point of the game depends upon what *usually* happens.

Point of a game.

But doesn't the word "seeing red" mean to me a particular process /certain (private) experience/ or (mental) event, a *fact* in the realm of primary experience—which surely is utterly different from saying certain words?

The words "'seeing red' means a particular experience" are useless unless we can follow them up by: "namely this ↗ (pointing)." Or else they may say experience as opposed to physical object; but then this is grammar.

How does he know that he sees red /has the visual imp[ression]/ i.e. how does he connect the word 'red' with 'a particular colour'? In fact what does the expression 'a particular colour' here mean? What is the criterion for his connecting it /the word/ always to the same colour /experience/? Is it not often just that he calls it red?

In fact, if he is to play a lang[uage] game, the possibility of this will depend upon his own and the other people's reactions. The game depends upon the agreement of these reactions; i.e., they must describe the same things as 'red.'

"But if he speaks to himself, surely this is different. For then he needn't consult other people's reactions and he just gives the name 'red' now to *the same colour* to which he gave it on a previous ⟦288⟧ occasion." But how does he know that it is *the same colour?* Does he also recognise the sameness of colour as what he used to call sameness of colour, and so on ad inf[initum]? It is quite true he /connects/ uses, in agreement with or[d]ina[r]y use, the word "red" /and the same colour/ and that he would not say that he saw now the colour he had seen before, that that colour is red but that what he sees now is not red etc.

It is quite true he connects the word and the exp[erience].

But I could use language just for making entries in my diary and without ever having learned it. I could have invented a name for the particular colour sensation, say, the name "red" and then used this name to note down whenever I had that colour sensation. That means, you (would) play a private language game with yourself. But let's see, how are we to describe this game?—Christening. The words

" 'seeing red' means a part[icular] experience" are senseless unless we can follow them up by namely this → (pointing) or else they may say experience as opposed to phy[sical] obj[ect], but then this is grammar.

When you say "the expression '_______' means to you a certain private exp[erience]" you are (indeed) supplementing this statement by imagining a colour /red/ or looking at a red object (which supply the 'namely this') but how do you use /make use of/ the expression and the experience you thus connect with it? For what we call the meaning of the word lies in the game we play with it.

But it seems to me that I either see red or don't see red. Whether I express it or not.

Picture we use here.

This picture not questioned but its application.

Other cases of tautologies.

"Surely seeing is one thing, and showing that I see is another thing."—This certainly is like saying "skipping is one thing and jumping another." But there is a supplement to this statement—"skipping is this (showing it) and jumping [is] this (showing it)." Now how about this supplement in the first case? "Seeing red is this (showing it) and showing that we see red [is] this (showing it)." The point is just that there just isn't a 'showing that I see' except showing that I see. "But can't I say 'seeing red is what I'm doing now' (looking at something red)? And although in a sense the other man can't directly see what I'm talking about /be aware of the activity/, I certainly know what it is that I'm talking about. That is, although for him I can't point directly to my seeing red, for myself I can point to it; and in this sense I can give an ostensive definition of the expression to myself." But an ostensive definition is not a magic act. If I explain to someone [the] use of . . . by . . . giving the o[stensive] d[efinition] simply consists in . . .

One might be inclined to say that castling was not just the act of. . . . But it is the game of which it is part . . .

So what does giving myself the ostensive def[inition] of red consist in?—Now how am I to describe it? shall I say: seeing red and saying to myself 'I see red,'—or is it "seeing a certain colour sensation and saying 'I see red' "? The first (version) it seems won't do as /doesn't account for the fact that/ it isn't essential to us that when I do what I for myself call 'seeing red,' that should necessarily be what we then mean by 'seeing red.' /The first version I don't like. It assumes that the other knows the very same private impression which I am having./ So I would rather leave it open what colour I am concentrating my attention on. But then how can I call it a colour? Isn't it just as uncertain that I mean by 'colour' what they mean as that I mean by 'red' what they mean? And the same applies of course to 'seeing' (for what here I mean by this word is not an activity of the human eye). (The second version is justified only if I wish to say that it does not matter here to which of the colours (say, red green blue yellow) he assigns the name 'red' and so we might have said "he sees some colour, say, blue and says 'I see red' ").

"But it's a blatant error to mix up 'seeing red' with showing that you see red! I know what seeing red is and I know what showing . . . is." Couldn't we say that knowing what showing . . . is is seeing showing? Now what is knowing what seeing is?

In knowing what seeing red is you seem to say to yourself 'seeing red is this'—you seem to give yourself a sample but you don't because the usual criteria for the sameness of the sample ⟦289⟧ don't apply. I can say I call 'red' always the same colour, or whenever I explain 'red' I point to a sample of the same colour.

Consider the prop[osition]: He makes sure what it means *to him* by. . . . Would you say the word had meaning to him if it meant something else every time? And what is the criterion of the same colour coming twice?

If we describe a game which he plays with himself, is it relevant that he should use the word 'red' [for] the same colour in our sense, or would we also call it a lang[uage] game if he used it anyhow? Then what is the criterion for using it in the same way? Not merely the connection between "same," "colour," and "red."

Which is the same colour as that I saw? Not the one to which I apply the words 'this is the same colour'?

"Let me see if I still know which of these colours is red?—(Looking about.) Yes I know." (Here I could have said "is called red.")

So he can be sure, in this private way, of what t[oothache] means by having a pri[vate] sens[ation]?!

Making sure that you know what 'seeing red' means, is good only if you can make use of this knowledge in a further case. Now what if I see a colour again, can I say I made sure I knew what 'red' was /meant/ so now I shall know that I'll recognise it correctly? In what sense is having said the words 'this is red' before a guarantee that I now see the same colour when I say again I see red?

We can indeed imagine a Robinson [Crusoe] using a language for himself but then he must *behave* in a certain way or we shouldn't say that he plays lang[uage] games with himself.

The grammar of 'private sense data.'

What's interesting is not that I don't have to pay attention to my behaviour in order to know that I have toothache, but rather that my behaviour says nothing at all to me.[58]

"I sent him to the doctor because he moans" is just as correct as "I sent him to the d[octor] because he has toothache".

"I moan because I have pain".—Are you sure that that's why you moan?

"But d[amn it] a[ll] the nucleus of our language remains untouched whatever we might imagine our behaviour to be!" The nucleus is the word together with its meaning.

"'Toothache' is a word which I use in a game which I play with other people, but it has a private meaning to me."

"Christen toothache".

Changing the meaning of a word.
Meaning connected with the use of the ostens[ive] def[inition].

58. Das Interessante ist nicht, daß ich nicht auf mein Benehmen achten muß, um zu wissen, daß ich Zahnschm[erz] habe, sondern daß mir mein Benehmen gar nichts sagt.

In the use of the word 'meaning' it is essential that the same meaning is kept throughout a game.

Consider a game in which this isn't so. Would you call this sort of activity a game?

"Are you sure that you call 'toothache' always the same private experience?"

"I recognise it as being the same". And are you also recognising the meaning of the word the same, so you can be sure that "recognising it to be the same" now means the same to you which it did before?

"But in ostensively defining a word for myself I impress its meaning on me so as not to forget it later on". But how do you know that this helps? Do you know later on whether you remember it rightly or wrongly?

Can you recognise something to be red which isn't red?

To be sure that so-and-so is the case. To know. Does 'p' follow from 'I know p'?

The normal case of being sure, of a strong conviction.

Does it make sense to say, that what you see is green, and you recognise it to be red?

"It seems to me to have sense." You are undoubtedly using a picture, therefore it 'seems to you to have sense'. But ask yourself what use you are making of that picture? We shall have to talk about sense and nonsense later.

What's the use here of being sure, if it doesn't follow that it is so and if your being sure is the only criterion there is for its being so?

That means: This isn't at all a case of being sure, of conviction.

The [phrase] 'recognising as . . .' is used where you can be wrong in recognising.

⟦287⟧ Sometimes these bodies change their weight, and then we look for the cause of the change and find, say, that something's come off the body. Sometimes however the weight of a body changes and we can't account for the change at all. But we nevertheless don't say that weighing it had lost its point "because now the body really doesn't have any weight." Rather we say that the body had changed somehow—that this was the cause of the change of weight—but that hitherto we have not found this cause. That is, we will go on playing the game of weighing, and we try to find an explanation for the exceptional behaviour.

We use the form of expression "the weight of this body" to designate something inherent in the body, something which could only be diminished by destroying part of the body. The same body—the same weight. (And this is a gramm[atical] prop[osition].)

Grocer.

Supposing what in fact is the rule became the exception. Under certain peculiar circ[umstance]s indeed a body kept on weighing the same; say, iron in the presence of mercury. A piece of cheese, on the other hand, though keeping its size, calories, etc., weighed different weights at different times unaccountably. Would we still. . . .

On the one hand it seems that if there wasn't the behaviour of t[oothache] . . .

⟦289⟧ "So-and-so has excellent health, he never had to go to the dentist, never complained about toothache; but as toothache is a ⟦290⟧ private experience, we can't know whether he hasn't had terrible toothache all his life."

How does one assume such and such to be the case? What is an assumption that, e.g., '*A* has t[oothache]'? Is it saying the words "*A* has t[oothache]"? Or doesn't it consist in doing something with these words?

"A game of assumption."—

Assuming: a state of mind. Assuming: a gesture.

"But the point is just that we don't *assume* that *we* have t[oothache]. Therefore, even if we have no ground to assume that anyone else has t[oothache] we may nevertheless know that we have". But would we in this case at all talk of a (particular) behaviour as a symptom of pains? "Suppose no one knew pains except I, and I just invented a name 'abracadabra' for it!"

Showing his grief,—hiding his grief.

Certain behaviour under certain circumst[ances] we call showing our toothache, other behaviour hiding our t[oothache]. Now would we talk about this behaviour in this way if people didn't ordinarily behave in the way they do? Suppose I and they described my behaviour without such a word as pain, would the description be incomplete? The question is: do *I* consider it incomplete? If so, I will distinguish between two cases of my behaviour, and the others will say that I use two words alternately for my behaviour and thereby they will acknowledge that I have t[oothache].

"But can't he have t[oothache] without in any way showing it? And this shows that the word 't[oothache]' has a meaning entirely independent of a behaviour connected with t[oothache]."

The game which we play with the word 't[oothache]' entirely depends upon there being a behaviour which we call the expression of t[oothache].

"We use 't[oothache]' as the name of a personal experience."—Well, let's see how we *use* the word!

"But you know the sensation of t[oothache]! So you can give it a name, say, 't[oothache]'."

But what is it like to give a sensation a name? Say it is pronouncing the name while one has the sensation and possibly concentrating on the sensation,—but what of it? Does this name thereby get magic powers? And why on earth do I call these sounds the 'name' of the sensation? I know what I do with the ⟦291⟧ name of a man or of a number, but have I by this act of "definition" given the name a use?

"I know what t[oothache] is". But how do I know that I know it? Because something comes before my mind? But /and/ how do I know that that is the right thing? Because I recognise it? But then it doesn't matter what *it is,* as long as I recognise it as t[oothache]! . . .

"But when you ask me 'do you know what t[oothache] is?' I answer 'yes' after having brought before my mind a certain sensation". But how is this *certain* sens[ory] characte[rization] used? Only by that, that it comes when you say the word 't[oothache]'? Or that it comes and you are in some way satisfied?

"To give a sensation a name" means nothing unless I know already in what sort of a game this name is to be used.

---

We describe certain behaviour by: "it is obvious that he was hiding his pain," or: "I think he was hiding his pain," or: "I don't know at all whether he was hiding pain."

But can't I just assume with some degree of certainty that he has pain although I have no reason whatever for it? I can say "I assume . . . ," but if I sent them all to the doctor although they showed no sign of illness /pain/, I should just be called mad.

That we try to account for something is due to the fact that we often can account for it. If I saw no regularity whatever I should not be inclined to say that there is one which I haven't as yet discovered. What usually happens makes me take this point of view.

The 'private definition' is not *binding.*

---

In our priv[ate] lang[uage] game we had, it seemed, given a name to an impression—in order, of course, to use the name for this impr[ession] in the future. The def[inition], that is, should have determined on future occasions for what imp[ression] to use the name and for which not to use it. Now we said that on certain occ[asions] after having given the defin[ition] we did use the word [and] on others we didn't; but we described these occ[asions] only by saying that we had 'certain impr[essions]'—that is, we didn't describe them at all. The only thing that characterized them was that we used such and such words. What seemed to be a definition didn't play the role of a def[inition] at all. It did not justify one subsequent use of the word; and all that remains of our priv[ate] lang[uage] game is therefore that I sometimes without justification, without /any particular reason/ write the word 'red' in my diary without any justif[ication] whatever.

"But surely I feel justified when normally I use the word 'red' although I don't think of a def[inition] while doing so." Do you mean that whenever normally you use the word 'red' you have a particular feeling which you call a feeling of justificat[ion]? I wonder if that is true. But anyhow by 'justific[ation]' I didn't mean a feeling. But I think I know what makes you say that on saying, e.g., 'this book is red' you have a feeling of being justified in using the word. For you might ask: isn't there an obvious difference between the case in which I use a word in its well known meaning ⟦292⟧—as when I say to someone "the sky is blue today"—and the case in which I say any arbitrary word on such an occasion, e.g., "the sky is moo." In this case, you will say, I either know that I am just *giving* a meaning to the word 'moo,' or else I shall feel that there is no justification whatever for using the word. The word is just *any* word and not the appropriate word. I quite agree that there is a difference in experience between the cases of 'using the name of the colour,' 'giving a new name to the colour,' and 'using some arbitrary word in place of the name of the colour.' But that doesn't mean that it is correct to say that I have a feeling of appropriateness in the first case which is absent in the third. "But 'red' somehow seems to us to fit this colour." We certainly may be inclined to say this sentence on certain occasions, but it would be wrong to say that therefore we had a feeling of fitting when ordinarily we said that something was red.

"But do you mean that one man couldn't play a game of chess with himself and without anyone else knowing that he did?"—What would you say he should do to be playing a private game of chess? Just anything?

I suppose you would say, e.g., that he imagines a chessboard with the chessmen on it, that he imagines certain moves, etc. And if you were asked what it means to imagine a *chessboard,* you would explain it by pointing to a real chessboard, or say to a picture of one, and analogously if you were asked what does it mean to imagine the king of chess, a pawn, a knight's move etc. Or should you have said: he must go through certain . . . ? But what private experiences are there? and would any of them do in this case? For instance, feeling hot? "No! The private exp[erience] I am talking of must have the multiplicity of the game of chess." But again, does he recognise two private exp[eriences] to be different by a further priv[ate] exp[erience] and this to be the same in different cases? (Priv[ate] exp[erience] in fiction.) Mustn't we say in this case that we can't say anything whatever about private experiences and are in fact not entitled to use the word 'experiences' at all? What makes us believe that we are is that we really think of the cases in which we can describe his priv[ate] exp[eriences], describing different ways of playing chess in one's imagination.

How can we say he may see red although nobody may be able to find it out?

If we go through with this idea of a private experience which we don't know, we can't talk of a certain private experience either, because this expression is taken from the case in which it alludes to a certain class of experiences which we know—though we don't know which one of its members he has. Rather, the private experiences /impressions/ which we imagined as the background to the foreground of our actions, dissolve into a mist/ which we wished to talk about and imagined to be back of our actions, dissolve into a mist./ Rather, the private experiences which we imagined as an unknown x, y, z etc. behind our actions dissolve into a mist and into nothing.

One might suggest . . .: the word 't[oothache]' stands on the one hand for a behaviour and on the other hand for a private experience. The connection is that when a man has the priv[ate] exp[erience] he tends to behave in the particular way.

But why should you talk of *a* priv[ate] exp[erience] and not 100 priv[ate] experiences as you don't know whether there is only one or whether there are 100?

What is so confusing here is to talk of the meaning of the word instead of the use.

The idea of different kinds of objects.

Why should you know better what experiencing is like with the other person than what seeing red is like? If you were very careful you would say "a certain something".

⟦293⟧ What is it that happens when in one case I say "I have toothache /see red/" and mean it, and am not lying, and on the other hand I say the words but know that they are not true; or say them not knowing what exactly they mean, etc.?

The criteria for it being the truth have to be laid down beforehand in common *language.* /are laid down in *language* (in rules, charts, etc.)./ "But how am I to know how in the particular case to apply them? For in so far as they are laid down in common lang[uage], they join the rest of the rules of common language; i.e., they do not help me in my particular case. Is there such a thing as justifying what in the particular case I do, just by what then is the case and not by a rule? Can I say I am now justified in using the sentence . . . just by what is now the case?" No!

Nor /can I say/ does it help me to say /"I am justified—when I *feel* justified." For about feeling justified the same thing can be said as about feeling t[oothache].

My criteria for having t[oothache] /saying I have t[oothache]/ are the same as /no other than/ for the other to say I have toothache; for I can't say that feeling or having t[oothache] is my criterion for having a right to say it.

Examine: 'These two operations bring about the same pain'. The pain which they all bring about I shall call 't[oothache]'.

What does this show??

Did I call a *behaviour* "having toothache"?

Did I call a behaviour "having the same pain"?

Did I give the name "t[oothache]" to a behaviour?

But showing toothache can never be lying.

I must assume an expression which is *not* lying.

I believe that I wanted to say that 'toothache' is here not given as name of a behaviour and that one does not point to an experience behind the behaviour either.[59]

59. Ich glaube, ich wollte sagen, daß 't[oothache]' hier nicht als Name eines Benehmens gegeben wird und daß man auch nicht auf eine Erfahrung hinter dem Benehmen zeigt.

When are we to say that they do? It could be when the patient /subject/ says: I have the same pain now as . . . I imagine that he says this spontaneously having been taught the word the same . . .
Now do I say that there is not the experience of t[oothache] but only the behaviour?!?

When I say that moaning is the expression of t[oothache], then under certain circ[umstance]s the possibility of it being the expression without the feeling behind it mustn't enter my game.

It is nonsense to say: the expression may always lie.[60]
The language games with expressions of feelings (private experiences) are based on games with expressions of which we don't say that they may lie.

"But was I when a baby taught that 'toothache' meant my expression of toothache?"—I was told that a certain behaviour was called expression of toothache.

"But isn't it possible that a child should behave just as a normal child when it has t[oothache] and not have t[oothache]?"

But does, if we speak of the baby, "having t[oothache]" mean the same as "behaving such-and-such"?

We say "poor thing, it moans."

Can't I, in the child too, separate the moaning from the pain? Can't I say that I pity it because it has pain, not because it moans?

You ought, I suppose, to say that you pity it because you believe that it has pains. But what is believing that it has pains like, as opposed to believing /just seeing/ that it moans? It doesn't here consist in believing that he doesn't cheat but in a different experience.

"Something clicked in my brain /mind/ when I came to this colour." (This is a picture.) But did you know from the clicking that it was red? Supposing looking at this colour your eyes opened wider and you gave a jerk,—was it *by* its producing this reaction that you recog-

60. Es ist Unsinn zu sagen: der Ausdruck kann immer lügen.

nised the colour as being red? Indeed, this is the phenomenon we call recognition, but we call it that because it happens under circumstances where we have other criteria for saying that we've recognised the object.

I saw a particular colour, concentrated on it and the word red came without tension.

"But surely there's a case in which I'm justified to say 'I see red,' where I'm not lying, and one where I'm not justified in saying so!" Of course I can be justified by the ostensive def[inition] or by asking the others "now isn't this red?" and they answer that it is. But you didn't mean this justification, but one which justifies me privately, whatever others will say.

"But do you mean to say that the truth or falsehood of my saying 'I see red' does not consist in there being red before my mind's eye in one case and not in the other; but that it depends on such things as whether I say it in this or that tone of voice?" /with a certain tension?"/

⟦294⟧ If I say "I see red" without reason, how can I distinguish between saying it with truth and saying it as a lie?

It is important here that there is no such case /that I exclude the case/ of saying the untruth by mistake.

Here there is no comparing of proposition and reality! (Collating.)[61]

Don't I know, when I say 'I see red' and am lying that I am lying?—When do I translate my experience into the words expressing my knowledge? One might say: knowing that I am lying doesn't mean saying that I do but being ready to say it.

I could say: Lying is characterised by a peculiar /an experience of/ tension. What is it like to know that I don't see red and to say that I do?

61. Hier haben wir keinen Vergleich des Satzes mit der Wirklichkeit! (Kollationieren.)

"Well, it is simply not seeing red and saying 'I see red'! There is nothing problematic about this, as seeing and saying something are utterly independent".

"What I now call . . ."

(We never dispute the opinions of common sense but we question the expression of common sense.)

Suppose I said "I see red" and was lying, for I actually saw red—but had made a slip of the tongue.

But which lie was it I had said, or (rather) thought? Of course I may say later "I wanted to say 'I see green' " but did anything corresp[ond] to these words while I said 'I see red'?

But suppose that he felt that he was lying but never said so,—did he know that he was lying or not?

"Did he know that he was doing what we call lying?" "Did he know that he was doing what, on other occasions, he called lying?"

What is his criterion for saying—wanting to speak the truth—that he was lying? Is there a criterion?

Do these two sentences say the same: "He says he sees red and really sees red" and "He says he sees red with conviction?" /and has the experience of not lying"?/

"So you think seeing red consists in saying 'I see red' in a certain tone of voice?"—No, but saying 'I see red' and seeing it might be saying it in a particular tone of voice.

How do I imagine myself seeing red? Isn't it by imagining red?! But how do I imagine myself addressing a meeting?

Imagine a Robinson [Crusoe] lying to himself.—Why is this difficult to imagine?

Look at something red and say to yourself 'I see green', a) meaning by 'green' what usually you mean by 'red' (i.e. speaking the truth), b) lying.

But one might call it lying to oneself if one, e.g., turns one's watch forward to make oneself get up earlier.

Falsifying an account. I add up numbers, arrive at 273 s[hillings], then rub out 3 and put a 5 instead.

When in this discussion we talk of lying, it ought always to mean *subjectively* lying, and subjectively lying to the other person and not to oneself.

If I see green without saying I see green, in what way can these words be said to describe what I see?

One could imagine someone constantly lying *subjectively* but not objectively.

Imagine this case: Someone has a particular way of lying, he always lies calling red 'green' and green 'red,' but as a matter of fact what he says agrees with the usage of the other people and so his lying is never noticed. //taken notice of.//

Supposing one said: To see red means to see that which makes me inclined to describe it by saying ". . .". "To know that I am lying means to have that experience which *I should* describe by the words '. . .'."

(Our language on the one hand has very much more possibilities of expression than logicians admit /dream of/ /imagine/, and on the other hand, the uses of these modes of expression are very much more limited than logicians /they/ imagine).

What makes 'I see red' into lying? The private experience of not seeing red or the private experience of feeling a certain tension?

Is it wrong to say that lying in such-and-such cases consists in saying so-and-so and feeling a tension?

One could very well say that sometimes lying is characterised by the fact that I only am conscious that things are otherwise, and sometimes not that way but by the fact that I sense the tension of bad conscience, etc.[62]

62. Man könnte sehr wohl sagen daß manchmal die Lüge dadurch charakterisiert ist, daß ich nur bewußt bin, daß es sich anders verhält, und manchmal nicht so, sondern dadurch, daß ich die Spannung des schlechten Gewissens spüre, etc.

If I now say "a person who says 'I see red' and sees green lies", then that's not right, for I ought to say "a person who says 'I see red' and knows (or believes) he sees green lies".[63]

"He is lying who says 'I see red' and who sees the colour that he himself *would call* 'green.'" But this means: he would call it that if he were speaking *truthfully*. Or can we say, "would call it that *to himself*"?

Hence the idea that one may lie by saying one thing out loud and something else softly—and what one says out loud is the lie.[64]

"It is the person who knows which colour he sees who *could express* it in some way or other". What is the criterion that he *could* do it?[65]

⟦295⟧ What could be meant by: truthfully calling a colour impression "red"? Does the word fit one impression better than another?[66]

We might even say here: one ought not to talk of the subjective truth of the sentence. The truth of the sentence "I have a toothache" would have to be judged only objectively.[67]

"The right word comes differently from the wrong one."[68]

One can say: "All these words came in the same way".[69]

The word which you utter is a reaction. *The* reaction which we translate into the proposition "he sees . . ."—But isn't it true that the

63. Wenn ich nun sage „der lügt, der sagt ‚ich sehe rot' und sieht grün", so stimmt das nicht, denn ich müßte sagen „der lügt, der sagt ‚ich sehe rot' und weiß (oder glaubt), er sieht grün."

64. „Der lügt, der sagt ‚ich sehe rot' und sieht die Farbe, die er selbst mit dem Worte ‚grün' *bezeichnen würde.*" Aber das heißt doch, *wahrheitsgemäß* so bezeichnen würde. Oder können wir sagen, „*für sich* so bezeichnen würde"?

Daher ist die Idee, daß man lügen kann, indem man laut das eine und leise das andere sagt—und was man laut sagt, ist hier die Lüge.

65. „Der weiß, welche Farbe er sieht, der es irgendwie *ausdrücken könnte.*" Was ist das Kriterium dafür, daß er es *könnte*?

66. Was soll es dann heißen: einen Farbeneindruck wahrheitsgemäß mit „rot" bezeichnen? Paßt das Wort denn einem Eindruck besser als dem andern?

67. Man könnte hier auch sagen: man solle gar nicht von subjektiver Wahrheit des Satzes sprechen. Die Wahrheit des Satzes „ich habe Zahnschmerz" habe nur objektiv beurteilt zu werden.

68. „Das wahre Wort kommt anders als das falsche."

69. Man kann sagen: „Alle diese Worte sind in derselben Weise gekommen".

other doesn't need to know that my reaction occurs in such-and-such a way? He thinks that I tell him *'straight out'* what I see and it isn't so, rather, I concoct a lie.[70]

"He doesn't know what I see until I tell him, I know it already //*before* he learns of it//". Could it also be the other way around?[71]

I have now been writing with a pencil for a long time: did I know that the writing is grey and the paper white?

Did I know *that*? or did I simply know that it is as it is?[72]

"I know that I didn't tell it to him straight out."—"Yes, but wasn't something *of* this 'reaction' already there, namely the experience, that I didn't tell him straight out?"[73]

"Still, can't we say that something visible to all happens (externally) and something further 'in me', that only I can recognise?"[74]

"How am I justified in saying that I see this apple [is] red?" You are not justified. But isn't it true that when I'm lying I am not justified and that when I say the truth I am justified?

How is a lie possible in a case where there is no justification?

Supposing one said: Lying (here) consists in applying one word to the colour and not another? A misleading word instead of a not misleading one?

70. Das Wort, welches Du sprichst, ist eine Reaktion. *Die* Reaktion, die wir in den Satz übersetzen „er sieht . . . "—Aber ist es nicht wahr, daß der Andere nicht wissen braucht, daß meine Reaktion in dieser und dieser Weise vor sich geht? Er meint, ich sage ihm ‚*geradeheraus*', was ich sehe, und es ist nicht so sondern ich erfinde eine Lüge.

71. „Er weiß nicht, was ich sehe, bis ich es ihm sage, ich weiß es schon vorher, //*ehe* er es erfährt//". Könnte es auch umgekehrt sein?

72. Ich habe jetzt lange mit einem Bleistift geschrieben: wußte ich, daß die Schrift grau und das Papier weiß ist?

Wußte ich *daß*? oder wußte ich bloß, daß es ist, wie es ist?

73. „Ich weiß, daß ich es ihm nicht geradeheraus gesagt habe."—„Ja, aber war nicht *von* dieser ‚Reaktion' schon etwas da, nämlich eben das Erlebnis, daß ich es ihm nicht geradeheraus gesagt habe?"

74. „Können wir nicht doch sagen, daß etwas, jedem sichtbar (äußerlich), geschieht und etwas weiteres, nur mir erkennbar, ‚in mir'?"

I am justified if the word comes in one way and not justif[ied] if it comes in another way.—But in which way?—If it comes in the straightforward way, I'm justified. But which is the straightforward way?—I know but can't explain as the paradigm of it is in me.—But as far as it's in you it serves no purpose in the future application of the word. (Priv[ate] ostens[ive] def[inition]).

How do I know that it comes in the straightforward way? What the st[raightforward] way is must be fixed by a paradigm.

"Why on earth should it be wrong to use a word not in the simple ('straightforward') way?" Couldn't it not even be my duty to use the word which doesn't come straightforwardly? Imagine the case where we had laid down a code in which 'red' meant green.

"I said the word with a bad conscience".

What troubles me are the prop[osition]s in which an action is described accompanied by a 'state of mind'.

"Lying when you say 'I see red' consists in saying those words and having a private experience which I call 'feeling unjustified', or 'seeing green' etc."—"But suppose that I call the feeling of being justified 'feeling unjustified'!?"—Now this last sentence, though it sounds absurd, had sense.

"What you say comes to this: when I truly say 'I see red' I am not justified in saying this by a fact, that I see red."—No, I should say— — —

"You either have a feeling of being unjustified or you don't!"

"But surely there is a case in which I say 'I see red' and am telling the (subjective) truth, and one in which I lie!"—Yes, that is, *we distinguish* between a case of telling the truth and not telling the truth.—But what does lying, in such a case, consist in? We may try all sorts of explanations: "It consists in saying . . . and seeing green" "It consists in saying . . . and knowing that I see . . ." "It consists in saying . . . and feeling that I'm not justified in saying this" and others. Now, let us ask: do all these expl[anations] come to the same or do they describe different facts? We can say, if they describe different facts, the differences are quite unimportant to us (here). For our purpose they can all be said to describe the same case. (We might have said lying consists in saying 'I see red' and having stomach ache but as stomach ache is a priv[ate] sens[ation], why not rather consider the priv[ate] sens[ation] of seeing a colour other than red?) We may say therefore that these explanations, for our purpose, *were no explanations at all.* They left us just where we were, and they only (seem to) say that the cases of lying and saying the truth are distinguished by the private experience accompanying the sentence. So let us put our question like this: Lying, in our case, consists in saying 'I see red' and seeing green; what does seeing green consist in? As an answer we immediately give ourselves a sample for 'green'. But is it essential that this sample should be what the others also call green? No, it might be what they call yellow or blue. But are you inclined to say it might be what they call hot, cold or tepid? Then, after all, you are thinking of games played with others though you left a certain latitude. . .

When we talk of the *private* experience which the others don't know, we don't originally mean to talk of a shapeless nothing but of a variable with a certain definite value.

It is said sometimes that if I and someone else are looking at some objects I can never know what colour the other really sees. But with what right do we here use 'colour' and 'seeing'? Some philosophers (e.g. Driesch) would here be inclined to think that they can save the situation by using the senseless phrase "We can't know *what* the other *has*." Compare Driesch: . . . But as long as 'to have' here has any meaning at all it can't help us and when it has no meaning at all I think it can't help us either.

'We distinguish between . . . and . . .' That means: We sometimes use the expression "I lied when I said that I saw green" as opposed to "I told the truth when I said '. . .'". But isn't this enough?—"But *under what circumstances* do you use the expression '. . .'?" But must I necessarily stop giving you circumstances when I have given you a sample? Why not when I have given you a word, a verbal expression? Is the use of such an expression necessarily indefinite as compared with the use of a sample? Can't a sample be used, compared with objects in many different ways?

The word 'lying' is taught us in a part[icular] way in which it was fastened to a certain behaviour, to the use of certain expressions under certain circumstances. Then we use it, saying that we have been lying, when our behaviour was not like the one which first constituted the meaning.

But in the same way we were taught the word 'red' in a game, say like No. 1, and then we use it when the conditions are different (compare the past in the description of a dream) (and of course it isn't just the word 'red' we use but the whole imagery connected with it.)

"But you talk as though there was only the expression 'I see red' but not an impression corresponding to it." On the contrary, I don't say that when a man says . . . he also has the impression.

But is all that happens that you *say* "I see red"? Isn't there something else being the case, happening, when you say this and it is true? But if you ask, isn't there something else happening, you don't mean just anything else, e.g. that it's raining. So after all you have to give a description of what it is you mean is happening and insofar as you give a description of it you must know what it is that happens, and it is not an X. And keeping it partly unknown does not help you either. On the other hand, there is no reason why you should always stop with giving a sample and not with giving an expression (in this sense one can say that an expression acts as a picture).

The philosophical puzzle seems insoluble if we are frank with ourselves, and *is* insoluble. That is, till we change our question.

'Expressions can always be lying.' How can we say this of the expressions to which we fasten our words?

"But I always know whether I'm lying or not!"—You are just now obsessed with the use of the word 'lying.' In general you talk without thinking of lying and of whether you lie or not.

But (then) I'm always either lying or not lying! (Whether I always know it or not.)

(Is there always a link between reality and our expression?)

Suppose a child learned the word 'toothache' as an equivalent for its moaning, and noticed that whenever it said the word or moaned the grown-ups treated it particularly well. The child then uses moaning or the word 't[oothache]' as a means to bring about the desired effect: is the child lying?

You say: "Surely I can moan with toothache and I can moan without toothache; so why shouldn't it be so with the child? Of course I only see and hear the child's behaviour but from my own experience I know what toothache is (like) //I know toothache apart from behaviour// and I am led to believe that the others sometimes have the pains I have."—The first sentence already is misleading. It isn't the question whether I *can* moan with [or] without toothache, the point is that I distinguish 'moaning with toothache' and 'moaning without toothache' and now we can't go on to say that of course in the child we make the same distinction. In fact we don't. We teach the child to use the words "I have toothache" to replace its moans, and this was how I too was taught the expression. How do I know that I've learned the word ⟦296⟧ 't[oothache]' to mean what they wanted me to express? I ought to say I *believe* I have!

Now one can moan because one has pain, or, e.g., one can moan on the stage. How do I know that the child, small as it is, doesn't already act, and in this case I teach it to mean by 'toothache' something I don't intend it to mean?

I have taught the child to use the expression 'I have toothache' under certain circumstances. And now it uses the words under these circumstances.—But what are these circumstances? Shall I say "the circumstances under which it moaned," and what are these?

But now I also teach the child to moan on the stage! That is to say, I even *teach* it to use this expression in a different game. I also teach it to read out the sentence 'I have toothache' from a book, when it hasn't toothache. In fact I could teach it to lie, as a separate language game. (In fact we often play this kind of game with children.)

"But doesn't what you say come to this: that it doesn't matter what the persons feel as long as only they behave in a particular way?"

"Do you mean that you can define pain in terms of behaviour?"

But is this what we do if we teach the child to use the expression 'I have toothache'? Did I define: "Toothache is such and such a behaviour"? This obviously contradicts entirely the normal use of the word! "But can't you, on the other hand, at least for yourself give an *ostensive* def[inition] of 'toothache'? Pointing to the place of your pain and saying 'this is . . .'?" Can't I give a name to the pain I've got? Queer idea to give one's pain a name! What's it [to] do with a name? Or what do I do with it? What do I do with the name of a person whom I *call* by the name? I mean to say, what connection is the name to have with the pain? The only connection so far is this: that you had toothache, pointed to your cheek, and pronounced the word 'moo.' "So what?" Remember what we said about priv[ate] ost[ensive] def[inition].

"But aren't you neglecting something—the experience or whatever you might call it—? Almost *the world* behind the mere words?"

⟦297⟧ But here solipsism teaches us a lesson: It is that thought which is *on the way* to destroy this error. For if the *world* is idea it isn't any person's idea. (Solipsism stops short of saying this and says that it is my idea.) But then how could I say what the world is if the realm of ideas has no neighbour? What I do comes to defining the word 'world.'

'I neglect that which goes without saying.'

"What is seen *I* see" (pointing to my body). I point at my geometrical eye, saying this. Or I point with closed eyes and touch my breast and feel it. In no case do I make a connection between what is seen and a person.

Back to 'neglecting'! It seems that I neglect life. But not life physiologically understood but life as consciousness. And consciousness not physiologically understood, or understood from the outside, but consciousness as the very essence of experience, the appearance of the world, the world.

Couldn't I say: If I had to add the world to my language it would have to be one sign for the whole of language, which sign could therefore be left out.

How am I to describe the way the child learns the word 'toothache'—like this?: The child sometimes has t[oothache], it moans and holds its cheek, the grown-ups say ". . . ," etc. Or: The child sometimes moans and holds its cheek, the grown-ups . . . ? Does the first description say something superfluous or false, or does the second leave out something essential? Both descriptions are correct.

"But it seems as if you were neglecting something." But what more can I do than *distinguish* the case of saying 'I have t[oothache]' when I really have t[oothache], and the case of saying the words without having t[oothache]. I am also /further/ ready to talk of any *x* behind my words so long as it keeps its identity.

Isn't what you reproach me of as though you said: "In your language you're only *speaking!*"

⟦298⟧ But why should I say "*I* have t[oothache] in his tooth"? I would insist on his tooth being extracted. Who is supposed to cry out if it is?

What does it mean: distributing primary experience over all subjects? Imagine that they have all *real* toothache in their teeth. The one which you only have. I now describe certain facts. (Not metaphysical ones, but facts about the coincidence of certain experiences.)

He gets a blow and cries—I think: "no wonder for it really hurts." But wouldn't I say to myself: Queer that *he* cries, for *I* feel the pain all right,—but he?!

What does it consist in, that *I* have pain, *I* feel myself crying, *I* hear that *I* am crying, *my* mouth cries?

It seems there is a phenomenon which in general I refer to as 'my toothache,' which, experience teaches me, is always connected with one particular person (not 'I' but) L.W. I now imagine facts other than they are and connect up this phenomenon to all sorts of persons so as to make it not at all tempting to call this phenomenon "my toothache."

Isn't it a particular phenomenon *to hear myself speak* (not, 'to hear LW speak').———

"I see so-and-so" does not mean "the person so-and-so, e.g., L.W., sees so-and-so."

A lang[uage] game in which everybody calls out what he sees but without saying "I see . . . ." Could anybody say that what I call out is incomplete because I have left out to mention the person?!

A lang[uage] game in which everybody (and I too) calls out what *I* see without mentioning *me.*

They always know what I see. If they don't seem to, I misunderstand what they say.

I am tempted to say: "It seems at least a fact of experience that at the source of *the visual field* there is mostly a small man with gray flannel trousers, in fact L.W."—Someone might answer this to me: It is true you almost always wear gray flannel trousers and often look at them.

⟦299⟧ "But I *am* in a favored position. I am the center of the world." Suppose I saw myself in the mirror saying this and pointing to myself. Would it still be all right?[75]

When I say I play a unique role I really mean the geometrical eye.

On the other hand, if I describe the usual appearance of my body around the geometrical eye, this is on the same level as saying that in the middle of the visual field there is in general a brown table and at the edges a white wall (as I generally sit in my room).

Now suppose I described this in the form: The visual world in general is like this: (follows the description). Would this be wrong?—Why should it be wrong?! But the question is, what game I intend to be played with this sentence; e.g., who is allowed to say it and in what way are those to whom it is said to react to it? I should like to say, that it's I who is to say it, not L.W., but the person at the source of the vis[ual] field. But this I seem not to be able to explain to anyone but

75. „Ich bin *doch* bevorzugt. Ich bin der Mittelpunkt der Welt.“ Denken wir uns ich sähe mich in einem Spiegel das sagen und auf mich zeigen! Wäre es noch richtig?

me /anyone/. (Queer state of affairs.) The game played might be the one which is in general played with "I see so-and-so."

Can't I say something to nobody, neither to anybody else *nor* to myself? What is the criterion of saying it to myself?

If I see a fire he runs to extinguish it.

At intervals I paint what I see. But can't someone else paint it for me? Or the picture be presented to me somehow, already finished?

What if I see before me a picture of the room as I am seeing the room? Is this a lang[uage] game?

I want to say: "the visual world is like this . . ."—but why *say* anything?

But the point is that I don't establish a relation between a person and what is seen. All I do is that alternately I point in front of me and to myself.

Solipsism. //The conception of solipsism// does not stretch to games. The other can play chess as well as I.[76]

I.e., when we play a lang[uage] game we are on the same level.

"I am in the lucky position of being in the source of the visual world /field/. It is I who see it!" I have a comfortable feeling while saying this although the statement isn't one of the class of statements which in general give me this kind of feeling. I said it as though I had said "I have more money than anyone else in this place".

But what I now see, this view of my room, plays a unique rôle, it is the visual world!

⟦300⟧ (The solipsist flutters and flutters in the flyglass, strikes against the walls, flutters further. How can he be brought to rest?)[77]

76. Der Solipsismus. //Die Auffassung des Solipsismus// erstreckt sich nicht auf Spiele. Der Andere kann Schach spielen so gut wie ich.

77. (Der Solipsist flattert und flattert in der Fliegenglocke, stößt sich an den Wänden, flattert weiter. Wie ist er zur Ruhe zu bringen?)

"Description: this is what I now see". Leave out the "see" leave out the "now" and leave out the "I".[78]

"(Description): this is the visual world". But why do you say visual and why do you say that it's the world?

"A red patch is (now) at the centre." All others must say "*I see* . . .". But is this distinction necessary, as I know anyhow who's saying it, whether I or one of the others?

But the real question for me here is: How am *I* defined? Who is it that is favoured? *I.* But may I lift up my hand to indicate who it is?—

Supposing I constantly change and my surrounding does: is there still some continuity, namely, by it being *me* and *my surrounding* that change?!

(Isn't this similar to thinking that when things in space have changed entirely there's still one thing that remains the same, namely space.) (Space confused with room.)

But is *my* hand favoured as compared to someone else's hand I see? This is ridiculous. Then either nobody is favoured or I am, that is, the person L.W. whose hand lifted.

All right, —then I, L.W., see what's seen!

Where is *my* toothache? I.e. how is its place determined?

---

"What I now see justif[ies] me in saying that I see red". And what do you now see? The answer may be "this ↗" but by this answer I don't tell myself what it is I see. I don't see what I see more definitely if at the same time I see my finger pointing to it. (The question ought to have been: what are you now looking at?) I don't tell myself what it is I see by seeing my finger pointing to something.

Suppose I said "What I now see justif[ies] me in saying 'I see red' because it is the same colour as this sample", this is a justific[ation]

78. The original draft includes the words 'leave out the "this"' but they have been crossed out.

only if I use the expression 'the same colour' in a *fixed* way. That is, when we judge how this word is used on the ordinary grounds of behaviour etc.

Is the criterion for my playing a private game of chess my being however strongly inclined to say that I am playing one?

How does one tell whether I am *strongly* inclined?

What would I say if I, in my priv[ate] judgements, came into contradiction with all other people? I.e., if I could no longer play a lang[uage] game with them. Or if all the facts around me became extraordinary? Would I stick to my judgements?

Suppose someone asked me, "What does it mean to play a private game of chess with oneself?" and I answered: "Anything, because if I said I was playing a game of chess I would be so sure that I was that I would stick to what I said, whatever anyone else might say."

Suppose someone painted pictures of the landscape which surrounds [him]. He sometimes paints the leaves of trees orange, sometimes blue, sometimes the clear sky red, etc. Under what circumstances would we agree with him that he was portraying the landscape?

Under what circ[umstance]s would we say that he did what we call portraying, and under what circ[umstance]s that he called something portraying which we didn't call that? Suppose here we said: "Well I can never know what he does inwardly"—would this be anything [more] than resignation?

We call something a calculation if, for instance, it leads to a house being built.

We call something a lang[uage] game if it plays a particular rôle in our human life.

"But can't he play a game with the colour names, against whatever anybody else says?" But why should we call it a game with the colour names? ⟦301⟧ "But if *I* played it I would stick to saying that I was playing a game with the colour names." But is that all I can say about it; is all that I can say for its being this kind of game that I stick to calling it so?

Under what circumstances do I say I am entitled to say that I'm seeing red? The answer is showing a sample, i.e., giving the rule. But if now I came into constant contradiction with what anybody else said, should I not say that I am applying the rule in a way which prevents me from playing the game? That is: is all that is necessary that the rule I give should be the rule they give, or isn't besides this an agreement in the application necessary?

If "having the same pain" *means* the same as "saying that one has the same pain," then "I have the same pain" means the same as "I say that I have the same pain" and the exclamation "Oh!" means "I say 'Oh!' "

Roughly speaking: The expression 'I have t[oothache]' stands for a moan but it does not mean 'I moan.'

But if 'I have t[oothache]' stands for a moan, what does 'he has t[oothache]' stand for? One might say: it, too, stands for a moan, that of compassion.

"T[oothache], seeing, etc. I only know from myself and not from the other."

"I never *know* that he has t[oothache], I only know when I have it."

"I can only believe that he has it, that he has what I have."

"Has 't[oothache]' then a different meaning in my case and in his?"

"Isn't it possible that everybody should have t[oothache] but without expressing it?"

"If it is possible that sometimes one can have 't[oothache]' without expressing it, it is possible that always this should be so."

"If my personal experience is all I know, how can I even assume that there is any other besides?"

"Does 't[oothache]' in the other mean behaviour?"

"I only know what I mean by 't[oothache]'."

"I was taught the word 't[oothache]' in connection with my behaviour but interpreted it to mean my pain."

"Only my t[oothache] is real t[oothache]".

"What justifies me in saying that the other has t[oothache] is his behaviour, what just[ifies] me in saying that I have is the experience of t[oothache]".

"Is there only the expression of t[oothache] and not the t[oothache]?"

"I know what it means to say that the other has 't[oothache]' even if I have no means to find out whether he has."

"Only he knows whether he has t[oothache], we can never know".

"Does the *I* enter into the personal experience or not?"

If I say we must assume an expression which can't lie, this can't be explained by saying that pain really corresponds to this expression.

We aren't lying, we are speaking the truth, if a fact corresponds to the sentence. This is no explanation at all but a mere repetition unless we can supplement it by 'namely this →' and a demonstration; and then the whole explanation lies just in this demonstration. The whole problem here only arose through the fact that in this case the demonstration of 'I see red,' 'I have t[oothache],' seems indirect.

⟦302⟧ "But aren't you saying, that all that happens is the moaning, and that there is nothing behind it?"—I am saying that there is nothing *behind* the moaning.

"Do you deny that the moaning is the expression of something?" No, that is, I too should call moaning an expression (or even an expression of something, though this is misleading). But the word 'expression' here only characterises the lang[uage] game played with it. I react differently . . .

"So you don't really have pain, you just moan?!"—There seems to be a *description* of my behaviour, and also, in the same sense, a description of my experience, my pain! The one, so to speak, the description of an external, the other of an internal fact. This corresponds to the idea that in the sense in which I can give a part of my body a name, I can give a name to a private experience (only indirectly).

And I am drawing your attention to this: that the lang[uage] games are very much more different than you think /it appears/.

You couldn't call moaning a description! But this shows you how far the prop[osition] 'I have t[oothache]' is from a 'description,' and how far teaching the use of the word 't[oothache]' is from teaching the word 'tooth.'

One could from the beginning teach the child the expression "I think he has toothache" instead of "he has t[oothache]," with the corresponding uncertain tone of voice. This mode of expression could be described by saying that we can only believe that the other has t[oothache].

But why not in the child's own case? Because there the tone of voice is simply *determined* by nature.

In "I have t[oothache]" the expression of pain is brought to the same form as a description "I have a matchbox /5 shillings/."

We teach the child to say "I have been lying" when it has behaved in a certain way. (Imagine here a typical case of a lie.) Also this expression goes along with a particular situation, facial expressions, say of shame, tones of reproach, etc.

"But doesn't the child know that it is lying before ever I teach him the word /verbal expression/?" Is this meant to be a metaphysical question or a question about facts? It doesn't know it in words. And why should it know it at all?—"But do you assume that it has only the facial expression of shame, e.g., without the *feeling* of shame? Mustn't you describe the inside situation as well as the outside one?"—But what if I said that by facial exp[ression] of shame I ⟦303⟧ meant what you mean by 'the fac[ial] exp[ression] + the feeling,' unless I explicitly distinguish between genuine and simulated fac[ial] expressions? It is, I think, misleading to describe the genuine expression as a *sum* of the expression and something else, though it is just as misleading—we get the function of our expressions wrong—if we say that the genuine expression is a particular behaviour and nothing besides.

We teach the child the use of the word "to speak."—Later it uses the expression "I spoke to myself."—We then say "We never know whether and what a person speaks to himself."

Surely the desc[ription] of the facial exp[ression] can be meant (used) /is used/ as a description of feelings and can be meant /used/ otherwise. We constantly use such expressions as "when he heard that, he pulled a long face" and don't add that the expression was genuine. In other cases we describe the acting[79] of a person in the same words, or again we wish to leave it open whether the expression

79. On the stage.

was genuine or not. To say that we describe the feeling indirectly by the descr[iption] of expressions is wrong!

Imagine a lang[uage] in which toothache is called "moaning" and the difference between just moaning and moaning with pain is expressed by the moaning or dry tone in which the word is pronounced. People would not say in this lang[uage] that it became clear later on that *A* didn't really have pain, but they would perhaps in an angry tone say that at first he moaned and then he suddenly laughed.

Suppose he says to himself "I lie," what is to show that he means it? But we would any day describe this lying by saying: "He said . . . , and told himself at the same time that he was lying." Is this too an indirect description of lying?

But couldn't one say that if I speak of a man's angry voice, meaning that he was angry, and again of his angry voice, not meaning that he was angry, in the first case the meaning of the description of his voice was much further reaching than in the second case? I will admit that our description in the first case ⟦304⟧ doesn't *omit* anything and is as complete as though we had said that he really was angry,—but somehow the meaning of the expression then reaches below the surface.

But how does it do that? The answer to this would be an explanation of the two uses of the expression. But how could this explanation reach *under the surface?* It is an explanation about symbols and it states in which cases these symbols are used. But how does it characterize these cases? Can it in the end do more than distinguish two expressions? i.e., describe a game with two expressions?

"Then is there nothing under the surface?!" But I said that I was going to distinguish two expressions, one for the 'surface' and one for 'what is below the surface'—only remember that these expressions themselves correspond just to a *picture,* not to its usage. It is just as misleading to say that there is just surface and nothing underneath it, as that there is something below the surface and that there isn't just the surface. Because once we make use of the picture of the 'surface' it is most natural to express with it the distinction as on and below the surface. //Because we naturally use this picture to express the distinction between 'on the surface' and 'below the surface.'// But we misapply the picture if we ask whether both cases are or aren't on the surface.

Now in order that with its normal meaning we should teach a child the expression "I have lied" the child must behave in the normal way. E.g., it must under certain circ[umstance]s 'admit' that it lied, it must do so with a certain facial expression etc., etc., etc. We may not always find out whether he lied or not, but if we never found out, the word would have a different meaning. "But once he has learned the word he can't be in doubt whether he is lying or not!"—Consider the case of the person who finds that his subjective lies are, judged by the ordinary criteria, truths. He says that he has been to school feeling that it's a lie but the teacher and the boys confirm that he has been etc. etc. You might say: "But surely he can't doubt that he said a *subjective* lie".

This of course is like saying that he can't be in doubt about whether he has toothache or whether he sees red, etc. On the one hand: doubting whether I have the experience *E* is not like doubting whether someone else has it. Remember what we said about the asymmetry of the game No. 1. On the other hand: one can't say "surely I must know what it is I see" unless 'to know what I see' is to mean 'to see whatever I see.' The question is what we are to call "knowing what it is I see," "not being in doubt about what ⟦305⟧ it is I see." Under what circumstances are we to say that a person is in no doubt (or is in doubt) about this? (Such cases as being in no doubt about whether this looks red to the normal eye, and analogous ones, of course don't interest us here.) I suppose that the knowledge of what it is I see must be the knowledge that it is so-and-so I see; 'so-and-so' standing for some expressions, verbal or otherwise. (But remember that I don't give myself information by pointing to something I see with my finger and saying to myself I see this.) 'So-and-so' in fact stands for a word of a lang[uage] game. And doubting what it is I see is doubting, e.g., what to call what I see. Doubting, e.g., whether to say 'I see red' or 'I see green.' "But this is a simple doubt about the appellation of a colour, and it can be settled by asking someone what this colour (pointing) is called." But are all such doubts removable by this question (or which comes to the same, by giving a definition: "I shall call this colour so-and-so")?

"What colour do you see?"—"I don't know, is it red or isn't it red; I don't know what colour it is I see."—"What do you mean? Is the colour constantly changing, or do you see it so very faintly, practically black?" Could I say here: "don't you see what you see?"? This obviously would make no sense.

Colour: black and white /red and blue/ chequered.

"What colour do you call: a, e, i, o, or u?"—"I don't know what colour I see?"

"Primary colours are those used in flags."

It is queer that one never uses brown on a flag and says it is a blend of yellow, black, and red although nobody can really produce a proper brown by mixing these colours.

Is there a *reason* for not admitting brown as a primary colour?
Is it not enough that we refuse to group it with red, blue, green, etc?

One sometimes thinks the reason is that we see transitions from brown to pure yellow, red, black; but we do in the case of red etc.

Imagine all objects around us were iridescent, I mean of the appearance of a white paper on which the sun is shining, you would see the surface covered with tiny specks of red, blue, green, yellow.

Shall we say that a pointillist sees the objects as he paints them?

It seems as though, however the outward circ[umstance]s change, once the word is fastened to a particular personal experience it now retains its meaning; and that therefore I can now use it with sense whatever may happen.

To say that I can't doubt whether I see red is in a sense absurd, as the game I play with the expression 'I see red' doesn't contain a doubt of this form.

It seems, whatever the circumstances I always know now whether to apply the word or not. It seems, at first it was a move in a special game but then it becomes independent of this game.

(This reminds one of the way the idea of length seems to become emancipated from any particular method of measuring it.)[80]

80. Wittgenstein marked this paragraph and the preceding three as unsatisfactory and wrote "vague" in the margin.

⟦306⟧ We are tempted to say: "damn it all, a rod has a particular length however I express it." And one could go on to say that if I see a rod I always see (know) how long it is, although I can't say how many feet, meters, etc.—But suppose I just say: I always know whether it looks tiny or big!

But can't the old game lose its point when the circ[umstance]s change, so that the expression ceases to have a meaning, although of course I can still pronounce it.

He sticks to saying that he has been lying although none of the usual consequences follow. What is there left of the lang[uage] game, except that he says the expression?

We learn the word 'red' under part[icular] circ[umstance]s. Certain objects are usually red, and keep their colours; most people agree with us in our colour judgments. Suppose all this changes: I see blood, unaccountably sometimes one sometimes another colour, and the people around me all make different statements. But couldn't I in all this chaos retain my meaning of 'red,' 'blue,' etc., although I couldn't now make myself understood to anyone? Samples, e.g., would all constantly change their colour—'or does it only seem so to me?' "Now am I mad or have I really called this 'red' yesterday?"

The situations in which we are inclined to say "I must have gone mad!"

"But we could always call a colour-impression 'red' and stick to this appellation!"

The atmosphere surrounding this problem is terrible. Dense mists of language are situated around the problematic point. It is almost impossible to get through to it.[81]

Suppose I had before me drawings of what I and other people now see and I said of the drawing of what I see "there is something unique about this picture."

81. Die Atmosphäre, die dieses Problem umgibt, ist schrecklich. Dichte Nebel der Sprache sind um den problematischen Punkt gelagert. Es ist beinahe unmöglich, zu ihm vorzudringen.

If *I* can speak about 'what is seen', why shouldn't anyone else speak about it? —But I have a feeling that only I can; and if I assume that others also speak about what normally I should call my visual image there seems to me to be something wrong with this assumption.

If 'what I see' has nothing to do with a particular person, why should I feel that there's something wrong in assuming that anybody might talk about it? i.e. *mean it* when he speaks? Then of course I can't tell them what I see nor they me what they see, any more than I can tell myself what I see.

But they could make conjectures as to what might happen in future, in our visual field.

In the normal game I say: "I don't know what *they* see, they've got to say what they see",—but in the game I'm considering they could as much know what I see as my hand can write down what my mouth can say.

And their different conjectures would be like conjectures made by myself at different times.

Can my mouth tell my hand what I see in order that my hand should be able to write it down?

Do I by painting what I see tell myself what I see?

"This picture is unique, for it represents what is really seen." What justification do I have to say this? //What is my *justification* for saying this?//

⟦307⟧ I see two spots on this wall and lift two fingers. Do I tell myself that I see two spots? But on the other hand couldn't this be the sign for my seeing two spots?!

Is it a special picture or do I give it special attention?[82]

"Today he points to *me*; and yesterday he pointed to *me* also."

The meaning of: "He points at me."

"I see that he points at *A*."
"I see that he points at me."

82. Ist das Bild ausgezeichnet, oder zeichne ich es aus?

You seem to be able to give yourself a sort of ostensive explanation of what the expression 'what is seen' refers to.

Imagine a game: One person tells the other what he (the other) sees; if he has guessed it rightly he is rewarded. If *A* hasn't guessed correctly what *B* sees, *B* corrects him and says what it is he sees. This game is more instructive if we imagine the persons not to say what is seen but to paint it or to make models of it.—Now let me imagine that I am one of the players.

Wouldn't I be tempted to say: "The game is asymmetrical, for only what I say I see corresponds to a visual image."

The problem lies thus: This ↗) is what's seen; and this is also what I see.

Ask yourself: Can only *I* see this ↗), or can someone else see it too? Why only I?[83]

There is no difference, for me, between *I* and *this* ↗; and for me the word "I" is not a signal calling attention to a place or a person.[84]

I am trying to bring the whole problem down to our not understanding the function of the word "I" (and "this ↗").[85]

⟦308⟧ When I stare at a coloured object and say "this is red," I seem to know exactly to what I give the name red. As it were, to that which I am drinking in.

It is as though there was a magic power in the words "*this is*. . . ."

I can bring myself to say: There is no toothache there ↗ (in the man's cheek who says he has toothache). And what would be the

83. Frage Dich: Kann das ↗) nur *ich* sehen, oder kann es auch ein Andrer sehen? Warum nur ich?

84. Für mich existiert kein Unterschied zwischen *ich* und *das* ↗; und das Wort „ich" ist für mich kein Signal, das einen Ort oder eine Person hervorhebt.

85. Ich versuche das ganze Problem auf das nicht-Verstehen der Funktion des Wortes „Ich" (und „das ↗") zu reduzieren.

expression for this in ordinary language? Wouldn't it be *my* saying that *I* have no toothache there?

"But who says this?"—"I!" And who says *this?*—"I!"—

Suppose I give this rule: "Whenever I said 'I have t[oothache]' I shall from now on say 'there is t[oothache].' "

I tell the waiter: Bring me always clear soup, and thick soup to all the others. He tries to remember my face.

Suppose I change my face (body) every day entirely, how is he to know which is me? But it's a question of the *existence* of the game. "If all chessmen were alike, how should one know which is the king?"

Now it seems that, although *he* couldn't know which is me, *I* still would know it.

Suppose now I said: "it wasn't so-and-so, it was I who asked for clear soup"—couldn't I be wrong? Certainly. I.e., I may think that I *asked* him, but didn't. Now are there *two* mistakes I can make: one, thinking that I *asked* him, the other, thinking that *I* asked him? I say: "I remember having asked you yesterday," he replies: "You weren't there at all yesterday." Now I could say either: "well then I suppose I remember wrongly," or: "I was here only I looked like him yesterday."

It seems that I can *trace* my identity, quite independent of the identity of my body. And the idea is suggested that I trace the identity of something dwelling in a body, the identity of my mind.

"If anybody asks me to describe *what I see,* I describe *what's seen.*"

What we call a description of my sense datum, of what's seen, independent of what is the case in the physical world, is still a description for the other person.

⟦309⟧ If I speak of a description of *my* sense datum, I don't *mean* to give a particular person as its possessor.

(No more do I want to speak about a particular person when I moan with pain.)

It must be a serious and deep-seated disease of language (one might also say 'of thought') which makes me say: "Of course this ↗) is what's really seen."

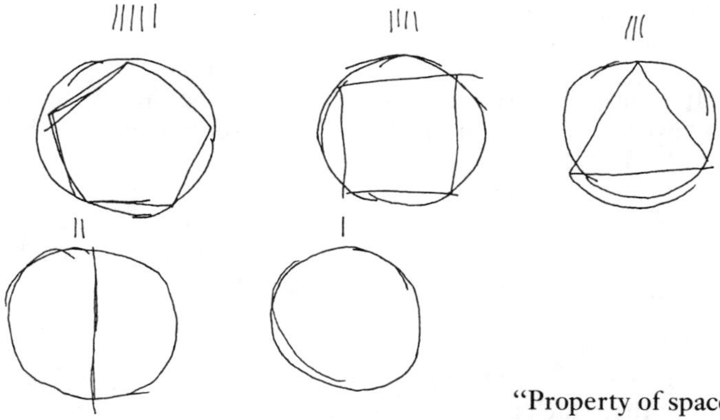

"Property of space"

I can tell you the fact *p* because I know that *p* is the case. It has sense to say "it rained and I knew it," but not "I had toothache and knew that I had." "I know that I have toothache" means nothing, or the same as "I have toothache."

This, however, is a remark about the use of the word "I," whoever uses it.

$(q)\ p \supset \sim q$
$(y)\ f(a) \supset \sim f(y)$

Examine the sentence: "There is something there," referring to the visual sensation I'm now having.

Aren't we inclined to think that this is a statement making sense and being true? And on the other hand, isn't it a pseudo-statement?

But what (what entity) do you mean (refer to) when you say that sentence?—Aren't we here up against the old difficulty, that it seems to us that meaning something was a special state or activity of mind? For it is true that in saying these words I am in a special state of mind, I stare at something,—but this just doesn't constitute meaning.

Compare with this such a statement as: "Of course I know what I am referring to by the word 'toothache.'"

Think of the frame of mind in which you say to yourself that $p \cdot \sim p$ does make sense and by repeating a statement of this form you are, as it were by introspection, trying to find out what it means.

The phenomenon of *staring* is closely bound up with the whole puzzle of solipsism.

"If I am asked 'what do you see?,' I describe the visual world."—Couldn't I say instead of this ". . . I am describing what is there ↗" (pointing before me)?

⟦310⟧ But now consider the case of someone having a picture before him of the part of his room he is seeing, and he says: "This in the picture is like *this* (a part of his visual field as he is looking at his room)."

Thus one can, for example, compare parts of the afterimage with parts of that which is seen with open eyes.[86]

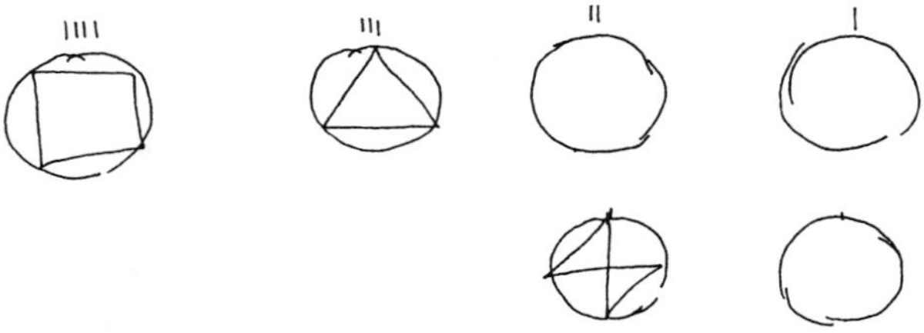

It would be a genuine mathematical problem: 'Construct the 2-gon.' And a mathematician might solve the problem i.e. devise a construction which on such and such grounds we could hardly help calling 'construction of the 2-gon.'

We may *or we may not* feel a discomfort about it.[87]

Supposing I said "there is something there"; and being asked, "What do you mean?," I painted a picture of what I see. Would this justify saying that statement?—Wouldn't this picture have to be understood 'in a system'? And mustn't *I* understand it as an expression within a system?

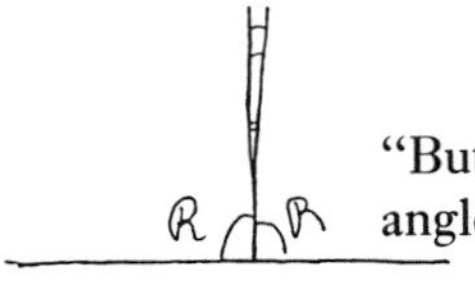


"But then, how are we to account for the angle $\alpha$? Are we to say that $R + \alpha = R$?"

86. So kann man z.B. Teile des Nachbildes mit Teilen des mit offenen Augen Gesehenen vergleichen.

87. There is an arrow from this sentence, pointing to the circle with a square inside it.

'Look at the geometrical proposition as a member of the whole system of geometrical prop[ositions], then you shall see whether you really want to accept this proposition!'

$$p . \sim\sim p = p = \sim\sim p$$

"It's no use saying that the other person knows what he sees and not what I see and that therefore all is symmetrical, because there is just nothing else corresponding to my visual image, my visual image is unique!"[88]

A geometry in which two straight lines which form an angle start out by running together for a while; to be compared with a [device] in which a body on which no force is acting moves with slowly decreasing velocity.[89]

"Obviously this ↗) is what's seen!"

If one says to the solipsist John Smith "So you say that of all people only John Smith really sees?" he doesn't really recognise this to be his view. He didn't mean that if you regard him as one person out of many he had any special privilege.—He would be inclined to say: "Not John Smith has any particular privilege (it would be ridiculous to say this), but *I* have, as seen by myself."

Couldn't one assume that all those persons had a right to talk about what's seen who were being seen. I.e. all those who were [in] a picture could talk about the picture.

"But I can persuade myself that nobody else has pains even if they say they have, but not that I haven't."

*It makes no sense* to say "I persuade myself that I have no pain," *whoever* says this. I don't say anything about myself when I say that I can't persuade myself that I haven't pain, etc.

88. In the margin: "*sehr wichtig, wenn auch schlecht gesagt.*" (Very important, although badly expressed).

89. Geometrie, in welcher zwei Geraden, die einen Winkel bilden, erst ein Stück mit einander laufen; zu vergleichen einer [Klecbank], in der ein Körper, auf den keine Kräfte wirken, sich mit langsam abnehmender Geschwindigkeit bewegt.

"Can't I use the word 'to see' in such a way that I call only this → 'seen'?" But how do I act according to this decision? Do I e.g., admit that someone else besides me can see it, or do I say that only I can see it?

Suppose everybody talked only about what we should now describe as "what's seen by me, LW". But they all know what I see; they don't ask me. And if anybody describes it wrongly we say that he doesn't speak properly, expresses himself wrongly. There is no such thing as deceiving someone about what I see.—Can't I even then imagine a temptation to say "I can only know what *I* see, not what the others see"?

If I say "*I* see this ↗" I am liable to tap my chest to show which person I am. Now suppose I had no head and pointing to my geometrical eye I would point to an empty place above my neck, wouldn't I still feel that I pointed to the person who sees, tapping my chest? Now I might ask "how do I know in this case who sees this?" But what is *this?* It's no use just pointing ahead of me, and if, instead, I point to a description and tap both my chest and the description and say '*I see this*'—it has no sense to ask "How do you know that it's *you* who sees it?," for I don't *know* that it's this person and not another one which sees before I point, but one could, in certain cases, say I know *because* I point.—This is ⟦311⟧ what I meant by saying that I don't choose the mouth which says "I have toothache."

The, if I may so put it, pathological character of solipsism shows itself if we try to draw the consequence that only I, *N.N.*, really see, since we immediately shrink back from this consequence. We immediately see that we didn't want to say that at all.[90]

Isn't it queer that if I look in front of me and point in front of me and say "this!," I should know what it is I mean. "I mean just these shades of colour and shapes, the *appearance.*"

(A scientist says that he only pursues empirical science/or a mathematician, only mathematics/and not philosophy—but he is subjected

90. Der, wenn ich so sagen darf, krankhafte Charakter des Solipsismus zeigt sich, wenn wir die Konsequenz zu ziehen versuchen, daß nur ich *N.N.* wirklich sehe, da wir vor dieser Konsequenz sofort zurückschrecken. Wir sehen sofort, daß wir das gar nicht sagen wollten.

to the temptations of language like everyone else, he is in the same danger and must be on guard against it.)[91]

If I say "I mean the appearance," it seems I am telling you what it is I am pointing to or looking at, e.g., the chair as opposed to the bed, etc. It is as though by the word "appearance" I had actually *directed your attention* to something else than, e.g., the physical objects you are looking at. And indeed there corresponds a particular stare to this 'taking in the appearance.' Remember here what philosophers of a certain school used to say so often: "*I believe* I mean something, if I say '. . . .'"

It seems that the visual image which I'm having is something which I can point to and talk about; that I can say of it, it is unique. That I am pointing to the physical objects in my field of vision, but not meaning them but the *appearance.* This object I am talking about, if not to others then to myself. (It is almost like something painted on a screen which surrounds me.)

This object is inadequately described as "that which I see," "my visual image," since it has nothing to do with any particular human being. Rather I should like to call it "what's seen." And so far it is all right, only now I've got to say what can be said about this object, in what sort of language game "what's seen" is to be used. For at first sight I should feel inclined to use this expression as one uses a word designating a physical object, and only on second thought I see /it appears/ that I can't do that.—When I said that here [there] seems to be an object I can point to and talk about, it was just that I was comparing it to a physical object. For only on second thought it appears that the idea of "talking about" isn't applicable here. (I could have compared the 'object' to a theatre decoration.)

Now when could I be said to speak about this object? When would I say I did speak about it?—*Obviously* when I describe—as we should say—my visual image. And perhaps only if *I* describe it, and only if I describe it to myself.

⟦312⟧ But what is the point, in this case, of saying that when I

91. (Ein Wissenschaftler sagt, er betreibe nur empirische Wissenschaft /oder ein Mathematiker nur Mathematik/ und nicht Philosophie,—aber er ist den Versuchungen der Sprache unterworfen wie Jeder, er ist in der gleichen Gefahr und muß sich vor ihr in Acht nehmen.)

describe to myself what I see, I describe a (peculiar) /an/ object called "what is seen"? Why talk of a particular object here? Isn't this due to a misunderstanding?

Imagine a game played on a kind of chessboard. You can teach the game to 64, 81, 100, etc. squares, and the situation which is losing in the 64-game is winning in the 81-game, losing in the 100-game, winning in the 121-game etc. . . .

If you are asked "What did 'meaning what he said' consist in" you will describe facts which, supplemented by certain other facts, would be characteristic of his *not* meaning what he said,—and so on.

"Can I imagine $10^{10^{10^{10}}} = \mu$ soldiers in a row?"
"Can I imagine an endless row of soldiers?"
Why shouldn't I say, I can imagine an endless row of soldiers? The image is something like a row the end of which I can't see and a gesture and the words "on and on for ever—" said in a particular tone of voice. And suppose I said: $\mu$ soldiers would reach from here halfway to the sun if we placed them a yard apart! Isn't this too 'imagining the row'?

It is a very remarkable and most important fact that there are numbers which all of us should call "large numbers".

There is a particular way of explaining the sense (meaning) of an expression which we may call . . .

In philosophy we often say that people wrongly imagine a certain state of affairs, e.g. "they imagine that a law of nature in some way compels things to happen" or "they imagine that it's a question of psychology how a person can know a certain fact, whereas it is one of grammar" etc. etc. But it is necessary in these cases to explain what it means "to imagine so too", what kind of image is it they are using. It often sounds as though they were able to imagine the logically impossible and it is not easy to straighten out our description of the case and to say what in this case they actually imagine.

E.g.: People treat the question "how do we know that so-and-so is the case" as a question of psychology, which has nothing to do with the sense of the prop[osition] which we say is known. But first: where do they take this idea from, how do they come by it? Which really psychological question are they thinking of?

Obviously, there is a case in which the question "How does he find this out?" is a personal and, perhaps, psychological one. "How did he find out that N was in his room?"—He saw him through the window or he was hidden under the bed.—"How did he find out that the glass was cracked?" He saw the crack with his naked eye or he saw it through the magnifying glass, etc. We say he finds out the same thing in different ways and not that what he finds depends upon how he finds it.

When do we say that he finds out the same thing in two ways? Imagine language games: Somebody is asked a question —"A?"— and trained to answer "yes" if he sees a person, A, in the next room, "no" if he doesn't. He is trained to answer the question "A?" by "yes" also if he hears A's voice from the next room. "What right have we to ask the same question in these two cases?" or "What right has he to use these two different tests to answer the same question?" Or suppose someone asked: "Now is this really one and the same question or do we have two different questions, only expressed in the same words?"

Now consider the ostensive definition: "This man is called 'A'" and ask yourself whether this definition tells us if we are to regard seeing A from a different side or in a different position or hearing his voice as criteria of his being there?—Here we are tempted to say: "But surely I just point to this man, so there can't be any doubt what object I am meaning!" But that's wrong though the doubt of course is not whether I mean this ↗ or that → thing.

One may say that the 'object' I am inclined to say I am pointing to in the ostensive definition is not determined by the act of pointing but by the use I make of the word defined. And here one must beware of thinking that after all the pointing finger pointed to a different object in the sense in which the arrow ———> $\overset{A}{\bullet}\ \overset{B}{\bullet}$ may be said to point to A or to B, so that by a different way of pointing I might have distinguished the cases.

"But we conceive of objects, things, different from our sense data, e.g. the table as opposed to the view we get of it." But what does conceiving of this object consist in? Is it a peculiar 'mental act' occurring whenever, say, we talk about the table? Isn't it using the word 'table' in the game we do use it [in]? using it as we do use it?

We are tempted to say that the word "toothache" is the 'name of a feeling of which I don't know whether anybody except me ever has it'. But even I can be said not to *know* whether I always mean the same by this word.

"I always thought that holding one's cheek was having toothache; then he knocked out a tooth of mine, then I knew what 'toothache' meant." Well, what does it mean?—And what was it like "to know what 'toothache' means"?

"Now I know what 'pain' means".

A faked moan of pain isn't necessarily a moan without something and a real moan of pain a moan with something.

But we would like to say "the surrounding circumstances are different". But there is something incorrect in that.[92]

You say, in this case the expression corresponds to the experience. But how does it correspond?

Imagine, you were wrong about the correspondence, then what would remain? That you said these words and that you did not cheat, but now cheating and not cheating are not 'private experiences'? It's no good saying "I recognise this experience as . . ." as I don't know whether I recognise the experience of recognising rightly.

We are using the word "to cheat" in two different ways. In one way, whether I do it can be verified by the other person, in the other sense we say "only I know whether I cheat".

"I knew all the time that I had cheated".

Quite true, we distinguish simple acting and acting prompted by feeling, and feeling with expression. These are distinctions in our language. "But are you saying that all these distinctions are distinctions in mere behaviour?"—

Can one by multiplying 2 with itself obtain 12?

"*Mere behaviour.*" "There is only behaviour" would seem to say that there was no life, that we (or I) acted as automatons, as unconscious machines.

I wish to say: "The difference between me and a machine doesn't

92. Aber wir möchten sagen „Die Begleitumstände sind andere". Aber daran ist etwas Unrichtiges.

just consist in the difference of our actions but in this, that I am conscious and the machine isn't".

But oughtn't I say that this only distinguishes a machine from *me*, not from a human being? For why shouldn't I say that the difference between a human being, animal, sewing machine, etc., lies in their actions, if I except myself. But then I don't even except my body.

"I know consciousness only from myself, I don't *know* whether anybody else has consciousness, but it makes *sense* to assume it, and I do make the assumption in a class of cases."

What worries me is the idea of 'behaviour + experience.'—We might think that it was possible to talk of behaviour without there being experience. 'Could I talk about moaning if there was no such thing as hearing the moaning?' Or: Isn't talking of behaviour[93] talking of experience and *therefore* what we call "talking of private experience" a special case of "talking about 'behaviour' "?

One might put it by saying: "Experience is at the bottom of everything we say about phenomena; so if we call anything in particular talking about direct experience it must be just a special case of talking about phenomena in the *ordinary* way."

If we say "toothache is nothing but behaviour" we seem to say that it is not so-and-so, we seem to wish to exclude something. But that's obviously what we mustn't do.

Our job is obviously not to reduce anything to anything, but *only* to avoid certain misleading ways of expression.

"Toothache is not a behaviour but an experience". "We distinguish between 'behaviour' and 'experiences'". Dancing is a behaviour, toothache an experience." These are grammatical statements. About the use of the words "dancing" and "toothache".

("This form of words seems to mean something but means nothing." That is: We connect a certain image with this expression or we are inclined to use it because it sounds analogous to other expressions and we connect a certain attitude, state of mind etc. with it; but

93. At this point in the manuscript, the discussion jumps over a little over eight pages of notes on the philosophy of mathematics and then resumes in mid-sentence.

if we then ask ourselves how we are going to use it we find that we have no use for it or a use of a totally different kind from that which we at first vaguely imagined (expected).)

First of all it seems that we are partial for 'behaviour,' that we wish to explain everything in terms of *it. Now why should we be biased in this way?* Is it because of some kind of materialism? What axe have we to grind?

There is an ordinary (and unproblematic) way of using such a word as "toothache," but we are inclined on philosophizing about it to give it a different use, finding out, however, that we can then do away with it entirely, because that proposed use as a matter of fact makes it into a useless symbol.

"We use the expression 'x has toothache' when we perceive a certain behaviour in others, or, on the other hand, when we ourselves have toothache." What does it mean: "I say 'I have toothache' when I feel toothache"? What does this explain? It could, of course, be an explanation in several ways: I say to someone: "Now, if I have stomach ache I'll always say 'I have toothache' in order to make Smith believe so-and-so," "I won't lie again, I will only say 'I have t[oothache]' when I really have it," or I say "I say 'I have t[oothache],' when I feel a pain here (pointing)".

I wish to say that we can't adduce the 'private experience' as a justification for expressing it.

We can't say "he is justified in moaning because he has pains" if we call pain *the* justification for moaning.—We can't say "he is justified in expressing pain, because he has pain" unless we wish to distinguish this case of being justified in expressing pain from another way of justification, e.g., that he is on the stage and has to act [as] a sick man.

If I am tempted to say "my justification for moaning is having pain," it seems I point—at least for myself—to something to which I give expression by moaning.

The idea is here that there is an 'expression' for everything, that we know what it means 'to express something,' 'to describe something.'

Here is a feeling, an experience, and now I could say to someone "express it!" But what is to be the relation of the expression to what it expresses? In what way is this expression the expression of this feeling rather than another?! One is inclined to say "we *mean* this feeling by its expression," but what is meaning a feeling by a word like? Is this quite clear if, e.g., I have explained what "meaning this person by the name '*N*'" is like?

"We have two expressions, one for moaning without pain, and one for moaning with pain." To what states of affairs am I pointing as explanations of these two expressions?

"But these 'expressions' can't be mere words, noises, which you make; they get their importance only from what's *behind* them (the state you're in when you use them)!"—But how can this state give importance to noises which I produce?

Suppose I said: The expressions get their importance from the fact that they are not used coolly but that we can't help using them. This is as though I said: laughter gets its importance only through being a *natural* expression, a natural phenomenon, not an artificial code.

⟦313⟧ Now what makes a 'natural form of expression' natural? Should we say "An experience which stands behind it"?

If I use the expression "I have toothache" I may think of it as 'being used naturally' or otherwise, but it would be wrong to say that I had a *reason* for thinking either.—It is very queer that *all* the importance of our expressions seems to come from that *X, Y, Z,* the private experiences, which forever remain in the *background* and can't be drawn into the foreground.

But is a cry when it is a cry of pain not a mere cry?

Can one say: "If I teach the child the use (meaning) of the word 'toothache' I can only hope that it really feels toothache, (or, that it feels real toothache) for if it doesn't then I've taught him a wrong meaning"?

Why should I say that the 'expression' derives its meaning from the feeling behind it—and not from the circumstances of the lang[uage] game in which it is used? For imagine a person crying out with pain alone in the desert: is he using a language? Should we say that his cry had *meaning*?

We labour under the queer temptation to describe our language and its use, introducing into our descriptions an element of which we ourselves say that it is not part of the language. It is a peculiar phenomenon of iridescence which seems to fool us.

"But can't you imagine people behaving just as we do, showing pain etc., etc., and then if you imagine that *they don't feel pain* all their behaviour is, as it were, dead. You can imagine all this behaviour *with* or *without* pain.—"

The pain seems to be the atmosphere in which the expression exists. (The pain seems to be a *circumstance.*)

Suppose we say that the image I use in the one case is different from that which I use in the other. But I can't point to the two images. So what does it come to, to say this, except just to saying it, using *this* expression.

We are, as I have said, tempted to describe our language by saying that we use certain elements, images, which however in the last moment we again withdraw.

Isn't the expression *in its use* an image,—why do I refer back to an image which I can't show?

⟦314⟧ "But don't you talk as though (the) pain wasn't something terribly real?"—Am I to understand this as a prop[osition] about pain? I suppose it is a prop[osition] about the use of the word 'pain,' and it is one more utterance, and essential part of the surrounding in which we use the word 'pain.'

Feeling justified in having expressed pain.

I may *concentrate on the memory of pain.*

Now what's the difference between using my expressions as I do but yet not using "toothache" to mean real pain, and the proper use of the word?—

The private experience is to serve as a paradigm, and at the same time admittedly it can't be a paradigm.

The 'private experience' is a degenerate construction of our grammar (comparable in a sense to tautology and contradiction). And this grammatical monster now fools us; when we wish to do away with it, it seems as though we denied the existence of an experience, say, toothache.

What would it mean to deny the existence of pain?!

"But when we say we have toothache we don't just talk of expressing toothache in this or that way!"—Certainly not,—we express toothache!—"But you admit that the same behaviour may be the expression of pain or may not be that."—If you imagine a man cheating—cheating is done secretly but this secrecy is not that of the 'private experience.' Why shouldn't it be considered wrong in him to use language in this way?

We say "only he knows whether he says the truth or lies." "Only you can know if what you say is true."

Now compare secrecy with the 'privateness' of personal experience! In what sense is a thought of mine secret? If I think aloud it can be heard.—"I have said this to myself a thousand times but not to anyone else."

"Only you can know what colour you see." But if it is true that only you can know, you can't even impart this knowledge nor can you express it.

⟦315⟧ Why shouldn't we say that I know better than you what colour you see if you say the wrong word and I can make you agree to my word, or if you point to the wrong sample, etc.?

"I didn't know that I was lying."—"You *must* have known!"

Examine: "If you don't know that you're having toothache, you don't have toothache."

"I don't just *say* 'I've got toothache,' but *toothache makes me say this.*" (I deliberately didn't write 'the feeling of toothache,' or 'a certain feeling.')

This sentence distinguishes between, say, saying it as an example of a sentence, or on the stage, etc., and saying it as an assertion. But it is no explanation of the expression "I have toothache," of the use of the word "toothache."

"I know what the word 'toothache' means, it makes me concentrate my attention on one particular thing." But on what? You're now inclined to give criteria of behaviour. Ask yourself: "what does the word 'feeling,' or still better 'experience,' make you concentrate on?" What is it like to concentrate on experience? If *I* try to do this I, e.g., open my eyes particularly wide and stare.

"I know what the word 'toothache' means, it produces one particular image in my mind." But *what* image? "That can't be explained."—But if it can't be explained what was the meaning of saying that it produced one particular image? You could say the same about the words "image in your mind." And all that it comes to is that you are using certain words without an explanation. "But can't I explain them to myself? or understand them myself without giving an explanation? Can't I give a private explanation?" But is this anything you can call an explanation? Is staring a private explanation?

But how does this queer delusion come about?!

Here is language,—and now I try to embody something in language as an explanation, which is no explanation.

We decide to say that the triangle *a* has half the area of the rectangle

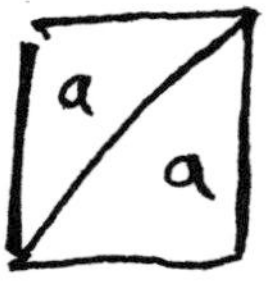


Can't you imagine that the question 'how big is the area of the triangle 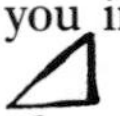 ?' should make no sense to you at all as you only talked of areas of rectangles. One might be inclined to say, that the triangle had not *really* one particular area; perhaps that there was a series of areas which could be said to approach filling the triangle.

⟦316⟧ Privacy of sense data. I must bore you by a repetition of what I said last time. We said that one reason for introducing the idea of the sense datum was that people, as we say, sometimes see different things, colours, e.g., looking at the same object. Cases in which we say "he sees dark red whereas I see light red." We then are inclined to talk about an object other than the physical object which the person sees who is said to see the phys[ical] obj[ect]. It is further clear that we only gather from the other person's behaviour (e.g., what he tells us) what that obj[ect] looks like, and so it lies near to say that he has this object before his mind's eye and that we don't see it. Though we can also say that we might have it before our mind['s] eye as well, without however knowing that he has it before his mind's eye. The 'sense datum' here—the way the physical object appears to him. In other cases no phys[ical] object enters.

Now I must draw your attention to one particular difficulty about the use of the 'sense datum.' We said that there were cases in which we should say that the person sees green what I see red. Now the question suggests itself: if this can be so at all, why should it [not] be always the case? It seems, if once we have admitted that it can happen under peculiar circumstances, that it may always happen. But then it is clear that the very idea of seeing red loses its use if we can never know if the other does not see something utterly different. So what are we to do: Are we to say that this can only happen in a limited number of cases? This is a very serious situation.—We introduced the expression that *A* sees something else than *B* and we mustn't forget that this had only use under the circumstances under which we introduced it. Consider the prop[osition]: "Of course we never know whether new circ[umstance]s wouldn't show that after all he saw what we see." Remember that this whole notion need not have been introduced. "But can't I *imagine* all blind men to see as well as I do and only behaving differently; and on the other hand imagine them really blind? For if I can imagine these possibilities, then the question, even if never answerable makes sense." Imagine a man, say W., now blind, now seeing, and observe what you do? How do these images give sense to the question? They don't, and you see that the expression stands and falls with its usefulness.

The idea that the other person sees something else than I, ⟦317⟧ is only introduced to account for certain expressions: whereas it seems that this idea can exist without any reference to expressions. "Surely what I have he too can have."

"And remember that we admit that the other may have pain without showing it! So if this is conceivable, why not that he never shows that he has pain; and why not that everybody has pain constantly without showing it; or that even things have pain?!" What strikes us is that there seem to be a few useful applications of the idea of the other person's having pain without showing it, and a vast number of useless applications, applications which look as though they were no applications at all. And these latter applications seem to have their justification in this, that we can imagine the other person to have what we have and in this way the prop[osition] that he has toothache seems to make sense apart from any expression at all. "Surely," we say, "I can imagine him to have pain or to see, etc." Or, "As I can see myself, so I can imagine him to do the same." In other words I can imagine him to play the same role in the act of seeing which I play. But does saying this determine what I mean by "he sees"?

We arrive at the conclusion that imagining him to have pain (etc.) does not fix the sense of the sentence "he has pain."

"He may all along mean something different by 'green' than I mean." Evidence (verification). But there is this consideration: "Surely I mean something particular, a particular impression, and therefore he may have another impression; surely I know what that would be like!" "Surely I know what it is like to have the impression I call 'green'!" But what is it like? You are inclined to look at a green object and to say "it's like *this!*" And these words, though they don't explain anything to anybody else, seem to be at any rate an explanation you give yourself. But are they?! Will this explanation justify your future use of the word 'green'? In fact seeing green doesn't allow you to make the substitutions of someone else for you and of red for green.

"The sense datum is private" is a rule of grammar, it forbids use [of] such expressions as "they saw the same sense datum"; it may (or may not) allow such sentences as "he guessed that the other had a sense datum of this . . . kind." It may only allow expressions of the form: "The other looked round, ⟦318⟧ had a sense datum and said. . . ." You see that this word in such a case has no use at all. But if you like to use it, do!—

"But surely I distinguish between having toothache and expressing it, and merely expressing it; and I distinguish between these two in myself." "Surely this is not merely a matter of using different expressions, but there are two distinct experiences!" "You talk as though the case of having pain and that of not having pain were only distinguished by the way in which I expressed myself!"

But do we always distinguish between 'mere behaviour' and 'experience + behaviour'? If we see someone falling into flames and crying out, do we say to ourselves: "there are of course two cases: . . ."? Or if I see you here before me do I distinguish? Do you? You can't! That we do in certain cases, doesn't show that we do in all cases. This to some of you must sound silly and superficial; but it isn't. When you see me do you see one thing and conjecture another? (Don't talk of conjecturing subconsciously!) But supposing you expressed yourself in the form of such a supposition, wouldn't this come to adopting a '*façon de parler*'?

Can we say that 'saying that I lie is justified by a particular experience of lying'? Shall we say '. . . by a particular priv[ate] experience'? or '. . . by a part[icular] priv[ate] exp[erience] of lying'? or 'by a part[icular] priv[ate] exp[erience] characterized in such and such ways'?

"But what, in your opinion, *is* the difference between the mere expression and the expression + the experience?"

"Do you know what it means that W. behaves as he does but sees nothing; and on the other hand that he sees?"

If you ask yourself this and answer 'yes' you conjure up some sort of image. This image is, it seems, derived from the fact of your seeing or not seeing (if you close your eyes), and by this derivation, it seems, it must be the picture we interpret to correspond to our sentence "he sees," "he doesn't see."—As when I substitute for my body, his body, and for holding a match, holding a pen.—But substituting his body for my body might mean that my body has changed so as to be now like his, and perhaps vice ⟦319⟧ versa. It seems a direct and simple thing to understand "thinking that he has what I have," but it isn't at all. The case is simple only if we speak, e.g., of physiological processes. "I know only indirectly what he sees, but directly what I see" embodies an absolutely misleading picture. I can't be said to know that I have toothache if I can't be said not to know that I have toothache. I can't be said to know indirectly what the other has if I can't be said to know it directly. The misleading picture is this: I see my own matchbox but I know only from hearsay what his looks like. We can't say: "I say he has t[oothache] because I observe his behaviour, but I say that I have because I *feel* it." (This might lead one to say that 't[oothache]' has two meanings, one for me and one for the other being.)

"I say 'I have t[oothache]' because I *feel* it" contrasts this case with, say, the case of acting on the stage, but can't explain what 'having t[oothache]' means because having t[oothache] = feeling t[oothache], and the explanation would come to: "I say I have it because I have it" = I say I have it because it is true = I say I have it because I don't lie. One wishes to say: In order to be able to say that I have t[oothache] I don't observe my behaviour, say in the mirror. *And this is correct,* but it doesn't follow that you describe an observation of any other kind. Moaning is not the description of an observation. That is, you can't be said to *derive* your expression from what you observe. Just as you can't be said to derive the word '*green*' from your *visual impression* but only from a sample.—Now against this one is inclined to say: "Surely if I call a colour green I don't just say that word, but the word comes in a particular way," or "if I say 'I have toothache' I don't just use this phrase but it must come in a particular way!" Now this means nothing, for, if you like, it always comes in a particular way. "But surely seeing and saying something *can't be all!*" Here we make the confusion that there is still an object we haven't mentioned. You imagine that there is a *pure* seeing and saying, and one + something else. Therefore you imagine all distinctions to be made as between *a*, *a* + *b*, *a* + *c*, etc. The idea of this addition is mostly derived from consideration of our bodily organs. All that ought to interest you is whether I make all the distinctions that you make: whether, e.g., I don't distinguish between cheating and telling the ⟦320⟧ truth.—"There is something else!"—"There is nothing else!"—"But what else is there?"—"Well, this ↗!"

"But surely I know that I am not a mere automaton!"—What would it be like if I were?—"How is it that I can't imagine myself not seeing, /experiencing/ hearing etc.?"—We constantly confuse and change about the commonsense use and the metaphysical use.

"I know that I see."—

"I see."—you seem to read this off some fact; as though you said: "There is a chair in this corner."

"But if in an experiment, e.g., I say 'I see,' why do I say so? surely because I see!"

It is as though our expressions of personal experience needn't even spring from regularly recurrent inner experiences but just from *something.*

*Confusion of description and samples.*

The idea of the '*realm of consciousness.*'

# 11

*Rush Rhees arrived in Cambridge in September of 1935 to study philosophy as a postgraduate student under G. E. Moore. He soon became one of Wittgenstein's closest friends and loyal students. After leaving Cambridge in 1938 Rhees went on to teach philosophy at University College of Swansea in Wales until his retirement in 1966. Wittgenstein, near the end of his life, designated Rhees along with G. H. von Wright and G. E. M. Anscombe as his literary executors. They were given the right and responsibility to decide, after Wittgenstein's death, what was to be published of his extensive notes and manuscripts, and in what form it was to be published.*

*Rhees's lecture notes cover roughly the second half of Wittgenstein's course of lectures for the academic year 1935–36. The material in these lectures is quite similar to Wittgenstein's own writings published in Chapter 10 of this volume. Wittgenstein's writings were presumably preparatory for these lectures. It was Rhees's hope that his own notes would be read in a study of Wittgenstein's writings and not otherwise.*[1]

*Notes for Wittgenstein's lectures during the whole academic year were also taken by Margaret Macdonald (and, though they remain unpublished, they have been edited by Cora Diamond). We have used Macdonald's notes to indicate dates for the lectures recorded by Rhees. If the order and dating of Macdonald's notes are accurate, Rhees, in his editing of the material, has changed the order of some of it (i.e., lectures VI–VIII should precede lecture I). Lectures I–IX were all given in the Lent term; lectures X–XIX constituted the lectures for Easter term.*[2]

1. See Rhees's "Introductory Note" to the original publication of these lecture notes (*Philosophical Investigations*, vol. 7, 1984, pp. 1–2). In this "Note" Rhees also summarized what Wittgenstein had been discussing in classes before these lecture notes commence.

2. What Rhees has indicated as a separate lecture III was, according to Macdonald's notes, simply part of the March 3rd lecture. Rhees's notes for lecture XIII do not correspond to anything in Macdonald's notes—presumably she was absent that day. We have conjectured the date based on the Monday–Wednesday schedule Wittgenstein seemed to be keeping.

# The Language of Sense Data and Private Experience

*(Notes taken by* Rush Rhees *of Wittgenstein's Lectures, 1936)*

## I

[February 26, 1936]

I want to talk about the idea of the *privacy* of sense data.

The suggestion arises from the fact that I and another man may look at something and I may say "he sees it a different colour from what I do". I might do this in the case where one of us has put on coloured glasses. Or suppose I teach a person colour names in a certain light. He is then able to bring me red objects in the room when asked. Suppose then I bring him into the light of day, and he calls rose petals green and grass red, and so on. If then we bring ⟦3⟧ him back into the artificial light and he behaves as before, then we might say "He sees red where we see green".

Here the *criteria* for my saying "He sees green where I see red" are very complicated, although the *meaning* is very simple.

Take the instance of a man whom we call blind. On the other hand we might say he still sees something: it might be that when he is cured he says "When before someone knocked me, I saw what I now call lights". Then did he not see?—Couldn't we then say "Perhaps he saw every sort of thing we see, but behaves differently"? Could we not say this of any man whom we call blind? Then we would seem to have no idea whether the man sees or not: we know only what he behaves like.

But then we would distinguish cases where we can't know but can make a conjecture, and other cases where we can't even make a conjecture.—Take the first case: What would we call grounds for a conjecture? Suppose we said "He behaves like all of us, therefore he probably sees". Then we should have to say in our case also "we probably see". "He behaves like me, therefore he probably sees."

Whether a statement is a conjecture or not seems to be determined
1) by the tone of voice in which it is said,
2) by the use made of the expression.

It is the tone of voice not only in which you say one sentence but also the tone of voice of the surrounding expressions. We associate certain words with this—words like "perhaps" or "probably". I say "Watson probably sees" and this is a conjecture. But whether it *acts* as a conjecture or not is a totally different question. We might *use* the expression otherwise than as a conjecture, rhetorically to state a matter of fact.

If I say "I can never know whether he sees or not"—we might say this is a case of being utterly doubtful.

We have to consider two cases:

a) the case where we say "we never know whether he sees red where we do":—Note that we don't say "perhaps he sees a stomach-ache". We'd say "of course we know whether he understands what we do by '*colour*' ". But why should we? Have we more ground for this than we have for saying he doesn't understand what ⟦4⟧ we mean by "green"?

b) The clearer case is where one of us has put on coloured spectacles and we say that one person doesn't see the same colour as the other person—where he *does* understand what we mean by "green".

There is a difference between
"This is the same colour as this", and
"He sees the same colour as I do".

Can one say: "Either he sees the same or he does not see the same. I may not know it, but there is no alternative: either he sees what I see here or he does not."?

Consider the momentary impression which I have and which I call green. There is a question about the "I *have*". There is an inclination to say "I'll give this impression a name, say the name 'alpha', and I know then what the name 'alpha' means".—Here again we have the problem of what it is like to christen an impression.

Suppose you are giving a person a name. Is there a difference between making a blue dash on his forehead and making a dash which I read as "Watson"? Is simply making the dash the giving of a name? You might answer yes or no according to what is meant. A word which we connect with a thing can have all sorts of different functions. The name of a diamond, Koh-i-noor, does not have the same function as the name of a person. I can *call* a person by his name, as I can't with the name of a diamond. To give a person a name I must give a scratch in *connexion* with conventions of its use.

Now if I call a particular *impression* "alpha" it seems as if I had performed an act of christening. But here, whatever might have happened when I gave it does not very much matter. Of course I do have a particular state of mind. I stare at the impression. But I seem only to have stared and uttered the word "alpha". We don't know at all what to do with the word, and consequently it can't be said to have a meaning.

One is inclined to say I can't know whether another person can have this impression. There's a tendency to say also that it makes no *sense* to say another might have this impression.

Supposing I said "Only this chair *can* be green"—this means it has no sense to say of another chair it is green.

⟦5⟧ We say the same colour can be in different places. But someone might say it is really not the *same* colour—though it looks like it. Then he is trying to give to a colour the same kind of identity which we give to a physical object. We have a criterion for what we call the identity of a physical object. We can imagine also someone saying a colour can't travel.

But then why say "This *chair* is green"? why not just "there is green"?

If we say "Green can't be in two places", this would mean we are going to use a word differently from the way in which we use it now. And then we can't go on to say "This chair is green" and use "green" as we do now use it.

Thus (to the question about "I *have*") if I have an impression which I call "alpha", then I can't say "I see alpha" without being redundant.

The proposition that "Only I can see" or "Only I can have this sense datum" is not a statement of a fact of experience, an empirical generalization. It means: to say that he and I have the same sense datum is senseless. *Therefore* I can't use the expression that I *have* it.

Suppose a language which did not divide shapes and colours as we do: in which a white circle would be an 'alpha', a white square a 'beta'. We might say that such people did not notice a similarity. We are then inclined to say "We separate two things and these people treat them as one".—But do we separate two things? The inclination is to treat a white circle as a *complex* in the sense in which a tricolour is. What complex would it be? Of whiteness and circularity? But why not of two semicircles?

Imagine a picture language in which I wish to convey that someone drew a white circle. I could do two different things: ((Wittgenstein was drawing with white chalk on a blackboard.))

1) 

2) 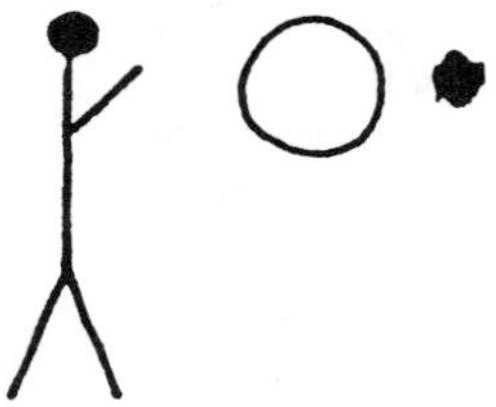

⟦6⟧ We are accustomed to taking things to pieces in the way of (2) here. But we say of this chair it is green and of that chair it is green—and this does not analyse the chair or take it to pieces.

Can another person have my toothache? You could say "Yes of course: same intensity, same throbbing etc." I might object, "That means exactly alike, but not the same". Then you answer, "Aha, by 'my toothache' you mean an identity like that of a physical object". Then if I say he can't have the same toothache, that is now a proposition of grammar.

People say he and I can't have the same pain, because he has his pain and I have my pain. But then we should not talk of "his pain" or "my pain"—or rather of "*having* my pain"; we should say only "There is my toothache".

If asked "What is your sense datum?" I should answer "My sense datum is *this*". The "*this*" is not merely pointing for his benefit. I am taking together myself and what I see—but not in the sense in which "myself" is "Wittgenstein". I am not identifying myself or recognizing myself.

## II [March 3, 1936]

I want to continue with 'the privacy of sense data'. Last time I imagined the case in which we tried to show a man what we meant by "green", and he had really seen it as red and called it green.

We might be inclined to say here that for some time we did not *know* he saw red where we saw green, and then later we found out. Then it seems as though it would be possible we should *never* have found out. And then one may say: If this happened once, why should it not *always* happen: ((so that other people never see the colour that I see, although they use the same word to describe it)).

Again, we say this particular man has pain now without showing it. Why should we not say that perhaps everyone has pain all the while, without showing it?

You might try to get rid of this difficulty by saying: This notion of seeing green where I see red has application only in special cases such as we have described, and can be used only in such a case.— ⟦7⟧ The answer to this is: that at any rate I can *imagine* his seeing green where I see red in other cases as well. Without ever imagining an artificial case, I can easily imagine a case where he sees red while I see green. What is artificial is only the way in which I might *find out* that he saw red when I saw green.

Now the question is: what is meant by "imagining that another man sees a certain colour"? What do you do when you imagine me seeing red? You might do what you would do if you *painted* me with my eyes open and a red object before me.

This has similarities to the primitive language of a savage tribe.

Or you may think of yourself seeing a red object, and then say "he does the same thing". But in a sense this does not make "*him*". To imagine me *looking* at a red object is an easy thing. To imagine me *seeing* red is difficult.

One says, "I can imagine him to have a toothache, for I can imagine that he has what I have." When I have a shilling, I can imagine him to have what I have. So also if I have a black eye. But is it the same sort of transition when we take '*seeing*' or '*toothache*'? "Having" is used in an entirely different sense when we speak of 'having a toothache' and 'having a black eye'.

What is meant by: "I have only to substitute him for myself"?

I can imagine pain in his jaw rather than in mine. But is this the same as imagining his having a toothache? Is it not rather *my* having toothache in his jaw then?

Is it clear what is meant by "substitute him for me in having a toothache"?

Imagining consists
1) in having a certain image,
2) in using it in a certain way.

I don't mean I can't imagine him having a toothache; I can.—I know what is meant by "image of him having a toothache".—But having this image does not mean the sentence has sense.

There are only certain circumstances in which "He has pain but does not show it" has any sense. And to say "*Everyone* has pain but does not show it" does not have sense.

⟦8⟧ "But apart from consideration of verification, the sentence has sense from another source, *because* we can imagine it."

If you say: 'Surely we can say it makes sense to say "he sees red where I can see green" because I can imagine it,' then I reply that the fact that you can imagine it does not tell us what sense it has unless we know how you are going to use it.

There is no objection to adopting a way of expression in which we say: "He looked at the sky, had a sense datum, and said 'It's a blue sky, let's go for a walk'." Or again, "He had a sense datum, said 'Go to hell'," etc.—But what is the use of "had a sense datum" in this case? Has it any meaning? We can *imagine what it means* to say "had a sense datum" but in countless cases it has no use.

We spoke of "a private language". We might say: "Even if no one else knows what I call 'toothache', at least *I* know."

"I know what it is like if *I* imagine red."

Well, what is it like?

"I can't explain to another person, but I can explain this to myself. I do this by imagining red."

Does this play the rôle of an explanation?

What's the criterion for this now being red? That I remember giving that name to this colour before? You might say "Surely I just recognise this as the same colour." But could we then ask: whether you recognise the use of "the same" in the same way?

I cannot remind myself in my private language that this was the sensation I called red. There is no question of my memory's playing me a trick—because (in such a case) there can be no criterion for its playing me a trick. If we lay down rules for the use of colour words in ordinary language, then we can admit that memory plays tricks regarding these rules. But it is essential here that certain things should be the rule, and that tricks of memory should be exceptions.

If we use such a phrase as "he sees this green where I see red"—we must not think that here we have to do with *indirect* criteria, whereas there is a *direct* criterion which we can't get hold of or can't use. As a matter of fact we know no such direct criterion. We call ⟦9⟧ others *indirect* criteria, because for what *I* see I don't need this sort of criterion: I know what I see directly, I know what he sees indirectly.

(If "having pain" and "knowing that you have pain" are not the same, then you might have pain and not know that you had pain. And then you might *know* that you had pain *indirectly.*)

We are inclined to say that for the statement that I have a toothache there is a certain *justification,* which consists in my having a toothache; and we say that this justification is private.—I say: If the justification is private, then you can't *call* it private—meaning: it has no *sense* to say that anyone could know it. Pepys had a private language, but one that *could* be divulged.

To say "sense data are private" would give a rule of grammar: you must not say "I have the same sense datum as he", and also you must not say "I have a different sense datum from his".

## III [March 3 continued]

Take the case "Now I know what 'toothache' means." This seems *prima facie* just the introduction of a *sample.* But really you have not got a sample, since you cannot answer "Well, what is it like?" by pointing to it.

Supposing now the next day he also said "Now I have a toothache, I know what it is like, etc." Could you then ask, "What if he has something entirely *different* today?"?

What did he have that made him understand it?

"He had a toothache."—Yes, but this doesn't help.

"Toothache is having a certain sensation."—But does this help at all? How do you know what he means by "a certain sensation"?

For "having a sensation" and "having a toothache" you use the normal criteria.

If you don't want to use behaviouristic criteria—Suppose we were very cautious and thought you could not understand, and I said just "I have an x, and I know what it means". This obviously is not what you wanted.

⟦10⟧ Is toothache a behaviour, or is it something more than a behaviour?

We could use "behaviour" as a grammatical term: we call jumping, running, smiling etc. *behaviours,* as opposed to *bodies,* for example.

I would not put 'toothache' in this category. But there is a behaviour which we call "*expression* of toothache".

Apart from these behaviours, we may have "personal experiences".

"If a man moans with pain, then surely there is not just the moaning, but something besides."—Does one always regard this as an *addition*? Is it "behaviour *plus* experience"?

Suppose one says "I'll be delighted to see you". Distinguish between (a) speaking it and meaning it, and (b) speaking it and meaning the opposite.—"When is the next train to London?" "3:33." Did you mean what you said? "Yes." But what went on here?—We are almost inclined to say: Nothing went on when I meant it, and something went on when I *lied.*

Suppose I talk always in a monotone, always on C. Is this 'talking plus something' or 'talking minus something'?—You might say "Talking plus a note". But might it not more reasonably be called 'talking *minus*'?

You might take 'moaning without toothache' as *two,* and 'moaning with toothache' as *not* two.

What misleads here is the notion of "outside plus the inside".

"When I look at the wall, there is not only the wall but also the *way* in which I see it." But this is misleading if it suggests that a distinction is made by putting two things together.

"Toothache is not a behaviour"—this is a grammatical sentence.

On the other hand, we have said that the word "toothache" would have no use in such sentences as "Possibly everyone has toothache and does not show it."

We must not look for 'toothache' as something independent of behaviour. We cannot say: "Here is toothache, and here is behaviour—and we can put them together in any way we please."

⟦11⟧ You might say, '"toothache" is a description of what goes on inside us.' But is moaning a description of behaviour? "I moan" is a description of behaviour, but moaning is not. The word "toothache" is like moaning, not like "I moan".

"I have a toothache" is no more the description of behaviour than moaning is. To call it a description is misleading in a discussion like this.

What we call the description of a feeling is as different from the description of an object as "the name of a feeling" is different from "the name of an object".

Of course "toothache" is not *only* a substitute for moaning. But it is *also* a substitute for moaning, and to say this shows how utterly different it is from a word like "Watson".

We can distinguish moaning in pain and moaning in the theatre and moaning for fun. But it is a mistake to say that one of these is distinguished as 'moaning *plus* something'. For then: "moaning plus *what*?" And we find this cannot be answered.

In order to be sure that he knows what "pain" means, he pinches his finger. Why does he do this? How does he know it produces *pain* now? Suppose he made a mistake: he pinched his finger and had a most agreeable sensation. How would he know he felt a most agreeable sensation?

## IV [March 4, 1936]

Do you know what is meant by saying "Wisdom behaves just as he does and sees", and also

"Wisdom behaves just as he does and does not see"?

If you are inclined to say "yes", you conjure up some image of what it is like for him to see and for him not to see. You do this first from acquaintance with your own seeing, and then: "I imagine he does what I do".

If we have a system of sentences, and images corresponding to these.—

"Wittgenstein holds a book in his left hand", etc.—

⟦12⟧ We then say, "This is Skinner", and we go on

"Skinner holds a book in his left hand."

It seems easy to understand this.

It seems as if it were equally easy to substitute "him" for "me" in the case of *seeing* and *not-seeing*.—Suppose I make the substitution of his body for mine. Then why should not the image be that of my body having changed into this shape? It might be the image of my seeing through Wisdom's eyes.

Does the image I get by first having an image of seeing something, and then substituting in some way him for me—does this necessarily correspond to the proposition "He sees"? May it not mean just: "I see and I appear as he appeared an hour ago"?

In many cases we *might* say "nothing is easier than to imagine that he does what I do". But in this case the language of images has no such simple relation to the language of propositions. When we talk of "seeing" we generally refer to something like activity of our eyes. Here the substitution is quite simple.

If you say "surely you can imagine him seeing, no matter what his behaviour might be"—then you *don't* mean by "seeing" an activity of the eyes.

When you do imagine him as seeing, you always imagine some reference to his eyes, and you don't imagine he can see behind his head.

On the one hand we are inclined to say that your behaviour is the only *clue* to whether you see or not.

On the other hand inclined to say: Whether you see or not is independent of your behaviour.

I say there is a contradiction here.

Suppose you say, "The eye turns yellow when the liver is out of order." This we know from the correlation of two experiences. And here the clue is independent of the sense of the proposition "the liver is out of order". But we can say it is a clue because we have the correlation of the two experiences.

But in the other case we have not the two experiences to correlate. And if (a) the two are independent, and if (b) we have *ex hypothesi* no experience correlating them, how could we say one was a clue to the other?

In the case of a new disease, "flu", we might say "Having flu is ⟦13⟧ simply defined by his having fever etc."—But in our case we say he might be blind and behave as if he were not blind. And you might say this shows that *seeing* and *behaving* are independent.

But this does not follow.

The question is of what your imagery has to do with the sentences 'I see' and 'he sees'.

It makes no sense to say "I know that I see" if it makes no sense to say "I don't know that I see".

To say "I know directly that I see, but only indirectly that he sees"—is a consequence of a misleading simile: e.g., "I know what is in my pocket by directly feeling it, but I know what is in his pocket only by hearsay."

*If* it makes no sense to say "I know directly that he sees", it makes no sense to say "I know indirectly that he sees".

Suppose one said "The barber cuts hair only indirectly, because he uses his hand." If you ask "What would it be like to cut hair directly?", we might answer "That makes no sense."—But the use of "indirectly" suggests that the two opposites are significant. And so it is confusing.

Of course I do say "Now don't tell me what I feel", and also "I don't know what you feel."

It is misleading if you say "I know that he has pain because I see how he behaves, but I know that I have pain because I feel it." The latter comes to: "I know that I have pain because I have it, i.e. because it is true, i.e. because I don't lie."

It seems as though we could say I derive an expression like "I have pain" from my personal private sensation. I wish to say this is not so.

If I give an ostensive definition of 'red', and then say of an object "*This* is red", I can be said to derive this from the ostensive definition.—We might say, in this case: in a sense I must derive the word from what I see, since I say it is red only because it *is* red.

But if you think you can derive "red" from what you see, then this contradicts the notion of private personal experience. For if it is ⟦14⟧ private you see what you see and say "red" for *no* reason.—You can derive it from an ostensive definition, but not from a private sensation.

You might say that can't be *all* that happens—that you look at a colour and say a word—but you have to say the word comes in a particular way. There is a difference between

a) looking and saying the name of the thing, and
b) looking and saying just *any* word.

But if you look at a thing and give it a name, do you recognize the word to be the name of the thing by the way it comes? You might or you might not. Actually no one pays any attention to the way the word comes.

What is the difference between calling the colour 'John', and looking at the colour and calling John to me?

Supposing we have the word "green", and I show you a series of colours (and ask you to tell me if one is green), and a bell rings in your head when you see green. But this just pushes the question further back—for how did you recognize the bell as a sign? There *may* be a special way in which the word comes; but it is no explanation.—His saying "green" is really all that happens. Of course he may *cheat.* But this does not mean that that can't be all.

Suppose:

The first might be said to be purely visual, the second not purely visual. A further case:

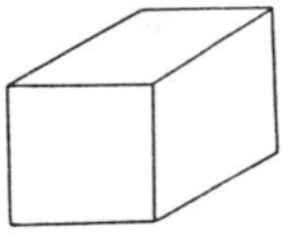

⟦15⟧ This notion of "seeing *and* something else" is partly derived from our body. "Seeing" is what the eye alone does, and I might see and smile at the same time.

If you wish to say there are distinctions which are not shown in "He sees that" I quite agree. But the "and something else" is nevertheless misleading.

If we want to ask "is it all, or is it not?"—I say this is a question about your notation. How do you introduce the differences?

The general question of "What do we regard as the simple, and what do we regard as the complex?" (('seeing plus something', 'seeing simply'. . . ))

In certain cases there is no doubt. It is often clear what is meant by "This isn't all". If you mean there is a table as well as 2 chairs, then it is clear.—If you mean "It isn't all: the chairs also stand on their feet", then I answer that we don't generally use an additive for this.

What does "comes in a particular way" mean? Don't all words come in a particular way? All we can do is to distinguish between cases in which we may say, for example, "He cheats", or "he just says any word that comes into his mind."

You mustn't think of "the way" as some medium.

The question is just: "Do I distinguish between having a toothache and moaning, not having a toothache and moaning, and having a toothache and not moaning?" I should answer, Yes, I do distinguish. But can you ask any more of me?

One way of making yourself feel "This isn't all" is to look at something and say: "There is something more: I see." Here it seems as though I gave a description of something which I observe; and if you tell yourself you see, then you could say "That's what I really mean."

In this sentence ("I see") the word "I" is really a signal. It is like lifting one's hand. This is not a name for your body, and it is also not a name for anything in your body.—And if I say to *myself* "I see", then I'm using an English sentence, but this has no use, because I signal no one.

⟦16⟧ I could say "I see" to an oculist. And it seems as if, when I say "I see" to myself, the sentence must retain its sense.

We speak of "attaching sense to a sentence". We often do speak, for example, of *images* attached to a sentence, but not written. But from this we have the notion that meaning is some nebulous, shadowy thing attached to sentences.—Some images are characteristic for the words, and we can say it is characteristic for the use of the sentence that such images are attached to it.

The notion of informing myself: "I've a toothache and I must go to the dentist." Suppose we asked where this proposition derives its sense: is it from a game I play with myself, or from a game I play with others? If I leave out the second clause—"I must go to the dentist"—what is the difference between saying these words, "I've a toothache", (to myself) and making any other noise (to myself)?

You might answer "They have been used before". Then it is clear that I am informing myself of something only because I am using that phrase which I use to inform someone else.

Suppose I knew no word for a new pain and I said "I'll call it toothache", and I also say how it is used, "I *have* a toothache". But you could not say then that you inform yourself of anything here. Where could the information come in?—Really you had not even invented a name for anything; it only seemed as if you had.

So in the sentence "I see" I seem to inform myself of something.

We take *staring* to be an ostensive definition, as though we were pointing at something by staring. We can of course point by staring: I can stare at someone and say "He's a fool". But then I am pointing not in visual space but in common space. If someone said "By staring you direct your attention", we could ask the question "To what?" And the answer might be: "To him."

## V [March 9, 1936]

If we see an object and say to ourselves "red", there may be a question how this is *justified* ((what justifies the use of this word ⟦17⟧

here)). It may be justified by an ostensive definition—this is a *rule.*—A particular impression is not a rule, and can't *justify* usage.

We may ask the further question whether all that happens is that we look at this and say "red". If I look at it and say "John"—I would not thereby be calling it "John". This leads to the assumption that "this can't be all".

But this latter statement is not clear. In what case would we say "This is all"? Some cases are clear: I say "There are two chairs in the room" and you ask "Is that all?" We are accustomed to cases in which the question can be answered without trouble. But here is a case in which it is not at all clear: Could one say "There is more than the two chairs, there is a noise going on"? Sometimes we would even take the absence of a noise as "something".

You might say 2 is a mere face, but 3 is a very impressive face.

Again: draw R. We may say we have here not merely a visual impression—meaning that we can never forget that it is the letter R.

People speak of "recognition". They say it is not enough that you *say* "red", you must also *recognize* it.

There are all sorts of experiences which we call 'recognition'. I recognize that as a cap, and further as my cap. I go home, go up to my table and sit down, etc. If a philosopher asks you "Do you recognize your table?", you would probably say "yes".

Again, I meet a man whom I suddenly recognize as So-and-so. Suppose I meet some utter stranger. Could one say I recognize him as a human being? This is certainly vastly different from what we were speaking of in the other case.

When I look at this chair as I repeatedly do, do I recognize this as brown? To say so would seem to mean nothing but that I don't ask myself "What is this?"

⟦18⟧ Why should the recognition of this as red not be just the experience of saying "red" when asked?

"Is this all?"

What does happen?

Suppose Wisdom met an old friend in the street and told me of it, and I asked him "How did it happen?" He would say some such thing as "He came nearer, and I thought 'Surely this must be Smith' etc." The narrative he would give would be something of this sort.

Take this narrative as a model. And now tell me how you recognized me as you came in just now. The other is a full-fledged case of recognition. You recognized me, didn't you. But you could say *nothing* corresponding to that narrative.

"Did nothing happen?" can be taken as a question of experience or as a question of grammar. We say sometimes "nothing happened" when we could say "It happened that I walked, my height didn't vary, my hair kept its colour, I walked at a certain rate, etc." Is this latter something, or is it nothing? If you once leave a certain standard, you could say all sorts of things.

I tell you I saw a collision of buses in the street. "Did anything happen when *you* were there?" "Nothing happened"—i.e., taking the collison as an example, nothing happened.

And now the question whether when you say "red" you call this "all" or not is a mere question of grammar.

The example, say in a psychological laboratory, in which one person says various words to you one after the other, and you say "yes" when you understand. There is then a difference between what happened when you understood the word "thermoscope" and said "yes", and when you understood "tree" and said "yes". You would say in the latter case, quite likely, nothing happened—as compared with the other case. Although as a matter of fact you had, e.g., looked at the floor.

The difference between the case where I say a word and *mean* it, and the case where I say it *lying*. We are inclined to say it must "come in a particular way". The example of "I believe it will rain tomorrow". You might say there must be some experience ⟦19⟧ accompanying the sentence—one the experience of sincerity, the other the experience of lying.

There are certainly gestures of conviction. It is clear there is not *one* gesture of conviction; but there are many which are more or less similar. We could make a Galtonian composite photograph of 100 expressions of conviction. We might get cases of very *strong* expression of conviction, and cases around it which were more or less mild.

It is analogous in a *feeling* of conviction. There is no *one* feeling of conviction.

I would say there is no *one* experience of *lying,* but many. There might be a certain feeling of discomfort; or saying the opposite to oneself; etc., etc. A "polite lie" is different from a malicious lie, etc.

Is there a feeling of sincerity which is present when you tell a man who comes to your room you are delighted to see him and also when you tell him ((in answer to his question)) the time the train leaves?

Suppose there is a particular feeling of sincerity and this is present when you say "red". Does the feeling continue all the while?—Suppose immediately after it you have a feeling of lying, then a feeling of sincerity, then another of lying. What *was* this? Was it a lie? Do we use the word "lying" in such a way that it could be a lie for 30 seconds and then not?

When we talk of a person lying or not lying we use certain criteria and he uses them with us. I ask someone to tell me the colour of the sky: something has happened to my eyes, and I want to go out. If he says "blue" I'll go out, if "grey" not. He has reasons for wanting me to go out and he lies: the sky is grey and he says "blue". Here I am speaking of motives. There could be thousands of stories of this sort. Yet they would be closely knitted. Many would be excluded. They will all turn round our human life and refer to definite sets of connexions.—And then it is clear that his *feeling* of lying plays hardly any part in the story. What we call a lie is characterized by two different things: 1) circumstances under which it is said, 2) a peculiar experience of lying. If in the story just given the man had an alternation of the feeling of truth and a feeling of lying, and we were then asked "What did he do?", we would say "he told a lie".

⟦20⟧ When we talk of 'lying' we mean not only what the person concerned could describe at the moment. I don't deny there are experiences characteristic for the situation of having told a lie. But if you assume there is *one* experience of sincerity or of lying—you get queer results.

Does one always know when he is telling a lie?

We are inclined to think there *must* be a peculiar experience of lying. Yet we can't find that one, and find all sorts of others which aren't peculiar.

## VI [February 17, 1936]

There are different ways of talking about "the nature" of an object.

One way is by giving its properties; as when I say "Anthracite is hard"—where "hard" is not one of the defining criteria of anthracite.

But we may also talk of the nature when we do mention one of the defining criteria.

One might say that space and colour have different properties: what is true of colour is not true of space. But the *nature* of the objects in this case is not determined by properties which we can attribute to them truly as opposed to those which we can't. It is determined by the grammar of the word which denotes it. "The colour green has a different nature from a cubic foot": this is an expression of the fact that a different grammar applies.

We have the idea that the grammar of "1 cubic foot" *must* be different from the grammar of "green", because what we call '1 cubic foot' has a different nature. We have the idea that the grammar is determined by the meaning of the word and so we can't give it any grammar we please. But this is a misleading or wrong way of putting it. I want to show that the grammar determines the meaning of the word.

The meaning of a word *seems* to be determined in two different ways: 1) by pointing, 2) by giving rules. But when you point to the colour of an object, and when you point to its shape, you don't ⟦21⟧ move your arm in a different direction. And *which* you point to is determined by the way in which you use the word.

"Pointing" may be any of a variety of different things. I don't point to the colour green just by pointing to one object. I point to a variety of objects so that you can guess (grasp) what they have in common.

Could one say "I know what I *mean* to point to"—as though the *arm* might be pointing to any of a variety of properties, but the *mind* points to only one of them.—Certainly we can take steps to avoid misunderstandings.

Take the notion of connecting the right idea with the word. What would "the right idea" be? What he expresses by "The meaning suddenly dawned" might be just an association of an image with a scratch. It will show he has understood (our explanation) if he goes on to act in future as we said he would act. But might he not have had this image and *not* have gone on to act as we said he would act?—Is "understanding" something that happens only in one moment?

By "understanding" we sometimes mean a state of mind at a moment. But we mean this only in conjunction with a certain behaviour in the future. Unless we have *both* we would not say he has understood.

If we mean something which happened in a single moment, it might be that he suddenly got hold of an idea—say, of an algebraic expression. What happened when he *suddenly understood*? He had not applied it in all future cases. The algebraic expression in itself in his mind does not constitute the understanding. So we say it must be *more* than the algebraic expression before you. As if some queer thing called "the mind" had the property of crossing all (the) bridges before it gets there.

We have the notion that "he has understood" is something that did happen whether we know it or not at a particular time.

You *can* say he has understood if he has given the algebraic expression. You *might* say he has understood if he developed 5 places and no more. It depends on your criterion.

You might say "Understanding is something going on from 5 to 5:05". And again, you might say it is something which is shown in action and behaviour.—If we say "He suddenly understood me", what happened was like the coming into mind of a picture. But this did not contain the future application of the picture.

⟦22⟧ We bring in 'time': he knows what he wants from 5 to 5:05. But this is nothing like a note going on, or like a sentence which has a beginning and an end.

We regard a picture as an *equivalent* for a certain way of action.

Our use of the word "understand" is very flexible. When he understands '1, 4, 9, 16 . . .' and then goes on to write '25, 36' etc.—this may consist just in the fact that he went on to write. Or he may say only "Of course", and not have imagined any further number.—We describe all these very different processes with the same word because they hang together with a certain way of future action.

What is meant by "seeing what there is in common" among things pointed to? It might mean all sorts of different things. If we say "Anyway *he* must know what he means", this assumes that besides having this picture he has also something else in his mind. But what can this be except another picture?

We assume that he must have an "interpretation" in his mind, as something which can't be further interpreted.

So we have the idea that he would have the *use* of a symbol as something given in a lump.

When you see the king of chess, you may say you understand the function of the king. This does not mean going through all the rules that apply to the king. The temptation is to imagine that the whole use of the king of chess is in some way in the background when you see the king of chess.

Suppose I say we have two processes, "drinking in the colour" and "drinking in the shape". Drinking in the colour might then be looking about and saying "white"; and drinking in the shape could mean making a movement with my finger. But *either* of these processes could be applied in the future—e.g., he might make the movement of his finger as we would apply the word "white". But it is more likely that he would apply it to what we should call *shape.*

If I eliminate misunderstandings on his part by giving a series of objects, this does not mean that by these means I determine how he is to use the word—except that he will *probably* use it that way.

Here there are two sorts of misunderstandings. Giving a certain ⟦23⟧ number of objects will produce understanding by giving an image of which we could say that all these objects have this in common. But we might forget: a) that this image can be used in different ways, or b) that by examples different images may be produced.

The question: what it would be like if anything *did* determine how he is going to use the word? Suppose I wrote a very simple series down for a child—first a series of cardinals, then a series of squares, etc.—always letting him go on. Then I write '2, 4, 6,' and let him go on '8, 10,' etc. There is something which we may call drawing his attention to the fact that he *needn't* go on in that way. Instead of the series of squares he might go on 1, 4, 7, 10, etc. (always adding 3). This is another game.

Often we are puzzled by a certain uniqueness, and the puzzle is removed by giving several examples. Perhaps people were puzzled by the fact that our earth, inhabited by human beings, should be in the centre of the universe. Then it is different when we look at it in the Copernican way.

People have spoken of a "basic intuition" in connexion with numbers: we go to 100 and then to 101. But then we may say this is just another game—and there is another way in which one *could* go on. And I say, "Oh now I see I *could* have gone on otherwise." And the temptation to speak of "basic intuition" then vanishes.

We cannot say what it would be like if a picture determined the application. But the point is that whereas we might before have felt inclined to go on only in one way, we now see other possibilities—and we have not the same inclination.

This is connected with the point: people have an idea that the application is contained in the picture itself.

Don't be misled by the use of "understand" where on the one hand it seems to be taking place in a moment or two, and on the other hand it seems to extend over future actions. Don't say "in a sense he must have already done them".

(All this comes to the question, "What happens when you are philosophically puzzled?"

Take the puzzlement over "the rose is red". The puzzle was ⟦24⟧ solved by introducing two different signs: "=" and "ε". We say then "don't imagine 'rose' and 'red' are the same." But what is being said here? What happens when you are puzzled is that you say the same thing over and over again. The philosophical puzzlement stops when you stop saying it.)

When you get the picture of "being determined" out of your mind, then you get rid of the puzzle.—But still one can say the algebraic expression determines his actions—and perfectly correctly. But now you have got rid of the cramp.

We need only remember that here we could use 2 different words instead of "understanding".

There is a suggestion that by pointing we put grammar under an obligation. What we mean is, however, in one sense determined by pointing, and in another sense determined by grammar. ((Taking hold of the canvas of a deck-chair)) I say "I'm going to call this here *pea green.*" If I then used "pea green" in the way in which we use "canvas", you would be surprised. What I meant was determined both by pointing and the rest of the grammar of it—because it is a colour word.

Imagine colour words used so: People have 7 colour words and they have 7 days in a week; and they use the words in a cycle, so that they use "blue" on Tuesdays for that for which they used "red" on Monday, etc. Does one then use the word in a different sense each day? They mean the same. But they do not mean the same *colour.* "Tomorrow" *means* the *same* every day. But it does not mean the same *date*—it means a different date. So they go on with the word "blue" to a different *colour* every day. But does "blue" always mean "blue"?—yes, of course. What else could it be?

They might give an ostensive definition of "blue", and then they would go on automatically to call this other colour "blue" tomorrow.—They might on occasion ask, "but you said *yesterday* that was blue, how can it be today?"

To ask "does he mean the same object or different objects?" should be reserved for things to which we can point separately—the same man, or a different man.

⟦25⟧ VII [February 19, 1936]

((Reply to a question raised at the end of previous lecture:))

Whether the grammar employed depends on what is actually the case.

Suggestion that under certain conditions language games lose their point.

(Drawing a line on the blackboard:)
"This is the Greenwich foot", as must be distinguished from "This is 1 foot long".
The latter depends on measurement, the first does not.

If we found that the mark in question did not remain constant, we should not be inclined to measure by reference to it.

This is the way in which grammar depends on facts. If so-and-so were not the case—if it were not constant—then we should not be inclined to do with it what we do.

Similarly, for example, with weighing. Suppose one said "If the weight varied erratically, then no one would speak of the weight of a body." This seems stupid. Like saying "If the foot constantly changed its length, it would have no sense to speak of one foot." What is *meant* is, If the *rod* changed its length, we would not be inclined to *measure* with it.

If we take the grammar of colour, then colour appears as the *word* 'colour' in inverted commas.

I can produce a certain patch and say "this is red". This is a rule of grammar. But then the patch enters (in my explanation) as a *sample.* The patch enters as a symbol or sign also. This does not mean that the grammar after all treats of those objects the names of which it mentions. Here "This is red" does not treat of red as "This chair is green" treats of green.

I want to go on to the question as to the nature of sense data.

The word "sense datum" really means the same as "appearance". But the term introduces a particular way of looking at appearance. We might call it "*objectification*". If "personification" means, e.g., using the word "time" as though it were the name of a person, then ⟦26⟧ objectification is talking of it as though it were a thing. No puzzles arise out of personification. No one actually thinks that the ship is female.

I might say, for example: "This suit seemed to me dirty, but it was not dirty." Suppose I then said "The *appearance* of the suit *is* dirty". In the first case I would be ready to say "I was wrong". The other seems to be connected with "I was right".

Suppose I say, "If this coat appeared grey, then something must have been grey". This is objectification. We assimilate the grammar of appearance to the grammar of physical objects.

"If 2 lines *seem* convergent, then something must be convergent." Suppose we said instead, ". . . then something must seem convergent". Or: ". . . then I must be able to transform the sentence into one in which I say of something that it is convergent."

$$\text{f(a) seems to be the case} = \text{f}(\alpha) \text{ is the case.}$$

It is better not to say "If . . . , then . . .", but simply to treat it as the same sentence.

Take the case

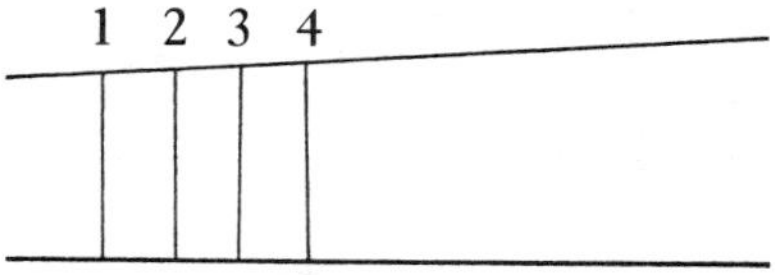


where we seem to have the conclusion: that as applied to sense data the equality of length is not transitive: length 1 = length 2, length 2 = length 3, length 1 ≠ length 3.

Take the case of dizziness, where "I see the room revolving round me". Really I don't see it revolving. I don't stand and see the articles of furniture in regular succession go past me.

The lines 1 and 2 seem equal. But when we speak of "the appearance" we say "*is* equal".

We often say "Oh this is an ellipse, but I *saw* it as a *circle.*" Or, "I looked at a circle and saw it as an ellipse."

⟦27⟧ We may say "The visual circle has something in common with its tangent", or "the visual circle consists of straight bits". It is natural to speak in this way of "a visual circle". Is it a circle which is also a polygon, then?

The difficulty about sense data begins with the notion of the *privacy* of them.

I want to talk about the view that perhaps sense data alone are real.

Objectification leads people to compare an 'appearance' with a *picture.* The idea is that we not only look at a chair, but also *look at* (not merely see) something else.

"Look at" means doing something, not merely seeing—opening one's eyes, turning one's head, etc. But I can't turn my head round to see a sense datum.

The question of the reality of sense data comes first with the idea of our senses *cheating* us. The suggestion that we never see the real thing: we only get pictures which are more or less correct.

The next step was: dissatisfaction with the simile—we seem to have pictures which we compare with nothing.

We then go to say: The picture is the only thing which is real, nothing else exists.

Thus we first objectify, and then go on to talk of existence and non-existence.

(We are often told that when I shut or cover over one eye, I "see everything flat". What does this mean? We can speak of a diagram which I sometimes see flat and sometimes not; ((sometimes a hexagon, sometimes a cube)). But what of seeing a human face flat?)

Take the suggestion that a physical object is a construction from sense-data.

We could introduce a notation in which instead of talking of a pencil we would talk of *views* of the pencil—but not in such a way that we substitute "view of pencil" for "pencil". Instead of "I put the pencil down here" we say "I'm changing the view of the pencil from so-and-so to so-and-so". As, e.g., we speak of 3 projections ⟦28⟧ from a cylindrical body. This does not mean I have projected the pencil onto the wall. It means only that I have altered my expression, and instead of saying "pencil" I use the words "projection A, B, etc.".

What is meant by saying it is a *construction out of these projections*?

We might actually see pictures on 3 walls. It would be natural then to describe a plane shape moving in three planes. Suppose we then found that we could describe this by using the word "the pencil" and say "the pencil goes up, rotates, etc.". *Then* you could say "The pencil is a construction".

Here we talk of 2 things: a) seeing the pencil move, where it is not a construction; b) seeing the pencil move, where we say we don't really see the pencil move, it is only a construction from the 3 images.

What then could have led people to say a pencil is only a construction from sense data? If people say "all that we have is the sense data"—and not what? It is a reaction against saying "the sense data are only pictures of *something*". And it suggests that, in order to justify my speaking about the pencil, I must show how the pencil is constructed from sense data which I have.

Then is it not quite true to say "I see a pencil move"? In *some* cases, where there are hallucinations, etc., we are wrong. But in our grammar we account for this (our grammar provides for this)—we say "Oh, I was wrong".

We can actually *transform* a statement about a pencil into a statement about appearances of a pencil—even when no one is there: "if someone *were* there, he would see . . . etc". One is often tempted: always to use the picture of someone seeing the pencil, and then to talk of "a pencil somewhere else" as a pencil seen by someone.

The use of *pointing* is misleading here. There is a temptation to introduce the idea of "pointing to an appearance". Like "looking at an appearance"—as one can point to or look at a picture.

A primitive form of describing a body is to draw or paint it. This describes the body in terms of the *appearance* of it. And you might say "all I've got is the *appearance*—namely, that which I can paint."

⟦29⟧ You can say "all I've got now is an appearance of this chair—as opposed to what I will get when I touch it or move it about." But if I say "All I've got is the appearance as opposed to the real object", . . . what then?

There are two opposing tendencies of our language: In one symbolic system we would say *this,* in another *that* . . . and then we use both, forgetting that they belong to two different systems.

We may say "The chair is a fiction". This is a sentence taken from a context explaining that it is not a real chair but is a cake, etc. The sentence is an old sentence of our language meaning something entirely different.

If we think of contemplating the appearance of a (human) foot, we are inclined to make an error: the idea that the word "foot" would really be used in the same way as "*appearance* of a foot", which we could substitute for it—although we find that we *can't.* This then is the appearance,—then where is the foot?—We don't use the word "foot" as one of the arguments in a function of which some arguments are "*appearances* of the foot".

"I don't see the foot, I see the appearance". This does *not* mean I should put, instead of "foot", "appearance of the foot" in the sentence. There is a temptation to do this because we do speak of "seeing a circle" and of "looking at a circle and not seeing it *as* a circle".

To say "what really exists is the foot" means just as little as "what really exists is the appearance".

(The expression "metaphorical"—which usage is metaphorical? One criterion is: what comes first to our mind when we hear, say, the word "flight"? The flight of a bird? or the flight of thought?—Or again: "*inside*"—inside a box, or inside my mind?

We might speak of "the *surrounding* of an idea". Understanding words. There is a game in which someone reads out words and you are to answer "yes" if you understand, "no" if not. He reads out "hygrometer", "identification", "chair", "columbine", etc. Then we ask what happens when you say "yes". There would be various processes. You might do no more than say "yes". But the word is ⟦30⟧ *surrounded* with various ideas, of which you would think on further stimulus. What we often take to be momentary understanding is: that you begin immediately to move in the surrounding of that word.

I say: "Had he asked me, I *would* have answered him so-and-so"—A form of language which is not subjunctive and refers to something that actually happened: You speak of Napoleon. I ask, "Did you mean the man who won the battle of Austerlitz?" and you say "Yes, I meant him". Suppose I ask then, "*When* did you mean it?" What answer? Presumably when you said it—

So also: in the case when someone adds 2 to 100—I say "That is not what I meant him to do", although I may never have thought of 100 when I gave the rule.

It is a form of experience which uses the idea of "disposition". We speak of 'having a disposition'—*when* do I *have* the disposition? What does it consist in? Might one answer: "It consists in having one's brain constructed in such and such a way"?)

## VIII [February 24, 1936]

The question "Are physical objects real?" would never be asked in ordinary life. But the expressions involved in it are taken from ordinary life—*essentially* from ordinary life. From circumstances in which we may say "that is not real"—for instance: "This on the stage is not a real house, but a piece of scenery". A tram conductor is not likely to use language about electrons or helium. But he does use the language in which we ask questions about physical objects.

Our attention is drawn to the fact that our senses can cheat us. And since I can be wrong in one case, why should I not be wrong always?

People say sometimes "We only believe in the reality of physical objects, we don't know it." Or again someone might say "we don't even believe in them": he might say they are *fictions*. But what is meant by this? A centaur is a fiction. King Lear is a fiction. But what would it be like to invent 'physical objects'?

If you are impressed by the fact that the senses may cheat, this may incline you to say the chair is not real.

⟦31⟧ Dr. Johnson's kicking the stone. This shows that the uncertainty of "real" and "unreal" has some connexion with seeing: the examples are generally taken from vision. The notion of 'idealism' hangs together chiefly with *visual* sense data. For example, we see only one side of a physical object, whereas we can get hold of it all round.

Seeing a cube . We say "A cube is symmetrical". But what you really see is this, and this is not symmetrical.

"Seeing a penny as an ellipse." The difference between seeing it as an inclined circle and seeing it as a level ellipse. But if you *draw* it from that angle, then you draw it as an ellipse.

"Has the cube 12 edges? or has it 9 real edges and 3 imaginary edges?"

The difficulty about saying that what you see is a *view* of the object: we are tempted to say that this view is *private*—it is only *my* view. I may then go on to say: what is real is only the view which I have *now*—but I cannot describe the view that I have *now* because there is no time.

Some of the considerations in favour of idealism are *arguments*. But some are not. One is sometimes inclined to say "All that is real is *this*" where you would say "I'm pointing at the sense datum".

Suppose you are trying to make clear to yourself the sense of the Law of Identity. You point ((say, to a pencil you are holding)) and say: "*This* is the same as *this*" ((pointing with each 'this')). "This is not the same as this"—is something you could say to explain that the object had altered—although it isn't a natural expression.—Generally we'd use the expression ("this is the same as this") in pointing to *two* objects. The other case is a degenerate form of expression. But not merely that.

You would never have the temptation to say it if the object pointed to changed colour. One might then say: if you could reduce the time in which you said it, so that the change of colour had not gone far enough, then the more rapidly you say it, the nearer you get to the truth.

We get something similar when we write a tautology like "$p \supset p$".

⟦32⟧ We formulate such expressions to get something in which there is no doubt—even though the sense also has vanished with the doubt.

Take the case then of "All that is real is this". Or: "Only *I* really see."

Or the case of having a toothache. It is said that I can never know for certain that another person has a toothache; I can only infer it from the way he acts. Whereas I know my own toothache directly. Perhaps this is the only toothache. Not only this, but it seems that it only makes *sense* to say that I have a toothache, and one ought to say something else about other people. So also with '*seeing*'.

This can't be right. For then why say at all that I have a toothache and another person has not. I ought to say that what I call "my toothache", I shall call simply "toothache"—and say something else of the other person.

But then there is no sense in saying "I have a toothache", but only "*there is a toothache*". Then about another person I'd have to say something quite different—since I can't say "there is a toothache" in his case.

There is no objection to saying that for me, Wittgenstein, different words are to be used than for anyone else. This is all right if you can get other people to do it—everyone will then understand. Then only for me would it be correct to say "there is a toothache"; and if Watson has a toothache we must not say "there is a toothache", since Wittgenstein could answer "there is not".

If I am a solipsist in this way there is no objection to it. But that does not satisfy me. For you would be taught my identity by pointing out my body. Now I want that my body should not come in at all. What if I changed bodies with Watson. I'd still want this arrangement, but no one would understand me now.

It seems as though you don't anyway understand me. The only one who understands is me. If I said to myself "*I* only see" . . . I don't see my body. And I don't wish to point to Wittgenstein at all. What do I mean by "I" in this case?

The problem of solipsism hangs together with a wrong idea of the use of the word "I".—Recall what we said about ostensive definition; and our suggestion that the use of the word is its meaning.

⟦33⟧ Take the expressions "I", "here", "now". What is "now"? A moment of time. But which moment of time is it?—So also: What is "here"? Which place is it?

Who is "I"? A person. But which person is it?

We can use "here" as an argument in functions into which you can put the description of a place. So, "here—i.e., on the chair". "Here" is generally not used at all by itself alone, but with some gesture of pointing.

"On this chair" is a place. "Here" is also a place. But they don't mean the same. Are there then two places? No. We just have two words which are used differently.

How is "I" used? The mere fact that we point to a certain thing in explaining a word, does not explain the use of the word. So with "I" and "Wittgenstein".

You say "Who wants a drink?" and I say "I". Or I might answer by raising my arm. If I raise my arm I don't point to a human body, although I attract attention to a human body—in a different way from pointing.

We have an idea that when we give (something) a name, this is psychological, and the name is in some mysterious way connected with the object. You might write a name on an object.

You cannot write a name on a toothache. But giving toothache a name is a queer thing. It seems as though no one would know what I give the name to. It seems as if I (would) give the name privately—only for my own use. But what is meant by 'giving a name' in such a case? what is the point of giving it a name? Training myself to say "toothache" in certain circumstances is not what is meant by giving a name. How do we *use* this word at all?

If we know what it is to give a name to a physical object, we don't yet know what it means to give a name to a pain. We can give a name to a pain—but we can only do this in cases where the pain is not private—where the word is to be used by all of us.

There is then the temptation to think "I ought to have two words for my toothache—the one which I use to myself, the other to someone else." For someone else gets only the skeleton of my toothache, not the real timbre of it.

⟦34⟧ We might say something similar with regard to the use of "red". And here again it may seem to me that I ought to use two different words.

But actually such a private language game does not exist.

I may feel inclined to say that no one really understands what I mean by red, but that *I do* know what I mean by it. And so I might consider a language I talk only to myself.

Robinson Crusoe may have held soliloquies. And then he talks to himself alone. But he talks the language he has talked with people before.

But imagine him *inventing* a *private* language. Imagine that he gives a name to a sensation of his. What then does he do with it?—Suppose he kept a diary, and that in this diary he put x against each day when he had a toothache. We must assume that what he wants to say no one understands anyway, and he can't explain it. How are we to describe what he does?

"He had a toothache, and he remembers and puts a cross." How does he know he remembers? In the end we have to say just "He puts crosses"—we must not use the word "toothache", for it is not used as we generally use "toothache", and he is not using 'x' for this.

Suppose he put into the diary an ostensive definition of "red" by means of a sample; and whenever the sun sets red he writes "red". Or we should say rather: "When it *seems to him* that the sun sets red". For we might ask how he uses the sample, or which way seems to him the right one? You might say "He will be justified in writing 'red' by looking at the sample and seeing whether it (the sunset) is red". But I don't know how he will apply this (("seeing whether" etc.)), I know only that he writes "red" on certain days.

I may be with him and I stare at what he has written and if it *agrees* with the red sunset, then I say "I know what he means by 'red' ". But if it does not agree? "Then I don't know what he means." But he has written down what he means. The point is that if I don't know how he uses it, then it would cease to us to be a language at all. You could say "I should normally say he means 'red' ", but we must forget this, because he is not using it for a language. His language is a language only in so far as it might be used among human beings.

⟦35⟧ It would be absurd to speak of translating his 'language' into English—or into any other language.

The situation in which I'm inclined to say "I can know only that I have a toothache, and maybe no one else has." We can imagine a condition in which other people are perfectly healthy and have no pain. Then I have pain, and I invent a name (for it). What then do I do with it? You might say this question is foolish: you can't make yourself understood to anyone—just as you can't buy if there are no shops.

Say I have given my sensation the name "pain". It seems as if I had done something with which we are familiar, like saying "I have given him the name Smith". Here there is more than the noise, since there is the use—what will be done with it. But how is it in the case of giving the name "pain"? what else is there besides the noise? We might say "he *meant* the sensation". But how do you *mean* the sensation?—For whose benefit do I point? Do I intend to make people do so and so, etc.? Could I train them to extract a tooth when I say "pain"? Then and thereby would the word get a meaning.

Can one say "toothache" is the name of a sensation?

One can't talk of a private justification for expressing our pain.

When you learn the word—you hold your cheek, make moans etc., and people say to you "You have a toothache". Then you *guess* the meaning of the word by reference to the particular sensation which you have. But this latter (the sensation) is not a justification of your saying "I have a toothache". Of course you might *lie* in using the expression. But I can't say that when I tell the truth this is justified by my having the sensation. For I don't *give* any justification.

What would a justification for his *moaning* be? We can distinguish various forms: "He is justified in moaning because he is in pain."

"He is justified in moaning on the stage, because he has to earn his living by it." Etc.

Suppose someone who has never had a toothache, but has heard the word. Then one day he has a toothache, and says "Now I know what 'toothache' means".

⟦36⟧ But then suppose I ask him, "Well, what *does* it mean?" Or: "Does it mean what I had?"

When I have a sample of red, then if you ask me "Well, what *does* 'red' mean?", I can answer "It means *this*". In the case of toothache, the temptation is to say "Well, I know, although I can't express it". There is a suggestion that you have a private ostensive definition. And I say you have not got one.

Just as there is an inclination to say that the ostensive definition of 'red' might be secret—recorded in my diary (which no one else sees); but further, that it is *essentially* secret.

One is inclined to say: If he can *transmit* his toothache, then in this way he divulges what it means.—If this is how he used "Now I know what 'toothache' means", then it is on a footing with 'red'. But he'll say this is impossible: he can give someone else a toothache, but not transmit *his* toothache.

The suggestion is that "He can't see what I see, because I am I and he is he."

If someone asks, "What do you see?", I am tempted to say "I see *this*". This may mean different things.

## IX [March 11, 1936]

The notion of "talking about" something.

I talk about Smith. What happens? I say words, and perhaps I have an image of him; but this is inadequate as an account of what happens. How do you know what it is an image of? ((cf. "What makes the mental image an image of *him*?")) An image might play the same rôle as a picture. And I might be using a picture of Smith as a type for a man, or of a posture. Or might not the mental image be the image of a portrait?

An image might help you in the sense in which pointing to something helps you to understand a word.

What happens, then? You might say: I just use his name; and the relation of this to the man here is just that this man is normally called this; etc.

Suppose we talk about a thunderstorm. Well, what is the relation ⟦37⟧ between the word "thunderstorm" and what we talk about? And what part does the *image* of a thunderstorm play in talking about a thunderstorm—an image which is probably quite vague?

Or take the case in which I am talking about tomorrow. I can't point to tomorrow, of course. Neither can I point to a thunderstorm now.

Suppose now we use a certain word and point to a picture on the wall. We say all sorts of things and at intervals we point. Then at the end we say: "Therefore he must be hanged and we will lead him to the gallows." This might show that we were talking about Smith.

But while the conversation is still going on . . . what is the answer to the question "What are we talking about?" Suppose we had used the word "Smith" several times, and then someone asks "What are you talking about?", and we answer "Well, Smith". But is this satisfactory?

Suppose we are talking about a house which is not yet built, but which will be built tomorrow. Tomorrow we can say: "We were talking about this". This is an explanation which we cannot give today. Yet today we were using words in such a way that we shall be able to give that explanation tomorrow.

It seems as if there must be some queer relation between me and what I am talking of. If I say "We talked of *this*", this is not a description of what we were doing; ((as "we put our hands on this" would be)). If I say "We hanged Smith" you might ask "How could you, when he wasn't there?" But we can *talk* about something which is not there.

Now apply this to talking about toothache.—People seem to have a notion of talking about it, as though one talked and at the same time did something to it. Whereas we talk about toothache, and we say words.

Problem: It seems as though what-we-were-talking-about is fixed by something like an image. But the image shows no more clearly what I am talking about than mere words do. For the ⟦38⟧ *connexion* is made in applying what we say—it is not something which is given all at once . . .

There is a certain regularity in that *often* when I speak of Smith I have an image of Smith, of course. And I am liable to say "While I speak I know what I am talking about". But in what sense? What is the criterion of 'knowing' in this sense? There seems to be a criterion which is something like an image while we speak.

It seems as if what we spoke about is something we concentrate on. "It is round and hard": If I say this touching the edge of the stove, and at the same time concentrate on the impression . . . But did saying the words plus concentrating in this way determine what I was talking about?

How about an image of pain? Does this image not play the same role as the impression of touch played in the other case?

Why is it that when I touch this and concentrate on it there can be no doubt what I am talking about? It seems as though I were talking about something in a more direct way than when I am talking about Smith.—In what sense can one say that this concentrating does show what I am talking about, and in what sense doesn't it?

If I say "This is round" and stare at a knob ((an unfixed brass doorknob he was holding in his hand)), it seems as though I had almost done something to the thing I stared at when I talked about it. I say I know what I'm talking about when I say "*It* is etc.". And it seems as if in the very way of talking I made some queer connexion other than that in the case of talking about Smith, where the relation is one which appears in the whole application.

In ordinary cases of pointing, and cases where we speak of Smith, etc., the relation is not one which is there in the moment when I speak. But in the case of the pressure sensation there seems to be some such relation present at the moment.

In certain cases we are inclined to think that what we talk about is that on which we concentrate attention. This is sometimes the case. It seems to us sometimes that concentrating attention really is a kind of pointing at it. If I concentrate on this chair by staring at it, this may replace pointing at it *for you.* But this does not mean it is a pointing from *my* point of view.

⟦39⟧ I am inclined to say: "I know what impression I call 'green' ", and I stare at a green object and concentrate my attention on it.

But concentrating attention on the colour of this canvas here does not come to: giving an explanation of the meaning of the word "green". Explanation is something which shows us how to use a word at some other time as well.—Could we say "staring at this and saying 'green' could give me a lead how to use the word 'green' another time"? What is missing is the comparison. The next time again I stare and say "this is green" because it does not matter *what* I stare at. It is not an explanation, because it doesn't oblige me to do anything. I do not give the rule and follow it.

I might always say "green" for the same colour. But what is meant by "the same colour"?

The question is as to what makes these gestures of staring, etc., a *rule*? Answer: that this (what makes them a rule) is just the rôle they play in the normal game.

Suppose one is talking about toothache, and says he knows what he is talking about. He checks to make sure by "recalling an image of pain".

There is a difference between an image of pain and an image of a man holding his cheek. If I talk about having an image of a man holding his cheek, I can show another person what my image is like. But if I say that I imagine toothache or pain—you might ask "How did you learn the expression 'imagining pain'?" How does one learn the meaning of: "imagining something"? You could not *point* at an image.

Take the case where a child learned to use the words "I dreamed so and so". What happens is that the child wakes up and says "I drank milk last night"—having learned the word "drink" by ostensive definition—and he is then taught to say "I dreamt I drank etc.".

You tell a dream in the past tense. This is a reason for saying you aren't having the dream whilst you are telling it. I don't say that this (the past tense) is a *sign* for anything. I can't say the child observes that he had the dream in the past. I don't know what he observes—but I do know he uses the past tense. *He uses that picture.*

It is a similar case in our example ("imagining pain", "imagining red"). I can point out a red object. But I cannot point out a red ⟦40⟧

after-image. Might one ask whether this latter is a new use of "red"?—The point is that after having been taught to use the words in the ordinary way, the child then *uses* the words in this new way *without* being taught.

In analogous ways we are taught such phrases as "imagining so and so". We do not teach the child the word "imagine" by pointing to an imagination. But he uses language in certain circumstances after having used it under other circumstances. *Then* we teach him such words as "I imagine". (If the child says "There is a dog here" when there is not. We ask "Can you see it?" and the child says "Yes".)

Suppose a child has been taught to use the words "imagining so and so". There is an inclination to say: "then the child will say under certain circumstances 'I imagine that there is a cat', etc." The question here is about "under certain circumstances". What is one talking about? "If a certain thing happens . . ." But if *what* happens? The expression is taken from a case when you *point* to something. But here there is *nothing* you point to.

Can we say then only that under certain *external* circumstances he reacts in a certain way? He looks at the sun, and then says "I have a red after-image". We may feel inclined to say "It does not matter what he says—what matters is what goes on inside".—Does this mean: "What is important is the unknown x?"

But why should I say that what is important is what goes on inside, if it is always what is important anyway? We are supposed to be talking of something for which we can have no external criteria.

## X [April 27, 1936]

((Wittgenstein began his lecture by reading a passage "from one of my detective story magazines". He said it is much more revealing and important when you find this sort of confusion in something that's said "in a silly detective story than it is when you find it in something that's said by a silly philosopher". The scene is of the narrator, the detective, alone on the deck of a ship in the middle of the night, with no sound except the ticking of the ship's clock. He thinks to himself:))

⟦41⟧ "A clock is a bewildering instrument at best: measuring a fragment of infinity; measuring something which does not exist perhaps."

Here you might say "obviously a clock is not a bewildering instrument at all".—If in some situation it strikes you as a bewildering instrument, and you can then bring yourself round to saying that of course it is not bewildering—then this is the way to solve a philosophical problem.

The clock becomes a bewildering instrument here because he *says* about it "it measures a fragment of infinity, measuring something which does not exist perhaps." What makes the clock bewildering is that he introduces a sort of entity which then he can't find: he says it is to measure '*time*'—and this we can't see, and it seems like a ghost.

The connexion between this and what we were saying about sense data: What is bewildering is the introduction of something we might call "intangible". It seems as though there is nothing intangible about the chair or the table, but there is about the fleeting personal experience.

But if we try to avoid the intangible by referring to the clock and not to 'time', we may want to ask "but is time the movement of the clock hand? Doesn't that happen *in* time?"—The answer is that I don't direct your attention to the clock in order to substitute for the word "time" the word "clock-hand", but rather to take your attention entirely off the word "time".

It is similar in the case of numbers and numerals. When we want to speak of numbers, then we turn to investigate the use of numerals. But it is a fallacy to say that the number is the numeral. The word "the number one" cannot be replaced by "the numeral 1". You don't get rid of the ghost by saying "The word doesn't mean a ghost, it means this concrete thing here".

We have discussed the way in which we learn to use such an expression as "*imagine* a red patch". We don't learn the meaning of this expression in the same way as we learn the expression "red". And now it looks as if I wished to say, "There isn't really a red image, there is only this reaction." It seems as if I wished to explain away certain experiences.

I have suggested that the expression "I have a toothache" is like a ⟦42⟧ *moan*; and this seems to be wrong.—Expressions like "I have pain" are *taught* to a child to *replace* a moan. You might say that a moan does not say "I have pain", for this is something articulate, whereas the moan is not meant to say anything definite. The man who moans may lead you to guess that he has pain, but he does not say it. But I think this objection is misleading. A moan is as direct and clear an expression as there is. You might ask "What does a moan mean?" And someone might answer "It means that you have pain". But is that an explanation? How would you explain (the meaning of) "I have pain"? The next explanation would be a moan again.

You might say the expression "having pain" refers to a certain phenomenon. But to which? Can you point to it? And what do we call pointing to the phenomenon of pain? How am I to explain to *myself* the meaning of "pain" by pointing to it? Especially if I have no pain now. You may *imagine* pain. But then how do you know what the image is an image of?

This leads to the question of "talking about" something. What is it like to talk *about* pain if pain does not exist?

When it is said that "'pain' means a certain phenomenon", this is on the model of "'falling' means a certain phenomenon"; and this refers to a sort of ostensive definition. Saying *what* phenomenon it is, is a rule of grammar—it is giving an explanation. But *what* explanation in the case of "toothache"? I might put my hand to my cheek and make a grimace and say "it's that". This *is* an explanation. But I can't say now I have pointed to the *phenomenon* of pain and am preserving that. As I might have a photograph of me in that position and use this photograph as an explanation.

Suppose I give an explanation of "red" by putting a red strip beside the word "red". I can't say that I am preserving here the *impression* of red. Just as it makes no *sense* to say I have painted the impression of red. In the same way, I could not say "I am showing you the impression of toothache".

It is no use saying "pain is a certain phenomenon" unless—

It is like "A table is a certain thing". This may or may not be an explanation. If I use "thing" in a certain way, you may know that "table" is a word like "chair" or "clock" and not like "and" or "but"—it is the name of a physical object. But compare "Pain is a certain phenomenon" or "a certain mental phenomenon". If I used "mental ⟦43⟧ phenomenon" for things like "joy" etc., then you know that "pain" does not stand for that which the French call "la table", etc.

It might seem as if, when I said the word "pain" and said to you "Well now I don't know what to point to", you could reply "But surely someone has pain".

Take the proper name 'Watson', and you ask me "To whom does this refer?" I say "It refers to him here"; and if he goes out of the door it still refers to him, and if he goes to America it refers to him in America, or if he is dead it refers to him in the past. It seems as if there were some sort of string by which the word refers to him wherever he is.

(All this is connected with pointing and "talking about".)

If now I described the use of my language, part of my language *may* be: "*This* is Watson." But if I write down rules, then Watson must be there in the book for this rule. If he is not there, I might use a photograph. But now the photograph alone is there. I can say the photograph "refers to someone". But to whom does it refer?

Suppose you have been told about Watson by reference to the photograph and by words, but have not seen him. Then one day he comes along and I say "This is Watson". Shall I say that only now you understand what I am talking about?

"There is a connexion between the photograph and him." But what is "a *connexion*" here? There is a sort of superstition about "the connexion of meaning".—This hangs together with expressions like "I think of him": these words express exactly that connexion.

Suppose I had been talking of Watson when I had only a photograph here. Do I mean that the word Watson is the proper name for a piece of paper? Yet it is not true that there must be somewhere a body to which this name refers.

It is just the same with an *image* of a toothache, the word "toothache", and a real toothache.—If I say that this gesture is an explanation of the word "toothache", this does not mean that I call this gesture a toothache.

I say "Smith" is not the name of the photograph—if I throw the photograph into the fire, I don't say Smith is burning.—If you ask ⟦44⟧ then "What meaning does the word 'Smith' have?"—I say it is not the name of that to which I point; I say it is the name of a man, and the man is not here.—Do you understand the sentences? Yes, of course.

So when I make this gesture ((grimacing, holding my cheek)) and say "This is a toothache", this is a kind of pointing to the gesture, but the gesture is not the meaning of "toothache".

I want to return to the question whether we have explained away the existence of mental phenomena. You might ask, "Do you wish to say there is only moaning, and not the real pain at all?"

As a child you had pain and moaned, etc., and you were taught to say just "pain". Next you learn to say "I have pain". Then you learn a whole language: "I had pain", "Perhaps I shall have pain", "He had pain". And then, ((when you have learned this language)) if you now say "I have pain", has this a different meaning now—which affects its use at the moment while you're saying it?

Suppose you were asked "What were the phenomena which were pointed out when you learned the word 'pain'?" There would be certain noises in other people and then one's own. Then one replaces the moan by "I have pain". The rest of it: "He has pain", "he had pain", etc., is not puzzling. The new phenomenon is the moaning—the *expression* of pain.

Suppose we asked "Does 'I have pain' *analyse* what was expressed in the moan?"

To "What does the moan stand for?", the answer is: Nothing at all. "But you don't just wish to say that you moan?" No; but the moan is not the statement "I moan".

If moaning stands for "I have pain", then it must refer to something, for everyone would say that the sentence "I have pain" refers to something. If we say "the moan expresses something", this does not mean just: "is caused by something". Therefore we say rather: ". . . referred to something".

"I have pain" is syntactically like "I have a match box" or "The chair has a hole". This is a description of something. And "I have pain" sounds like a description of something. When I say it is like a moan, I want to say the words are used in an utterly different way. ⟦45⟧ In one form it replaces a moan.

If I want to explain "The table has a hole", the natural way is to show you what a table is and what a hole is. But I can do nothing of the sort with "I have pain". Where then do we get the equivalent of an ostensive definition? If "pain" is explained by reference to a moan, which in turn *expresses* something—how are we to say what a moan expresses? I can't point at anything and say "the moan expresses *this*". Does it then help to say the moan expresses *something*?

⟦101⟧ XI [April 29, 1936]

The use of: "the impression so-and-so".

We are tempted to say, e.g.: We can define the word "green" by pointing to a sample. But it seems that the "impression which this gives me now" has a different meaning from the word "green".

I might say "This is green, and this is boo", but "this is boo" is taken to be giving a name to the impression which the thing gives me, as opposed to giving a name to the colour. It seems in this case as though I pointed to a different object—that I point just to the impression. I seem to *look* at something different. And I seem to define this by *staring* at or *concentrating* on the sample.

You might say you define the colour in a different way from the way in which you define the shape. You use a different action for defining. And here ((in connexion with 'the impression')) if you use a particular way, e.g. of gazing, this seems to imply that you know now how to use the word.

Gazing is of course connected with pointing. In a particular sense it can replace pointing. I can point out something to *you* by looking at it.—We often mix up *looking* and *seeing.* Gazing qua *looking* can stand for pointing, but qua *seeing* it *can't* stand for pointing.

Suppose I said "I am now drinking in a certain impression".—*What* impression?—"*This* impression."—Pointing to it with my finger would not tell me what impression. What I see is my finger.

Take the case of two objects in my field of vision. I look at *this* as opposed to *that.* But it would have no sense to say I *see* this as opposed to that, for I always see both.

⟦102⟧ The whole problem of solipsism arises from a situation like "I'm looking at *this*".—(You could define a solipsistic position by beginning every sentence with "I think . . .".)—But then you carry this use of "impression" to the point that you want to say "I see only my impressions"; etc.

Think of the state of mind in which I stare and say "*This* equals *this*" ((pointing twice to the same object)), or "This colour is *this* colour". This would be like uttering the sentence "This is here". It is like comparing something with itself.—It is natural to make sentences for which we have no use at all.

It is almost as though we were talking *to* a thing as opposed to *about* it.

We can of course look at things which do not change.

I might say "I don't know if he has the same impression of this as I have", and go on to suggest that he sees dark green where I see light green. Here we make it clear what the *impression* we talk about is by reference to samples etc.

Here the difference between *pointing* and *concentrating* is important.

It is the use of "*this*" where you don't point to 'this' as opposed to 'that', but say "this" and—"I'm drinking in *this*."

Here I don't wish to say "I'm drinking in *green*". For to use "green" does not characterise what I'm drinking in.

"I'm drinking in *this*, and what I'm drinking in I'm calling 'bah'."

Consider the case of a person who says "I think I mean something by this sentence". We should ask: What use does he make of it? But I might say also "he *does* mean something"—i.e., he has got himself into a state of mind in which it is natural to say that, although he would not say it in ordinary life.

We imagined the example of a boy who invented the name "pain" or "toothache". It does not *prima facie* sound absurd to say ⟦103⟧ he invents the word "toothache" and makes private use of it.—I wish to say he makes no use of it whatever, and that the whole business of 'christening the sensation' is all off.

How do I *connect* the word "green" with a certain impression? I might say just: I look at this cloth and say "green, green". But suppose one objected that this "gives only the outside of it. There must always be the same impression." But then I might answer: I don't even know whether it is the same impression; or even whether "the same" is used in the same way on a different occasion.

We may talk about "impressions" as subjective if we can give a criterion to show that he has this impression and I have that, from this thing here.

But the other sense of "impression" arises from a confusion about definition by means of *gazing.* It is a definition of a particular state of mind.

There is the same confusion in what we try to say about 'toothache'. There seem to be two things: There is the word "toothache". And we are then inclined to say "I could use *another* word for my present *sensation*". And this (("using a word *for* my sensation")) would consist in *concentrating* on something. If I am asked "on *what*?" the only correct answer would be "on making this grimace".

If I can say "I concentrate on *this*", isn't it clear that pointing and concentrating must be two different things?—What I should like to have is that concentrating and pointing should be the same. But in the present case this would be like pointing at what I am pointing at—which would be quite empty.

You might say all this sounds as if I had denied the existence of an *impression.*

But what have I denied the existence of?

In certain connexions it is useful to use a different form of expression for a while; and then we may go back and use the old form without feeling that it is unsatisfactory.—The first thing is a dissatisfaction with something in our normal forms of expression.

⟦104⟧ Suppose we call a man "Smith". And then I suggest that this must be objectionable because he is constantly changing shape—he sits, stands, bends etc. There is a dissatisfaction arising from the belief that we ought not to give two different objects the same name—for then there is confusion. And someone might then say it is wrong to give him the same name, because he is constantly changing.

What is the answer to this? First: "It works all right, so why object?"

We speak of birds singing. When I was a boy I was bothered in listening to birds, because it obviously isn't *singing.* Finally someone said to me, "All right, don't call it singing, call it something else". And soon I could listen to birds and enjoy it.

Suppose you get into the habit of mind which says you can't call *this* "Smith" and also call *another* shape "Smith".—Suppose someone were accustomed to call only *statues* names. Then he would find it queer to give *names* to human beings. "Surely you can't give this a name." Then I say "Well never mind, don't call it a name". Or: "if you don't want to give it one name, give it fifty names." The person would now see the relation between this and the other ((normal sense of)) name, and would not be tempted to think they are really the same.

## XII [May 6, 1936]

There is a sentence,

"I see this",

when by "this" I do not mean the physical object, but rather the *impression.*

We can use the phrase if we point to a spot and ask "Do you see this?" and he answers "No, I don't see that, but I see this" pointing to something else. But also, if we want to point out an impression, we can of course say "I see this". If I look through a telescope and someone asks me what I see, I can then draw three dots and say "I see this"—meaning I see three dots in this arrangement. But this may seem to be indirectly pointing; and suppose one can point *directly* and say "I see this".

⟦105⟧ a) I can say "I see this"—as opposed to what is on the other side of the blackboard.

b) "I see this" can be of just the same nature as "A is A" or "I am here".

If I point to something and use a name, I either (1) designate that which I point to as a sample which I am going to use in my language in future. "I am going to call what I see now 'green' "—"I am going to call this 'green' ". This is not attributing the property 'green' to something but saying I am going to use it ((what I point to)) as a sample.

I can then (2) look over there and say "I see this colour" ((pointing to the same object as before)). Then I am already *using* it as a sample.

But the temptation is to do something between these two, and use it as a sample of itself, so to speak.

We use the expression "a certain . . .". "I have a certain feeling." "A certain" is all right in "I met a certain man—*namely* Smith". But "a certain experience"—if you concentrate on your toothache and say you are concentrating on a certain experience, then you have the idea that you have pointed to something,—as though when you say "toothache is a certain experience" you have defined the word "toothache".

You may say "I see this" where after the words "I see" the "this" points either (1) to the physical object, or else (2) to some sort of description.—But if you don't do either of these and try to use it to point to an *impression,* then you might say anything you like about your impression—perhaps that your impression never varies at all.

Compare the sort of view which says "All that is real is my present experience". Here the "present experience" is taken to be something like a flash of what he sees. If you say this you can't talk of a *change* of your experience. You can't say "In the next moment it changes".—I don't want to say that a man who does this does anything *wrong.* Only, if he gives his impression a name, there is no reason why he should ever use any other name. If I call my ⟦106⟧ impression "A" and say "this is A", then we might say "Well if it is always 'this', then it is always A".

It has been said that "this" and "that" are the only real proper names. One could have said rather that the word "Hello" or "Cheerio" is the real proper name. Suppose you stand before something which impresses you—e.g. a flower—and say "Aha!" or "Ah!". You might thus have said that "ah!" is the only real proper name—for just the same reasons as led people to say "this" is the only real proper name.

We might say a proper name is a kind of *greeting* of an object. Concentrate on this chair and say the word "green"—but where the word "green" is said as one might say the word "hello". If you use 'proper name' in *this* way, then it would be quite *natural* that your impressions should have the same proper name.

We can't say "If I look at this I see this". I may say "If I look at this I see . . ."—But then there must be "the chair" or "this colour". What you point to as an explanation of what you see, is a sample. And a sample is something used in language.

Suppose I said, "Since I don't know what impressions other people have of things, all that matters is their behaviour or what they say." But can't I say this of myself as well?

Suppose I call this green and then say "how do I know this is what I call green?" Answer: "It is the same." But how do I know I am using "the same" in the same way? The fact is that I am *using* it.

Imagine a cinema where we have names for the pictures on the screen, a, b, c, etc., and we say "c is now"—meaning by "c" the picture on the film and saying that this is being projected. Now imagine someone who thought he could use "c" not to refer to pictures on the film but saying it of what is on the screen simply—*pointing* to *that,* calling that c, and saying "c is now". He might equally well have said *any*thing was "c".

When a person says "This is now" etc., he looks at things in a way in which he would look if he were giving them names for ⟦107⟧ future use. He mixes up (1) the use in which we would give a sample with (2) the attitude in which we *predicate* something.

In our everyday talk we speak of an impression being kept in memory. If someone says "Only the impression of the present moment is real", he cannot talk of a change in that impression. He cannot use a name for a past impression—unless the name were a word like "now". As though, instead of writing at the top of the page "Date, 2 July", I wrote just "Date".

The temptation to say that only the present is real is like the temptation by the word "date". It is like a person saying "The *real* date is *now*" and "the real place is *here*". One could say to this person, "Well, the two words 'now' and 'here' do correspond to what you might find on a form to be filled in, namely the word 'place' and the word 'date'."

"Only the present is real" is not, in one sense, just equivalent to "the present is the present". It is more like putting the present on a pedestal, like crowning it—("real" in a laudatory sense).

It is not to the point to say "It is absurd to say the present sensation alone is real, because the past sensation *was* real." This is not to the point. It is like trying to answer the solipsist who says "Only my toothache that I feel is real" by saying "You feel yours, but he also feels his". His mistake is in the function which our words have. It is like thinking that the word "date" is actually the date, or that the word "this" is the name.

If someone says "Only my present sensation is real" and if he then goes on to say that he doesn't want to say that you and other people are automatons etc.,—his "only my present sensation is real" was just an innocuous noise.

When we say "the past does not exist" we think of the past as *different* from the present, and we say that *that* doesn't exist: if I at one time sat like that, and I now sit like this . . . But if I sit always in the same way—does the past exist in this case, or doesn't it?—We have the false view that the present is being destroyed.

⟦108⟧ Memory. Has memory "a certain specific character"? What does one think of, when one thinks of the specific character of memory? You think of some examples. But suppose someone asked you, "How do you know you are not mistaken about your example? How do you know this really is an example of memory?—apart from the fact that you are calling it such? How do you know your example does not change in just that 'essential respect'?"

You may say that you can think of *other* cases of memory, perhaps of cases which have the same 'specific character', and which differ from cases of imagining which are not memory in the same way in which this case does.—But what does "in the same way" mean here? We can't use this phrase interchangeably with "*a certain* way".—And suppose someone were to ask you to give the way in which they all differ from imagining?

Now of course I might use the notion of something's "happening in the same way", when I want to use it as a model to myself. I may say, "it moves in this way, or in that way", where I can produce specific examples. But the case of the "certain specific character of memory" is of just the same sort as "I see this". You are talking about your impression only, and you are using it as a sample of itself. You take something as a *sample* of memory, and you call this having an *example* of memory before one's mind.

## XIII [May 11 (?), 1936]

When I say "I see this", if I point to something it is a sample.—There is the case in which I say "I see this" meaning "I see the table". But where it doesn't mean "I see the table" one imagines one is pointing to a sample.

Suppose I recall something; and I say, "Memory is a specific experience". Can one supplement this? "It is an experience in which we feel something is past"—and one is tempted to say "namely *this*", without giving any further description. In fact one would like to say "I know what it is but I can't say it".

Suppose you are learning the word "Gedächtnis". You learn the word, read it, and remember sitting in the garden. You impress ⟦109⟧ something on yourself.—But in this case there is such a thing as right and wrong remembering. In the other case there does not seem to be any such possibility. It is just a question of how it seems to you.

It is the question of how words are used.

We talk of giving someone or something a name. I may give a name by saying so and so and pointing. We are likely to think this is *all* that is involved in giving a name. But giving a name should show the way in which I am going to use it.—How am I going to use a name in such a way that it might be said that it is the name of an impression?

Generally I fix a sample: and this is what we call giving an impression a name. But if this is naming an impression, then I can't say I point to an impression and say "I see this".

We can't say "all that happens is that you use the word 'green'". I may see green and it may be green, and then this is not all. Or I may see green and may have my eyes closed, and then it is all.

It is not clear what we mean by "there is more". Is it more that there is a toothache than that there isn't a toothache? When he says there is a toothache and there is, then if you say "there is more" this is unobjectionable so long as it is taken to be just a transformation of what is said before.

I may say "There is more, there is *this*" if "this" means a *sample.* This is not objectionable.

If we give this creature a name, then we cannot give the time atom a name in the normal sense.

The question "What is it made of?" is different when it is a physical question, and when it is a question of logical analysis.

Suppose I say a man is made up of a number of time atoms. Suppose I said "at 5 o'clock there was this  present, and I call this A". If I then say that at 5 minutes past 5 there was B, which was exactly the same as this which I called A—well, then why use "A" and "B"? ((Application to: this time atom, and later *this* time atom.))

Compare William James's view that there is "an 'if' sensation", "an 'and' sensation", "a 'but' sensation". . . .

⟦110⟧ I may draw your attention to something by saying "If it rains, we'll go out" and then asking: "Well, don't you feel some sensation?"—"Yes."—"Well, that's the 'if' sensation."

We might say "There is a peculiar 'if' gesture, namely *this*"—and give a sample of a gesture. So you might say also "there is a specific 'not' gesture". But as soon as you say this you see that one doesn't always make the same gesture.

"Do you wish to say there *isn't* a particular 'if' sensation? Do you wish to say there is only an 'if' gesture?"

Whenever we make statements which seem to be behaviouristic statements, the essence is that we give a *sample.* What is behaviouristic is the *sample* which I give. Someone asks me "What is *pain*?" and I pinch him. I've given a sample of pain.

Now what was the sample? Was it the *pinching,* or was it the particular sensation which you gave him?—In the sense in which you say (a) that only he knows what the sensation was, and (b) the sensation was that which was *present*—the sensation couldn't have been the sample. The sample is part of our language; it is like a word in this respect. We use samples differently from words, and words sometimes as samples and sometimes not. But what I meant was: a sample is, just as a word is something which lasts—I show you the sample, you see it, I see it, we look at it for five minutes. The grammar of '*sample*' and the grammar of '*word*' are similar in a way in which the grammar of 'word' and the grammar of 'impression' are not.

(("Was it the pinching, or was it the particular sensation you gave him?"—)) You can say both. I can say, "Yes, it is that peculiar sensation"—pinching him again.—"It's that sensation, it's not only the pinch." This could mean: if he were anaesthetised he would not understand me.

Suppose someone says: "The sensation passes, and then later on you recognize it again". I would say no, if you say that, then the sensation is not the sample. You can't talk of *recognizing* it, because you have no criterion of recognizing correctly or incorrectly.

It is the same case with speaking of atoms of 'Smiths'. Imagine that the sensation were something like a body which moved about ⟦111⟧ and disappeared. Suppose there were a way of tracing the sensation's movements: you can see it move about away from him, move around, and then it comes back and you say "Ah yes, he has it again". Here you can say "He recognizes it".—But clearly this is a wrong picture. And it makes plain that there is in our case no such thing as *recognizing* it, since there is no criterion for recognizing it wrongly or rightly.

I gave him the sample by pinching him. I can say the sample is the pinch, or I can say it is "this sensation"—and then I have to say "this sensation" whilst I pinch him.

We might say that Formalism in mathematics is behaviourism in mathematics. I could draw '2' and say "That is the number two". This is exactly the same as pinching and saying "This is pain".—Mathematicians say "Surely it is not just the numeral, it is something more." Yes, something more if you like.—Suppose one said: "What one says about the number 2, one could express in terms of the numeral 2." It is just the same in the case of "this pain".

Of course one says the expression can always lie. "If we just used behaviouristic criteria, we should certainly take something for granted." Yes. But not as though, if we looked we should see something more.

We have to talk of behaviour if we talk of our language and its use.

We talk of *recognizing* rightly and wrongly. "It is the same and he recognized it." But here the criterion is *that* you recognize it—that you say "pain" again. This really means that it is impossible to recognize it wrongly—in fact that there is not any such thing as recognition here.

With regard to a man who comes into the room, you would not say "he is the same if you say he is the same". But in the case in which the only criterion is that he says "green" or moans. . . .

We use "recognize" where we can say "it *is* the same and he *recognized* it". Here it is used only where there is a distinction ⟦112⟧ between appearance and reality. But in this other case there is no such distinction.—Can you say "He has a toothache but he doesn't recognize it"? or "he had no toothache, but it seemed to him he did, and he got along all right"?

You can be *wrong* only in the game you play with other people. Suppose I ask, "Why do you again say it is *pain*?"—"Because it is the same experience."—"But why do you call it the *same* now?"

If you imagine that pinching him is an indirect way of calling his attention to something else, A, and that this recurs and he recognizes it, then I say this is wrong. For ((in what you are imagining)) there can't be a case in which it recurs and he didn't recognize it; and if it didn't recur and he thought he recognized it, it would do just as well. You are talking of a "something".

You can say "I've got the same sensation now". But not: "This is the same sensation again, and therefore I recognize it". Is it something different to recognize it as the same and to recognize it as red?

You can say: "recognized" = "it is the same".
Then "I recognize this sensation" = "I have the same sensation".
Therefore you cannot say "I have the same sensation *and* I recognize it".

Suppose you do say that when, for example, I pinch you to show you what pain is, I draw your attention to a certain something in an indirect way; and "If that certain something recurs then I recognize it and say that is pain".

If so, then the pinching was something unessential—I might just as well have said "ha ha". Then I have no idea what I am drawing his attention to. He may now say he recognizes it and say: "I have pain here and what a joke!". Is he then using it correctly and playing our language game with the word "pain"?

Suppose we gave a man a definition of pain by pinching. Then we stuck pins in him and he laughed; then we gave him a sweet and he said "pain".—Should we then say he recognized pain? Should we say he meant by pain what we mean?

If by "pain" we mean something *private,* then we ought not to say it means a certain *feeling,* for "feeling" is not a private word—it refers to a certain grammar in our language. We should have to say that by "pain" we mean, not the pinching, but "a certain something". Then it becomes absurd.

## ⟦113⟧ XIV [May 13, 1936]

The delusion both of the behaviourists and of their opponents can be explained thus:

"This has this colour" (where I point twice to the same thing). You can say this is no sentence.

An opponent of the behaviourist might say, "Then are you going to say that it has no colour at all—that there is only the sentence and the sample?"

No, it has a colour, namely *this* (pointing to something *else*). We can use the phrase "this colour" when we say, for example, "this colour is the same as this" (comparing two pieces of material); but we can't use it in that sentence ("This has this colour", pointing to the same thing).

We are inclined to think we give a name to a sensation if we have the sensation and say, for example, "This is A" and "This is red".

If I take this patch to be the *sample* of what we call "blue", then there is no sense in saying of it "this is blue".

Regarding sensations: Suppose he has it again and says "This is A".—But what is meant by "if he has *it* again"? Is it the sample or isn't it? If it isn't, then where is the sample? He might say the sample is my memory image; that this is what persists.

But it isn't necessary that the *perception* should be interrupted; it could also go on. Then he would need no memory image. He says "This I call green". At another moment "There is green" means just "The sensation which I have persists". (If then you were to ask him what "persisting" meant, he would have to give a similar definition: "This I call persisting". Then after a time he goes on and says "It persists".)

Does it say that I have no impression, if I call it senseless to say "I have this impression"? You might accuse me of saying that there is only the words and the sample to which I can point, and therefore of denying that there is an impression.

I can say "The impression I have in looking at this chair I call *ba*". But this is not a definition; the chair is then the sample.

⟦114⟧ If you wanted to support behaviourism you could say: A definition is a piece of behaviour; it must say "This is pain". It does not follow that pain is a behaviour.

If someone were to ask "Is that all?", then I should answer: In the realm of *language* that is all.

Similarly, it is a definition to grimace and say "This is a toothache", but none to *say simply* "This is a toothache"; not even a definition for yourself.

Sometimes when someone looks at something and says "This is red" it *is* a definition; for then *looking* is a kind of pointing—directing my attention. But *seeing* and saying "This is red" is *no* definition.

It is all bound up with the notion of *'recurring'* and the word "the same"; with the words "already" and "again".

What do we *define* as being a recurrence? How do we *use* the word "recur"?

Suppose that Adam when he was naming the animals said "This is the lion again"—is this a definition of "lion", or of "again"?

Suppose someone just learns by heart the names of colours, without using a colour chart—"impressing them on his memory". If you say he *learns* this, then you distinguish between a correct and a wrong remembering; if not, there is no learning. He has colours in a row and says "blue, green, yellow . . ." etc. Perhaps he asks himself, "Do I *know* it now?". If he can know it, it must be possible for him to be wrong.

After a bit he says "Now I know it. Therefore what I call blue is now blue. There is no further criterion for checking up."—Then he is not using any language at all. He simply goes about and makes noises.

If he and I played the game *together*, then it would become a language; for then I could say, "No, you were wrong".—Otherwise we can't say "he calls blue what *is* blue". He just makes a noise which he has made three times before. The point of repeating it is to "get it right"—otherwise it has no point: he said the word three times and later said it again.

⟦115⟧ You might object, "He said the word and it was the same". But what is 'being the same' here?

He would be using a language just as much and just as little as if he were to go about and say "Hello" to various objects. But it would not be a case of using the word "blue" correctly, as we may do in our language. The nearest thing to it in our language would be "Ah!". Just as, when I say "I have a peculiar sensation" it is like "Ah!" or "Hm".

Regarding memory:

If I see something actually pass by ((a race horse, a log being carried down stream . . .)) then I can say "That has passed" or "That's past". Then we can use the word "past" where nothing has 'passed'. This is not a peculiarity of memory. We also use the words "clearly" and "unclearly"—which have been used in such and such a fashion—and speak of remembering clearly or unclearly. This *is* a peculiar character of memory.

Remember Hume's description of "ideas" as "faint copies". If he had said "When I drink beer I see things fainter", he would have described an experience. Whereas he didn't.

Suppose I couldn't make you see what I meant by the word "idea", and in order to do so I showed you a cartoon in which I had a blue picture, and said "That is an idea". You might of course misunderstand.

Or I might say "Time is more ethereal than a chair", or "The passage of time is more ethereal than the passage of a train".—But this is not a matter of experience.

The non-behaviouristic element in an account of memory will consist of the use of words like "feeling", "attitude of mind" and so on. You get finally to a definition which is in terms of behaviour—even though you may say "This sensation I call pain, and this behaviour I call pinching". This is like "This numeral I call 'two', this number I call 'toe'."—Whether the words describe a behaviour or describe a sensation is not shown by simply saying "This I will call pain" (pinching). And when I say "*This* I will call pain, this sensation", I am outlining a *use* for this definition.—Suppose I say "There is a sensation 'long, long ago' . . .", giving ⟦116⟧ certain gestures. The *definition* is a piece of behaviour, and the word "sensation" referred to a peculiar *use* of that definition.—We might say, "The sensation of '*pastness*' is: (with a gesture) '*long, long ago*'."

I can say "Of course I have given a behaviouristic explanation—i.e., I have behaved in a certain way.—And on the other hand I *haven't* given a behaviouristic explanation, for I was defining a *sensation*."

I said earlier: When you think of "if-feelings", substitute for the feelings the gestures. The feelings are not the gestures. But if I said "There is a 'perhaps-feeling'" and you asked me "What is it?", I would answer: "It is the *feeling* 'perhaps' (making a gesture)."

We come on the question of what is describable and what is indescribable. You can describe a face. But you might say, "What I really saw when I looked at him, I can never describe". Or, "One can never describe the exact impression one has had."

But what do you call "describing an impression"?

We understand the expression "giving Watson a name". But what is: "giving the sensation of looking at him a name"?

We speak of directing your attention to something by the definition. But does this mean "*pointing* to something"? You can't point to a sensation—it means nothing. When I say the sensation of pastness is: (gesture) 'long, long ago', this is not a way of *pointing* to something.

## XV [May 18, 1936]

Part of our philosophical difficulties can be cleared up if we use samples instead of words.

I talk to myself. This is an interesting phenomenon. But does it mean I inform myself of something? Does it, for instance, if I whistle to myself?

Look at a bright colour and say: "Surely there is such a thing as ⟦117⟧ an impression." But now ask yourself: "But why did you make a noise along with it?"

"Use samples instead of words." We can do this because the use of the word "red" is actually connected with a sample.

Using a sample in this way, for instance: If you don't see this chair and I wish to describe its colour, I say "The chair is like this" and point to a sample. Or another use in a psychological experiment: a current is sent through you and you are asked to say what colours you see. You might answer then . . . (just pointing to a coloured patch).

Our use of words like "impression", "mental state" etc. centres round a double use of the symbols.

Generally if I point to a sample there is a way of checking whether I am right or wrong. It is different in the psychological experiment, where I can't point to anything. This is not because I can't open my inside. There isn't anything to point to.

We are inclined to say: the difference is that in the one case I can point, because the object is outside, in the other case I cannot, because it is inside.

Compare this with the case where we say of low notes in music that they are "dark". We can then say "The bumble bee produces a dark sound". But if I say "The middle C is dark" that is using "dark" in a different way, and I could say "It gives me the impression of darkness".

In the first case I use the word "dark" as I use "deep". In the other case not.

We may talk of the man called Beethoven. I can say of Smith "He is a Beethoven". Here I am making a fuss of him. But when I say of Beethoven "This is Beethoven", I am not.

When you say "Toothache is something *internal*", this may be used in either of two ways.—Your assertion does not contain the element of time: we can't ask "When?" You think it *cannot* be anything else. You are using the picture "external—internal" in the same way in which one uses "dark" and "bright" in the case of ⟦118⟧ notes of the piano. You don't want to say that subcontra C is dark *now*. Or if you do, you mean it gives you a dark impression.

You don't say of a toothache *that it is internal*. You *compare* moaning and a toothache with 'external' and 'internal'.

I want to speak of the danger of saying that in the psychological experiment there is an object which you cannot point to.

I can of course imagine myself giving a definition without giving it. If you think of *'pointing inwardly'* what you do is to imagine pointing *outwardly*.—If you imagine pointing to the image of red, you can explain what you were doing by pointing outwardly.

You might ask, "Do you say then that all that happens in the experiment is that you show the experimenter the sample?"

If the subject is not ready to point to samples, why should he have used words? What is the good of the word "green" if he can't point to a green sample?

Suppose a man learned the names of colours, and he said "green". Then I ask him "What did you see just now?", and he answers "red"; after another moment "green"; and after another "red" . . . etc. Could he use our language at all?

This means that our use of words is dependent on the phenomenon of remembering, and if all our answers were different we should have no reason to say anything.

The question then: "Do you mean nothing happens in him?"

He gives you the sample. You may suggest that ((in doing this)) he matches the sample with a picture before his mind's eye.—I say it is wrong to say this, because you have here the idea of matching, and the word "match" could also be represented by a sample.

But it is also incorrect to say "nothing happens except that he has shown a sample".

It is wrong to say "I show this sample *because* it matches the picture before my mind's eye". It's wrong—i.e., he says no more by showing the sample than when he says "This matches the picture before my mind's eye". Compare what we said about the fact that the sentence

"I moan" is not a moan, and to moan is not to ⟦119⟧ say "I moan". It seems as though "I have a toothache" were an explanation of the moan. Whereas it is really the other way about. If you then ask "What does the moan mean?", there is no answer.

Suppose someone said, "It is not just that you point to the sample but you *refer* to something by pointing to it."—What did the sample refer to? In the case of an after-image you could say "I see two red dashes". But does one of these refer to the other?

Could I have said in any *clearer* way what I really saw? It seems as if I could, and that it was not just pointing to the sample.—But what *is* the impression which justifies me in pointing to the sample? Is it the impression which I see projected, or is it the sameness between these two impressions?

"You didn't just show the sample" = "You had a justification for doing so". I say you had none. A justification refers to a *rule*: I can't say "what I see here is a justification".—The chain of reasons has an end. Finally the reason can only be a *rule*: 'You do *that*'—and there is no reason for it.

Is there a reason for calling these // the same colour?

If someone said, "In the psychological experiment all that happens is that the subject points to the samples", the "all that happens" would mean only that he has no reason. But if you said "Oh you don't mean to say he sees red?", then you'd be wrong—just the opposite. *Pointing* was just the translation of "I see red".

Objection: He can tell us a lie. This means he can show us a sample which does not agree with what he sees before his mind's eye.

This is misleading.

Suppose I give an example. I say: "For instance I lie if I say this is red (pointing to this)."

But "He lies if he points to what does not agree" just means "He lies when he lies".—You can go on and explain, "He lies if he says he sees this when he sees that", pointing in both cases.

"He must know when he lies." What does it mean, to know when you lie?

⟦120⟧ This question is connected with another question. Each of us can obey an order of the form "Imagine so and so". He says, "Yes, I am imagining a red spot".—How did he know he was imagining? How does he know what to do, or whether he has obeyed the order? You might say: all that happens is that a colour comes into his mind.

You may want to add, "It must come in a particular way". Or perhaps, "when it comes you have a good conscience".

How does he know he is lying? Here again you might say just, "He has a bad conscience".

I would say, there is not one but many different feelings of lying: which correspond to different behaviours. And we have to say further, these alone *don't* constitute a case of lying.

Turn to the case of reading. How do you know you are reading? Is all that happens that you see the scratches on the paper? Or do sounds come in a particular *way*? and is this what is meant by reading it?

Suppose 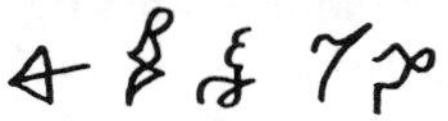

A man sees this and he has the same experience as I have when I read

ABOVE

Would we then say he is reading?

What we call reading is connected with certain experiences: but *with* these experiences in certain cases I would not say I read, and in others *without* them I *would* say I read.

Similarly with lying. *When* does one say that he lies? *When* does he know that he lies? Does he know it when it is done, and then suddenly? (Compare: "When does he understand the sentence? How long does it take to understand?")

Lying is not *one* process, but masses of different processes.

Suppose you always said an aside when you lied. We would call this lying because of the role which it plays in ordinary life.

What happens at the moment of lying may be what makes us say that he lies, but this is not what is characteristic of *lying*.

"He knew the whole time that he was lying." But this is not a ⟦121⟧ question of some accompaniment that is happening, that you are doing concomitantly.

"Every expression may lie." Therefore it can't be just that I tell myself in an aside the opposite. It must be that I *mean* the opposite.

There is no question of *knowing* that it is lying. It is a question of the role which certain statements play.

There is no one 'full fledged' case of lying. I am inclined to say there are cases where you lie with knowledge, and others where you do it automatically.

Compare also statements about 'a full fledged case of volition'. ((*The Brown Book*, p. 150))

With reference to the psychological experiment, where we say "What happens is that he knows what he sees, and then points to the sample." But what does he know? Does he know he sees *this*? Then this is just pointing to the sample. What is it like to know what he sees?

When someone says "he knows what he sees", we generally think of words. But why should he have used words at all?

Samples and words: this has to do with the point that we don't wonder enough about the use which language has.—This is connected with the point about "He is a Beethoven".

Our use of colour words is connected with a use of samples. But if I say "I see red" when there is no sample present, and this has sense—then why should one not say it has sense without any connexion with a sample? I say no, you cannot say that; the expression has sense in that game in which we use samples.

One can look at the words as samples themselves; which means I don't *gain* anything by avoiding samples. You can see a connexion between this and reading sounds from written letters. "How does one read off sounds?"

Someone might say "In a psychological experiment we don't need samples, and samples tie us down to something. I don't know what is before his mind's eye. But he uses the word with sense. ⟦122⟧ And therefore ((without samples)) he uses it with greater freedom".—

But insofar as the word "green" doesn't tie him down to anything, it is no good at all.

The word "green" *seems* to have two different kinds of connexion: a) the connexion with a sample ((e.g. in a colour chart)); b) a connexion which is made with an image before the mind's eye. This latter need not be the same at different times, since all that is needed is that he says "green" with a good conscience. It is a tie with something else, of which it doesn't matter what it is.

You could say there are samples outside, but also inside. He combines the word "green" with a sample inside. But it doesn't matter what, so long as he is *bona fide.* Therefore the use of "green" is here more loose.

But how do you fix the "internal function"?

Imagine that you use "the same" and "boo" and "bah", and that you mustn't say, "boo; now it's the same again, it's bah", but rather "it's the same again, it's boo".—Here we have a rule but no samples. But what use would it be?

## XVI [May 20, 1936]

What is meant by *describing* a certain state of affairs?

In what sense can it be said of a person in a psychological experiment that he *describes* his experience?

"I believe he is there." Does this describe a mental experience?—"I am certain he is there." Does this?—Does one *always* describe a mental experience when he talks?

Avoid the notion that it is a less complete statement when he points to a sample than when he says "I see red".

One might say: His statement "I see red" may be true or false—agree or disagree with what he sees.

Do two red dashes agree with each other, and do a red dash and a blue dash disagree? I might say they are the same. I might suppose ((the red and the blue dash together)) as a sample for "the same".

⟦123⟧ One might think that to use a dark red patch as a sample for light red would be no good. But it might be that it is easier to copy into a lighter shade; or that it is easier to copy a red patch blue.

I will write: 1, 1 + 1, . . . . Now go on in the same way.

What is the same way? Is it 1 + 1 + 1, or (1 + 1) + (1 + 1)?

You might say the common factor here is "+1", and not "1 + 1", and it is with the use of this common factor that you should go on. But would that compel you to go on in *this* way?

"Surely there must be a right way and a wrong way?"—Well, *we* do go on in a certain way. If a man doesn't do this, we may not be able to teach him. But we can't say "it leads to anarchy" to say the opposite. We might say we can't bring him to do arithmetic, or we can't bring him to do arithmetic *right.* But "right" here doesn't mean there is no difference between playing another game and playing no game at all.—"But you know what you want."—Well yes, if this means just that if you ask me I'll give you an answer. It does not mean that anything is going on at the time.

"How do we control the game?" By the rules.—But do we control the application of the rules?—No.—What then does it mean to control by the rules?—Just that people do in fact act in certain ways.

"Go on adding one." And what is adding one? To 'know how to go on' is much more complicated than one would think.

It is the same sort of thing with the grammar of "Point to the same colour".

What makes a description which the person gives in the psychological experiment right or wrong? You might say, "If his way of expression is to point to the sample, then the sample has to agree with what he sees." And what is that? Might it not agree in one moment and in another disagree?

"Doesn't this lead to anarchy?"

No, for the police ((law enforcement)) which stops the anarchy acts in the public language.

"Is it *winning* to put one piece of wood on another?" Only in a game.

Only within a language game is there a right or wrong in it. You couldn't say, "for the other person it could not have been wrong, ⟦124⟧ but for him it is wrong". There is no question of right or wrong until you have fixed certain rules.

As regards *'going on'*: (1) there is no sharp line between plausible and less plausible ways. (2) You are more familiar with certain ways, and less familiar with others.

"But examples don't define a rule. You use *'the same'* in a different way: if you define the way in which you use it, all will be well."

But this really does not help, since how *is* one to define or explain the way you use it?

(3) Surely you know yourself in what way you use 'the same'.

"So you say *everything's* all right?" No, I don't. We do draw a line. We say in certain cases, "Then he is doing no arithmetic at all, he is obeying no rule".

Suppose each of us possesses a private object, which no one else has seen or can see. Then we make (up) a game comparing our private objects—say in respect of colours. We teach people colour names.

Suppose a man plays the normal colour game. But when he looks into his private box and sees a blue object there, he says "red" or points to a red sample. He does this entirely *bona fide*.—Would you say he was wrong? Might he not say "those rules were for common objects, but this is my *private* object"? I should say he was *neither* right nor wrong.

"Play the same game with your private object." But which *is* the same, in this case? (The question will then arise, what sense it *had* to say: it was blue and he said it was red.)

"But the fact that it is internal shall make no difference." Answer: Yes, that is just it, it *doesn't* make any difference.

The case is so: I first of all use normal language to describe a certain case—until it becomes apparent that part of my description has no use at all. I say "it is blue but he says it is red". But what is this? I have described no game played with this internal object, and I pretend to describe a certain phenomenon.

Or differently: There is a certain object before him and he has to say the colour. But other people don't see it, and so everyone says ⟦125⟧ "Of course I can't know".—I first make this statement that the object is in a peculiar position in our game. *Then* I use the normal language with reference to it. So if you go through the example you see that you really talk rubbish.

"Go on the same." But there *isn't* one thing which is the same and the other is contradicting.—And in the special case there is no question of "is it the same or not?" or "is he right or wrong?"

In the example of the 'private object', how can I explain either to you or to myself, that although I really see red I say blue? Can I even say to myself that although the object is the same as the red patch, I say blue "*because it is internal*"? What does this mean?

You might say "Surely I can imagine blue and say 'red'". Yes; I may imagine that I see *that,* and say *this* (red patch). But in what sense can I imagine that I see the internal object?

I want to talk about 'right' or 'wrong' in the continuation of: 1, 1 + 1, . . . . I don't say there is no right or wrong at all. If I say "Add 1" then it is wrong to go on: (1 + 1) + (1 + 1), but right to go on: 1 + 1 + 1. The question is whether I could give you a reason for this: "Why is it right?". I might just say "That is what I meant", or just "Well you've got to do that".—"It is right" is a *decision* which I make. I can't give reasons *ad infinitum.*

Take the table:

| | | | | |
|---|---|---|---|---|
| a | I | | | |
| b | II | | | |
| c | III | | | |
| d | IV | | | |

etc.

You then look up what corresponds to b, and find II. But why go on in just that way? Why not diagonally down from b, or diagonally up from b? I say there was a rule (for 'corresponds in such a table'). But I can't give you a reason for it.

⟦126⟧ "Do you mean that:

to say: 2 + 1 = 3

is the same as to say: that you *say* 2 + 1 = 3, or write it?"

No. The words "I write so and so" have a different application.

"But it *agrees* with the rule which you have given when you write 1 + 1 + 1." Well, this just means that you have to do this—that's what the rule is for.

Return to the psychological experiment and the example of the private object. Suppose you found that I said "red" but then said to Smith when we were alone, "Between you and me, I saw blue, but said red". Is this nonsense, or does it make sense?—Should we say, "Then you told a lie"? Supposing people who did this were in general rather bad characters, then it would play the rôle of a lie.

If he tells himself or tells someone else (("between you and me")), he does it by pointing to samples: "I see this, and say I see that". Here one could speak of two disagreeing statements. But could one ask, "Now which of these statements agrees with the thing itself?"—unless we can say that if he said to himself "I see this, but say I see that", then he saw *this*.

"Surely he knows what he sees." How does he do this? Suppose it consists in pointing to one of these samples. So I could know that I see this, and tell the other person I see that—and then I should have told a lie.

"How do I know my image is red?"—I told you: if it is like *this*.—"How do I know it is like that?"—If things are thus related, they are like one another.—"How do I know that this and my image stand in the same relation?" Etc.

The question "How do I know my image is red?" is like "How do I know my image has the colour it has?" (cf. the point above "He knows what he sees". He himself knows in terms of symbols: what he knows, he could say.)

We are inclined to say there must be a reason when there *is* no reason. If I say "How do you know that you see red?"—there *is* no justification. But then the temptation is to say: "So all it comes to is that you say it (say the words)". As though pointing meant the same as the words "to point".

⟦127⟧ I want to go on to the example of 'projection'. "He projects his image . . ." If you ask "What sort of projection did the child use?", this makes no sense. We have explained the use of the word 'projection' in certain cases and not in others. We could say that a certain mode of projection took place in his imagination—i.e., he imagined such a projection. But not a projection from his imagination into reality.

## XVII [May 25, 1936]

It was suggested that you might speak of "projecting" a private image into the sample which you use. The point of this was to make clear how far the use of the term "describe" was justified in connexion with the psychological experiment.—It showed that the word "same" may be used in many different ways.

Suppose we learned to describe a geometrical figure which we see by drawing a certain geometrical figure which is connected with the figure seen by a certain mode of projection.—This would roughly correspond to using a *scale* in making a map.

Suppose then that someone in a psychological experiment were to describe what he sees, and he points to a certain triangle. If we asked "What method of projection did you use?" . . .

Suppose it was by colour: he makes (draws) a red dash. What is the relation between the colour drawn and that imagined?—I don't mean this is nonsense. You would probably answer "the same". But I ask what you mean by "the same", and you give the sample //. So I say, "Aha, so you tell me you imagined this colour according to this mode of projection."

But is this really more explicit? If you give me a mode of projection 'by the complementary (colour)', I can transform this into another, that of equality. And then the mode of projection adds nothing. I say: "Oh you imagine according to that mode of projection,—so you imagine *this* (red dash)."

One is inclined to say, "Although I give you a sample of what I see, and connect it in all sorts of different ways—still I must *know* what I see." There are two possibilities: he may say

⟦128⟧ 1) "I know what I see, namely *this* (giving a sample, not pointing to what I see)."

2) "I know what I see—yes, I just told you."

But people have an idea that he points to what he sees—that he knows that he sees what he sees, or that he knows that he sees *this.*

We are tempted to use the grammar which we use for a word designating a physical object—we are tempted to use this grammar for words that designate impressions. In our primitive language most substantives relate to some physical object or other. When then we begin to talk of impressions, we have a temptation to use the same kind of grammar. This produces a puzzle which doesn't look as though it were a grammatical puzzle.

Suppose you see a film. You can imagine it going slowly enough so that you can follow the movements; or again so rapidly that you cannot follow the movements: you can't catch up.

There is a puzzlement from feeling that our language can in no case catch up with events. . . But here it is not because of rapid movements. Even if you are standing still you have the same puzzle.—

If I say this is a grammatical puzzle,—it seems to be a metaphysical puzzle.

You could have a *physical* puzzle regarding movements—e.g., what curves do horses' hoofs describe? You solve it by taking a cinematograph film.—But here you can't solve it in this way.

It is here a grammatical puzzle. We talk of "running away" where there *is* no running away. Nor is there any question of catching up with anything. The picture we use makes us pant without running. As soon as you remember this and stop applying the word here, the feeling disappears.

We can say the same thing about the *grammatical* delusion of "I see this". Again one would be inclined to call this a metaphysical delusion.—The puzzle is that one is inclined to say "I *know* what I see", and not to be satisfied with "namely this (pointing to a sample)"; as though he sees something which you *don't* know. We have an idea that he can say "namely this"—pointing to *what he sees.*

Our craving is to make the *grammar* of the sense datum similar to ⟦129⟧ the grammar of the physical body. That is why the term 'sense datum' was introduced—it being the "private object" corresponding to the "public object".

Suppose we have taught someone the use of colour words for describing not only the objects which we can all see but also for objects which we don't see but he does. Suppose that after he has learned this we perform an experiment: we send a current through him, and we find that "he sees the colours differently". We find that, in normal circumstances, when he sees a red object and we ask him "What colour?" he answers "red". Then we send the current through him and he answers "green". Now shall we say he has the same impression but uses a different word? or shall we say his impression changes? Most of us would say his impression changes.

Note that if he had to say what his impression is, he would again point to the old sample. Suppose we had never given him a word language but only a sample language. In this case the experiment would never have succeeded at all. When the current goes off we might ask him "What was the change like?" and he could say "like the change from this to this (pointing to two different colours)".

"Yes, that's necessary for us: we don't know whether his impression changed. But *he* knows it changed."—But what does this mean? Not "he knows his impression did what it did". He knows it did *this.* If he *knows* something, it is no longer private. Where we have a *sample* of the change, we can say "Yes, then his impression is changed". It would have done if he had said "it is just the change of the traffic light from stop to go".

He knows no more than he tells us. But in this case we have enough to enable us to say "He is not only changing names, he also has a change of impression".—One is tempted to say "We may not know, but *he* knows whether it is the name or the impression that has changed." But he knows only what we can know.

People have been tempted to make an ideal language. Everyone uses proper names, every day. A philosopher comes along and says "The real proper name is '*this*'". Why does he say this, when it isn't a proper name at all?

It comes from the consideration that a horse, for example, may be "imperfect" in some way or other—that it has a broken leg, etc. But if we extend this to talking of "the real horse", this means ⟦130⟧ that we have altered the point of view—it is an expression of an aesthetic point of view. People make the same sort of change in referring to "the real atom", or in saying "Elements are what is real", "The real change is quantitative", etc. And so it is with "the real proper name".

We have a similar case in "We can't really describe anything". This suddenly means that they have an unreachable ideal of a description. Otherwise we should just answer, "Some of us can describe it and some can't".

In the case of "the real horse" and some others there may be some practical importance—e.g. an ideal for breeders. But "the real description" and "the real proper name" have no practical importance.

This type of puzzle can be removed by actually adopting a particular expression which alters nothing. "Don't ever say you saw a horse: say only that you saw an approximation to a horse." This expresses a certain mood. It is like adding "if nothing unforeseen happens"—which does not express a doubt, like doubt about the weather, etc.

So the person who talks about an impression as something we can't describe might say, "I have an indescribable impression which we call red". If he wants to say this, then all right.

There are people today ((1936)) who say "the only real human beings are those that have blonde hair and blue eyes". It is difficult for many people to escape this notion of *an ideal.* This in some cases is (has become) a strictly practical matter.

If a person says "Surely I don't just point to a sample: something else is going on"—I cannot say this is *wrong,* but it is misleading.

If I say "This statement has no sense", I could just point out statements with which we are inclined to mix it up, and point out the difference. This is all that is meant.—If I say "It seems to convey something and doesn't", this comes to "it seems to be of this kind, and isn't". The statement becomes senseless only if you try to compare it with what you can't compare it with. What is wrong is to overlook the difference.

⟦131⟧ "Couldn't he say 'I knew what I could say, although I didn't say it'?" Does this mean a process was going on? Then no.

"Because he sees this colour he knows what it is."—What sort of argument is this? He may see the colour without knowing what it is, if, say, he does not point to a sample and say "it is *this* colour". The deception consists in saying: He says "it is this colour" in pointing to what he *sees.* It is like: "I see it, therefore I *must* know what it is."

What we have here is: taking the same thing as a sample and as what is described by the sample. Like the game of trying to catch your own thumb.

## XVIII [May 27, 1936]

If we really wished to go through with the analogy made by saying that there is a private object, the impression—we should have to say that *anything* could be a description of this private object.

Suppose you and I are learning to play chess. Each of us has a little chess board of his own, and there is another on which we both play. Each makes a move first on his own board, and then on the common board. This is the way it is taught. Someone can check up to see whether I (or you) make the same move here and there, and if not he tells me "that's wrong".

Suppose another case where the instructor says "Always make the *same* move on the private and on the common board". He sometimes checks what we do, sometimes not.

A third case, where we are given the same instructions but he *never* corrects us.

Suppose I make a move which he sees. Then there is a misunderstanding, so that I don't make the same move but one correlated in a different way. If I once start this deviation, I can do *anything* as correlation. So now I do anything or nothing. In the game now anything is right.

We would say, "Well now, as far as the game is concerned it must be just what is played on the common board".

I have started with a description of two private games and a common game. Then I loosened the connexions in such a way that it is ridiculous to speak any longer of two private games and a ⟦132⟧ common game.—Here there is an exact analogy to the case of 'description of private experience': He might have anything or nothing, which he can describe in any way—he can always call it the same, and he is never corrected. Nor would there be any point in correcting him. (It was misleading to talk of the private object and then make it appear that it had no use.)

The misunderstanding was connected with the idea of a man knowing what he sees and knowing whether he sees it or not.

"Is it possible that a man who is not blind should look at this table and not know what colour it has?" In a sense, yes.

If we imagine that *knowing* is a process which is then translated into the language which we speak—we imagine this process of knowing is some sort of language, possibly different from the spoken one. Translation can take place only between different *languages.* In a sense in which knowing is not some process translatable into words, he may see the table and not know what colour it is. Which does not mean that he is in any doubt.

"Is it possible to see a face and not know what expression it has?"

Surely I do know.

"And what expression does it have?"

You could answer sensibly, or not.

Sensibly: "It has a cheerful expression" or "the expression of the Duchess in *Alice in Wonderland.*"

Nonsensically: "It has an expression which can't be described."

Why does one say this latter? We compare words, say, with a drawing, and then say of words "we can't describe it". In the drawing the "stupidly smiling face" would correspond to *many different* symbols.

If you say you know what it is, you can't just explain "Well, it's this". This is the temptation to take the "what it is" that you know as consisting just in seeing it.—One may come to this view also when someone says "Please look at it and get hold of the expression". This does not mean describing it at all. It means just looking at it carefully. (The confusion between staring and pointing to a sample.)

⟦133⟧ "Get hold of an impression", does not mean that you '*know*' in the other sense at all—that you know what the impression is. It means just "look carefully".

When we consider the confusion between the use of words for physical objects and the use of words for impressions, this leads to another. When we make such an analogy, we say things like: "We can't do so and so". "We can transmit only the gesture", because we can't transmit the feeling. We can never know what the other man feels.

How do we come by the idea of transmitting feelings, if we then say that it can't be done?

We do talk of knowing what the other man feels. Then suddenly we talk of a sense of "knowing" and of "feeling" in which we say we *can't*.

First we extend our language by means of some analogy to include a certain expression. Then we *exclude* this expression and say "can't".

We might then say, "Well, let's not make this analogy. Cut out this other sense of 'know'." When we say "*can't* be done" what we are really saying is "it is nonsensical". We use an *analogy* in *saying* "we can never . . ."; what we really do is to exclude this phrase.

But we have yielded to the temptation *in that* we introduce the phrase. And thus we cannot say it is nonsensical.—Don't abolish the phrase "know the other person's feelings", because we want it in the ordinary sense. And in the other sense we exclude it anyway.

(The notion of "*impossibility*" is varied.

We can say: "We can never draw an exact circle." We measure the diameter and the circumference; divide the circumference by the diameter, and get a few places of $\pi$. We might say "it is impossible to get $\pi$"—which is grammatical; meaning it makes no sense to 'get $\pi$', but it does make sense to get an approximation of $\pi$.

Mathematics here enters into the grammar of the word '*accurate*'. In order to get a degree of accuracy, we develop $\pi$. We can then say: "Of course we can never get an exact circle"—meaning it has no sense to talk of getting an exact circle, but it *has* sense to speak of getting an approximation. Which is, of course, an approximation to nothing.)

⟦134⟧ If we take such an idea as 'thinking' or 'understanding', we are inclined to say that understanding a sentence is a very complex state of mind. I say, perhaps: "I can't explain 'understanding' except by reference to examples"; or "I can draw a trapezoid and thus explain what I am talking about". But these are *grammatical* statements, not statements about the *nature* of feeling or the nature of a trapezoid.

This is connected with the problem of what is meant by saying: that if you alter the face drawn a very little the expression alters a great deal. "What is it that changes? For *ex hypothesi* the lines change very little."—Well, it altered from a stupid to an intelligent expression; or from laughing to crying. The only answer to "*What* altered?" is: the *expression.*

In one sense the expression altered a little, in another it altered a lot. *Measured* it altered 2 millimetres; but it altered from sad to gay.

We say the expression is something very intricate or very complicated. We might say the dashes are very simple. But we might also say they are very complicated—meaning that each little bit of them matters. So if one says the state of mind is something complicated, it does not mean he perceives many parts: but in the sense in which a *gesture* is complicated. Let the gesture be slightly different and it alters the whole expression.

The temptation is to say that '*hoping*' or '*believing*' are subtle states of mind, practically indescribable. But in one sense it *is* describable—one can make a gesture which describes very vividly what the state of mind is. And then you might say the gesture is complicated in the sense mentioned.

Suppose someone says: "We can find by experience that moaning is caused by a toothache."

—How can you find this out? What experiences, what phenomena which you see make you say this?—

"With *others,* I can only connect their utterances. But *I* know that when I have a toothache I moan."

Imagine the way in which he observes himself and finds out that moaning is the expression of his toothache. He might write down: "I moaned and I had a toothache on this day". What he correlates will then be two expressions. What then is the difference between his own case and that of others whom he observes?

⟦135⟧ The words used don't matter, of course; they could be 'X' and 'Z'. But what must we do with the words to give them some sort of life? We must explain them, *use* them. And I can give a sample of X, which is moaning. But what of Z, which is my toothache?

Of course there are criteria for another person's having a toothache whereas there are none for my having a toothache. I could give you my evidence for saying that he has a toothache; but there would be no sense in saying "I know I have a toothache because I am acting in a certain way". There is a difference. But it does not mean that I know the toothache in myself by introspection, pointing in myself at something.

As regards the notion of pointing in oneself: I point at Skinner. Could one say the impression of my arm points at the impression of Skinner?

((Skinner was seated in the front row, as Watson and Wisdom were.))

But the game played with impressions is not a game played with Skinner.—Suppose I stab Wisdom and you take a photograph. "Doesn't the picture of the dagger stab the picture of Wisdom?" You can say this if you mean just that it is a picture of a dagger going into him. But the picture of Wisdom doesn't fall down. What is perceived in a picture depends on the picture.

## XIX [June 1, 1936]

I was discussing the notion that I *observe* that moaning is caused by a toothache.

We use 'observe' in two different ways: 1) I observe *this* (pointing); 2) I observe *that so and so is the case.*

'1)' tells you what I direct my attention to. It does not tell you what the physicist tells us when he says he observes *that* something is going on. If we ask "What is going on?" he would not answer "I observe *this*" unless he is actually showing us what he is observing. He might answer by giving a sample or giving a description, i.e. a symbol. This is different from directing your attention to so and so.

What is "observing that I moan when I have a toothache" like?

I could say "I observed that he moaned: i.e., I observed *this* ⟦136⟧ (sample)". This is different from the case where "this" directs your attention to what I observe.

To "What is it you observe?", I answer either by "a toothache" (i.e. by a word); or by "I observe *this*" (giving a sample).

This is connected with the notion of '*talking about*'. The temptation is to think that my talking in some way envelops what I talk about: similar, it *seems,* to directing attention.—"Whom did you talk about?"—"I talked about *him* (pointing)".—But when I *was* talking about him, he need not have been there, nor any connexion established.

"I'm talking about the pain in my leg" seems to establish a relation. This is the relation established by pointing. But it *seems* as if it must be some such relation as looking at it. Actually it is a relation as made in ostensive definition.

So when I talk about my toothache, the relation established is not a sort of concentrating on it.

Often, if asked "Do you know what a robin is?", you may, in order to be certain that you know, call up a picture before your mind. I say "in order to be sure you know what the word means . . ." But now I ask, "Do you know what you are calling up?" Or will you call *anything* that comes to mind a robin?

Take the analogy when I talk about Smith who is not here: I have a lot of photographs with names, and I go through them to know what Smith is. Here I am just dependent on what the album will show me.—In the case of calling up a colour before your mind's eye—You seem to call it, and it comes. If you knew what (colour) you are calling, you would not need to call it. So perhaps you call the name, and something comes—and whatever comes is what has that name. Or perhaps you would say no, you can tell *when it comes* whether it is that or not.

This seems to make you dependent on some mechanism: either a mechanism which makes something appear when you call its name, or else a mechanism which makes you say "yes" when you see it.

This seems unsatisfactory. If what I call "Skinner" is the person who comes when you shout "Skinner"—then if Redpath comes is it Skinner?

⟦137⟧ The point is, that if you say "crimson" and an image comes to your mind, we can ask "and what colour did come?"—and you can give a sample.

The confusion is expressed in the analogy which enters when we say "we call up a *picture* of him". This is the same as when we say that *ideas* are pictures of things: the whole point is that we can *compare* it with a thing. In *some* ways the grammar of '*idea*' is comparable with the grammar of '*picture*', and in other ways *not.*

"If I imagine a robin, then for all intents and purposes this is giving myself a picture of a robin."—Suppose the "picture" here is very vivid indeed. Why then don't you say you give yourself a *robin*, instead of a picture? We can distinguish both from a photograph: I can have an image of a picture of a robin just as I have an image of a robin.

(Suppose he says "It seems to me as though I saw a picture of a robin". Then you could ask him to draw what he saw, and you could say whether it really was a picture of a robin.)

What we call the image of a robin is not a picture. "I see" is wrongly applied when applied to the *image*—but not when applied to the picture.

This is why some have suggested that one should say not "I think" but "it thinks". If I talk of *seeing*, then as a rule I think of a subject which sees an object—I think of a human body and before his eyes a certain object. The case is different when I say "I imagine". Where is the subject and where the object? (If the subject is the person who speaks, then he could actually say "it imagines".)

The point is that there aren't such things as "your minds' eyes". There is no possibility of saying with what organ I imagine.

When we talk of the image as a picture, we mean "a picture of the *robin* before my mind's eye".

This is connected with the point that: "When something seems to me green, then something *is* green." First of all we have sentences such as "The table is green"; or it may be, "The table seems green to me". If in this latter case you say "then there is *something* which is really green"—this is a change of mode of expression, so that we no longer have the idea of *seeming* but of *being*.

⟦138⟧ We are tempted to make this transition again when we say "One may see something which is not there". Take the case of the optical illusion:

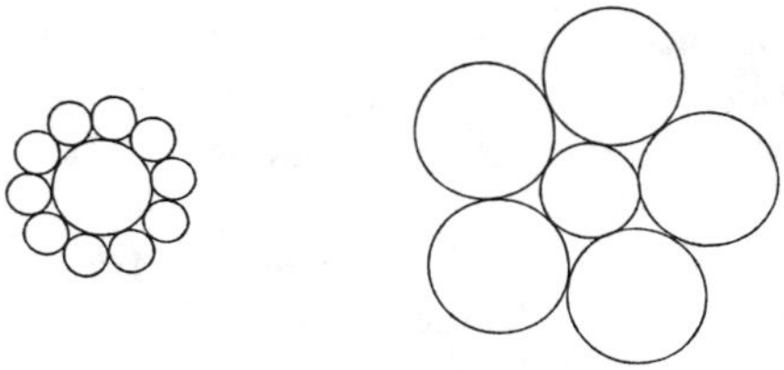

I II

Here the centre circle in (II) seems smaller than the centre circle in (I).

But what *is* the relation which you observe between the centre circles I and II? "The relation of smaller and bigger."—But can you please give me a sample of this?

"May the sample given not be an illusion?"—It doesn't matter.—"Well then, why could one not have used I and II as samples straight away? When I say 'this (II) is smaller than this (I)', I seem almost to be pointing to a sample. If you ask me 'What are you talking about?' I say I am talking about *this*."

But then why use the word "smaller" and not "equal"?

We'd be inclined to say you were talking about I and II and their relation. But if we are asked to say what *is* smaller, we must not say it is II, but something else.

"They seem unequal but they are equal." And with each "they" we point to the same thing.

What we have talked about this year are problems which begin in the way in which we feel that "impressions", "mental states" etc. are something rather queer. We may feel shy of talking about them. This is not feeling a problem, but is already making a *mistake*. Just as it is making a mistake to say "What a queer thing *time* is!"

⟦139⟧ This is the essence of a philosophical problem. The question itself is the result of a muddle. And when the question is removed, this is not by answering it.

If you put the metaphysical problem and stick to it in the form in which it first arises—"What is the nature of impressions?"—you feel it is insoluble.

One attitude is that you have to *analyse* something: we are inclined to say that the notions are unanalysed and we have to analyse them. The idea of analysis is taken from the sciences. And often we can say that something is made clearer by analysis, where the analysis is giving a definition.

A philosopher may say there is something puzzling about our calling things "*good*". This is all right. But the mistake comes from asking then "What is the *nature* of goodness?" And it is no removal of the puzzle to say it is indefinable. Why "indefinable" rather than "undefined"? The ". . . able" says you may try as much as you like and you won't define it. (Russell calls "or" indefinable, although he says it *could* be defined by means of "and" and "not". He should say "undefined".)—If we are puzzled by the use of "good" it is not because we have no definition of it. It is all right to say "Now, don't define it". But to say it is indefinable solves nothing.

The first mistake is to ask "What is 'good'?" The second mistake is to give a definition or say it is indefinable.

What you should do is to give those separate cases in which it is puzzling. A man who is unselfish we call good. Is he good *because* he is unselfish? . . . etc. We might solve certain puzzles by pointing out that we mustn't look for one common property to be found in all cases: a kinship may be there, but with no common property to which you can point.

We have the feeling that the ordinary man, if he talks of "good", of "number" etc., does not really understand what he is talking about. I see something queer about perception and he talks about it as if it were not queer at all. Should we say he knows what he is talking about or not?

You can say both. Suppose people are playing chess. I see queer problems when I look into the rules and scrutinise them. But Smith and Brown play chess with no difficulty. Do they understand the game? Well, they play it. And they understand the rules in the sense ⟦140⟧ of following them. But if you ask, "Would they not become confused if one drew their attention to certain questions about these rules?", I would say yes.

A philosopher has temptations which an ordinary person does not have. You *could* say he knows better what a word means than others do. But in fact philosophers generally know *less.* Because ordinary persons have no temptations to misunderstand language.

It seems as though the sentence "I am conscious" (after being knocked out) had a peculiar use. Suppose I stare at something and say "I am conscious" and then pass on to: "And in particular I see this". In fact "I am conscious" is only a different form of "I see this". Here again you have the feeling that you know what you are talking *about.*

"An automaton can *use* a word, but only a *conscious* being can *mean* something." Here, if you mean "conscious" as equivalent to "not knocked out", then granted. But if we talk of "consciousness" or "I am conscious" as marks of 'conscious being', then we have a misuse of the subject, and "consciousness" seems something gaseous.

# 12

*For roughly the first ten years after his return to philosophy in 1929, Wittgenstein kept his first-draft writing in a series of volumes that he numbered from I to XVIII (MSS 105–22 in von Wright's catalogue), though portions of these volumes were used for other purposes as well. From these notebooks he would select remarks for inclusion into more topical typescripts, grouping and regrouping, adopting or reformulating them in further typescripts. MS 119, for example, contains a considerable variety of remarks, pursuing a variety of ongoing concerns. While a few remarks are private and written in a coded script, the majority deals with mathematical and various fundamental philosophical questions. From among the 295 pages of handwritten remarks in MS 119, many of the remarks were selected, reformulated, and regrouped by Wittgenstein for inclusion ultimately in the* Philosophical Investigations. *When Wittgenstein's literary executors compiled the* Remarks on the Foundations of Mathematics, *it turned out that many of those remarks as well had originated from the reflections of MS 119. Rush Rhees noticed, however, that though MS 119 had been mined at least twice by Wittgenstein for apparently different purposes, there still remained a number of interesting passages, especially a section beginning with a bracketed title "[On cause and effect, intuitive awareness]".*[1] *Rhees edited and published this passage, along with a few others, in 1976 under that title.*

*This material, written between the end of September and the end of October 1937, is interesting not only for its philosophical content, but also because it is one of only a few cases in which Wittgenstein's first-draft writing from the eighteen Roman-numbered volumes has been published in its original form and context.*[2]

*Rhees begins with a series of remarks from the very beginning of the manuscript (roughly pages 1–5 of the manuscript, beginning with the second remark on page 1). He then inserts just one remark, dated September 26th (1937), which he takes from an extended discussion (roughly pages 5–99 of the manuscript), most of which had found its way into the two volumes mentioned above. A variant of that remark later appeared as part of Wittgenstein's* Zettel *(a not-yet-assembled*

1. „[*Zu Ursache und Wirkung, intuitives Erfassen*]", see p. 376/377 below.

2. The only other first-draft material published directly from these volumes is Parts II and III of the second edition of the *Remarks on the Foundations of Mathematics.*

*typescript that consisted of a collection of cut-out remarks from previous typescripts), but in the later context it had a different point. Rhees then skips to the bracketed title and thus the main section of this collection (roughly pages 99–150 of the manuscript). At the end he adds three further passages from pages 5–99 of the manuscript, the first of which was also written on September 26th. Rhees includes this passage even though it also occurs in the* Philosophical Investigations *(section 193) and the* Remarks on the Foundations of Mathematics *(Part I, section 122). He may have done so in order to underscore the interconnectedness of Wittgenstein's various concerns as they first appear in a single manuscript volume.*

*Finally, Rhees added three appendices that contain some related material, apparently preparatory for lectures, from MSS 159 and 160. The German passage in Appendix B is from MS 160; the rest is from MS 159. The material in these pocket notebooks apparently dates from the years 1937–38. We restored a few of the English remarks from MS 159, at least as far as they belonged with the remarks originally selected by Rhees. As commentary, Rhees included in the appendices some of his own lecture notes from Cambridge in 1938.*

*The very first remark of MS 119 ultimately became section 415 of the* Philosophical Investigations. *Since the following collection begins with the second remark of MS 119, and in order to underscore the close relation between all these texts, here is that programmatic statement as it appears in the* Investigations:

> *What we are supplying are really remarks on the natural history of human beings; we are not contributing curiosities however, but observations which no one has doubted, but which have escaped remark only because they are always before our eyes.*[3]

3. „Was wir liefern, sind eigentlich Bemerkungen zur Naturgeschichte des Menschen; aber nicht kuriose Beiträge, sondern Feststellungen, an denen niemand gezweifelt hat, und die dem Bemerktwerden nur entgehen, weil sie ständig vor unsern Augen sind."

# Ursache und Wirkung: Intuitives Erfassen

24.9.37

Wenn man sagt: „ich fürchte mich, weil er so finster dreinschaut" — so wird hier scheinbar eine Ursache unmittelbar erkannt, ohne wiederholtes Experiment.

Russell sagte, man müsse, ehe man etwas als Ursache durch wiederholte Erfahrung erkenne, etwas durch Intuition als Ursache erkennen.

---

1. This refers, I think, to Bertrand Russell's paper, "The Limits of Empiricism," in *Proceedings of the Aristotelian Society,* 1935/36.—"Intuition" is not Russell's word. He says we must be able to "perceive" a causal relation, or "see" a relation of producing. This is an uncommon use of each of these words; and much of what Wittgenstein says of "intuition" would apply to this use of them.

Here are a few passages from "The Limits of Empiricism":

p.137: If I say: 'I said "cat" because I saw a cat', I am saying more than is warranted. One should say: 'I willed to say "cat" because there was a visual occurrence which I classified as feline.' This statement, at any rate, isolates the 'because' as much as possible. What I am maintaining is that we can know this statement in the same way in which we know that there was the feline appearance, and that, if we could not, there would be no verbal empirical knowledge. I think that the word 'because' in this sentence must be understood as expressing a more or less causal relation, and that this relation must be *perceived,* not merely inferred from frequent concomitance. "Cause", accordingly, must mean something other than "invariable antecedent" [ . . . ]

p.136: [ . . . ] the word "because" seems to take me beyond what an empiricist ought to know.

pp.148f: [. . .] We have reason to believe: That if any verbal knowledge can be known to be in any sense derived from sense experience, we must be able, sometimes, to "see" a relation, analogous to causation, between two parts of one specious present. [ . . . ]
It is not necessary to maintain that we can arrive at knowledge in advance of experience, but rather that experience gives more information than pure empiricism supposes. [ . . . ]

# Cause and Effect: Intuitive Awareness

24.9.37

If someone says: "I am frightened, because he looks so threatening"—this looks as if it were a case of recognizing a cause immediately without repeated experiments.

Russell said that before recognizing something as a cause through repeated experience, we would have to recognize something as a cause by intuition.[1]

---

pp.149f: When I am hurt and cry out, I can perceive not only the hurt and the cry, but the fact that the one 'produces' the other. When I perceive three events in a time-order, I can perceive that preceding is transitive—a general truth of which an instance is contained in the present sense-datum [ . . . ]

If we can sometimes *perceive* relations which are analogous to causation, we do not depend wholly upon enumeration of instances in the proof of causal laws. [ . . . ] When we come to matters which must be at best probable, the apparatus of perceived general propositions may suffice to give an *a priori* probability, which is necessary for the satisfactory working of probable inference. I do not profess to know, in detail, how this is to be done, but at any rate it is no longer, as in pure empiricism, an obvious logical impossibility.

Russell returned to some of the questions in this paper in another called "On Verification" (*Proceedings of the Aristotelian Society,* 1937/38) and in a symposium on "The Relevance of Psychology to Logic" *(Aristotelian Society Supplementary Volume,* 1938) and in Chapter 3 of *An Inquiry into Meaning and Truth* (London 1940). On page 46 of the 1938 symposium he said:

> I must insist that the relation I intend is quasi-causal, not causal. I am inclined to think that the relation of cause and effect, as ordinarily understood, is a smoothly logical relation manufactured from cruder materials, in the same sort of way in which the spatial relations of geometry are manufactured from the less regular relations between percepts. [ . . . ]

Ist das nicht ähnlich, als sagte man: Man muß, ehe man etwas als 2m durch Messung anerkennt, etwas durch Intuition als 1m erkennen?

Wie nämlich, wenn jener Intuition durch wiederholte Experimente widersprochen wird? Wer hat dann recht?

Und was ist es, was uns die Intuition über die Erfahrung sagt, die wir ‚als Ursache erkennen'? Handelt sich's da um etwas andres, als eine Reaktion unserseits gegen den Gegenstand: die Ursache?

Erkennen wir nicht unmittelbar, daß der Schmerz von dem Schlag herrührt, den wir erhalten? Ist er nicht die Ursache und kann ein Zweifel sein, daß er es ist? — Aber läßt es sich nicht ganz gut denken, daß wir in gewissen Fällen hierüber getäuscht werden? Und später die Täuschung erkennen. Es scheint uns etwas zu schlagen und dabei wird ein Schmerz in uns hervorgerufen. (Man glaubt manchmal einen Lärm durch eine gewisse Bewegung zu verursachen und kommt dann drauf, daß er von uns unabhängig ist.)

Und freilich, es ist hier eine echte Erfahrung, die man ja ‚Erfahrung der Ursache' nennen kann. Aber nicht, weil sie uns unfehlbar die Ursache zeigt, sondern weil hier, im Ausschauen nach einer Ursache, *eine* Wurzel des Ursache-Wirkung Sprachspiels liegt.

*Wir reagieren auf die Ursache.*

Etwas „Ursache" nennen, ist ähnlich, wie, zeigen und sagen: „*Der* ist schuld!"

Wir stellen instinktiv die Ursache ab, wenn wir die Wirkung nicht wollen. Wir schauen instinktiv vom Gestoßenen auf das Stoßende. (Ich nehme an, wir tun es.)

Wie nun, wenn ich sagte, wir vergleichen, wenn wir von Ursache und Wirkung reden, alles dem Fall des Stoßes; der ist das Urbild der Ursache einer Wirkung? Hätten wir da den Stoß ⟦393⟧ als Ursache *erkannt*? Denk eine Sprache, in der statt ‚Ursache' immer ‚Anstoß' gesagt wird!

26.9.37

Denke Dir zwei verschiedene Pflanzenarten, A und B, man erhält von beiden Samen; und die Samen der beiden Arten sehen ganz

Isn't that like saying: Before recognizing something as 2m long by measuring it, we have to recognize something as 1m long by intuition?

For what if that intuition is contradicted by repeated experiments? Who is right then?

And what does the intuition tell us about the experience which we recognize as the cause? Is there anything more to it than a reaction of ours to the object: the cause?

Don't we recognize immediately that the pain is produced by the blow we have received? Isn't this the cause and can there be any doubt about it?—But isn't it quite possible to suppose that in certain cases we are deceived about this? And later recognize the deception? It seems as though something hits us and at the same time we feel a pain. (Sometimes we think we are causing a sound by making a certain movement and then realize that it is quite independent of us.)

Certainly there is in such cases a genuine experience which can be called 'experience of the cause'. But not because it infallibly shows us the cause; rather because *one* root of the cause-effect language-game is to be found here, in our looking out for a cause.

⟦410⟧ *We react to the cause.*

Calling something 'the cause' is like pointing and saying: '*He's* to blame!'

We instinctively get rid of the cause if we don't want the effect. We instinctively look from what has been hit to what has hit it. (I am assuming that we do this.)

Now suppose I were to say that when we speak of cause and effect we always have in mind a comparison with impact; that this is the prototype of cause and effect? Would this mean that we had *recognized* impact as a cause? Imagine a language in which people always said 'impact' instead of 'cause'.

26.9.37

Think of two different kinds of plant, A and B, both of which yield seeds; the seeds of both kinds look exactly the same and even after

gleich aus und die genaueste Untersuchung kann keinen Unterschied zwischen ihnen feststellen. Aber aus den Samen einer A-Pflanze kommen wieder A-Pflanzen, aus den Samen einer B-Pflanze, B-Pflanzen. Wir können nur dann voraussagen, was für eine Pflanze aus einem solchen Samenkorn entstehen wird, wenn wir wissen, von welcher Pflanze es gekommen ist. — Sollen wir uns nun damit zufrieden geben; oder sollen wir sagen: „Es *muß* ein Unterschied in den Samen selber sein, oder sie *könnten* nicht verschiedene Pflanzen erzeugen; ihre Vorgeschichte allein *kann* nicht die Ursache ihrer weiteren Entwicklung sein, wenn die Vorgeschichte nicht Spuren im Samen selbst zurückgelassen hat."

Wenn wir nun aber keinen Unterschied in den Samen finden! Und es ist nun Tatsache: Wir sagen die Entwicklung nicht aus den Eigentümlichkeiten des Samens voraus, sondern aus seiner Vorgeschichte. — Wenn ich sage: diese könne nicht Ursache der Entwicklung sein, so heißt das also nicht, ich könne aus der Vorgeschichte nicht die Entwicklung vorhersagen, das tue ich ja, wohl aber heißt es, daß wir *das* nicht ‚ursächlichen Zusammenhang' nennen, daß wir eben hier nicht aus der Ursache die Wirkung vorhersagen.

Und die Beteuerung: „Es *muß* ein Unterschied in den Samen sein, auch wenn wir ihn nicht finden" ändert an den Tatsachen nichts, drückt aber aus, wie mächtig in uns der Drang ist, alles durch das Ursache und Wirkung Schema zu sehen.[1]

Wenn von Graphologie, Physiognomik und dergleichen die Rede ist, hört man immer wieder den Satz: „. . . es muß freilich der Charakter sich *irgendwie* in der Schrift ausdrücken . . ." ‚Es muß', d. h.: dieses Bild wollen wir unter allen Umständen anwenden.

(Es wäre nicht ganz unsinnig zu sagen, die Philosophie sei die Grammatik der Wörter „müssen" und „können"; denn so zeigt sie, was a priori und a posteriori ist.)

⟦394⟧ Und so kannst Du Dir vorstellen, daß der Same einer Pflanze A eine Pflanze B hervorbringt und der Same dieser Pflanze, der gleich ist dem Samen der ersten, wieder eine A-Pflanze usf. abwechselnd — obwohl wir nicht wissen ‚warum'. Etc.

Und nimm nun an, im vorigen Beispiel wäre es Jemandem endlich gelungen, einen Unterschied zwischen den Samen einer A- und

1. Variant: „. . . wie mächtig in uns das Ursache und Wirkung Schema ist."

the most careful investigation we can find no difference between them. But the seeds of an A-plant always produce more A-plants, the seeds of a B-plant, more B-plants. In this situation we can predict what sort of plant will grow out of such a seed only if we know which plant it has come from.—Are we to be satisfied with this; or should we say: "There *must* be a difference in the seeds themselves, otherwise they *couldn't* produce different plants; their previous histories on their own *can't* cause their further development unless their histories have left traces in the seeds themselves."?

But now what if we don't discover any difference between the seeds? And the fact is: It wasn't from the peculiarities of either seed that we made the prediction but from its previous history.—If I say: the history can't be the cause of the development, then this doesn't mean that I can't predict the development from the previous history, since that's what I do. It means rather that we don't call *that* a 'causal connection', that this isn't a case of predicting the effect from the cause.

And to protest: "There *must* be a difference in the seeds, even if we don't discover it", doesn't alter the facts, it only shows what a powerful urge we have to see everything in terms of cause and effect.[2]

When people talk about graphology, physiognomics and suchlike they constantly say: ". . . clearly character must be expressed ⟦411⟧ in handwriting *somehow* . . ." 'Must': that means we are going to apply this picture come what may.

(One might even say that philosophy is the grammar of the words "must" and "can", for that is how it shows what is a priori and what a posteriori.)

And then you can imagine that the seed of a plant A produces a plant B and that the seed of this, which is exactly like that of the first, produces an A-plant, and so on alternately—although we don't know '*why*', etc.

And now suppose that in the foregoing example someone had at last succeeded in discovering a difference between the seed of an

2. Variant: ". . . how powerful the cause-effect schema is in us."

einer B-Pflanze zu finden: der würde doch gewiß sagen: „nun sehen wir, daß es eben doch nicht möglich ist, daß *ein* Same zu dieser und zu jener Pflanze wird.“ — Wenn ich nun entgegnete: „Woher weißt Du, daß das Merkmal, das Du entdeckt hast, nicht rein zufällig ist? Woher weißt Du, daß *das* etwas damit zu tun hat, daß einmal jene Pflanze aus dem Samen wird?“ —

12.10.
[Zu Ursache und Wirkung, intuitivem Erfassen]:

Ein Klang scheint mir von dorther zu kommen, auch ehe ich untersucht habe, wo (physikalisch) seine Quelle ist. Im Kino scheint der Laut des Sprechens vom Mund der Figur auf der Leinwand zu kommen.

Worin besteht diese Erfahrung? Etwa darin, daß wir unwillkürlich den Blick auf eine bestimmte Stelle — die scheinbare Quelle des Lauts — heften, wenn wir einen Laut hören. Und niemand blickt im Kino dorthin, wo das Mikrophon angebracht ist.

Die *Grundform* unseres Spiels muß eine sein, in der es den Zweifel nicht gibt. — Woher diese Sicherheit? Es kann doch nicht eine historische sein.

‚Die Grundform des Spiels kann den Zweifel nicht enthalten.‘ Wir *stellen* uns da vor allem eine Grundform *vor*; eine Möglichkeit, und zwar eine *sehr wichtige* Möglichkeit. (Die wichtige Möglichkeit verwechseln wir ja sehr oft mit geschichtlicher Wahrheit.)

13.10.

„Der Zweifel — könnte ich sagen — muß einmal irgendwo enden. Irgendwo müssen wir — ohne zu zweifeln — sagen: *das* geschieht aus *dieser* Ursache.“

⟦395⟧ Ähnlich: Wir sagen: „Nimm diesen Sessel!“ und es kommt uns nie in den Sinn, daß wir uns irren könnten, daß es vielleicht eigentlich kein Sessel ist, daß spätere Erfahrung uns etwas anderes lehren könnte. Ein Spiel wird hier gespielt ohne die Möglichkeit des Irrtums, und ein anderes komplizierteres mit dieser Möglichkeit.

A-plant and the seed of a B-plant: he would no doubt say: "There, you see, it just isn't possible for *one seed* to grow into two different plants." What if I were to retort: "How do you know that the characteristic you have discovered is not completely irrelevant? How do you know *that* has anything to do with which of the two plants grows out of the seed?"—

12.10.
[On cause and effect, intuitive awareness:]

A sound seems to come from over there, even before I have investigated its (physical) source. In the cinema the sound of speech seems to come from the mouth of the figures on the screen.

What does this experience consist in? Perhaps in the fact that we involuntarily look towards a particular spot—the apparent source of the sound—when we hear a sound. And in the cinema no one looks towards where the microphone is.

*The basic form* of our game must be one in which there is no such thing as doubt.—What makes us sure of this? It can't surely be a matter of historical certainty.

'The basic form of the game can't include doubt.' What we are doing here above all is to *imagine* a basic form: a possibility, indeed a *very important* possibility. (We very often confuse what is an important possibility with historical reality.)

⟦412⟧
13.10.

"Doubting—I might say—has to come to an end somewhere. At some point we have to say—without doubting: *that* happens because of *this* cause."

Similarly: we say "Take this chair" and it doesn't occur to us that we might be mistaken, that perhaps it isn't really a chair, that later experience may show us something different. Here one game is played that does not include the possibility of a mistake, and another more complicated one which does include it.

Ist es nicht *so*: Es ist dem Spiel, welches wir spielen, sehr wesentlich, daß wir gewisse Worte aussprechen und regelmäßig nach ihnen *handeln.*

Der Zweifel ist ein ritardierendes Moment und ist, sehr wesentlich, eine Ausnahme von der Regel.

Man könnte sagen: Es ist dem Verkehr auf unsern Straßen wesentlich, daß die allermeisten Wagen und Fußgänger jeder in gleichbleibender Richtung einem Ziele zugehen, und nicht gehen, wie Einer, der sich jeden Augenblick anders besinnt, erst in der Richtung von A nach B geht, dann umkehrt und einige Schritte zurück macht, dann wieder umkehrt, usw. — Und „dies ist ein wesentlicher Zug des Verkehrs auf unsern Straßen“ heißt: es ist ein wichtiger und charakteristischer Zug; wäre dies anders, so würde sich ungeheuer viel ändern.

Was heißt es nun, wenn man sagt: das Spiel müsse erst einmal *ohne* Zweifel anfangen; der Zweifel könne nur nachträglich hinzutreten? — Ja warum soll man nicht von Anfang an zweifeln? Aber halt — wie sieht der Zweifel dann aus? — Ja, wie immer nun sein Gefühl oder dessen Äußerung ist, er hat nun eine ganz andere *Umgebung,* als die, welche wir kennen. (Denn als Ausnahme hat der Zweifel die Regel zur Umgebung.) (Haben diese Augen einen Ausdruck, wenn sie nicht in einem Gesicht stehen?)

Die *Gründe* des Zweifels sind jetzt Gründe, ein eingefahrenes Geleise zu verlassen.

Unsere Welt erscheint ganz, ganz anders, wenn man sie mit andern Möglichkeiten umgibt.

Wir lehren ein Kind: „*Das* ist ein Sessel.“ Konnten wir es von Anfang an den Zweifel daran lehren, ob dies ein Sessel sei? Man wird sagen: „Unmöglich! es muß doch zuerst wissen, was ein Sessel ist, um daran zweifeln zu können, daß dies einer ist.“ — Ist es aber nicht denkbar, daß das Kind von Anfang an lernt zu sagen: „Das schaut aus wie ein Sessel — ob es aber wirklich einer ⟦396⟧ ist? — “ Oder doch, daß es von Anfang an lernte, in zweifelndem Ton zu sagen: „Ich *glaube,* hier steht ein Sessel“ und nicht in behauptendem Ton: „Hier steht ein Sessel.“

Was ist nun daran — „man kann nicht mit dem Zweifel anfangen?“ So ein „kann“ ist immer verdächtig.

Isn't this how it is: It is very fundamental to the game we play that we utter certain words and regularly *act* according to them.

Doubt is a moment of hesitation and is, *essentially*, an exception to the rule.

We might say: It is essential to street traffic that in the great majority of cases a car, or a pedestrian, travels in a constant line towards a destination and does *not* move about like somebody who is changing his mind at every moment, going first from A towards B, then turning round and taking a few steps back, then turning round again, and so on . . .—And to say "This is an essential feature of street traffic" means: it is an important and characteristic feature; if this were different, then a tremendous amount would change.

So what does it mean to say: at first the game has to start *without* including doubt; doubt can only come into it subsequently? Why *shouldn't* doubting be there right from the start? But wait a minute—what does doubting look like? The point is—whatever it feels like or however it is expressed, its *surroundings* are quite different from those we are familiar with. (For, since doubt is an exception, the rule is its environment.) (Do these eyes have any expression if they are not part of a face?)

As things are, the *reasons* for doubting are reasons for leaving a familiar track.

Our world looks quite different if we surround it with different possibilities.

We teach a child: "*That's* a chair". Could we teach him right at the start to doubt whether this is a chair? Someone will say: "That's impossible. He must first know what a chair is if he is to ⟦413⟧ be in a position to doubt whether this is one." But isn't it conceivable that the child should learn right from the start to say: "That looks like a chair—but is it really one?—" Or at any rate that he should learn from the beginning to say in a doubting tone of voice: "I *think* there's a chair here" and not in an affirmative tone: "There's a chair here."

Now what about this remark: "We can't begin with doubting"? A 'can't' of this sort is always fishy.

14.10.

Man kann dann sagen: Der Zweifel kann kein *notwendiger* Bestandteil des Spiels sein, ohne den das Spiel offenbar unvollständig und unrichtig ist. Denn es gibt in Deinem Spiel Kriterien für die Berechtigung des Zweifels *nicht anders* wie es Kriterien für sein Gegenteil gibt. Und das Spiel, welches den Zweifel einschließt, ist also nur ein noch komplizierteres, als eines, welches ihn nicht einschließt.

Man denkt leicht: der Zweifel mache es erst — *naturgetreu.*
(Wenn man auf einer Eisenbahn für lange und kurze Fahrstrecken den gleichen Fahrpreis bezahlen müßte — wäre das eine offenbar ungerechte, unsinnige, Bestimmung?)

„Man kann nicht wissen, ob Einer Schmerzen hat? — *Doch,* man kann es *wissen*!" — Das sagt doch nicht: „wir haben ein ‚intuitives Wissen' dieser Schmerzen!" Es ist nur eine — berechtigte — Auflehnung gegen die, die sagen: „Man kann nicht *wissen* . . ." Es behauptet aber nicht ein Naturvermögen, das jene leugnen. —

„Das Spiel kann nicht mit dem Zweifel anfangen." — Es sollte heißen: das Spiel *fängt* nicht mit dem Zweifel an. — Oder auch: das „kann" hat dieselbe Berechtigung wie in dem Satz: „Der Verkehr auf Straßen kann nicht damit anfangen, daß Alle zweifeln, ob sie da- oder dorthin gehen sollen; d. h., es käme dann nie zu dem, was wir ‚Verkehr' nennen, und das Schwanken würden wir dann wohl auch nicht ‚Zweifel' nennen."

Die philosophische Beteuerung, „Wir *WISSEN,* daß dort ein Sessel ist!" beschreibt ja bloß ein Spiel. Aber sie *scheint* zu sagen, daß Gefühle der felsenfesten Überzeugung mich bewegen, wenn ich Einem sage: „bring mir den Sessel dort."

⟦397⟧ Das Spiel beginnt nicht mit dem Zweifel, ob Einer Zahnweh hat, denn das entspräche — sozusagen — nicht der biologischen Funktion des Spiels in unserm Leben. Seine primitivste Form ist eine Reaktion auf die Klagelaute und Gebärden des Andern, eine Reaktion des Mitleids, oder dergleichen. Wir trösten, wollen helfen. Man kann denken: weil der Zweifel eine Verfeinerung, in gewissem Sinne,

14.10.

We may say: Doubting can't be a *necessary* element without which the game is obviously incomplete and incorrect. For in your game the criteria for justifying a doubt aren't applied any *differently* than the criteria for the opposite. And the game which includes doubt is simply a more complicated one than a game which does not.

It is easy to think: only the game which includes doubt is *true to nature.*

(If the same fare were charged for both long and short railway journeys—would that be an obviously unjust, absurd arrangement?)

"We can't know whether somebody is in pain?—Oh yes we *can,* we can *know* it!"—But that is not to say: "We have 'intuitive knowledge' of these pains". It is simply a—justified—objection against those who say: "We can't *know*. . ." But it isn't to claim the existence of a natural capacity which the others deny.

"The game can't start with doubting"—What we ought to say is: the game *doesn't* start with doubting.—Or else: the "can" has the same justification as it has in the assertion: "Street traffic can't begin with everybody doubting whether to go in this, or rather in that direction; in that case it would never amount to what we call 'traffic' and then we shouldn't call their hesitation 'doubting' either."

A philosopher who protests, "We *KNOW* there's a chair over there!" is simply describing a game. But he *seems* to be saying that I am moved by feelings of unshakeable conviction if I say to someone: "Fetch me that chair."

⟦414⟧ The game doesn't begin with doubting whether someone has a toothache, because that doesn't—as it were—fit the game's biological function in our life. In its most primitive form it is a reaction to somebody's cries and gestures, a reaction of sympathy or something of the sort. We comfort him, try to help him. We may think that because doubt is a refinement, and in a certain sense too an improvement of

Verbesserung des Spiels ist, so wäre es wohl das allerrichtigste, mit dem Zweifel gleich anzufangen. (Ähnlich wie man denkt, weil es oft gut ist, wenn ein Urteil begründet ist, so müßte zur vollkommenen Rechtfertigung eines Urteils die Kette der Gründe ins Unendliche weitergehen.)

Denken wir uns den Zweifel und die Überzeugung nicht durch eine Sprache, sondern bloß durch Handlungen, Gebärden, Mienen, ausgedrückt. So könnte es etwa bei sehr primitiven Menschen, oder bei Tieren sein. Denken wir also eine Mutter, deren Kind schreit und sich dabei die Wange hält. *Eine* Art der Reaktion ist also die, daß die Mutter das Kind zu trösten trachtet und es, auf irgend eine Art und Weise, pflegt. Hier ist nichts, was dem Zweifel daran entspricht, ob das Kind wirklich Schmerzen habe. Ein anderer Fall wäre der: die Reaktion auf die Klage des Kindes ist für gewöhnlich die eben beschriebene, unter gewissen Umständen aber verhält sich die Mutter skeptisch. Sie schüttelt dann etwa mißtrauisch den Kopf, unterbricht das Trösten und Pflegen des Kindes, ja: äußert Unwillen und Teilnahmslosigkeit. Nun aber denken wir uns die Mutter, die von vornherein skeptisch ist: Wenn das Kind schreit, zuckt sie die Achseln und schüttelt den Kopf; manchmal sieht sie es prüfend an, untersucht es; ausnahmsweise macht sie auch vage Versuche des Tröstens oder Pflegens. — Sähen wir ein solches Verhalten, so würden wir es durchaus nicht das der Skepsis nennen, es würde uns nur seltsam und närrisch anmuten. „Das Spiel kann nicht mit dem Zweifel anfangen" heißt: wir würden es nicht ‚Zweifel' nennen, wenn das Spiel damit anfinge.

Denk Dir diese Frage: „Kann die Partie eines Spiels damit *anfangen,* daß einer der Spieler gewinnt (oder verliert) worauf dann das Spiel eigentlich angeht?" Warum soll nicht ein spielähnlicher Vorgang dann mit dem anfangen, was für gewöhnlich unmittelbar bei dem Gewinnen und Verlieren in einem Spiel vor sich geht? Es wird einem z. B. Geld ausbezahlt, er wird zu seinem Erfolg beglückwünscht, und anderes mehr. Nur werden wir dies dennoch nicht „im Spiel gewinnen" nennen und vielleicht das Ganze kein ⟦398⟧ „Spiel". Wenn wir so einen Gebrauch sähen, so wäre er uns ‚unverständlich' und wir würden wahrscheinlich nicht sagen: „diese Leute gewinnen und verlieren zu *Anfang* des Spiels."

the game, the correct thing would surely be to start straight off with doubt. (Just as we may think that, because it is often good to give the reasons for a judgement, the complete justification of a judgement would have to extend the chain of reasons to infinity.)

Let us imagine that doubt and conviction, instead of being expressed in a language, are expressed rather through actions, gestures, demeanour. It might be like this with very primitive people, or with animals. So imagine a mother whose child is crying and holding his cheek. *One* kind of reaction to this is for the mother to try and comfort her child and to nurse him in some way or other. In this case there is nothing corresponding to a doubt whether the child is really in pain. Another case would be this: The usual reaction to the child's complaints is as just described, but under some circumstances the mother behaves sceptically. Perhaps she shakes her head suspiciously, stops comforting and nursing her child—even expresses annoyance and lack of sympathy. But now imagine a mother who is sceptical right from the very beginning: If her child cries, she shrugs her shoulders and shakes her head; sometimes she looks at him inquiringly, examines him; on exceptional occasions she also makes vague attempts to comfort and nurse him.—Were we to encounter such behaviour, we definitely wouldn't call it scepticism; it would strike us as queer and crazy.—"The game can't begin with doubting" means: we shouldn't call it 'doubting', if the game began with it.

Consider this question: "Can a match *start* with one of the players winning (or losing) and the game going on from there?" Why shouldn't a procedure that looks like a game start with what usually happens when a game is won or lost? For instance, one of the participants is paid money, congratulated on his success, and so on. However, we won't call this "winning the game" and perhaps we won't call the whole thing a "game". If we were to meet such a practice, it would be 'incomprehensible' to us and we should probably not say: "these people win and lose at the *start* of the game".

„*Kann* das geschehen?" — Gewiß. Beschreib es nur bis in die Einzelheiten und Du wirst schon sehen, daß der Vorgang den Du beschreibst sich zwar leicht vorstellen läßt, daß Du aber freilich die und die Ausdrücke nicht auf ihn anwenden wirst.

„Könnte der Reim in einem Gedicht an den Anfang statt ans Ende der Verszeilen fallen?"

„Es kommt also in Deinem primitiven Spiel kein Zweifel vor — aber ist es denn *sicher,* daß er Zahnschmerzen hat?" — *So* ist das Spiel. — Und daraus kannst Du, wenn Du willst, entnehmen, wie das Wort „Zahnschmerzen" gebraucht wird; also, welche Bedeutung es hat.

„Wie, wenn er betrügt?" — Aber er kann gar nicht betrügen, wenn, was er tut, in dem Spiel nicht *Betrügen* ist.

15.10.

„Ist es denn sicher, daß ein Sessel hier steht?" — Ja kann ich nicht beides tun: sicher sein, und zweifeln? Hängt es nicht davon ab, ob mir etwas als Rechtfertigung des Zweifels gilt?

Wir sagen: wenn das und das nicht eintrifft: wir haben uns *geirrt,* eine falsche Annahme gemacht. Der Irrtum ist ein Fehler; wir werden seinetwegen getadelt, tadeln uns selbst.

Vergleiche damit folgendes: Wir bestimmen die Mitte zwischen zwei Stellen im Raum, A und B,

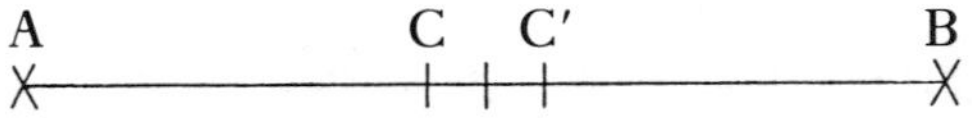


durch mehrmalige Schätzung auf *die* Weise: wir sagen „Ich nehme an, sie liegt bei C" und machen, mehr oder weniger in der Mitte, einen Punkt. — Tragen dann $\overline{AC}$ von B aus auf und erhalten C′. Dann wiederholen wir den Vorgang gegen die Mitte von $\overline{CC'}$ hin. — War die erste Annahme ein Irrtum? Du kannst sie so nennen — aber dieser ‚Irrtum' wird hier nicht als Fehler behandelt.

⟦399⟧ Wenn wir nicht zweifeln, so betrachten wir das als einen Fehler, eine Dummheit — der Zweifel ist die tiefere Einsicht in die Natur der Sache, so scheint es uns.

⟦415⟧ "*Can* that happen?!"—Certainly. Just describe it in detail and you will then see that the procedure you describe can perfectly well be imagined, although you will clearly not apply such and such expressions to it.

"Could the rhyme in a poem come at the beginning of the lines instead of at the end?"

"All right, doubting doesn't have any place in your simple game—but does that mean it is *certain* that he has toothache?" *That* is the game.—And you can, if you want, gather from it how the word "toothache" is being used: what it means.

"What if he is shamming?" But he can't be shamming if the way he acts doesn't count as *shamming* in the game.

15.10.

"So is it certain there's a chair here?"—Well, don't I have two alternatives: to be certain or to doubt? Doesn't it depend on whether I count something as justifying doubt?

If something doesn't happen as we expected we say: we have *made a mistake,* a wrong assumption. The mistake is a fault; we are reproached for it, reproach ourselves.

Compare that with the following: We determine the mid-point between two places A and B,

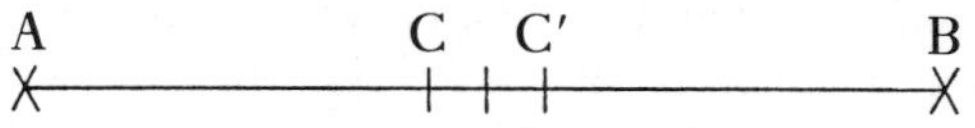


by making repeated estimates in this way: we say "I assume it lies near C" and make a mark more or less near the centre.—Then we take the length $\overline{AC}$ starting at B and get point C′. The procedure is then repeated, taking a point roughly halfway between C and C′.—Was the first assumption a mistake? You can call it that if you like—but here this 'mistake' is not treated as a fault.

If we don't doubt, we regard this as a fault, something stupid—doubting is a deeper insight into the nature of the matter: or so it seems.

Die perspektivische Darstellung der Menschen (etc.) erscheint uns als die richtige verglichen mit der ägyptischen Art. Selbstverständlich; so schauen doch die Menschen nicht aus! — Aber muß das ein Argument sein? Wer sagt, daß ich auf dem Papier den Menschen so sehen will, wie er wirklich ausschaut?

„Wer nicht zweifelt, übersieht doch einfach die Möglichkeit, daß es sich anders verhalten kann!" Durchaus nicht, — wenn es diese Möglichkeit in seiner Sprache gar nicht gibt. (Wie der nichts übersehen muß, der für lange und kurze Arbeitszeit den gleichen Lohn gibt oder fordert.) „Aber der bezahlt dann eben nicht die Arbeitsleistung!" — So *ist* es. —

Warum nennt man das, was man unmittelbar erkennt, ebenso wie das, was uns wiederholte Erfahrung der Koinzidenz lehrt? *Inwiefern* ist es denn dasselbe? (Aus einer andern Erkenntnisquelle fließt eine andere Erkenntnis.)

„Man kann die Existenz eines Mechanismus auf zwei Arten erkennen: erstens dadurch, daß wir ihn *sehen,* zweitens dadurch, daß wir seine Wirkung sehen." Könnte man nicht sagen: Man gebraucht die Aussage ‚es existiere hier ein Mechanismus der und der Art' auf zweifache Weise: a) wenn ein solcher Mechanismus gesehen werden kann — b) wenn man Wirkungen erkennt, wie ein solcher Mechanismus sie hervorrufen würde.

Es gibt eine Reaktion, die man „Reaktion gegen die Ursache" nennen kann. — Man redet auch davon, daß man der Ursache ‚nachgeht'; in einem einfachen Fall geht man etwa einer Schnur nach, um zu sehen, wer an ihr zieht. Wenn ich ihn nun finde — wie weiß ich, daß er, sein Ziehen, die Ursache davon ist, daß sich die Schnur bewegt? Stelle ich das durch eine Reihe von Experimenten fest?

16.10.

Wer nun der Schnur nachgegangen ist und den findet, der an ihr zieht, macht der noch einen weiteren Schritt indem er schließt: also war das die Ursache, — oder ist nicht alles, was er finden wollte, ob jemand, und wer an ihr zieht. Stellen wir uns ⟦400⟧ eben wieder ein einfacheres Sprachspiel vor, als das, was mit dem Wort „Ursache" gespielt wird.

Representing people (etc.) in perspective strikes us as correct compared with the Egyptian way of drawing them. Of course; ⟦416⟧ after all, people don't really look like that!—But must this count as an argument? Who says I want people on paper to look the way they do in reality?

"Anyone who doesn't doubt is simply overlooking the possibility that things might be otherwise!"—Not in the least—if this possibility doesn't exist in his language. (Just as someone who gives or asks for the same wages for long and short periods of work needn't be overlooking anything.) "But then he is just not paying for the work performed!"—That's how it *is.*—

Why do we call what we recognize immediately by the same name as the one we apply to what we learn from repeated experience of conjunctions? To what extent *is* it the same? (Knowledge which flows from a different source is different knowledge.)

"There are two ways of becoming aware of the existence of a mechanism: first, by *seeing* it, secondly by seeing its effects." Might we not say: the assertion 'there is a mechanism of such and such a sort here' is used in two different ways (a) if such a mechanism can be seen—(b) if effects can be discerned of a kind which such a mechanism would produce.

There is a reaction which can be called 'reacting to the cause'.—We also speak of 'tracing' the cause; a simple case would be, say, following a string to see who is pulling at it. If I then find him—how do I know that he, his pulling, is the cause of the string's moving? Do I establish this by a series of experiments?

16.10.

Someone has followed the string and has found who is pulling at it: does he make a further step in concluding: so that was the cause—or did he not just want to discover if someone, and if so who, was pulling at it? Let's imagine once more a language-game simpler than the one we play with the word "cause".

Denken wir uns zwei Vorgänge: der eine besteht darin, daß ein Mensch, wenn er den Zug an einer Schnur fühlt, oder eine Erfahrung ähnlicher Art hat, der Schnur — dem Mechanismus — nachgeht, in diesem Sinne die *Ursache* findet, — und etwa beseitigt. Er möge auch fragen: „warum bewegt sich diese Schnur?" oder dergleichen. — Der andre Fall sei der: Er hat bemerkt, daß seine Ziegen, seit sie das Futter auf diesem Abhang fressen, wenig Milch geben. Er schüttelt den Kopf, fragt „warum" — und macht nun Versuche. Er findet, daß das und das Futter die Ursache der Erscheinung ist.

„Aber sind diese Fälle nicht von der gleichen Art: er hätte ja auch Experimente darüber machen können, ob der Mensch, der an der Schnur zieht, wirklich die Ursache der Bewegung sei, ob nicht *er* am Ende durch die Schnur bewegt werde und diese durch eine andere Ursache!" — Er hätte Experimente machen können — aber ich nehme an, er macht *keine. Dies* ist das Spiel, welches er spielt.

Was ist es denn, was ich in solchen Fällen immer tue? Die Vernunft — möchte ich sagen — gibt uns sich als Gradmesser *par excellence,* an welchem alles, was wir machen, alle Sprachspiele, sich selber messen und beurteilen. — Wir können sagen: wir sind mit der Betrachtung des Maßstabes so präoccupiert, daß wir unsre Blicke nicht auf gewissen Erscheinungen oder Bildern *ruhen* lassen können. Wir sind, sozusagen, gewöhnt diese damit ‚abzutun', sie seien unvernünftig, entsprechen einem niedrigen Stande der Intelligenz, etc. Unser Blick wird von dem Maßstab gefangen gehalten und durch ihn immer wieder von diesen Erscheinungen, gleichsam nach oben hin, abgezogen. — Wie wenn uns ein gewisser Stil — Baustil oder Stil des Benehmens — so gefangen hält, daß wir unsere Blicke nicht *voll* auf einen andern richten, nur schief nach ihm blicken können. (Damit verwandt: eine hübsche Betrachtung, die Eddington über die Demonstration des Trägheitsgesetzes anstellt.)

In einem Fall heißt nun „*Der* ist die Ursache" einfach: *der* hat an der Schnur gezogen. Im andern Falle, etwa: *das* sind die Umstände, die ich ändern müßte, um diese Erscheinung abzustellen.

„Aber wie ist es denn — wie konnte er überhaupt auf die Idee kommen, einen Umstand abzuändern, *um* die und die Erscheinung abzustellen? Das setzt doch voraus, daß er vor allem einmal einen ⟦401⟧ Zusammenhang wittert! Einen Zusammenhang für möglich hält; wo kein Zusammenhang zu sehen ist. Er muß also vorher schon die Idee

Consider two procedures: in the first somebody who feels a tug on a string, or has some similar sort of experience, follows the string—the mechanism—in this sense finds the *cause*, and perhaps removes it. He may also ask: "Why is this string moving?", or something of the sort.—The second case is this: He has noticed that, since his goats have been grazing on that slope, they give less ⟦417⟧ milk. He shakes his head, asks "Why?"—and then makes some experiments. He finds that such and such a fodder is the cause of the phenomenon.

"But aren't these cases both of the same kind: after all he could have made some experiments to determine whether the man who is pulling at the string is really the cause of the movement, whether *he* is not really being moved by the string and this in its turn by some other cause!"—He could have made experiments—but I'm assuming that he does *not*. *This* is the game he plays.

Now what is it I constantly do in such cases? Reason—I feel like saying—presents itself to us as the gauge *par excellence* against which everything that we do, all our language games, measure and judge themselves.—We may say: we are so exclusively preoccupied by contemplating a yardstick that we can't allow our gaze to *rest* on certain phenomena or patterns. We are used, as it were, to 'dismissing' these as irrational, as corresponding to a low state of intelligence, etc. The yardstick rivets our attention and keeps distracting us from these phenomena, as it were making us look beyond.—Suppose a certain style of building or behaviour captivates us to such an extent that we can't focus our attention *directly* on another one, but can only glance at it obliquely. (Connected with this: a nice remark of Eddington's about the demonstration of the law of inertia.)

In one case "*He* is the cause" simply means: *he* pulled the string. In the other case it means roughly: those are the conditions that I would have to change in order to get rid of this phenomenon.

"But then how did he come by the idea—how was it even possible to come by the idea—of altering a condition *in order to* get rid of such and such a phenomenon? Surely that presupposes that he first of all senses there is some connection. Thinks there may be a connection: where no connection is to be seen. So he must already have got the

eines solchen, ursächlichen, Zusammenhangs erhalten haben." Ja, man kann sagen, es setzt voraus, daß er sich nach einer Ursache umschaut; daß er von dieser Erscheinung — auf eine *andere* schaut. —

17.10.

Intuition. Die Ursache durch Intuition wissen. Welches Spiel spielt man mit dem Wort „Intuition"? Was für ein Kunststück soll damit gemacht werden?

Wir haben da die Auffassung: Das Wissen dieses Sachverhalts ist ein Zustand des Geistes; und *wie* es zu diesem gekommen ist, ist gleichgültig, wenn uns nur interessiert, daß Einer das und das *weiß*. Wie Kopfschmerzen aus mancherlei Ursache entstehen können, so auch das Wissen. Daß wir uns in der Logik überhaupt für diesen Zustand interessieren ist dann freilich merkwürdig. Was gehn uns solche Zustände an? — Erinnere Dich an die Frage: „*Wann* weiß Einer, daß (z. B.) jemand im Nebenzimmer ist?" — Während er den Gedanken denkt? Und wenn er ihn denkt: während aller Glieder (Wörter) des Gedankens?

Wenn ich sage: „ich weiß, daß jemand im Zimmer ist" und es stellt sich heraus, daß ich mich geirrt habe, so *wußte* ich's also nicht — habe ich mich da bei der Introspektion in meinem Geisteszustand geirrt? ich sah hinein und hielt etwas für ein *Wissen,* was keines war! — Oder kann ich so etwas nicht *eigentlich* wissen? sondern nur solche Tatbestände wie: „ich sehe etwas Rotes", „Ich habe Schmerzen" und dergleichen. Also nur dort sollte man das Wort „wissen" anwenden, wo es niemand anwendet; wo nämlich „ich weiß, daß p" nichts heißt wenn nicht etwa das gleiche wie „p", und die Form „ich weiß nicht, daß p" ein Blödsinn ist.

Schau nur ja nicht auf den tatsächlichen Gebrauch der Worte „ich weiß . . ."! schau nur auf die Worte und spekuliere, zu welchem Gebrauch sie passen möchten. —

Wie geht denn das Sprachspiel — wann sagen wir denn, wir ‚*wissen*'? Wirklich wenn wir uns in einem bestimmten Zustand finden? — Nicht, wenn wir eine gewisse Evidenz haben? — Und da kommt es also auf die Evidenz an und ist ohne sie kein Wissen!

Was ist nun die Intuition? Ist sie eine uns aus dem gewöhnlichen Leben bekannte Art und Weise, wie wir Dinge erfahren, uns Wissen aneignen? Oder ist sie eine Schimäre, von der wir bloß in der Philosophie Gebrauch machen? — Ist die Meinung, in dem und ⟦402⟧

idea of such a causal connection." Yes, we can say it presupposes that he looks round for a cause; that he doesn't attend to this phenomenon—but to *another* one.—

17.10.

Intuition. Knowing the cause by intuition. What game is being played with the word "intuition"? What sort of feat is it supposed to achieve?

⟦418⟧ The underlying idea is this: Knowing this state of affairs is a state of mind; and *how* this state of mind has come about is irrelevant if all that interests us is that somebody *knows* such and such. Just as headaches can be caused in all sorts of ways, so too with knowing. That such a state should interest us at all in a logical investigation is certainly remarkable. Why should such states concern us?—Remember the question "*When* does a man know that (e.g.) someone is in the next room?"—While he is thinking the thought? And if he does think it: throughout all the phases (words) of the thought?

If I say: "I know there is someone in the room" and it turns out that I have made a mistake, then I didn't *know* it—have I made a mistake in introspecting my state of mind then? I looked inside and took something to be a *knowing,* when it wasn't.—Or can't I *really* know something like that, but only such facts as: "I see something red", "I am in pain", and the like. That is, we are supposed to use the word "know" only in situations where nobody does use it; in other words, where "I know that p" means nothing, unless perhaps it means the same as "p", and the expression "I don't know that p" is nonsense.

Whatever you do, don't look at the actual use of the words "I know. . ." just look at the words and speculate what might be a fitting use of them.

How does the language-game work then—when do we say we '*know*'? Is it really when we ascertain that we are in a certain state of mind? Isn't it when we have evidence of a certain sort?—And then it's a matter of the evidence, without which it isn't knowing.

What is intuition then? Is it a way of experiencing things so as to attain knowledge which we are familiar with in common life? Or is it a chimera, which we make use of only in philosophy?—Is the belief that intuition is involved in such and such circumstances comparable

dem Fall sei Intuition im Spiel, vergleichbar der Meinung, die und die Krankheit werde durch den Stich eines Insekts erzeugt? (Diese Meinung kann richtig oder falsch sein, aber wir kennen jedenfalls Fälle dieser Art.) Oder haben wir hier einen Fall, wo das Wort gilt:

> Denn eben wo Begriffe fehlen,
> Da stellt ein Wort zur rechten Zeit sich ein.

(Man könnte sich einen Sprachgebrauch denken, in welchem nicht gesagt wird, „es ist nicht bekannt, wer dies getan hat", sondern: „Herr Unbekannt hat es getan" — um nicht sagen zu müssen, man wisse etwas nicht.)

18.10.

Was wissen wir denn von der Intuition? Welchen Begriff haben wir von ihr? Sie soll wohl eine Art Sehen sein, ein Erkennen auf *einen* Blick; mehr wüßte ich nicht. — „Also weißt Du ja doch, was eine Intuition ist!" — Etwa so, wie ich weiß, was es heißt „einen Körper mit einem Blick von allen Seiten zugleich sehen". Ich will nicht sagen, daß man diesen Ausdruck nicht auf irgend einen Vorgang, aus irgend einem guten Grund, verwenden kann — aber weiß ich darum, was er bedeutet? —

‚Die Ursache intuitiv erkennen' heißt: die Ursache, *irgendwie, wissen* (sie auf andere Weise erfahren, als die gewöhnliche). — Es weiß sie nun Einer — aber was nützt das, — wenn sich sein Wissen nicht *bewährt*? Nämlich, in der gewöhnlichen Weise mit der Zeit bewährt. Aber dann ist er ja in keinem andern Fall, als der, der die Ursache auf irgend eine Weise *richtig erraten* hat. Das heißt: — wir haben ja keinen Begriff von diesem besondern *Wissen* der Ursache. Wir können uns ja vorstellen, Einer sage mit den Zeichen der Inspiration, er *WISSE* nun die Ursache; aber das hindert nicht, daß wir nun *prüfen*, ob er das Rechte weiß.

Das Wissen interessiert uns nur im Spiel.

(Es ist, wie wenn jemand behauptete, er besitze die Kenntnis der Anatomie des Menschen durch Intuition; und wir sagen: „Wir zweifeln nicht daran; aber wenn Du Arzt werden willst, mußt Du alle Prüfungen ablegen, wie jeder Andere.")

to the belief that such and such an illness is produced by an insect sting? (This belief may be true or false, but anyway we are familiar with kinds of cases produced like that). Or is this a case where we can say:

> For where concepts are lacking,
> We shall always find a word in good time.[3]

(One could imagine a use of language in which people say: "Mr. Unknown did it" instead of: "It isn't known who did this"—so that they don't have to say there is something they don't know.)

⟦419⟧
18.10.

What do we know about intuition? What idea have we of it? It's presumably supposed to be a sort of seeing, recognition at a *single* glance; I wouldn't know what more to say.—"So you do after all know what an intuition is!"—Roughly in the same way as I know what it means "to see a body from all sides at once". I don't want to say that one cannot apply this expression to some process or other, for some good reason or other—but do I therefore know what it means?

'Knowing the cause intuitively' means: *somehow or other* knowing the cause, (experiencing it in a way different from the usual one).—All right, somebody knows it—but what's the good of that,—if his knowing doesn't *prove its worth* in the usual way in the course of time? But then he's no different from someone who has somehow *correctly guessed* the cause. That is: We don't have any concept of this special *knowing* of the cause. We can certainly imagine someone saying, with signs of inspiration, that now he *KNOWS* the cause; but this doesn't prevent us from testing whether what he claims to know is right.

Knowing interests us only within the game.

(It is just as if somebody claimed to have knowledge of human anatomy by intuition; and we say: "We don't doubt it; but if you want to be a doctor, you must pass all the examinations like anybody else.")

3. Goethe, *Faust I,* Mephistopheles and the student in the *Studierzimmer.*

20.10.

Warum ‚muß der Zweifel einmal irgendwo enden'? — Weil das Spiel nie anfinge, wenn es mit dem Zweifel anfinge?

⟦403⟧ Denk doch, es finge damit an, daß er sich den Kopf darüber zerbricht, was die Ursache von dem und dem ist. Wie müßte man dieses Kopfzerbrechen denken, diese Überlegungen? Doch in einer einfachen Weise. Es ist also etwa ein *Suchen,* und endlich ein Finden irgend eines Gegenstandes (der Ursache). Was ist also daran, daß das Spiel nicht mit dem Zweifel anfangen kann?

Der Zweifel muß irgendein Gesicht haben. Wenn er zweifelt, so ist die Frage: wie schaut sein Zweifel aus? Wie schaut, z.B., die Untersuchung aus, die er anstellt? — Will man nur sagen: das Spiel kann nicht damit anfangen, daß Einer sagt: „Man kann nie *wissen,* was die Ursache von etwas ist?" — Aber warum soll er nicht auch das sagen; wenn er dann nur einen beherzten Schritt macht. — Aber dann brauchen wir ja nicht von den *Anfängen* des Spiels zu reden, sondern wir können sagen: Das Spiel ‚die Ursache aufsuchen' *besteht* vor allem und hauptsächlich in einer gewissen Praxis, in einer gewissen Methode. Es herrscht darin auch etwas, was wir Zweifel und Unsicherheit nennen können, aber dies ist ein Zug zweiter Größe. Wie es charakteristisch für das Funktionieren der Nähmaschine ist, daß sich ihre Teile abnützen und verbiegen, und die Achsen in den Lagern schlottern können, aber doch ein Charakteristikum zweiter Ordnung verglichen mit dem normalen Gang der Maschine.

Denk Dir diese seltsame Möglichkeit: Wir hätten uns bisher immer in der Multiplikation 12 × 12 verrechnet. Ja, es ist unbegreiflich, wie es geschehen konnte, aber es ist so. Also ist alles falsch, was man so ausgerechnet hat! — Aber was macht es? Es macht ja gar nichts! — Da muß also etwas falsch sein in unserer Idee von Wahrheit und Falschheit der arithmetischen Sätze.

21.10.

Der Ursprung und die primitive Form des Sprachspiels ist eine Reaktion; erst auf dieser können die komplizierteren Formen wachsen.

Die Sprache — will ich sagen — ist eine Verfeinerung, ‚im Anfang war die Tat'.

20.10.

Why is it that 'doubt must come to an end somewhere'?—Is it because the game would never get started if it were to begin with doubt?

But suppose it began with someone's racking his brains about what the cause is of something or other. How should we have to conceive this brain-racking, these reflections? Well, quite simply. It's just a matter of *searching* for, and eventually finding some object (the cause). So what's the point of saying that the game can't begin with doubt?

Doubt has to have some physiognomy. If someone doubts, the question is: what does his doubt look like? What, e.g., does the inquiry that he initiates look like?—Do you merely want to say: the game can't begin with someone's saying: "We can never *know* what ⟦420⟧ the cause of something is"?—But why shouldn't he say *that* too; as long as he confidently makes the next step?—But in that case there's no need to speak of the *beginnings* of the game, and we can say: The game of 'looking for the cause' *consists* above all in a certain practice, a certain method. Within it something that we call doubt and uncertainty plays a role, but this is a second-order feature. In an analogous way it is characteristic of how a sewing machine functions that its parts may wear out and get bent, and its axles may wobble in their bearings, but still this is a second-order characteristic compared with the normal working of the machine.

Imagine this strange possibility: up to now we have always made a mistake in calculating $12 \times 12$. Yes, it's quite incomprehensible how it could happen, but that's how it is. So everything that we've calculated like that is wrong!—But what does it matter? It doesn't matter at all!—So there must be something wrong here in the idea we have of the truth and falsity of arithmetical propositions.

21.10.

The origin and the primitive form of the language game is a reaction; only from this can more complicated forms develop.

Language—I want to say—is a refinement. "In the beginning was the deed."[4]

4. Goethe, *Faust I,* opening scene in the *Studierzimmer.*

Erst muß ein fester, harter Stein zum Bauen da sein, und die Blöcke werden *unbehauen* auf einander gelegt. *Dann* ist es freilich wichtig, daß er sich behauen läßt, daß er nicht gar zu hart ist.

⟦404⟧ Die primitive Form des Sprachspiels ist die Sicherheit, nicht die Unsicherheit. Denn die Unsicherheit könnte nicht zur Tat führen.

Ich will sagen: es ist charakteristisch für unsere Sprache, daß sie auf dem Grund fester Lebensformen, regelmäßigen Tuns, emporwächst.

Ihre Funktion ist *vor allem* durch die Handlung, deren Begleiterin sie ist, bestimmt.

Wir haben eben einen Begriff davon, welcherlei Lebensformen primitive sind, und welche erst aus solchen entspringen konnten. Wir glauben, daß der einfachste Pflug vor dem komplizierten da war.

Die einfache Form (und das ist die Urform) des Ursache-Wirkung Spiels ist die der Bestimmung der Ursache, nicht des Zweifels.

(„. . . Irgendwo müssen wir — ohne zu zweifeln — sagen: *das* geschieht aus *dieser* Ursache.") Im Gegensatz, etwa, *wozu*? Im Gegensatz dazu wohl, daß man den Knoten nie *anzieht,* sondern immer zweifelhaft bleibt, was die Ursache der Erscheinung wirklich sei; als hätte es einen Sinn zu sagen: strenggenommen könne man nie mit Sicherheit *wissen.* So daß es also der *Wahrheit* am strengsten entspreche, die Frage *nicht* zu entscheiden. Welche Idee auf einem gänzlichen Mißverstehen der Rollen beruht, die der Genauigkeit und dem Zweifel zufallen.

22.10.

Die Grundform des Spiels muß eine sein, in der gehandelt wird.

„Wie sollte der Begriff ‚Ursache' auf die Beine gestellt werden, wenn immer gezweifelt würde?"

„Die Ursache muß ursprünglich etwas Handgreifliches sein."

First there must be firm, hard stone for building, and the blocks are laid rough-hewn one on another. *Afterwards* it's certainly important that the stone can be trimmed, that it's not *too* hard.

The primitive form of the language game is certainty, not uncertainty. For uncertainty could never lead to action.

I want to say: it is characteristic of our language that the foundation on which it grows consists in steady ways of living, regular ways of acting.

Its function is determined *above all* by action, which it accompanies.

We have an idea of which ways of living are primitive, and which could only have developed out of these. We believe that the simplest plough existed before the complicated one.

⟦421⟧ The simple form (and that is the prototype) of the cause-effect game is determining the cause, not doubting.

(". . . At some point we have to say—without doubting—: *that* happens because of *this* cause.")[5] As opposed to *what* for instance? As opposed surely to never *tightening* the knot, but remaining constantly uncertain what the cause of the phenomenon really is; as if it made sense to say: strictly speaking no one could ever *know* the cause with certainty. So that it would correspond most strictly to the *truth not* to settle the question. This idea is based on a total misunderstanding of the role played by exactitude and doubt.

22.10.

The basic form of the game must be one in which we act.

"How could the concept of 'cause' be set up if we were always doubting?"

"Originally the cause must be something palpable."

5. See above, p. 376/377.

Heißt es nicht eigentlich: mit der *philosophischen Spekulation* kann man nicht anfangen — ?

⟦405⟧ Wenn ich nie wüßte, was die Ursache von etwas ist, wie wäre ich dann zu diesem Begriff gekommen? — Das heißt doch: wie hätte ich mich wundern können, was von dem und dem wohl die Ursache ist, wenn ich nicht schon eine Ursache von etwas gesehen hätte? — Ja nun, dieses ‚können' muß wohl ein logisches sein — denn sonst könnte man sich ja alle möglichen Erklärungen denken. Dann heißt es aber bloß: Gib bei der Beschreibung dieses ‚Wunderns' acht, daß Du wirklich etwas beschreibst!

Das Wesentliche des Sprachspiels ist eine praktische Methode (eine Art des Handelns) — keine Spekulation, kein Geschwätz.

* * *

26.9.

Die Maschine (ihr Bau) als Symbol für ihre Wirkungsweise: Die Maschine — könnte ich zuerst sagen — ‚scheint ihre Wirkungsweise schon in sich zu haben'. Was heißt das?

Indem wir die Maschine kennen, scheint alles Übrige, nämlich die Bewegungen, die sie machen wird, schon ganz bestimmt zu sein.

„Wir reden so, als *könnten* sich diese Teile nur so bewegen, als könnten sie nichts Andres tun."

Wie ist es — : vergessen wir also die Möglichkeit, daß sie sich biegen, abbrechen, schmelzen können, etc.? *Ja*; wir denken in *vielen* Fällen gar nicht daran. Wir gebrauchen eine Maschine, oder das Bild einer Maschine, als Symbol für eine bestimmte Wirkungsweise. Wir teilen z. B. Einem dieses Bild mit und setzen voraus, daß er die Erscheinungen der Bewegung der Teile aus ihm ableitet. (So wie wir jemand eine Zahl mitteilen können, indem wir sagen, sie sei die fünfundzwanzigste der Reihe: 1, 4, 9, 16, . . .)

„Die Maschine scheint ihre Wirkungsweise schon in sich zu haben" heißt: Du bist geneigt, die künftigen Bewegungen der Maschine in ihrer Bestimmtheit Gegenständen zu vergleichen, die alle schon in einer Lade liegen und von uns nun herausgeholt werden.

Isn't the real point this: we can't start with *philosophical speculation*?—

If I never knew the cause of anything how would I ever have arrived at this concept?—But that means: how could I ever have wondered what was the cause of this or that event if I hadn't already seen the cause of something? But, don't forget, this 'could' has to be taken in a logical sense,—because otherwise one might start thinking of all sorts of possible explanations. Whereas the point is simply: When you give a description of this 'wondering', take care that you really are describing something.

The essence of the language game is a practical method (a way of acting)—not speculation, not chatter.

* * *

26.9.[6]

The machine (its structure) as symbol of its mode of operating: The machine—I might start by saying—already seems to have its mode of operating within itself. What does this mean?

⟦422⟧ According to our knowledge of the machine, all the rest, that is, the movements it will make, seem already to be completely determined.

"We talk as though these parts *could* move only in this way, as though they couldn't do anything different."

How is that—are we forgetting the possibility that they may bend, break off, melt, etc.? *Yes;* in *many* cases we don't think of that at all. We use a machine, or the picture of a machine, as a symbol for a particular mode of operation. For example, we give someone this picture and assume he will conclude from it how the parts will move. (Just as we can give someone a number by telling him it's the twenty-fifth in the series 1, 4, 9, 16 . . .).

"The machine already seems to have its mode of operating within it" means: You are inclined to compare the details of the machine's movements with objects which are already in a drawer and which we then take out.

6. For the following nine paragraphs, cf. *Remarks on the Foundation of Mathematics,* Part I, §122; see also *Philosophical Investigations,* §193.

So aber reden wir nicht, wenn es sich darum handelt, das wirkliche Verhalten einer Maschine vorauszusagen; da vergessen wir, im allgemeinen, nicht die Möglichkeiten der Deformation der Teile etc.

⟦406⟧ Wohl aber, wenn wir uns darüber wundern, wie wir denn die Maschine als Symbol einer Bewegungsweise verwenden können — da sie sich doch auch ganz *anders* bewegen könne.

Nun, wir könnten sagen, die Maschine, oder ihr Bild, stehe hier als Anfang einer Bilderreihe, die wir aus diesem Bild abzuleiten gelernt haben.

Wenn wir aber bedenken, daß sich die Maschine auch anders hätte bewegen können, so erscheint es uns leicht, als müßte in der Maschine als Symbol ihre Bewegungsart noch viel bestimmter enthalten sein, als in der wirklichen Maschine. Es genüge da nicht, daß dies die erfahrungsmäßig vorausbestimmten Bewegungen sind, sondern sie müßten eigentlich — in einem mysteriösen Sinne — bereits *gegenwärtig* sein. Und es ist ja wahr: die Bewegung des Maschinensymbols ist in anderer Weise vorausbestimmt, als die einer gegebenen wirklichen Maschine.

Die Schwierigkeit aber entsteht hier in allen Fällen durch die Vermischung von „ist" und „heißt".

28.9.

Man sagt: „Es ist schwer zu wissen, ob diese Medizin wirklich hilft oder nicht, weil man nicht weiß, ob der Schnupfen länger gedauert hätte oder ärger gewesen wäre, wenn man sie nicht genommen hätte." Wenn man dafür wirklich keinen Anhaltspunkt hat, ist es dann bloß schwer zu wissen?

Ich hätte eine Medizin erfunden; ich sage: diese Medizin einige Monate hindurch genommen verlängert das Leben *jedes* Menschen um einen Monat. Hätte er sie nicht genommen, so wäre er einen Monat früher gestorben. „Man kann nicht *wissen,* ob es wirklich die Medizin war; ob er nicht ohne sie ebenso lang gelebt hätte." — Ist diese Ausdrucksweise nicht irreführend? Sollte es nicht besser heißen: „Es heißt nichts, von dieser Medizin zu sagen, sie verlängere das Leben, wenn eine Prüfung der Behauptung in dieser Weise ausgeschlossen wurde." Nämlich: Wir haben hier zwar einen richtigen deutschen Satz nach Analogie oft gebrauchter Sätze gebildet, aber

But we don't talk like that when what interests us is predicting the actual behaviour of a machine; then we don't usually forget that it's possible for the parts to get deformed, etc.

On the other hand this is what we may do if we are wondering how we can use the machine as a symbol of a way of moving—since it may after all in fact move quite *differently.*

Well, we might say that the machine, or its picture, is the first member of a series of pictures which we've learnt to derive from it.

But if we reflect that the machine could have behaved differently, we easily get the impression that the machine as symbol contains its own mode of operation much more determinately than does the real machine. In that case we're not satisfied that the movements should be those which experience has taught us to expect; on the contrary we feel they must really—in a mysterious sense—already be *present* in the machine. And it's quite true: the operation of the machine symbol is predetermined in a different way from that of some real machine.

But in all these cases the difficulty comes from confusing "is" and "is called".

28.9.

We say: "It is hard to know whether this medicine helps or not, because we don't know if the cold would have lasted longer or got ⟦423⟧ worse if we hadn't taken it." If we really have no evidence concerning this, is it simply hard to know?

Suppose I have invented a medicine and say: *Every* man who takes this medicine for a few months will have his life extended by one month. If he hadn't taken it, he would have died a month earlier. "We can't *know* whether it was really the medicine; or whether he wouldn't have lived just as long without it." Isn't this a misleading way to speak? Wouldn't it be better to say: "It is meaningless to say this medicine prolongs life, if testing the claim is ruled out in this way." In other words, we are indeed dealing with a correct English sentence constructed on the analogy of sentences which are in common use, but you are not clear about the *fundamental* difference in the use of these

Du bist Dir nicht klar über den *grundlegenden* Unterschied in den Verwendungen dieser Sätze. Diese zu überblicken ist nicht leicht. Der Satz liegt Dir vor Augen, aber nicht eine übersichtliche Darstellung seiner Verwendung.

Mit „Es heißt nichts . . ." will also gesagt werden: dies sind Worte, die Dich etwa irreführen, sie spiegeln einen Gebrauch vor, ⟦407⟧ den sie nicht haben. Sie rufen wohl auch eine Vorstellung hervor (der Verlängerung des Lebens, etc.), aber das Spiel mit dem Satz ist so eingerichtet, daß es die wesentliche Pointe nicht hat, die dem Spiel mit ähnlich gebauten Sätzen seinen Nutzen gibt. (Wie der ‚Wettlauf zwischen dem Hasen und dem Igel' zwar aussieht wie ein Wettlauf, aber keiner ist.)

Du mußt Dich fragen: was nimmt man als Kriterium dafür, daß eine Medizin geholfen hat? Es gibt verschiedene Fälle. In welchen Fällen sagt man: „Es ist schwer zu sagen, ob sie geholfen hat"? In welchen Fällen ist die Redeweise als sinnlos zu verwerfen: „Man kann natürlich nie sicher sein, ob es die Medizin war, die geholfen hat"?

Wann nennen wir zwei Körper gleich schwer? Wenn wir sie gewogen haben, oder während wir sie wägen.

Wenn Wägen das einzige Kriterium für das Gewicht wäre — *wann* hat nun ein Körper sein Gewicht geändert, wenn er bei einer Wägung mehr wiegt als bei der vorhergehenden? Der Sprachgebrauch könnte *so* sein: der Körper hat das und das Gewicht, bis er beim Wägen ein anderes zeigt; auf die Frage: „Wann hat er sein Gewicht geändert?" gibt man den Zeitpunkt dieser Wägung an. — Oder: man sagt: „Man kann nicht wissen, wann er sein Gewicht geändert hat, wir wissen nur: bei der ersten Wägung hatte er dieses, bei der zweiten jenes Gewicht." — Oder: „Es ist sinnlos, zu fragen, wann er sein Gewicht geändert hat, man kann nur fragen, wann sich die Gewichtsänderung gezeigt hat."

29.9.

„Aber der Körper hatte doch zu jeder Zeit irgend *ein* Gewicht, also war doch die Antwort die richtige: wir *wüßten* nicht, wann er es geändert habe." —

sentences. It isn't easy to have a clear view of this use. The sentence is there before your eyes, but not a clear overall representation of its use.

So to say "It is meaningless . . ." is to point out that perhaps you are being misled by these words, that they make you imagine a use which they do not have. They do perhaps evoke an idea (the prolongation of life, etc.), but the game with the sentence is so arranged that it doesn't have the essential point which makes useful the game with similarly constructed sentences. (As the 'race between the hare and the hedgehog' looks like a race, but isn't one.[7])

You must ask yourself: what does one accept as a criterion for a medicine's helping one? There are various cases. In which cases do we say: "It is hard to say whether it has helped"? In what cases should we reject as senseless the expression: "Of course we can never be certain whether it was the medicine that helped"?

When do we say that two bodies weigh the same? If we have weighed them or whilst we are weighing them?

Suppose weighing were our sole criterion of something's weight;—if a body registers a greater weight at one weighing than at the previous one, *when* did its weight change? It might be established usage to say: the body weighs so and so much until a new weighing gives a different result. We answer the question: "When did its weight change?", by giving the time of this weighing.—Or: we say it's impossible for us to know when it changes its weight, we only know that it has one weight at the first weighing and another at the second."—Or: "It's senseless to ask when it changed its weight, we can only ask when the change in weight was registered."

⟦424⟧
29.9.

"Still, the body had *some* weight at any given time, so the right answer was: we *don't know* when it changed."—

7. See "The Hare and the Hedgehog," #187 in Grimms' *Tales.* (eds.)

Und wie, wenn wir sagten, ein Körper habe gar kein Gewicht, außer dann, wenn es sich irgendwie zeigt, oder, er habe kein *bestimmtes* Gewicht, außer wenn es gemessen wird? Könnten wir nicht auch dieses Spiel spielen?

Denke, wir verkauften ein Material ‚nach dem Gewicht' und das Herkommen ist so: Wir wägen das Material alle fünf Minuten und berechnen dann den Preis nach dem Resultat der letzten Wägung. Oder ein anderes Herkommen: Wir berechnen den Preis auf diese Weise nur wenn das Gewicht bei der Wägung nach dem ⟦408⟧ Kauf das gleiche ist, hat es sich dann geändert, berechnen wir den Preis nach dem arithmetischen Mittel der beiden Gewichte. Welche Art der Preisbestimmung ist die richtigere? –

(Wenn sich der Preis einer Ware von gestern auf heute geändert hat, *wann* hat er sich geändert? Wie hoch stand er um 12 Uhr Mitternacht, als niemand kaufte?)

Resultat: Die Verbindung der Ausdrücke: „der Körper hat jetzt das Gewicht . . .", „der Körper wiegt jetzt ungefähr . . .", „ich weiß nicht, wieviel er jetzt wiegt", mit den Ergebnissen der Wägung ist keine ganz einfache, hängt von diversen Umständen ab, wir können uns leicht verschiedene Rollen denken, die die Wägung in den Verrichtungen des Lebens spielen könnte, und also verschiedene Rollen für die Ausdrücke, die das Wägespiel begleiten.

And what if we said that a body doesn't have any weight at all except when it is being registered somehow, or that it doesn't have any *definite* weight, except when it is being measured? Couldn't we play this game too?

Imagine we sell some material 'by weight' and the custom is as follows: We weigh the material every five minutes and then calculate the price according to the result of the last weighing. Or another custom: we calculate the price in this way only if the weight is the same when the material is weighed after the sale; if it has changed, we calculate the price according to the arithmetic mean of the two weights. Which way of fixing the price is the more correct?

(If the price of a commodity has changed between yesterday and today, *when* did it change? How much was it at midnight when nobody was buying?)

Conclusion: The expressions "the body now has a weight of. . .", "the body now weighs roughly. . .", "I don't know how much it weighs now", aren't connected quite straightforwardly with the results of the weighing, but this depends on a variety of circumstances; we can easily imagine different roles which weighing could play among the institutions within which we live and different roles for the expressions which accompany the game of weighing.

⟦429⟧

# Appendix A
## Immediately Aware of the Cause

*Roughly half the notes in the small pocket notebook MS 159 are written in German and refer to Gödel's proof (subject of Wittgenstein's lectures in the autumn of 1937). The English notes seem to be memoranda for lectures in the winter and spring of 1938. (He never had notes with him when lecturing.)*

"Immediately aware."

"I'm immediately aware of that which I can't be wrong about."

"I'm not sure whether a man went into this room, but I am sure that it seemed to me that one did, that I saw that[1] image."

If I painted my impression instead of just describing it in words, I could now point to my picture and say: "I'm sure that this was what I saw." (Of course the "I'm sure" is really superfluous.) But further: I have painted, portrayed my impression—but have I portrayed, projected it correctly? All justifications you might try to give are idle wheels, they don't drive anything.—Now this is why the expressions "immediate awareness" or "knowledge" are in this sort of case misleading.

The proposition is not unquestionable because it rests so securely on something but there is no question of its resting on anything. To say that we are *certain* that we have this impression is like saying that the earth rests on something that is firm in itself.

"I am immediately aware that my exclamation is caused by something."—So I'm immediately aware that the word "cause" fits the case? But remember that *words* are public property.

⟦430⟧ Private language: Playing a game of chess in the imagination. Playing a soccer match in the imagination.

What if I said: The word 'cause' fits my impression privately?—But "to fit" is a public word.

Ask yourself: What do we make this noise of words for?

1. Variant: "such an".

"You are immediately aware . . ." makes one think that you are *right* about something, that you can be shown to be right about; whereas the point is that there is no *right* (or wrong) about it. (And of course no one would say: I'm sure I'm right that I have pain.)

Being *immediately aware* of the cause when you say: "That's where it hurts!"

Being *immediately aware* of the cause of terror, pleasure etc.

Being *immediately aware* of the cause in a mechanism.
Causal 'nexus'.
'Cause-reaction'

"Cause isn't just temporal coincidence but influence."

"You can't go on having one thing resting on another; in the end there must be something resting on itself." (The *a priori*) Something firm in itself.

I propose to drop this mode of speech as it leads to puzzlements.

"If a stone could think he would think that he wished to drop."

'immediately aware of motive.'

Immediately aware of what makes me laugh in a joke.

[. . .]

*Notes taken by Rush Rhees during one of Wittgenstein's lectures, Lent Term, 1938*

Consider what we have called an "utterance"—e.g., "I am in pain", as opposed to "he is in pain".

"If one makes an utterance, one is immediately aware that it is caused." This "immediately aware" seems a cheap explanation.—So you are immediately aware that the word 'cause' fits. And this is queer; because where it fits or not is not for you to decide (unless you are making a definition). It is a matter of public property.

You may say, "Well, it fits anyway subjectively, fits my idea." Then what about the idea of *fitting*? If you say the word fits your idea, what can we do with it? I don't know what your idea is nor what 'fitting' is. You have told me nothing.—

⟦431⟧ I see a man walking into the room. What am I sure of? There are cases where I'd say only: "I'm sure it seemed to me a man walked in." This comes to "I'm sure of an impression".—One could, instead of describing the impression, *paint* it and then say: I am sure that this was my impression. But are you aware that it (the picture) fits your impression? and in what way does it fit? You might have various scales or projections.

It is no use at all trying to go beyond that picture. Anything of the sort is just an idle wheel.

The expressions "know", "be immediately aware" in such cases are misleading. (Normally of course one does not say "I know that I have pain" or "I know that I am right that I have pain", etc.)—We might say that the expression marks the end of a certain chain. And to say "all I know is that I have a toothache" comes to just the same as: " 'I have a toothache' is an utterance." But it is misleading. Suppose you said: "one thing must rest on another—the cushion on the chair, the chair on the earth . . . but in the end something must rest on itself." You can say this, but it produces puzzlement because it is not a normal statement. One would rather say "it rests on nothing"; but this gives a feeling of insecurity, whereas the other gives a sense of security. "If the earth rests on nothing, you might as well have no foundation to your house."—This is the source of the idea of '*a priori*'.

Consider Russell's point that we don't always arrive at the proposition "this is the cause of that" by observing regular sequences. One has first to recognize certain causes intuitively—I am immediately aware that this is the cause.

We *do* use the word in cases where 'ascertaining the cause' does not mean making experiments or working with statistics or anything like that.

I start. Someone asks "Why do you start?"—"Because I saw a light there."—Here no sort of experiment is involved. But what would be meant by "I perceive the cause directly" here? How do I *learn* the word 'cause' or 'because' in such a case?

If I start at someone's entering the room, how is this different from jumping when pricked? It actually involves *looking* at him: the person who causes me to start is the person at whom I look with terror in my eyes. I learned to use the word in this way.

You threaten me with a dagger and I make a gesture—which could

be called a reaction against a cause. 'The cause' here is what I am pushing away. To say "immediately aware" gives the wrong impression. I *call* "cause" that which I push away.
⟦432⟧ "What are you so pleased about?"—This and that.—"Are you sure?"—You might be foolish enough to say "of course I'm sure".

Russell's classifying an appearance as "cat". What would *classifying* consist of? He sees  and classifies it. This might mean just giving it the name "cat". But it probably means putting it into a category table in one's mind. Something like drawing a line from appearance to model.

But why should he go through this ceremony?—One might say "but here you have the word 'cat', and you draw a line to the picture which has on top of it the word 'cat'." But it doesn't matter what is on top of what. The word 'cat' might have been on top of another picture.

Two people playing chess. I say this is not all that happens. The truth is that each one plays a private game himself. Before every move each one of them carries out some mental operation in an imaginary note book. You might say, "What are these private games like? Have you any reason to suppose this rather than anything else? If not, have you any reason to call it a game at all? It might be anything."

Similarly with "classifying".

Suppose you have an entirely private table which you consult to see whether it is a cat. Have we any reason to think it is ordered in this way rather than another? We know nothing about it.

| | Pictures | |
|---|---|---|
| Dog | | |
| Cat | | |
| Elephant | | |

Why should I not assume that he changes the rules about, etc.?

Thus the table comes to nothing at all. If I know nothing about the table, why call it a table? It might be *anything*—or nothing.—We start with the idea of a table which we know well. But finally it turns out that there's no reason to assume anything, and what matters is the result, namely whether he calls a cat what we call a cat.

⟦433⟧ One thing we call "detecting a cause" is *following a particular kind of mechanism.* I feel a pull on a string; I go along the string and detect the cause. This again is not by doing experiments.

When I turn this wheel, then *this* wheel turns and the lever will strike the bell.—"Could we not have made experiments here?"—Yes; but you didn't. You were taught to use the word "cause" here in *following the mechanism.*—It is from this, by the way, that we have the idea of a '*causal nexus*'.

The idea that cause is not mere sequence, but is a *connexion.* But the connexion is a string or cogwheels.

"Tracing the cause" is an entirely different process here from making frequent experiments.

The reaction of *looking from one thing to another thing.*—Someone touches me with a pole, I look along the pole. Someone throws a stone, I feel it and I see him in a particular position, I throw back. This is reaction against a *cause.*

*Impact:* in mechanics we are inclined to explain by this. If a thing has been explained by impact, it has been *explained.* Finding what strikes. "Etwas gibt den Anstoss." ["Something gives an impulse."]

In the bell example it would be misleading to say I am "immediately aware of the cause". Say rather: this is what I call "cause" in such a case.—We use both experiments and also such observations to *predict* what will happen. And so we use the same word.

Suppose someone said: "I'm immediately aware of the cause of lifting my arm when I will to do it."—No one ordinarily says he "wills" to do something. He lifts his arm, that's all. But one can generally predict the movements of one's body.

Imagine we had seeds which came from two plants. We find that the two plants have exactly the same seed. But if it comes from a poppy, the seed produces a poppy again; if it comes from a rose it produces a rose. We are then inclined to say there must be some difference in the seed itself. But if we did discover a difference, we should not know whether it was a relevant difference (whether it affected the outcome).

"I know what this seed will give: it will give a poppy."
"Why?"

"Because it came from a poppy."

To say "It will give a poppy because it came from a poppy" ⟦434⟧ would be disagreeable. Whereas "I know it will, because it came from a poppy" is not so.

There is something like action at a distance here—which shocks people. The idea would revolutionize science. "A seed that has come from a poppy will produce a poppy"—this is all right. But not: "It will produce a poppy *because* it came from a poppy."

Today, in case we actually discovered two seeds which we could not distinguish, but one producing a poppy and the other a rose, we should look frantically for a difference.—But in other circumstances we might give this up—give up looking for a difference. This would be a tremendous thing to do—as great as recognizing indeterminacy. We would no longer *look* for the difference, and so we would no longer say there *must* be a difference. *Now* (today) we have every reason to say there must be a difference. But we could imagine circumstances where we would break with this tradition.

"Of course the character of a person *must* be exhibited in some way in his handwriting." It is important to be able to say, "no; this needn't be."

There is an ideal—a direction in which investigations are constantly pushed. "There *must* be" corresponds to this ideal.

# ⟦435⟧ Anhang B
## Können wir etwas außer den Daten erkennen?

*Wittgensteins Aufzeichnungen*

You know what I mean by 'sense datum': *this!* —

And how do you know that you mean *it*; how do you know that you hit it with the meaning?

Eine Lokomotive durch die Sinneseindrücke, die wir von ihr erhalten, definieren. — Tun wir das nicht ohnehin, wenn wir jemandem eine Lokomotive zeigen und sagen: dies ist eine Lokomotive?

Statt zu sagen: „Das ist eine Lokomotive" — könnte ich Dir nicht sagen: „Was diese Sinneseindrücke erzeugt ist eine Lokomotive"? [. . .]

Die Sprache wird verwendet, — ob sie sich der Wörter für physikalische Gegenstände bedient, oder für Sinneseindrücke.

Aber sind nicht die Sinneseindrücke das unmittelbar Wahrgenommene? Die unmittelbaren Gegenstände, auf die sich alles, was wir sagen, am Schluß beziehen muß?

Das Bild von den Bausteinen. Alles was wir bauen besteht endlich aus diesen Bausteinen. Aber das Bild ist falsch, da wir ‚*diese*' Bausteine nicht andern entgegensetzen.

Wie weißt Du, welchem Gegenstand Du den Namen gegeben hast?

Ja, wie weißt Du, daß Du überhaupt irgend etwas diesen Namen gegeben hast? [. . .]

Es ist hier gar keine Frage darüber, daß der Name des physikalischen Gegenstands den einen und der Name des Eindrucks einen andern Gegenstand bezeichnet, wie wenn man nacheinander ⟦436⟧

# Appendix B
# Can We Know Anything but Data?

*Notes by Wittgenstein in pocket notebook MS 160.*

You know what I mean by 'sense datum': *this!*—

And how do you know that you mean *it*; how do you know that you hit it with the meaning?

Defining a locomotive by means of the sense impressions we get from it.—Don't we do that anyway if we show someone a locomotive and say: this is a locomotive?

Instead of saying: "That's a locomotive"—couldn't I say to you: "What produces these sense impressions is a locomotive"? [. . .]

Language is being used,—whether it utilizes words for physical objects or words for sense impressions.

But aren't sense impressions what we are immediately aware of? Aren't they the immediate objects to which everything we say must finally refer?

The picture of building blocks. Everything we build consists ultimately of these blocks. But it is a false picture since we are not contrasting '*these*' building blocks with any others.

How do you know which object you gave the name to?

For that matter, how do you know you gave this name to anything at all? [. . .]

There is no question of its being the case here that the name of the physical object refers to one object and the name of the impression to another, as when someone points successively at two different objects

auf zwei verschiedene Gegenstände zeigt und sagt, „ich meine diesen Gegenstand, nicht diesen". Das Bild von den verschiedenen Gegenständen ist hier ganz falsch gebraucht.

Nicht, das eine ist der Name für den unmittelbaren Gegenstand, das andere für etwas andres; sondern die zwei Wörter werden einfach verschieden verwendet. Wir zeigen bei der Namenerklärung nicht einmal auf den unmittelbaren Gegenstand und einmal auf den physikalischen.[. . .]

„Du redest vom Ding, willst aber eigentlich von Sinneseindrücken reden." — Ich will reden, wie ich rede und Du kannst sagen, ich rede von Sinneseindrücken. Nur sieht von Sinneseindrücken reden nicht so aus, wie Du es Dir vorstellst.[. . .]

Die Technik des Gebrauchs der Worte beschreiben wir in Worten.[. . .]

Es gibt ja immer noch eine *Technik* der Anwendung einer Erklärung.

Und wenn ich die beschreibe, so gibt es eine Technik der Anwendung dieser Beschreibung.

Der Dreher erhält die Werkzeichnung, ein sehr einfaches Bild des Körpers, den er zu drehen hat. Könnte er sich nichts anders denken, nicht etwas ganz anderes nach ihr erzeugen? auch gegeben seine Abrichtung, das Herkommen etc., etc.

Wenn Du etwas von einem Ding aussagst, willst Du natürlich etwas von Erscheinungen aussagen. Also kannst Du, statt von dem Ding zu reden geradezu von den Erscheinungen reden. Aber wie soll ich von den Erscheinungen reden?

Ich erwarte z.B. jemand und weiß natürlich nicht, genau welche Erscheinungen er mir bieten wird. Angenommen nun, ich hätte eine ungeheure Menge von Bildern — entspricht es nun wirklich dem, was ich beim Erwarten tue, wenn ich alle diese Bilder durchsähe und mir sagte, daß eines davon treffen wird? Wäre es da nicht besser ich benützte *ein* Bild des Menschen und sagte dazu, daß er ungefähr so aussehen werde? Ich will sagen: warum soll ich den Namen des

and says, "I mean this object, not that one". The picture of the different objects is being used quite wrongly here.

It is not that one is the name of the immediate object and the other of something else; rather, the two words are simply being used differently. In explaining the names we do not point first at the immediate object and then at the physical object. [. . .]

"You speak about the thing, but really want to speak about sense impressions."—I want to speak as I do speak, and you can say that I am speaking about sense impressions. The only trouble is that speaking about sense impressions does not look the way you imagine it does. [. . .]

The technique of using words is described in words. [. . .]

There is, at the same time, a *technique* of applying an explanation.

And if I describe the technique, there is a technique of applying this description.

A lathe operator is given a blueprint, a very simple picture of the body he is to turn. Couldn't he think differently, produce something quite different from the blueprint?—even given his training, background etc., etc.

When you speak about a thing of course you mean to say something about appearances. So, instead of speaking about the thing, you can speak directly about the appearances. But how am I supposed to speak about the appearances?

I am for example expecting someone and I don't of course know exactly what appearances he will present me with. Now suppose that I had an enormous quantity of pictures—does it really correspond to what I do when I expect someone if I look through all these pictures and say to myself that one of them will be right? Wouldn't it be nearer the mark if I were to use *one* picture of the person and say that he will look roughly like this? What I mean is: why do I have to replace the

Dings durch *alle* seine Erscheinungen ersetzen, und nicht durch *eine* und das Übrige der Verwendung dieses Bildes überlassen?

[. . .]Aber wie spricht man unmittelbar von Erscheinungen — Was nennt man „unmittelbar von Erscheinungen sprechen"? Ist ⟦437⟧ es: von Bildern sprechen — statt von Dingen? Und von *allen* Bildern der Dinge?

Wenn ich sage: ich werde in den Garten gehen und mich unter den großen Nußbaum setzen — welche Bilder entsprechen diesem Satz? Nun, ich könnte den Satz wohl durch ein Bild illustrieren. Aber was wäre die Beziehung dieses Bildes zu meinen Eindrücken von dem Baum? [. . .]

15.9.38

„Wenn ich von diesem Baum rede, will ich natürlich so oder so von Erscheinungen reden. So laß mich also direkt von Erscheinungen reden und nicht über den Umweg des Baumes." Aber das ist so, als hätte man eine Menge Erscheinungen (‚des Baumes') vor sich, von denen man reden will, und bediente sich des Wortes „Baum" in einer Art abgekürzter Redeweise.[. . .]

„Aber was mich interessiert, wenn ich von physikalischen Gegenständen spreche, ist doch, was ich sehe und höre, rieche, schmecke und fühle. Also sind es die Sinneseindrücke, was mich interessiert; also kann ich doch *gleich* von diesen reden." — Wenn es so ist, so *rede* ich also ‚von Sinneseindrücken', indem ich von physikalischen Gegenständen rede.

„Von etwas reden" kann eben so manches heißen. (Reden wir von Zukünftigem oder Gegenwärtigem, wenn wir auf den Himmel zeigen und sagen „es wird bald regnen"?)

* * *

name of the thing with *all* its appearances? Can't I use just *one*, and then leave everything else to the application of this picture?

[. . .] But how does someone speak immediately about appearances—What do we call "speaking immediately about appearances"? Is it: speaking about pictures—instead of about things? And about *all* pictures of things?

If I say: I shall go into the garden and sit under the big nut tree—what pictures correspond to this sentence? Well, I suppose I could illustrate the sentence with a picture. But what would be the relation between this picture and my impressions of the tree? [. . .]

15.9.38

"If I speak about this tree, of course I mean in one way or another to speak about appearances. So let me speak directly about appearances without making a detour round the tree." But that is as though one had before one a number of appearances ('of the tree') that one wanted to talk about and used the word "tree" as a sort of abbreviation. [. . .]

"But what interests me if I speak of physical objects is what I see, hear, smell, taste and feel. So it is the sense impressions that interest me; so I can after all speak about these *straight off*."—But if this is the case I *do* speak 'about sense impressions' when I speak about physical objects.

"Speaking about something" can just mean so many things. (Are we talking about something in the future or something in the present if we point at the sky and say "It will rain soon"?)

* * *

*Notes by Wittgenstein in pocket notebook MS 159.*

The unity of grammar and experience.

"You can't have the relation of 'knowing' to a fact of this sort."[1] The relation of knowing does not fit such a fact it has not the right number of valences, as O can't combine with one atom of H. "A cube can't lie in a plane or be cut by a straight line in two—." A fact of this sort hasn't the right structure for being known.

"Or else—if you call *this* knowing, it's something else than knowing that you have a sense datum."

Collecting the evidence; distinguishing between evidence and surmise. "Now what did you actually see?"—Did you actually touch it?—No—"Then it might also have been a———"

We take one *particular* game and make it into *the* game always played.

"The logical structure of the universe."

[. . .]

"You can't 'know' it *in the same sense* . . ."

Can you deny in the same sense that 20 × 20 = 400 and that it rains?

"We can't be directly aware of. . . ."

'To be directly aware of the direction the sound comes from.'

[. . .]

"You can't *know.*"

⟦438⟧ *Knowing* is here like having; having in yourself.

You *know* only the data, everything else is conjecture.

We identify knowing and data.

1. Wittgenstein had earlier been writing in German about scrutinizing a conjurer's (*Taschenspieler*) trick. (eds.)

*Notes taken by Rush Rhees during one of Wittgenstein's lectures (following that referred to on p. 407)*

"One can know only that there is a red patch, etc. One cannot know that there's a chair there."

This sort of statement comes from ordinary life. Suppose you see a conjuring trick, and you tell someone what you saw. The hearer may doubt and say, "Well, all you know is that you had this sort of image."—You would like to give one a film of such a case and say, "Well, that's what I saw: now you explain it."

Or: "Whatever you know, you know through your senses. Thus you can *know* only what your senses tell you. All else is conjecture."—This is the sort of talk about "sense evidence"—in which one is not aware that one is using a metaphor.

The first sense we think of is the eye; then the ear, then . . .—"The eye gives us pictures." But surely not: then they are pictures which don't last—like evidence which is destroyed at once.

We compare what actually happens with some process in which the first thing we get hold of is something like painted pictures, and then we draw conclusions about the existence of certain bodies.—This might happen, but generally it does not.

If we think experience gives us pictures, then it does not give us the sentences which express these pictures, or the pictures which express these pictures. The evidence is *private*; and the doubt is whether you are using "blue" in the right way, if you say "all I know is that I see a blue patch".

The confusion is in the idea that the senses give evidence—as if it were, "This sense says so and so". But the sense says nothing. Nothing is said but what I say.

We have the idea that senses give evidence but in a *picture* language—although actually they don't. Primitive languages are picture languages. And the idea is then that we translate these pictures into words.

⟦439⟧ *But nobody sees or hears the evidence of the senses.* If you say, "I do myself" . . . the point is that nobody can tell whether you are translating correctly.—If you draw, and say "I saw this", then the picture is what's *drawn*—and it is a metaphor to say the *senses* provide us with pictures.

The idea is that although no doubt is possible in the case of what the senses tell us, there is always a doubt possible as to interpretation. . . .

*The whole game we play depends just as much on not doubting every physical fact as on not doubting whether we use "red" or "blue" correctly.*

You might think that although doubting whether we were using words correctly would make the whole game impossible, a doubt whether this is a sofa would not make the game impossible, it would only make it more accurate.

At first it seems as though I were a judge, who before passing judgment scrutinized the evidence of witnesses most carefully.—But actually it is something wholly different.

Suppose we made experiments which give us data expressed by

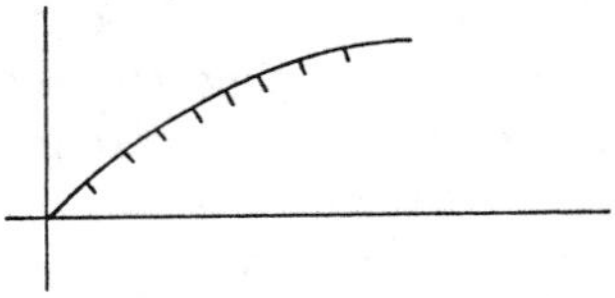

After we have the points, we draw a curve.—Suppose I ask, "is it always rash to draw a curve?"—Could it not be, in a particular case, no more rash to draw a curve than it is to make a dot here?

It seemed as though we could play a game more cautiously or less cautiously: and as though there was an ideal of cautiousness—like looking up every word in the dictionary when translating German into English. Supposing then I began to doubt the dictionaries; there are good and bad dictionaries, but suppose I began to doubt The Oxford English Dictionary? What should I do?—It looked at first as though there were one correct way to play the game: this is true only in a certain limited field.

⟦440⟧ To say it is rash to draw this curve would be like saying, "You must not draw any curve." *If* EVER *there is evidence enough there is now.*

One might say that to the curve a different kind of doubt adheres than to the points—meaning that, given that these are the points, it might still have been an oscillating curve between one point and another.—But if by "a different kind of doubt" you mean "degree of doubtfulness"—then this is wrong. Like saying that to the sentence "I see a blue patch" a different kind of doubt adheres than to "I see a blue waistcoat". This is actually wrong if it refers to a doubtful state of mind. And what is *correct* is that we play a different game. If we are doubtful of the one we do something different about it.—So, if I am doubtful about a dot, then I see if the experiment is wrong.—If I doubt "I see a blue patch", I am doubting if English people use the word in this way; if I doubt whether that's a blue waistcoat, I go and feel it. But it does not mean that the state of doubtfulness is different.

Suppose I wish to say what a man means when he says "Jones passed me in the street". Suppose I then show a colour film and say, "This is what one means".—Is this an explanation of what one means by the sentence? Yes and no. It would be supplemented in a thousand different ways. We don't learn these words just by being shown this picture.

No ostensive definition gives me anything like a *full* explanation of the use of the word. It could still be used in all sorts of ways.

We can *imagine* a game in which "Such and such a body is there" is a shorthand for "I have had such and such impressions". But to take this as the general rule is to simplify our language—construct a game which is not the one played. Not just a simplification, a falsification, and there is hardly any similarity between the game described—having "views" and then concluding—and the game actually played.

But what tempts one to do this sort of thing? There is a tendency to say that everything must be "well grounded". The game we play with the word "sofa" must be well grounded: and we imagine there is unshakable evidence in what our senses tell us. When we see that we *can* attach doubt also to sense-data statements, this reasoning falls away.

[[441]]

# Appendix C
# How Can "Knowing" Fit a Physical Fact?

*Notes by Wittgenstein in a small pocket notebook MS 159.*

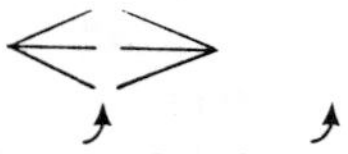

"This fits this "

Not *any // every //* sequence of puzzles is beneficial.

Language idles.

(Socrates is mortal)

Information.

"This colour matches this very nicely."

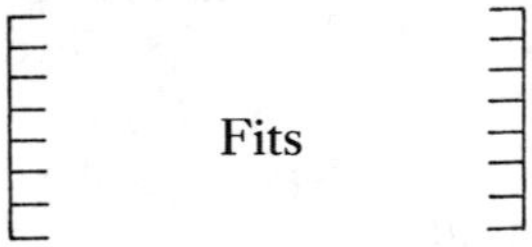


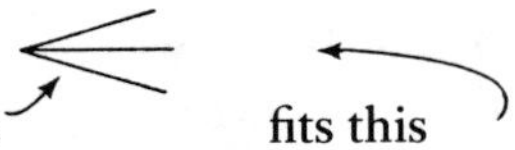

this fits this

"Things being what they are"
'Can we imagine it not fitting?'

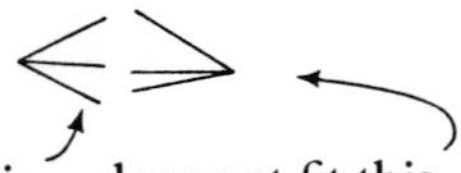

"This does not fit this "

How do you know whether this is a statement or a rule?

Is it *meant* as one or the other?

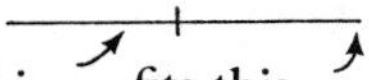

This fits this

This fits this *now*.

Everything fits itself.

'Does this fit?'—Make an experiment!

'Are we to call this a fit?'

⟦442⟧ *Notes taken by Rush Rhees during one of Wittgenstein's lectures, Cambridge, 1938.*

. . . It seems as if the *ideal* case of 'knowing' were that of knowing a sense datum; others are only approximate. But if you admit this, then there is the problem: How can 'knowing' fit a physical fact if it fits entirely the fact that you have a certain impression?

Can one have a bad tooth in the same sense in which one has a toothache?

Here we make the mistake of confusing subject and predicate.

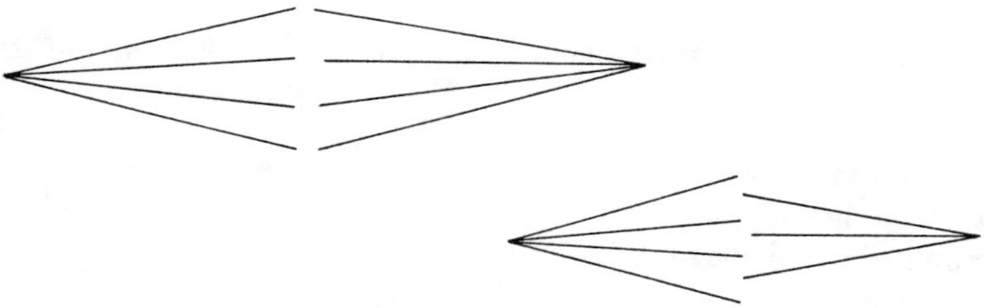

Suppose we have such figures, and we call it 'fitting' when the left hand fork matches the right hand one.

"Surely a four-pronged fork can never fit a three-pronged fork in the sense in which a four-pronged fits a four-pronged." (Or we could say '*joined*' or '*correlated*'.)—The question of *structure* enters.

Say we distinguish 'join$_1$' and 'join$_2$': when they are not 'joined$_1$' they may be 'joined$_2$'; for example:

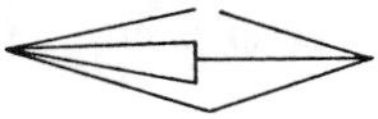

We could then use the two figures in this way: We say of a combination of a four-pronged and a three-pronged "it is joined$_2$". To know what this means, look at the illustration. If you said "they are joined$_1$"—then I might not know what this was to mean. I *could* give it sense, but I may not have done this.

If someone were to say of two four-pronged forks "they are joined$_2$", I would ask "What's this like? I don't know how it is to be applied." Or if you now ask, "*Can* two four-pronged forks be joined$_2$?", then I don't know. If we use this picture as an illustra⟦443⟧tion for joining of two four-pronged forks, then it is a very *impractical* picture. This is important.

We are inclined to say "This is not a mere matter of words: it is in the *nature* of the two forks that they can be joined in this way."

"*In the nature* . . ."

Supposing in this drawer there are two forks. Someone asks "Are they joined$_1$?", and you answer, "No, it is their nature that they can't be joined in way$_1$."—This might mean "They have a different number of prongs." This is a piece of information—not about paradigms, but about the two forks.

"These two forks can't be joined$_1$" = "They can't be joined in this way."

If you say "this fork" and "this fork"—what does it mean? the fork which is in this place?—Suppose when we try to join them, a new prong grows on one of them—is it then the same fork?

You may say "we wish to talk not about an external relation but an *internal* relation." In fact "nature" and "internal relation" always go together.

"These two forks have different natures."—But when you've referred to these two forks, you can't refer to the paradigm of *having different natures.* If  is our illustration of *having* different natures . . . then we can't say of this paradigm that the figures have different natures.

It seemed like a sham *experiment*—to see if they have different natures.

Obviously these two could be joined$_1$—if, e.g., a prong grows when they are brought together. But one has the idea that this is in fact the illustration of a case of *not being capable of being joined.*

If you say of two forks in this room they can't be joined—this might mean anything: one prong might vanish.

If we ask "In what way incapable?", and the answer is, "In this way: ",—then one uses this in a way both as subject and as predicate. ((Saying of what is *drawn* that they can't be joined; and explaining "can't be joined" by what is drawn.))

These are *predicates.* What is it you say this about? You may say it about the two forks here. You can say, "They can't be ⟦444⟧ joined, they look like this ." But you can't say of this drawing on the paper "this looks like this".

In philosophy language *idles.* No one asks how it is used.

What we mean by "fitting" in connexion with 'knowing' is *logical* not experimental fitting. Whether it fits or not, is not determined by putting two things together. But it is the nature of the two that they don't fit. This can't be determined by experiment. Nothing that happens by bringing them together could convince me that they fit or don't fit.

Suppose I had given  as an explanation of '*fitting*'; and I then go on to make a statement pointing to : This fits this.

A queer statement.

Where I have before me pieces of a jig-saw puzzle I can say such a thing—then I bring the two pieces together and see. This is giving information, part of a language game. But in the case of the forks we had drawn on paper this is not so. In this case to say "this fits this" may be true, or false, or a definition, or anything. We don't know what you're saying.

Take: "This coincides with this."—One question would be: Do you mean *now,* or at another time? In five minutes what would it be like; what would it be like if it *didn't* coincide then—would it be the same shape? or not?

The same applies to 

"This does *not* fit this"—which could be a paradigm of not fitting, for example.

There is a case where we say "fit" in *order* to see whether they have the same number: 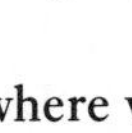

We put them together and say, "Oh yes, they fit."

When you talk of *fitting logically,* you imagine two things which fit and are actually parts of the paradigm for fitting.—You have the case which you represent as a picture of fitting: *knowing* (fits) *some fact.*

You now seem to be able just to concentrate on this fact—knowing that you have pain—and see the fitting. I want to say the concentration doesn't help at all: it does not help to determine how the word "fitting" is used—although it seems as though it did.

⟦445⟧ If you look at a picture and the picture suggests fitting, and you then say, "this fits this"—you still don't know what to do with it. What would it be like, for instance, if knowing did not fit the physical fact? or did not fit having pain?—We don't concern ourselves about the language game played with "fitting", we concern ourselves with a picture. But we could not merely by contemplating it see that one thing fits another thing.

"Why do you call it 'fitting'?"—"Because this is the picture of two things which fit."

# 13

*Yorick Smythies was a close friend and loyal student of Wittgenstein's who never became an academic philosopher. Wittgenstein was not usually happy about people taking notes at his lectures, but he made an exception for Smythies. One of Wittgenstein's students recalls that "Wittgenstein disliked us to take notes during his classes, and he would prevent anyone foolhardy enough to try. He did, however, allow Smythies to take notes."*[1]

*The circumstances of these two lectures have not so far proved possible to reconstruct. Smythies made an untitled typescript with handwritten corrections of his notes of Wittgenstein lecturing on freedom of the will. A copy of this was included in the Cornell microfilm of the Wittgenstein Papers prepared in 1967 at Oxford by Norman Malcolm and G. H. von Wright. Norman Malcolm prepared a handwritten cover-sheet stating: "Notes taken by Y. Smythies of a lecture on Freedom of the Will, delivered in Cambridge. Probably [1939 blotted out] 1945–46. Oxford". When these notes were published in 1989, an editor changed this conjecture to 1945–1946 or 1946–1947.*

*In fact, the notes come from two lectures, not one. Though this is not indicated in the typescript under consideration, when Smythies subsequently made a fuller collection of his own lecture notes, this item was listed as two lectures, with the break coming where we have placed it in the text.*[2]

*We will never know why Malcolm changed "1939" to "1945–46", but there are good reasons for thinking the lectures were not given in 1945–46 (or in 1946–47). G. E. M. Anscombe, who was at Cambridge with Wittgenstein from 1942 to 1947, has no recollection of the lectures; nor does Stephen Toulmin, who was there from January, 1946 to Summer, 1947. The lectures had to have occurred when Smythies and Casimir Lewy (who is mentioned as asking questions during the second lecture) were at Cambridge. A "Mr. Malcolm" (presumably Norman Malcolm) and a "Moore" (presumably G. E. Moore, but possibly his son Timothy Moore) are also referred to by Wittgenstein, though that does not prove they were present. In fact, all of this cast of characters were*

1. Wolfe Mays, "Recollections of Wittgenstein," in *Ludwig Wittgenstein: The Man and His Philosophy,* ed. K. T. Fann, New York: Dell, 1967, p. 81.

2. This discovery is due to Brian McGuinness, who was able to consult this fuller version of Smythies' notes.

*present in Cambridge in 1939.*[3] *Thus, 1939 may have been the better conjecture as to the date of the lectures.*

*From the sound of the first few paragraphs, the lectures seem to be part of a larger course of lectures. Anscombe and Toulmin, who attended the lectures in 1945–46, do not recall them, and they are not mentioned in the record of his 1946–47 lectures.*[4] *Students' notes of Wittgenstein's lectures on the foundations of mathematics in Lent and Easter terms of 1939 show him briefly discussing free will in terms roughly similar to the lectures on freedom of the will.*[5] *While the discussion is too brief to* be *the lectures on freedom of the will, it may well be echoing or prefiguring these lectures from another contemporary context. Wittgenstein does not seem to have addressed the Cambridge Moral Sciences Club on the topic of freedom of the will.*[6] *It seems most likely that these were part of Wittgenstein's regular course of lectures for the Michaelmas term of 1939.*[7]

3. See Malcolm's *Ludwig Wittgenstein: a Memoir,* 2nd edition, 1984, p. 30. In fact Malcolm first arrived in Cambridge in the Fall of 1938, which therefore constitutes the earliest possible date for the lectures. However, Malcolm did not attend regular lectures by Wittgenstein until Lent term of 1939, and seems not to have gotten to know Wittgenstein until then. Since Wittgenstein refers to Malcolm three times by name in the second lecture on freedom of the will, it is very unlikely they were given in 1938.

4. See *Wittgenstein's Lectures on Philosophical Psychology: 1946–47,* edited by Peter Geach, Chicago: University of Chicago Press, and Hemel Hempstead: Harvester Wheatsheaf, 1989. This consists of notes by Geach, Shah, and Jackson.

5. See *Wittgenstein's Lectures on the Foundations of Mathematics: Cambridge, 1939,* edited by Cora Diamond, Ithaca, N.Y.: Cornell University Press, and Sussex: Harvester Press, 1976, p. 242. This was compiled from notes taken by Bosanquet, Malcolm, Rhees, and Smythies. A pirated version of Malcolm's notes was separately published in 1954 in San Francisco as "*Math Notes* by [sic] Ludwig Wittgenstein". On p. 57 they contain a similar brief discussion of free will.

6. In the period from 1939 to 1948 Wittgenstein gave five talks to the club. The minutes indicate topics for all of them except 22 February 1945, when "Professor L. Wittgenstein opened a discussion."

7. We have found no other record of that term's lectures to compare with these. But see Wittgenstein's disturbing comment to von Wright in a letter of September 13, 1939 (reprinted in Chapter 15) concerning that term's lectures. And compare with that Wittgenstein's remarks about one's failing to be a hero (perhaps in the face of the Nazis?) in the second lecture, below.

# Lectures on Freedom of the Will

*By* LUDWIG WITTGENSTEIN
(Notes by YORICK SMYTHIES)

## I

Could one say that the decision of a person was not free because it was determined by natural laws?—There seemed to be a point in saying that if it is determined by natural laws, if the history of people can be determined, if we know their anatomy etc., then a decision can't be said to be free.

It is on the face of it extremely curious to them that natural laws were after all general descriptions of what has happened, what is going to happen should compel things to happen as they do.

We said you could explain the way people looked at natural laws by saying they regarded them as if they were rails, along which things had to move. The expression of a natural law was in some way such a rail.

I said: 'One can't in a general way say that rails determine the track of something along it. Rails don't generally change their shape when something travels along them. If so, it would be impossible to prophesy where the train is going to get to'.

Looking at the natural law does the same if the natural law holds. If it doesn't hold, all we could do is compare it with a rail which had changed its shape, or say that we had not known the exact shape of the rail.

Therefore to say that the natural law in some way compels the things to go as they do is in some way an absurdity.

Suppose I said: 'A certain natural law compels them to move as they do move, under the influence of gravity'. Is *this* all I should say? Or should I say *what* natural law compels them? If I said it is the law of gravity, then I might be wrong. Then someone else may say: 'All right Wittgenstein, it's not the Newtonian Law of Gravitation, it's another law "q"'. 'Give it me'.

⟦86⟧ Suppose it doesn't hold, could he say: 'We don't know the law. Some law holds.'?

If I say the law of gravitation holds, this means nothing less than that the body moves according to the law of gravitation. 'Suppose it isn't this, it is some other law. *Some* law of nature forces the thing to go as it does.' Does this say anything else than that it goes as it goes?

Suppose you see that the law of gravitation holds as far as you can see, then you see a [deviation]. I would say: 'So the Newtonian law of gravitation doesn't exactly hit the thing. A slight amendment of the law will hit it.'

If you say it is not the Newtonian law, it is some other law, you mean it is some law pretty near to that. And that of course is making a statement.

Of course, it may be you come across a case which doesn't follow the Newtonian law at all. Then what you said doesn't mean anything. It means some *other* description will be true if the other proves false. 'It is some other law.' What is opposed to this? No law at all? It is when we would say there is no law at all.

Suppose I said: 'Our decisions are determined by the circumstances of our education and our whole anatomy. We don't know in what way they are determined. We can't predict except in very rare circumstances and then very roughly. All the same it is reasonable to think they follow natural laws and are determined.' 'They follow natural laws' would only mean that one day we may, though it is most misleading and out of the question in fact, forecast a man's actions. But thinking this is no reason for our saying that if the decisions follow natural laws—that if we know the laws which they follow—they are therefore in some way *compelled*. What on earth would it mean that the natural law compels a thing to go as it goes. The natural law is correct, and that's all. Why should people think of natural laws at all as compelling events? If what I say is correct people would seem to have made a blunder.

First of all, the idea of compulsion already lies in the word 'law'. The word 'law' suggests more than an observed regularity which we take it will go on.

The usage of the word natural law connects, one might say, to a certain kind of fatalism. What will happen is laid down somewhere . . . if we got hold of the book in which the natural laws were really laid down.

⟦87⟧ The rules were laid down by a Deity—written in a book. Rules in physics are a guess: 'I suppose that is the law'.

There is the convention that the laws of nature must be found simple. You might say this is a very queer idea indeed. Where did people get it? Somewhere the rules are laid down. This (book) would really contain an authoritative description of those rails on which all these events run. What would encourage one to use this metaphor? To think about natural events in this way? . . .

Had the case always been that of the apple tree with the leaves dancing about, don't you think we would have had a different idea?—As things are now, you might say: if only we knew the velocity of the wind, the elasticity of the leaves etc. then we could forecast the movements of the leaves. But we would never dream of saying this if we hadn't already been successful, and colossally so.

You know that all science started afresh at the time of Galileo, with the laws of gravitation and the observation of the planets—with the discovery of the regularities which were the most obvious. The encouragement for all science was the observation of regularities when they were obvious. For instance, in shooting: there you see real regularity. This is what Galileo really started with, with ballistics.

We would never have said 'If we only knew the laws, then . . .' if we hadn't got science; and science could only start with obvious regularities, going on and on to less obvious regularities.

The idea of laws written down already, which we only guess at. What encourages one to make such a metaphor is that we have actually natural laws. There is a huge realm where we have not found natural laws. But there is a big realm, gradually increasing, where we have found natural laws. The simile only represents a certain way of looking at things, a certain way of acting, looking for regularities etc. If the exceptions were the rule . . .

There is no reason why, even if there was regularity in human decisions, I should not be free. There is nothing about regularity which makes anything free or not free. The notion of compulsion is there if you think of the regularity as compelled; as produced by rails. If, besides the notion of regularity, you bring in the notion of: 'It must move like this because the rails are laid like this.'

When we bring in the notion of compulsion this already shows one peculiar way of looking at events, in the sense that fatalism is a peculiar way of looking at things.

⟦88⟧ 'The thief who steals a banana moves as inevitably as a stone falling'. The stone moves this way, always has, and we are absolutely certain it will in the future. Is there anything else? . . . We might say: 'This bullet inevitably goes that way, as inevitably as if it moves on rails.' It goes this way—what do you mean, 'inevitably'?

How does this apply to the thief?—The whole point of the 'inevitability', I thought, lay in the regularity of the observations. And the point with the thief is that there is no such regularity.

You might ask: what are the points of similarity?

(1) In both cases things move.

(2) In the case of the thief, also, a *certain* regularity has been observed.

You might ask: 'Why don't we regard it in the light of indeterminism? Why do we still stick to determinism'?

We might look at it from the point of view of the bronchial hair, or from the point of view of the falling stone.

If we say 'There are also natural laws in the case of the thief', we have no clear idea at all. What is the point of saying this?

There is the point of view of the biologist and the psychologist, who more and more insist that they have made more and more progress; that it is only a question of time; only a question of degree.

Suppose I said: 'The difference (in greatness) between myself and Kant is only one of degree'? Would I say the difference between black and white is only one of degree?

'We shall find these regularities out too'. Who will? In 1,000 or in 10,000 years?—Is there really any reason to say they will find it out?

You might say (in the case of the thief): 'There is a mechanism here, but a very much more complicated one'.

In the case of electrons one simply gives up. 'No. There are no laws here'.

We have found out lots of things about the human body we didn't know before, and every day find out more. What things?

Who would insist on there being a similarity between the thief and the stone?

(1) Scientists. 'Go on . . .' ⟦89⟧

(2) Not to punish man. Stones can't be punished. No more can a murderer who lifted a heavy instrument. It is a question of holding him responsible or not holding him responsible.

(3) 'He was brought up in this way, [not] this way. It is all as inevitable as machinery.'

After feeling scandalised by thieves I get hungry, and steal. I might say: 'I am a blasted rascal too. I'm no better than them.'

This particular formula 'Inevitable as a stone' is nothing else than comparing his action with a stone.

The readiness is also a sign that you don't want to make him responsible, or be harsh in your judgement. Or it may mean nothing at all.

Imagine that we had a smooth plane with a motor car on it. We put no-one inside. Steering wheel and throttle might be fixed, so it might go in a straight line. We could imagine that the steering wheel and throttle were wobbly so that the motor car described a queer path. Or we could imagine that the steering and throttle moved not because anyone moved them or because the ground was uneven, but for some reason we didn't know.

It is clear that movements of the steering wheel and throttle will determine the movements of the car. I might say: Movement of the car is determined by movement of the motor and machinery. Movement of the front wheels is determined by the movement of the steering wheel. But the steering wheel moves about without being determined by anything.

Couldn't you compare this with what you imagine movements of human beings to be like? There is, you might say, a free element in the motor car. The steering wheel somehow does what it likes. What would make us say that the steering wheel moves freely?

(1) If we couldn't find any cause.

(2) If we couldn't find any law.

Are we compelled to say that the steering wheel is free? No. You might go on looking for some law. On the other hand, you might give up entirely and say the steering wheel is free.

One day you discover a regularity in its movements. Have you got to give up? You might say: 'It is free, but now it chooses to go regularly'. You might choose to look at it in this way or you might not do so.

You compare the case with that of a clock—mechanically determined.

⟦90⟧ I can't see why they should not have held that a human being is responsible, and yet held that his decisions are [. . .] determined—meaning that people may find natural laws (but nothing else).

It seems as if, if you are very strongly impressed by the responsibility which a human being has for his actions, you are inclined to say that these actions and choices can't follow natural laws. Conversely, if you are very strongly inclined to say that they do follow natural laws, then you are inclined to say I can't be made responsible for my choice. That you are inclined in this way, I should say, is a fact of psychology. [. . .]

# II

You sometimes see in a wind a piece of paper blowing about anyhow. Suppose the piece of paper could make the decision: 'Now I want to go this way.' I say: 'Queer, this paper always decides where it is to go, and all the time it is the wind that blows it. I know it is the wind that blows it.'

That same force which moves it also in a different way moves its decisions.

In this sense, there is a certain outlook: 'We are all the time being determined. We think we decide, but all the time we are being shoved about, our decisions too. This means that we are misled into thinking that we do what we want.'

Normally, unless we philosophise, we don't talk this way. We talk of making decisions. Is there a case in which we would actually say that a man thought he decided, but actually didn't decide?

In a prison you are normally locked in, said not to be free. I am in this room, free to go wherever I please. Suppose in the room below, there is a man, and he has certain people with him, and he says: 'Look, I can make Wittgenstein go exactly where I want.' He has a mechanism, and he regulates it with a crank, and you see (with a mirror) that I walk exactly as the man wants me to. Then someone comes up to me and says 'Were you dragged about? Were you free?' I say: 'Of course, I was free.'

Actually, there are cases which come pretty near to this.

Man who could make someone choose the card he wanted him to choose. This is of course a primitive case. Everyone would say he chose freely, and everyone would say he made him choose what he wanted him to choose.

People would say that the man in the room above thought he was free, and actually did any damn thing people below wanted him to do.

Suppose one said: 'Wittgenstein moved about freely, only did what they ⟦91⟧ wanted him to do.' Why not say, 'Wittgenstein moved about freely, only did what Professor Smith wanted him to do.'?

You can describe a case in which you would definitely say: He thinks he is free, but we are really regulating all his movements. And on the other hand this is really a rare case.

They could not only move my legs but also my arms, and make me kill someone. What would they say in a Law Court? Would they say I was responsible or not? Would the people downstairs be punished or would I; or both? The Law Court gives us some idea of what we call 'free', 'responsible'.

I should say they would say I was not responsible.

You probably imagine that they make me do rather queer things. Suppose I had had violent quarrels with a particular gentleman every day. Every reasonable person was expecting me to quarrel anyhow. I, who acted according to what they did, did only what everyone would have expected me to do. This is different from the case where I would have done something alien to my ordinary character. (If, for instance, the people downstairs moved their apparatus so as to make my actions [in]compatible with the actions I did every day.)[1]

We are comparing the case of a human being with those special cases where we *would* say that a man was decided: where we would say that he thought he was deciding freely, but was actually compelled. Why should anyone be inclined to compare ordinary cases with such a very special case?

When sometimes I have looked frantically for a key, I have thought: 'If an omniscient is looking at me, he must be making fun at me. What a joke for the Deity, seeing me look when he knows all the time.' Suppose I asked, Is there any good reason for looking at it in this way?

I want to impress on you that given a certain attitude, you may be, for reasons unknown, compelled to look at it in a certain way. A certain image can force itself upon you. Imagine, for instance, that you are not free; or that you are compelled.

*Must* you look at looking for something in this way? No. But it is one of the most important facts of human life that such impressions sometimes force themselves on you.

In general, this impression is connected with particular ways of ⟦92⟧ acting etc., but it need not be. For instance, Fatalism, or the idea that whatever may happen is somehow put down somewhere. Suppose someone could show you that what is going to happen is already written down. There is an escape by saying: When the time comes, whatever is written down may be interpreted in a different way.

'In three years Lewy may be a D.Sc.' Interpretation of '3' may be '6'. Suppose we interpret the book as a cipher with a key. Suppose I say: It is the same book; but the cipher has been changed.

1. There was an indication in the manuscript that this sentence should be inserted at this point. (eds.)

The idea that it is written down may be the expression of my lack of fear. But it isn't necessary that the picture of its being written down should be connected with courage.

Would it be unreasonable to think that the actions of a human being follow natural laws, but never the less hold him responsible for what he does?

Suppose you say: 'I don't hold a man responsible for lifting his hand and killing a man if his hand was guided this way.'

Suppose you say: 'If we really assume that his actions follow natural laws, let us assume that we knew these laws; knew the whole working of his cells acting on one another and were therefore able to calculate what he was going to do'. This should determine us into saying 'Now we see after all that he isn't responsible for his actions. Ought we to punish him? etc.'

Cf. the example of the kidney advertisement. 'There are 15 miles of kidney to clean' compares cleaning the kidneys with doing something extremely difficult—which it may not be at all.

I wanted to say that if really someone could perform this calculation (of what he was going to do), I don't see why we shouldn't still hold him responsible.

'To understand all is to excuse all'. 'If you understood the working of his mind and understood all the circumstances as well as you understand a piece of machinery you wouldn't hold him responsible for his actions.' I would say: 'how do you know?' It doesn't follow any more than that kidneys are difficult to clean.

I am not clear about calling the case of the falling stone analogous to that of the thief.

Suppose I know all and more than physicists and biologists know—why should I say that this makes him more analogous to machinery—except in so far as I mean that I can forecast better?

I don't know why I won't be led to an indeterminist view. 'So, ⟦93⟧ don't attempt to forecast movements of all the cells, but only the average movements'.

All these arguments might look as if I wanted to argue for the freedom of the will or against it. But I don't want to.

Suppose I had shown someone how it is impossible to resist certain temptations—showing how things worked—and how according to natural law he could do nothing but steal. Suppose someone said: 'But his choice was free. He could also have chosen to do the opposite. His guilt lies in the very fact that he chose in the way which seems so natural.'

What is the criterion for it being true to say that I could have done something else or have chosen otherwise?

In general, one doesn't wish to say: he ought not to be punished because he couldn't have chosen differently.

Unless you distinguish cases in which you say 'He could have chosen otherwise' and cases in which you say 'He couldn't have chosen otherwise'.[2] You could, for instance, say that if he was drunk he couldn't have chosen otherwise: 'Alcohol increases the temptation to do certain things colossally'. You might say: 'The man is not forced to do this. He chooses to do it. But I can't hold him responsible; the temptation under these circumstances is overwhelming'.

Certain circumstances will make it easy for me to be patient, other circumstances will make it very difficult. If I have a bad headache and there is a very tiresome person it may be very difficult.

One person may say 'Nevertheless you can choose the one or the other. Therefore you are responsible'. Another may say 'If you are drugged, that is too much'.

You can distinguish cases in which you say 'The man is free' and 'The man is not free', 'The man is responsible' and 'The man is not responsible'.

In this case, an argument is all right if it converts you.

There are cases in which you say 'Look how he has been brought up. He is not strong in character etc. What would you [do]?' Suppose I then think of myself 'What would I have done under his circumstances? Of course, exactly the same thing'. But I could also ⟦94⟧ have said 'Yes, he is a rascal and so am I. I am to blame and so is he'.

'He hasn't given himself weakness and strength' etc. This is generally, though not always, the beginning of a plea of not guilty. It is the way in which we look at a case when we don't want to judge.

St. Paul says that God has made you a vessel of wrath or a vessel of grace, and yet that you are responsible.[3]

I was going to say: 'It is clear that if you think the Deity knows what is going to happen then there is no absurdity in supposing that a human being might discover wholly or partly the laws of a human being.'

2. An incomplete sentence which starts a new paragraph in the manuscript; it is perhaps qualifying the sentence that precedes it.

3. Cf. Romans 9:21–23. (eds.)

Suppose you said: 'Whether the will is free or not, only experience can teach us'. Another thing that has been said 'If we look into ourselves, we experience there or see there a freewill'. How does one look into oneself and experience a freewill in oneself?

(1) If I am quite cool, I am inclined to walk about in my room and move my head in various ways, and say 'Yes. I can do this. I can do that' etc. I walk about, as it were, to prove to myself that I can walk as I like. Although it is obvious, no-one is compelling me.

One reminds oneself of cases where there is a free choice as apart from cases where there isn't. In one of the many ordinary senses of 'free choice'. This is a trivial case and in a way a stupid case I have described.

(2) Suppose I were about to do something of great consequence to myself and to someone else. I may get a very strong sense of what I may call freedom of will. I may say: 'I can't say that I am forced to do this or not to [do] it. I choose freely to do it if I do do it.' And I could also imagine saying to myself 'I am not free. What can I do? I haven't chosen these circumstances. Why should I do this? No-one would. I am not a hero.' In this case, what actually am I saying to myself? Am I saying something about scientific law, or about what will probably be found when they discover more about the human mind?

*Lewy.* Is the feeling of being free a sufficient ground for saying you are free?

*Witt.* I don't know what feeling you are talking about. Instead of these words 'He had the feeling' I might just as well say 'He had the thoughts'. ⟦95⟧

*Lewy.* Suppose I ask: what are the grounds for his conviction of being free?

*Witt.* I might say: There are no grounds. And as for feelings, you can choose whatever you consider most interesting.

I said that it was puzzling what he meant by it. In fact, if a particular kind of physicist should have the particular kind of thought I described, it may well associate for him with other thoughts he has had about science. His ideas on science may serve, in this case, as a prop, but they may not.

If you said: 'What is the meaning?', how should we set about to describe the meaning of a sentence at all? Do you mean by 'the circumstances under which it is said', the contemporary circumstances, or the circumstances contemporary and before, or the circumstances contemporary, before and after?

Suppose a man makes a resolution and says 'I shall from now on be more charitable', and then throws the next person he is talking to out of the room—does his action affect what he meant?

How would you characterise the meaning of 'I am damned if I shall do such and such'?

Cf. 'God be willing'.[4] Sometimes it means nothing at all. But the Epistle obviously doesn't mean it in this sense.

When he says the words he does say he seems to take the responsibility on himself. You might associate saying the one thing on the whole with different attitudes to saying the other thing. You might say that the one man will probably blame himself more than the other.

The two may disagree greatly, little, or hardly at all. It depends.

Suppose you heard them saying what they were saying, then you might say they disagree in feeling. It would depend on the way in which it was said.

'I am wholly responsible for what I am doing' I hear someone saying. But for all I know this may be a mere phrase he had heard when he was a child.

Cf. If when I am marching against the enemy I say 'We have got to fight' in a stirring tone, and then immediately run away.

If you want to characterise the meaning of these words ('I am responsible' etc.), you've got to say, for one thing, whether the words are the result of a struggle. Isn't this part of saying what the meaning of these words is?

Suppose I said some such thing as 'I am only like a machine'. ⟦96⟧ You might ask: What do these words mean? How, 'like a machine'? I'd say 'Well, he is comparing himself to a falling stone'. In 'What do they mean?' I might include 'What is the point of his words?'

He might be brooding about something he had done and be feeling very uncomfortable, and at a certain moment, to dispel his discomfort say 'My God, I am like a falling stone'. I'd say 'I see exactly what he means. This is a process of describing what he means in this case'.

Suppose someone who had been under a pressure one day said 'Now I am free to do what I want', is he giving himself the information that he is free?

If someone who was making a grave decision said 'I shall do what I choose myself', I'd say: if you want to give his meaning you'll have to

4. Cf. Romans 15:32, I Corinthians 4:19 and 16:7, Hebrews 6:3, and James 4:13–15. (eds.)

give thoughts akin to this, thoughts preceding his utterance, and the circumstances under which it is said.

Suppose I said: he is making a comparison of his situation with one thing rather than with another. He says 'I am not a hero' as he might say 'This is a cake. How could it be anything else?' Where is this comparison taken from? What sort of analogy is he making? How does he know he is not a hero? Because he has always acted in this way? In the case of the hero, there is nothing analogous to the case of the cake. Why are you making a point of this analogy at all?

One thing is: not to be made responsible.

Another might be: a particular attitude of seeing what is tragic in a human being. You may be driving at this if you say 'What do you want? That is how he is made.'

Among other things, saying this rules out certain expectations. I might expect Mr. Lewy to act in different cases in different ways. Then someone says 'What do you want? He just is this way.'

This is no analogy. He is *what* way? The reason it is said is in general in order to say: Rule out any hope at all; this is out of the question.

If you say 'The character does not change', what is the object of saying this? What is it which belongs to the 'character'? It is never said.

In certain cases, it is perfectly all right to say it. You assume certain things which won't change and call them the character.

'I can assure you that what [you] now find in Smith you will find two years hence'. You might say: 'When something arises in two ⟦97⟧ years' time, his character not having changed, he acts differently.' Cf. 'The character of a face does not change'.

Can you forecast what things will not change?

My point was that these statements were not scientific statements, not corrected by experience.

These statements are not used as scientific statements at all, and no discovery in science would influence such a statement. This is not quite true. What I mean is: we couldn't say now 'If they discover so and so, then I'll say I am free'. This is not to say that scientific discoveries have no influence on statements of this sort.

Scientific discoveries partly spring from the direction of attention of lots of people, and partly influence the direction of attention.

Cf. Evolution.

Two mistakes are made in such a case (of a new discovery): At the moment a new explanation is produced which is in at least some cases successful, it has happened again and again that many people become ever so optimistic, saying 'It is only a question of time . . .' There exist two camps, optimists and pessimists. The pessimists don't see the point of the hypothesis at all. The optimists see it clearly, but . . .

Cf. Evolution of mathematics. Not a solution of mathematical puzzlement.

If your attention is drawn for the first time to the fact that economic states of affairs have enormous and obvious consequences, whereas such things as general states of mind of people do not: or that it is much more easy to prophesy from economic states of affairs than from the state of mind of a nation; it is very natural to think that *all* explanations can and should be given like economic explanations of historic states of affairs. 'A wave of religious enthusiasm swept over Europe', whereas actually this is a mere metaphor. 'The Crusades had their origin in the state of soul of chivalry'. And you may for instance think of what is happening now-a-days.

The papers now write something entirely different every 6 months. Suppose someone tried to explain events by saying 'Why, just read the Times etc. and see the spirit of the nation'. Someone might say: 'this is only the foam and the froth on top of what is important'.

You may be misled entirely about the facts from which it is safe ⟦98⟧ to make a forecast. Suppose you are a meteorologist, 'If you want to make a forecast don't look at the clouds *here*, but do have a station in Greenland'. You can't make a forecast on this (the papers). It is froth. You might feel: 'One thing I know: if people are hungry they want to eat. Cold nearly always produces a reaction of wanting to get warm etc.' You might for instance now say: 'What the newspapers now say is nothing at all. It is the economic condition of the people which is important.' Once you find this out, or hear it from someone, the natural reaction is to think 'Now it's all done'. It is as if you have explained everything, when all you have done is get hold of an explanation which may not have explained anything at all. The discovery dazzles you.

A discovery might influence what you say on the freedom of the will. If only by directing your attention in a particular way.

I think one can say that propositions of which one is inclined to say that they express feeling are generally said with feeling.

'Constant and inevitable experience teaches me that I have freedom of choice'—Bishop Barnes.[5]

He could have said: 'that I have choice'.

If he had said this we'd agree. We say that human beings choose things; we often say they choose to do one thing or another thing.

He might have said: 'Constant experience teaches me that I can choose what I like'.

No-one would say: 'Now choose to choose so and so'. 'I choose to choose to go for a walk'—I take it this would come to exactly the same thing as to say 'I choose to go for a walk'.

He doesn't only say that he can choose, but that the fact he can choose contradicts the fact his actions can be predicted.

One might either include his choices among his actions or not. I don't see why one shouldn't reckon his choices as part of his actions.

'The statement that he can choose contradicts the statement that his actions can be predicted.'—It is in one way rubbish to say 'If my actions can be predicted I can't choose'.

I now make a prediction as to what Mr. Malcolm will choose.

The idea that you can connect predicting what a man will choose with materialism is rubbish. Prediction doesn't mean you will predict from *material* data.

Prediction is incompatible with choice in the case where you yourself predict what you will choose, or I predict and then tell ⟦99⟧ you. You can imagine that today I predict what I will choose tomorrow, and that I will actually choose this. There is the possibility that when choosing I will remember what I predicted and the possibility that I will not remember. People would be inclined to say that the situation in which a difficulty lies is that in which when choosing I remember the fact that I predicted my choice.

The difficulty I feel comes to something like this: Can there be both certainty and uncertainty? One might say: Aren't you in your description presupposing two contradictory states of mind in this person at the same time, that of not knowing and that of knowing?

As a matter of fact, it is possible we know the whole time what we are going to choose and that nevertheless a process of choice is going on.

5. Presumably E. W. Barnes (1874–1953), Bishop of Birmingham 1924–1953, Fellow and tutor at Trinity College, Cambridge, and, in 1912, tutor in Trinity of Wittgenstein's friend David Pinsent. (eds.)

Suppose someone said: 'Not only can I predict and tell Mr. Malcolm what he is going to choose tomorrow but I can also predict the whole process of choosing'.

(a) I predict what I am going to do and do not remember my prediction when I choose.
(b) I predict what I am going to do and remember my prediction when I choose.
(c) Someone predicts my exact process of choosing and I read it a few minutes before I choose.
(d) Someone predicts my exact process of choosing and writes it down, and I read what he has written while I am going through the process of choosing.

Cf. Reading a novel and applying it to a situation in your own life.

You thought that the situation I had brought about was no longer a situation of deliberating. You might say: 'Wittgenstein, you haven't actually described any state of affairs at all'. When we talk of choosing and someone says this is not compatible with calculating our choice, we might say: 'Then our choice simply depends on our ignorance. If we weren't as ignorant as we are we should have no choice.' You might say: 'Our apprehension of freewill is only due to our ignorance of the laws of nature.' It looks as if, if we knew these laws, we should know we have no freewill. On the other hand we could say: 'if we knew these laws then our will wouldn't be free', in the sense in which one might say: 'If I had prophesied to Mr. Malcolm what he was going to choose ⟦100⟧ tomorrow and he had read my prophecy, then he would not deliberate.'

The knowledge of these laws would simply change the business. There is truth in that. One might say: being able to calculate things we can't calculate now would indeed change the whole situation; (and if I could calculate things I still might be said to calculate the facts of choice).

If Moore and I play chess or roulette and someone else could predict what was going to happen (telling us), we would just give up playing roulette. Suppose someone said: 'This is no game of chance at all. What makes us think it is a game of chance is only our ignorance', I could contradict this and say: 'No. It is a game of chance now that we are ignorant; if in the future we were no longer ignorant it would no longer be a game of chance.'

We can't even say that if prediction was possible Moore and I would not play the game. You might say: the point of the game would then be different. And the point of choosing would be changed if we had a prediction of it.

I would say: You can call it a different game or not call it a different game.

# 14

*This is a transcription of a previously unpublished manuscript of Wittgenstein's, composed almost entirely in English, MS 166 in von Wright's catalogue. While no dates are recorded in the body of the text, von Wright originally assigned it a date of "Probably 1935–6." Although he did not state his reasons, a number of considerations lend support to this date. First, the ideas set out here seem to be very much of a piece with the "Notes for Lectures on 'Sense Data' and 'Private Experience'" which were mostly written during the 1935–36 academic year. As the exposition in this piece is more clear-cut and didactic than most of the "Notes for Lectures," it seems unlikely that it was written before the "Notes." Second, Wittgenstein usually wrote in German during the 1930s and 1940s, except for the 1934–35 and 1935–36 academic years, when he made a sustained effort to write in English. The first drafts of many of the remarks on private language in the* Philosophical Investigations, *written down in German during 1937–38 (MSS 119–121) show no sign of being directly based on this manuscript or the "Notes for Lectures."*

*On the other hand, the manuscript's title, which Wittgenstein wrote at the very top of the first page, suggests that it was written for the British Academy's "Philosophical Lecture," an annual public lecture on a philosophical topic. While Wittgenstein never gave a lecture in the series, the minutes of the committee which chooses the Philosophical Lecturer record, under the date April 16th 1941, that "the section recommended that Professor Wittgenstein be invited to deliver the lecture for 1942. . . ." Later the minute book records "Professor Wittgenstein accepted, but was obliged to withdraw by pressure of other work."*[1] *Of course, it is possible that the notes were written earlier and the title added in 1941. But the fact that Wittgenstein went to unusual lengths to explain his methods in this piece and assumed that his audience would take nothing for granted, without the asides in German and the extensive digressions characteristic of the "Notes for Lectures," strongly suggests that it was written for a general audience, rather than for his regular classes. In any case, it is clear that the manuscript must have been written by 1942, at the very latest, and it seems very likely that it was composed with the Philosophical Lecture in mind.*

1. These discoveries are due to the work of James Klagge and especially the research of Dr. Anthony Kenny, President of the British Academy.

*Very few editorial alterations have been made; they have mainly been a matter of correcting spelling and grammar and completing abbreviated words. Material that was crossed out has been omitted, but where Wittgenstein wrote in an alternative above the original text and crossed out neither, both are shown, with the later alternative enclosed in single slashes: "/". Occasionally, Wittgenstein used double slashes to mark alternatives within the body of the text: "//". Material that Wittgenstein later inserted has simply been included in the main text without comment.*[2]

DAVID G. STERN

2. The transcription was originally prepared in 1984 from a microfilm of the Wittgenstein papers at the University of California, Berkeley, and revised in 1988 after I had consulted Professor von Wright's photocopy of the manuscript. I would like to acknowledge the support of a Killam postdoctoral fellowship at the University of Alberta, which made it possible for me to visit Helsinki, and to thank Professor von Wright for his assistance and encouragement.

# Notes for the 'Philosophical Lecture'

Privacy of experiences. This privacy a superpr[ivacy]. *Something like* privacy. What seems to be the essential characteristic of pr[ivacy]? Nobody but I can see it, feel it, hear it; nobody except myself knows what it's like. Nobody except I can get at it. Language game with the colour-chart. Let us imagine each man has a private chart (perhaps *besides* having a public one.) Imagine he points to green on his pr[ivate] ch[art] when "red" is said—why should we say he means by "red" the colour we mean by "green"? Privacy of feelings can mean: nobody can know them unless I show them, or: I can't really show them. Or: if I don't want to, I needn't give any sign of my feeling but even if I want to I can only show a sign and not the feeling.

---

Meaning consisting of the word referring to an object.

How a kind of object is hypostatized for a technique of use. This word refers to this → object that word to that → object. Explanation of the object referred to not by pointing but by explaining a technique. Colour-words, shape-words, etc.

Under what circumstances pointing can explain i.e. convey the use of a word. Not to a baby. *It* learns by being drilled. There is therefore no occult act of *naming* an object that in itself can give a word a meaning.

Words for colour and shape. Words for colour on one side of a line. What does "now" refer to or "this" or "I"? The private object. The naming of the private object. The private language. The game someone plays with himself. When do we call it a *game*? If it resembles a public game. The diary of Robinson Cr[usoe].

So we mustn't think that we understand the working of a word in lang[uage] if we say it is a name which we give to some sort of pr[ivate] experience which we have. The idea is here: we *have* something it is as it were before the mind's eye (or some other sense) and we give it a name. What could be simpler? One might say /could put it roughly this way/: All ostensive definition explains the use of a word only when it makes one last determination, removes one last indeterminacy.

The relation between name and object. Lang[uage] game of builders. What is the relation between names and actions names and shapes? The relation of ostensibly defining. That's to say, in order to establish a name relation we have to establish a technique of use. And we are misled if we think that it is a peculiar process of christening an object which makes a word the word for an object. This is a kind of superstition. So it's no use saying that we have a private object before the mind and give it a name. There is a name only where there is a technique of using it and that technique can be private; but this only means that nobody but I know about it, in the sense in which I can have a private sewing machine. But in order to be a private sewing machine, it must be an object which deserves the name "sewing machine," not in virtue of its privacy but in virtue of its similarity to sewing machines, private or otherwise.

Now why do we say: My feelings are my private property? Because only I am directly aware of my pain. But what does that mean. I suppose to be aware of pain means to feel it, and isn't it "my" pain because I feel it? So what does it mean to say only I feel my pain? We have, so far, not given any sense to the phrase "I feel his pain" (except in the sense I feel the same kind of pain, or perhaps I vividly imagine his pain) and therefore no use to the phrase "I feel my pain" either. (I don't say that we couldn't arrange for a sense for these phrases.) We could of course use the prop[osition] "A person is directly aware of his pain only and indirectly aware of the other man's" as a grammatical rule /determination[1]/ to the effect that if I say of N "N, directly aware of pain," this means "N has pain," whereas "N is indir[ectly] aware of pain" is to mean: "N is aware of the fact that someone else has pain." (And this I'm inclined to call the healthy use of these phrases.)

Here too however the expressions "directly aware" and "indir[ectly] aware" are *extremely* misleading. What gives us the idea that the person who feels pain is aware of an object, as it were, sees it, whereas we are only told that it's there but can't see it? It is the peculiar function of the verbs like feeling, seeing etc. But before explaining what I mean I must make a preliminary remark. For I know that some of you will think this is the worst kind of verbalism. So I must make a general remark about grammar and reality. Roughly

1. Bestimmung.

speaking, the relation of the grammar of expressions to the facts which they are used to describe is that between the description of methods and units of measurement and the measures of objects measured by those methods and units. Now I could describe the shape and size of this room by giving its length, breadth and height in feet and just as well by giving them in meters. I could also give them in microns. In a way, therefore, you might say that the choice of the units is arbitrary. But in a most important sense it is not. It has a most important reason lying both in the size and in the irregularity of shape and in the use we make of a room that we don't measure its dimensions in [microns][2] or even in m[illi]m[eters]. That is to say, not only the prop[osition] which tells us the result of measurement but also the description of the method and unit of measurement tells us something about the world in which this measurement takes place. And in this very way the technique of use of a word gives us an idea of *very* general truths about the world in which it is used, of truths in fact which are so general that they don't strike people, I'm sorry to say, and philosophers, too. And so I will turn to some points in /features of/ the technique of use of expressions like "feeling pain." The first point is this: that this verbal expression is, in the first person, used to replace an *expression* of pain. So that if some people say that "having pain" in the end refers to pain behaviour we can answer them that "I have pain" does not refer to pain behaviour but *is* a pain behaviour. It corresponds to a cry of pain, not to the statement "I am crying." "But surely you distinguish between my pain behaviour when I just behave that way and have no pain and my pain behaviour in the opposite case." If you mean, do I admit the fact that people sometimes behave as though they have pain whereas they haven't, I do. But I wish to say that you can't explain that difference by saying that if he has pain there is behind his expression /behaviour/ a certain something present which he expresses by his behaviour. If instead of "a certain something" or some such phrase you're bold enough to say "pain," then the statement becomes tautologous. If you want to avoid the mention of pain because this already presupposes that we know what is behind his expression then it doesn't help you to say "a certain feeling" or "a certain something" for how do you know that you are allowed to call it a feeling or even a something? For the word "something" has a public meaning if it means anything at all.

2. Here Wittgenstein uses the Greek letter mu, $\mu$, the standard scientific abbreviation for a micron (a millionth of a meter).

And then if you risk saying that he *has something* you might as well say all you know /mean/ and say that he has pain. The point is that an essentially private object can't *justify* the use of a word, neither for the others *nor* for him. The private object does not only not enter the public game but it can't enter a private *game* either. You can see this, e.g., if you replace the one private object which is to justify his use of a pain expression by a series of different objects which he *has* at different times when he says he has pain. "But surely the use of the word pain is based on the fact that he 'recognises' his private object as always being the same on those occasions!" What's he mean in this case by being the "same," or by "recognising"? Neither he nor we have ever learnt to apply these words to his private object. Supposing instead of "he recognises the object" we said more cautiously "he believes he recognises"—but then we ought to say that he believes that he believes he recognises and so on ad inf[initum]. In other words: if this object is as private as we want it to be we have no reason to call it one object rather than 100 objects, we have no reason to apply the word object at all, and no more has he.

(This paper if it is in the least as I think it ought to be, should at first sight be very confusing indeed. For in this case it apparently consists of a mixture of trivialities and paradoxes and why I should say them seems pretty unclear.)

For to say that he has a private object means that we shall regard no description which he may give of it as really telling us what it's like. We assume that when he was taught our language the privacy of the object made it impossible to teach him the application of language to this object. "But what if he just had *guessed* the right application?" But which *is* the right application? There is nothing to guess at. "But couldn't he, if only by chance, have stumbled on the application analogous to the public one?" But what are we in this case to call analogous?

If you cheat others, at least don't cheat yourself; and if you don't cheat yourself—why should you cheat the others?[3]

3. This sentence was originally written in a simple letter-substitution code (a = z, b = y, etc.). While the autobiographical coded passages quoted by Brian McGuinness in *Wittgenstein: A Life* (Berkeley and Los Angeles: University of California Press, and London: Duckworth, 1988) and Ray Monk in *Ludwig Wittgenstein: The Duty of Genius* were presumably written in code with the aim of concealing them from a casual reader (see McGuinness, p. 212), in this case it is more likely that the point of the device was to indicate that this passage was not intended as part of his lecture.

In fact the private object is one about which neither he who has it nor he who hasn't got it can say anything to others or to himself.

"But what you say always sounds as though you wished to deny the existence of pain, as opposed to that of pain behaviour." But what could it mean to deny the existence of pain, except to deny that people have ever felt pain; or to deny that it makes sense to say that someone has pain? What I do deny is that we can construe the grammar of "having pain" by hypostatising a private object. Or: The private object functions all right only as long as its grammar is entirely constructed to suit the grammar of the common objects in question. And it becomes an absurdity if its nature is supposed to explain that grammar.

We can express this as follows: There is no *justification* for an utterance of pain in the sense in which there is for my saying that someone else is in pain. There is no essentially private justification for I couldn't know whether anything that is essentially private *is* a *justification.* There is something in front of me which justifies me in saying there is a table in front of me.

---

As introduction:

Word referring to an object. Using a word analogously to certain cases. Equality and the criteria of equality. Imagining making an image and making *use* of the image.

Recognising the object as the same you had before. But if we use the words "recognise" and "same" he must be *justified* in saying that he recognises the object as the same. Can his recognition be infallible? No, for he may be /can go/ wrong in the use of the word "same." // No, for we may say that he goes wrong in the application of the word "same." // He recognises; but suppose he went wrong, would it make any difference? But what is it like to be right in this case?

We can't, e.g., discuss the question, when he is justified to use the *same* utterance twice. If we imagine anything that we should call a justification, some private regularity, it seems to be something which, if we saw it, we should call a regularity. But what would, in our case, mean "seeing his private regularity"? We haven't given it any sense. That is, we have indeed given the expression "to feel what he feels" sense, but with particular criteria for the identity. If we now talk of identity and don't wish to use *these* criteria we are left without any, unless we give fresh ones. And of course I know perfectly well that we are thinking of criteria similar to the ones of physical objects, only we can't apply any such criteria in our case and *that's* what we mean by talking of the privacy of the objects. Privacy here really means the absence of means of comparison. Only we mix up the state of affairs when we are prevented from comparing the objects with that of not having fixed a method of comparison. And in the moment we would fix such a way of comparing we would no longer talk of "sensations."

But suppose I say: "I have the same sensation now as five minutes ago"—what criterion of identity am I using?—What criterion am I using for determining that what I feel is pain, or that what I see is red? None. There are criteria which can convince me that I am using the word "red" or "pain" as they are normally used in English. I can point to something and say: "The colour of this you do call 'mauve,' don't you?" etc.

That's to say: In "I feel what I felt 5 min[utes] ago" I have no justification analogous to the case for calling the sensations identical apart from my justification of my use of the words employed in *other* contexts. And this means: I can't justify my saying this, either to others or to myself. Or rather it's better to say that I can justify saying this in such and such a sense but not in one analogous to. . . . It is as when we compare games and say: "In this ball game there is nothing corresponding to the net in tennis."

Memory can be compared with a storehouse only so far as it fulfills the same purpose. Where it doesn't, we couldn't say whether the things stored up may not constantly change their nature and so couldn't be said to be stored at all.

"But don't we say two sensations are equal when we find them equal and isn't finding them so the justification for saying it?" But how do we recognise "finding two sensations equal"?

He learns to use the word, and then, whenever . . . . , he says ". . . ." What are the circumstances under which he then says ". . . ."? Could we then say: . . .and then whenever he feels pain he says ". . . ."? or: . . . and then, whenever he has a certain feeling he says [". . . ."]? or: . . . and then, whenever he has a something particular he says ". . . ."?

"But if he is truthful, why shouldn't we take his word for it that he sees red?" But we do! That's to say, we believe that he is not telling us a lie. —"But if he is intelligent as well, why shouldn't we believe that what he has before his mind's eye is red." We do,—according to the method of comparison applicable in this case. "Then where do you disagree with us?" —When you talk about something incommunicable, private.

"You seem to deny the existence of something; on the other hand you say you don't deny any existence: why should it *seem* as if you did? You seem to say 'There is *only*. . . .' You deny, it seems, the background of the expression of sensations. Doesn't the expression point to something beyond itself?" —If we see the feeling as a background to the expression then we can always assume that we are wrong in thinking that this background doesn't change; we can assume that our memory at each instant cheats us and that we use the expression bona fide to express something different each time. So that one might say: It doesn't matter *what* is behind the expression so long as it is a bona fide expression of it.

Our answer is: Why do you think that a cry would be the *expression* of the background if there were one? In what sense would the cry *for me* point to such a background? Aren't you assuming a *language game* which in this case is not played? You bring in the idea of expression and background because you look at the game that's actually played through the schema of another game.

"A cry *with* and a cry *without* something."

The grammar of an expression can't be investigated by transforming the expressions, particularly when they all make use of the same picture. You have to remind yourself of the use to get out of the rut in which all these expressions tend to keep you.

The whole point of investigating the "verification," e.g., is to stress the importance of the use as opposed to that of the picture.

In this way we have to *investigate* the use of "cry with . . ." and "cry without . . ." although of course there are plenty of pictures ready taken from other uses of "with" and "without" but the pictures which come most readily in our mind are just the ones which confuse us.

Comparing measuring time with measuring lengths. To get rid of the confusing picture remind yourself exactly *how* we measure time. The difficulty here is that those pictures are terribly insistent, forcing us to see everything in their likeness.

Words with and without sense.

The application of a word (say "with") compares *this* case with other cases. But we're just questioning how far this comparison holds. So we must remind ourselves of facts which these words don't suggest. "But, surely, I know what pain is and that I always have just that when I say 'I have pain.'" Doesn't it strike you as odd that you should know so well what pain is, now, when you haven't got it?! This rather suggests that you don't need to recognise any private object to know the meaning of pain. Nor can you say: To understand the word "pain" it's necessary to recognise pain when it does come. For who is to say whether you do recognise it, unless recognising here means feeling (uttering) recognition, not recognising rightly. In this sense I could be said to recognise Smith as being Jones.

"But you can't *describe* the phenomenon of people feeling pain by describing their pain behaviour. You *do* know there is more to it than that. In your own case you know that all that happens isn't that under certain *external* circumstances you do and say such and such things." —In your own case you know that what's meant by feeling pain is entirely independent of external circumstances, and as to internal ones the only one that matters is *feeling pain.*

How would I justify my pain-behaviour in order to show to someone that I wasn't just acting in this way? I would add more expressive behaviour.

"But when I in my own case distinguish between, say, pretending that I have pain and really having pain, surely I must make this distinction on some grounds!" Oddly enough—no!—I do distinguish but not on any *grounds.*

"But if you say this aren't you saying that all the phenomenon of human pain is a phenomenon of behaviour?"

If we assume a justification behind the expression of feeling and if we then try to describe this justification, it turns out that it isn't a justification after all, that we have to say things about it which take away its character of justification.

It is as though I said: this man is N's guardian and then said things about the way he functions which are incompatible with his being a guardian to N.

"This feeling of mine, however you call it, justifies my behaviour." —This already presupposes that you can use the word "feeling."

Common idea: a word has meaning by referring to something.

There is a connection between a w[ord] and an object. What sort of connection? Is it something like this: The w[ord] reminds us of the obj[ect]? What happens when a thing reminds me of something? Seeing M reminded me of his father. Let's say, roughly, seeing M produces in me thoughts about his father, or images of M's father.

(Remark) The sentence "I imagine so-and-so" is not a *description* of a picture before my mind's eye. Ask yourself: do you recognise him from the picture before your mind's eye? Would you say: "I see a man with white hair etc., I suppose I'm imagining N but perhaps it's only someone who looks very much like him"? There is (however) a use we make of pictures which resembles much more that which we make of the product of our imagination: E.g. we describe the position of objects in a street accident and say while drawing: "This (line) is [the] street, this (square) is the overturned car, this (cross) the policeman at the corner, etc." Here too we are using sentences of the same form as those which would describe what we believe a picture represents, whereas their use is to give a picture an interpretation. —It is useful here to imagine that a man imagines by means of drawing or painting, sketching or even by producing a cartoon film. If you said that in order to draw he must already have a mental picture which he copies, the answer is that the mode of projection used to copy his mental picture is not determined and the latter therefore might be *anything,* so that in fact all that gives us a right to speak about a mental picture is the fact that we are inclined to call a (non-mental) picture a representation of a mental one.

"Is there then no such thing as a mental picture?" The proper answer to a question thus worded would be //is//: "People at times have mental pictures /images/." But this isn't really the sort of answer we wanted. We meant to ask: have we a right, under the circumstances under which it is normally said that a person /man/ has a mental image, to say that he has such an image or picture? Have we a right to say that someone married money? This may mean did he "marry money" or is the expression an appropriate one. Think of the ways in which such a question is decided? —Suppose we ask the question: are people murdered in tragedies or aren't they? One answer is: In *some* tragedies some people are murdered. Another answer: "people aren't *really* murdered on the stage and they only pretend to murder and to die." But the use of the word pretend here is again ambiguous for it may be used in the sense in which Edgar pretends to have led Gloucester to the cliff. //But you may say: Oh no! Some people really die in tragedies, e.g., Juliet at the end of the play, whereas before she pretended to have died. //"Oh no, they don't all pretend; Edgar pretends to lead Gloucester to the edge of the cliff /be a peasant/ he is really Gloucester's son //Gloucester is *really* blind."// We shall say the words "really," "pretend," "die," etc., are used in a peculiar way when we talk of a play and differently in ordinary life. Or: the criteria for a man dying in a play aren't the same as those of his dying in reality. But are we *justified* to say that Lear dies at the end of the play? Why not. And, analogously, that there is no reason for objecting to saying we have /see/ mental pictures does not mean that we [know] the criteria for the existence of a non-mental picture are the same as those for the existence of a mental picture. One may even say that the former and the latter criteria need not even be similar, as one may say that the criteria for the death of a person in the play and outside a play are utterly dissimilar, though there is of course a connection.

Back to the function of words! We could imagine a use of language in which the words were used to bring images before our minds, an image for each word, or some thought concerning the object mentioned. As when we read a list of names of people whom we know and reading, imagine them or think various thoughts about them. And to amplify the idea, I can assume that the person who reads the list actually sketches the people or writes down sentences about them. This is obviously not the way the words in a sentence normally work. For again we might imagine a particular use of sentences in which their purpose is to make the reader draw a certain picture. One is inclined to think that understanding a sentence must consist in something at least *similar* to having a picture of the "fact the sentence refers to" before one's mind. What is true in this is that there is a connection between the capability to produce such a picture and understanding. But the idea that understanding means producing such a picture or something similar, is quite wrong. When we philosophise we are constantly bound to give an account of our technique of the usage of words and this technique we know in the sense that we master it, and we don't know it in the sense that we have the very greatest difficulty in surveying it and describing it. Thus we are inclined to look for an activity when we are to give an account of the meaning of a verb. And if some /an/ activity is closely connected with it we tend to think that the verb stands for this activity. The use of the word "understanding," however, is such that it is very misleading to say it refers to an activity. Lots of activities are signs that we have understood. The technique of use of the verb "understanding" is most similar to the technique of use [of] the verb "to be able to." In particular in such cases as: "to be able to play chess." "Aren't you trying to make the distinction between understanding as a disposition and u[nderstanding] as an action?"[4]

A philos[ophical] problem can be solved only in the right surrounding. We must give the problem a new surrounding, we must compare it to cases we are not used to compare it with.———

If we describe the lang[uage] game of fetching coloured things, it might seem that we only describe it superficially, because the real game is played with impressions, and these we haven't mentioned at all in our description. It seems as if we hadn't really gone to the bottom of it.

We always forget that "impression" is a peculiar grammatical form, and that we could describe phenomena without using just this form.

Talking about impressions already means to look at phenomena in one particular way, i.e., to *think* about them in one particular fashion.

"What does green look like to me? —It looks like this → to me."—

"This is the colour impression which I'm calling 'green.' "
Am I *sure* I'm talking about my private *impression*? And how can I be sure—? Do I *feel* that I'm talking about the impression? What happens? I look at a green patch, I concentrate my attention on such a patch and I say these words. But on what kind of a patch? Not on a green one. On one which seems to deserve the name "green"?
It is not true that I see impressions before me and that they are the primary objects.

In the sense in which I can't explain "what green looks like to me," I can't say that I know what it looks like either.

Swapping experiences.

Having a particular use of the word in mind.

4. Here, the word "No" follows immediately in the text, but it has been crossed out.

The difference between "Now I know the formula" and "Now I can go on."

The difference between saying the formula and saying "Now I know the formula."

The importance of the if-feeling.

The "conditional feeling" not unlike seeing a vowel coloured.[5]

5. The last nine pages of this notebook contain transcriptions, in Russian, of five poems by Pushkin; the titles of the poems are usually translated as "Elegy," "Prophet," "The Upas Tree," "Demons," and "Remembrance." See A. S. Pushkin, *Sobranie sochinenii v 6-ti tomakh* Izdatel'stvo "Pravda" (Moscow, 1969), vol. 1, pp. 330, 257, 293, 328, 285. English translations can be found in *Pushkin: A Laurel Reader,* ed. E.J. Simmons (New York: Dell, 1961) pp. 55, 41, 44, 55, and 47.

James Klagge has suggested that Wittgenstein may have written out these poems as a personal response to the sudden death, on October 11, 1941, of his dear friend Francis Skinner. Skinner had studied Russian with Wittgenstein and had taken a special interest in Pushkin. For more information on their study of Russian, see the account by their Russian teacher, Fania Pascal, in "A Personal Memoir," *Recollections of Wittgenstein,* ed. R. Rhees, esp. pp. 15–21. For more on their interest in Pushkin, see Theodore Redpath, *Ludwig Wittgenstein: A Student's Memoir* (London: Duckworth, 1990) pp. 28–29.

# 15

*As one can discover by reading these letters, Georg Henrik von Wright arrived in Cambridge as a student early in 1939. He attended Wittgenstein's lectures and became a good friend as well. After Wittgenstein resigned as Professor of Philosophy at Cambridge in 1947, he urged von Wright to apply for the position. Von Wright was appointed in 1948 and held the position until his resignation at the end of 1951. Wittgenstein designated von Wright along with Rush Rhees and G.E.M. Anscombe as executors of his literary estate. Since 1961 von Wright has been Research Professor at the Academy of Finland.*

# Letters from Ludwig Wittgenstein to Georg Henrik von Wright

1.

81, East Road
Cambridge
9.3.39

Dear Sir,
I'm sorry I caused you the trouble of writing to me. I shall try to explain why the presence of two new people in my class, the other day, greatly disturbed me.—I am, in my classes, doing my utmost to explain a *very* difficult matter to the students who have been attending my classes this term. I know that it is quite impossible for any one coming in in the middle, or at *the end,* of the term to get any idea of what we really are driving at. In fact he must necessarily get wrong ideas. I hope you will understand this, and if you do you will also understand why being aware of this fact disturbs me a lot when I should be concentrating entirely on my subject. If I could, as many other people can, prepare my lectures in writing and then read them off in front of the class the presence of new people would not disturb

me. But as I'm unable to do this and have to think things out afresh while I'm talking I am very easily disturbed.

In answer to your letter I suggest, therefore, that if you wish to come to my classes you should begin at the beginning of next term; but please don't come to the last few lectures (2 or 3) in this term. I hope you will see my point and not think me unfriendly in suggesting this.

Yours sincerely
L. WITTGENSTEIN

P.S. If you like, come round to my rooms (at the above address) at 4.30 p.m. tomorrow. It may be easier for me to explain the matter to you when I see you than by writing. If you can't come don't bother to reply. I shan't wait for you longer than until 4.45 p.m.

*1.* 'greatly disturbed me'—This refers to my first, rather dramatic encounter with Wittgenstein when I went to his class without previous permission from him. I had just arrived at Cambridge and got permission from the chairman of the faculty, C. D. Broad, to attend lectures and classes in philosophy.

'come round to my rooms'—I accepted Wittgenstein's kind invitation and the conversation we then had may be said to have laid the foundation for our mutual friendship and understanding.

2. [POSTCARD]

81, East Rd.
Cambr.
20.4.[39]

My first lecture will be on Monday 24th Apr. in Smythies' room at 5 p.m.

L. WITTGENSTEIN

*2.* 'Smythies' room'—Wittgenstein's lectures were then held in the rooms of his pupil and friend Yorick Smythies in King's College.

3.

81, East Rd.
Cambridge
13.9.39

Dear v. Wright,

Thank you so much for your letter, dated Aug. 27th. I was *very* glad to get it. I wish I were in that landscape of yours. It must be similar to the landscape in Norway, which I love. I wish you were here and could help me with my discussion classes. They should start in about 3 weeks; but I can't imagine how I shall be able to lecture. I feel as though, under the present shameful and depressing circumstances, I ought to do anything but discuss philosophical problems, with people who aren't really deeply interested in them anyway.

I should very much like to send you the M.S. of what would be the first volume of my book. I have an idea that it shall never be published in my lifetime and might perhaps be entirely lost. I should like to know that you had read it and had a copy of it. Write to me if you like to have it; and if it can be sent I'll send it to you.

⟦57⟧ I think it goes without saying that I shall always be exceedingly glad to hear from you. I myself am a *bad* correspondent, especially now that everything that I do seems to me futile and I don't know what sort of life I ought to lead.

Let me hear from you before long.

Yours
LUDWIG WITTGENSTEIN

*3.* 'that landscape of yours'—An island in the archipelago off the South shore of Finland.

'send you the M.S.'—I arranged for the thing to be sent by diplomatic mail from England to Finland but Wittgenstein evidently considered dispatching it too unsafe. Finland got involved in a war with the Soviet Union later that Autumn.

'the first volume of my book'—This means, roughly, the first 188 sections of Part I of the *Philosophical Investigations* as printed. The second volume was to deal with the philosophy of mathematics.

4.

Trinity College
Cambridge
21.2.47

Dear Professor von Wright,

Thank you for your letter of Feb. 14th. My lectures vary a great deal. They are sometimes satisfactory, sometimes very unsatisfactory. My mind, for reasons I don't know, often feels very exhausted. (I am, by the way, in perfectly good health.) This equilibrium of mine is so labile that, before long, my lectures *may* become hopelessly inadequate and that, after a struggle, I may have to give up teaching. Why do I write you all this? Because, if I should feel sterile and exhausted next Easter Term, I'll ask you not to come to my classes; for your presence, in that case, might make things more difficult for me. Otherwise I shall be glad if you will attend.

I'm glad that you are going to lecture here, and I know that by attending your lectures I could learn a very great deal. In spite of this I will not come to them—for the *sole* reason that, in order to *live* and to *work,* I have to allow no import of foreign goods (i.e., philosophical ones) into my mind. For the same reason I haven't read your book, though I am convinced of its excellence. If you think that I'm getting old—you're right. So long! and good luck!

Yours sincerely,
LUDWIG WITTGENSTEIN

*4.* In 1947, April through July, I visited Cambridge again and gave a series of lectures on induction at the invitation of the Moral Science Faculty.

5. Trin. Coll.
Wednesday

Dear Prof v. Wright,
I had your letter this morning. If only you had mentioned that you wished to see me yesterday at the gate!!—I'll be at home today from 1 to 3 p.m. and also after 6 p.m. So, if you like to see me then, please come to my room (Whewell's Ct. K 10). I could also see you tomorrow morning after 11 a.m. If you'd like to see me either this evening, or tomorrow morning please send me a note to that effect; address it to me, *don't* stamp it, and give it to the porter at the main lodge; he'll send it up to me. If you want to see me today between 1 and 3 don't trouble to let me know; I'll be in my room anyhow.

So long!
LUDWIG WITTGENSTEIN

*5.* The exact date of this letter is 23 April 1947. I saw Wittgenstein in his rooms later that same day.

6. Saturday
Dear v. Wright,
Thanks for your letter. *Sorry* you weren't able to come to my class! Not that you lost anything.—The two items I bring along with this letter are not meant to be looked at, but to be eaten. Of the vitamin B, you take a tablet a day. It *can't* do you any harm but *may* do you a lot of good; it has helped me when I was run down. The black currant

puree was given to me as a present. I pass it on because I REALLY don't need it; *you do!* Don't make any fuss but eat it.—I was very glad to read the kind words you said in your letter about Kreisel and Miss Anscombe. (I, too, respect both of them very much.) You made a "?" over Miss Anscombe's name,—I wonder, why. You couldn't possibly have mistaken Mrs Braithwaite for her, could you?—I shall expect you on Monday morning betwen 9.30 and 10.30 in my room. I very much hope you'll soon recover.

So long!
L. WITTGENSTEIN

*6.* The date of this letter is 24 May 1947.

7.

Trinity College
Cambridge
6.6.47

Dear v. Wright,
This is only to thank you for your letter. I'm glad you liked Smythies. I didn't doubt, you would. I feel extremely run down and tired myself and, therefore, shan't write any more today. I hope to see you after the middle of June. Take good care of my typescript—whatever you think of it. I have two more copies of it, but in your copy there are some corrections and additions which don't appear in the other copies.

I very much hope you'll have a good, if short, rest.

Yours,
L. WITTGENSTEIN

*7.* 'my typescript'—Wittgenstein had given me the typescript of what evidently is now Part I of the printed *Investigations* to take with me to Oxford where I was lecturing at the end of May and beginning of June.

8.

Wednesday

Dear v. Wright,
Thanks for your letter. I was very glad to get it. Could you come to see me tomorrow (Thursday), say, at 3 p.m.? If you can don't bother to reply. If you can't just ring up Trinity Coll. Porters Lodge and leave a message to that effect. I am pretty deadly as I've been a bit ill all last week and feeling altogether *very* run down, consequently I'll be dull.

So long!
LUDWIG WITTGENSTEIN

*8.* The date evidently is 18 June 1947.

9. 27.8.47

Dear v. Wright

Thank you very much for your letter. It meant a great deal to me to have you in Cambridge for a term. I, too, ⟦58⟧ wish it had been for longer. I've been to Ireland and I intend to go to Vienna on Sept. 10th and to return to England about Oct. 7th. I believe that I'll then resign my professorship and go somewhere where I can be alone for a longish time in order to think and, *if possible,* to finish a part of my book. I thought of going to Norway for that purpose but may go to Ireland instead. I'm not sure. I haven't told the Cambridge authorities anything about it so far, as it's not yet *absolutely* certain. (Though just now I can't see how it can be avoided, I mean, my leaving Cambridge.) My mind just now is in *great* disorder. It's partly due to this, that I dread seeing Vienna again after all that's happened and, in a way, I also dread chucking my job at Cambridge. But I'll get over it. May I see you again some day!! I wish you all good luck for your outer life, but by far more for your inner life; and I wish myself the same. My case is *much* more hopeless, I feel, than yours.—I like to think of our time at Cambridge. Let me remain in contact with you.

Yours

LUDWIG WITTGENSTEIN

*9.* 'a part of my book'—The meaning of this phrase is not clear to me. What Wittgenstein then was actually writing has later been published under the title *Remarks on the Philosophy of Psychology,* Volume I (Oxford: Basil Blackwell, 1980). These remarks may be regarded as a kind of preliminary studies for Part II of the posthumously printed *Investigations.* It is possible, however, that by 'my book' Wittgenstein meant a projected work in two parts, the second part of which was to deal with the philosophy of mathematics (cf., comment on letter 3). On *this* second part he wrote extensively in the years 1937–44 but then he gave up further work on it.

10. 6.11.47

Dear v. Wright,

Thanks for you letter. I have resigned but my professorship ends on December 31st. I shall stay here for another 3 weeks, I'm dictating some of the stuff which I wrote during the last 2–3 years. It's mostly bad but I've got to have it in a handy form, i.e. typewritten, because it may possibly give rise to better thoughts when I read it. I don't know where in Ireland I shall be but the address "Trinity College" will always find me. I am in *no* way optimistic about my future but as soon as I had resigned I felt that it was the only natural thing to have done.—In dictating my stuff I am using up the paper you were so *very* nice to bequeathe to me.—"Der Schmetterling" I don't like as much as "Eduards Traum", but it's wonderful in parts. Especially the homecoming. You are quite right, I found the book by an extraordinary chance in a shop in Vienna.

I hope to hear from you often if you're not too busy. I wish you luck!

Yours
LUDWIG WITTGENSTEIN

*10.* 'dictating some of the stuff'—This is material published in *Remarks on the Philosophy of Psychology,* Volume I.

'"Der Schmetterling"'—By Wilhelm Busch. Wittgenstein had given me a copy as a present. "Eduards Traum" by the same author was one of his favourites.

11. [XMAS CARD]

My present address is:
c/o Mrs Kingston
Kilpatrick House
Red Cross
Wicklow
*Eire*
but if you should write to me in about 2 months use this:
c/o Dr Drury
St. Patrick's Hospital
James's Street
Dublin

There isn't much to write just now, but I shall when there is.

Good wishes,
from
LUDWIG WITTGENSTEIN

12.

c/o Mrs Kingston
Kilpatrick House
Red Cross
Wicklow
Eire
22.12.47

Dear v. Wright,
Thank you for your X-mas letter. A day or two ago I sent you a card. As you see from the above address I'm not solitary. This is a big sort

of farm and they take guests in summer but not during the winter, and so I'm alone with the family. They are very quiet, I have my meals in my room and am very little disturbed. Still, I could do with greater loneliness and I intend to exchange this place for a more lonely one later in the year. Red Cross is a village, but the farm is about 2 miles outside it and fairly isolated. I am working a fair amount. Not too bad—and not too good. Heaven knows if I'll ever publish this work, but I should like you to look at it after my death if you survive me. There is a good deal of hard thinking in it. I feel *a good deal* better here than in Cambridge.

What you write about not intending to apply for the professorship in Cambridge I understand perfectly, and I had assumed before you wrote to me that you'd not apply. The chief reason why *I* thought it was, that the prospect of becoming English, or a refugee in England, seemed to me anything but attractive in our time, and I thought that you would *certainly* not wish to bring up your children in England. I hope for your sake you won't be compelled to do so; though for Cambridge it would be lucky, unless Cambridge were to drag you down, which, however, I don't assume.

'Der Schmetterling' is, in part, marvelous e.g. the end when he comes home—"*Es war ein lustiges Schneegestöber bei nördlichem Winde . . .*".

I read hardly anything: a few detective stories and some other things I've already read many times. Real reading is always bad for me.

I have a close friend in Dublin (about 2½–3 hours journey from here) whom I can see about once a month. Whether I'll go to Norway again I don't know at all.—Thanks for the cutting. I think I know where the *Steinlawine* must have gone down. I hope nothing has happened to any of the people I know!

I wish you good thoughts and good feelings and that nothing shall make you shallow. I hope somehow to see you again some day before so very long.

LUDWIG WITTGENSTEIN

P.S. On looking at your address I see that I made a mistake on the envelope of my X-mas card I wrote 77 instead of 7. I wonder if you'll get it.

*12.* 'working a fair amount'—What Wittgenstein was then writing were still 'preliminary studies' for Part II of the *Investigations* as printed. The actual writing is included in *Remarks on the Philosophy of Psychology,* Volume I.

'apply for the professorship'—When I was at Cambridge in 1947 Wittgenstein had told me of his plans of resigning his chair and also that he would have liked to see me as his successor. (See comment to the next letter.)

'a close friend in Dublin'—Dr M. O'C. Drury.

'the cutting'—I had seen in a paper the news of a 'stone avalanche' near the place in Norway where Wittgenstein had his hut and sent him a cutting. The drawing on the postcard must be a chart of the place concerned. The drawing on the other side showing a church tower I do not recognise from our correspondence or conversations. ⟦59⟧

13.

Kilpatrick House
Redcross
Wicklow
Eire
23.2.48

Dear von Wright,

Miss Anscombe wrote to me a few weeks ago that you had put in for the professorship. I shall write the recommendation in a few days and send it to the Registrary as you suggest. May your decision be the right one! I have *no* doubt that you will be a better professor than any of the other candidates for the chair. But Cambridge is a dangerous place. Will you become superficial? smooth? If you don't you will have to suffer terribly.—The passage in your letter which makes me feel particularly uneasy is the one about your feeling enthusiasm at the thought of teaching in Cambridge. It seems to me: if you go to Cambridge you must go as a SOBER man.—May my fears have no foundation, and may you not be tempted beyond your powers!

If I wanted to play providence I'd write a luke-warm recommendation; but I won't. I'll write you as good a one as you can possibly wish for. For what can I know about the future?

Good luck!

Yours
LUDWIG WITTGENSTEIN

*13.* 'put in for the professorship'—When, after long hesitation, I applied for the professorship Wittgenstein wrote a recommendation in support of my application. (I have, incidentally, never seen the document.) I later withdrew my application but, when the Electors met on 15 May they nevertheless offered me the chair—and I accepted. After Wittgenstein's death three years later I decided to give up the chair and move back to Finland. My resignation was effective as from 31 December 1951.

14.

Kilpatrick House
Redcross
Wicklow
Eire
17.3.48

Dear v. Wright,
Thanks for your letter of March 3rd. About 2 weeks ago I sent the recommendation to the Registrary and a copy of it to Broad, just in case something should happen to the originals. I think I can say that, if you don't get the job, it's not because my recommendation wasn't warm enough—though I didn't say anything in it that I don't strictly believe to be the truth.—My work is progressing very slowly and very painfully. I often believe that I am on the straight road to insanity: It is difficult for me to imagine that my brain should stand the strain very long. That I dread this end I needn't say. You're not the only one who needs more courage. May our fate not be too terrible! and may we be given courage.

Yours,
LUDWIG WITTGENSTEIN

15.

Rosro Cottage
Renvyle P.O.
C^O Galway
Eire
26.5.48

Dear von Wright
Thank you for your two letters. I'm glad that you've accepted. May things go well!!—My life here is very strenuous as I'm living completely alone. The cottage is on the West coast of Ireland, right on the sea. I arrived here a month ago and don't yet know how things will shape as time goes on. At present I get tired, bodily and mentally, very easily. That's bad, but perhaps it'll mend.

Perhaps we shall see each other before too long!

Lots of good wishes!
LUDWIG WITTGENSTEIN

*15.* 'accepted'—See comment to letter 13.

16.

c/o Richards
40 Swakeleys Rd.
Ickenham,
Uxbridge
2.9.48

Dear von Wright,

Thanks for your letter. I am near London right now and am leaving for Vienna on Wednesday next. I'm coming back on Sept. 29th and then should like to spend a fortnight or so in Cambridge to dictate some stuff of mine. I am looking forward to seeing you then. I shall not try to see you before leaving as I'm not in the right frame of mind for a conversation; but I hope we'll have *good* talks after my return from Austria.

I shan't write more now. I'm feeling *very* stupid.

All good wishes!
So long!
LUDWIG WITTGENSTEIN

*16.* 'dictate some stuff'—Wittgenstein was in Cambridge the first two weeks of October and we met a number of times. The stuff he then dictated is the last of his preserved dictations and has later been published as Volume II of *Remarks on the Philosophy of Psychology* (Oxford: Basil Blackwell, 1980).

17. [POSTCARD]

IV. Argentinierstr. 16
Wien
Austria

Dear v. Wright,

This is just to thank you for your last short letter from Cambridge. I shall be back in London on the 29th and I intend to go to Cambridge on the 30th, or October 1st. I'm looking forward to seeing you. There are many things I should like to talk to you about. So long.

LUDWIG WITTGENSTEIN

18. [XMAS CARD WITH PRINTED TEXT] 1948

To v. Wright
from
LUDWIG WITTGENSTEIN

19.

IV. Argentinierstr. 16
Wien
Austria
29.4.49

Dear v. Wright,
Thanks for your letter. It was forwarded to Vienna. This ⟦60⟧ is only to say that I'm unable at present to write a proper letter. I am here because my eldest sister is ill. I intend to fly to England in 2 or 3 weeks. I'm very much looking forward to seeing you before long.

Yours
LUDWIG WITTGENSTEIN

*19.* 'my eldest sister'—Hermine Wittgenstein. Wittgenstein was deeply attached to her. She died in February 1950. See letter 29.

20.

Ross's Hotel
Parkgate Street
Dublin
24.5.49

Dear v. Wright,
Thanks a lot for your letter. I'd love to stay with you and I hope I'll be able to. My plans are all very wobbly right now. After I had felt illish for about four months I had my blood examined a few days ago and it appears that I am very anaemic and there is likely to be some inner cause for that. I'm going to hospital today to have it investigated. So I wonder now if I shall really see you in June.

Good wishes!
LUDWIG WITTGENSTEIN

21.

Ross's Hotel
Parkgate Street
Dublin
1.6.49

Dear v. Wright,
Thanks a lot for your letter. The X-ray and the test-meal have shown that there is nothing wrong with my alimentary canal. The doctor says that my anaemia is a-typical and something between an ordinary and a pernicious anaemia. He thinks that, if I respond well to the iron and liver which I'm getting, I should feel an improvement in a fortnight and that, if I then feel up to it, I might go to Cambridge. In

about 2 months he thinks I might be all right again, if everything goes well.—It's very kind of you to say that you'll let me have two rooms, but one room is *ample.* There is one thing that I'm afraid of: I may not be able to discuss philosophy. Of course it's possible that things will have changed by then, but at present I'm quite incapable of even thinking of philosophical problems. My head is *completely* dull.—I hope that you will soon get some rest, once the Term is over and I'm looking forward to seeing you even if I feel that I may be a bad companion.

Please give my good wishes to Miss Anscombe and to Smythies via Miss Anscombe. I want to write to them soon.

So long!
Yours
LUDWIG WITTGENSTEIN

22.

Ross's Hotel
Parkgate Street
Dublin
8.6.49

Dear v. Wright,
Thanks for your card. I'm afraid I have to bother you with another question. I don't quite know yet whether I'm getting better, but if so, it's a very slow process. Now I'd like to come to Cambridge on Monday, or Tuesday the week after next (i.e. June 20th or 21st) and although I think I'll be a good deal stronger by then I may still not be able to walk about a lot, and hence, to go to restaurants for my meals *may* not be possible for me. That means that I *may* have to stay in a place where they give me all my meals. Now I don't know if that wouldn't be more than your household could do and if it wouldn't be, at least, a frightful nuisance to your family. Please write me a line about it and be VERY frank. I'm sorry that there should be all these difficulties and you know that I'm not happy about them, either, but I can't change them.

Wish me luck! and the same to you!

Yours,
LUDWIG WITTGENSTEIN

P.S. In case you see Kreisel, please give him my good wishes and tell him to ask Gitta Deutsch if she can do some typing for me when I come to Cambridge. She's the girl that's typed for me in the past and she is a friend of Kreisel's.

23.

Ross's Hotel
Dublin
Tuesday

Dear v. Wright,
Thanks for your letter, I'm glad to say that I got *much* better in the last 3–4 days. I'm sorry Miss Deutsch can't give me more time. It means that I'll have to try to get someone else, either besides her, or instead of her. I used to dictate to a typist in Huntingdon Rd. who was pretty efficient though personally not very agreeable. Trouble is—I don't remember her name, only the house in which she lived (and not even the number). So, when I get to Cambridge, I'll look her up. If you heard of anyone who can type German well it would of course be grand, but that's *most* unlikely. Don't bother about it.—I shall write day and time of my arrival.

Looking forward to seeing you soon.

Yours
LUDWIG WITTGENSTEIN

24.

c/o Dr Richards
40 Swakeleys Rd.
Ickenham
Uxbridge
3.7.49

Dear v. Wright,
This is just to ask you a favour. As you may remember I ⟦61⟧ gave you ration cards for two weeks (they are marked in ink "5" and "6"). Now I want you to take *all* the rations available by these cards and then to send me what remains of the *cards*, i.e., just the bit of paper that remains when *all* coupons are cut away. I need these bits for a purpose which it would be too long to explain in a letter. Of course it's possible that these bits may already have been thrown away, in which case there is nothing one can do about it, and it's *no* tragedy.—I want to thank you and your wife again for all the great kindness you've shown me. My health is sofar unchanged, not particularly good. I don't know as yet how things will go here and won't know for some days.

Give my regards to all your family.

Yours
LUDWIG WITTGENSTEIN

*21–24.* Wittgenstein came to Cambridge on 20 June and stayed until 2 July. Then he went for a few days to London (see letter 24) but returned to Cambridge on 7 July and left again on the 12th. During his stay in Cambridge Wittgenstein occupied a separate apartment of two rooms in the house ('Strathaird') which we rented in Lady Margaret Road and he had his meals regularly with the family. It was presumably then that he dictated the typescript for the second part of the *Investigations.* This was, for all I know, his last dictation of a philosophic typescript. The typescript was used for printing the book but is now unfortunately lost, probably destroyed. The same holds true of the printing typescript of Part I of the *Investigations.*

25.

40, Swakeleys Road
Ickenham
Uxbridge

Dear v. Wright
I'm afraid I shan't see you before I sail (on Wednesday). This book might help your children learn English.

*Good luck!*
LUDWIG WITTGENSTEIN

*25.* 'before I sail'—This letter, with the book for my two children, aged 5 and 4, was received on 20 July. This was presumably the day when Wittgenstein set out on his voyage to the United States where he visited Norman Malcolm and his wife at Ithaca, New York. Wittgenstein returned from the United States early in November. On 4 November he telephoned me from London and on the 9th he came to Cambridge to stay with us in Lady Margaret Road. He was feeling very ill and we immediately called on our family doctor, Edward Bevan, to see and examine him. The final diagnosis was given on 25 November: cancer of the prostate. Wittgenstein stayed with us until 22 December when he left for Vienna.

26. [Telegram]

WIEN
26.12.49

ARRIVED VIENNA EXCELLENT HEALTH AND SPIRITS NOTIFY FRIENDS
LUDWIG WITTGENSTEIN

*26.* 'excellent health and spirits'—This, of course, is an euphemism. Wittgenstein did not wish his illness to be disclosed to members of the family.

27. IV. Argentinierstrasse 16
Wien
1.1.50

Dear v. Wright,
First I'd like to say that my health isn't too bad at all. Unfortunately I caught a cold some days ago, but it's gradually getting better. The main reason I'm writing is this: I have an idea that last summer, before leaving for America, I gave you a book to read, the letters of Wilhelm Busch to a Frau Marie Anderson. I wanted to lend you the book and to give it as a Christmas present to Rhees. I forgot to ask you about it before I left. Please, if you can, look for it in your room, etc., and if you find it, please send it to Rhees with a note. If you still have some Christmas paper around I'd be grateful if you wrapped it in that. I'm sorry to trouble you with it.—I *hope* you're all well by now! and that you had a pleasant Christmas. Please give your wife my kindest regards and to Eva also.

Yours ever
LUDWIG WITTGENSTEIN

Happy New Year!
P.S. Rhees's Address is 96 Bryn Rd. Swansea

*27.* 'Eva'—Eeva Ede, *née* Haataja, a young lady from Finland who was living in our house, helping my wife with the children. Later, when Wittgenstein was staying in the house of Dr Bevan, Mrs Ede used to go and read aloud to him.

28. IV. Argentinierstr. 16
Wien
19.1.50

Dear v. Wright,
Thanks for your letter and Hijab's Christmas card. I'm glad you had a good Christmas. Thank you for sending the book to Rhees. I'm sorry you had no time to read it. It's very remarkable.—Things are going very well with me. I'm much stronger and my nerves are all right. I have very good nights without using much of my sedatives. Please let Dr Bevan know about me and give him my thanks for his last (very kind) note. I am completely acclimatized and don't feel the cold as I did at first when I arrived.

I haven't been to a concert so far but I hear a fair amount of music. A friend of mine plays the piano to me (very beautifully) and one of my sisters and he play piano duets. The other day they played two string quartets by Schumann and a sonata written for 4 hands by Mozart.

The last two weeks I read a great deal in Goethe's "Farbenlehre". It's partly boring and repelling, but in some ways also *very* instructive and philosophically interesting. You might take it out of your book case and look at what he wrote about Lord Bacon in the *historical* part.

Give my good wishes to everybody, particularly to your wife.

Yours
LUDWIG WITTGENSTEIN

*28.* 'A friend of mine'—Rudolf Koder, a close friend of Wittgenstein since the time they both worked as schoolmasters at Puchberg am Schneeberg in Lower Austria in the 1920s.

'one of my sisters'—Frau Helene Salzer, *née* Wittgenstein.

'Lord Bacon'—Refers to discussions we had in Cambridge concerning Bacon's place in the history of thought. Cf. the remarks in *Culture and Value,* pp. 54, 61, 68.

29.

IV. Argentinierstrasse 16
Wien
12.2.50

Dear v. Wright,
My eldest sister died very peacefully yesterday evening. We had expected her end hourly for the last 3 days. It wasn't a shock.

I'm in very good health. I see Miss Anscombe 2–3 times a week, and we even had a discussion the other day which wasn't too bad.—I was very glad indeed to hear that Geache's lectures are good. Frege was just the right food for him!

Please give my love to all my friends.

Yours
LUDWIG WITTGENSTEIN

*29.* 'Miss Anscombe'—Elizabeth Anscombe was that Winter in Vienna to improve her German. She was living with the family of Ludwig Hänsel, a close friend of Wittgenstein.

'Geache's lectures'—Peter Geach gave a course of lectures at Cambridge on Frege which I attended.

30. IV. Argentinierstrasse 16
Wien
15.3.50

Dear v. Wright,
I'm arriving in London on Thursday (23rd) evening. I'd like to stay in London for about a week and then to go to Cambridge for a week or two. I don't know if you'll be away just then. If not, I wonder whether you can put me up. Perhaps you could write a line to me c/o Mrs. Rhees, ⟦62⟧ 104 Goldhurst Terrace, London N.W. 6., that's where I'm staying. I'm very much looking forward to seeing you and Mrs v. Wright again.—By the way, thanks for your letter. The news about ****** being offered a professorship in 'Christian Religion' is indeed almost unbelievable. But then everything is that happens these days.—Thanks for keeping my parcel for me.

I hope to see you pretty soon anyway. Lots of good wishes!

Yours
LUDWIG WITTGENSTEIN

*30.* 'stay in London'—Wittgenstein seems to have arrived in London on 27 March. I went there to see him on the 30th. On 3 April my wife and I went on a holiday to the Lake District from where we returned a week later. In the meantime Wittgenstein had moved into our Cambridge house. He stayed with us until the 25th with an interruption for a weekend in London. From us he moved to Elizabeth Anscombe and her family in Oxford. In June he came for another week to stay with us at Cambridge. The asterisks are substituted for a name.

31. 27 St. John Street
Oxford
28.4.50

Dear von Wright,
Thank you very much indeed for the Grimm. When the parcel from Deighton Bell arrived I was sure at first that it must have been sent to me by mistake as I had never ordered any books; but when I opened it I had a very pleasant surprise and I enjoy reading in the books.—The above address is where I live. I don't yet feel acclimatized at all. The house isn't very noisy but not very quiet, either. I don't know yet how I shall get on. The lodgers seem all to be rather nice, and one of them even very nice.

*Thanks again!* Give my good wishes to everybody.

Yours
LUDWIG WITTGENSTEIN

*31.* 'the Grimm'—I had picked up a copy of the first edition of Jacob Grimm's famous work *Geschichte der deutschen Sprache* and sent it to Wittgenstein to Oxford as a birthday present.

32.

27 St. John Street
Oxford
Tuesday

Dear v. Wright,

Thanks for the shoes which arrived the day after I did. I enjoyed what talks we had and I liked to see Kreisel again. I hope you still saw him after I left. I hope your journey to Finland won't be too unpleasant and that you'll spend your time there *profitably.* Let me hear from you if you've nothing better to do. Give all my good wishes to your wife and to Bevan if you see him. I'm pretty well and pretty stupid.

Yours
LUDWIG WITTGENSTEIN

*32.* The date of this letter presumably is 13 June 1950. Wittgenstein had been staying for another week with us in Cambridge.

'the shoes'—Wittgenstein apparently forgot and left a pair of shoes with us.

'journey to Finland'—In mid-June I and the family went to Finland. After six terms at Cambridge I had a sabbatical leave and remained the Autumn in Helsinki. On my return alone in January I moved into Trinity College. I did not see Wittgenstein again until 9 February. (See comments to letter 35.)

33.

27 St. John Street
Oxford
6.9.50

Dear v. Wright,

Thanks for two letters. I haven't written for such a long time because there isn't anything to write about me. My trip to Norway hasn't come off. Richards failed his exam and decided to take it again in September; so he has to cram and can't have any holidays until the beginning of October. We plan to go to Norway then. I did some work, though not good work, for quite a time, but I've hardly done anything for the last 3 weeks, and anyhow my ability for philosophical work seems to have practically vanished.—I was very sorry to hear about your accident. I hope you'll get better soon.—What you write about Spengler agrees with what I think of him. I looked at Toynbee the other day and found him *very* stupid. But perhaps he's amusing.—Give my kind regards to your wife and to her mother.

Good wishes!
Yours
LUDWIG WITTGENSTEIN

*33.* 'I did some work'—A part of the work done in this period is presumably identical with writings which have been published as Part III in *Remarks on Colour* (Oxford: Basil Blackwell, 1977). See also letter 28 on his reading Goethe's *Farbenlehre.* When Wittgenstein was staying in Cambridge in April and June 1950 colour concepts was a main topic of our conversations.

'Spengler'—I was at that time writing a study on Spengler and Toynbee. Spengler was a topic which we had often touched upon in our discussions. See also Wittgenstein's reflexions on Spengler in *Culture and Value.*

34.

27 St. John Street
Oxford
7.12.50

Dear v. Wright,
Thanks for several letters. I'm sorry I didn't write before now. In Norway there was for a time a lot of trouble: Ben Richards fell ill *twice* with asthma and bronchitis. In spite of all this we enjoyed our stay enormously. We had excellent weather the whole time and were surrounded by the greatest kindness. I decided then and there that I'd return to Norway to work there. I get no *real* quiet here. If all goes well I shall sail on Dec. 30th and go to Skjolden again. I don't think I'll be able to stay in my hut because the physical work I've got to do there is too heavy for me, but an old friend told me that she'd let me stay at her farmhouse. Of course I don't know whether I'm able any more to do decent work, but at least I'm giving myself a real chance. If I can't work there I can't work anywhere. By the way, I'd rather you didn't talk about that plan of mine *just yet.*—I had a letter from Malcolm a few days ago in which he asks me to remember him to you.

Please give Mrs. v. Wright and her mother my very kind regards, and to Eva, too, if she is with you.

Good wishes!
Yours
LUDWIG WITTGENSTEIN

*34.* 'an old friend'—Must refer to Miss Anna Rebni, teacher in the village school at Skjolden. Wittgenstein made friends with her when he was living in his hut in Norway 1936–37. It seems to me very remarkable that Wittgenstein should have thought of moving back to Norway as late as in December 1950, not many months before his death.

35.

27 St. John Street
Oxford
29.1.51

Dear von Wright,
Thanks for your letter. I have been rather ill for the last month, or so, and though I'd like to see you, it wouldn't be worth your while to come to Oxford. All the more as I shall, in all likelihood, come to Cambridge sometime next week. I'll stay with Dr Bevan and will let you know when I'm there. The last few days I've been feeling pretty good, but I still stay in bed for part of the day.

I'm looking forward to seeing you.

Yours
LUDWIG WITTGENSTEIN

*35.* 'come to Cambridge'—Wittgenstein came to Cambridge early in February to stay until his death with Dr and Mrs Edward Bevan in 76 Storey's Way. During that time I saw him on and off in the house of the Bevans. On one occasion he came to see me in college. This was on 21 April—our last encounter. I sat in my rooms immobile because of a broken cartilage. Wittgenstein entered unannounced. Seeing him greatly surprised me. He said, jokingly, that it was not him I saw but his 'astral body' walking round. He brought me some flowers. He then sat down for a short while and we talked about Aksakov's 'Family Chronicle' which I was reading. Then he left. He died eight days later. It then struck me that he had actually come to say goodbye.

# APPENDICES

# The Wittgenstein Papers

*By* GEORG HENRIK VON WRIGHT

## Historical Notes on the *Nachlass* [legacy]

Early in February 1951, Wittgenstein moved to the house of Dr Edward Bevan at Cambridge, where he died on 29 April. During the last six weeks of his life he was working continuously. He had with him a number of manuscript notebooks containing his last writings. Other manuscripts and typescripts he had left in the house of Miss Anscombe at Oxford, where he had been living, with minor interruptions, since April 1950.

At the time of Wittgenstein's death his literary executors did not know for certain whether there existed papers other than those just referred to. We knew, however, that Wittgenstein on his last visit to Vienna, from Christmas 1949 to March 1950, had ordered a great many papers, belonging to all periods of his work, to be burned.[1] We also knew that, when living in Ireland after giving up his chair at Cambridge, Wittgenstein destroyed old material which he considered useless for his work. It was therefore not without surprise that we gradually realized that our initial estimate of the scope of the *Nachlass* was much mistaken.

In December 1951, the executor of Wittgenstein's will, Mr Rush Rhees, received a box which had been left by Wittgenstein in Trinity College. It was thought to contain some of his books, but turned out to contain a huge number of manuscripts. Professor G. E. Moore returned to us a typescript which Wittgenstein had left with him, probably in 1930, and showed us verbatim notes of dictations made in Norway in 1914. From Bertrand Russell we received copies of Wittgenstein's letters to him and of the 1913 'Notes on Logic'.[2] An early inquiry addressed to Dr Friedrich Waismann produced no answer,

1. See Editors' Preface to the first edition of *Notebooks 1914–1916*, Basil Blackwell, Oxford, 1961 (2nd edition, 1979).

2. Published as an Appendix in ibid.

but after Dr Waismann's death in 1959 much material consisting of notes on conversations and also of some verbatim dictations came to light.[3]

In the summer of 1952 the literary executors visited Austria. At Gmunden in the house of Wittgenstein's sister, Mrs M. Stonborough, we were shown some manuscripts and typescripts, among them the three notebooks (1914–16) from the time of the germination of the *Tractatus*. Later the same year seven big manuscript volumes were discovered at the family estate, Hochreit. The literary executors had photographic copies made for them in England of the pre-*Tractatus* notebooks and of the Hochreit manuscripts.

Thirteen years later I revisited Vienna with the purpose of checking the Austrian material and obtaining copies of some of the items which, in addition to the 1914–16 notebooks, had been at Gmunden in 1952. Of this last material I found, alas, no trace. But in addition to the manuscript volumes 1 to 7 (items 105–111 of the catalogue), I found also volumes 8 and 9 (items 112 and 113). This filled the gap which had up to then existed between the Austrian material and the manuscript volumes in England, the earliest of which was numbered 10. An entirely unexpected discovery was that of a manuscript book containing a complete early version of the *Tractatus*.[4] A typescript of the *Tractatus* was also discovered.

Further searching for the missing items in the Gmunden material was without result. But in the course of this search a number of hitherto unknown typescripts were found in 1967.

In 1976 and 1977 further typescripts came to light. They are listed here as items 235–245 of the catalogue. The most interesting one among them is a revision of the first half of the pre-war version of the *Philosophical Investigations*.

In the summer of 1967 the part of the *Nachlass* which was then known to exist in England was temporarily collected at Oxford and microfilmed for Cornell University. The process was supervised by Professor Norman Malcolm and myself. Later in the same year copies of papers in the Austrian part of the *Nachlass* were filmed at Cornell.

3. For an account of this material see the Preface by B. F. McGuinness to F. Waismann, *Wittgenstein and the Vienna Circle*, Basil Blackwell, Oxford, 1979 (German edition, 1967). Cf. also the comment on items 302–308 of the catalogue below.

4. Published under the title *Prototractatus*, with a facsimile of the author's manuscript, Routledge and Kegan Paul, London, 1971.

The material thus filmed is available to students and scholars. Some items belonging to the *Nachlass* that were found after 1967 are not on the film.

In May 1969 Wittgenstein's literary executors gave all their originals of the Wittgenstein papers to Trinity College, Cambridge. The originals are kept in the Wren Library. Wittgenstein himself had deposited his papers there during the Second World War; and later he indicated to one of us that he regarded the Library as a suitable place for their permanent custody. The typescripts that were found after 1969 are now also in Trinity.

Seven manuscript books of the Austrian *Nachlass* have been donated to the Wren Library. These are items 101, 102, 103, 108, 109, 110, and 111 in the catalogue. The early *Tractatus* manuscript (104) was sold to the Bodleian Library, Oxford, and items 105, 106, 107, 112, 113, and 203 to the Österreichische Nationalbibliothek in Vienna.

On a visit to Israel in 1964, I met Mr Paul Engelmann. He showed me a typescript, from which apparently Wittgenstein's *Logisch-philosophische Abhandlung* [*Tractatus Logico-Philosophicus*] had first been printed (in Germany in 1921). This typescript too is now in the Bodleian.

## Classification and Description of the Papers

The papers of which this essay gives an account can be divided into three main groups: manuscripts, typescripts dictated to a typist or otherwise prepared by Wittgenstein himself, and verbatim records of dictations to colleagues or pupils. Comprising a fourth group are the notes, more or less verbatim, of conversations and lectures, of which there exist a good many. Wittgenstein's correspondence constitutes a fifth group of papers.

Nearly all the manuscripts are written in bound manuscript books and only a few on loose sheets. The manuscript books I have classified in the catalogue given below as either 'volumes', 'large notebooks', 'notebooks', or 'pocket notebooks'. All the volumes are solidly bound in hard covers. They vary considerably in size. Some of the biggest are ledgers measuring 21 by 31 cm; a few of the smaller ones measure 18 by 21 cm. What I have called large notebooks are all of uniform size (22 by 29 cm) and have soft covers. The pocket notebooks normally measure 10 by 16 cm, and most of them have hard covers.

One can, broadly speaking, distinguish two strata of writings in manuscript form. I shall refer to them as 'first drafts' and 'more finished versions'. But the distinction between the strata is by no means clearcut, and there is no one-to-one correlation between them. Some of the more finished writings are revisions of earlier, draftlike material, but others are revisions of material itself classified here as 'more finished'. Some of the most finished manuscripts have the nature of 'fair copies' of remarks which have been extracted from earlier writings. Others definitely have the character of manuscripts for a planned book.

All manuscripts here classified as 'volumes' are of the more finished type, but to the same category belong also some notebooks, pocket notebooks, and writings on loose sheets. Particularly difficult to classify are some of the manuscripts from the last two years of Wittgenstein's life.

In the more finished manuscripts the entries are often dated. This makes a chronological arrangement of these manuscripts relatively easy. In many cases the books are running diaries in which apparently every day on which an entry was made is recorded. In other manuscripts of this category there are only a few dates and large sections are undated. Some of the manuscript volumes contain parts separated by long intervals of time. (A case in point is 116 which spans the period from the mid-1930s to 1945.) Sometimes two or more manuscript volumes have been written during the same, or during largely overlapping, periods (114 and 115 are one example; another is 117, the first half of which stretches over roughly the same time as 118–121). The chronological order of the volumes is thus not entirely linear.

The more draftlike notebooks sometimes have a date at the beginning and sometimes dates in the text. But often they contain no dates at all. The chronology of the manuscripts of this kind and their relations to the more finished writings are to some extent a matter for conjecture.

The main bulk of the more finished manuscripts can be divided into two 'series'. The first series consists of 18 volumes written in the years 1929–40. Wittgenstein referred to them as *Bände* [volumes] with a number. Usually he also gave them a title—for example, '*Philosophische Bemerkungen*' ['Philosophical Remarks'].

The second series consists of 16 manuscript books, some few of which are pocket notebooks and not 'volumes'. It is impossible to tell exactly which writings should count as belonging to this series and whether it, like the first, is complete. It covers the years 1940–49. The books are not numbered. The last three in the series Wittgenstein called '*Band Q*', '*Band R*', and '*Band S*'. One of the earlier members in the series, a pocket notebook, he marked '*F*'. I have not found any indications that Wittgenstein thought of the unnamed members of the series as volumes *A, B, C,* and so forth. But if one arranges the existing manuscript books in a chronological order and assigns to each of them a letter, one is struck by the following fact. The notebook called '*F*' becomes correlated with the letter *E* and the volume called '*Q*' with the letter *N.* If we assume that *one* of the first five manuscript books of the series,[5] and *two* books after the one called '*F*',[6] are lost or have been destroyed, then we have a perfect alphabetical order for the manuscripts in the second series. This observation is of some interest in connection with the conjectured existence of, and the search for, missing manuscripts.

Not all of the more finished manuscripts have a place in either series.

From the more finished manuscripts Wittgenstein dictated to typists. In the course of dictation he evidently often altered the sentences, added new ones, and changed the order of the remarks in the manuscripts. Usually he continued to work with the typescripts. A method which he often used was to cut up the typed text into fragments [*Zettel*] and to rearrange the order of the remarks. Conspicuous instances of this method of work are items 212, 222–224, and 233 of the catalogue. A further stage was the production of a new typescript on the basis of a collection of cuttings. One case of this procedure is represented by item 213, a typescript of 768 pages, evidently made in 1933. In an outward sense it is one of the most finished of all Wittgenstein's writings after the *Tractatus.* It is divided into 19 main chapters which are themselves subdivided into larger sections. Each chapter and section has a heading—a unique occurrence in Wittgenstein's literary output. The literary executors used to refer to this item as the Big Typescript. It was in our hands from 1951. But it was not until 1967 that the *Zettel* from which it was made and the typescripts from which these fragments are cut were discovered.

The typescript of the *Philosophical Investigations* probably had a

5. But see the comment on item 163 of the catalogue.
6. It is also possible that there never was a '*Band J*' or a '*Band O*'.

similar history. The beginning of the book as we have it, up to Section 189, is a revision of a typescript (220 of the catalogue) which was composed probably in 1937 on the basis of a manuscript volume (142) now lost. The history of the origin of the final typescript for the book remains to a certain extent obscure.[7] It is reported that there existed in September 1944 a typescript of Part I consisting of cuttings (perhaps partly from the 1937 typescript) clipped together in bundles.[8] The final typescript of Part I was probably finished in the academic year 1945–46. Part II of the *Investigations* has a more straightforward history. Its first version was a manuscript extracted by Wittgenstein from the manuscripts which were themselves of the kind here called 'more finished'. From this manuscript he composed, with some omissions, the typescript from which the book was printed.

The papers listed as verbatim dictations to colleagues and pupils can be regarded as on a level with the rest of Wittgenstein's own writings. Eleven (or twelve)[9] items of this kind are known: the dictations to G.E. Moore in Norway in 1914; seven (or eight) dictations to Schlick; and the so-called Blue and Brown and Yellow books. It is important to distinguish these verbatim dictations from the more or less verbatim notes taken by various people of conversations and lectures.[10] Many of these notes are of great interest and evidently very faithful to their source. Several of them have been published.

## Catalogue

To make reference easier I have numbered the items in the catalogue as follows: manuscripts beginning at 101, typescripts at 201, and dictations at 301. In some cases several items are grouped under the same number and distinguished as a, b, c, and so forth. The names in quotation marks are Wittgenstein's own titles. Names invented by the editors and executors are not enclosed in quotation marks and are prefixed 'called' or 'so-called'. The language of the writings is German, except when otherwise indicated. For each manuscript and typescript the number of pages it contains is also given. The actual

7. See 'The Origin and Composition of the *Philosophical Investigations*' in my book *Wittgenstein,* Basil Blackwell, Oxford, 1982.
8. Report by R. Rhees.
9. See the comment on items 302–308 below.
10. See the comment on item 311 below.

pagination is not always by Wittgenstein himself. There is some vacillation; sometimes, for example, the title page has a number, sometimes it has not. Also errors occasionally occur. Some comments on individual items follow after the catalogue.

MANUSCRIPTS

101 Notebook. 9 August–30 October 1914. 106 pp.
102 Notebook. 30 October 1914–22 June 1915. 265 pp.
103 Notebook. 7 April 1916–10 January 1917. 118 pp.
104 Notebook. The so-called *Prototractatus.* 1918. 122 pp.
105 Volume I. '*Philosophische Bemerkungen.*' Begun 2 February 1929. 135 pp.
106 Volume II. Undated, 1929. 298 pp.
107 Volume III. '*Philosophische Betrachtungen*' [Philosophical Considerations]. Last entry 15 February 1930. 300 pp.
108 Volume IV. '*Philosophische Bemerkungen.*' 13 December 1929–9 August 1930. 300 pp.
109 Volume V. '*Bemerkungen*' [Remarks]. 11 August 1930–3 February 1931. 300 pp.
110 Volume VI. '*Philosophische Bemerkungen.*' 10 December 1930–6 July 1931. 300 pp.
111 Volume VII. '*Bemerkungen zur Philosophie*' [Remarks Concerning Philosophy]. 7 July–September 1931. 200 pp.
112 Volume VIII. '*Bemerkungen zur philosophischen Grammatik*' [Remarks Concerning Philosophical Grammar]. 5 October–28 November 1931. 270 pp.
113 Volume IX. '*Philosophische Grammatik*' [Philosophical Grammar]. 28 November 1931–23 May 1932. 286 pp.
114 Volume X. '*Philosophische Grammatik.*' First entry 27 May 1932. 288 pp.
115 Volume XI. '*Philosophische Bemerkungen.*' First entry 14 December 1933. '*Philosophische Untersuchungen*' [Philosophical Investigations]. August 1936. 292 pp.
116 Volume XII. '*Philosophische Bemerkungen.*' Autumn 1937; May 1945. 347 pp.
117 Volume XIII. '*Philosophische Bemerkungen.*' 1937; 1938; 1940. 263 pp.
118 Volume XIV. '*Philosophische Bemerkungen.*' 13 August–24 September 1937. 238 pp.

119 Volume XV. 24 September–19 November 1937. 295 pp.
120 Volume XVI. 19 November 1937–26 April 1938. 293 pp.
121 Volume XVII. '*Philosophische Bemerkungen.*' 26 April 1938–9 January 1939. 186 pp.
122 Volume XVIII. '*Philosophische Bemerkungen.*' 16 October 1939–3 February 1940. 238 pp.
123 Notebook. '*Philosophische Bemerkungen.*' 25 September–23 November 1940; 16 May–6 June 1941. 138 pp.
124 Volume. 6 June–4 July 1941; 5 March–19 April 1944; 3 July 1944–?. 292 pp.
125 Pocket notebook. 28 December 1941–16 October 1942. 156 pp.
126 Pocket notebook. 20 October 1942–6 January 1943. 155 pp. (Missing.)
127 Pocket notebook. '*F. Mathematik und Logik*' [Mathematics and Logic]. 6 January–4 April 1943; 27 February–4 March 1944; undated part. 175 pp. (Missing.)
128 Volume. *Circa* 1944. 52 pp.
129 Volume. First entry 17 August 1944. 221 pp.
130 Volume. Undated part; 26 May–9 August 1946. 294 pp.
131 Volume. 10 August–9 September 1946. 206 pp.
132 Volume. 9 September–22 October 1946. 212 pp.
133 Volume. 22 October 1946–28 February 1947. 190 pp.
134 Volume. 28 February 1947–?. 184 pp.
135 Volume. 12 July–18 December 1947. 192 pp.
136 Volume. '*Band Q.*' 18 December 1947–25 January 1948. 288 pp.
137 Volume. '*Band R.*' 2 February 1948–9 January 1949. 286 pp.
138 Volume. '*Band S.*' 15 January–20 May 1949. 66 pp.
139a The Lecture on Ethics. 1929. Written in English on loose sheets. 23 pp.
b The same. (Missing.)
140 '*Grosses Format*' [Large Format]. Approximately 1934. Large sheets. 42 pp.
141 The beginning of an early version in German of the Brown Book. Large sheets. 1935 or 1936. 8 pp.
142 Volume. '*Philosophische Untersuchungen.*' November–December 1936. (Missing.)
143 Notes on Frazer's *The Golden Bough.* Loose sheets of varying size. 1936 or later. 21 pp.
144 Volume. Fair manuscript copy containing Part II of the *Investigations.* 1949. 118 pp.

145 Large notebook. Called *C*1. 1933. 96 pp.
146 Large notebook. Called *C*2. 1933–34. 96 pp.
147 Large notebook. Called *C*3. 1934. 96 pp. Partly in English.
148 Large notebook. Called *C*4. 1934–35. 96 pp. Mainly in English.
149 Large notebook. Called *C*5. Immediate continuation of 148. 1935–36. 96 pp. Mainly in English.
150 Large notebook. Called *C*6. 1935–36. 96 pp. Mainly in English.
151 Large notebook. Called *C*7. 1936. 47 pp. Mainly in English.
152 Large notebook. Called *C*8. 1936. 96 pp.
153a Pocket notebook. '*Anmerkungen*' [Annotations]. 1931. 339 pp.
b Pocket notebook, immediately continuing 153a. 122 pp.
154 Pocket notebook. 1931. 190 pp.
155 Pocket notebook. 1931. 189 pp.
156a Pocket notebook. *Circa* 1932–34. 121 pp.
b Pocket notebook, immediate continuation of 156a. 116 pp.
157a Pocket notebook. 1934; 1937. 142 pp.
b Pocket notebook, immediate continuation of 157a. 1937. 81 pp.
158 Pocket notebook. 1938. 94 pp. Partly in English.
159 Pocket notebook. 1938. 80 pp. Partly in English.
160 Pocket notebook. 1938. 63 pp. Partly in English.
161 Pocket notebook. 1939–?. 140 pp. Partly in English.
162a Pocket notebook. Begun and probably also completed in January 1939. 103 pp.
b Pocket notebook, immediate continuation of 162a. Ends in August 1940. 140 pp.
163 Pocket notebook. 22 June–29 September 1941. 156 pp.
164 Pocket notebook. *Circa* 1941–44. 172 pp.
165 Pocket notebook. *Circa* 1941–44. 230 pp.
166 Pocket notebook. 'Notes for the "Philosophical Lecture".' Written in English. Probably 1941–42. 65 pp. (At the end, transcriptions of some poems in Russian.)
167 Pocket notebook. Probably 1947–48. 64 pp.
168 Notebook. Fair manuscript copy of some remarks from the years 1947–49 on general subjects. 12 pp.
169 Pocket notebook. Probably first half of 1949. 161 pp.
170 Pocket notebook. Probably 1949. 10 pp.
171 Pocket notebook. 1949 or 1950. 14 pp.
172 Manuscript on loose sheets. Probably 1950. 24 pp.

173 Notebook. 24 March–12 April 1950; undated part. 200 pp.
174 Notebook. 1950. 78 pp.
175 Pocket notebook. 1950; 10–21 March 1951. 156 pp.
176 Notebook. 1950; 21 March–24 April 1951. 160 pp.
177 Notebook. 25–27 April 1951. 21 pp.
178 Undated fragments:
a '*Man könnte die (ganze) Sache. . . .*' [The (whole) matter could be . . .] 10 pp.
b '*Ich verstehe es. . . .*' [I understand it . . .] 9 pp.
c '*Das Bild der Cantorschen Überlegung. . . .*' [The picture of Cantor's consideration . . .] 6 pp.
d '*Unter Logik versteht man. . . .*' [Logic is considered . . .] 6 pp.
e '*darfst Du Dich nicht. . . .*' [you may not . . .] 4 pp.
f '*Ich möchte sagen. . . .*' [I would like to say . . .] 2 pp.
g '*Diese Sicherheit ist eine empirische. . . .*' [This kind of certainty is empirical . . .] 2 pp.
h '*folgt? ist das Verstehen? . . .*' [follows? is that understanding? . . .] 1 p.
179 Notebook. 1944 or 1945. 72 pp.
180a Notebook. 1944 or 1945. 80 pp.
b Notebook. 1944 or 1945. 56 pp.
181 'Privacy of sense data.' Probably 1935–36. Loose sheets. 6 pp. In English.
182 List of the remarks from TS 228 which were included in the final version of Part I of the *Investigations*. Loose sheets. 2 pp.

TYPESCRIPTS

201a 'Notes on Logic.' September 1913. The so-called Russell Version. English. 7 typescript pages dictated by Wittgenstein and 23 manuscript pages in Russell's hand.
b The same. The so-called Costello Version. English.
202 The so-called Engelmann TS of the *Tractatus*. 1918. 53 pp.
203 The so-called Vienna TS of the *Tractatus*. 1918. 56 pp.
204 The so-called Gmunden TS of the *Tractatus*. 1918. (Missing.)
205 '*Geleitwort zum Wörterbuch für Volksschulen.*' [Preface to the Dictionary for Elementary Schools]. 1925. 6 pp.
206 An Essay on Identity. English. 1927. 3 pp.

207 The Lecture on Ethics. 1929. 10 pp.
208 Typescript based on 105, 106, 107, and the first half of 108 (MS Volumes I, II, III, and IV). 1930. 97 pp.
209 '*Philosophische Bemerkungen.*' Typescript based on 208. 1930. 139 pp.
210 Typescript based on the second half (p. 133 ff.) of 108. *Circa* 1930. 87 pp.
211 Typescript based on 109, 110, 111, 112, 113, and the beginning of 114. Probably 1932. 771 pp.
212 Typescript consisting of cuttings from 208, 210, and 211. 1932 or 1933.
213 The so-called Big Typescript. Probably 1933. viii + 768 pp.
214 Three essays. Probably 1933. 15 pp.
a '*Komplex und Tatsache*' [Complex and Fact].
b '*Begriff und Gegenstand*' [Concept and Object].
c '*Gegenstand*' [Object].
215 Two essays. Probably 1933. 20 pp.
a '*Unendlich lang*' [Infinitely Long].
b '*Unendliche Möglichkeit*' [Infinite Possibility].
216 An essay, '*Gleichungen und Ungleichungen sind Festsetzungen oder die Folgen von Festsetzungen*' [Equations and Nonequations Are Conventions or Consequences of Conventions]. Probably 1933. 6 pp.
217 An essay, '*Allgemeinheit einer Demonstration*' [Generality of a Demonstration]. Probably 1933. 5 pp.
218 An essay, '*Wie kann uns ein allgemeiner Beweis den besonderen Beweis schenken?*' [How can a general proof yield us a particular proof?]. Probably 1933. 3 pp.
219 Typescript beginning '*Muss sich denn nicht. . .*' [Must not. . . .]. Probably 1932 or 1933. 24 pp.
220 Typescript, probably based on 142, of approximately the first half of the prewar version of the *Investigations.* 1937 or 1938. 137 pp.
221 Typescript, based on 117–120 (MS Volumes XIII–XVI) and 162a of the second half of the prewar version of the *Investigations.* 1938. 134 pp.
222 Typescript composed of cuttings from 221.
223 Typescript beginning '*Man kann sich leicht eine Sprache denken. . . .*' [One can easily conceive a language . . .], composed of cuttings from 221. 10 pp.

224 Typescript beginning '*Das Überraschende in der Mathematik . . .*' [The surprise in mathematics . . .], composed of cuttings from 221. 7 pp.
225 Typescript of Preface to the prewar version of the *Investigations.* August 1938. 4 pp.
226 Translation into English by R. Rhees with corrections by Wittgenstein, of the beginning of the prewar version of the *Investigations.* 1939. 72 pp.
227 Typescript of Part I of the final version of the *Investigations.* (1944)–45–(46). 324 pp.
228 '*Bemerkungen* I.' 1945 or 1946. 185 pp.
229 Typescript, being a continuation of 228. 1947. 272 pp.
230 '*Bemerkungen* II.' Probably 1945 or 1946. 155 pp.
231 Two lists of corresponding remarks in '*Bemerkungen* I' and '*Bemerkungen* II'. Probably 1945 or 1946. 8 pp.
232 Typescript based on MS Volumes 135–137. 1948. 174 pp.
233 '*Zettel.*' Cuttings from various typescripts from the period 1929–48, but mostly from 1945–48 (items 228–230 and 232).
234 Typescript of Part II of the final version of the *Investigations.* Probably dictated in 1949. (Missing.)
235 Typescript of a Table of Contents to an unidentified work. Date unknown. 9 pp.
236 Typescript consisting of 17 non-consecutive pages from 210 and one page from 211. 18 pp.
237 Typescript of fragments, partly as cuttings, from pp. 80–92 of 220, with additions and changes. 5 pp.
238 Typescript of revisions of pp. 77–93 of 220. 1942 or 1943. 16 pp.
239 Typescript of a revised version of 220. 1942 or 1943. 134 pp.
240 Typescript of fragments, partly as cuttings, from 221 with changes. 3 pp.
241 Typescript based on 129. 1944–45. 33 pp.
242 Typescript of pages between pp. 149–195 of the so-called Intermediate Version of the *Investigations.* 1944–45. 23 pp.
243 Typescript of a Preface to the *Investigations,* dated 'Cambridge im Januar 1945'. 4 pp.
244 Typescript of an 'overlapping' part of 228 and 229. 11 pp.
245 Typescript beginning in the middle of remark 689 of 244 and containing the rest of 244 and the whole of 229. Date unknown. 192 pp.

DICTATIONS

301 Notes dictated to G.E. Moore in Norway, April 1914. English. 31 pp.
302 The so-called *Diktat für Schlick* [Dictation for Schlick]. Approximately 1931–33. 42 pp.
303 Dictation to Schlick beginning '*Die normale Ausdrucksweise. . . .*' [The normal mode of expression . . .]. Date uncertain. 11 pp.
304 Dictation to Schlick beginning '*Hat es Sinn zu sagen. . . .*' [Does it have sense to say . . .]. Date uncertain. 4 pp.
305 Dictation to Schlick beginning '*Fragen wir diese. . . .*' [If we ask this . . .] Date uncertain. 1 p.
306 Dictation to Schlick beginning '*Was bedeutet es denn. . . .*' [For what does it mean . . .] Date uncertain. 2 pp.
307 Dictation to Schlick. The so-called *Mulder* II. 6 pp.
308 Dictation to Schlick. The so-called *Mulder* V. 57 pp.
309 The so-called Blue Book. English. Dictated to the class at Cambridge in the academic year 1933–34. 124 pp.
310 The so-called Brown Book. English. Dictated to Alice Ambrose and Francis Skinner at Cambridge in the academic year 1934–35. 168 pp.
311 The so-called Yellow Book. Dictated to Margaret Masterman, Alice Ambrose, and Francis Skinner in the year 1933–34.

## Comments on Individual Items in the Catalogue

**105 and 106.** Only the first few entries in 105 are dated; they are from 2 to 6 February 1929. In 106 there are no dates. It is, however, apparent that the left-hand pages numbered 8, 10, and so forth up to 132, and from there to the end (p. 135) of 105 continue the text of 106. The text in 106 again first runs through the right-hand pages up to 296 and then continues on the left-hand pages up to and including right-hand page 298.

**107 and 108.** The first date occurs on page 87. The date is 11 September 1929. The next date, 6 October 1929, is on page 153. From here on dating is regular. After the entry made on 4 December 1929, which ends on page 229, the writing continues in 108 (Volume IV), pages 1–64. Wittgenstein was in Vienna during the Christmas vacation and did not bring 107 (Volume III) with him from Cambridge. The writing in 107 (p. 229) was resumed on 10 January 1930 and continued to 15 February, which is the date of the last entry in 107. On the next day the writing continues in 108 on page 64.

**109 and 110.** The same sort of 'jump' from one manuscript volume to the next, and back, occurs in 109 and 110. The reason is probably the same as in the case of 107 and 108. Pages 1–31 of 110 were written in the period 10 December 1930–28 January 1931. These pages follow chronologically after page 271 of 109. The writing in 109 from page 272 to the end are from 29 January to 3 February 1931. Then the writing continues on page 31 in 110.

**111.** The last date in this volume is 13 September. It is on page 166.

**114 and 115.** These each fall into two parts. The first part of 114 consists of 60 pages, not paginated by the author, and written in the period from 27 May to 5 June 1932. The second part of 114 is paginated by the author 1–228. There are no dates at all in it. It may be regarded as of one piece with the first part (pp. 1–117) of 115 and with MS 140 on large sheets ('*Grosses Format*'). 115 was commenced on 14 December 1933, but there are no further dates in the first part of 115, either. 140 is essentially a revision of pages 1–56 of the second part of 114. Numerous passages from the first part of 115 need to be inserted into the second part of 114. The revisions and 'jumps' back and forth between the manuscripts mean that the reading of them is not easy. From the point of view of their content, however, they form a close unity. It is clear that Wittgenstein is here attempting to write a *book*, to give a consecutive and coherent statement of his philosophical position at the time. It is a plausible conjecture that this piece of writing dates from the academic year 1933–34 and that it is at least partly contemporary with the dictation of the so-called Blue Book.

The second part of 115 (pp. 118–292) is dated as of the end of August 1936 and called '*Philosophische Untersuchungen. Versuch einer Umarbeitung*' [philosophical investigations, attempt at a revision]. It is an attempt at a revision, in German, of the so-called Brown Book. It ends with the words '*Dieser ganze "Versuch einer Umarbeitung" von Seite 118 bis hierher ist* NICHTS WERT.' [this entire "attempt at a revision" from page 118 up to here is NOT WORTH ANYTHING]. A little later in the same year (1936) Wittgenstein wrote a first version of what are now sections 1–188 of the *Investigations* (MS 142).

**116.**[11] In 116—the largest volume in the series—four parts can be distinguished. The first (pp. 1–135) begins as a selection and revision of material in the early portions of 213 (the Big Typescript), but becomes more and more unlike 213, moving, so to speak, in the direction of the *Investigations.* In places there are strong similarities to the Blue Book. The second part of 116 (pp. 136–264) contains revisions of writings from the academic year 1937–38, and the third (pp. 265–315) seems related to some writings which presumably date from 1944. Finally, the fourth part (pp. 316–347) contains a good many remarks which occur at the very end of Part I of the printed version of the *Investigations.*

The manuscript volume 116 is from Bergen, Norway. After his return to philosophy, Wittgenstein visited Norway in 1931, and then again in 1936 when he remained there, with two interruptions, nearly to the end of the following year.

When did Wittgenstein begin writing MS 116? The selected and revised passages from TS 213 in the first part of the manuscript often appear less "revised" and closer to TS 213 than the revisions in MS 140 which Wittgenstein wrote around 1934.[12] This circumstance baffled me for a long time. It seemed to indicate that Wittgenstein had acquired the manuscript book and started writing in it years before his long séjour in Norway, beginning in 1936. For this reason I declared in the first edition of my book *Wittgenstein* that the chronological problems connected with MS 116 puzzled me but that I "would not despair of the possibility of eventually solving them".[13]

My optimism proved to be warranted. The problems have indeed been solved and credit for this goes to S. Stephen Hilmy. Mainly through a comparative analysis of 116 and 119 (which definitely originated between 24 September and 19 November 1937) he established beyond doubt that the first part of MS 116 was written during

11. For a fuller account of this volume and the problems connected with it, see 'The Origin and Composition of the *Philosophical Investigations*', op. cit., pp. 122–125.

12. See Anthony Kenny, "From the Big Typescript to the Philosophical Grammar", Jaakko Hintikka (ed.), *Essays on Wittgenstein in Honour of G.H. von Wright,* Acta Philosophica Fennica *28,* 1976, p. 52.

13. At that time I was unaware of the fact that Wittgenstein had been in Norway already in 1931. This added to my mystification. Yet I believe I was right in thinking that Wittgenstein acquired the manuscript book only in 1936 when he went to live in his hut at Skjolden.

the academic year 1937–38 and most probably stems from the same period as the text of MS 119. Also, the opening part of 116 is not so much a further *revision* of the content of the Big Typescript (as such comparable with earlier revisions in manuscripts 114, 115, and 140), but rather a *selection* (with some revisions) of remarks that Wittgenstein still considered useful for the task he was dealing with at the time in 1937.

The only date in MS 116 stands at the beginning of the fourth part and reads (in English) 'May 1945'. There is every reason for thinking that the whole of the fourth part dates from 1945. This is, incidentally, the only preserved writing in manuscript form which is known with certainty to be from this year.

**117.** Several parts of 117 can be distinguished. Pages 1–97 is manuscript material for 222 and 223—that is, Part I of the *Remarks on the Foundations of Mathematics.* The first entry is dated 11 September 1937; there are no further dates in this part of the volume. Pages 97–110 are headed '*Ansätze*' [approaches]. They are printed in Part II of the *Remarks* (the revised edition). There are no dates. Pages 110–126 contain three drafts of a Preface to the *Investigations.* The third is dated Cambridge, August 1938. Pages 127–148 are undated but were probably written in the second half of 1938. In this section there are references to a typescript which is evidently item 213, from which Wittgenstein was then making excerpts for his current project (the *Investigations*). Pages 148–273, finally, are an immediate continuation of the material in 122. The entries are dated 3 February–18 April 1940. There is a gap in the pagination between pages 209 and 220, evidently due to a mistake.

**118–121.** This is manuscript material from the same period, and dealing with much the same topics, as pages 1–148 of 117. Roughly the second half of 121 was written in the period 25 December 1938–9 January 1939.

**122.** This is the last in the series that Wittgenstein called '*Bände*' (volumes), giving each a number. But it is continued in 117 (pp. 148–273). Thus it is there, on 18 April 1940, that the writings in the numbered '*Bände*' which had begun on 2 February 1929 come to an end (not counting the section from 1945 in 116). There are no manuscripts preserved from the period 18 April–25 September 1940, when Wittgenstein began 123. This is the first volume in the series of manuscripts, some of which were called by Wittgenstein '*Bände*' and given a letter from the alphabet.

**125–127.** These are pocket notebooks written during the war when Wittgenstein was working first at Guy's Hospital in London, from November 1941 to April 1943, and later in a medical laboratory in Newcastle. In the autumn of 1944 he resumed his teaching at Cambridge. The general character of the notebooks makes it reasonable to classify them with the second series of manuscript volumes of a more finished kind. (Cf. the comment on 163 below.) Photocopies exist of 126 and 127; the originals are missing.

**128.** This volume contains no dates and its classification is problematic. Near the end there is a draft of what eventually became the Preface to the final version of the *Investigations.* This links 128 with the next volume in the catalogue.

**129.** This begins with several undated drafts of the preface to the *Investigations.* In these drafts, as also in the draft at the end of 128, Wittgenstein speaks of the results of his philosophical investigations in 'the last 16 years'. The same phrase occurs in the printed Preface to the *Investigations* which is dated Cambridge, January 1945. The drafts therefore seem to be from the same period as the final version (in 227) of the Preface—that is, late 1944 or early 1945. Since the drafts in 129 are written on special sheets at the beginning of the volume, it is quite possible that they were written *after* the rest of the material in the volume, for the first entry (after the drafts of a preface) is dated 17 August 1944. There are no other dates in the volume.[14]

**130.** The first dated entry here, of 26 May 1946, is halfway through the book. The entries after that are dated. The undated first half of the book could have been written, or at least begun, one or two years earlier.

**134.** The last dated entry in this volume is of 27 June 1947. There are a few entries at the end which are presumably later.

**138.** The consecutive writings in this volume end on 22 March 1949, but there is a single additional entry dated 20 May.

**139.** Two manuscripts of this lecture are known to exist or to have existed. The one listed as 139a differs in some interesting respects from the typescript (207) from which the lecture was posthumously

14. In the printed Preface of the *Investigations* it is said: 'Four years ago I had occasion to re-read my first book (the *Tractatus Logico-Philosophicus*) and to explain its ideas to someone.' This sentence makes reference to conversations that Wittgenstein had been having in 1943 with Nicholas Bachtin, linguist and classical scholar (d. 1950). The typescript has, correctly, 'Vor zwei Jahren' [two years ago].

printed in the *Philosophical Review* **74**, 1965. The manuscript listed as 139b is now missing. It was in Gmunden in 1952.

**140.** See comments on 114 and 115 above.

**142.** This manuscript volume, dedicated to Wittgenstein's sister, Mrs M. Stonborough, was in Gmunden in 1952. It is now missing.

**143.** This was published, together with some other comments on Frazer in 110, under the title 'Bemerkungen über Frazers *The Golden Bough*' in *Synthese* **17**, 1967, 233–253, with an Introductory Note by R. Rhees. The editor's comment on the date is 'not earlier than 1936 and probably after 1948'. (Reedited and republished in book form as *Remarks on Frazer's* Golden Bough, ed. by Rush Rhees, Brynmill, Retford, 1979.)

**145 and 146.** These contain material in draft form for 114 and 115 (Volumes X and XI).

**147.** Commenced in February 1934. The latter part of this notebook consists of drafts for the Blue Book.

**148.** Mainly notes for lectures in the academic year 1934–35.

**149.** Mainly notes for lectures, 1935–36.

**150.** Mainly notes for Part II of the Brown Book.

**151.** Largely notes for lectures, 1936.

**152.** Drafts for the beginning of the *Investigations.* Probably written in Norway in the second half of 1936.

**153a and b.** Drafts for 111 (Volume VII). Notebooks have been grouped, a and b, under the same item, when the second book is an immediate continuation of the material in the first.

**154 and 155.** These contain no dates. They contain draft material for 111 and 112 (Volumes VII and VIII), and probably date from 1931.

**156a and b.** These likewise contain no dates.

**157a.** This pocket notebook begins with an entry dated 4 June 1934 and has (p. 90) an entry dated 9 February 1937. The first entry in 157b is dated 27 February 1937.

**159.** This pocket notebook ends with what is evidently the first draft of the Preface to the (pre-war version of the) *Investigations.* Cf. the comment on 117.

**161.** This falls into two distinct parts. Pages 1–32 are written in English, the rest in German. The first part contains drafts for Wittgenstein's lectures on the philosophy of mathematics given in the winter and spring of 1939. The second half seems to consist of drafts written in 1941 for the first part of MS 124.

**163.** The entries in this pocket notebook are dated throughout. It is arguable that it should perhaps be placed after 124 in the second series of more finished manuscripts. The draftlike nature of the contents, however, speaks against this classification. (Cf. the comment on 125–127 above).

**168.** The remarks, entered in the reverse order (1949–47), are from 136–138 (MS volumes Q–S).

**172.** These manuscript pages—dealing with the topics of colour and of certainty—were probably written by Wittgenstein during his last visit to Vienna in the early months of 1950.

**201.** There exist two versions of these notes. Both are in English and both date from the autumn of 1913. Their origin and mutual relation were for a long time obscure, but have eventually been clarified in what seems a conclusive manner by Brian F. McGuinness in 'Bertrand Russell and Ludwig Wittgenstein's "Notes on Logic"', *Revue Internationale de Philosophie* **26,** 1972. What is called the Russell Version in the catalogue consists of a 'Summary' evidently dictated by Wittgenstein (in English) and four 'Manuscripts' which Russell had translated into English from notes in German by Wittgenstein. The so-called Costello Version is apparently a subsequent rearrangement of the text made by Russell alone.

**202.** In all probability, this is the typescript from which Wittgenstein's *Logisch-philosophische Abhandlung* was printed by Ostwald in Germany in 1921. (The printing of the book in England seems to have been from an offprint of the publication by Ostwald.) The manuscript was later given by Wittgenstein to his friend, the architect Paul Engelmann. (See p. 482 above.)

**203.** This is not a second copy of 202, but a different typescript. The last page is lost.

**204.** This typescript was in Gmunden in 1952. With it was also a typescript of Russell's Introduction. They are now missing. (Cf. p. 481 above.) It is not possible to tell at present whether 204 is a second copy of 202 or 203.

**206.** This 'essay' on identity is an extract from a communication from Wittgenstein to Ramsey in June 1927. The extract exists in a carbon copy of a typescript, found among Waismann's papers. The copy is headed '*Wittgenstein an Ramsey, Juni 1927. Durchschlag*' [Wittgenstein to Ramsey, June 1927, carbon copy]. The communication was evidently a letter which is now lost. There is some evidence that the letter had, in fact, been written by Schlick. The extract, and probably the rest of the communication, is in English. It is possible that the communication was dictated by Wittgenstein to Schlick (in German) and that Schlick translated the dictation into English. One hesitates therefore over whether to classify this item among the typescripts or among the dictations. There can be no doubt, however, that the thoughts stem directly from Wittgenstein.

**208.** The typescript originally had 144 pages. The missing ones were used by Wittgenstein himself, chiefly for the composition of 211.

**209.** The original, which is now lost but of which there exist photocopies, was put together from cuttings from a carbon copy of 208 pasted into a black ledger book.

**210.** A few pages at the end of this typescript seem to be missing.

**211.** A few pages are missing, but can be identified in 213. Photocopies of the missing pages have been inserted.

**212.** The cuttings from the 'underlying' typescripts are arranged and clipped together in chapters. The chapters are grouped in 'parts' and enclosed in folders.

**213–218.** These represent the content of 212 typed out, following the arrangement into chapters and parts. The reason for separating, in the catalogue, 214–218 (what I have called the Essays) from 213 (the Big Typescript) is that the essays are already placed apart in 212 and that their pagination does not follow on from the pagination of 213. The reason again for separating the essays from each other in the manner done in the catalogue is that the pagination of the three essays in 214 and of the two in 215 is consecutive, whereas the three essays 216, 217, and 218 are three distinct typescripts.

**220 and 221.** The pagination of the two typescripts is consecutive from 1 to 271. TS 220 ends with page 137. The page numbered 1 is lost and has been replaced in the typescript, as we have it, by three pages with Roman numerals i, ii, and iii. The actual number of paginated sheets in the existing typescript 220 is thus 139.

It is possible but not certain that the two typescripts were typed at the same time. The manuscript material for 220 must already have existed in the first half of 1937; that for 221 was not ready until some time in 1938. (A few remarks at the very end of 221 are from January 1939.)

Roughly the second half of 220 is a top copy; the first half a second copy. The remainder of the top copy is actually preserved in the typescript with the catalogue number 239, found in 1977. Of TS 221 two copies exist more or less intact. Neither of them is a top copy. The top copy was evidently used for composing 222.

**222–224.** The reason for distinguishing these as three different items, although they all stem from 221, is that Wittgenstein himself separated 223 and 224 from the main body of cuttings comprising 222.

**228 and 229.** The pagination is consecutive from 1 to 457, and the remarks are numbered consecutively from 1 to 1804. The typescript nevertheless clearly falls into two parts. Wittgenstein made some corrections and revisions to the remarks (1–698) of the first part; the second part is unrevised. At the beginning of the second part there seems to be some confusion in the numbering of the remarks. The first remark has the number 699. Then follows 670, which probably is a mistake and ought to be 700. Thus the total number of remarks in 228 and 229 together is not 1,804 but 1,834. An additional typescript of the remarks with overlapping numbers 670–698 (in 229) was found later, in 1976. It was given the catalogue number 244.

**230.** This is a collection of 542 numbered remarks, practically all of which are in 228 ('*Bemerkungen* I'). There is a complete list of correspondence between the remarks in the two collections in 231.

**232.** This is a collection of 736 numbered remarks written in the period 9 November 1947–23 August 1948. The pages of the typescript are numbered 600–773. The explanation for this pagination is not known.

**233.** Concerning the arrangement of the cuttings, see the Editors' preface to *Zettel* (Basil Blackwell, Oxford, 1967).

**302–308.** Eight typescripts are known of dictations by Wittgenstein to Schlick. One of them, however, is essentially a typescript version of 140 (the manuscript to which Wittgenstein referred by the name '*Grosses Format*'). This typescript I have not listed in the catalogue. (Cf. also the comment on 206 above.) The dictations cannot be dated with accuracy. None, however, can be earlier than 1926. It is improbable that any of the listed typescripts is later than 1933.

**309–310.** The Blue Book was dictated in the period from 8 November 1933 to the first week in June 1934, the Brown Book in the period from mid-October 1934 to late April or May 1935. Of the first, a number of copies were taken and circulated to friends and pupils by Wittgenstein himself. The second was not meant for circulation and originally existed in only three copies. Clandestinely made copies of both dictations came into circulation against Wittgenstein's wishes. In some of the original copies of the Blue Book, which Wittgenstein gave away, he inserted minor corrections. In future scholarly editions of the text, attention should be paid to variations

between the copies. I am indebted to Professor Ambrose-Lazerowitz for information concerning the origin and history of 309 and 310.
**311,** also known as the Yellow Book, consists of verbatim notes taken by Margaret Masterman, Alice Ambrose, and Francis Skinner in 1933–34. It is doubtful whether it should be classified with the other dictations or with the notes of conversations and lectures (cf. p. 485 above).

## The Posthumous Publications

In his will, dated 29 January 1951, Wittgenstein gave to Mr R. Rhees, Miss G.E.M. Anscombe, and myself the copyright in all his unpublished writings with the intention that we should publish from the papers as many of them as we considered fit.

Wittgenstein did not give us specific instructions concerning the publication and preservation of his unpublished writings. (It was, in fact, not until after his death that I learned that he had named me in his will as one of his literary executors.) We knew, of course, that he had for many years been writing a major work to which he had never been able to give an absolutely finished form but which he certainly wanted to be published and read. Of this work, the *Investigations,* there had, moreover, existed an earlier version from the late 1930s, the second half of which dealt with the philosophy of mathematics. This second half Wittgenstein had later 'laid aside' and it formed no part of the book in the final form he gave it.[15] Yet it somehow belonged there, perhaps after the discussion of the philosophy of psychology in Part II of the *Investigations.*[16] To have published the most mature fruits of Wittgenstein's labours after his return to philosophy in 1929, but none of his writings on the philosophy of mathematics, would have been to give to the world a seriously truncated picture of his life's work. When Anscombe and Rhees had finished their work as editors of the text of the *Investigations* in 1951, the literary executors therefore immediately proceeded to supplement it with a volume of Wittgenstein's writings on the philosophy of mathematics from the period 1937–44.

15. See Editors' Preface to *Remarks on the Foundations of Mathematics* (Basil Blackwell, Oxford, 1956; revised edition, in German, 1974, and in English, 1978).
16. Cf. the concluding remark in Part II, section xiv, of the *Investigations.*

The *Remarks on the Foundations of Mathematics* occupy a nearly unique, and not altogether happy, position among the posthumous publications. In addition to the relatively finished Part I, corresponding to typescripts 222, 223, and 224 of the catalogue and constituting the second half of the pre-war version of the *Investigations*, the *Remarks* contain *selections* from several manuscripts (117, 121, 122, 124, 125, 126, and 127). In the revised edition of 1974 (English translation 1978) the selections from those manuscripts were somewhat enlarged and a further manuscript (164) which was not known to the editors at the time of the first edition was added, practically without omissions. A publication of the manuscripts *in toto*, however, seemed to us excluded even at the time of preparing the new edition.

The 1930 typescript (209) called *Philosophische Bemerkungen (Philosophical Remarks)*, which had been in the custody of G.E. Moore, was a nearly completed work. It could be published (1964) with a minimum of editorial interference. As Appendices to it, 214a and 215a and 215b were included.

A much more complicated case was presented by the so-called Big Typescript (213) of 1933 (cf. p. 484 above). The last third of it, on the philosophy of mathematics, existed in a relatively finished form. But on the earlier parts Wittgenstein had started to make extensive revisions. The revisions were first made in the typescript, but the work was continued in new manuscripts from the years 1933 and 1934, and perhaps even later (see comment on item 116 above).

Rush Rhees, the editor of the *Philosophische Grammatik*, which was published in German in 1969 and in English translation as *Philosophical Grammar* in 1974, decided to include the part on the philosophy of mathematics (five chapters in all) and two chapters dealing with logic practically unchanged from TS 213. They form Part II of the printed book. Four chapters of the typescript were omitted altogether and the remaining ones printed in the revised form that Wittgenstein gave to them, mainly in new manuscripts (114, 115, 140). TS 214 was now included *in toto* in an Appendix between the two parts of the volume.

From the time of the composition of the *Investigations* (1936–49) there were several typescripts in addition to the two which embodied the final versions of Part I and Part II of Wittgenstein's *chef d'oeuvre.* Among Wittgenstein's papers there was also a box containing a huge collection of cuttings from various typescripts but mainly from the time after 1945. The fragments were partly loose, partly clipped in bundles. An arrangement of the cuttings made by Peter Geach was published in 1967 under the title *Zettel*. A much-needed improvement of the German text of *Zettel* was incorporated into the second edition in English (1981), but the German text still awaits publication.[17]

From May 1946 to May 1949 Wittgenstein wrote consecutively on the philosophy of psychological concepts (MSS 130–138). Three typescripts of his were based on these writings, the last of the three being the now lost typescript for Part II of the *Investigations*. The other two can with some justification be regarded as preliminary studies for Part II of Wittgenstein's main work. They were published in two volumes in 1980 under the title *Remarks on the Philosophy of Psychology* in German and English parallel texts.

Wittgenstein's writings in the last two years of his life (after May 1949) never advanced to the typescript stage. In these writings three main themes can be clearly distinguished. The one which is treated most fully concerns knowledge and certainty, and what Wittgenstein wrote on this theme was published under the title *On Certainty* in 1969. A second main theme was the philosophy of colour concepts. A small volume *Remarks on Colour* appeared in print in 1977. The remaining bulk of the writings can be placed under the heading 'The "Inner" and the "Outer"' and appeared in 1992 as the second of two volumes of *Last Writings on the Philosophy of Psychology* (the first volume, containing manuscript material from the years 1948 and 1949, was published in 1982).

In nearly all Wittgenstein's manuscripts, from 1914 to 1951, there occur scattered remarks which do not directly belong to his philosophical work but deal with art, religion, philosophy of history, questions of value, *Lebensweisheit*, and other 'general topics'. It was long clear to us that a collection of these remarks had to be published. I was entrusted with the task of compiling it. The *Vermischte Bemerkungen* [Miscellaneous Remarks] eventually appeared in German in 1977, and three years later in a bilingual edition with the title *Culture and Value*. In the Preface to the book I have explained the principles I followed in making the selections.

17. Dr Maury traced the manuscript material (probably) used by Wittgenstein in the dictation of the typescripts leading up to the remarks in *Zettel*. A. Maury, 'Sources of the Remarks in Wittgenstein's *Zettel*', *Philosophical Investigations* 4, 1981.

It has taken us 30 years to make the full body of Wittgenstein's philosophy accessible to the public.[18] All the works of major interest have, in my view, now been published (save for the Big Typescript, perhaps). The availability of copies of the Cornell film in public libraries has opened the door to research by everybody who is interested in the details of the development of Wittgenstein's thought and the relation between the various 'layers of composition' of his works. The student will also be able to judge, by comparing the published texts with the originals, the editors' choices between variants in the formulations and the selections they have made when, as in the *Remarks on the Foundations of Mathematics,* the complete manuscripts have not been published.

In the course of continued and careful study of the manuscripts and typescripts, corrections and improvements to the editions have turned out to be necessary.[19] Sometimes the editors have misread words or been too rash in the choice of alternative readings or interfered, in a way that now seems unwarranted, with Wittgenstein's own punctuation or with details of his spelling of words. A thorough revision of the bulk of already published writings seems to me called for. Although I think we adopted a basically sound policy in avoiding, as much as possible, editorial and scholarly comments on the texts, a few more indications of variants and explanations of otherwise obscure references would, in my opinion, now be appropriate.

18. When I wrote this sentence I did not foresee the unfortunate ten-year delay in publication of the second volume of the *Last Writings.*

19. The texts that the literary executors have edited and published so far are 'clean' in the sense that they do not usually show variant readings, words crossed out or changed or added, the author's indications of a change in the order of the remarks, variants and changes made by Wittgenstein in the underlying typescripts or manuscripts. In order to prepare a rather more critical edition of the *Investigations,* Heikki Nyman and I edited typescripts 220, 221, 239, 227 (Part I) and Part II of the *Investigations.* A special apparatus of notes, or 'comments', records *all* differences between the typed text and the printed, 'final' text of the book. Copies of the edited and commented material have been deposited in the University Libraries of Cambridge and of Cornell, in the Wren Library of Trinity College, Cambridge, and in the Bodleian Library, Oxford. Compare pp. 7 to 10 and 111 to 136 of Georg Henrik von Wright, *Wittgenstein,* Basil Blackwell, Oxford, 1982. Another example of Heikki Nyman's exemplary editorial skills is his preparation of 'Philosophie', an excerpt from Big Typescript 213, in the present volume, pp. 160–199.

For some time there have been plans for a *complete* publication of the *Nachlass*. This would record all information which the manuscripts and typescripts provide about deletions and insertions, variant readings, and the author's own comments, cross-references, and other textual marks.[20]

## Appendix I. The Writings of Ludwig Wittgenstein Published by Him in His Lifetime

Review of P. Coffey, 'The Science of Logic', *Cambridge Review* **34,** No. 853 (6 March 1913).

*Logisch-philosophische Abhandlung, Annalen der Naturphilosophie,* edited by Wilhelm Ostwald, *Band* XIV, *Heft* 3/4, 1921.

*Tractatus Logico-Philosophicus,* with an Introduction by Bertrand Russell, Kegan Paul, London, 1922.

*Wörterbuch für Volks- und Bürgerschulen,* Hölder-Pichler-Tempsky, Vienna, 1926. An introduction to this dictionary, 'Geleitwort zum Wörterbuch für Volksschulen' (TS 205 of the catalogue), was published posthumously in a reprint of the *Wörterbuch* issued by the original publishing firm in 1977, edited with an Introduction by A. Hübner and W. and E. Leinfellner.

'Some Remarks on Logical Form', *Proceedings of the Aristotelian Society,* Supp. Vol. 9 (1929), pp. 162–171.

A Letter to the Editor, dated Cambridge, 27 May 1933, *Mind* **42,** No. 167 (July 1933), pp. 415–416.

## Appendix II. Wittgenstein's Letters

Over the years the following collections of letters by Wittgenstein have been published:

W. Eccles, 'Some Letters of Ludwig Wittgenstein', *Hermathena* **97,** 1963.

Paul Engelmann, *Letters from Ludwig Wittgenstein. With a Memoir,* trans. by L. Furtmüller, ed. by B.F. McGuinness, Basil Blackwell,

20. I am particularly indebted to Mr Rush Rhees and Mr Brian McGuinness for their invaluable help in my efforts to make accurate both the catalogue and the comments on individual items in it. I shall be grateful for any additional information and corrections that students of the Wittgenstein papers might wish to suggest.

Oxford, 1967. The German original, *Ludwig Wittgenstein, Briefe und Begegnungen,* ed. by B.F. McGuinness, was published by R. Oldenbourg, Vienna and Munich, 1970.

Ludwig Wittgenstein, *Briefe an Ludwig von Ficker,* ed. by G.H. von Wright in collaboration with W. Methlagl, Otto Müller Verlag, Salzburg, 1969.

Ludwig Wittgenstein, *Letters to C.K. Ogden with Comments on the English Translation of the Tractatus Logico-Philosophicus,* ed. with an Introduction by G.H. von Wright and an Appendix of Letters by Frank Plumpton Ramsey, Basil Blackwell, Oxford, and Routledge & Kegan Paul, London, 1973.

Ludwig Wittgenstein, *Letters to Russell, Keynes and Moore,* ed. with an Introduction by G.H. von Wright assisted by B.F. McGuinness, Basil Blackwell, Oxford, 1974, 2nd edit. with corrections 1977.

Ludwig Wittgenstein, *Briefwechsel mit B. Russell, G.E. Moore, J.M. Keynes, F.P. Ramsey, W. Eccles, P. Engelmann und L. von Ficker,* ed. by B.F. McGuinness and G.H. von Wright, Suhrkamp Verlag, Frankfurt am Main, 1980. This volume also contains all the letters that have been preserved to Wittgenstein from his correspondents.

At least from his return to Cambridge in 1929 Wittgenstein preserved letters from his friends—except casual communications and notes. It should therefore be possible to publish, at some future date, a more complete collection of exchanges of letters than the collection already published by Suhrkamp.

# Addendum to "The Wittgenstein Papers"

The following information is designed to supplement von Wright's account of the publication history of Wittgenstein's work. It simply fills in some gaps left by von Wright's account. Some things are not mentioned here because they are already adequately discussed in his paper, others because we have been unable to provide additional information.

The following information supplements the final section, "The Posthumous Publications":

MS 101, 102, & 103 were published in a bilingual edition as *Notebooks: 1914–1916* (pp. 1–21, partway through the remarks for 30.10.14, are MS 101; pp. 21–71 are MS 102; and pp. 71–91 are MS 103). The coded personal remarks from these notebooks were omitted in the publication of these manuscripts (as well as in most copies of the Cornell microfilm of them), but have become available in presumably unauthorized editions: Wilhelm Baum (ed.) "Diarios Secretos de Ludwig Wittgenstein," *Saber* (Barcelona), 1985, no. 5, pp. 24–52, and no. 6, pp. 30–59. A scholarly edition was recently published as *Geheime Tagebücher: 1914–1916,* edited and documented by Wilhelm Baum (Vienna: Turia & Kant, 1991). Selected excerpts from the coded remarks have also been published in a variety of biographical pieces.

MS 104 was published in a bilingual edition as the *Prototractatus.*

MS 114: Material from this (i.e., pp. 45–51, 59–118, 121–22, and 132–44), as well as from MSS 115 (pp. 1–31), 116 (p. 80), 140 (pp. 1–39), and TSS 213 (pp. 100–101, 113–42, 294–353, and 530–768) and 214 (pp. 1–15), was published as *Philosophische Grammatik,* edited by R. Rhees, and later translated as *Philosophical Grammar.* For a complete discussion of the correspondences, see Anthony Kenny, "From the Big Typescript to the Philosophical Grammar," *Essays on Wittgenstein in Honour of G. H. von Wright, Acta Philosophica Fennica,* vol. 28, 1976, pp. 41–53.

The second half (i.e., pp. 118–292) of MS 115 has been published as pp. 117–237 of "Eine Philosophische Betrachtung" in *Schriften 5* (Frankfurt: Suhrkamp, 1970).

A selection (pp. 97–110) from the first half of MS 117 was included in Part II of the revised edition of *Bemerkungen über die Grundlagen der Mathematik* in *Schriften 6* (Suhrkamp, 1974) and later translated as *Remarks on the Foundations of Mathematics* (hereafter RFM 2). The second half of MS 117 (pp. 148–273) was included in Part III of RFM 2.

Selections from MS 119 (basically pp. 1–5, 99–150, and three excerpts from pp. 5–99) were published in a bilingual edition as "Cause and Effect: Intuitive Awareness," *Philosophia*, vol. 6, 1976, pp. 392–425, and are included in this volume.

Selections from MS 121 were included in Part II of RFM 2.

Selections from MS 122 were included in Part III of RFM 2.

Selections from MS 124 were published as Part VII of RFM 2.

Selections from MS 125 were published as Part IV of RFM 2.

Selections from MSS 126 and 127 were published as Part V of RFM 2.

The second half of MS 137 plus MS 138 have been published in a bilingual edition as *Last Writings on the Philosophy of Psychology, volume I,* except some material that was included in *Vermischte Bemerkungen,* 1977 (later expanded and published in a bilingual edition as *Culture and Value,* 1980). A full account of all the manuscript sources for the collage of remarks published in *Culture and Value* can be found in Alois Pichler, *Ludwig Wittgenstein, Vermischte Bemerkungen: Liste der Manuskriptquellen,* Schriftenreihe des Wittgenstein Archivs, University of Bergen, Norway, Nr. 1, 1991.

MS 140: See comments on MS 114.

MS 143 has been published as Part II of "Bemerkungen über Frazers *The Golden Bough,*" *Synthese,* vol. 17, 1967, and is included in this volume.

MSS 148, 149, and 151 were the source for the material published as "Notes for Lectures on 'Private Experience' and 'Sense Data'," originally published in *Philosophical Review,* vol. 77, 1968, pp. 275–320. Save for forty-seven pages of notes on the philosophy of mathematics that come in the middle of MS 148 and eight pages of draft notes for a lecture on the philosophy of mathematics that come in the middle of MS 151, these three MSS are now published in their entirety in this volume (pp. 202–226 come from MS 148, pp. 226–272 constitute MS 149, and pp. 272–288 come from MS 151).

Brief selections from MS 159 have been published as part of appendices A, B, and C of "Cause and Effect: Intuitive Awareness" and are included with minor additions in this volume.

An excerpt from MS 160 has been published as part of appendix B to "Cause and Effect: Intuitive Awareness" and is included in this volume.

Part of MS 164 was published as Part VI of RFM 2.

MS 166 is published for the first time in this volume.

MS 169 was published as the first section of the bilingual volume *Last Writings on the Philosophy of Psychology, volume 2: The Inner and the Outer, 1949–1951* (hereafter LW 2).

MS 170 was published as the second section of LW 2.

MS 171 was published as the third section of LW 2.

Part of MS 172 (i.e., pp. 1–4) was published as Part II of the bilingual volume *Remarks on Colour*; the rest (i.e., pp. 5–24) was published as sections 1–65 of the bilingual volume *On Certainty.*

Most of MS 173 (i.e., pp. 1–63 and 95–200) was published as Part III of *Remarks on Colour* (sections 1–130 and 131–350 respectively); the rest (as well as some material already published as sections 296–350 of *Remarks on Colour*) was published as the fourth section of LW 2.

Part of MS 174 (i.e., pp. 1–14) was published as the fifth section of LW 2; the rest (p. 15 to the end) was published as sections 66–192 of *On Certainty.*

MS 175 was published as sections 193–425 of *On Certainty* (pp. 1–35 of MS 175 constitute sections 193–299, and p. 35 to the end constitutes sections 300–425).

Part of MS 176 (pp. 1–22) was published as Part I of *Remarks on Colour,* part (pp. 22–81) was published as sections 426–637 of *On Certainty,* and the rest (pp. 82–160) was published as the final section of LW 2.

MS 177 was published as sections 638–76 of *On Certainty.*

TS 201a was published as Appendix I: "Notes on Logic" in the 2nd edition of *Notebooks: 1914–1916,* 1979.

TS 201b was published as Appendix I: "Notes on Logic" in the 1st edition of *Notebooks: 1914–1916,* 1961.

TS 207 was published as "The Lecture on Ethics," *Philosophical Review,* vol. 74, 1965, pp. 3–12, and is included in this volume.

Portions of TS 211 (pp. 313–22 *et passim*) were published as Part I of "Bemerkungen über Frazers *The Golden Bough*," *Synthese,* vol. 17, 1967, and are included in this volume.

TS 213: In addition to the material that was incorporated into *Philosophische Grammatik* (see comments on MS 114), a section called "Philosophie" (pp. 405–35) has been published in *Revue Internationale de Philosophie,* vol. 43, 1989, pp. 175–203, and is included in this volume.

TS 214: See comments on MS 114.

TS 222 was published as Part I and Appendix I of Part I of RFM 2.

TS 223 was published as Appendix III of Part I of RFM 2.

TS 224 was published as Appendix II of Part I of RFM 2.

TS 229 and 232 were published as volumes I and II (respectively) of the bilingual *Remarks on the Philosophy of Psychology.*

D 301 was published as Appendix II: "Notes Dictated to G. E. Moore in Norway" of *Notebooks: 1914–1916.*

D 309 and 310 were published together as *The Blue and Brown Books.*

D 311: Portions of this were published as pp. 43–73 of *Wittgenstein's Lectures: Cambridge, 1932–1935,* edited by Alice Ambrose.

The following information supplements Appendix II: "Wittgenstein's Letters":

"Some Hitherto Unpublished Letters from Ludwig Wittgenstein to Georg Henrik von Wright," *Cambridge Review,* vol. 104, 1983, pp. 56–65 (reprinted in this volume).

"Wittgenstein's Letters to Norman Malcolm," in Norman Malcolm, *Ludwig Wittgenstein: A Memoir,* 2nd edition, 1984, pp. 85–134.

"Letters to Ludwig von Ficker," translated by Bruce Gillette, edited by Allan Janik, in *Wittgenstein: Sources and Perspectives,* Ithaca, N.Y.: Cornell, 1979, edited by C. G. Luckhardt, pp. 82–98.

Letters from Wittgenstein to Ludwig Hänsel, published as Part 3 (pp. 295–341) of Konrad Wünsche, *Der Volksschullehrer Ludwig Wittgenstein, mit neuen Dokumenten und Briefen aus den Jahren 1919-1926,* Frankfurt: Suhrkamp, 1985.

Three additional letters from Wittgenstein to Russell, as well as all of Russell's recently discovered letters to Wittgenstein, have been published in "Unpublished Correspondence between Russell and Wittgenstein," *Russell,* vol. 10, Winter 1990–1991, pp. 101–24.

All of Frege's recently discovered letters to Wittgenstein have been published as "Gottlob Frege: Briefe an Ludwig Wittgenstein," in *Wittgenstein in Focus,* eds. B. McGuinness and R. Haller, Amsterdam: Rodopi, 1989, *Grazer Philosophische Studien,* vol. 33/34, 1989, pp. 5–33.

# Additions and Corrections to the Texts

There are a large number of changes that have been made to the texts that are too trivial to detail. Some previous editors of these texts had attempted to preserve Wittgenstein's spelling and grammar, even when they were obviously mistaken. But since other errors inadvertently crept in, it was impossible to tell which were Wittgenstein's and which were the editors' errors. (And it was not always possible to consult original manuscripts to distinguish the source of the errors.) We have judged that misspellings and obvious grammatical mistakes have so little scholarly value that they are rarely worth preserving. We corrected the ones we noticed that made no difference to the sense of the passage, unless the errors had some special interest (as, for instance, in the case of the German text of the *Geleitwort*). In some cases we made changes for the sake of uniformity within a text, or between texts, but we did not pursue that goal with vigor.

Each of the translations has been modified at points, none extensively. Modifications have almost always been done in consultation with the original translator. These changes are not detailed either, especially since the original German is there to consult directly.

Where noteworthy changes have been made, this has always been done after examination of microfilm of the original manuscripts or typescripts. Such microfilm is not always easy to read, either because of the poor state of the original material or occasionally because of poor microfilming. Even where the microfilm is clear, it is not always obvious how to interpret it or render it into text. Some editing is inevitably conjectural, sometimes in ways that are impossible to indicate (or not worth indicating) adequately.

In what follows, passages are referred to by page number, paragraph number (treating the first full paragraph on a page as the first paragraph), and/or line number in this volume.

## Chapter 3

p. 24, bottom paragraph: Elisabeth Leinfellner pointed out that the difference between Wittgenstein's various handwritten signs for 'ss' had been overlooked in the previous edition prepared by her. The distinction is preserved and discussed here.

## Chapter 7

A number of improvements were possible in light of the revised edition of the German text that was first published in Ludwig Wittgenstein, *Vortrag über Ethik und andere kleine Schriften* (Frankfurt: Suhrkamp, 1989). Of these, two are significant:

p. 128, paragraph 5 is new.

p. 144, lines 26–27: "Interpretation" was changed to "Introspektion".

The Brynmill edition *lacks* the following (marked by brackets in our text):

p. 136, paragraph 4 through p. 140, paragraph 3;

p. 140, paragraphs 5, 6, and 7; and

p. 150, paragraph 3 to the end of the chapter.

## Chapter 10

As Rhees did not use broken underlining and very rarely included variant wordings, there are many minor revisions, not listed here, that can be identified by looking for slashes, double slashes, and broken underlining. (For the purpose of identifying paragraphs on each page, diagrams have been counted as paragraphs here.)

p. 202, paragraphs 3 and 5–9 are new.

p. 203, paragraphs 1–4 and 6–8 are new.

p. 204, paragraphs 8–12 are new.

p. 205, paragraphs 1–9 and 11 are new.

p. 206, paragraphs 4–12 are new.

p. 207 is new.

p. 208, paragraphs 4–6 are new.

p. 209, paragraphs 2–8 are new.

p. 210, paragraphs 3–7 are new.

p. 211, paragraphs 1–2 and 4–5 are new.

pp. 212–214 are new.

p. 215, paragraphs 1–3 are new.

p. 216, paragraphs 3–9 are new.

pp. 217–218 are new.

p. 219, paragraphs 1–2 and 4–8 are new.

p. 220, paragraphs 1–6 are new.

p. 221, paragraphs 1–3 and 8–10 are new; paragraph 4 is substantially revised.

p. 222, paragraphs 1–6 are new.

p. 223, paragraphs 8–9 are new.

p. 224, paragraph 9 is new.

p. 225, paragraph 6 is substantially revised; paragraphs 7–8 are new.

p. 226, paragraphs 2 and 4–6 are new.

p. 227, paragraphs 2–8 are new.

p. 228, paragraphs 2–11 are new.

p. 229, paragraphs 2 and 4–11 are new.

p. 230, paragraphs 1–9 are new.

p. 231, paragraph 5 is new.

p. 232, paragraph 4 is new.

p. 234, paragraphs 1 and 7–8 are new; paragraph 2 is substantially revised; and the last sentence of paragraph 6 is new.

p. 235, paragraphs 1 and 7 are new; the last sentence of paragraph 6 is new; and the fourth and last sentences of paragraph 8 are new.

p. 236, paragraph 5 is new.

p. 237, paragraphs 1, 3, 5–8, and 10–12 are new.

p. 238, paragraphs 2, 4–10, and 13 are new.

p. 239, paragraphs 5 and 10 are new; the last sentence of paragraph 2 is new.

p. 240, paragraphs 1 and 8 are new.

p. 241, paragraphs 1 and 5–6 are new; the last sentence of paragraph 7 is substantially revised.

p. 243 is new.

p. 244, paragraphs 1, 5–10, and 13 are new.

p. 245, paragraphs 1–2 and 7–12 are new.

p. 246, paragraphs 1, 3, and 7–8 are new.

p. 247, paragraphs 1–11 and 13 are new.

p. 248, paragraphs 4 and 7–11 are new; paragraph 6 is substantially revised.

p. 249, paragraphs 1, 4, and 7–9 are new.
pp. 250–252 are new.
p. 253, paragraphs 2–5 and 7–9 are new.
p. 256, paragraphs 6 and 8 are new.
p. 258, paragraphs 2–4 and 7–9 are new.
p. 259, paragraphs 1–3 and 7–11 are new.
p. 260, paragraphs 1–3 are new.
p. 261, paragraphs 4–16 are new.
p. 262, paragraphs 1–4 and 8 are new.
p. 263, the last three sentences of paragraph 1 are new.
p. 265, the third sentence of paragraph 2 is new.
p. 266, paragraphs 1–9 are new.
p. 267, paragraph 8 is new.
p. 268, paragraphs 1–6 are new.
p. 269, paragraph 1 is new.
p. 271, paragraphs 1–2 and 5–6 are new.
p. 272, paragraphs 4–7 and 9–10 are new.
p. 273, paragraphs 2 and 4–7 are new.
p. 274, paragraphs 1–2, 4, and 6 are new; the fifth sentence of paragraph 3 is substantially revised.
pp. 276–279 are new.
p. 280, paragraphs 1–3 are new.
p. 281, paragraph 7 is new.
p. 284, paragraphs 5–7 are new.

CHAPTER 12

Appendix A:

p. 407, paragraphs 10, 11, and 12 are new.

Appendix B:

p. 418, paragraphs 1, 7, 8, 9, and 10 are new; paragraph 2 is all new, save for the first sentence; and paragraph 5: "have" was changed to "take".

Appendix C:

p. 422, we have invented the title.

CHAPTER 13

p. 433, paragraphs 10 and 11 are altered. Smythies's notes contain two versions of these paragraphs. The previous edition used the other version, which, however, Smythies seems to have crossed out. The version printed here contained an infelicitous (and clearly accidental) "not" which we've replaced with a bracketed ellipsis. The other version does not contain the "not" but is inferior in other respects.

p. 435, paragraph 2, the parenthetical sentence has been relocated in conformity with Smythies's indication which the previous edition inadvertently ignored. The "[in]" has no basis in the manuscript but seems required by the context.

# German Index

This index is to aid non-German speakers in reconstructing Wittgenstein's taxonomy of terms. For example: a reader who wants to find out what Wittgenstein says about 'mind' will find in the English index that the word 'mind' has been used to translate the German terms 'Geist' and 'Seele'. Turning to the German index, the reader will find that 'Geist' has been translated into English not only as 'mind' but also as 'spirit'. Likewise, 'Seele' has been translated into English as 'mind' and 'soul'. Given that 'Seele' usually and literally means 'soul' the reader may now rephrase her original question: she may decide to restrict her attention to 'mind' in the sense of 'Geist'. Accordingly, she will no longer consider all occurrences of the English word 'mind' but will exempt all translations of 'Seele'. By the same token, she will now include in her considerations some occurrences of the English word 'spirit', at least where they correspond to 'Geist'. She can use this knowledge further when approaching the bilingual editions (and indices) of, say, the *Tractatus* or of the *Philosophical Investigations*. The German index does not contain names of persons or places, nor does it cross-reference between entries.

# English Index

This is not a systematic index referring the reader to passages in which Wittgenstein gives sustained discussions of certain theoretical concepts or issues. Instead it is more like a record of terms. In conjunction with the German index, it allows the reader to trace Wittgenstein's use of these terms. It also serves as an index of names. Families of words (adjectives, adverbs, nouns, and verbs) are grouped together according to somewhat less stringent considerations than those that governed Wittgenstein's *Wörterbuch*.